Christopher T.S. Ragan | Richard G. Lipsey
McGill University
Professor Emeritus,
Simon Fraser University

Twelfth
Canadian
Edition

MICROECONOMICS

PEARSON
Addison
Wesley
Toronto

Library and Archives Canada Cataloguing in Publication

Ragan, Christopher
Microeconomics/Christopher T. S. Ragan, Richard G. Lipsey.—12th Canadian ed.

Includes index.
Authors' names in reverse order on Canadian 10th ed.
ISBN-13: 978-0-321-31491-8
ISBN-10: 0-321-31491-3

1. Microeconomics—Textbooks. I. Lipsey, Richard G., 1928– . II. Title.

HB172.R35 2008 338.5 C2006-904887-8

Pearson Addison Wesley. Previous editions were published by HarperCollins Publishers (formerly Harper & Row Publishers) in 1994, 1991, 1988, 1982, 1979, 1969, and 1966. Portions of the work were first published in the United Kingdom as *An Introduction to Positive Economics*, © 1963 by Richard G. Lipsey.

ISBN-13: 978-0-321-31491-8
ISBN-10: 0-321-31491-3

Editor-in-Chief: Gary Bennett
Marketing Manager: Eileen Lasswell
Developmental Editor: Maurice Esses
Production Editor: Marisa D'Andrea
Copy Editor: Ann McInnis
Proofreader: Catharine Haggert
Production Coordinator: Andrea Falkenberg
Indexer: Belle Wong
Photo and Permissions Researcher: Mary Rose MacLachlan
Compositor: Nelson Gonzalez
Art Director: Julia Hall
Interior and Cover Design: Opus House Inc/Sonya Thursby
Cover Image: Getty Images/David Gould

1 2 3 4 5 12 11 10 09 08

Printed and bound in the United States.

PEARSON
Addison Wesley

Brief Contents

Contents

List of Boxes

Applying Economic Concepts

Extensions in Theory

Lessons From History

Additional Topics on MyEconLab (www.myeconlab.com)

Chapter 1	A Brief Introduction to Graphing
	Challenges Facing the Developing Countries
Chapter 2	How Economists Choose Their Theories
	What the S&P/TSX Really Measures
	A Brief Introduction to Graphing
Chapter 3	Economic Data and the Identification Problem
	A Primer on the Market for Crude Oil
Chapter 4	Some Further Details About Demand Elasticity
	Who Really Pays for Payroll Taxes?
Chapter 5	Linkages Between Markets
	When Rent Controls Work and When They Don't
	Agriculture and the Farm Problem
Chapter 6	What Makes People Happy?
	Do Taxes Discourage Work Effort and Saving?
Chapter 7	Multinational Enterprises and Foreign Direct Investment
	Do Firms Really Maximize Profits?
Chapter 8	Explaining Different Concepts of Efficiency
	Understanding and Addressing Canada's Productivity Challenges
Chapter 9	An Example of Loss Minimization as Profit Maximization
	The Long-Run Industry Supply Curve
Chapter 10	The Growing Battle Over Online Prescription Drugs
Chapter 11	The Nature of Globalization
	A Sequential Game in Fibre Optics
	Oligopoly and Contestable Markets
Chapter 12	Ontario's Troubled Electricity Sector
Chapter 13	Is Canada Suffering a Brain Drain?
Chapter 14	Do Government Job-Creation Programs Really Create Jobs?
Chapter 15	A Beginner's Guide to the Stock Market
	Investment and Saving in Globalized Financial Markets
	Interest Rates and the Extraction of Natural Resources
Chapter 16	Externalities and the Coase Theorem
	How Excessive Regulation Hobbles Development
Chapter 17	A Market for SO_2 Emissions in the United States
	Climate Change, Energy Use, and the Kyoto Emissions Targets
Chapter 18	Debate More Healthy than Health Care
	Who Are Canada's Poor?
Chapter 33	Who Are Canada's Trading Partners?
	Does Third-World Growth Harm First-World Prosperity?
Chapter 34	The Continuing Saga of Softwood Lumber
	Farm Subsidies and the World Trade Organization

To the Instructor

Economics is a living discipline, changing and evolving in response to developments in the world economy and in response to the research of many thousands of economists throughout the world. Through twelve editions, *Microeconomics* has evolved with the discipline. Our purpose in this edition, as in the previous eleven, is to provide students with an introduction to the major issues facing the world's economies, to the methods that economists use to study those issues, and to the policy problems that those issues create. Our treatment is everywhere guided by three important principles:

1. Economics is *scientific,* in the sense that it progresses through the systematic confrontation of theory by evidence. Neither theory nor data alone can tell us much about the world, but combined they tell us a great deal.
2. Economics is *useful* and it should be seen by students to be so. An understanding of economic theory combined with knowledge about the economy produces many important insights about economic policy. Although we stress these insights, we are also careful to point out cases where too little is known to support strong statements about public policy. Appreciating what is not known is as important as learning what is known.
3. We strive always to be *honest* with our readers. Although we know that economics is not always easy, we do not approve of glossing over difficult bits of analysis without letting readers see what is happening and what has been assumed. We take whatever space is needed to explain why economists draw their conclusions, rather than just asserting the conclusions. We also take pains to avoid simplifying matters so much that students would have to unlearn what they have been taught if they continue their study beyond the introductory course. In short, we have tried to follow Albert Einstein's advice:

   Everything should be made as simple as possible, but not simpler.

CURRENT ECONOMIC ISSUES

In writing the twelfth edition of *Microeconomics,* we have tried to reflect the major economic issues that we face in the early twenty-first century.

Living Standards and Economic Growth

One of the most fundamental economic issues is the determination of overall living standards. Adam Smith wondered why some countries become wealthy while others remain poor. Though we have learned much about this topic in the past 230 years since Adam Smith's landmark work, economists recognize that there is still much we do not know.

The importance of technological change in determining increases in overall living standards is a theme that permeates both the microeconomics and macroeconomics halves of this book. Chapter 8 explores how firms deal with technological change at the micro level, and how changes in their economic environment lead them to create new products and new production processes. Chapters 11 and 12 discuss how imperfectly competitive firms often compete through their innovative practices, and the importance for policymakers of designing competition policy to keep these practices as energetic as possible.

We are convinced that no other introductory economics textbook places as much emphasis on technological change and economic growth as we do in this book. Given the importance of continuing growth in living standards and understanding where that growth comes from, we believe this emphasis is appropriate. We hope you agree.

Globalization

Enormous changes have occurred throughout the world over the last few decades. Flows of trade and investment between countries have risen so dramatically that it is now common to speak of the "globalization" of the world economy. Today it is no longer possible to study any economy without taking into account developments in the rest of the world.

Throughout its history, Canada has been a trading nation, and our policies relating to international trade have often been at the centre of political debates. International trade shows up in many parts of this textbook, but it is the focus of two chapters. Chapter 33 discusses the theory of the gains from trade; Chapter 34 explores trade policy, with emphasis on NAFTA and the WTO and its current Doha round of negotiations.

For some time, many Canadians have been worried about a possible "brain drain" to the United States. The fear is that Canada's "best and brightest" are leaving in increasing numbers, in pursuit of greater employment prospects, lower income taxes, and higher living standards available south of the border. How mobile is labour across international borders? Does such labour mobility imply that Canada's policies cannot diverge significantly from those in other countries? We explore these issues at various points throughout the book, especially in Chapters 13, 14, and 18.

The forces of globalization are with us to stay. In this twelfth edition of *Microeconomics,* we have done our best to ensure that students are made aware of the world outside Canada and of how events elsewhere in the world affect the Canadian economy.

The Role of Government

The political winds appear to have shifted in Canada, the United States, and many other countries over the past two decades. Political parties that once advocated a greater role for government in the economy now argue the benefits of proscribed government. But has the fundamental role of government really changed? In order to understand the role of government in the economy, students must understand the benefits of free markets as well as the situations that cause markets to fail. They must also understand that governments often intervene in the economy for reasons related more to equity than to efficiency.

In this twelfth edition of *Microeconomics,* we continue to incorporate the discussion of government policy as often as possible. Here are but a few of the many examples that we explore:

- tax incidence (in Chapter 4)
- the effects of minimum wages and rent controls (in Chapter 5)
- economic regulation and competition policy (in Chapter 12)
- pay equity policy (in Chapter 13)
- environmental policies (in Chapter 17)
- disincentive effects of income taxes (in Chapter 18)
- trade policies (in Chapter 34)

THE BOOK

Economic growth, globalization, and the role of government are pressing issues of the day. Much of our study of economic principles and the Canadian economy has been shaped by these issues. In addition to specific coverage of growth and internationally oriented topics, growth and globalization appear naturally throughout the book in the treatment of many topics once thought to be entirely "domestic."

Most chapters of *Microeconomics* contain some discussion of economic policy. We have two main goals in mind when we present these discussions:

1. We aim to give students practice in using economic theory, because applying theory is both a wonderfully effective teaching method and a reliable test of students' grasp of theory.

2. We want to introduce students to the major policy issues of the day and to let them discover that few policy debates are as "black and white" as they often appear in the press.

Both goals reflect our view that students should see economics as useful in helping us to understand and deal with the world around us.

Structure and Coverage

To open Part 1, Chapter 1 presents the market as an instrument of coordination. We introduce the issues of scarcity and choice and then briefly discuss alternative economic systems. The problems of converting command economies to market economies will be with us for some time, and comparisons with command economies help to establish what a market economy is *by showing what it is not.* Chapter 2 makes the important distinction between positive and normative inquiries and goes on to an introductory discussion of the construction and testing of economic theories. We also discuss graphing in detail.

Part 2 deals with demand and supply. After introducing price determination and elasticity in Chapters 3 and 4, we apply these tools in Chapter 5. The case studies are designed to provide practice in applying the tools rather than a full coverage of each case. Chapter 5 also has an intuitive and thorough treatment of economic value and market efficiency.

Part 3 presents the foundations of demand and supply. The theory of consumer behaviour is developed via marginal utility theory in Chapter 6, which also provides an introduction to consumer surplus and an intuitive discussion of income and substitution effects. The Appendix to Chapter 6 covers indifference curves, budget lines, and the derivation of demand curves using indifference theory. Chapter 7 introduces the firm as an institution and develops short-run costs. Chapter 8 covers long-run costs and the principle of substitution, and goes on to consider shifts in cost curves due to technological change. The latter topic is seldom, if ever, covered in the micro part of elementary textbooks, yet applied work on firms' responses to changing economic signals shows it to be extremely important.

The first two chapters of Part 4, Chapters 9 and 10, present the standard theories of perfect competition and monopoly with a thorough discussion of price discrimination and some treatment of international cartels. Chapter 11 deals with monopolistic competition and oligopoly, which are the market structures most commonly found in Canadian industries. Strategic behaviour plays a central part in the analysis of this chapter. The first half of Chapter 12 deals with the efficiency of competition and the inefficiency of monopoly. The last half of the chapter deals with regulation and competition policy.

Part 5 begins in Chapter 13 by discussing the general principles of factor pricing and how factor prices are influenced by factor mobility. Chapter 14 then examines the operation of labour markets, addressing issues such as wage differentials, discrimination, labour unions, and the "good jobs–bad jobs" debate. Chapter 15 discusses investment in physical capital, the role of the interest rate, and the overall functioning of capital markets.

The first chapter of Part 6 (Chapter 16) provides a general discussion of market success and market failure and outlines the arguments for and against government intervention in a market economy. Chapter 17 deals with environmental regulation with a detailed discussion of market-based policies. Chapter 18 analyzes taxes, public expenditure, and the main elements of Canadian social policy. These three chapters expand on the basics of microeconomic analysis by providing current illustrations of the relevance of economic theory to contemporary policy situations.

We hope you find this menu both attractive and challenging; we hope students find the material stimulating and enlightening. Many of the messages of economics are complex—if economic understanding were only a matter of common sense and simple observation, there would be no need for professional economists and no need for textbooks like this one. To understand economics, one must work hard. Working at this book should help readers gain a better understanding of the world around them and of the policy problems faced by all levels of government. Furthermore, in today's globalized world, the return to education is large. We like to think that we have contributed in some small part to the understanding that increased investment in human capital by the next generation is necessary to restore incomes to the rapid growth paths that so benefited our parents and our peers. Perhaps we may even contribute to some income-enhancing accumulation of human capital by some of our readers.

SUBSTANTIVE CHANGES TO THIS EDITION

We have done a major revision and update of the entire text with guidance from an extensive series of formal reviews and other feedback from both users and nonusers of the previous editions of this book. As always, we have strived very hard to improve the teachability and readability of the book. We have focused the discussions so that the major point is emphasized as clearly as possible, without the reader being distracted by non-essential points. We have removed some material from the textbook and placed it in the *Additional Topics* section of the book's MyEconLab (www.myeconlab.com). The MyEconLab also includes new material that has been written especially for this edition. (A complete listing of the *Additional Topics* on MyEconLab is provided following the List of Boxes.) As in recent editions, we have kept all core material in the main part of the text. The three boxes (Applying Economic Concepts, Lessons From History, and Extensions in Theory) are used to show examples or extensions that can be skipped without fear of missing an essential concept. But we think it would be a shame to skip too many of them, as there are many interesting examples and policy discussions in these boxes.

What follows is a brief listing of the main changes that we have made to the textbook.

The *structure* of our microeconomics treatment has not changed from the previous edition because we feel that the current structure is more logical than any alternative. Following an introductory part, we first examine the basic theory of demand, supply, equilibrium, and elasticity, together with a chapter illustrating several applications of basic price theory. We then turn to the details of consumer and producer theory. Once production and costs are in hand, we turn to an examination of the four main market structures as well as a discussion of economic efficiency.

The next part of the book examines factor markets in detail, including separate chapters on labour markets and capital markets. The final part of the microeconomics treatment provides a detailed discussion of the role of government in the economy. We begin with a discussion of market failures, then provide a separate chapter on the economics of environmental protection, and finish off with an examination of taxation and public expenditure in Canada.

Though the overall structure of our micro treatment has not changed, we have tried to anticipate in earlier chapters the important issues of market failures and deadweight loss that do not get fully explained until later in the book. In this way, readers obtain a glimpse of some important and interesting economic issues early on, even though they must wait a while to see the full treatment.

Part 1: What Is Economics? Chapter 1 introduces the central ideas of scarcity, choice, and opportunity cost. It also examines the idea behind the "invisible hand." We have combined the former discussions on central planning and alternative economic systems, and they now appear as the final major section.

Chapter 2 explores how economists build and test their theories. It discusses different kinds of data, what index numbers mean and how they are constructed, and the basics of graphing. We have clarified the discussion of correlation and causation, and also clarified the discussion of slopes of lines.

Part 2: An Introduction to Demand and Supply
The basics of demand, supply, and market price are developed in Chapter 3. In the box showing the algebra of market equilibrium, we have added a numerical example that should make the box more accessible to students. To the box examining weather shocks, we have added a discussion of the effects of Hurricane Katrina on the world price of oil.

Chapter 4 examines elasticity. We have changed the hypothetical data in Tables 4-1 and 4-2 to simplify the computations of elasticity. The former Appendix examining details about elasticity now appears as an *Additional Topic* on MyEconLab. We have added more examples to illustrate the relationship between elasticity and total expenditure. The box on payroll taxes has been moved to MyEconLab, and the section on income elasticity has been rewritten.

Chapter 5 offers many examples of markets in action, and helps the students to use the principles they have learned in the previous two chapters. We have removed the long section on agriculture and it now appears as a full-length *Additional Topic* on MyEconLab. In its place, we have created an entirely new discussion that introduces the reader to economic value and market efficiency. We begin by interpreting demand as "value" and supply as "cost," and go on to discuss the surplus generated through transactions. We then review the basics of price floors and price ceilings, highlighting the effects on total surplus and market efficiency. We have made this important change to this chapter in response to many reviewers' comments that revealed a desire to introduce the issue of market efficiency early on in the micro half of the book.

Part 3: Consumers and Producers Chapter 6 examines marginal utility theory and uses it to motivate the discussion of consumer surplus. We have streamlined the discussion of income and substitution effects of price changes. The box on taxes and work effort has been moved to MyEconLab, where it is expanded to include the effects of taxes on saving. The discussion on consumer surplus has been shortened, as it now relates back to the new discussion in Chapter 5. The material on indifference curves remains in the Appendix.

Production and costs are the focus of Chapter 7. Our opening discussion of the organization of firms now leads to a new box on corporate social responsibility, a popular and important current topic. We have clarified the discussion of fixed and variable costs, and how these costs change when the firm's plant size increases. The former box on Ronald Coase's view of why firms exist has been removed, and the Appendix on whether firms really do maximize profits now appears as an *Additional Topic* on MyEconLab.

Chapter 8 examines firms' choices in the long run, when there are no fixed factors, and in the very long run, when technology changes. We have clarified our discussion of the condition for cost minimization, and used the rise in the use of ATMs to illustrate the principle of substitution. The material on isocost and isoquant analysis remains in the Appendix.

Part 4: Market Structure and Efficiency The theory of perfectly competitive markets is developed in Chapter 9. We have used recent data on wheat production to improve the discussion of firm-level versus industry-level demand elasticity. We have added a new table to illustrate a situation where a firm makes losses but nonetheless chooses to produce positive output; we also illustrate the shut-down decision. The former discussion of long-run industry supply curves now appears as an *Additional Topic* on MyEconLab.

Chapter 10 examines monopoly, price discrimination, and cartels. We have rewritten the discussion of the inefficiency of monopoly, referring back to the new material in Chapter 5. In the discussion of price discrimination, we have added a numerical example and figure illustrating the greater profitability of charging different prices across segmented markets.

Imperfect competition and strategic behaviour are examined in Chapter 11. The former box on globalization now appears as an *Additional Topic* on MyEconLab, where it is expanded to include data on the ongoing reductions in transportation and communications costs. We have shortened the discussion of why firms are (often) so large, and have added several examples of firm innovation to maintain entry barriers.

Chapter 12 examines in more detail the concepts of efficiency that were first introduced in Chapter 5. We begin by making the distinction between productive and allocative efficiency, and relating both concepts to the production possibilities boundary. We have streamlined the discussion of marginal-cost and average-cost pricing for natural monopolies, and have added a discussion about the recent CRTC ruling outlining the conditions under which the telecommunications industry would be deregulated. In the section on Canadian competition policy, we have added a new box outlining the cases for and against bank mergers.

Part 5: Factor Markets Chapter 13 offers a general discussion of factor mobility and the operation of factor markets. We have streamlined the discussion of the demand for factors, and the former box on the possible "brain drain" has been moved to MyEconLab. In our treatment of economic rent, we have added a discussion of Alberta's oil royalties.

Several aspects of labour markets are examined in Chapter 14. We have enriched the discussion of labour-market discrimination, and have clarified the nature of the service sector in the discussion of "good" jobs and "bad" jobs. We now make the point that the service sector has many high-income jobs that are excellent in many respects. But it also has many low-paying jobs that are the source of concern in this debate.

Capital markets and the interest rate are examined in Chapter 15. We have modified the discussion of the demand for and supply of capital by expressing both demand and supply in terms of *flow* concepts. Thus, the model becomes one of an ordinary loanable-funds model in which the interaction of investment demand and saving supply determines the equilibrium interest rate.

Part 6: Government in the Market Economy Chapter 16 offers a detailed treatment of market failures and the role of government in the economy. The section on the Coase theorem now appears as an *Additional Topic* on MyEconLab, where it is expanded to include a numerical example. The former box on elephants and buffaloes has been removed. We have updated the discussion of declining fish stocks and have added some recent FAO data on the state of the world's fish stocks. The short discussion of missing markets has been removed.

Policies for environmental protection are the topic of Chapter 17. We have clarified the explanation for the inefficiency of direct pollution controls, and have added some relevant examples. The box on charging for garbage by the bag has been completely rewritten with up-to-date data drawn from recent Canadian experience. The former box on the Kyoto Protocol has been moved to MyEconLab where it provides an expanded discussion of the economic and social consequences of global warming, and the relationship between economic growth, energy use, and greenhouse-gas emissions.

Taxation and public expenditure are the central topics of Chapter 18. In our discussion of the tax system, we have clarified the message that an evaluation of the *system* is preferable to an evaluation of any individual tax. Several parts of the discussion of public expenditure have been rewritten to reflect recent developments in federal–provincial transfers, the alleged fiscal imbalance, and developments in the health-care debate.

Part 12: Canada in the Global Economy Chapter 33 explores the gains from trade, and emphasizes that the gains arising from trade between individuals are the same as the gains that arise from trade between countries. We have sharpened the discussion of the importance of economies of scale and learning by doing, and have also put a little more emphasis on the idea that comparative advantages can be acquired as well as lost. This is the important idea that comparative advantage is a *dynamic* concept.

Trade policy is the topic of Chapter 34. In restating the case for free trade, we have argued that protection may have the effect of reducing the amount of innovation by protected firms, thus leading to an eventual loss of relative living standards. We have improved the discussion of the protection of infant industries, due either to scale economies or learning by doing, and we have also sharpened the discussion of strategic trade policy. We have updated the discussion of the WTO negotiations, and added a new box that outlines the debate about the success or failure of the WTO. The former box on headline trade disputes has been removed, but there is now a full-length item on MyEconLab about the history, politics, and economics of the softwood lumber dispute.

If you are moved to write to us (and we hope that you will be!), please do. You can send any comments or questions regarding the text (or any of the supplementary material, such as the *Instructor's Manual*, the *Study Guide*, the *TestGen*, or web-based *Additional Topics*) to:

Christopher Ragan
Department of Economics
McGill University
855 Sherbrooke St. West
Montreal, Quebec H3A 2T7
e-mail: christopher.ragan@mcgill.ca

To the Student

Welcome to what is most likely your first book about economics! You are about to encounter what is for most people a new way of thinking, which often causes people to see things differently than they did before. But learning a new way of thinking is not always easy, and you should expect some hard work ahead. We do our best to be as clear and logical as possible, and to illustrate our arguments whenever possible with current and interesting examples.

You must develop your own technique for studying, but the following suggestions may prove helpful. Begin by carefully considering the Learning Objectives at the beginning of a chapter. Read the chapter itself relatively quickly in order to get the general run of the argument. At this first reading, you may want to skip the boxes and any footnotes. Then, after reading the Summary and the Key Concepts (at the end of each chapter), reread the chapter more slowly, making sure that you understand each step of the argument.

With respect to the figures and tables, be sure you understand how the conclusions that are stated in boldface at the beginning of each caption have been reached. You should be prepared to spend time on difficult sections; occasionally, you may spend an hour on only a few pages. Paper and pencil are indispensable equipment in your reading. It is best to follow a difficult argument by building your own diagram while the argument unfolds rather than by relying on the finished diagram as it appears in the book.

The end-of-chapter Study Exercises require you to practise using some of the concepts that you learned in the chapter. These will be excellent preparation for your exams. To provide you with immediate feedback, we have posted Solutions to Selected Study Exercises on MyEconLab (www.myeconlab.com). The end-of-chapter Discussion Questions require you to apply what you have studied. We advise you to outline answers to some of the questions. In short, you should seek to understand economics, not to memorize it.

The bracketed boldface numbers in the text refer to a series of mathematical notes that are found starting on page M-1 at the end of the book. For those of you who like mathematics or prefer mathematical argument to verbal or geometric exposition, these may prove useful. Others may disregard them.

In this edition of the book, we have incorporated many elements to help you review material and prepare for examinations. A brief description of all the features in this book is given in the separate section that follows.

We encourage you to make use of the brand new MyEconLab for the book (www.myeconlab.com) at the outset of your studies. MyEconLab contains a wealth of valuable resources to help you. MyEconLab provides Solutions to Selected Study Exercises. It also includes many additional practice questions, some of which are modelled on Study Exercises in the book. The MyEconLab icon myeconlab identifies those Study Exercises that are reformulated online for you. In the book, the MyEconLab icon also directs you to online discussions of *Additional Topics*—these represent material written especially for this textbook, and include many interesting theoretical, empirical, and policy discussions. For more details about the resources provided on the MyEconLab, please see the description in the section on Supplements.

We strongly suggest you make use of the excellent *Study Guide* written expressly for this text. The *Study Guide* is closely integrated with the book. In fact, special references in the margins of the textbook will direct you to appropriate practice questions and exercises in the *Study Guide*. They will test and reinforce your understanding of the concepts and analytical techniques stressed in each chapter of the text and will help you prepare for your examinations. Explanations are provided for the answers to some of the Multiple-Choice Questions to facilitate your independent study. The ability to solve problems and to communicate and interpret your results are important goals in an introductory course in economics. The *Study Guide* can play a crucial role in your acquisition of these skills.

Over the years, the book has benefited greatly from comments and suggestions we have received from students. Please feel free to send your comments to christopher.ragan@mcgill.ca. Good luck, and we hope you enjoy your course in economics!

Features of This Edition

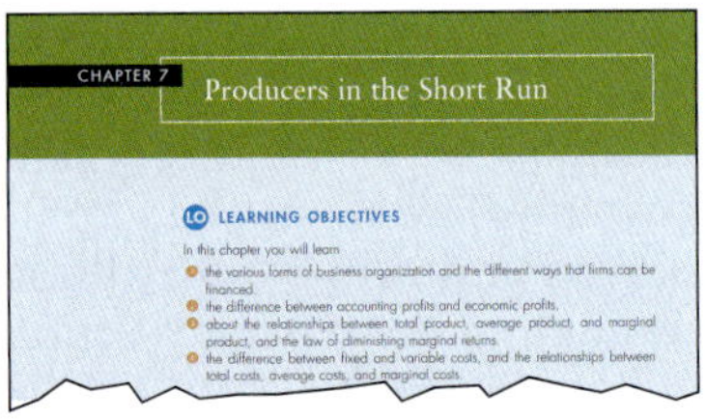

We have made a careful effort with this edition to incorporate features that will facilitate the teaching and learning of economics.

- A set of **Learning Objectives** at the beginning of each chapter clarifies the skills and knowledge to be learned in each chapter. These same learning objectives are used in the chapter summaries, as well as in the *Study Guide*.

- **Major ideas** are highlighted in red in the text.
- **Key terms** are boldfaced where they are defined in the body of the text and they are restated with their definitions in the margins. In the index at the back of the book, each key term and its page reference to its definition are boldfaced.
- **Weblinks** to useful Internet addresses are given in the margins. Each weblink presents a URL address, along with a brief description of the material available there. Some links are to government home pages where much data can be obtained. Other links are to organizations such as OPEC, the UN, and the WTO.
- **Study Guide** references in the margin direct students to appropriate questions in the *Study Guide* that reinforce the topic being discussed in the text.

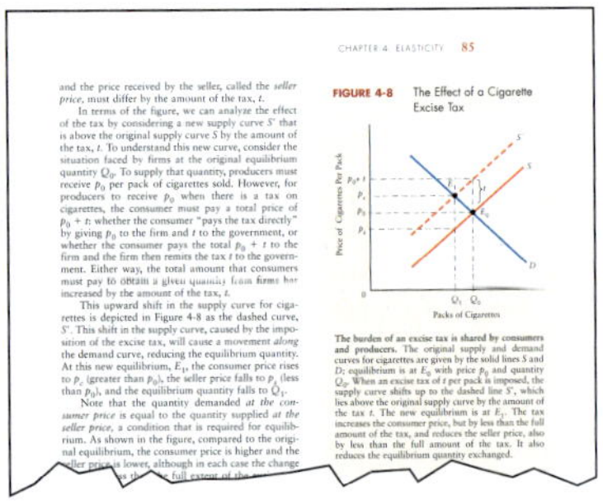

- **A caption for each Figure and Table** summarizes the underlying economic reasoning. Each caption begins with a boldfaced statement of the relevant economic conclusion.
- The **colour scheme for Figures** consistently uses the same colour for each type of curve. For example, all demand curves are blue, whereas all supply curves are red.

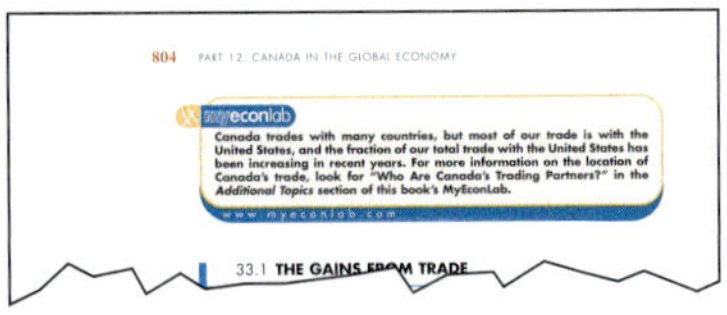

- **Additional Topics on MyEconLab (www.myeconlab.com)** are referenced in special boxes inserted at the appropriate place in the body of the relevant chapter. The *Additional Topics* include the entire online Chapter 36W, Challenges Facing the Developing Countries.

- **Applying Economic Concepts** boxes demonstrate economics in action, providing examples of how theoretical material relates to issues of current interest.
- **Extensions in Theory** boxes provide a deeper treatment of a theoretical topic that is discussed in the text.

- **Lessons From History** boxes contain discussions of a particular policy debate or empirical finding that takes place in a historical context.
- **Photographs with short captions** are interspersed throughout the chapters to illustrate some of the arguments.

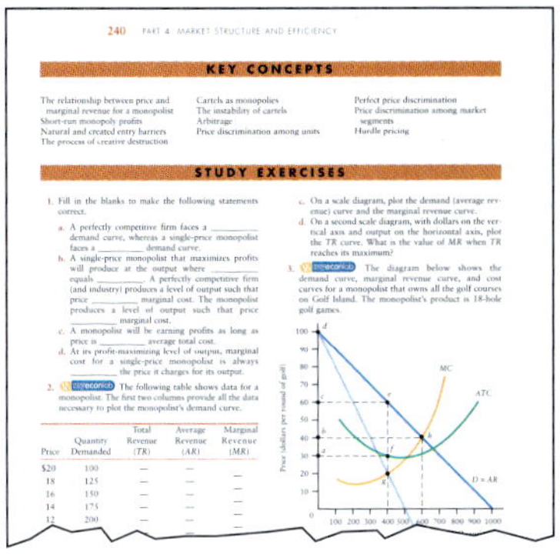

- **Chapter Summaries** are organized using the same numbered heading as found in the body of the chapter. The relevant learning objectives (LO) numbers are given in orange next to each heading in the summary.
- **Key Concepts** are listed near the end of each chapter.
- A set of **Study Exercises** is provided for each chapter. These often quantitative exercises require the student to analyze problems by means of computations, graphs, or explanations.
- **MyEconLab icons** tie certain Study Exercises in the book to exercises on MyEconLab (www.myeconlab.com).

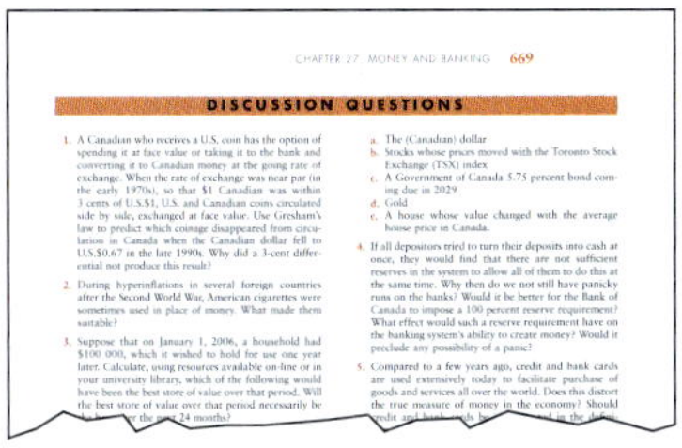

- A set of **Discussion Questions** is also provided for each chapter. These questions require the student to synthesize and generalize. They are designed especially for discussion in class.

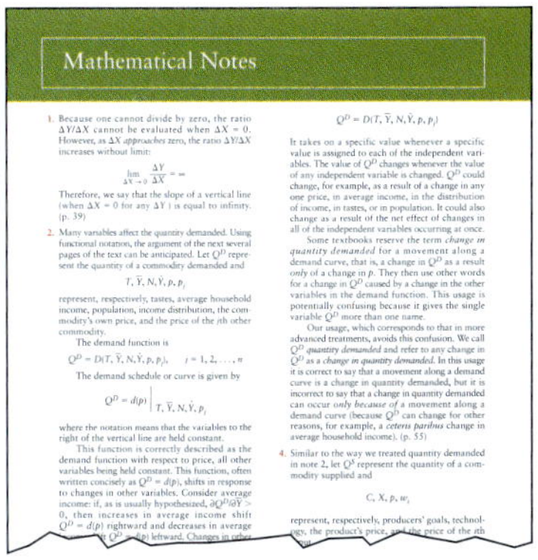

- A set of **Mathematical Notes** is presented in a separate section near the end of the book. Because mathematical notation and derivations are not necessary to understand the principles of economics but are more helpful in advanced work, this seems to be a sensible arrangement. References in the text to these mathematical notes are given by means of boldfaced numbers in square brackets.

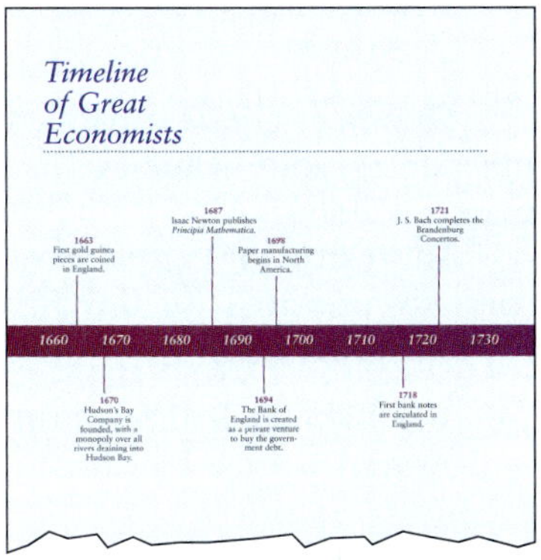

- A **Timeline of Great Economists,** running from the mid-seventeenth century to the late-twentieth century, is presented near the end of the book. Along this timeline we have placed brief descriptions of the life and works of some great economists, most of whom the reader will encounter in the textbook. Along this timeline we have also listed some major world events in order to give readers an appreciation for when these economists did their work.
- **Economists on Record,** given on the inside of the back cover, quotes some classic excerpts that are relevant to the study and practice of economics.
- For convenience, a list of the **Common Abbreviations Used in the Text** is given on the inside of the front cover.

Supplements

A comprehensive set of supplements has been carefully prepared to assist students and instructors in using this new edition.

A thoroughly revised and expanded **Study Guide,** written by Paul T. Dickinson and Gustavo Indart, is designed for use either in the classroom or by students on their own. The *Study Guide* offers additional study support and reinforcement for each text chapter. It is closely integrated with the textbook. Special notes in the margins of the textbook direct students to appropriate practice exercises in the *Study Guide.* For this edition, we have increased the number of questions and exercises. And to facilitate independent study, we have provided explanations for more of the solutions to the Additional Multiple-Choice Questions. For each chapter, the *Study Guide* provides the following helpful material:

- Learning Objectives matching those in the textbook
- Chapter Overview
- Hints and Tips
- Chapter Review consisting of Multiple-Choice Questions, organized into sections matching the numbered sections in the textbook
- Short-Answer Questions
- Exercises
- Extension Exercises
- Additional Multiple-Choice Questions
- Solutions to all of the Questions and Exercises above
- Explanations for the solutions to at least 50 percent of the Additional Multiple-Choice Questions

The *Study Guide* is available as a cumulative volume or as split volumes for microeconomics and macroeconomics.

An **Instructor's Resource CD-ROM** has been specially prepared for this new edition. It contains the following items:

- An *Instructor's Manual* (in both Word and PDF format) written by Christopher Ragan. It includes full solutions to all the Study Exercises and suggested answers to all the Discussion Questions.
- *PowerPoint Slides* prepared by Christopher Ragan. Instructors can readily adapt these slides for lecture presentations.
- A thoroughly revised *TestGen*, written by Ingrid Kristjanson and Christopher Ragan, with contributions from Bogdan Buduru and Burc Kayahan. The testbank has been substantially expanded and now consists of more than 3600 multiple-choice questions. For the new edition, more emphasis has been placed on applied questions (as opposed to recall questions), quantitative questions (as opposed to qualitative questions), and questions with graphs or tables. Approximately 60 percent of the questions now test applied skills, about 20 percent of the questions are quantitative, and about 20 percent of the questions have a graph or table. All the questions have been carefully checked for accuracy. For each question, the authors have provided the correct answer, identified the relevant section number in the textbook chapter, specified the concept being tested, assigned a level of difficulty (easy, moderate, or challenging), identified the skill tested (recall or applied), noted whether the question is qualitative or quantitative, and noted whether the question involves a graph or table. *TestGen* enables instructors to search for questions according to any of these attributes and to sort questions into any order desired. With *TestGen,* instructors can easily edit existing questions, add questions, generate tests, and print the tests in a variety of formats. *TestGen* also allows instructors to administer tests on a local area network, have the tests graded electronically, and have the results prepared in electronic or printed reports.

MYECONLAB

MyEconLab—the online homework and tutorial system packaged with every new copy of the text—puts you in control of your own learning with study and practice tools directly correlated to the textbook content. Within MyEconLab's structured environment, you can practise what you learn, test your understanding, and pursue a personalized study plan that MyEconLab generates for you based on your performance on practice tests.

To register your access code, or to get more information about MyEconLab, visit the MyEconLab website at **www.myeconlab.com**.

If you do not have an access code, you can purchase one from your bookstore:

Economics MyEconLab Student Access Kit: ISBN 978-0-321-46880-2
Microeconomics MyEconLab Student Access Kit: ISBN 978-0-321-46881-9
Macroeconomics MyEconLab Student Access Kit: ISBN 978-0-321-46882-6

MyEconLab is also available in CourseCompass. If your instructor is teaching with CourseCompass, he or she will provide you with the Course ID you will need to access your course.

MyEconLab: Problem Solving for Students

MyEconLab gives you the tools you need to learn from your mistakes whenever you might be struggling.

Personalized Study Plan A Study Plan is generated from each student's results on Sample Tests and instructor assignments. Students can clearly see which topics they have mastered and, more importantly, which they need to work on. The Study Plan links to additional practice problems and tutorial exercises to help with those topics.

Unlimited Practice Most Sample Test and Study Plan exercises contain algorithmically generated values, ensuring students get as much practice as they need. Every problem links students to learning resources that further reinforce concepts they need to master.

Learning Resources In the lower left-hand corner of each practice problem is a link to the eText page, which discusses the very concept being applied. Students also have access to guided solutions that take them step by step through many of the more complex problems. MyEconLab has a suite of graphing tools for practice and current news articles that tie chapter topics to everyday issues.

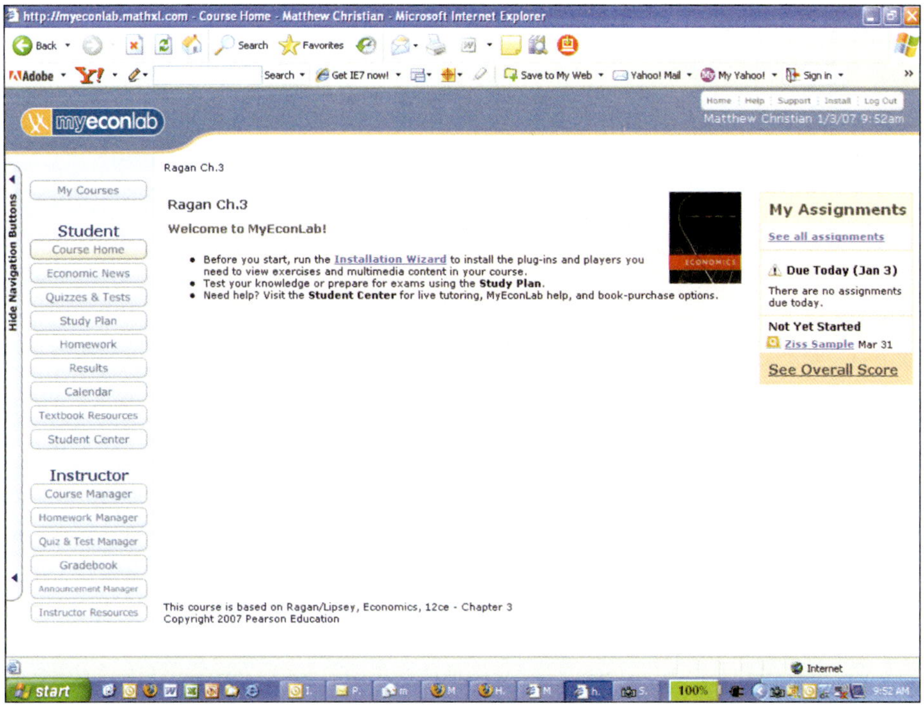

Tests and Other Assignments MyEconLab comes with two pre-loaded Sample Tests for each chapter so students can assess their understanding of the material themselves. Instructors can assign these Sample Tests or create assignments using a mix of publisher-supplied content and their own custom exercises.

MyEconLab: Solving Problems for Instructors

You decide the level of your own participation. Students benefit from full access to MyEconLab regardless of your choice. Full faculty involvement is possible in MyEconLab, and also in MyEconLab in CourseCompass, which is available to you if you choose.

Tutorial Help No instructor setup is needed at all for students to get two pre-loaded assessments per chapter, Study Plans, tutorial help, and more.

Ready-to-Use Assignments Use pre-loaded Sample Tests or create your own assignments using a mix of MyEconLab problems, the book's Testbank, and questions written using the Econ Exercise Builder. Assign problems as tests, quizzes, or homework, and student results will be captured in MyEconLab's powerful online Gradebook.

Automatic Grading MyEconLab grades every homework and quiz question—even those with graphing. Students get unlimited graphing practice and immediate feedback with links to specific learning tools for each question. At any time, instructors can check on students' progress in their online Gradebook.

Individual Student Settings Instructors can modify assignment settings for individual students, without other students seeing the changes or being affected by them. From either the Homework and Test Manager or a student's results page in the Gradebook, instructors can change any of the following assignment settings for individual students: due dates and times, number of attempts, time limit, whether to show remaining time during a test, whether a password is required (and what it is), whether a homework assignment is available to be worked on past its due date, and whether the work is assigned or unassigned.

MyEconLab can also be made available on request through Blackboard and WebCT. Contact your Pearson Education Canada sales representative for more information about these two course-management systems.

Acknowledgments

It would be impossible to acknowledge here by name all the teachers, colleagues, and students who contributed to the development and improvement of this book over its previous eleven editions. Hundreds of users have written to us with specific suggestions, and much of the credit for the improvement of the book over the years belongs to them. We can no longer list them individually but we thank them all sincerely.

For the development of this twelfth edition, we are grateful to the many people who offered informal suggestions. We would also like to thank the following instructors who provided us with formal reviews of the textbook. Their observations and recommendations were extremely helpful.

- Morris Altman (University of Saskatchewan)
- Soham Baksi (University of Winnipeg)
- Michael Benarroch (University of Winnipeg)
- Ugurhan G. Berkok (Queen's University)
- Ryan Compton (University of Manitoba)
- Yolina Denchev (Camosun College)
- Livio Di Matteo (Lakehead University)
- Oliver Franke (Athabasca University)
- Shahidul Islam (Grant MacEwan College)
- Alok Johri (McMaster University)
- Rafal Kosztirko (Mount Royal College)
- Carol Chui Ha Lau (Concordia University)
- Stephen Law (Mount Allison University)
- Ambrose Leung (Bishop's University)
- A. Gyasi Nimarko (Vanier College)
- Derek Pyne (Memorial University)
- Neil Roberts (Kwantlen University College)
- Francisco J. Santos-Arteaga (York University)
- Rob Scharff (Kwantlen University College)
- Jim Sentance (University of Prince Edward Island)
- Prakash Sharma (University of Ottawa)
- Maurice Tugwell (Acadia University)
- Jane Waples (Memorial University)

We would like to express our thanks to the many people at Pearson Education Canada involved in the production of this textbook. Through several editions, we have been privileged to work closely with Gary Bennett (Editor-in-Chief), Maurice Esses (Developmental Editor), and Marisa D'Andrea (Production Editor), and are grateful for their experience, professionalism, and diligence and care in guiding this book through the publication process. Eileen Lasswell joined the team on this edition as the Marketing Manager and has brought a great deal of energy, enthusiasm, and creativity to this project. These individuals have been a pleasure to work with each step along the way and we are deeply grateful for their presence and their participation, and delighted to consider them friends as well as professional colleagues.

Our thanks also to the many people at Pearson with whom we work less closely but who nonetheless toil behind the scenes to produce this book, including Matthew Christian, Andrea Falkenberg, Julia Hall, Nelson Gonzalez, and Mary Rose MacLachlan.

Thanks also to Ann McInnis for copyediting, Kit Pasula for the technical review, and to Catharine Haggert and Hallie Benjamin for proofreading, all of whom provided an invaluable service with their attention to detail.

In short, we realize that there is a great deal more involved in producing a book than *just* the writing. Without the efforts from all of these dedicated professionals, this textbook simply would not exist. Our sincere thanks to all of you.

Finally, we would like to express our appreciation to Ingrid Kristjanson, who is deeply involved in all of the detailed work of the revision of the textbook. She discusses the revision ideas, reads first and second drafts, does her fair share of rewriting, and carefully handles the often-complex transcription process. In addition, for this edition she has played a central role in our complete rewriting and expansion of the *TestGen*. Without her, the revision of the textbook would be far less pleasant and efficient than it now is.

Christopher Ragan
Richard Lipsey

PART 1: WHAT IS ECONOMICS?

CHAPTER 1

Economic Issues and Concepts

LEARNING OBJECTIVES

In this chapter you will learn

1. to view the market economy as a self-organizing entity in which order emerges from a large number of decentralized decisions.
2. the importance of scarcity, choice, and opportunity cost, and how all three concepts are illustrated by the production possibilities boundary.
3. about the circular flow of income and expenditure.
4. that all actual economies are mixed economies, having elements of free markets, tradition, and government intervention.

If you want a litre of milk, you go to your local grocery store and buy it. When the grocer needs more milk, he orders it from the distributor, who in turn gets it from the dairy, which in its turn gets it from the dairy farmer. The dairy farmer buys cattle feed and electric milking machines, and gets power to run all his equipment by putting a plug into a wall outlet where the electricity is supplied as he needs it. The milking machines are made from parts manufactured in several different places in Canada, the United States, and overseas. The parts themselves are made from materials mined and smelted in a dozen or more different countries.

As it is with the milk you drink, so it is with everything else that you buy. When you go to the appropriate store, what you want is normally on the shelf. Those who make these products find that all the required components and materials are available when they need them—even though these things typically come from many different parts of the world and are made by people who have no direct dealings with each other.

1.1 THE COMPLEXITY OF THE MODERN ECONOMY

Your own transactions are only a small part of the remarkably complex set of transactions that takes place every day in a modern society. Shipments arrive daily at our ports, railway terminals, and airports. These shipments include: raw materials, such as iron ore, logs, and oil; parts, such as automobile engines, transistors, and circuit boards; tools, such as screwdrivers, lathes, and digging equipment; perishables, such as fresh flowers, coffee beans, and fruit; and all kinds of manufactured goods, such as washing machines, computers, and personal DVD players. Railways and trucking lines move these goods among thousands of different destinations within Canada. Some go directly to consumers. Others are used by local firms to manufacture their products—some of which will be sold domestically and some exported to other countries.

Most people who want to work can find work. They spend their working days engaging in the activities just described. In doing so, they earn incomes that they then spend on goods and services produced by others. Other people own firms that employ workers to assist in the many activities described above, such as importing, making, transporting, and selling things. They earn their incomes as profits from these enterprises.

economy A system in which scarce resources are allocated among competing uses.

An **economy** is a system, typically a very complex one, in which scarce resources—such as labour, land, and machines—are allocated among competing uses. Decisions must be made about: which goods are produced, and which are not; who works where and at what wage; and who consumes which goods at what times. While each of these individual decisions may seem simple, the entire combination is remarkably complex, especially in modern societies.

The Self-Organizing Economy

Early in the development of modern economics, thoughtful observers wondered how such a complex set of dealings gets organized. Who coordinates the whole set of efforts? Who makes sure that all the activities fit together, providing jobs to produce the things that people want and delivering those things to where they are wanted? The answer is, surprisingly, no one!

The great insight of economists is that an economy based on free-market transactions is *self-organizing.*

By following their own self-interest, doing what seems best and most profitable for themselves, and responding to the incentives of prices determined in open markets, people produce a spontaneous economic order. In that order, literally thousands of millions of transactions and activities fit together to produce the things that people want within the constraints set by the resources that are available to the nation.

The great Scottish economist and political philosopher Adam Smith (1723–1790),[1] who was the first to develop this insight fully, put it this way:

> *It is not from the benevolence of the butcher, the brewer, or the baker, that we expect our dinner, but from their regard to their own interest. We address ourselves, not to their humanity but to their self-love, and never talk to them of our own necessities but of their advantages.*

Smith is not saying that benevolence is unimportant. Indeed, he praises it in many passages. He is saying, however, that the massive number of economic interactions that characterize a modern economy cannot all be motivated by benevolence. Although benevolence does motivate some of our actions, often the very dramatic ones, the vast majority of our everyday actions are motivated by self-interest. Self-interest, not benevolence, is therefore the foundation of economic order.

Adam Smith wrote An Inquiry into the Nature and Causes of the Wealth of Nations *in 1776. Now referred to by most people simply as* The Wealth of Nations, *it is considered to be the beginning of modern economics.*

[1] Throughout this book, we encounter many great economists from the past whose ideas shaped the discipline of economics. At the back of the book you will find a timeline, beginning in the 1600s, that contains brief discussions of many of these thinkers and places them in their historical context.

Efficient Organization

Another great insight, which was hinted at by Smith and fully developed over the next century and a half, was that this spontaneously generated economic order is relatively *efficient.* Loosely speaking, efficiency means that the resources available to the nation are organized so as to produce the largest possible amount of the goods and services that people want to purchase, and to produce them with the least possible amount of resources.

An economy organized by free markets behaves almost as if it were guided by "an invisible hand," in Smith's now-famous words. This does not literally mean that a supernatural presence runs a market economy. Instead it refers to the relatively efficient order that emerges spontaneously out of the many independent decisions made by those who produce, sell, and buy goods and services. The key to explaining this market behaviour is that these decision makers all respond to the same set of prices, which are determined in markets that respond to overall conditions of national scarcity or plenty. Much of economics is devoted to a detailed elaboration of how this market order is generated, and to how efficiently that job is done.

Main Characteristics of Market Economies

What, then, are the main characteristics of market economies that produce this spontaneous self-organization?

Self-Interest. Individuals pursue their own self-interest, buying and selling what seems best for themselves and their families.

Incentives. People respond to incentives. Sellers usually want to sell more when prices are high; buyers usually want to buy more when prices are low.

Market Prices and Quantities. Prices and quantities are determined in free markets in which would-be sellers compete to sell their products to would-be buyers.

Institutions. All of these activities are governed by a set of institutions largely created by government. The most important are private property, freedom of contract, and the rule of law. The natures of private property and contractual obligations are defined by laws passed by legislatures and enforced by the police and the courts.

1.2 SCARCITY, CHOICE, AND OPPORTUNITY COST

All of the issues discussed so far would not matter much if we lived in an economy of such plenty that there was enough to satisfy all of everyone's wants. But such an economy is impossible. Why?

The short answer is, because we live in a world of *scarcity.* Compared to the known desires of individuals for such products as better food, clothing, housing, education, holidays, health care, and entertainment, the existing supplies of resources are clearly inadequate. They are sufficient to produce only a small fraction of the goods and services that people desire. This gives rise to the basic economic problem of choice under conditions of scarcity. If we cannot have everything we want, we must choose what we will and will not have.

One definition of *economics* comes from the great economist Alfred Marshall (1842–1924), whom we will encounter at several points in this book: "Economics is a study of mankind in the ordinary business of life." A more penetrating definition is the following:

Economics is the study of the use of scarce resources to satisfy unlimited human wants.

Scarcity is inevitable and is central to economic problems. What are society's resources? Why is scarcity inevitable? What are the consequences of scarcity?

Resources

A society's resources are often divided into the three broad categories of land, labour, and capital. *Land* includes all natural endowments such as arable land, forests, lakes, crude oil, and minerals. *Labour* includes all mental and physical human resources, including entrepreneurial capacity and management skills. *Capital* includes all manufactured aids to production such as tools, machinery, and buildings. Economists call such resources **factors of production** because they are used to produce the things that people desire. We divide what is produced into goods and services. **Goods** are tangible (e.g., cars and shoes), and **services** are intangible (e.g., haircuts and education).

People use goods and services to satisfy many of their wants. The act of making them is called **production,** and the act of using them to satisfy wants is called **consumption.** Goods are valued for the services they provide. An automobile, for example, helps to satisfy its owner's desires for transportation, mobility, and possibly status.

factors of production Resources used to produce goods and services; frequently divided into the basic categories of land, labour, and capital.

goods Tangible commodities, such as cars or shoes.

services Intangible commodities, such as haircuts or medical care.

production The act of making goods or services.

consumption The act of using goods or services to satisfy wants.

Scarcity and Choice

For almost all of the world's six billion people, scarcity is real and ever present. As we said above, relative to people's desires, existing resources are inadequate; there are enough to produce only a fraction of the goods and services that are wanted.

But are not the advanced industrialized nations rich enough that scarcity is nearly banished? After all, they have been characterized as affluent societies. Whatever affluence may mean, however, it does not mean the end of the problem of scarcity. Canadian households that earn $64 000 per year, the average Canadian household income in 2004 but a princely amount by *world* standards, have no trouble spending it on things that seem useful to them and they would certainly have no trouble convincing you that their resources are scarce relative to their desires.

Because resources are scarce, all societies face the problem of deciding what to produce and how much each person will consume. Societies differ in who makes the choices and how they are made, but the need to choose is common to all. Just as scarcity implies the need for choice, so choice implies the existence of cost. A decision to have more of something requires a decision to have less of something else. The less of "something else" can be thought of as the cost of having the more of "something."

Scarcity implies that choices must be made, and making choices implies the existence of costs.

Opportunity Cost To see how choice implies cost, we look first at a trivial example and then at one that affects all of us; both examples involve precisely the same fundamental principles.

Consider the choice David faces on a Saturday night when he goes out for pizza and beer with his friends. Suppose that he has only $16 for the night and that each beer costs $4 and each slice of pizza costs $2. Since David is both hungry and thirsty, he would like to have four slices of pizza and three beers, but this would cost $20 and is therefore unattainable given David's scarce resources of $16. There are several combinations, however, that are attainable: 8 slices of pizza and 0 beers; 6 slices of pizza and 1 beer; 4 slices of pizza and 2 beers; 2 slices of pizza and 3 beers; and 0 slices of pizza and 4 beers.

FIGURE 1-1 Choosing Between Pizza and Beer

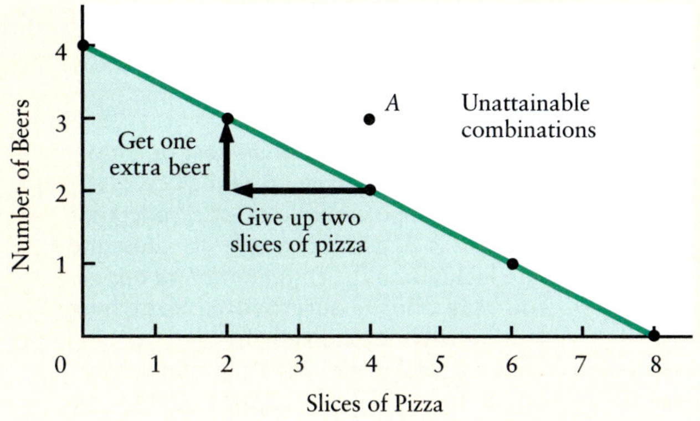

Limited resources force a choice among competing alternatives. Given a total of $16 to spend on $2 slices of pizza and $4 beers, some choices are unattainable, such as point *A*. The five points on the green line show all combinations that are attainable by spending the $16. If it were possible to buy parts of a beer and parts of a slice of pizza, then *all* combinations on the line and in the green area would be attainable. If the entire $16 is to be spent, the choice between more pizza and more beer involves an opportunity cost. The *slope* of the green line reflects opportunity costs. The opportunity cost of one extra slice of pizza is half of a beer; the opportunity cost of one extra beer is two slices of pizza.

David's choices are illustrated in Figure 1-1, which graphs the combinations of beers and slices of pizza that David considers buying. The numbers of pieces of pizza are shown on the horizontal axis; the numbers of beers are shown on the vertical axis. The downward-sloping line connects the five possible combinations of beer and pizza that use up all of David's resources—$16. Notice that point *A* shows a combination—4 slices of pizza and 3 beers—that lies outside the line because its total cost is more than $16. Point *A* is *unattainable* to David. If David could buy fractions of a beer and of a piece of pizza, *all* points that lie on or inside the line would be *attainable* combinations.

In this setting David can ask himself, "What is the cost of one beer?" One answer is that the cost is $4. An equivalent answer, assuming that he wished to spend all of this $16 on these two items, is that the cost of one beer is the two slices of pizza he must give up to get it. In fact, we say in this case that two slices of pizza is the *opportunity cost* of one beer since it is the opportunity David must give up to get one extra beer.

Practise with Study Guide Chapter 1, Exercise 3.

Every time a choice is made, opportunity costs are incurred.

The idea of opportunity cost is one of the central insights of economics. Here is a precise definition. The **opportunity cost** of using resources for a certain purpose is defined to be *the benefit given up by not using them in the best alternative way.* That is, it is the cost measured in terms of other goods and services that could have been obtained instead. If, for example, resources that could have produced 20 km of road are best used instead to produce one hospital, the opportunity cost of a hospital is 20 km of road; looked at the other way round, the opportunity cost of 1 km of road is one-twentieth of a hospital.

opportunity cost The cost of using resources for a certain purpose, measured by the benefit given up by not using them in their best alternative use.

See *Applying Economic Concepts 1-1* for an example of opportunity cost that should seem quite familiar to you—the opportunity cost of getting a university degree.

Production Possibilities Boundary Although David's choice between pizza and beer may seem to be a trivial consumption decision, the nature of the decision is the same whatever the choice being made. Consider, for example, the choice that any country must face between producing military and civilian goods.

APPLYING ECONOMIC CONCEPTS 1-1

The Opportunity Cost of Your University Degree

As discussed in the text, the opportunity cost of choosing one thing is what must be given up as the best alternative. Computing the opportunity cost of a college or university education is a good example to illustrate which factors are included in the computation of opportunity cost. You may also be surprised to learn how expensive your university degree really is!*

Suppose that a bachelor's degree requires four years of study and that each year you spend $6000 for tuition fees—approximately the average at Canadian universities in 2007—and a further $1500 per year for books and materials. Does this mean that the cost of a university education is only $30 000? Unfortunately not; the true cost of a university degree is much higher.

The key point is that the opportunity cost of a university education does not just include the out-of-pocket expenses on tuition and books. You must also take into consideration *what you are forced to give up* by choosing to attend university. Of course, if you were not studying you could have been doing any one of a number of things, but the relevant one is *the one you would have chosen instead*—your best alternative to attending university.

Suppose that your best alternative to attending university was to get a job. In this case, the opportunity cost of your university degree must include the earnings that you would have received had you taken that job. Suppose that your (after-tax) annual earnings would have been $20 000 per year, for a total of $80 000 if you had stayed at that job for four years. To the direct expenses of $30 000, we must therefore add $80 000 for the earnings that you gave up by not taking a job. This brings the true cost of your university degree—the opportunity cost—up to $110 000!

*This box considers only the cost *to the student* of a university degree. For reasons that will be discussed in detail in Part Six of this book, provincial governments heavily subsidize post-secondary education in Canada. Because of this subsidy, the cost *to society* of a university degree is generally much higher than the cost to an individual student.

Notice that the cost of food, lodging, clothing, and other living expenses did not enter the calculation of the opportunity cost in this example. The living expenses must be incurred in either case—whether you attend university or get a job.

If the opportunity cost of a degree is so high, why do students choose to go to university? The simple answer is that they believe that they are better off by going to university than by not going (otherwise they would not go). Maybe the students simply enjoy learning, and thus are prepared to incur the high cost to be in the university environment. Or maybe they believe that a university degree will significantly increase their future earning potential. (In Chapter 14 we will see that this is true.) In this case, they are giving up four years of earnings at one salary so that they can invest in their own skills in the hope of enjoying many more years in the future at a considerably higher salary.

Whatever the reason for attending college or university, the recognition that a post-secondary degree is very expensive should convince students to make the best use of their time while they are there. Read on!

The opportunity cost to an individual completing a university degree in Canada is large. It includes the direct cost of tuition and books as well as the earnings forgone while attending university.

Practise with Study Guide Chapter 1, Exercise 4.

If resources are fully and efficiently employed, it is not possible to have more of both. However, as the government cuts defence expenditures, resources needed to produce civilian goods will be freed up. The opportunity cost of increased civilian goods is therefore the forgone military output. Or, if we were considering an increase in military output, the opportunity cost of increased military output would be the forgone civilian goods.

production possibilities boundary A curve showing which alternative combinations of commodities can just be attained if all available resources are used efficiently; it is the boundary between attainable and unattainable output combinations.

The choice is illustrated in Figure 1-2. Because resources are scarce, some combinations—those that would require more than the total available supply of resources for their production—cannot be attained. The negatively sloped curve on the graph divides the combinations that can be attained from those that cannot. Points above and to the right of this curve cannot be attained because there are not enough resources; points below and to the left of the curve can be attained without using all of the available resources; and points on the curve can just be attained if all the available resources are used efficiently. The curve is called the **production possibilities boundary.** (Sometimes the word "boundary" is replaced with "curve" or "frontier.") It has a negative slope because when all resources are being used efficiently, producing more of one kind of good requires producing less of the other kind.

A production possibilities boundary illustrates three concepts: scarcity, choice, and opportunity cost. Scarcity is indicated by the unattainable combinations outside the boundary; choice, by the need to choose among the alternative attainable points along the boundary; and opportunity cost, by the negative slope of the boundary.

FIGURE 1-2 A Production Possibilities Boundary

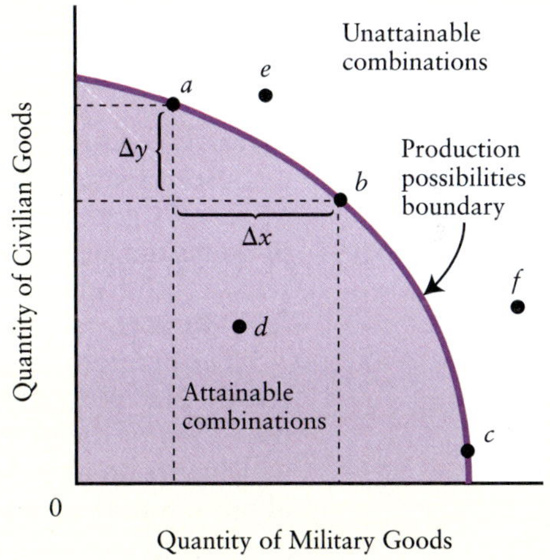

The negatively sloped boundary shows the combinations that are attainable when all resources are efficiently used. The production possibilities boundary separates the attainable combinations of goods, such as *a*, *b*, *c*, and *d*, from unattainable combinations, such as *e* and *f*. Points *a*, *b*, and *c* represent full and efficient use of society's resources. Point *d* represents either inefficient use of resources or failure to use all the available resources. If production moves from point *a* to point *b*, an opportunity cost is involved. The opportunity cost of producing Δx more military goods is the necessary reduction in the production of civilian goods equal to Δy.

The shape of the production possibilities boundary in Figure 1-2 implies that an increasing amount of civilian production must be given up to achieve equal successive increases in military production. This shape, referred to as *concave* to the origin, indicates that the opportunity cost of either good increases as we increase the amount of it that is produced. A straight-line boundary, as in Figure 1-1, indicates that the opportunity cost of one good in terms of the other stays constant, no matter how much of it is produced.

The concave shape in Figure 1-2 is the way in which economists usually draw a country's production possibilities boundary. The shape occurs because each factor of production is not equally useful in producing all

Practise with Study Guide Chapter 1, Exercise 2.

goods. To see why differences among factors of production are so important, suppose we begin at point *c* in Figure 1-2, where most resources are devoted to the production of military goods, and then consider gradually shifting more and more resources toward the production of civilian goods. We might begin by shifting nutrient-rich land that is particularly well suited to growing wheat. This land may not be very useful for making military equipment, but it is very useful for making certain civilian goods (like bread). This shift of resources will therefore lead to a small reduction in military output but a substantial increase in civilian output. Thus, the opportunity cost of producing a few more units of civilian goods, which is equal to the forgone military output, is small. But as we shift more and more resources toward the production of civilian goods, and therefore move along the production possibilities boundary toward point *a*, we must shift more and more resources that are actually quite well suited to the production of military output, like aerospace engineers or the minerals needed to make gunpowder. As we produce more and more civilian goods (by having more and more resources devoted to producing them), the amount of military output that must be forgone to produce one *extra* unit of civilian goods rises. That is, the opportunity cost of producing one good rises as more of that good is produced.

Four Key Economic Problems

Practise with Study Guide Chapter 1, Exercise 1.

Modern economies involve thousands of complex production and consumption activities. Although this complexity is important, many of the basic kinds of decisions that must be made are not very different from those made in primitive economies in which people work with few tools and barter with their neighbours. Whatever the economic system, whether modern or primitive, there are four key economic questions.

resource allocation The allocation of an economy's scarce resources of land, labour, and capital among alternative uses.

What Is Produced and How?

This question concerns the *allocation* of scarce resources among alternative uses. Such **resource allocation** determines the quantities of various goods that are produced. Choosing to produce a particular combination of goods means choosing a particular allocation of resources among the industries or regions producing the goods. What determines which goods get produced and which ones do not?

Furthermore, because resources are scarce, it is desirable that they be used efficiently. Hence, it matters which of the available methods of production is used to produce each of the goods. What determines which methods of production get used and which ones do not? Any economy must have some mechanism by which these decisions about resource allocation are made.

What Is Consumed and By Whom?

What is the relationship between an economy's production of goods and the consumption enjoyed by its citizens? Economists seek to understand what determines the distribution of a nation's total output among its people. Who gets a lot, who gets a little, and why?

If production takes place on the production possibilities boundary, then how about consumption? Will the economy consume exactly the same goods that it produces? Or will the country's ability to trade with other countries permit the economy to consume a different combination of goods?

microeconomics The study of the causes and consequences of the allocation of resources as it is affected by the workings of the price system.

Questions relating to what is produced and how, and what is consumed and by whom, fall within the realm of microeconomics. **Microeconomics** is the study of the causes and consequences of the allocation of resources as it is affected by the workings of the price system and government policies that seek to influence it.

Why Are Resources Sometimes Idle? Sometimes many workers who would like to have jobs are unable to find employers to hire them. At the same time, the managers and owners of offices and factories could operate at a higher level of activity—that is, they could produce more goods and services. For some reason, however, these resources—labour, factories, and equipment—lie idle. Thus, in terms of Figure 1-2, the economy is operating inside its production possibilities boundary.

Why are resources sometimes idle? Should governments worry about such idle resources, or is there some reason to believe that such occasional idleness is appropriate in a well-functioning economy? Is there anything that the government can do to reduce such idleness?

Is Productive Capacity Growing? The capacity to produce goods and services grows rapidly in some countries, grows slowly in others, and actually declines in others. Growth in productive capacity can be represented by an outward shift of the production possibilities boundary, as shown in Figure 1-3. If an economy's capacity to produce goods and services is growing, some combinations that are unattainable today will become attainable in the future. Growth makes it possible to have more of all goods. What are the determinants of growth? Are there some undesirable side-effects of growth? Can governments do anything to influence economic growth?

FIGURE 1-3 The Effect of Economic Growth on the Production Possibilities Boundary

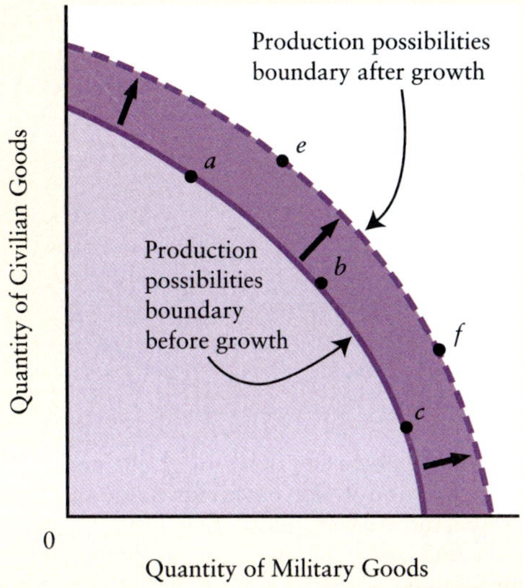

Economic growth shifts the boundary outward and makes it possible to produce more of all products. Before growth in productive capacity, points *a, b,* and *c* were on the production possibilities boundary and points *e* and *f* were unattainable. After growth, as shown by the dark shaded band, points *e* and *f* and many other previously unattainable combinations are attainable.

Questions relating to the idleness of resources and the growth of productive capacity fall within the realm of macroeconomics. **Macroeconomics** is the study of the determination of economic aggregates such as total output, total employment, the price level, and the rate of economic growth.

macroeconomics The study of the determination of economic aggregates such as total output, the price level, employment, and growth.

1.3 WHO MAKES THE CHOICES AND HOW?

So choices have to be made, but who makes them and how are they made?

The Flow of Income and Expenditure

Figure 1-4 shows the basic decision makers and the flows of income and expenditure that they set up. Individuals own factors of production. They sell the services of these factors to producers and receive payments in return. These are their incomes. Producers use the factor services that they buy to make goods and services. They sell these to individuals, receiving payments in return. These are the incomes of producers. These basic flows of income and expenditure pass through markets. Individuals sell the services of the factor that they own in what are collectively called *factor markets.*

FIGURE 1-4 The Circular Flow of Income and Expenditure

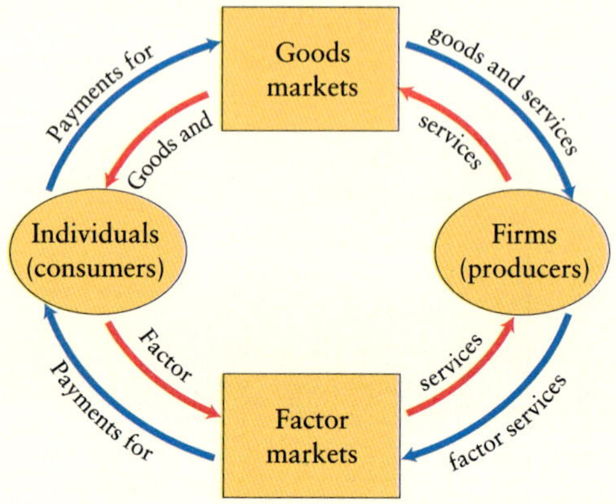

The red line shows the flows of goods and services; the blue line shows the payments made to purchase these. Factor services flow from individuals who own the factors (including their own labour) through factor markets to firms that use them to make goods and services. These goods and services then flow through goods markets to those who consume them. Money payments flow from firms to individuals through factor markets. These payments become the income of individuals. When they spend this income buying goods and services, money flows through goods markets back to producers.

When you get a part-time job during university, you are participating in the factor market. Producers sell their outputs of goods and services in what are collectively called *goods markets.* When you purchase a haircut or a new pair of shoes, for example, you are participating in the goods market.

The prices that are determined in these markets determine the incomes that are earned and the purchasing power of those incomes. People who get high prices for their factor services earn high incomes; those who get low prices earn low incomes. The income each person earns expressed as a fraction of all incomes that are earned in the nation shows the share of total income that each person can command. The *distribution of income* refers to how the nation's total income is distributed among its citizens. This is largely determined by the price that each type of factor service receives in factor markets.

Maximizing Decisions The basic decision makers in a market economy are individual consumers and producers. To these two groups we will shortly add a third, the government. The important assumption that economists usually make about how these two groups make their decisions is that everyone tries to do as well as possible for himself or herself. In the jargon of economics, people are assumed to be *maximizers.* When individuals decide how many factor services to sell to producers and how many products to buy from them, we assume that they make choices designed to maximize their well-being, or *utility.* When producers decide how many factor services to buy from individuals and how many goods to produce and sell to them, we assume that they make choices designed to maximize their *profits.*

Marginal Decisions Firms and consumers who are trying to maximize usually need to weigh the costs and benefits of their decisions *at the margin.* For example, when you consider buying an additional CD, you know the *marginal cost* of the CD—that is, how much you must pay to get one extra CD—and you need to weigh it against the *marginal benefit* that you will derive from that CD. If you are trying to maximize your utility, you will only buy that CD if you think that the benefit to you in terms of extra utility exceeds the marginal cost.

Similarly, a producer attempting to maximize its profits and considering whether to hire an extra worker must evaluate the *marginal cost* of the worker—the extra wages and benefits that must be paid—and weigh it against the *marginal benefit* of the worker—the increase in revenues that will be generated by the extra worker. A producer interested in maximizing its profit will only hire the extra worker if the benefit in terms of extra revenue exceeds the cost in terms of higher wages.

Consumers and producers who are maximizers are constantly making marginal decisions, whether to buy or sell a little bit more or less of the many things that they buy and sell.

Voting in an election is an example where decisions are *not* made on a marginal basis. When you vote in a Canadian federal election, you have only one vote and you must support one party over the others. When you do, you vote for everything that party stands for, even though you may prefer to pick and choose elements from each party's political platform. You cannot say "I vote for the Liberals on issue A and for the Conservatives on issue B." You must make a total, rather than a marginal, decision.

The Complexity of Production

Producers decide what to produce and how to produce it. Production is a very complex process in any modern economy. A typical car manufacturer assembles a product out of thousands of individual parts. It makes some of these parts itself. Most are subcontracted to parts manufacturers, and many of the major parts manufacturers subcontract some of their work out to smaller firms. This kind of production displays two characteristics noted long ago by Adam Smith—*specialization* and the *division of labour.*

Specialization In ancient hunter–gatherer societies, and in modern subsistence economies, most people make most of the things they need for themselves. However, from the time that people first engaged in settled agriculture and some of them began to live in towns, people have specialized in doing particular jobs. Artisan, soldier, priest, and government official were some of the earliest specialized occupations. Economists call this allocation of different jobs to different people the **specialization of labour**. There are two fundamental reasons why specialization is extraordinarily efficient compared with universal self-sufficiency.

specialization of labour The specialization of individual workers in the production of particular goods or services.

First, individual abilities differ, and specialization allows each person to do what he or she can do relatively well while leaving everything else to be done by others. Even when people's abilities are unaffected by the act of specializing, the economy's total production is greater when people specialize than when they all try to be self-sufficient. This is true for individuals but it is also true for entire countries, and it is one of the most fundamental principles in economics: the principle of *comparative advantage.* A much fuller discussion of comparative advantage is found in Chapter 33, in which we discuss the gains from international trade.

The second reason that specialization is more efficient than self-sufficiency concerns changes in people's abilities that occur *because* they specialize. A person who concentrates on one activity becomes better at it than could a jack-of-all-trades. This is called *learning by doing,* and was a factor much stressed by early economists; modern research shows that it is important in many modern industries.

The Division of Labour Throughout most of history each artisan who specialized in making some product made the whole of that product. Over the last several hundred years, many technical advances have made it efficient to organize production methods into large-scale firms organized around what is called the **division of labour**. This term refers to specialization *within* the production process of a particular product.

division of labour The breaking up of a production process into a series of specialized tasks, each done by a different worker.

Mass Production. In a mass-production factory, work is divided into highly specialized tasks using specialized machinery. Each individual repeatedly does one small task that is a small fraction of those necessary to produce any one product. This is an extreme case of the division of labour.

Artisans and Flexible Manufacturing. Two recent changes have significantly altered the degree of specialization found in many modern production processes. First, individual artisans have recently reappeared in some lines of production. They are responding to a revival in the demand for individually crafted, rather than mass-produced, products. Second, many manufacturing operations are being reorganized along new lines called "lean production" or "flexible manufacturing," which was pioneered by Japanese car manufacturers in the mid-1950s. It has led back to a more craft-based form of organization within the factory. In this technique, employees work as a team; each employee is able to do every team member's job rather than only one very specialized task at one point on the assembly line.

Globalization

Market economies constantly change, largely as a result of the development of new technologies. Many of the recent changes are referred to as *globalization,* a term often used loosely to mean the increased importance of international trade. International trade is, however, a very old phenomenon. The usual pattern over most of the last 200 years was manufactured goods being sent from Europe and North America to the rest of the world, with raw materials and primary products being sent in return. What is new in the last few decades is the globalization of manufacturing. Assembly of a product may take place in the most industrialized countries, but the hundreds of component parts are manufactured in dozens of different countries and delivered to the assembly plant "just in time" for assembly.

A major cause of globalization is the rapid reduction in transportation costs and the revolution in information technology that has occurred in the past 50 years. The cost of moving products around the world has fallen greatly over the last half of the twentieth century because of containerization and the increasing size of ships. Our ability to transmit and analyze data has been increasing even more dramatically, while the costs of doing so have been decreasing, equally dramatically. For example, today $1500 buys an ultra-slim laptop computer that has the same computing power as one that in 1970 cost $10 million and filled a large room. This revolution in information and communication technology has made it possible to coordinate economic transactions around the world in ways that were difficult and costly 50 years ago and quite impossible 100 years ago.

transnational corporations (TNCs) Firms that have operations in more than one country. Also called *multinational enterprises (MNEs).*

Globalization is as important for consumers as it is for producers. For example, as some tastes become universal to young people, spread by ever-increasing access to foreign television stations and global Internet chat lines, we can see the same clothes and hear the same music in virtually all big cities. And as tastes become more universal, many *corporations* are globalizing, as they become what economists call **transnational corporations (TNCs)**. McDonald's restaurants are as visible in Moscow or Beijing as in London, New York, Vancouver, or Montreal. Many other brands are also known around the world, such as Calvin Klein, Nike, Coca-Cola, Kellogg's, Heinz, Nestlé, Molson, Toyota, Rolls-Royce, Sony, and Mitsubishi.

The revolution in shipping and in computer technology has drastically reduced communication and transportation costs. This reduction in costs lies at the heart of globalization.

Through the ongoing process of globalization, national economies are ever more linked to the global economy, in which an increasing share of jobs and incomes is created.

The word *globalization* has recently become a focal point for an important and contentious set of policy debates and public protests. These debates are often very confusing to the observer. See *Applying Economic Concepts 1-2* for a brief outline of the key issues.

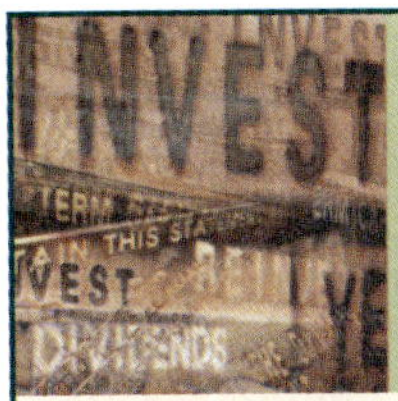

APPLYING ECONOMIC CONCEPTS 1-2

The Globalization Debate

Over the past several years, large public "globalization protests" have occurred in many cities around the world. These protests often occur when political leaders from many countries gather to discuss and negotiate agreements regarding international trade or finance. For example, in December 1999, the trade ministers from member countries of the World Trade Organization (WTO) met in Seattle to set the agenda for a new round of talks at which they would negotiate rules governing international trade. Thousands of angry protesters lined the streets of Seattle, throwing rocks and shouting slogans about the dangers of globalization and the undemocratic nature of the WTO talks. Thus, the "Battle of Seattle" was joined. Over the next few years, similar protests took place in Quebec City, Genoa, and several times in Washington, D.C. What are these protests about? What are the key issues?

The protesters, who generally refer to themselves as "anti-globalization activists," have two main arguments. First, they argue that increases in the flow of international trade and investment have been responsible for increasing global income inequality and worsening poverty in developing countries. Second, they argue that organizations such as the WTO, the World Bank, and the International Monetary Fund (IMF) operate in an undemocratic fashion and hold their meetings behind closed doors, out of view of and without critical input from the people whose lives their policies are so dramatically influencing. A related concern is that global economic agreements appear to give power to transnational corporations, taking power out of the hands of citizens. The anti-globalization activists are in favour of slowing down the process of globalization and reforming (if not eliminating) these international organizations.

On the other side of the barricades are the defenders of globalization and a rules-based approach to international trade. They argue that the process of globalization, far from being the cause of poverty in developing countries, is the best bet for *reducing* such poverty. They claim that freer trade between countries has been responsible for enormous advances in living standards over the past century, and that the developing countries of today will be much better off if trade is further liberalized. Indeed, some defenders of globalization argue that one of the problems has been the developed countries' unwillingness to permit genuinely free international trade with the developing countries—especially for products such as agricultural commodities and textiles in which the developing countries have a competitive advantage. According to this view, the biggest contributor to poverty in developing countries is too *little* trade, not too much.

Defenders of globalization also point out that the meetings held by the WTO and other international organizations are voluntary meetings held between the democratically elected leaders of the member countries, and that no agreements are legal until each of the member countries ratifies them in its parliament. Thus, the process is democratic.

Is there a middle ground in this debate? On the democratic issue, the defenders of globalization are probably correct, at least literally. The agreements do not come into force until they are passed by the respective parliaments. The political challenge for all countries involved is to improve communications so that these complicated international agreements—which often run to thousands of pages in length—are made clear enough that they can be effectively debated in the respective parliaments. With effective political debates within each member country, citizens will be more involved in the policy-making process.

The more subtle issue is the relationship between globalization and poverty. Most economists would argue, for reasons that we will explore in Chapters 33 and 34, that freer trade will lead to increases in *average* living standards within both developed and developing countries. A typical empirical finding is that an economy whose trade share increases from 20 percent to 40 percent of its GDP can expect to experience a 10-percent increase in per capita income. But there is no guarantee that, within any particular country, these gains in living standards will be shared among the various segments of society in a socially just way. One of the crucial challenges faced by governments negotiating international economic agreements is to ensure that the benefits from such agreements are spread throughout the population, thus increasing their public acceptability.

Markets and Money

People who specialize in doing only one thing must satisfy most of their wants by consuming things made by other people. In early societies the exchange of goods and services took place by simple mutual agreement among neighbours. In the course of time, however, trading became centred on particular gathering places called *markets*. For example, the French markets or trade fairs of Champagne were well-known throughout Europe as early as the eleventh century. Even now, many small towns in Canada have regular market days. Today, however, the term *market* has a much broader meaning. We use the term *market economy* to refer to a society in which people specialize in productive activities and meet most of their material wants through voluntary exchanges with other people.

Specialization must be accompanied by trade. People who produce only one thing must trade most of it to obtain all of the other things they desire.

barter An economic system in which goods and services are traded directly for other goods and services.

Early trading was by means of **barter**, the trading of goods directly for other goods. But barter is costly in terms of time spent searching out satisfactory exchanges. If a farmer has wheat but wants a hammer, he must find someone who has a hammer and wants wheat. A successful barter transaction thus requires what is called a *double coincidence of wants*.

Money eliminates the cumbersome system of barter by separating the transactions involved in the exchange of products. If a farmer has wheat and wants a hammer, he merely has to find someone who wants wheat. The farmer takes money in exchange. Then he finds a person who wishes to sell a hammer and gives up the money for the hammer.

Money greatly facilitates specialization and trade.

1.4 IS THERE AN ALTERNATIVE TO THE MARKET ECONOMY?

In this chapter we have discussed the elements of an economy based on free-market transactions—what we call a *market economy*. But are there any alternatives to this type of economy? The answer is no in one sense and yes in another. We answer no because the modern economy has no *practical* alternative to reliance on market determination. We answer yes because it is possible to identify other types of economic systems.

Types of Economic Systems

It is helpful to distinguish three pure types of economies, called *traditional, command,* and *market* economies. These economies differ in the way in which economic decisions are coordinated. But no actual economy fits neatly into one of these three categories—all real economies contain some elements of each type.

traditional economy An economy in which behaviour is based mostly on tradition.

Traditional Economies

A **traditional economy** is one in which behaviour is based primarily on tradition, custom, and habit. Young men follow their fathers' occupations. Women do what their mothers did. There is little change in the pattern of goods produced from year to year, other than those imposed by the vagaries of nature. The techniques of production also follow traditional patterns, except when the effects of an occasional new invention are felt. Finally, production is allocated among the members according to long-established traditions.

Such a system works best in an unchanging environment. Under such static conditions, a system that does not continually require people to make choices can prove effective in meeting economic and social needs.

Traditional systems were common in earlier times. The feudal system, under which most people in medieval Europe lived, was a largely traditional society. Peasants, artisans, and most others living in villages inherited their positions in that society. They also usually inherited their specific jobs, which they handled in traditional ways.

Command Economies In command economies, economic behaviour is determined by some central authority, usually the government, which makes most of the necessary decisions on what to produce, how to produce it, and who gets it. Such economies are characterized by the *centralization* of decision making. Because centralized decision makers usually lay down elaborate and complex plans for the behaviour that they wish to impose, the terms **command economy** and *centrally planned economy* are usually used synonymously.

command economy An economy in which most economic decisions are made by a central planning authority.

The sheer quantity of data required for the central planning of an entire economy is enormous, and the task of analyzing it to produce a fully integrated plan can hardly be exaggerated. Moreover, the plan must be continually modified to take account not only of current data but also of future trends in labour supplies, technological developments, and people's tastes for various goods and services. This is a notoriously difficult exercise, not least because of the unavailability of all essential, accurate, and up-to-date information.

Thirty years ago, more than one-third of the world's population lived in countries that relied heavily on central planning. Today, the number of such countries is small. Even in countries where central planning is the proclaimed system, as in Cuba, increasing amounts of market determination are being quietly permitted.

Free-Market Economies In the third type of economic system, the decisions about resource allocation are made without any central direction. Instead, they result from innumerable independent decisions made by individual producers and consumers. Such a system is known as a **free-market economy** or, more simply, a *market economy.* In such an economy, decisions relating to the basic economic issues are *decentralized.* Despite the absence of a central plan, these many decentralized decisions are nonetheless coordinated. As we discussed earlier in the chapter, the main coordinating device is the set of market-determined prices—which is why free-market systems are often called *price systems.*

free-market economy An economy in which most economic decisions are made by private households and firms.

In a pure market economy, all of these decisions are made by buyers and sellers acting through unhindered markets. The state provides the background of defining property and protecting rights against foreign and domestic enemies but, beyond that, markets determine all resource allocation and income distribution.

Mixed Economies Economies that are fully traditional or fully centrally planned or wholly free-market are pure types that are useful for studying basic principles. When we look in detail at any real economy, however, we discover that its economic behaviour is the result of some mixture of central control and market determination, with a certain amount of traditional behaviour as well.

In practice, every economy is a **mixed economy** in the sense that it combines significant elements of all three systems in determining economic behaviour.

mixed economy An economy in which some economic decisions are made by firms and households and some by the government.

Furthermore, within any economy, the degree of the mix varies from sector to sector. For example, in some planned economies, the command principle was used more often to determine behaviour in heavy-goods industries, such as steel, than in agriculture. Farmers were often given substantial freedom to produce and sell what they wished in response to varying market prices.

When economists speak of a particular economy as being centrally planned, we mean only that the degree of the mix is weighted heavily toward the command principle. When we speak of one as being a market economy, we mean only that the degree of the mix is weighted heavily toward decentralized decision making.

Although no country offers an example of either system working alone, some economies, such as those of Canada, the United States, France, and Hong Kong, rely much more heavily on market decisions than others, such as the economies of China, North Korea, and Cuba. Yet even in Canada, the command principle has some sway. Crown corporations, legislated minimum wages, rules and regulations for environmental protection, quotas on some agricultural outputs, and restrictions on the import of some items are just a few examples.

The Great Debate

As we saw earlier, in 1776 Adam Smith was one of the first people to analyze the operation of markets, and he stressed the relative efficiency of free-market economies. A century later, another great economist and political philosopher, Karl Marx (1818–1883), argued that although free-market economies would indeed be successful in producing high levels of output, they could not be relied on to ensure that this output would be justly distributed among citizens. He argued the benefits of a centrally planned system in which the government could ensure a more equitable distribution of output.

Beginning with the Soviet Union in the early 1920s, many nations followed Marx's thinking and adopted systems in which conscious government central planning replaced the operation of the free market. For almost a century, a great debate then raged on the relative merits of command economies versus market economies. Along with the Soviet Union, the countries of Eastern Europe and China were command economies for much of the twentieth century. Canada, the United States, and most of the countries of Western Europe were, and still are, primarily market economies. The apparent successes of the Soviet Union and China in the 1950s and 1960s, including the ability to mobilize considerable resources into heavy industries, suggested to many observers that the command principle was at least as good for organizing economic behaviour as the market principle. Over the long run, however, planned economies proved to be a failure of such disastrous proportions that they seriously depressed the living standards of their citizens. Within the last two decades of the twentieth century, these countries abandoned their central planning apparatus and began the difficult transition back toward market economies.

Lessons From History 1-1 discusses in more detail why the centrally planned economies failed. This failure suggests the superiority of decentralized markets over centrally planned ones as mechanisms for allocating an economy's scarce resources. Put another way, it demonstrates the superiority of mixed economies with substantial elements of market determination over fully planned command economies. However, it does *not* demonstrate, as some observers have asserted, the superiority of completely free-market economies over mixed economies.

There is no guarantee that completely free markets will, on their own, handle such urgent matters as controlling pollution or providing public goods (like national defence). Indeed, as we shall see in later chapters, much economic theory is devoted to explaining why free markets often *fail* to do these things. Mixed economies, with significant elements of government intervention, are needed to do these jobs.

Furthermore, acceptance of the free market over central planning does not provide an excuse to ignore a country's pressing social issues. Acceptance of the benefits of the free market still leaves plenty of scope to debate the most appropriate levels and types of government policies directed at achieving specific social goals. It follows that there is still considerable room for disagreement about the degree of the mix of market and government determination in any modern mixed economy—room enough to accommodate such divergent views as could be expressed by conservative, liberal, and modern social democratic parties.

So, the first answer to the question about the existence of an alternative to the market economy is no: There is no practical alternative to a mixed system with major reliance on markets but some government presence in most aspects of the economy. The second answer is yes: Within the framework of a mixed economy there are substantial alternatives among many different and complex mixes of free-market and government determination of economic life.

myeconlab

The debate regarding the appropriate roles of governments and free markets figures prominently in discussions of how today's developing countries can best bring about improvements in their citizens' living standards. For a detailed discussion of the "Challenges Facing the Developing Countries," see the *Additional Topics* section of this book's MyEconLab.

www.myeconlab.com

Government in the Modern Mixed Economy

Market economies in today's advanced industrial countries are based primarily on voluntary transactions between individual buyers and sellers. Private individuals have the right to buy and sell what they wish, to accept or refuse work that is offered to them, and to move where they want when they want.

Key institutions are private property and freedom of contract, both of which must be maintained by active government policies. The government creates laws of ownership and contract and then provides the institutions to enforce these laws.

In modern mixed economies, governments go well beyond these important basic functions. They intervene in market transactions to correct what economists call *market failures*. These are well-defined situations in which free markets do not work well. Some products, called *public goods*, are usually not provided at all by markets because their use cannot usually be restricted to those who pay for them. Defence and police protection are examples of public goods. In other cases, private transactors impose costs called *externalities* on those who have no say in the transaction. This is the case when factories pollute the air and rivers. The public is harmed but plays no part in the transaction. These market failures explain why governments sometimes intervene to alter the allocation of resources.

Also, important equity issues arise from letting free markets determine people's incomes. Some people lose their jobs because firms are reorganizing to become more

LESSONS FROM HISTORY 1-1

The Failure of Central Planning

The fall of the Berlin Wall in November 1989 was the beginning of the end of the Soviet system of central planning.

The Bolshevik Revolution in 1917 in Russia brought the world its first example of a large-scale communist society. With the rise to power of Joseph Stalin and the creation of the Soviet Union in 1922, communism and central economic planning began their spread throughout Eastern and Central Europe. This spread of central planning was accelerated by the Soviet Union's role following the Second World War in "liberating" several countries from Nazi domination, thus creating the group of countries that became known as the Eastern Bloc or the Soviet Bloc.

Despite the successful geographic spread of communism, the Soviet system of central economic planning had many difficulties. By 1989, communism had collapsed throughout Central and Eastern Europe, and the economic systems of formerly communist countries began the difficult transition from centrally planned to market economies. Although political issues surely played a role in these events, the economic changes generally confirmed the superiority of a market-oriented price system over central planning as a method of organizing economic activity. The failure of central planning had many causes, but four were particularly significant.

Failure of Coordination

In the centrally planned economies, a body of planners attempted to coordinate all the economic decisions about production, investment, trade, and consumption that were likely to be made by producers and consumers throughout the country. Without the use of prices to signal relative scarcity and abundance, central planning generally proved impossible to do with any reasonable degree of success. Bottlenecks in production, shortages of some goods, and gluts of others plagued the Soviet economy for decades.

efficient in the face of new technologies. Others keep their jobs, but the market places so little value on their services that they face economic deprivation. The old and the chronically ill may suffer if their past circumstances did not allow them to save enough to support themselves. For many reasons of this sort, almost everyone accepts some government intervention to redistribute income. Care must be taken, however, not to kill the goose that lays the golden egg. By taking too much from higher-income people, we risk eliminating their incentive to work hard and produce income, some of which is to be redistributed to those in need.

Failure of Quality Control

Central planners could monitor the number of units produced by any factory and reward plants that exceeded their production targets and punish those that fell short. Factory managers operating under these conditions would meet their quotas by whatever means were available, and once the goods passed out of their factory, what happened to them was someone else's headache.

In market economies, poor quality is punished by low sales, and retailers soon give a signal to factory managers by shifting their purchases to other suppliers. The incentives that obviously flow from such private-sector purchasing discretion were generally absent from centrally planned economies, where purchases and sales were organized by the body of planners and prices and profits were not used to signal customer satisfaction or dissatisfaction.

Misplaced Incentives

In market economies, relative wages and salaries provide incentives for labour to move from place to place, and the possibility of losing one's job provides an incentive to work diligently. This is a harsh mechanism that punishes job losers with loss of income (although social programs provide floors to the amount of economic punishment that can be suffered). In centrally planned economies, workers usually had complete job security. Industrial unemployment was rare, and even when it did occur, new jobs were usually found for all who lost theirs. Although the high level of security was attractive to many people, it proved impossible to provide sufficient incentives for reasonably hard and efficient work under such conditions.

Environmental Degradation

Fulfilling production plans became the all-embracing goal in centrally planned economies, to the exclusion of most other considerations, including the environment. As a result, environmental degradation occurred in the Soviet Union and the countries of Eastern Europe on a scale unknown in advanced Western nations. A particularly disturbing example (only one of many) occurred in central Asia where high quotas for cotton output led to indiscriminate use of pesticides and irrigation. Birth defects became very common, and the vast Aral Sea has been half-drained, causing major environmental effects.

This failure to protect the environment stemmed from the pressure to fulfill production plans and the absence of a "political marketplace" where citizens could express their preferences for the environment. Imperfect though the system may be in democratic market economies—and in some particular cases it has been quite poor—their record of environmental protection has been vastly better than that of the centrally planned economies.

These are some of the reasons all modern economies are mixed economies. Throughout most of the twentieth century in advanced industrial societies, the mix had been altering towards more and more government participation in decisions about the allocation of resources and the distribution of income. In the past three decades, however, there has been a worldwide movement to reduce the degree of government participation. The details of this shift in the market/government mix, and the reasons for it, are some of the major issues that will be studied in this book.

SUMMARY

1.1 THE COMPLEXITY OF THE MODERN ECONOMY

LO 1

- A market economy is self-organizing in the sense that when individual consumers and producers act independently to pursue their own self-interest, responding to prices determined in open markets, the collective outcome is coordinated.

1.2 SCARCITY, CHOICE, AND OPPORTUNITY COST

LO 2

- Scarcity is a fundamental problem faced by all economies. Not enough resources are available to produce all the goods and services that people would like to consume. Scarcity makes it necessary to choose. All societies must have a mechanism for choosing what goods and services will be produced and in what quantities.
- The concept of opportunity cost emphasizes the problem of scarcity and choice by measuring the cost of obtaining a unit of one product in terms of the number of units of other products that could have been obtained instead.
- A production possibilities boundary shows all of the combinations of goods that can be produced by an economy whose resources are fully and efficiently employed. Movement from one point to another along the boundary requires a reallocation of resources.
- Four basic questions must be answered in all economies: What is produced and how? What is consumed and by whom? Why are resources sometimes idle? Is productive capacity growing?

1.3 WHO MAKES THE CHOICES AND HOW?

LO 3

- The interaction of consumers and producers through goods and factor markets is illustrated by the circular flow of income and expenditure. Individual consumers sell factor services to producers and thereby earn their income. Similarly, producers earn their income by selling goods and services to individual consumers.
- Individual consumers are assumed to make their decisions in an effort to maximize their well-being or utility. Producers' decisions are assumed to be designed to maximize their profits.
- Modern economies are based on the specialization and division of labour, which necessitate the exchange (trading) of goods and services. Exchange takes place in markets and is facilitated by the use of money.
- Driven by the ongoing revolution in transportation and communications technology, the world economy is rapidly globalizing.

1.4 IS THERE AN ALTERNATIVE TO THE MARKET ECONOMY?

LO 4

- There are three pure types of economies: traditional, command, and free-market. In practice, all economies are mixed economies in that their economic behaviour responds to mixes of tradition, government command, and price incentives.
- In the late 1980s, events in Eastern Europe and the Soviet Union led to the general acceptance that the system of fully centrally planned economies had failed to produce minimally acceptable living standards for its citizens. All of these countries are now moving toward greater market determination and less state command in their economies.
- Governments play an important role in modern mixed economies. They create and enforce important background institutions such as private property and freedom of contract. They intervene to correct market failures. They also redistribute income in the interests of equity.

KEY CONCEPTS

The self-organizing economy
Scarcity and the need for choice
Choice and opportunity cost
Production possibilities boundary

Resource allocation
Specialization
The division of labour
Globalization

Traditional economies
Command economies
Free-market economies
Mixed economies

STUDY EXERCISES

1. What is the difference between microeconomics and macroeconomics?
2. List the four main types of economic systems and their main attributes.
3. Explain the three economic concepts illustrated by the production possibilities boundary.
4. myeconlab Consider an economy that produces only food and clothing. Its production possibilities boundary is shown below.

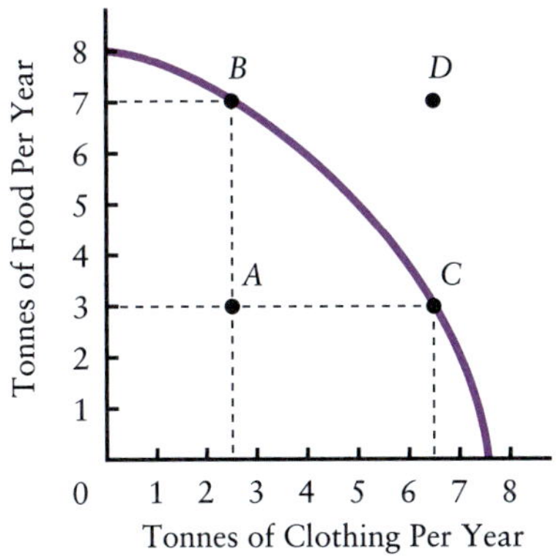

   a. If the economy is at point *A*, how many tonnes of clothing and how many tonnes of food are being produced? At point *B*? At point *C*?
   b. What do we know about the use of resources when the economy is at point *A*? At point *B*? At point *C*?
   c. If the economy is at point *B*, what is the opportunity cost of producing one more tonne of food? What is the opportunity cost of producing one more tonne of clothing?
   d. What do we know about the use of resources at point *D*? How would it be possible for the economy to produce at point *D*?
5. State and explain two reasons why the specialization of labour is more efficient than universal self-sufficiency.
6. Choiceland has 250 workers and produces only two goods, *X* and *Y*. Labour is the only factor of production, but some workers are better suited to producing *X* than *Y* (and vice versa). The table below shows the maximum levels of output of each good possible from various levels of labour input.

Number of Workers Producing *X*	Annual Production of *X*	Number of Workers Producing *Y*	Annual Production of *Y*
0	0	250	1300
50	20	200	1200
100	45	150	900
150	60	100	600
200	70	50	350
250	75	0	0

   a. Draw the production possibilities boundary for Choiceland on a scale diagram.
   b. Compute the opportunity cost of producing an extra 10 units of *X* if the economy is initially producing 60 units of *X* and 600 units of *Y*. How does this compare to the opportunity cost if the economy were initially producing 70 units of *X*?
   c. Suppose now that the technology associated with producing good *Y* improves, so that the maximum level of *Y* that can be produced from any given level of labour input increases by 10 percent. Explain (or show in a diagram) what happens to the production possibilities curve.
7. myeconlab Explain why a technological improvement in the production of one good means that a country can now produce more of *other* goods than it did previously. Hint: Draw a country's production possibilities boundary to help answer this question.
8. Consider your decision whether to go skiing for the weekend. Suppose transportation, lift tickets, and accommodation for the weekend costs $300. Suppose also that restaurant food for the weekend will cost $75. Finally, suppose you have a weekend job that you will have to miss if you go skiing, which pays you $120 (after tax) for the one weekend day that you work. What is the opportunity cost of going skiing? Do you need any other information before computing the opportunity cost?

9. Suppose you and a friend go wilderness camping for a week and must find your own food to survive. From past experience, you know that you and your friend have different abilities in fishing and hunting. If each of you were to work for one day either catching fish or trapping rabbits, the number of fish and rabbits that you could catch is given in the following table:

	Fish	Rabbits
You	6	3
Your friend	8	2

You and your friend decide that you should allocate the duties so that you get the most food for the least amount of effort. For simplicity, assume that one fish represents the same amount of food as one rabbit.

a. What is the opportunity cost for you to catch an additional rabbit? What is your friend's opportunity cost of catching an extra rabbit?
b. What allocation of tasks maximizes total output for the least amount of effort?
c. Suppose you both decide to work for two days according to the allocation in part (b). What is the total amount of output? What would it have been had you chosen the reverse allocation of tasks?

DISCUSSION QUESTIONS

1. What is the difference between scarcity and poverty? If everyone in the world had enough to eat, could we say that food was no longer scarce?

2. Evidence accumulates that the use of chemical fertilizers, which increases agricultural production greatly, damages water quality. Analyze the choice between more food and cleaner water involved in using such fertilizers. Use a production possibilities curve with agricultural output on the vertical axis and water quality on the horizontal axis. In what ways does this production possibilities curve reflect scarcity, choice, and opportunity cost? How would an improved fertilizer that increased agricultural output without further worsening water quality affect the curve? Suppose a pollution-free fertilizer were developed; would this mean that there would no longer be any opportunity cost in using it?

3. Discuss the following statement by a leading economist: "One of the mysteries of semantics is why the government-managed economies ever came to be called planned and the market economies unplanned. It is the former that are in chronic chaos, in which buyers stand in line hoping to buy some toilet paper or soap. It is the latter that are in reasonable equilibrium—where if you want a cake of soap or a steak or a shirt or a car, you can go to the store and find that the item is magically there for you to buy. It is the liberal economies that reflect a highly sophisticated planning system, and the government-managed economies that are primitive and unplanned."

4. Consider the market for doctors' services. In what way has this market taken advantage of the specialization of labour?

5. "It is not from the benevolence of the butcher, the brewer, or the baker, that we expect our dinner, but from their regard to their own interest. We address ourselves, not to their humanity but to their self-love, and never talk to them of our own necessities but of their advantages." Do you agree with this quotation from Adam Smith's classic, *The Wealth of Nations*? How are "our dinner" and "their self-interest" related to the price system? What does Smith assume to be the motives of firms and households?

6. In the chapter we used a simple idea of a production possibilities boundary to illustrate the concepts of scarcity, choice, and opportunity cost. We assumed there were only two goods—call them X and Y. But we all know that any economy produces many more than just two goods. Explain why the insights illustrated in Figure 1-2 are more general, and why the assumption of only two goods is a useful one.

CHAPTER 2

How Economists Work

LEARNING OBJECTIVES

In this chapter you will learn

1. to distinguish between positive and normative statements.
2. how economists use models to help them think about the economy.
3. about the interaction between economic theories and empirical observation.
4. to identify several types of economic data, including index numbers, time-series and cross-sectional data, and scatter diagrams.
5. that the slope of a relation between two variables, *X* and *Y*, is interpreted as the marginal response in *Y* to a unit change in *X*.

If you read the newspaper, watch television, listen to the radio, or surf Internet news sites you will often see or hear some economist's opinions being reported, perhaps about: unemployment, the exchange rate, or interest rates; some new tax; the case for privatization or regulation of an industry; or the possible reforms to Canada's health-care system. Where do economists' opinions come from? Are they supported by hard evidence, and if so, why do economists sometimes disagree with each other over important issues?

Economics is a social science, and in this chapter we explore what it means to be "scientific" in the study of economics. Along the way we will learn much about theories, hypotheses, data, testing, and graphing. We begin with the important distinction between positive and normative statements.

2.1 POSITIVE AND NORMATIVE ADVICE

Economists give two broad types of advice, called *normative* and *positive*. For example, they sometimes advise that the government ought to try harder to reduce unemployment. When they say such things they are giving normative advice; in this case, they are making judgements about the value of the various things that the government could do with its limited resources and about the costs and benefits of reducing unemployment. Advice that depends on a value judgement is normative—it tells others what they *ought* to do.

Another type of advice is illustrated by the statement, "If the government wants to reduce unemployment, reducing unemployment insurance benefits is an effective way of doing so." This is positive advice. It does not rely on a judgement about the value of reducing unemployment. Instead, the expert is saying, "If this is what you want to do, here is a way to do it."

normative statement A statement about what ought to be as opposed to what actually is.

positive statement A statement about what actually is (was or will be), as opposed to what ought to be.

Practise with Study Guide Chapter 2, Short-Answer Question 1.

Normative statements depend on value judgements and cannot be settled by recourse to facts. In contrast, **positive statements** do not involve value judgements. They are statements about matters of fact. The distinction between positive and normative is fundamental to scientific progress. Much of the success of modern science depends on the ability of scientists to separate their views on *what does happen* in the world from their views on *what they would like to happen*. For example, until the eighteenth century almost everyone believed that the Earth was only a few thousand years old. Evidence then began to accumulate that the Earth was billions of years old. This evidence was hard for most people to accept since it ran counter to a literal reading of many religious texts. Many did not want to believe the evidence. Nevertheless, scientists, many of whom were religious, continued their research because they refused to allow their feelings about what they wanted to believe to affect their scientific search for the truth. Eventually, all scientists came to accept that the Earth is about 4 billion years old.

Distinguishing what is actually true from what we would like to be requires distinguishing between positive and normative statements.

Examples of both types of statements are given in Table 2-1. All four positive statements in the table are assertions about the nature of the world in which we live. In contrast, the four normative statements involve value judgements. Notice two things about the positive/normative distinction. First, positive statements need not be true. Statement *C* is almost certainly false. Yet it is positive, not normative. Second, the inclusion of a value judgement in a statement does not necessarily make the statement normative. Statement *D* is a positive statement about the value judgements that people hold. We could conduct a survey to check if people really do prefer low unemployment to low inflation. We could ask them and we could observe how they voted. There is no need for the economist to rely on a value judgement in order to check the validity of the statement itself.

We leave you to analyze the remaining six statements to decide precisely why each is either positive or normative. Remember to apply the two tests. First, is the statement only about actual or alleged facts? If so, it is a positive one. Second, are value judgements necessary to assess the truth of the statement? If so, it is normative.

TABLE 2-1 Positive and Normative Statements

Positive		Normative	
A	Raising interest rates encourages people to save.	E	People should be encouraged to save.
B	High rates of income tax encourage people to evade paying taxes.	F	Governments should arrange taxes so that people cannot avoid paying them.
C	Lowering the price of tobacco leads people to smoke less.	G	The government should raise the tax on tobacco to discourage people from smoking.
D	The majority of the population would prefer a policy that reduced unemployment to one that reduced inflation.	H	The government ought to be more concerned with reducing unemployment than inflation.

Disagreements Among Economists

Economists often disagree with each other in the press or at conferences, but their debates are more often about normative issues than positive ones.

Economists often disagree with each other in public discussions, frequently because of poor communication. The adversaries fail to define their terms or their points of reference clearly, and so they end up "arguing past" each other, with the only certain result being that the audience is left confused.

Another source of disagreement stems from some economists' failure to acknowledge the full state of their ignorance. There are many things on which the evidence is far from conclusive. Informed judgements are then required in order to take a position on even a purely positive question. In such cases, a responsible economist will make clear the extent to which his or her view is based on judgements about the relevant facts.

Perhaps the biggest source of public disagreement between economists is based on the positive/normative distinction. Different economists have different values, and these normative views play a large part in most discussions of public policy. Many economists stress the importance of individual responsibility and argue, for example, that lower employment insurance benefits would be desirable because people would have a greater incentive to search for a job. Other economists stress the need for a generous "social safety net" and argue that higher employment insurance benefits would be desirable because human hardship would be reduced. In such debates, and there are many in economics, it is the responsibility of the economist to state clearly what part of the proffered advice is normative and what part is positive.

Because the world is complex and because no issue can be settled beyond any doubt, economists rarely agree unanimously on an issue. Nevertheless, there is an impressive amount of agreement on many aspects of how the economy works and what happens when governments intervene to alter its workings. A survey published in the *American Economic Review*, perhaps the most influential economics journal, showed strong agreement among economists on many propositions, including: "Rent control leads to a housing shortage" (85 percent yes), "Tariffs usually reduce economic welfare" (93 percent yes), "Large government budget deficits have adverse effects on the economy" (83 percent yes), and "A minimum wage increases unemployment among young workers" (79 percent yes). Other examples of these areas of agreement will be found in many places throughout this book.

2.2 **ECONOMIC THEORIES**

Economists seek to understand the world by developing *theories* and *models* that explain some of the things that have been seen and to predict some of the things that will be seen. What is a theory and what is a model?

Theories

Theories are constructed to explain things. For example, what determines the number of eggs sold in Winnipeg on a particular day, and the price at which they are sold? As part of the answer to questions such as these, economists have developed theories of demand and supply—theories that we will study in detail in the next three chapters. Any theory is distinguished by its variables, assumptions, and predictions.

variable Any well-defined item, such as the price or quantity of a commodity, that can take on various specific values.

Variables The basic elements of any theory are its variables. A **variable** is a magnitude that can take on different possible values.

In our theory of the egg market, the variable *quantity of eggs* might be defined as the number of cartons of 12 Grade A large eggs. The variable *price of eggs* is the amount of money that must be given up to purchase each carton of eggs. The particular values taken on by those two variables might be: 2000 cartons at a price of $1.80 on July 1, 2006; 1800 cartons at a price of $1.95 on July 1, 2007; and 1950 cartons at a price of $1.85 on July 1, 2008.

endogenous variable A variable that is explained within a theory. Sometimes called an *induced variable* or a *dependent variable.*

exogenous variable A variable that is determined outside the theory. Sometimes called an *autonomous variable* or an *independent variable.*

There are two broad categories of variables that are important in any theory. An **endogenous variable** is one whose value is determined within the theory. An **exogenous variable** influences the endogenous variables but is itself determined outside the theory. To illustrate the difference, the price of eggs and the quantity of eggs are endogenous variables in our theory of the egg market—our theory is designed to explain them. The state of the weather, however, is an exogenous variable. It may well affect the number of eggs consumers demand or producers supply but we can safely assume that the state of the weather is not influenced by the market for eggs.

Assumptions A theory's assumptions concern motives, physical relations, directions of causation, and the conditions under which the theory is meant to apply.

Motives. The theories we study in this book make the fundamental assumption that everyone pursues his or her own self-interest when making economic decisions. People are assumed to know what they want, and to know how to go about getting it within the constraints set by the resources at their command.

Physical Relations. If egg producers buy more chicks and use more labour, land, and chicken feed, they will probably produce more eggs. This is an example of one of the most important physical relations in economics. It concerns assumptions about how the amount of output is related to the quantities of factors of production used to produce it. This relation is called a *production function.*

A key assumption in economics is that firms make decisions with the goal of maximizing their profits.

Direction of Causation. When economists assume that one variable is related to another, they are assuming some causal link between the two. For example, when the amount of eggs that producers want to supply is assumed to increase when the cost of their chicken feed falls, the causation runs from the price of chicken feed to the supply of eggs. Producers supply more eggs because the price of chicken feed has fallen; they are not assumed to get cheaper chicken feed because of their decision to supply more eggs.

Conditions of Application. Assumptions are often used to specify the conditions under which a theory is meant to hold. For example, a theory that assumes there is "no government" usually does not mean literally the absence of government, but only that the theory is meant to apply when governments are not significantly affecting the situation being studied.

Although assumptions are an essential part of all theories, students are often concerned about those that seem unrealistic. An example will illustrate some of the issues involved. Much of the theory that we are going to study in this book uses the assumption that owners of firms attempt to maximize their profits. The assumption of profit maximization allows economists to make predictions about the behaviour of firms, such as, "firms will supply more output if the market price increases."

Profit maximization may seem like a rather crude assumption. Surely, for example, the managers of firms sometimes choose to protect the environment rather than pursue certain highly polluting but profitable opportunities. Does this not discredit the assumption of profit maximization by showing it to be unrealistic?

The answer is no; to make successful predictions, the theory does not require that managers be solely and unwaveringly motivated by the desire to maximize profits at all times. All that is required is that profits be a sufficiently important consideration that a theory based on the assumption of profit maximization will lead to explanations and predictions that are substantially correct. It is not always appropriate to criticize a theory because its assumptions seem unrealistic. A good theory abstracts in a useful way; a poor theory does not. If a theory has ignored some genuinely important factors, its predictions will usually be contradicted by the evidence.

All theory is an abstraction from reality. If it were not, it would merely duplicate the world in all its complexity and would add little to our understanding of it.

Predictions A theory's predictions are the propositions that can be deduced from it. They are often called *hypotheses*. For example, a prediction from our theory of the egg market is that, "if the price of chicken feed falls, producers will want to sell more eggs." Another prediction from the same theory is that "if the price of eggs declines, consumers will want to purchase more eggs."

Models

Economists use the term **economic model** in two different but related ways.

economic model A term used in several related ways: sometimes for an abstraction designed to illustrate some point but not designed to generate testable hypotheses, and sometimes as a synonym for theory.

First, a model may be an illustrative abstraction, not meant to be elaborate enough to generate testable hypotheses. The circular flow of income and expenditure in Chapter 1 is a model of this sort, as is the production possibilities boundary. Both models help us to organize our thinking and gain crucial economic insights, even though the real world is much more complex than the model. In some ways, a model of this sort is like a political caricature. Its value is in the insights it provides that help us to understand key features of a complex world.

Second, the term *model* is used as a synonym for a theory, as when economists speak of the Keynesian model of the determination of national income, or the demand-and-supply model of the Winnipeg egg market that we discussed earlier. In both cases, the word *model* could easily be replaced by the word *theory*. Sometimes economists use *model* to refer to a specific quantitative version of a theory. In this case, specific numbers are attached to the mathematical relationships embodied in the theory. The result is that the predictions are more precise. For example, rather than a prediction such as "a decrease in the price of chicken feed will lead to an increase in the quantity of eggs supplied," the prediction from the more specific model might be "a 10-percent reduction in the price of chicken feed will lead to an 8-percent increase in the number of eggs supplied."

2.3 TESTING THEORIES

A theory is tested by confronting its predictions with evidence. For example, is a decrease in the price of chicken feed *actually* followed by an increase in the amount of eggs producers want to sell? Generally, theories tend to be abandoned when they are no longer useful. A theory ceases to be useful when it cannot predict better than an alternative theory. When a theory consistently fails to predict better than an available alternative, it is either modified or replaced.

The old question "Which came first: the chicken or the egg?" is often raised when discussing economic theories. In the first instance, it was observation that preceded economic theories; people were not born with economic theories embedded in their minds. However, once economics was established as a scientific line of inquiry, theories and evidence interacted with each other. It has now become impossible to say that one precedes the other. In some cases, empirical evidence may suggest inadequacies that require the development of better theories. In other cases, an inspired guess may lead to a theory that has little current empirical support but is subsequently found to explain many observations. This interaction between theory and empirical observation is illustrated in Figure 2-1.

The scientific approach is central to the study of economics: Empirical observation leads to the construction of theories, theories generate specific hypotheses, and the hypotheses are tested by more detailed empirical observation.

myeconlab

Economists sometimes disagree about the usefulness of a theory or model. For a glimpse of one such debate between two Nobel Laureates, Milton Friedman and Ronald Coase, look for "How Economists Choose Their Theories" in the *Additional Topics* section of this book's MyEconLab.

www.myeconlab.com

Rejection Versus Confirmation

An important part of the scientific approach consists of setting up a theory that will explain some observation. A theory designed to explain observation X will typically generate a hypothesis about some other observable variables, Y and Z. The hypothesis about Y and Z can be tested and may be *rejected* by the data. If the hypothesis is rejected, the value of the theory is brought into question.

The alternative to this approach is to set up a theory and then look for *confirming* evidence. Such an approach is hazardous because the world is sufficiently complex that some confirming evidence can be found for any theory, no matter how unlikely the theory may be. For example, flying saucers, the Loch Ness monster, fortune-telling, and astrology all have their devotees who can quote confirming evidence in spite of the failure of many attempts to discover systematic, objective evidence of these things.

FIGURE 2-1 The Interaction Between Theory and Empirical Observation

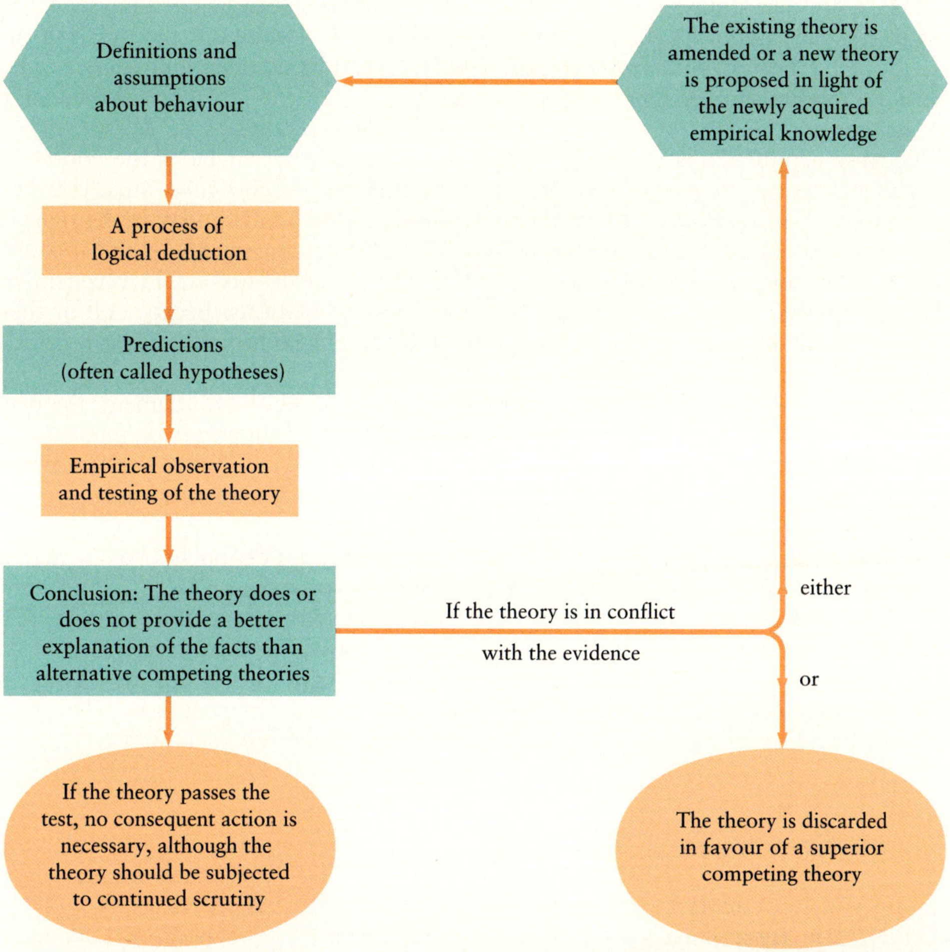

Theory and observation are in continuous interaction. Starting (at the top left) with the assumptions of a theory and the definitions of relevant terms, the theorist deduces by logical analysis everything that is implied by the assumptions. These implications are the predictions or the hypotheses of the theory. The theory is then tested by confronting its predictions with evidence. If the theory is in conflict with facts, it will usually be amended to make it consistent with those facts (thereby making it a better theory), or it will be discarded, to be replaced by a superior theory. The process then begins again: The new or amended theory is subjected first to logical analysis and then to empirical testing.

Statistical Analysis

Most theories generate a hypothesis of the form "if X increases, then Y will also increase." Another example is "if X falls, then Z will rise." Statistical analysis can be used to test such hypotheses and to estimate the numerical values of the function that describes the relationship. In practice, the same data can be used simultaneously to test whether a relationship exists and, if it does exist, to provide an estimate of the magnitude of that relationship.

Because economics is primarily a non-laboratory science, it lacks the controlled experiments central to sciences like physics and chemistry. Economics must therefore use millions of uncontrolled "experiments" that are going on every day in the marketplace. Households are deciding what to purchase given changing prices and incomes, firms are deciding what to produce and how, and governments are involved in the economy through their various taxes, subsidies, and regulations. Because all of these activities can be observed and recorded, a mass of data is continually being produced by the economy.

The variables that interest economists—such as the level of employment, the price of a DVD, and the output of automobiles—are generally influenced by many forces that vary simultaneously. If economists are to test their theories about relations among specific variables, they must use statistical techniques designed for situations in which other things *cannot* be held constant.

Fortunately, such techniques exist, although their application is usually neither simple nor straightforward. Later in this chapter we provide a discussion of some graphical techniques for describing data and displaying some of the more obvious relationships. Further examination of data involves techniques studied in elementary statistics courses. More advanced courses in econometrics deal with the array of techniques designed to test economic hypotheses and to measure economic relations in the complex circumstances in which economic evidence is often generated.

Correlation Versus Causation

Suppose you want to test your theory's hypothesis that "if X increases, Y will also increase." You are looking for a *causal* relationship from X to Y, because a change in X is predicted to *cause* a change in Y. When you look at the data, suppose you find that X and Y are positively correlated—that is, when X rises, Y also tends to rise. Is your theory supported? It might appear that way, but there is a potential problem.

Practise with Study Guide Chapter 2, Short-Answer Question 3.

A finding that X and Y are positively correlated means only that X and Y tend to move together. This correlation is *consistent* with the theory that X causes Y, but it is *not* direct evidence of this causal relationship. The causality may be in the opposite direction—from Y to X. Or X and Y may have no direct causal connection but may instead be jointly caused by some third variable, Z.

Here is a concrete example. Suppose your theory predicts that individuals who get more education will earn higher incomes as a result—the causality in this theory runs from education to income. In the data, suppose we find that education and income are positively correlated. This should not, however, be taken as direct evidence for the (causal) prediction. The data is certainly consistent with that theory, but it is also consistent with others. For example, individuals who grow up in higher-income households may "buy" more education, just as they buy more clothes or entertainment. This is a case of "reverse causality": income causes education, rather than the other way around. Another possibility is that education and income are positively correlated because the personal characteristics that lead people to become more educated—ability and motivation—are the same characteristics that lead to high incomes. In this case, the *causal* relationship runs from personal characteristics to both income and education.

Most economic predictions involve causality. Economists must take care when testing predictions to distinguish between correlation and causality. Correlation can establish that the data are consistent with the theory; establishing causality usually requires advanced statistical techniques.

2.4 ECONOMIC DATA

Economists seek to explain events that they see in the world. Why, for example, did the price of wheat rise last year even though the wheat crop increased? Explaining such observations typically requires an understanding of how the economy works, an understanding based in part on the insights economists derive from their theoretical models.

For data on the Canadian economy and many other quantifiable aspects of Canadian life, see Statistics Canada's website: **www.statcan.ca**

Economists also use real-world observations to test their theories. For example, did the amount that people saved last year rise—as the theory predicts it should have—when a large tax cut increased their after-tax incomes? To test this prediction we need reliable data for people's incomes and their savings.

Political scientists, sociologists, anthropologists, and psychologists often collect for themselves the data they use to formulate and test their theories. Economists are unusual among social scientists in mainly using data collected by others, often government statisticians. In economics there is a division of labour between collecting data and using it to test theories. The advantage is that economists do not need to spend much of their scarce research time collecting the data they use. The disadvantage is that they are often not as well informed about the limitations of the data collected by others as they would be if they had collected the data themselves.

Once data are collected they can be displayed in various ways, many of which we will see later in this chapter. They can be laid out in tables. They can be displayed in various types of graphs. And where we are interested in relative movements rather than absolute ones, the data can be expressed in *index numbers*. We begin with a discussion of index numbers.

Index Numbers

Economists frequently look at data on prices or quantities and explore how specific variables change over time. For example, they may be interested in comparing the time paths of output in two industries: steel and newsprint. The problem is that it may be difficult to compare the time paths of the two different variables if we just look at the "raw" data.

Table 2-2 shows some hypothetical data for the volume of output in the steel and newsprint industries, and reveals that because the two variables are measured in different units, it is not immediately clear which of the two variables is more volatile or which, if either, has an upward or downward trend.

index number An average that measures change over time of such variables as the price level and industrial production; conventionally expressed as a percentage relative to a base period, which is assigned the value 100.

It is easier to compare the two paths if we focus on *relative* rather than *absolute* changes. One way to do this is to construct some **index numbers**.

TABLE 2-2 Volume of Steel and Newsprint Output

Year	Volume of Steel (thousands of tonnes)	Volume of Newsprint (thousands of rolls)
1998	200	3200
1999	210	3100
2000	225	3000
2001	215	3200
2002	250	3100
2003	220	3300
2004	265	3100
2005	225	3300
2006	255	3100
2007	230	3200
2008	245	3000

Comparing the time paths of two data series is difficult when absolute numbers are used. Since steel output and newsprint output are measured in different units and have quite different absolute numbers, it is difficult to detect which time series is more volatile.

How to Build an Index Number We start by taking the value of the variable at some point in time as the "base" to which the values of the variable in other periods will be compared. We call this the *base period*. In the present example, we choose 1998 as the base year for both series. We then take the output in each subsequent year, called the given year, and divide it by the output in the base year, and then multiply the result by 100. This gives us an index number for the output of steel and a separate index number for the output of newsprint. For each index number, the value of output in the base year is equal to 100. The details of the calculations are shown in Table 2-3.

An index number simply expresses the value of some series in any given year as a percentage of its value in the base year. For example, the 2008 index of steel output of 122.5 tells us that steel output in 2008 was 22.5 percent greater than in 1998. In contrast, the 2008 index for newsprint output of 93.8 tells us that newsprint output in 2008 was only 93.8 percent of the output in 1998—that is, output was 6.2 percent lower in 2008 than in 1998. The results in Table 2-3 allow us to compare the relative fluctuations in the two series. It is apparent from the values in the table that the output of steel has shown significantly more percentage variability than has the output of newsprint. This is also clear in Figure 2-2.

TABLE 2-3 Constructing Index Numbers

	Steel			Newsprint		
Year	Procedure		Index	Procedure		Index
1998	(200/200) × 100	=	100.0	(3200/3200) × 100	=	100.0
1999	(210/200) × 100	=	105.0	(3100/3200) × 100	=	96.9
2000	(225/200) × 100	=	112.5	(3000/3200) × 100	=	93.8
2001	(215/200) × 100	=	107.5	(3200/3200) × 100	=	100.0
2002	(250/200) × 100	=	125.0	(3100/3200) × 100	=	96.9
2003	(220/200) × 100	=	110.0	(3300/3200) × 100	=	103.1
2004	(265/200) × 100	=	132.5	(3100/3200) × 100	=	96.9
2005	(225/200) × 100	=	112.5	(3300/3200) × 100	=	103.1
2006	(255/200) × 100	=	127.5	(3100/3200) × 100	=	96.9
2007	(230/200) × 100	=	115.0	(3200/3200) × 100	=	100.0
2008	(245/200) × 100	=	122.5	(3000/3200) × 100	=	93.8

Index numbers are calculated by dividing the value in the given year by the value in the base year, and multiplying the result by 100. The 2008 index number for steel tells us that steel output in 2008 was 22.5 percent greater than in the base year, 1998. The 2008 index number for newsprint tells us that newsprint output in 2008 was 93.8 percent of the output in the base year, 1998.

FIGURE 2-2 Index Values for Steel and Newsprint Output

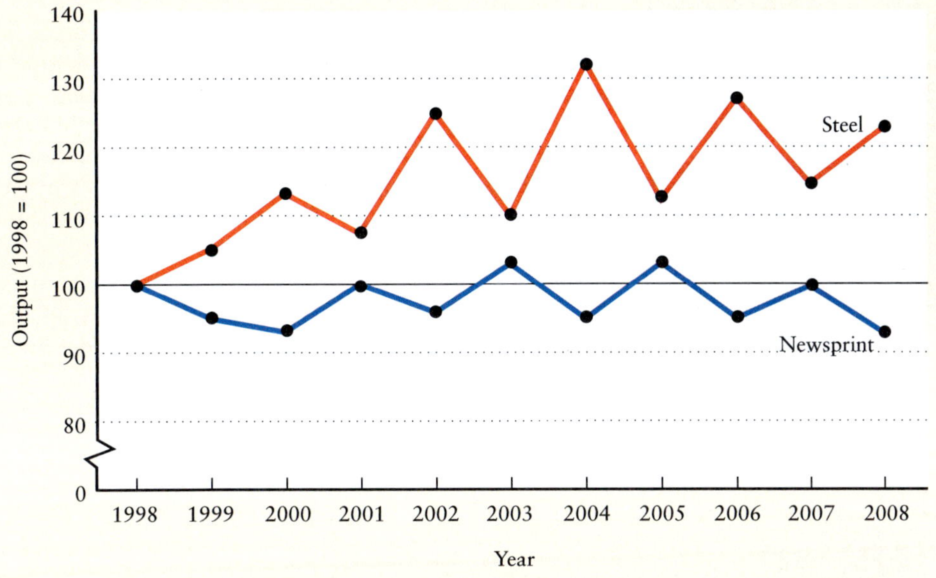

Comparing the time paths of two variables is much easier when index numbers are used. Since both index numbers are equal to 100 in the base year, relative volatility and trends become clear. Steel output is clearly more volatile in percentage terms than newsprint output. Steel output also has an upward trend, whereas newsprint output appears to have little or no trend.

The formula of any index number is:

$$\text{Value of index in any given period} = \frac{\text{Absolute value in given period}}{\text{Absolute value in base period}} \times 100$$

Care must be taken, however, when using index numbers. The index number always tells you the percentage change compared with the base year, but when comparing an index number across non-base years, the percentage change in the index number is *not* given by the absolute difference in the values of the index number. For example, if you want to know how much steel output changed from 2002 to 2004, we know from Table 2-3 that the index number for steel output increased from 125.0 to 132.5. But this is not an increase of 7.5 percent. The *percentage* increase in steel output is computed as (132.5 – 125.0)/125.0 = 7.5/125.0 = 0.06, or 6 percent.

More Complex Index Numbers Perhaps the most famous index number used by economists is the index of average prices—the consumer price index (CPI). This is a price index of the *average* price paid by consumers for the typical basket of goods that they buy. The inclusion of the word "average," however, makes the CPI a more complex index number than the ones we have constructed here.

Practise with Study Guide Chapter 2, Exercise 1.

With what you have just learned, you could construct separate index numbers for the price of beef, the price of coffee, and the price of orange juice. But in order to get the consumer price index we need to take the *average* of these separate price indexes (plus thousands of others for the goods and services we have ignored here). But it

The S&P/TSX is one of the best-known index numbers in Canada. Its fluctuations reflect changes in the market value of the largest publicly traded companies in Canada.

cannot be a simple average. Instead, it must be a *weighted* average where the weight on each price index reflects the relative importance of that good in the typical consumer's basket of goods and services. For example, since the typical consumer spends a tiny fraction of income on sardines but a much larger fraction of income on housing, the weight on the "sardines" price index in the CPI will be very small and the weight on the "housing" price index will be very large. The result is that even huge swings in the price of sardines will have negligible effects on the CPI, whereas much more modest changes in the price of housing will have noticeable effects on the CPI.

We will spend much more time discussing the consumer price index when we study macroeconomics beginning in Chapter 19. For now, keep in mind the usefulness of the simple index numbers we have constructed here. They allow us to compare the time paths of different variables.

myeconlab

Another famous index that is reported every day on the news is the S&P/TSX, an index number showing the average market value of a specific set of companies traded on the Toronto Stock Exchange. For more information about the S&P/TSX index, look for "What the S&P/TSX Really Measures" in the *Additional Topics* section of this book's MyEconLab.

www.myeconlab.com

Graphing Economic Data

A single economic variable such as unemployment, GDP, or the average price of a house can come in two basic forms.

cross-sectional data A set of observations made at the same time across several different units (such as households, firms, or countries).

time-series data A set of observations made at successive periods of time.

scatter diagram A graph of statistical observations of paired values of two variables, one measured on the horizontal and the other on the vertical axis. Each point on the coordinate grid represents the values of the variables for a particular unit of observation.

Cross-Sectional and Time-Series Data The first is called **cross-sectional data**, which means a number of different observations on one variable all taken in different places at the same point in time. Figure 2-3 shows an example. The variable in the figure is the average selling price of a house. It is shown for each of the ten Canadian provinces in 2006.

The second type of data is called **time-series data.** It refers to observations of one variable at successive points in time. The data in Figure 2-4 show the unemployment rate for Canada from 1978 to 2006. (Note that the Canadian unemployment rate is simply a weighted average of the ten provincial unemployment rates, where the weight for each province is the size of that province's labour force expressed as a fraction of the total Canadian labour force.) Time-series graphs are quite useful in economics because we often want to know how specific economic numbers are changing over time. As is clear in Figure 2-4, the Canadian unemployment rate is relatively volatile over long periods of time, but in recent years has been low by historical standards.

Scatter Diagrams Another way in which data can be presented is in a **scatter diagram.** This type of chart is more analytical than those above. It is designed to show the relation between two different variables, such as the price of eggs and the quantity of eggs purchased. To plot a scatter diagram, values of one variable are measured on the horizontal axis and values of the second variable are measured on the vertical axis. Any point on the diagram relates a specific value of one variable to a corresponding specific value of the other.

The data plotted on a scatter diagram may be either cross-sectional data or time-series data. An example of a cross-sectional scatter diagram is a scatter of the price of eggs and the quantity sold in July 2007 at two dozen different places in Canada. Each dot refers to a price–quantity combination observed in a different place at the same time. An example of a scatter diagram using time-series data is the price and quantity of eggs sold in Thunder Bay for each month over the last ten years. Each of the 120 dots refers to a price–quantity combination observed at the same place in one particular month.

FIGURE 2-3 A Cross-Sectional Graph of Average Housing Prices for Ten Canadian Provinces, 2006

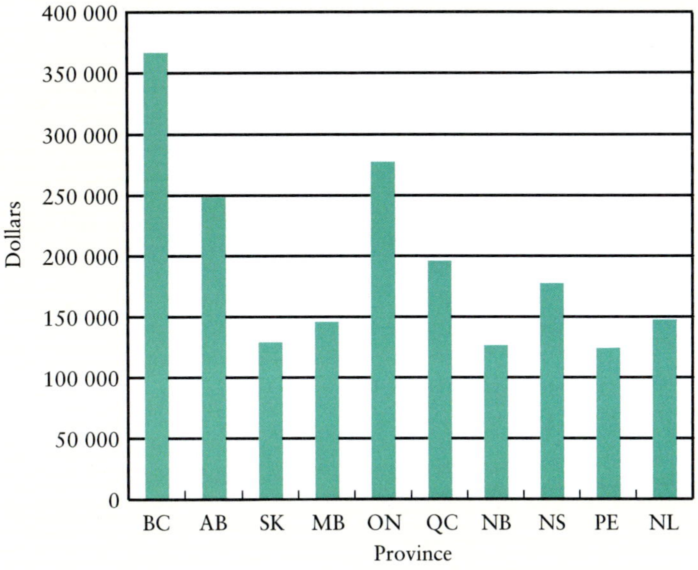

(*Source:* © 2007 The Canadian Real Estate Association. All Rights Reserved. These data are available at www.crea.ca/public/news_stats.)

FIGURE 2-4 A Time-Series Graph of the Canadian Unemployment Rate, 1978–2006

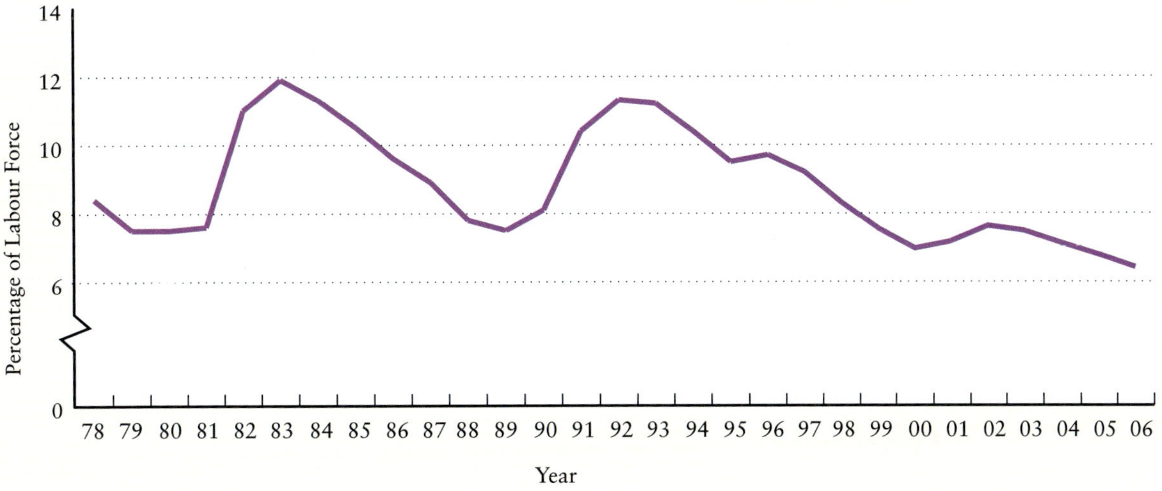

(*Source:* Annual average of monthly, seasonally adjusted data from Statistics Canada, CANSIM database, V2091177–282-0001 Canada; unemployment rate; both sexes; 15 years and over (monthly, 1978-01-01 to 2006-12-01). Reprinted with permission of Statistics Canada.)

The table in Figure 2-5 shows data for the income and saving of ten households in one particular year and these data are plotted on a scatter diagram. Each point in the figure represents one household, showing its income and its saving. The positive relation between the two stands out. The higher the household's income, the higher its saving tends to be.

FIGURE 2-5 A Scatter Diagram of Household Income and Saving

Household	Annual Income	Annual Saving
1	$ 70 000	$10 000
2	30 000	2 500
3	100 000	12 000
4	60 000	3 000
5	80 000	8 000
6	10 000	500
7	20 000	2 000
8	50 000	2 000
9	40 000	4 200
10	90 000	8 000

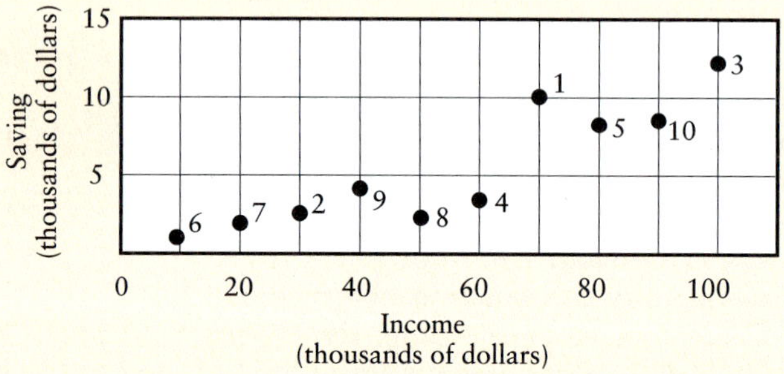

Saving tends to rise as income rises. The table shows the amount of income earned by ten selected households together with the amount they saved during the same year. The scatter diagram plots the income and saving for the ten households listed in the table. The number on each dot refers to the household in the corresponding row of the table.

myeconlab

If you need a quick refresher course on graphing, look for "A Brief Introduction to Graphing" in the *Additional Topics* section of this book's MyEconLab.

www.myeconlab.com

2.5 GRAPHING ECONOMIC THEORIES

Theories are built on assumptions about relationships between variables. For example, the quantity of eggs demanded is assumed to fall as the price of eggs rises. Or, the total amount an individual saves is assumed to rise as his or her income rises. How can such relations be expressed?

Functions

When one variable, X, is related to another variable, Y, in such a way that to every value of X there is only one possible value of Y, we say that Y is a *function* of X. When we write this relation down, we are expressing a *functional relation* between the two variables.

Here is a specific example. Consider the relation between an individual's annual income, which we denote by the symbol Y, and the amount that person spends on goods and services during the year, which we denote by the symbol C (for consumption). Any particular example of the relation between C and Y can be expressed several ways—in words, in a table or schedule, in a mathematical equation, or in a graph.

Verbal Statement. When income is zero, the person will spend \$800 a year (either by borrowing the money or by consuming past savings), and for every extra \$1 of income the person will increase expenditure by 80 cents.

Schedule. This table shows selected values of the person's income and consumption.

Annual Income	Consumption	Reference Letter
\$ 0	\$ 800	*p*
2 500	2 800	*q*
5 000	4 800	*r*
7 500	6 800	*s*
10 000	8 800	*t*

Mathematical Equation. $C = \$800 + 0.8Y$ is the equation of the relation just described in words. As a check, you can first see that when Y is zero, C is \$800. Further, you can see that every time Y increases by \$1, the level of C increases by 0.8(\$1), which is 80 cents.

Graph. Figure 2-6 shows the points from the preceding schedule and the line representing the equation given in the previous paragraph.

Comparison of the values on the graph with the values in the schedule, and with the values derived from the equation just stated, shows that these are alternative expressions of the same relation between C and Y. All four of these modes of expression refer to the same relation between the person's consumption expenditure and income.

FIGURE 2-6 Income and Consumption

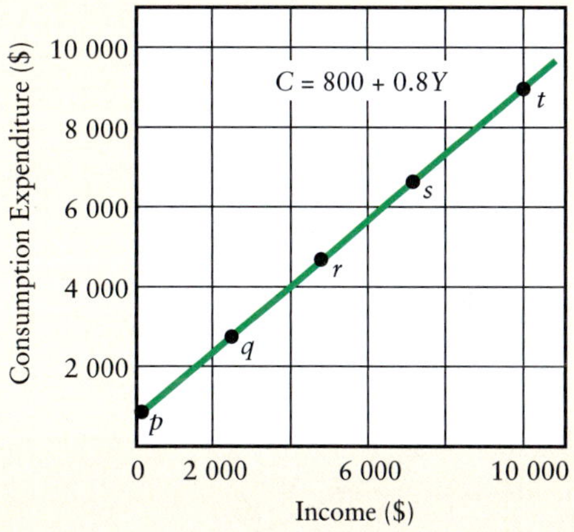

Consumption expenditure rises as income rises. The figure graphs the schedule and the equation for the functional relation discussed in the text.

More Detail About Functions Let us look in a little more detail at the mathematical expression of this relation between income and consumption. To state the expression in general form, detached from the specific numerical example above, we use a symbol to express the dependence of one variable on another. Using "f" for this purpose, we write

$$C = f(Y) \tag{2-1}$$

This is read, "C is a function of Y." Spelling this out more fully, we would say, "The amount of consumption expenditure depends upon the person's income."

The variable on the left-hand side is the dependent variable, since its value depends on the value of the variable on the right-hand side. The variable on the right-hand side is the independent variable, since it can take on any value. The letter "f" tells us that a functional relation is involved. This means that a knowledge of the value of the variable (or variables) within the parentheses on the right-hand side allows us to determine the value of the variable on the left-hand side. Although in this case we have used "f"

(as a memory-aid for "function"), any convenient symbol can be used to denote the existence of a functional relation.

Functional notation can seem intimidating to those who are unfamiliar with it. But it is helpful. Since the functional concept is basic to all science, the notation is worth mastering.

Functional Forms The equation $C = f(Y)$ states that C is a function of Y. It says nothing about the *form* of this function. The term *functional form* refers to the specific nature of the relation between the variables in the function. The example above gave one specific functional form for this relation:

$$C = \$800 + 0.8Y \qquad (2\text{-}2)$$

Equation 2-1 expresses the general assumption that consumption expenditure depends on the consumer's income. Equation 2-2 expresses the more specific assumption that C is equal to \$800 when Y is zero and rises by 80 cents for every \$1 that Y rises. An alternative assumption would be $C = \$600 + 0.9Y$. You should be able to say in words the behaviour implied in this relation. There is no reason why either of these assumptions must be true; indeed, neither may be consistent with the facts. But that is a matter for testing. What we do have in each equation is a precise statement of a particular assumption.

Notice that Equation 2-2 also specifies a *linear* consumption function—the relationship between C and Y is shown as a straight line in Figure 2-6. This is a very special case. Another possibility is that the relationship between C and Y is *non-linear*—so that the consumption function when graphed is not a straight line. This possibility takes us to our next discussion, of linear and non-linear functions, and of how to measure and interpret the *slopes* of functions.

FIGURE 2-7 Linear Pollution Reduction

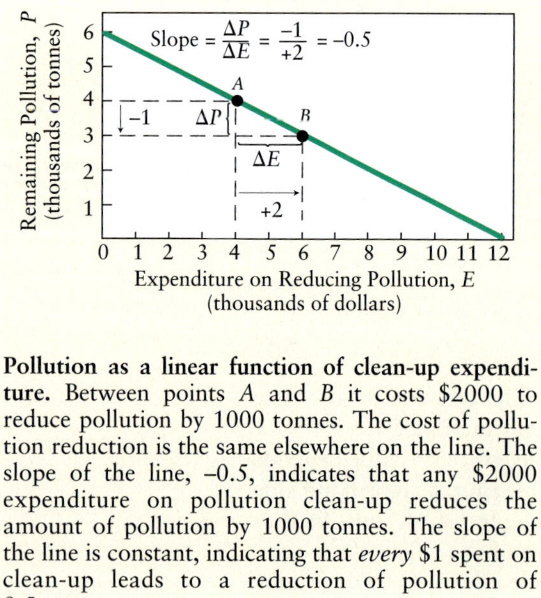

Pollution as a linear function of clean-up expenditure. Between points A and B it costs \$2000 to reduce pollution by 1000 tonnes. The cost of pollution reduction is the same elsewhere on the line. The slope of the line, –0.5, indicates that any \$2000 expenditure on pollution clean-up reduces the amount of pollution by 1000 tonnes. The slope of the line is constant, indicating that *every* \$1 spent on clean-up leads to a reduction of pollution of 0.5 tonnes.

Graphing Functional Relations

Different functional forms have different graphs, and we will meet many of these in subsequent chapters. Figure 2-6 is an example of a relation in which the two variables move together. When income goes up, consumption goes up. In such a relation the two variables are *positively related* to each other.

Figure 2-7 gives an example of variables that move in opposite directions. As the amount spent on reducing pollution goes up, the amount of remaining pollution goes down. In such a relation the two variables are *negatively related* to each other.

Both of these graphs are straight lines. In such cases the variables are *linearly related* to each other (either positively or negatively).

The Slope of a Straight Line Slopes are important in economics. They show you how much one variable changes as the other changes. The slope is defined as the amount of change in the variable measured on the vertical axis per unit change in the variable measured on the horizontal axis. In the case of Figure 2-7 it tells us how many tonnes of pollution, symbolized by P, are removed per dollar spent on reducing pollution, symbolized by E. Consider moving from point A to point B in the figure. If we spend $2000 more on clean-up, we reduce pollution by 1000 tonnes. This is 0.5 tonnes per dollar spent. On the graph the extra $2000 is indicated by ΔE, the arrow indicating that E rises by 2000. The 1000 tonnes of pollution reduction is indicated by ΔP, the arrow showing that pollution falls by 1000. (The Greek uppercase letter delta, Δ, stands for "the change in.") To get the amount of pollution reduction per dollar of expenditure we merely divide one by the other. In symbols this is $\Delta P/\Delta E$.

Practise with Study Guide Chapter 2, Exercise 2.

If we let X stand for whatever variable is measured on the horizontal axis and Y for whatever variable is measured on the vertical axis, the slope of a straight line is $\Delta Y/\Delta X$. [1][1]

The equation of the line in Figure 2-7 can be computed in two steps. First, note that when $E = 0$, the amount of remaining pollution, P, is equal to 6 (thousand tonnes). Thus, the line meets the vertical axis ($E = 0$) when P equals 6. Second, we have already seen that the slope of the line, $\Delta P/\Delta E$, is equal to -0.5, which means that for every one-unit increase in E, P falls by 0.5 unit. We can thus state the equation of the line as

$$P = 6 - (0.5)\,E$$

where both P and E are expressed as thousands of units (tonnes and dollars, respectively).

Non-Linear Functions Although it is sometimes convenient to simplify a real relation between two variables by assuming them to be linearly related, this is seldom the case over their whole range. Non-linear relations are much more common than linear ones. In the case of reducing pollution, it is usually quite cheap to eliminate the first units of pollution. Then, as the environment gets cleaner and cleaner, the cost of further clean-up tends to increase because more and more sophisticated and expensive methods need to be used. As a result, Figure 2-8 is more realistic than Figure 2-7. Inspection of Figure 2-8 shows that as more and more is spent, the amount of pollution reduction for an additional $1 of clean-up expenditure gets smaller and smaller. This is shown by the diminishing slope of the curve as we move rightward along it. For example, as we move from point A to point B, an increase in expenditure of $1000 is required to reduce pollution by 1000 tonnes. Thus, each tonne of pollution reduction costs $1. But as we move from point C (where we have already reduced pollution considerably) to point D, an extra $6000 must be spent in order to reduce pollution by 1000 tonnes. Each tonne of pollution reduction therefore costs $6.

Economists call the change in pollution when a bit more or a bit less is spent on clean-up the *marginal* change. The figure shows that the slope of the curve at each point measures this marginal change. It also shows that, in the type of curve illustrated, the marginal change per dollar spent is diminishing as we spend more on reducing pollution. There is always a payoff to more expenditure over the range shown in the figure, but the payoff diminishes as more is spent. This relation can be described as *diminishing marginal response*. We will meet such relations many times in what follows, so we emphasize now that diminishing marginal response does not mean that the *total* response is diminishing. In Figure 2-8, the total amount of pollution continues to fall as more and more is spent on clean-up. But diminishing marginal response does

1 Numbers in square brackets indicate mathematical notes that are found in a separate section at the back of the book.

FIGURE 2-8 Non-Linear Pollution Reduction

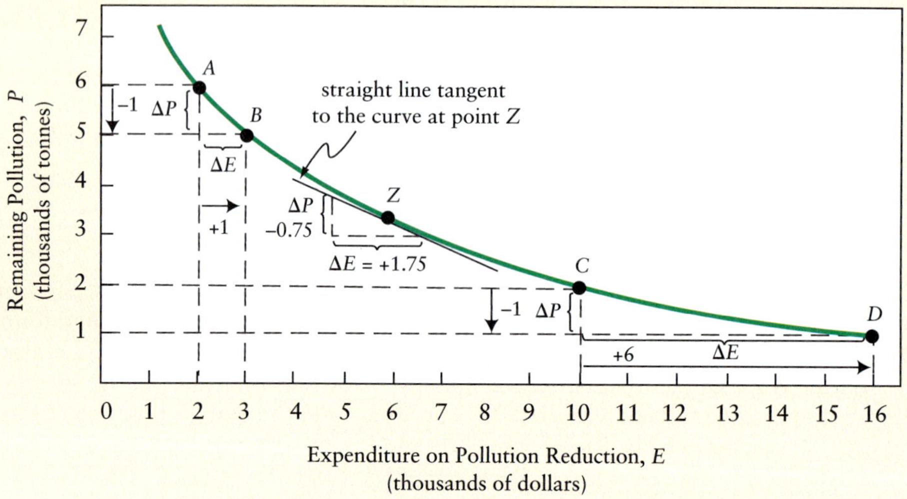

Pollution as a non-linear function of clean-up expenditure. The slope of the curve changes as we move along it. Between points *A* and *B*, it costs $1000 to reduce pollution by 1000 tonnes. Between points *C* and *D*, it costs $6000 to reduce pollution by 1000 tonnes. At point *Z*, the slope of the curve is equal to the slope of the straight line tangent to the curve at point *Z*. The slope of the tangent line is −0.75/1.75 = −0.43.

mean that the amount of pollution reduced per dollar of expenditure gets less and less as the total expenditure rises.

Figure 2-9 shows a graph where the marginal response is increasing. The graph shows the relationship between annual production costs and annual output for a firm that makes hockey sticks. Notice that the more hockey sticks produced annually, the higher the firm's costs. This is shown by the positive slope of the line. Notice also that as more and more hockey sticks are produced, the extra amount that the firm must pay to produce each extra hockey stick rises. For example, as the firm moves from point *A* to point *B*, annual costs rise by $30 000 in order to increase its annual output by 10 000 hockey sticks. Each extra hockey stick costs $3 ($30 000/10 000 = $3). But when the firm is producing many more hockey sticks, such as at point *C*, its factory is closer to its capacity and it becomes more costly to increase production. Moving from point *C* to point *D*, the firm's annual costs increase by $150 000 in order to increase its annual output by 10 000 hockey sticks. Each extra hockey stick then costs $15 ($150 000/10 000 = $15). This figure illustrates a case of *increasing marginal cost*, a characteristic of production that we will see often and learn more about later in this book.

Figures 2-8 and 2-9 show that with non-linear functions the slope of the curve changes as we move along the curve. For example, in Figure 2-8, the slope of the curve falls as the expenditure on pollution clean-up increases. In Figure 2-9, the slope of the curve increases as the volume of production increases.

How, exactly, do we measure the slope of a curved line? The answer is that we use the slope of a straight line *tangent to that curve* at the point that interests us. For example, in Figure 2-8, if we want to know the slope of the curve at point *Z*, we draw a straight line that touches the curve *only* at point *Z*; this is a tangent line. The slope of this line is –0.75/1.75 = –0.43. Similarly, in Figure 2-9, the slope of the curve at point *Z* is given by the slope of the straight line tangent to the curve at point *Z*.

For non-linear functions, the slope of the curve changes as *X* changes. Therefore, the marginal response of *Y* to a change in *X* depends on the value of *X*.

FIGURE 2-9 Increasing Production Costs

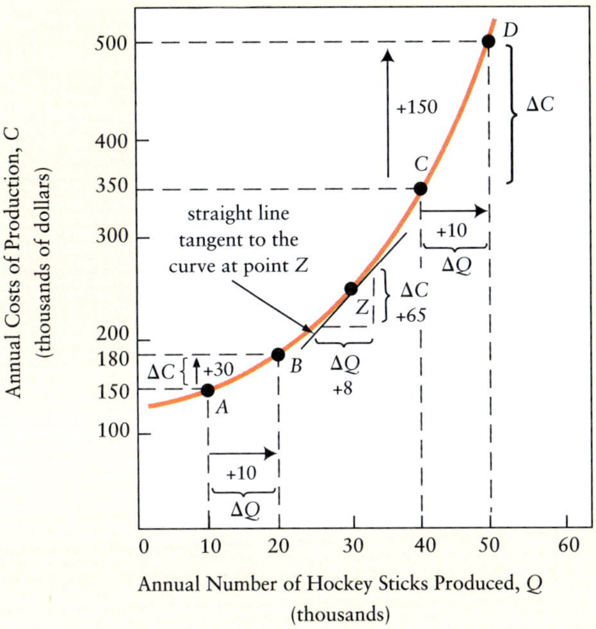

Production costs increase at an increasing rate as annual output rises. From point *A* to point *B*, an extra annual output of 10 000 hockey sticks increases annual costs by $30 000. Each extra hockey stick costs $3. From point *C* to point *D*, an extra output of 10 000 hockey sticks increases annual costs by $150 000. Each extra hockey stick then costs $15. This is a case of increasing marginal cost. At point *Z*, the slope of the curve is equal to the slope of the straight line tangent to the curve at point *Z*. The slope of the tangent line is 65/8 = 8.1.

Functions with a Minimum or a Maximum

So far, all the graphs we have shown have had either a positive or negative slope over their entire range. But many relations change directions as the independent variable increases. For example, consider a firm that is attempting to maximize its profits and is trying to determine how much output to produce. The firm may find that its unit production costs are lower than the market price of the good, and so it can increase its profit by producing more. But as it increases its level of production, the firm's unit costs may be driven up because the capacity of the factory is being approached. Eventually, the firm may find that extra output will actually cost so much that its profits will be *reduced.* This is a relationship that we will study in detail in later chapters, and it is illustrated in Figure 2-10. Notice that when profits are maximized at point *A*, the slope of the curve is zero (because a tangent to the curve at point *A* is horizontal) and so the *marginal response* of profits to output is zero.

Now consider an example of a function with a minimum. You probably know that when you drive a car the fuel consumption per kilometre depends on your speed. Driving very slowly uses a lot of fuel per kilometre travelled. Driving very fast also uses a lot of fuel per kilometre travelled. The best fuel efficiency—the lowest fuel consumption per kilometre travelled—occurs at a speed of approximately 95 kilometres per hour. The relationship between speed and fuel consumption is shown in Figure 2-11 and illustrates a function with a minimum. Note that at point *A* the slope of the curve is zero (because a tangent to the curve at point *A* is horizontal) and so the *marginal response* of fuel consumption to speed is zero.

At either a minimum or a maximum of a function, the slope of the curve is zero. Therefore, at the minimum or maximum, the marginal response of *Y* to a change in *X* is zero.

FIGURE 2-10 Profits as a Function of Output

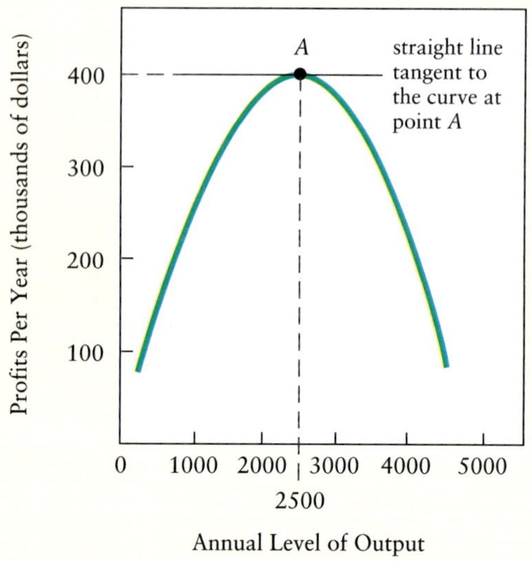

Profits rise and then eventually fall as output rises. When the firm is producing less than 2500 units annually, the marginal response of profit to output is positive—that is, an increase in output leads to an increase in profit. Beyond 2500 units annually, the marginal response is negative—an increase in output leads to a reduction in profit. At point *A*, profits are maximized and the marginal response of profit to output is zero. Because the tangent at point *A* is horizontal, the slope of the curve is zero at that point.

FIGURE 2-11 Average Fuel Consumption as a Function of Speed

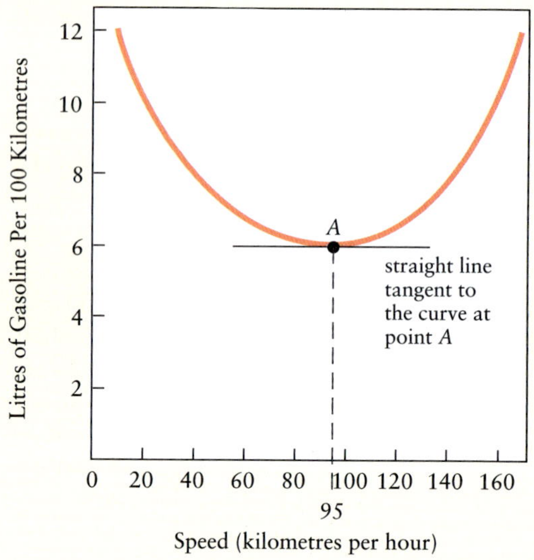

Average fuel consumption falls and then eventually rises as speed increases. Average fuel consumption in litres per kilometre travelled is minimized at point *A* at a speed of approximately 95 kilometres per hour (km/h). At speeds less than 95 km/h, the marginal response is negative—that is, an increase in speed reduces fuel consumption per kilometre. At speeds above 95 km/h, the marginal response is positive—an increase in speed increases fuel consumption per kilometre. At 95 km/h, the marginal response is zero and fuel consumption per kilometre is minimized.

A Final Word

We have done much in this chapter. We have discussed why economists use theory and how they build economic models. We have discussed how they test their theories and how there is a continual back-and-forth process between empirical testing of predictions and refining the theoretical model. Finally, we have devoted considerable time and space to exploring the many ways that data can be displayed in graphs and how economists use graphs to illustrate their theories.

Many students find themselves intimidated when they are first confronted with all of the details about graphing. But try not to worry. You may not yet be a master of all the graphing techniques that we have discussed in this chapter, but you will be surprised at how quickly it all falls into place. And, as is true for most skills, there is no substitute for practice. In the next three chapters we will encounter many graphs. But we will start simply and then slowly attempt more complicated cases. We are confident that in the process of learning some basic economic theories you will get enough practice in graphing that you will very soon look back at this chapter and realize how straightforward it all is.

SUMMARY

2.1 POSITIVE AND NORMATIVE ADVICE

LO 1

- A key to the success of scientific inquiry lies in separating positive questions about the way the world works from normative questions about how one would like the world to work.

2.2 ECONOMIC THEORIES

LO 2

- Theories are designed to explain and predict what we see. A theory consists of a set of definitions of the variables to be employed, a set of assumptions about how things behave, and the conditions under which the theory is meant to apply.
- A theory provides conditional predictions of the type "if one event occurs, then another event will also occur."
- The term "model" is often used as a synonym for theory. It is also used to describe an illustrative abstraction that is used to organize our thinking even though it may not generate testable hypotheses.

2.3 TESTING THEORIES

LO 3

- Theories are tested by checking their predictions against evidence. In some sciences, these tests can be conducted under laboratory conditions in which only one thing changes at a time. In economics, testing is almost always done using the data produced by the world of ordinary events.
- Economists make use of statistical analysis when testing their theories. They must take care to make the distinction between correlation and causation.
- The progress of any science lies in finding better explanations of events than are now available. Thus, in any developing science, one must expect to discard some existing theories and replace them with demonstrably superior alternatives.

2.4 ECONOMIC DATA

LO 4

- Index numbers express economic series in relative form. Values in each period are expressed in relation to the value in the base period, which is given a value of 100.
- Economic data may be graphed in three different ways. Cross-sectional graphs show observations taken at the same time. Time-series graphs show observations on one variable taken over time. Scatter diagrams show many points, each one of which refers to specific observations on two different variables.

2.5 GRAPHING ECONOMIC THEORIES

LO 5

- A functional relation can be expressed in words, in a schedule giving specific values, in a mathematical equation, or in a graph.
- A graph of two variables has a positive slope when they both increase or decrease together and a negative slope when they move in opposite directions.
- The marginal response of a variable gives the amount it changes in response to a change in a second variable. When the variable is measured on the vertical axis of a diagram, its marginal response at a specific point on the curve is measured by the slope of the line at that point.
- Some functions have a maximum or minimum point. At such points, the marginal response is zero.

KEY CONCEPTS

Positive and normative statements
Endogenous and exogenous variables
Theories and models
Variables, assumptions, and predictions
Correlation versus causation
Functional relations
Positive and negative relations between variables
Positively and negatively sloped curves
Marginal responses
Maximum and minimum values

STUDY EXERCISES

1. In the following examples, identify the exogenous (or independent) variable and the endogenous (or dependent) variable.
   a. The amount of rainfall on the Canadian prairies determines the amount of wheat produced in Canada.
   b. When the world price of coffee increases, there is a change in the price of your cup of coffee at Tim Hortons.
   c. If student loans were no longer available, there would be fewer students attending university.
   d. An increase in the tax on gasoline leads people to drive more fuel-efficient vehicles.

2. Use the appropriate graph—time-series, cross-sectional, or scatter diagram—to illustrate the economic data provided in each part below.
   a. Canada's prime interest rate in 2005:

January	4.25	July	4.25
February	4.25	August	4.25
March	4.25	September	4.50
April	4.25	October	4.75
May	4.25	November	4.75
June	4.25	December	5.00

   b. A comparison of average household expenditures across provinces in 2004:

British Columbia	64 266
Alberta	71 256
Saskatchewan	53 314
Manitoba	56 317
Ontario	71 583
Quebec	54 494
New Brunswick	51 531
Nova Scotia	54 559
Prince Edward Island	50 849
Newfoundland and Labrador	49 867

   c. Per capita growth rates of real GDP and investment rates for various countries, averaged over the period 1970–1990:

Country	Average Growth Rate (% per year)	Average Investment Rate (% of GDP)
Canada	2.6	22.0
Austria	2.6	25.5
Japan	3.6	31.0
United States	1.7	18.7
United Kingdom	2.1	18.2
Spain	2.5	23.0
Norway	3.2	28.2

3. myeconlab Use the following figure to answer the questions below.

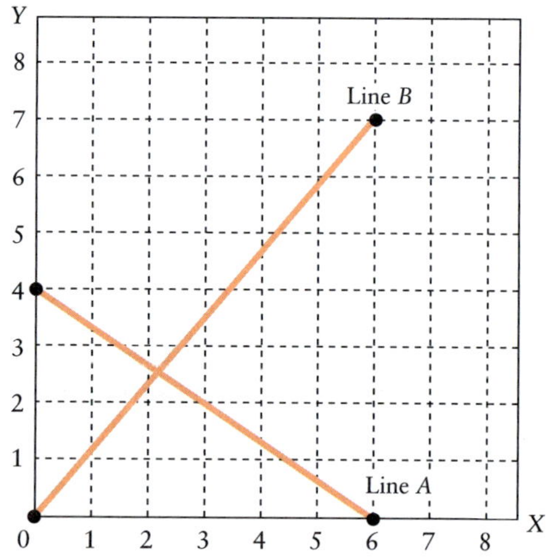

   a. Is the slope of Line *A* positive or negative? Line *B*?
   b. Calculate the slope of Line *A*. Write the equation describing the line in the form $Y = mX + b$ where m is the slope of the line and b is a constant term.
   c. Calculate the slope of Line *B*. Write the equation describing the line in the form $Y = mX + b$ where m is the slope of the line and b is a constant term.

4. myeconlab Suppose the relationship between the government's tax revenue (T) and national income (Y) is represented by the following equation: $T = 10 + 0.25Y$. Plot this relationship on a scale diagram, with Y on the horizontal axis and T on the vertical axis. Interpret the equation.

5. Consider the following three specific functional forms for a functional relation between X and Y:

   i) $Y = 50 + 2X$
   ii) $Y = 50 + 2X + 0.05X^2$
   iii) $Y = 50 + 2X - 0.05X^2$

   a. For the values of X of 0, 10, 20, 30, 40, and 50, plot X and Y on a scale diagram for each specific functional form. Connect these points with a smooth line.
   b. For each functional form, state whether the slope of the line is constant, increasing, or decreasing as the value of X increases.
   c. Describe for each functional form how the marginal change in Y depends on the value of X.

6. Suppose you want to create a price index for the price of pizza across several Canadian university campuses, as of March 1, 2007. The data are as follows:

University	Price Per Pizza
Dalhousie	$6.50
Laval	5.95
McGill	6.00
Queen's	8.00
Waterloo	7.50
Manitoba	5.50
Saskatchewan	5.75
Calgary	6.25
UBC	7.25
Victoria	7.00

   a. Using Calgary as the "base university," construct the Canadian university pizza price index.
   b. At which university is pizza the most expensive, and by what percentage is the price higher than in Calgary?
   c. At which university is pizza the least expensive, and by what percentage is the price lower than in Calgary?
   d. Are the data listed above time-series or cross-sectional data? Explain why.

7. For each of the functional relations listed below, plot the relations on a scale diagram (with X on the horizontal axis and Y on the vertical axis) and compute the slope of the line.

   i) $Y = 10 + 3X$
   ii) $Y = 20 + 4X$
   iii) $Y = 30 + 5X$
   iv) $Y = 10 + 5X$

8. Suppose we divide Canada into three regions—the West, the Centre, and the East. Each region has an unemployment rate, defined as the number of people unemployed, expressed as a fraction of that region's labour force. The table that follows shows each region's unemployment rate and the size of its labour force.

Region	Unemployment Rate	Labour Force
West	5.5%	5.3 million
Centre	7.2%	8.4 million
East	12.5%	3.5 million

   a. Compute an unemployment rate for Canada using a simple average of the rates in the three regions. Is this the "right" unemployment rate for Canada as a whole? Explain why or why not.
   b. Now compute an unemployment rate for Canada using weights that reflect the size of that region's labour force as a proportion of the overall Canadian labour force. Explain the difference in this unemployment rate from the one in part (a). Is this a "better" measure of Canadian unemployment? Explain why.

9. Draw three graphs in which the dependent variable increases at an increasing rate, at a constant rate, and at a diminishing rate. Then draw three graphs in which it decreases at an increasing, constant, and diminishing rate. For each of these graphs state a real relation that might be described by it—other than the ones given in the text of this chapter.

DISCUSSION QUESTIONS

1. What are some of the positive and normative issues that lie behind the disagreements in the following cases?

   a. Economists disagree on whether the government of Canada should try to stimulate the economy in the next six months.
   b. European and North American negotiators disagree over the desirability of reducing European farm subsidies.
   c. Economists argue about the merits of a voucher system that allows parents to choose the schools their children will attend.
   d. Economists debate the use of a two-tier medical system in Canada (whereby health care continues to be publicly provided, but individuals are permitted to be treated by doctors who bill the patient directly—"extra billing").

2. Much recent public debate has centred on the pros and cons of permitting continued unrestricted sale of cigarettes. Proposals for the control of cigarettes range from increasing excise taxes to the mandatory use of plain packaging to an outright ban on their sale. Discuss the positive and normative assumptions that underlie the national mood to reduce the consumption of tobacco products.

3. Economists sometimes make each of the following assumptions when they construct models. Discuss some situations in which each of these assumptions might be a useful simplification in order to think about some aspect of the real world.

   a. The earth is flat.
   b. There are no differences between men and women.
   c. There is no tomorrow.
   d. There are only two periods—this year and next year.
   e. A country produces only two types of goods.
   f. People are wholly selfish.

4. Untestable statements can often be reworded so that they can be tested by an appeal to evidence. How might you do this for each of the following assertions?

   a. Free-market economic systems are the best in the world.
   b. Unemployment insurance is eroding the work ethic and encouraging people to become wards of the state rather than productive workers.
   c. Robotics ought to be outlawed because it will destroy the future of working people.
   d. Laws requiring equal pay for work of equal value will make women better off.
   e. Free trade improves the welfare of a country's citizens.

5. There are hundreds of eyewitnesses to the existence of flying saucers and other UFOs. There are films and eyewitness accounts of Nessie, the Loch Ness monster. Are you convinced of their existence? If not, what would it take to persuade you? If you are already convinced, what would it take to make you change your mind?

PART 2: AN INTRODUCTION TO DEMAND AND SUPPLY

CHAPTER 3

Demand, Supply, and Price

LO LEARNING OBJECTIVES

In this chapter you will learn

1. what determines "quantity demanded," the amount of some product that consumers want to purchase.
2. to distinguish between a shift in a demand curve and a movement along a demand curve.
3. what determines "quantity supplied," the amount of some product that producers want to sell.
4. to distinguish between a shift in a supply curve and a movement along a supply curve.
5. about the forces that drive market price to equilibrium, and how equilibrium price is affected by changes in demand and supply.

How do individual markets work? We are now ready to study this important question. The answer leads us to what are called the laws of supply and demand. And though there is much more to economics than just demand and supply (as many following chapters will illustrate), this is an essential starting point for understanding how a market, and thus a market economy, functions.

As a first step, we need to understand what determines the demand for and the supply of particular products. Then we can see how demand and supply together determine the prices of products and the quantities that are bought and sold. Finally, we examine how the price system allows the economy to respond to the many changes that impinge on it. Demand and supply help us to understand the price system's successes and failures, and the consequences of many government policies.

This chapter deals with the basic elements of demand, supply, and price. In the next two chapters we use the demand-and-supply apparatus to discuss such issues as cigarette taxes, legislated minimum wages, price controls on rental housing, and the burden of payroll taxes.

3.1 DEMAND

What determines the demand for any given product? How have Canadian consumers responded to the recent declines in the prices of personal computers and cellular telephones? How will they respond to the next sudden change in the world price of oil or coffee? We start by developing a theory designed to explain the demand for some typical product.

What Is "Quantity Demanded"?

quantity demanded The amount of a good or service that consumers wish to purchase during some time period.

The total amount of any particular good or service that consumers wish to purchase in some time period is called the **quantity demanded** of that product. It is important to notice two things about this concept.

First, quantity demanded is a *desired* quantity. It is the amount that consumers wish to purchase when faced with a particular price of the product, other products' prices, their incomes, their tastes, and everything else that might matter. It may be different from the amount that consumers actually succeed in purchasing. If sufficient quantities are not available, the amount that consumers wish to purchase may exceed the amount that they actually purchase. (For example, think of standing in line to purchase tickets to a show, only to find out that the show is sold out before you get to the head of the line.) To distinguish these two concepts, the term *quantity demanded* is used to refer to desired purchases, and a phrase such as *quantity actually bought* or *quantity exchanged* is used to refer to actual purchases.

Second, quantity demanded refers to a *flow* of purchases. It must therefore be expressed as so much per period of time: 1 million units per day, 7 million per week, or 365 million per year. For example, being told that the quantity of new television sets demanded (at current prices) in Canada is 50 000 means nothing unless you are also told the period of time involved. Fifty thousand TVs demanded per day would be an enormous rate of demand; 50 000 per year would be a very small rate for a country as large as Canada. The important distinction between *stocks* and *flows* is discussed in *Extensions in Theory 3-1*.

The total amount of some product that consumers in the relevant market wish to buy in a given time period is influenced by the following important variables: [2]

- Product's own price
- Average income
- Prices of other products
- Tastes
- Distribution of income
- Population
- Expectations about the future

We will discuss the separate effects of each of these variables later in the chapter. For now, we focus on the effects of changes in the product's own price. But how do we analyze the distinct effect of changes in one variable when all are likely to be changing at once? Since this is difficult to do, we manage it in two stages. First, we consider the influence of the variables one at a time. To do this, we hold all but one of them constant. Then we let the selected variable vary and study how its change affects quantity demanded. We can do the same for each of the other variables in turn, and in this way we can come to understand the importance of each. Second, we then combine the separate influences of the variables to discover what happens when several things change at the same time—as they often do.

Holding all other variables constant is often described by the expressions "other things being equal," "other things given," or the equivalent Latin phrase, *ceteris paribus*. When economists speak of the influence of the price of eggs on the quantity

EXTENSIONS IN THEORY 3-1

The Distinction Between Stocks and Flows

An important conceptual issue that arises frequently in economics is the distinction between *stock* and *flow* variables. Economic theories use both, and it takes a little practice to keep them straight.

As noted in the text, a flow variable has a time dimension—it is so much *per unit of time*. For example, the quantity of Grade A large eggs purchased in Edmonton is a flow variable. No useful information is conveyed if we are told that the number purchased was 2000 dozen eggs unless we are also told the period of time over which these purchases occurred. Two thousand dozen eggs per hour would indicate a much more active market in eggs than would 2000 dozen eggs per month.

In contrast, a stock variable is a variable whose value has meaning *at a point in time*. Thus, the number of eggs in the egg producer's warehouse on a particular day—for example, 20 000 dozen eggs on September 3, 2007—is a stock variable. All those eggs are there at one time, and they remain there until something happens to change the stock held in the warehouse. The stock variable is just a number at a point in time, not a rate of flow of so much per unit of time.

The terminology of stocks and flows can be understood in terms of an analogy to a bathtub. At any moment, the tub holds so much water. This is the *stock*, and it can be measured in terms of the volume of water, say, 100 litres. There might also be water flowing into the tub from the tap; this *flow* is measured as so much water per unit time, say, 10 litres per minute.

The distinction between stocks and flows is important. Failure to keep them straight is a common source of confusion and even error. Note, for example, that a stock variable and a flow variable cannot be added together without specifying some time period for which the flow persists. We cannot add the stock of 100 litres of water in the tub to the flow of 10 litres per minute to get 110 litres. The new stock of water will depend on how long the flow persists; if it lasts for 20 minutes, the new stock will be 300 litres; if the flow persists for 60 minutes, the new stock will be 700 litres (or the tub will overflow!).

The amount of income earned is a flow; there is so much per year or per month or per hour. The amount of a consumer's expenditure is also a flow—so much spent per week or per month or per year. The amount of money in a bank account or a miser's hoard (earned, perhaps, in the past but unspent) is a stock—just so many thousands of dollars. The key test is always whether a time dimension is required to give the variable meaning.

The amount of water behind the dam at any time is the stock of water; the amount moving through the gate is the flow, which is measured per unit of time.

of eggs demanded, *ceteris paribus*, they refer to what a change in the price of eggs would do to the quantity of eggs demanded *if all other variables that influence the demand for eggs did not change.*

Quantity Demanded and Price[1]

We are interested in studying the relationship between the quantity demanded of a product and that product's price. This requires that we hold all other influences constant and ask, "How will the quantity demanded of a product change as its price changes?"

A basic economic hypothesis is that the price of a product and the quantity demanded are related *negatively,* other things being equal. That is, the lower the price, the higher the quantity demanded; the higher the price, the lower the quantity demanded.

The British economist Alfred Marshall (1842–1924) called this fundamental relation the "law of demand." In Chapter 6, we will derive the law of demand as a prediction that follows from more basic assumptions about individual consumer behaviour. For now, let's simply explore why this relationship seems reasonable. Products are used to satisfy desires and needs, and there is almost always more than one product that will satisfy any desire or need. Hunger may be alleviated by meat or vegetables; a desire for green vegetables can be satisfied by broccoli or spinach. The desire for a vacation may be satisfied by a trip to the ocean or to the mountains; the need to get there may be satisfied by different airlines, a bus, a car, or a train. For any general desire or need, there are many different products that will satisfy it.

Now consider what happens if income, tastes, population, and the prices of all other products remain constant and the price of only one product changes. As the price goes up, that product becomes an increasingly expensive means of satisfying a desire. Some consumers will stop buying it altogether; others will buy smaller amounts; still others may continue to buy the same quantity. Because many consumers will switch wholly or partly to other products to satisfy the same desire, less will be demanded of the product whose price has risen. As meat becomes more expensive, for example, some consumers will switch to meat substitutes; others may forgo meat at some meals and eat less meat at others. Taken together as a group, consumers will want to buy less meat when its price rises.

Conversely, as the price goes down, the product becomes a cheaper method of satisfying a desire. Households will demand more of it. Consequently, they will buy less of similar products whose prices have not fallen and as a result have become expensive *relative* to the product in question. When the price of tomatoes falls, shoppers switch to tomatoes and cut their purchases of many other vegetables that now look relatively more expensive.

Demand Schedules and Demand Curves

demand schedule A table showing the relationship between quantity demanded and the price of a commodity, other things being equal.

A **demand schedule** is one way of showing the relationship between quantity demanded and the price of a product, other things being equal. It is a table showing the quantity demanded at various prices.

The table in Figure 3-1 shows a hypothetical demand schedule for carrots. It lists the quantity of carrots that would be demanded at various prices, given the assumption that all other variables are held constant. We should note in particular that aver-

[1] In this chapter we explore the demand curve for some product for the market as a whole—what we often call the *market demand curve*. In Chapter 6 we discuss how this market demand curve is derived by aggregating the demands of different individuals.

FIGURE 3-1 The Demand for Carrots

A Demand Schedule for Carrots

Reference Point	Price Per Tonne ($)	Quantity Demanded When Average Household Income Is $50 000 Per Year (tonnes per year)
U	20	110
V	40	85
W	60	65
X	80	50
Y	100	40

A Demand Curve for Carrots

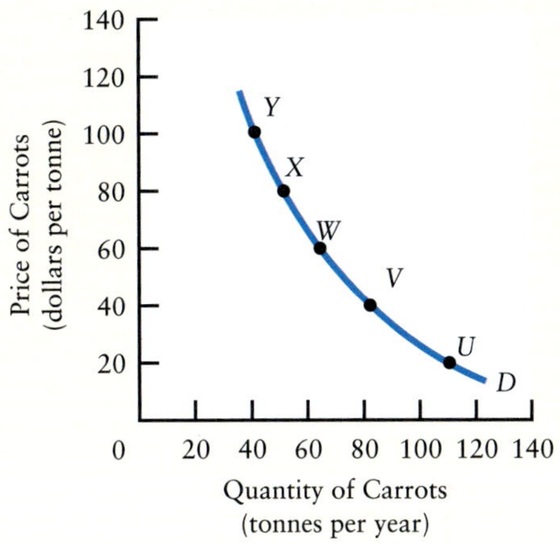

Both the table and the graph show the total quantity of carrots that would be demanded at various prices, *ceteris paribus*. For example, row *W* indicates that if the price of carrots were $60 per tonne, consumers would desire to purchase 65 tonnes of carrots per year, holding constant the values of the other variables that affect quantity demanded. The demand curve, labelled *D*, relates quantity of carrots demanded to the price of carrots; its negative slope indicates that quantity demanded increases as price falls.

age household income is assumed to be $50 000 per year because later we will want to see what happens when income changes. The table gives the quantities demanded for five selected prices, but in fact a separate quantity would be demanded at each possible price from 1 cent to several hundreds of dollars.

A second method of showing the relationship between quantity demanded and price is to draw a graph. The five price–quantity combinations shown in the table are plotted in Figure 3-1. Price is plotted on the vertical axis, and the quantity demanded is plotted on the horizontal axis.

The curve drawn through these points is called a **demand curve.** It shows the quantity that consumers would like to buy at each price. The negative slope of the curve indicates that the quantity demanded increases as the price falls. Each point on the demand curve indicates a single price–quantity combination. The demand curve as a whole shows something more.

demand curve The graphical representation of the relationship between quantity demanded and the price of a commodity, other things being equal.

The demand curve represents the relationship between quantity demanded and price, other things being equal.

When economists speak of demand in a particular market, they are referring not just to the particular quantity being demanded at the moment (i.e., not just to one point on the demand curve) but to the entire demand curve—to the relationship between desired purchases and all the possible prices of the product.

The term **demand** therefore refers to the entire relationship between the quantity demanded of a product and the price of that product. In contrast, a single point on a demand schedule or curve is the quantity demanded at that point. This distinction between "demand" and "quantity demanded" is an extremely important one and we will examine it more closely later in this chapter.

demand The entire relationship between the quantity of a commodity that buyers wish to purchase and the price of that commodity, other things being equal.

Shifts in the Demand Curve The demand curve is drawn with the assumption that everything except the product's own price is being held constant. But what if other things change, as they often do? For example, consider an increase in average household income while price remains constant. If consumers increase their purchases of the product, the new quantity demanded cannot be represented by a point on the original demand curve. It must be represented on a new demand curve that is to the right of the old curve. Thus, a rise in income that causes more to be demanded *at each price* shifts the demand curve to the right, as shown in Figure 3-2. This shift illustrates the operation of an important general rule.

A demand curve is drawn with the assumption that everything except the product's own price is held constant. A change in any of the variables previously held constant will shift the demand curve to a new position.

A demand curve can shift in two important ways. In the first case, more is desired at each price—the demand curve shifts rightward so that each price corresponds to a higher quantity than it did before. In the second case, less is desired at each price—the demand curve shifts leftward so that each price corresponds to a lower quantity than it did before.

We can assess the influence of changes in variables other than price by determining how changes in each variable shift the demand curve. Any change will shift the demand curve to the right if it increases the amount that households wish to buy at each price, other things remaining equal. It will shift the demand curve to the left if it decreases the amount that households wish to buy at each price, other things remaining equal.

FIGURE 3-2 An Increase in the Demand for Carrots

Demand Schedules

Price Per Tonne ($) p	Quantity Demanded When Average Household Income Is $50 000 Per Year (tonnes per year) D_0	Quantity Demanded When Average Household Income Is $60 000 Per Year (tonnes per year) D_1
20	110 *U*	140 *U′*
40	85 *V*	115 *V′*
60	65 *W*	95 *W′*
80	50 *X*	80 *X′*
100	40 *Y*	70 *Y′*

Demand Curves

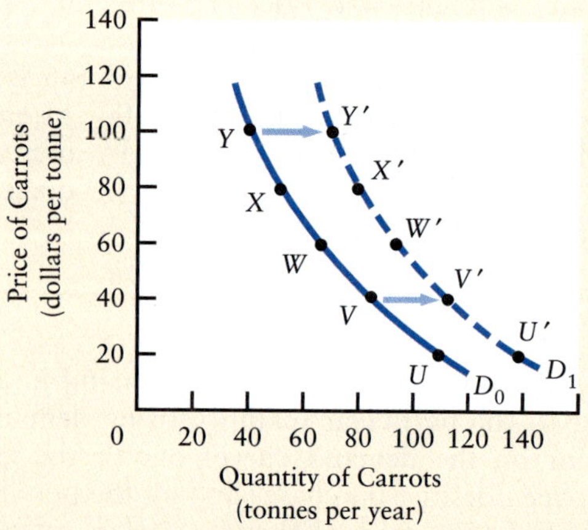

An increase in average household income increases the quantity demanded at each price (for all normal goods). This is shown by the rightward shift in the demand curve, from D_0 to D_1. When average income rises from $50 000 to $60 000 per year, quantity demanded at a price of $60 per tonne rises from 65 tonnes per year to 95 tonnes per year. A similar rise occurs at every other price.

1. Average Income. If average income rises, consumers as a group can be expected to desire more of most products even if prices don't change at all. Goods for which the quantity demanded increases when income rises are called *normal goods;* goods for which the quantity demanded falls when income rises are called *inferior goods.* The term *normal goods* reflects economists' empirical finding that the demand for most goods rises when income rises. We therefore expect that a rise in average consumer income shifts the demand curve for most products to the right, indicating that more will be demanded at any given price. Such a shift is illustrated in Figure 3-2.

2. Prices of Other Goods. We saw that the negative slope of a product's demand curve occurs because the lower its price, the cheaper the product becomes relative to other products that can satisfy the same needs or desires. These other products are called **substitutes**. Another way for the same change to come about is that the price of the substitute product rises. For example, carrots can become cheap relative to broccoli either because the price of carrots falls or because the price of broccoli rises. Either change will increase the amount of carrots that consumers wish to buy as some consumers substitute away from broccoli and toward carrots. Thus, a rise in the price of a substitute for a product shifts the demand curve for the product to the right. More will be demanded at each price. For example, Coke and Pepsi are substitutes. If the price of Pepsi increases, the demand curve for Coke will shift to the right.

substitutes Goods that can be used in place of another good to satisfy similar needs or desires.

Complements are products that tend to be used jointly. Cars and gasoline are complements; so are CD players and speakers, golf clubs and golf balls, electric stoves and electricity, and airplane flights to Calgary and ski-lift tickets in Banff. Because complements tend to be consumed together, a fall in the price of one will increase the quantity demanded of *both* products. Thus, a fall in the price of a complement for a product will shift that product's demand curve to the right. More will be demanded at each price. For example, a fall in the price of airplane trips to Calgary will lead to a rise in the demand for ski-lift tickets in Banff, even though the price of those lift tickets is unchanged. (So the demand curve for ski-lift tickets will shift to the right.)

complements Goods that tend to be consumed together.

3. Tastes. Tastes have an effect on people's desired purchases. A change in tastes may be long-lasting, such as the shift from fountain pens to ballpoint pens or from typewriters to computers, or it may be a short-lived fad as is common with many toys such as Pokémon cards and Beanie Babies. In either case, a change in tastes in favour of a product shifts the demand curve to the right. More will be demanded at each price. Of course, a change in tastes against some product has the opposite effect and shifts the demand curve to the left. The gradual but persistent reduction in demand for Camaro and Firebird cars eventually led General Motors in the late 1990s to close the plant at which those specific models were manufactured.

4. Distribution of Income. A change in the distribution of income will cause an increase in the demand for products bought most by consumers whose incomes increase and a decrease in the demand for products bought most by consumers whose incomes decrease. If, for example, the government increases the child tax credit and at the same time raises basic tax rates, income will be transferred from households without children to households with children. Demands for products more heavily bought by childless persons will decline, while demands for products more heavily bought by households with children will increase.

5. Population. Population growth does not create new demand unless the additional people have the means to purchase goods—that is, unless they have purchasing power. If there is an increase in population with purchasing power, the demands for all the products purchased by the new people will rise. Thus, we expect that an increase in

FIGURE 3-3 Shifts in the Demand Curve

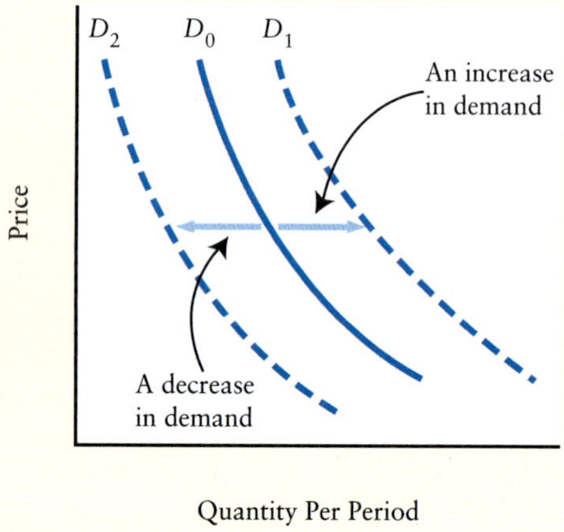

A rightward shift in the demand curve from D_0 to D_1 indicates an increase in demand; a leftward shift from D_0 to D_2 indicates a decrease in demand. An increase in demand means that more is demanded at each price. Such a rightward shift can be caused by a rise in income, a rise in the price of a substitute, a fall in the price of a complement, a change in tastes that favours that product, an increase in population, a redistribution of income toward groups that favour the product, or the anticipation of a future event that will increase the price.

A decrease in demand means that less is demanded at each price. Such a leftward shift can be caused by a fall in income, a fall in the price of a substitute, a rise in the price of a complement, a change in tastes that disfavours the product, a decrease in population, a redistribution of income away from groups that favour the product, or the anticipation of a future event that will decrease the price.

population will shift the demand curves for most products to the right, indicating that more will be demanded at each price.

6. Expectations About the Future. Our discussion has so far focused on how changes in the current value of variables may change demand. But it is also true that changes in people's *expectations about future values* of variables may change demand. For example, suppose you are thinking about buying a house in a small town in Nova Scotia, and you have learned that in the near future a large high-tech firm will be moving its head office and several hundred employees to this same small town. Since their future movement into your town will probably increase the demand for housing and drive up the *future* price of houses, this expectation will lead you (and others like you) to increase your demand *today* so as to make the purchase before the price rises. Thus, the demand curve for houses will shift to the right today in anticipation of a future event.

Figure 3-3 summarizes the reasons why demand curves shift.

Movements Along the Curve Versus Shifts of the Whole Curve Suppose you read in today's newspaper that a sharp increase in the world price of coffee beans has been caused by an increased worldwide demand for coffee. Then tomorrow you read that the rising price of coffee is reducing the typical consumer's purchases of coffee, as shoppers switch to other beverages. The two stories appear to contradict each other. The first associates a rising price with rising demand; the second associates a rising price with declining demand. Can both statements be true? The answer is yes—because the two statements actually refer to different things. The first describes a shift in the demand curve; the second describes a movement along the demand curve in response to a change in price.

Consider first the statement that the increase in the price of coffee has been caused by an increased demand for coffee. This statement refers to a shift in the demand curve for coffee—in this case, a shift to the right, indicating more coffee demanded at each price. This shift, as we will see later in this chapter, will increase the price of coffee.

Now consider the second statement—that less coffee is being bought because of its rise in price. This refers to a movement along the *new* demand curve and reflects a change between two specific quantities demanded, one before the price increased and one afterward.

Possible explanations for the two stories are:

1. A rise in population and income in coffee-drinking countries shifts the demand curve for coffee to the right. This, in turn, raises the price of coffee (for reasons we will soon study in detail). This was the first newspaper story.

2. The rising price of coffee is causing each individual household to cut back on its coffee purchases. The cutback is represented by an upward movement to the left along the new demand curve for coffee. This was the second newspaper story.

change in demand A change in the quantity demanded at each possible price of the commodity, represented by a shift in the whole demand curve.

change in quantity demanded A change in the specific quantity of the good demanded, represented by a change from one point on a demand curve to another point, either on the original demand curve or on a new one.

To prevent the type of confusion caused by our two newspaper stories, economists use a specialized vocabulary to distinguish between shifts of demand curves and movements along demand curves.

We have seen that demand refers to the *entire* demand curve, whereas quantity demanded refers to the quantity that is demanded at a specific price, as indicated by a particular *point* on the demand curve. Economists reserve the term **change in demand** to describe a change in the quantity demanded at *every* price. That is, a change in demand refers to a shift of the entire demand curve. The term **change in quantity demanded** refers to a movement from one point on a demand curve to another point, either on the same demand curve or on a new one.

A change in quantity demanded can result from a shift in the demand curve with the price constant; from a movement along a given demand curve due to a change in the price; or from a combination of the two. [3]

We consider these three possibilities in turn.

An increase in demand means that the whole demand curve shifts to the right; a decrease in demand means that the whole demand curve shifts to the left. At any given price, an increase in demand causes an increase in quantity demanded, whereas a decrease in demand causes a decrease in quantity demanded. For example, in Figure 3-2, the shift in the demand curve for carrots from D_0 to D_1 represents an increase in demand, and at a price of $40 per tonne, quantity demanded increases from 85 tonnes to 115 tonnes, as indicated by the move from V to V'.

A movement down and to the right along a demand curve represents an increase in quantity demanded; a movement up and to the left along a demand curve represents a decrease in quantity demanded. For example, in Figure 3-2, with the demand for carrots given by the curve D_1, an increase in price from $40 to $60 per tonne causes a movement along D_1 from V' to W', and quantity demanded decreases from 115 tonnes to 95 tonnes.

When there is a change in demand *and* a change in the price, the overall change in quantity demanded is the net effect of the shift in the demand curve and the movement along the new demand curve. Figure 3-4 shows the combined effect of an increase in demand, shown by a rightward shift in the whole demand curve, and an upward movement to the left along the new demand curve due to an increase in price. The increase in demand causes an increase in quantity demanded at the initial price, whereas the movement along the new demand curve causes a decrease in the quantity demanded. Whether quantity demanded rises or falls overall depends on the relative magnitudes of these two changes.

FIGURE 3-4 Shifts Of and Movements Along the Demand Curve

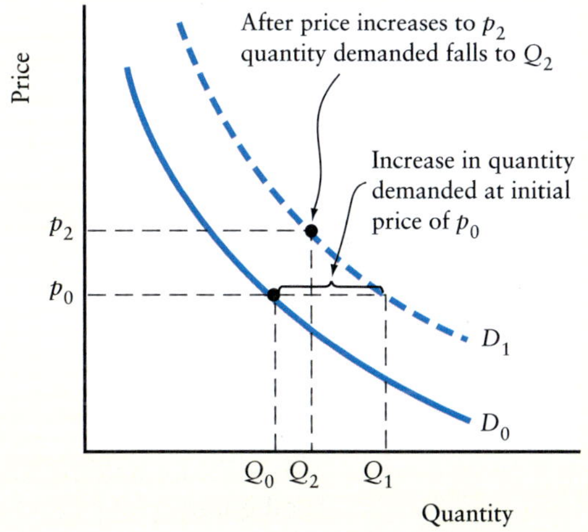

An increase in demand means that the demand curve shifts to the right, and hence quantity demanded will be higher at each price. A rise in price causes a movement upward and to the left along the demand curve, and hence quantity demanded will fall. The demand curve is originally D_0 and price is p_0, which means that quantity demanded is Q_0. Suppose demand increases to D_1, which means that at any particular price, there is a larger quantity demanded; for example, at p_0, quantity demanded is now Q_1. Now suppose the price rises above p_0. This causes a movement up and to the left along D_1, and quantity demanded falls below Q_1. As the figure is drawn, the quantity demanded at the new price p_2 is less than Q_1 but greater than Q_0. So in this case the combined effect of the increase in demand and the rise in price is an increase in quantity demanded from Q_0 to Q_2.

3.2 SUPPLY

What determines the supply of any given product? Why do Canadian oil producers extract and sell more oil when the price of oil is high? Why do Canadian cattle ranchers sell more beef when the price of cattle-feed falls? We start by developing a theory designed to explain the supply of some typical product.

What Is "Quantity Supplied"?

quantity supplied The amount of a commodity that producers wish to sell during some time period.

The amount of some good or service that producers wish to sell in some time period is called the **quantity supplied** of that product. Quantity supplied is a flow; it is so much per unit of time. Note also that quantity supplied is the amount that producers are willing to offer for sale; it is not necessarily the amount that they succeed in selling, which is expressed by *quantity actually sold* or *quantity exchanged*.

The quantity supplied of a product is influenced by the following variables: **[4]**

- Product's own price
- Prices of inputs
- Technology
- Government taxes or subsidies
- Prices of other products
- Expectations about the future
- Number of suppliers

The situation with supply is the same as that with demand: There are several influencing variables, and we will not get far if we try to discover what happens when they all change at the same time. Again, we use the convenient *ceteris paribus* assumption to study the influence of the variables one at a time.

Quantity Supplied and Price

We begin by holding all other influences constant and ask, "How do we expect the total quantity of a product supplied to vary with its own price?"

A rise in the price of wheat, other things being equal, will lead farmers to plant less of other crops and plant more wheat.

A basic hypothesis of economics is that the price of the product and the quantity supplied are related *positively*, other things being equal. That is, the higher the product's own price, the more its producers will supply; the lower the price, the less its producers will supply.

In later chapters we will derive this hypothesis as a prediction from more basic assumptions about the behaviour of individual profit-maximizing firms. For now we simply note that as the product's price rises, producing and selling this product becomes a more profitable activity. Firms interested in increasing their profit will therefore choose to increase their production.

Supply Schedules and Supply Curves

The general relationship just discussed can be illustrated by a **supply schedule**, which shows the relationship between quantity supplied of a product and the price of the product, other things being equal. The table in Figure 3-5 presents a hypothetical supply schedule for carrots.

supply schedule A table showing the relationship between quantity supplied and the price of a commodity, other things being equal.

A **supply curve**, the graphical representation of the supply schedule, is illustrated in Figure 3-5. Each point on the supply curve represents a specific price–quantity combination; however, the whole curve shows something more.

supply curve The graphical representation of the relationship between quantity supplied and the price of a commodity, other things being equal.

The supply curve represents the relationship between quantity supplied and price, other things being equal; its positive slope indicates that quantity supplied increases when price increases.

When economists make statements about the conditions of supply, they are not referring just to the particular quantity being supplied at the moment—that is, not to just one point on the supply curve. Instead, they are referring to the entire supply curve, to the complete relationship between desired sales and all possible prices of the product.

Supply refers to the entire relationship between the quantity supplied of a product and the price of that product, other things being equal. A single point on the supply curve refers to the *quantity supplied* at that price.

supply The entire relationship between the quantity of some commodity that producers wish to sell and the price of that commodity, other things being equal.

Shifts in the Supply Curve A shift in the supply curve means that at each price there is a change in the quantity supplied. An increase in the quantity supplied at each price is shown in Figure 3-6. This change appears as a rightward shift in the supply curve.

FIGURE 3-5 The Supply of Carrots

A Supply Schedule for Carrots

Reference Point	Price Per Tonne ($)	Quantity Supplied (tonnes per year)
u	20	20
v	40	45
w	60	65
x	80	80
y	100	95

A Supply Curve for Carrots

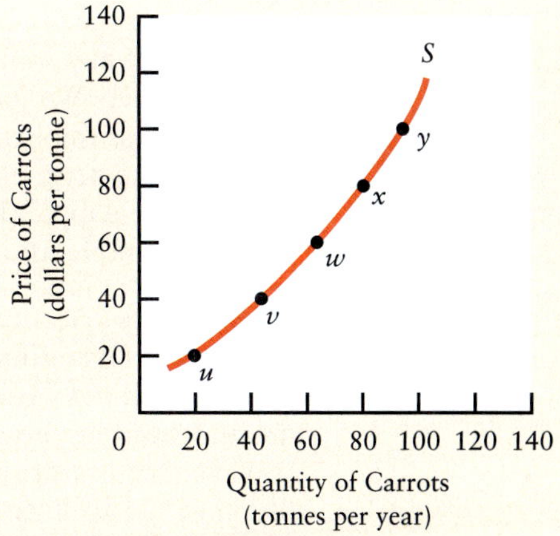

Both the table and the graph show the quantities that producers wish to sell at various prices, *ceteris paribus*. For example, row *w* indicates that if the price of carrots were $60 per tonne, producers would want to sell 65 tonnes per year. The supply curve, labelled *S*, relates quantity of carrots supplied to the price of carrots; its positive slope indicates that quantity supplied increases as price increases.

FIGURE 3-6 An Increase in the Supply of Carrots

Supply Schedules

Price Per Tonne ($) p	Quantity Supplied Before Cost-Saving Innovation (tonnes per year) S_0	Quantity Supplied After Innovation (tonnes per year) S_1
20	20 *u*	50 *u′*
40	45 *v*	75 *v′*
60	65 *w*	95 *w′*
80	80 *x*	110 *x′*
100	95 *y*	125 *y′*

Supply Curves

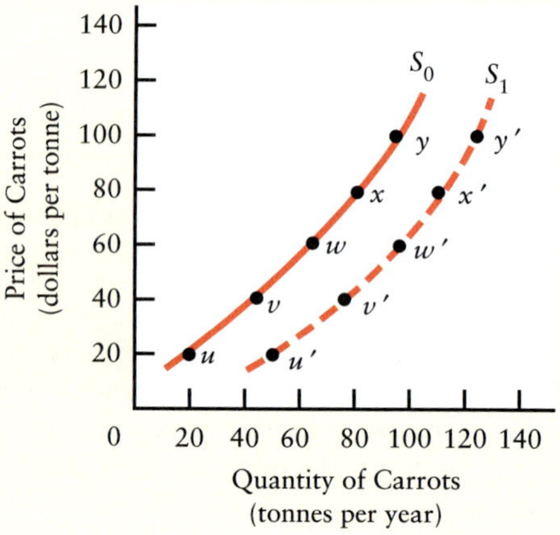

A cost-saving innovation increases the quantity supplied at each price. This is shown by the rightward shift in the supply curve, from S_0 to S_1. As a result of a cost-saving innovation, the quantity that is supplied at a price of $100 per tonne rises from 95 to 125 tonnes per year. A similar rise occurs at every price.

In contrast, a decrease in the quantity supplied at each price would appear as a leftward shift. For supply, as for demand, there is an important general rule:

A change in any of the variables (other than the product's own price) that affects the quantity supplied will shift the supply curve to a new position.

Let's now consider the possible causes of shifts in supply curves.

1. Prices of Inputs. All things that a firm uses to produce its outputs, such as materials, labour, and machines, are called the firm's *inputs*. Other things being equal, the higher the price of any input used to make a product, the less will be the profit from making that product. We expect, therefore, that the higher the price of any input used by a firm, the less the firm will produce and offer for sale at any given price of the product. A rise in the price of inputs therefore shifts the supply curve to the left, indicating that less will be supplied at any given price; a fall in the cost of inputs makes production more profitable and therefore shifts the supply curve to the right.

2. Technology. At any time, what is produced and how it is produced depend on what is known. Over time, knowledge changes. The enormous increase in production per worker that has been going on in industrial societies for about 200 years is due largely to improved methods of production. The Industrial Revolution is more than a historical event; it is a present reality. Discoveries in chemistry have led to lower costs of production for well-established products, such as paints, and to a large variety of new products made of plastics and synthetic fibres. Such inventions as silicon chips have radically changed products such as computers, televisions, and telephones, and the consequent development of smaller computers has revolutionized the production of countless other non-electronic products.

Any technological innovation that decreases the amount of inputs needed per unit of output reduces production costs and hence will increase the profits that can be earned at any given price of the product. Because increased profitability leads to increased willingness to produce, this change shifts the supply curve to the right.

3. Government Taxes or Subsidies. We have just seen that anything increasing firms' costs will shift the supply curve to the left, and anything decreasing firms' costs will shift the supply curve to the right. As we will see in later chapters, governments often levy special taxes on the production of specific goods, such as gasoline, cigarettes, and alcohol. These taxes make the production and sale of these goods less profitable. The result is that the supply curve shifts to the left.

For other goods, governments often subsidize producers—that is, they pay producers a specific amount for each unit of the good produced. This often occurs for agricultural products, especially in the United States and the European Union. In such situations, the subsidy increases the profitability of production and shifts the supply curve to the right.

4. Prices of Other Products. Changes in the price of one product may lead to changes in the supply of some other product because the two products are either *substitutes* or *complements* in the production process.

A prairie farmer, for example, can plant his field in wheat or oats. If the market price of oats falls, thus making oat production less profitable, the farmer will be more inclined to plant wheat. In this case, wheat and oats are said to be *substitutes* in production—for every extra acre planted in one crop, one fewer acre can be planted in the other. In this example, a reduction in the price of oats leads to an increase in the supply of wheat.

An excellent example in which two products are *complements* in production is oil and natural gas, which are often found together below the earth's surface. If the market price of natural gas rises, producers will do more drilling and increase their production of natural gas. But as more wells are drilled, the usual outcome is that more of *both* natural gas and oil are produced. Thus, the rise in the price of natural gas leads to an increase in the supply of the complementary product—oil.

5. Expectations About the Future. As in our discussion of shifts in demand curves, expectations about the future can play a role in shifting supply curves. This is especially important in agricultural markets in which farmers must make planting and production decisions several months ahead of when the output will actually be sold. In such cases, it is the expectation of the future price, and not just the current price, which guides farmers' decisions. A canola farmer who expects prices to be high in the fall will plant a large crop, even though actual prices in the spring may be low. Thus, other things being equal, an increase in the expected future price of a product leads to an increase in the supply of the product.

6. Number of Suppliers. For given prices and technology, the total amount of any product supplied depends on the number of firms producing that product and offering it for sale. If profits are being earned by current firms, then more firms will choose to enter this industry and begin producing. The effect of this increase in the number of suppliers is to shift the supply curve to the right. Similarly, if the existing firms are losing money, they will eventually leave the industry; such a reduction in the number of suppliers shifts the supply curve to the left.

change in supply A change in the quantity supplied at each possible price of the commodity, represented by a shift in the whole supply curve.

Movements Along the Curve Versus Shifts of the Whole Curve As with demand, it is important to distinguish movements along supply curves from shifts of the whole curve. Economists reserve the term **change in supply** to describe a shift of the whole supply curve—that is, a change in the quantity that will be supplied at every price. The

change in quantity supplied A change in the specific quantity supplied, represented by a change from one point on a supply curve to another point, either on the original supply curve or on a new one.

term **change in quantity supplied** refers to a movement from one point on a supply curve to another point, either on the same supply curve or a new one. In other words, an increase in supply means that the whole supply curve has shifted to the right, so that the quantity supplied at any given price has increased; a movement up and to the right along a supply curve indicates an increase in the quantity supplied in response to an increase in the price of the product.

A change in quantity supplied can result from: a change in supply, with the price constant; a movement along a given supply curve due to a change in the price; or a combination of the two.

An exercise you might find useful is to construct a diagram similar to Figure 3-4, emphasizing the difference between a shift of the supply curve and a movement along the supply curve.

Practise with Study Guide Chapter 3, Exercise 4.

3.3 THE DETERMINATION OF PRICE

So far we have considered demand and supply separately. We now come to a key question: How do the two forces of demand and supply interact to determine price?

The Concept of a Market

market Any situation in which buyers and sellers can negotiate the exchange of goods or services.

Originally the term *market* designated a physical place where products were bought and sold. We still use the term this way to describe places such as Granville Island Market in Vancouver, Kensington Market in Toronto, or Jean Talon Market in Montreal. Once developed, however, theories of market behaviour were easily extended to cover products such as wheat or oil, which can be purchased anywhere in the world at a price that tends to be uniform the world over. Today we can also buy and sell items in markets that exist in cyberspace—consider the online auction services provided by eBay—thus extending our viewpoint well beyond the idea of a single place to which consumers go to buy something.

eBay brings together buyers and sellers of thousands of different goods and services. It thus creates markets that exist only on the Internet.

For present purposes, a **market** may be defined as existing in any situation (a physical place or an electronic medium) in which buyers and sellers negotiate the exchange of some product or related group of products.

Individual markets differ in the degree of *competition* among the various buyers and sellers. In the next few chapters we will confine ourselves to examining markets in which the number of buyers and sellers is sufficiently large that no one of them has any appreciable influence on the market price. This is a very rough definition of what economists call *perfectly competitive markets.* Starting in Chapter 10, we will consider the behaviour of markets in which there are small numbers of either sellers or buyers. But our initial theory of markets will actually be a very good description of the markets for such things as wheat, pork, newsprint, coffee, copper, oil, and many other commodities.

Graphical Analysis of a Market

The table in Figure 3-7 brings together the demand and supply schedules from Figures 3-1 and 3-5. The quantities of carrots demanded and supplied at each price may now be compared.

There is only one price, $60 per tonne, at which the quantity of carrots demanded equals the quantity supplied. At prices less than $60 per tonne, there is a shortage of carrots because the quantity demanded exceeds the quantity supplied. This is a situation of **excess demand**. At prices greater than $60 per tonne, there is a surplus of carrots because the quantity supplied exceeds the quantity demanded. This is a situation of **excess supply**. This same story can also be told in graphical terms. The quantities demanded and supplied at any price can be read off the two curves; the excess supply or excess demand is shown by the horizontal distance between the curves at each price.

excess demand A situation in which, at the given price, quantity demanded exceeds quantity supplied.

excess supply A situation in which, at the given price, quantity supplied exceeds quantity demanded.

To examine the determination of market price, let's suppose first that the price is $100 per tonne. At this price, 95 tonnes are offered for sale, but only 40 tonnes are demanded. There is an excess supply of 55 tonnes per year. Sellers are then likely to cut their prices to get rid of this surplus. And purchasers, observing the stock of unsold carrots, will begin to offer less money for the product. In other words, *excess supply causes downward pressure on price.*

Now consider the price of $20 per tonne. At this price, there is excess demand. The 20 tonnes produced each year are snapped up quickly, and 90 tonnes of desired purchases cannot be made. Rivalry between would-be purchasers may lead them to offer more than the prevailing price to outbid other purchasers. Also, sellers may begin to ask a higher price for the quantities that they do have to sell. In other words, *excess demand causes upward pressure on price.*

FIGURE 3-7 Determination of the Equilibrium Price of Carrots

Demand and Supply Schedules

Price Per Tonne ($) p	Quantity Demanded (tonnes per year) D	Quantity Supplied (tonnes per year) S	Excess Demand (+) or Excess Supply (−) (tonnes per year) $D - S$
20	110	20	+90
40	85	45	+40
60	65	65	0
80	50	80	−30
100	40	95	−55

Demand and Supply Curves

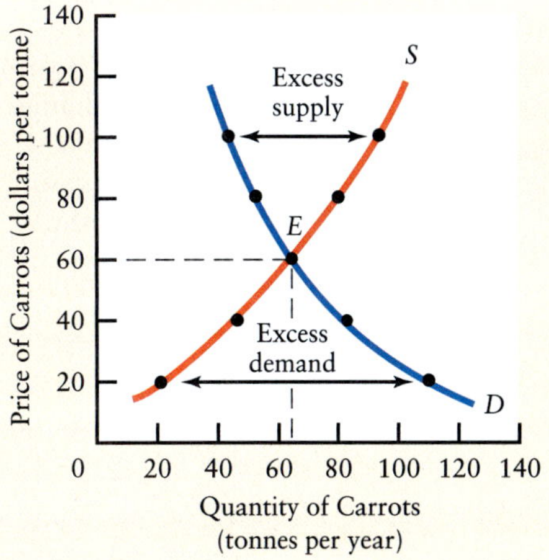

The equilibrium price corresponds to the intersection of the demand and supply curves. At any price above $60, there is excess supply and thus downward pressure on price. At any price below $60, there is excess demand and thus upward pressure on price. Only at a price of $60 is there no pressure for price to change. Equilibrium occurs at point *E*, at a price of $60.

Finally, consider the price of $60. At this price, producers wish to sell 65 tonnes per year, and purchasers wish to buy that same quantity. There is neither a shortage nor a surplus of carrots. There are no unsatisfied buyers to bid the price up, nor are there unsatisfied sellers to force the price down. Once the price of $60 has been reached, therefore, there will be no tendency for it to change.

equilibrium price The price at which quantity demanded equals quantity supplied. Also called the market-clearing price.

Equilibrium implies a state of rest, or balance, between opposing forces. The **equilibrium price** is the one toward which the actual market price will tend. Once established, it will persist until it is disturbed by some change in market conditions which shifts the demand curve, the supply curve, or both.

The price at which the quantity demanded equals the quantity supplied is called the equilibrium price, or the market-clearing price. [5]

disequilibrium price A price at which quantity demanded does not equal quantity supplied.

disequilibrium A situation in a market in which there is excess demand or excess supply.

Any price at which the market does not "clear"—that is, quantity demanded does not equal quantity supplied—is called a **disequilibrium price**. Whenever there is either excess demand or excess supply in a market, that market is said to be in a state of **disequilibrium**, and the market price will be changing.

Figure 3-7 makes it clear that the equilibrium price occurs where the demand and supply curves intersect. Below that price, there is excess demand and hence upward pressure on the existing price. Above that price, there is excess supply and hence downward pressure on the existing price.[2]

Changes in Market Prices

Changes in any of the variables, other than price, that influence quantity demanded or supplied will cause a shift in the demand curve, the supply curve, or both. There are four possible shifts: an increase in demand (a rightward shift in the demand curve), a decrease in demand (a leftward shift in the demand curve), an increase in supply (a rightward shift in the supply curve), and a decrease in supply (a leftward shift in the supply curve).

comparative statics The derivation of predictions by analyzing the effect of a change in some exogenous variable on the equilibrium.

To discover the effects of each of the possible curve shifts, we use the method known as **comparative statics**.[3] With this method, we derive predictions about how the *endogenous* variables (equilibrium price and quantity) will change following a change in some *exogenous* variable. We start from a position of equilibrium and then introduce the change to be studied. We then determine the new equilibrium position and compare it with the original one. The difference between the two positions of equilibrium must result from the change that was introduced because everything else has been held constant.

[2] When economists graph a demand (or supply) curve, they put the variable to be explained (the dependent variable) on the horizontal axis and the explanatory variable (the independent variable) on the vertical axis. This is "backwards" to what is usually done in mathematics. The rational explanation of what is now economists' odd practice is buried in the history of economics and dates back to Alfred Marshall's *Principles of Economics* (1890) [6]. For better or worse, Marshall's scheme is now used by all economists, although mathematicians never fail to wonder at this example of the odd ways of economists.

[3] The term *static* is used because we are not concerned with the actual path by which the market goes from the first equilibrium position to the second or with the time taken to reach the second equilibrium. Analysis of these movements would be described as *dynamic analysis*.

Each of the four possible curve shifts causes changes that are described by one of the four "laws" of demand and supply. Each of the laws summarizes what happens when an initial position of equilibrium is disturbed by a shift in either the demand curve or the supply curve. By using the term "law" to describe what happens, economists do not mean that they are absolutely certain of the outcome. The term "law" in science is used to describe a theory that has stood up to substantial testing. The laws of demand and supply are thus hypotheses that predict certain kinds of behaviour in certain situations, and the predicted behaviour occurs sufficiently often that economists continue to have confidence in the underlying theory.

The four laws of demand and supply are illustrated in Figure 3-8. Study the figure carefully. Previously, we had given the axes specific labels, but because it is now intended to apply to any product, the horizontal axis is simply labelled "Quantity." This means quantity per period in whatever units output is measured. "Price," the vertical axis, means the price measured as dollars per unit of quantity for the same product.

The four laws of demand and supply are as follows:

1. An increase in demand causes an increase in both the equilibrium price and the equilibrium quantity exchanged.
2. A decrease in demand causes a decrease in both the equilibrium price and the equilibrium quantity exchanged.
3. An increase in supply causes a decrease in the equilibrium price and an increase in the equilibrium quantity exchanged.

FIGURE 3-8 The Four "Laws" of Demand and Supply

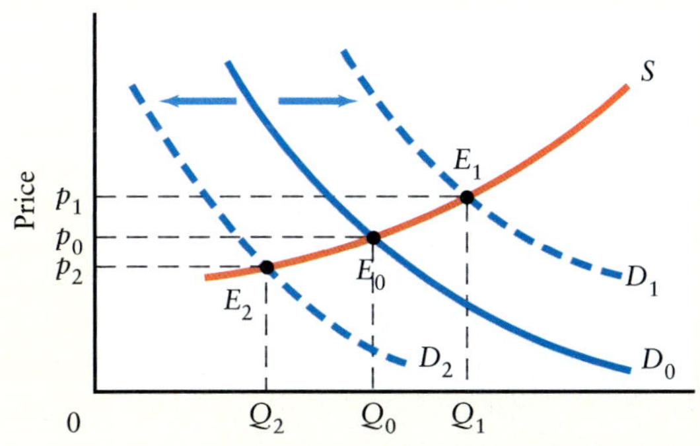

(i) The effect of shifts in the demand curve

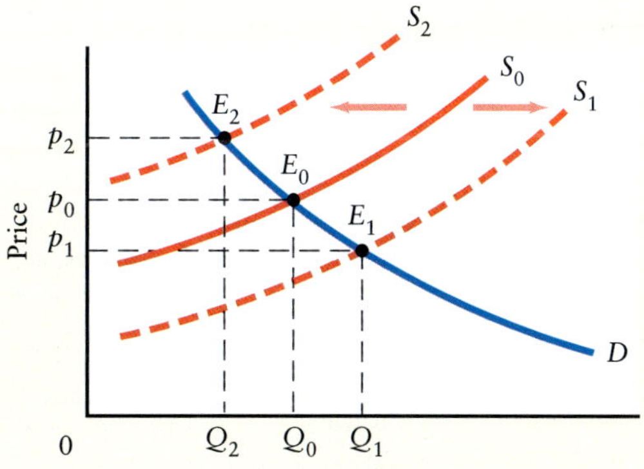

(ii) The effect of shifts in the supply curve

The effects on equilibrium price and quantity of shifts in either demand or supply are known as the laws of demand and supply. In part (i), suppose the original demand and supply curves are D_0 and S, which intersect to produce equilibrium at E_0, with a price of p_0 and a quantity of Q_0. An increase in demand shifts the demand curve to D_1, taking the new equilibrium to E_1. Price rises to p_1 and quantity rises to Q_1. Starting at E_0, a decrease in demand shifts the demand curve to D_0, taking the new equilibrium to E_2. Price falls to p_2 and quantity falls to Q_2.

In part (ii), the original demand and supply curves are D and S_0, which intersect to produce equilibrium at E_0, with a price of p_0 and a quantity of Q_0. An increase in supply shifts the supply curve to S_1, taking the new equilibrium to E_1. Price falls to p_1, and quantity rises to Q_1. Starting at E_0, a decrease in supply shifts the supply curve from S_0 to S_2, taking the new equilibrium to E_2. Price rises to p_2 and quantity falls to Q_2.

EXTENSIONS IN THEORY 3-2

The Algebra of Market Equilibrium

This box presents a specific model of demand and supply and the algebraic method for determining the equilibrium price and quantity. For simplicity, we assume that the demand and supply curves are linear relationships between price and quantity.

Consider the following demand and supply curves:

Demand: $Q^D = a - bp$
Supply: $Q^S = c + dp$

where p is the price, Q^D is quantity demanded, Q^S is quantity supplied, and a, b, c, and d are positive constants. Both relationships are plotted in the accompanying figure.

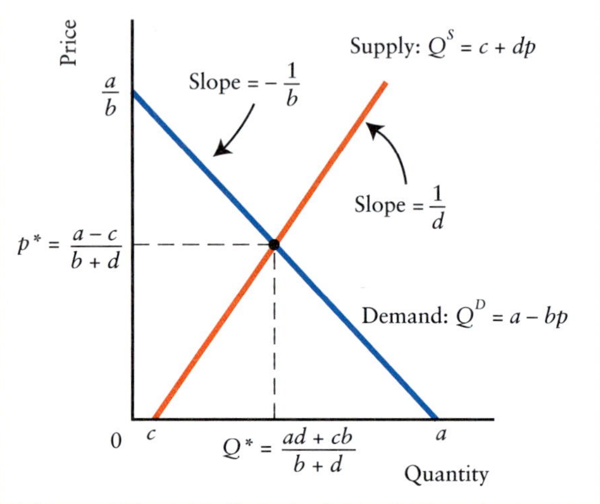

What is the interpretation of the demand curve and how do we plot it? First, at a price of zero, consumers will buy a units—this is the horizontal intercept of the demand curve. Second, if the price rises to a/b, consumers will buy zero units, so a/b is the vertical intercept of the demand curve. Finally, the slope of the demand curve is $-1/b$; the quantity demanded increases by b units for every $1 that price falls.

What is the interpretation of the supply curve, and how do we plot it? First, if the price is zero, suppliers will sell c units—this is the horizontal intercept of the supply curve. Second, for every $1 increase in price, the quantity supplied increases by d units. Thus, the slope of the supply curve is $1/d$.

Given these demand and supply curves, the market equilibrium can be determined in two ways. The first is to construct a scale diagram and plot the two curves accurately. If you do this carefully, you will be able to read the equilibrium price and quantity off the diagram. But your diagram will have to be very accurate for this to work!

A more precise method is to use algebra to solve for the equilibrium price and quantity. Here is how we do it. We know that in equilibrium quantity demanded equals quantity supplied, or $Q^D = Q^S$. We call the equilibrium quantity Q^*. But we also know that in equilibrium the price paid by the consumers will equal the price received by the producers—that is, there is only one equilibrium price, which we call p^*. Putting these two facts together we know that in equilibrium

Demand: $Q^* = a - bp^*$
Supply: $Q^* = c + dp^*$

4. A decrease in supply causes an increase in the equilibrium price and a decrease in the equilibrium quantity exchanged.

Demonstrations of these laws are given in the caption to Figure 3-8. The intuitive reasoning behind each is as follows:

1. **An increase in demand (the demand curve shifts to the right).** An increase in demand creates a shortage at the initial equilibrium price, and the unsatisfied buyers bid up the price. This rise in price causes a larger quantity to be supplied with the result that at the new equilibrium more is exchanged at a higher price.

We now have two equations and two unknown variables (p^* and Q^*) and can proceed to solve the system of equations. Since Q^* from the demand curve equals Q^* from the supply curve, it follows that

$$a - bp^* = c + dp^*$$

This implies

$$a - c = (b + d)p^*$$

which can be solved for p^* to get

$$p^* = \frac{a - c}{b + d}$$

This is the solution for the equilibrium market price. By substituting this value of p^* back into *either* the demand curve or the supply curve (it doesn't matter which) we get the solution for Q^*:

$$Q^* = a - bp^* = a - b[(a - c)/(b + d)]$$

which can be simplified to be

$$Q^* = \frac{(ad + bc)}{b+d}$$

We now have the precise solutions for the equilibrium price and quantity in this market. Notice that the solutions for p^* and Q^* naturally depend on those (exogenous) variables that shift the demand and supply curves. For example, an increase in demand for the product would be reflected by an increase in a. This would shift the demand curve to the right, increasing both p^* and Q^*. A decrease in supply would have a different effect. It would be reflected by a decrease in c that would shift the supply curve to the left, leading to an increase in p^* and a reduction in Q^*.

Now let's do the same thing but with even more specific demand and supply curves. Suppose we have the following relationships:

$$Q^D = 18 - 3p$$
$$Q^S = 2 + 5p$$

The equilibrium condition is that $Q^D = Q^S = Q^*$. And when quantity is equal to Q^*, price will be equal to p^*. Thus, in equilibrium we will have

$$Q^* = 18 - 3p^*$$
$$Q^* = 2 + 5p^*$$

Since Q^* from the demand curve obviously equals Q^* from the supply curve, we have

$$18 - 3p^* = 2 + 5p^*$$

which can be solved for p^* to get

$$8p^* = 16$$
$$p^* = 2$$

Putting this value of p^* back into the demand curve we get

$$Q^* = 18 - 3(2)$$
$$Q^* = 12$$

We have therefore solved for the equilibrium price and quantity in this specific numerical model of demand and supply.

Mastering the algebra of demand and supply takes a little practice, but is worth the effort. If you would like to practise, try the Study Exercises at the end of the chapter (and Chapters 4 and 5) that deal with the algebra of demand and supply.

2. **A decrease in demand (the demand curve shifts to the left).** A decrease in demand creates a surplus at the initial equilibrium price, and the unsuccessful sellers bid the price down. As a result, less of the product is supplied and offered for sale. At the new equilibrium, both price and quantity exchanged are lower than they were originally.

Practise with Study Guide Chapter 3, Exercise 3 and Short-Answer Question 4.

3. **An increase in supply (the supply curve shifts to the right).** An increase in supply creates a surplus at the initial equilibrium price, and the unsuccessful suppliers force the price down. This drop in price increases the quantity demanded, and the new equilibrium is at a lower price and a higher quantity exchanged.

4. **A decrease in supply (the supply curve shifts to the left).** A decrease in supply creates a shortage at the initial equilibrium price that causes the price to be bid up.

LESSONS FROM HISTORY 3-1

Ice Storms, Hurricanes, and Economics

Here are two simple examples of the demand and supply apparatus in action. Both examples show how the weather—something that changes in unpredictable and often dramatic ways—can have significant effects on either the demand or the supply of various products, with obvious implications for the observed market price.

The Weather and a Demand Shock

In January of 1998, Quebec, Eastern Ontario, and parts of the Northeastern United States were hit by a massive ice storm. So unprecedented was this storm in its magnitude that many electric power systems were devastated. Homes and businesses in the Montreal area went without power for as long as four weeks.

This electric power shortage had many economic effects, including lost factory production, damage to many businesses, the death of farm livestock, and the displacement of thousands of people into shelters. Another effect of the power shortage, as soon as it became clear that it would last for more than just a few hours, was a sudden and substantial increase in the demand for portable gas-powered electric generators. Within just a few days, all stores in the greater Montreal area were sold out of such generators, and the prices for newly ordered units had increased.

Furthermore, the shortages and price increases for electric generators were not confined to the area directly hit by the ice storm. As it became clear that there was an excess demand for generators in Quebec, sellers in other parts of the country began to divert their supply toward Quebec. This reduction in supply caused shortages, and thus price increases, in other parts of the country, as far away as Edmonton.

The Weather and a Supply Shock

In late August of 2005, Hurricane Katrina emerged from the Caribbean, gathered strength as it crossed the Gulf of Mexico, and unleashed its fury on New Orleans, Louisiana. The damage to New Orleans was massive, especially after the levee holding back Lake Pontchartrain broke and much of the city was flooded. Katrina was the worst natural disaster in U.S. history; the cost of the damage to buildings, bridges, houses, and other infrastructure was estimated to be close to 200 billion U.S. dollars.

Hurricane Katrina had an instant effect on the world market for oil. Over short periods of time, the

This rise in price reduces the quantity demanded, and the new equilibrium is at a higher price and a lower quantity exchanged.

In this chapter, we have studied many forces that can cause demand or supply curves to shift. By combining this analysis with the four laws of demand and supply, we can link many real-world events that cause demand or supply curves to shift with changes in market prices and quantities. *Lessons From History 3-1* shows how we can use demand-and-supply analysis to examine the effects of two real-world weather shocks: Quebec's 1998 ice storm and the effects of Hurricane Katrina in 2005.

Our discussion of demand, supply, and equilibrium has explained why equilibrium price and quantity are found at the intersection of the demand and supply curves. And we have shown diagrams (Figures 3-7 and 3-8) illustrating this in the general case. But we have not presented a specific example of demand and supply and "solved" precisely for the equilibrium price and quantity. This is a useful exercise but requires some algebra. See *Extensions in Theory 3-2* for an algebraic solution to a specific model of demand and supply.

STUDY GUIDE
Practise with Study Guide Chapter 3, Exercise 5 and Extension Exercise E1.

world demand curve for oil is relatively steep, reflecting the fact that users of oil reduce their purchases only slightly when the price rises. For the two years prior to Katrina, strong economic growth around the world had been shifting this relatively steep demand curve to the right. At the same time, the supply curve was also quite steep because most producers were operating close to their production capacity. Growing demand combined with a steep supply curve thus led to significant price increases—from just over U.S.$30 per barrel in June 2004 to about U.S.$60 per barrel in August 2005.

Hurricane Katrina interrupted the local production and distribution of oil, thereby causing a temporary reduction in world supply. Several large oil rigs in the Gulf of Mexico were damaged and were shut down or operating well below their capacity for several weeks. In addition, the major pipelines that transport this oil from the Gulf ports to the inland refineries were also seriously damaged. For both reasons, the supply curve for oil shifted to the left. And given the relatively steep demand curve, this reduction in supply caused a sharp increase in the equilibrium price. The price per barrel of oil reached U.S.$70.35 on August 29, 2005, and stayed above U.S.$65 for about a month. As the rigs and pipelines were repaired, and Gulf-area oil production began to approach its pre-Katrina levels, the supply curve shifted back to the right and the price returned to levels between U.S.$55 and U.S.$60 per barrel.

Hurricane Katrina in August 2005 damaged several oil platforms operating in the Gulf of Mexico and thus caused a temporary reduction in the supply of oil.

myeconlab

Economists often use data from market transactions to estimate demand and supply relationships. This is a difficult exercise, however, because the demand and supply curves in any given market are often shifting at the same time. To learn more about what is needed to identify a demand or supply curve using real-world data, look for "Economic Data and the Identification Problem" in the *Additional Topics* section of this book's MyEconLab.

www.myeconlab.com

Relative Prices and Inflation

The theory we have developed explains how individual prices are determined by the forces of demand and supply. To facilitate matters, we have made *ceteris paribus* assumptions. Specifically, we have assumed the constancy of all prices except the one we are studying. Does this mean that our theory is inapplicable to an inflationary world in which all prices are rising at the same time? Fortunately, the answer is no.

absolute price The amount of money that must be spent to acquire one unit of a commodity. Also called *money price*.

relative price The ratio of the money price of one commodity to the money price of another commodity; that is, a ratio of two absolute prices.

The price of a product is the amount of money that must be spent to acquire one unit of that product. This is called the **absolute price** or *money price*. A **relative price** is the ratio of two absolute prices; it expresses the price of one good in terms of (relative to) another.

We have been reminded several times that what matters for demand and supply is the price of the product in question *relative to the prices of other products;* that is, what matters is the relative price. For example, if the price of carrots rises while the prices of other vegetables are constant, we expect consumers to reduce their quantity demanded of carrots as they substitute toward the consumption of other vegetables. In this case, the *relative* price of carrots has increased. But if the prices of carrots and all other vegetables are rising at the same rate, the relative price of carrots is constant. In this case we expect no substitution to take place between carrots and other vegetables.

In an inflationary world, we are often interested in the price of a given product as it relates to the average price of all other products. If, during a period when all prices were increasing by an average of 5 percent, the price of coffee increased by 30 percent, then the price of coffee increased relative to the prices of other goods as a whole. Coffee became *relatively* expensive. However, if coffee had increased in price by 30 percent when other prices increased by 40 percent, then the relative price of coffee would have fallen. Although the money price of coffee increased substantially, coffee became *relatively* cheap.

In this chapter we have been assuming that changes in a particular price occur when all other prices are constant. We can easily extend the analysis to an inflationary setting by remembering that any force that raises the price of one product when other prices remain constant will, given general inflation, raise the price of that product faster than the price level is rising. For example, consider a change in tastes in favour of carrots that raises their price by 5 percent when other prices are constant. The same change would raise their price by 8 percent if, at the same time, the general price level were rising by 3 percent. In each case, the price of carrots rises 5 percent *relative to the average of all prices.*

In microeconomics, whenever we refer to a change in the price of one product, we mean a change in that product's relative price; that is, a change in the price of that product relative to the prices of all other goods.

myeconlab

The world price of oil increased from about U.S.$15 per barrel in 1998 to over U.S.$75 during 2006. For more details on the many recent developments in the world oil market, including the role of various geopolitical tensions, look for "A Primer on the Market for Crude Oil" in the *Additional Topics* section of this book's MyEconLab.

www.myeconlab.com

SUMMARY

3.1 DEMAND

LO 1 2

- The amount of a product that consumers wish to purchase is called *quantity demanded*. It is a flow expressed as so much per period of time. It is determined by tastes, average household income, the product's own price, the prices of other products, the size of the population, the distribution of income among consumers, and expectations about the future.
- The relationship between quantity demanded and price is represented graphically by a demand curve that shows how much will be demanded at each market price. Quantity demanded is assumed to increase as the price of the product falls, other things held constant. Thus, demand curves are negatively sloped.
- A shift in a demand curve represents a change in the quantity demanded at each price and is referred to as a *change in demand.*
- The demand curve shifts if:
  - average income changes
  - prices of other products change
  - consumers' tastes change
  - the distribution of income changes
  - population changes
  - expectations about the future are revised
- It is important to make the distinction between a movement along a demand curve (caused by a change in the product's price) and a shift of a demand curve (caused by a change in any of the other determinants of demand).

3.2 SUPPLY

LO 3 4

- The amount of a good that producers wish to sell is called *quantity supplied.* It is a flow expressed as so much per period of time. It depends on the product's own price, the costs of inputs, the number of suppliers, government taxes or subsidies, the state of technology, prices of other products, and expectations about the future.
- The relationship between quantity supplied and price is represented graphically by a supply curve that shows how much will be supplied at each market price. Quantity supplied is assumed to increase as the price of the product increases, other things held constant. Thus, supply curves are positively sloped.
- A shift in the supply curve indicates a change in the quantity supplied at each price and is referred to as a *change in supply.*
- The supply curve shifts if:
  - the prices of inputs change
  - technology changes
  - the government imposes taxes or subsidies
  - the prices of other products change
  - expectations about the future are revised
  - the number of suppliers changes
- It is important to make the distinction between a movement along a supply curve (caused by a change in the product's price) and a shift of a supply curve (caused by a change in any of the other determinants of supply).

3.3 THE DETERMINATION OF PRICE

LO 5

- The *equilibrium price* is the price at which the quantity demanded equals the quantity supplied. At any price below equilibrium, there will be excess demand; at any price above equilibrium, there will be excess supply. Graphically, equilibrium occurs where the demand and supply curves intersect.
- Price rises when there is excess demand and falls when there is excess supply. Thus, the actual market price will be pushed toward the equilibrium price. When it is reached, there will be neither excess demand nor excess supply, and the price will not change until either the supply curve or the demand curve shifts.
- Using the method of *comparative statics,* we can determine the effects of a shift in either demand or supply. An increase in demand raises both equilibrium price and equilibrium quantity; a decrease in demand lowers both. An increase in supply raises equilibrium quantity but lowers equilibrium price; a decrease in supply lowers equilibrium quantity but raises equilibrium price. These are called the laws of demand and supply.

- The absolute price of a product is its price in terms of money; its relative price is its price in relation to other products. In an inflationary period, a rise in the *relative price* of one product means that its absolute price rises by more than the average of all prices; a fall in its relative price means that its absolute price rises by less than the average of all prices.

KEY CONCEPTS

Ceteris paribus or "other things being equal"
Quantity demanded and quantity actually bought
Demand schedule and demand curve
Change in quantity demanded versus change in demand
Quantity supplied and quantity actually sold
Supply schedule and supply curve
Change in quantity supplied versus change in supply
Equilibrium, equilibrium price, and disequilibrium
Comparative statics
Laws of supply and demand
Relative price

STUDY EXERCISES

1. The following table shows hypothetical demand schedules for sugar for three separate months. To help make the distinction between changes in demand and changes in quantity demanded, choose the wording to make each of the following statements correct.

	Quantity Demanded for Sugar (in kilograms)		
Price/kg	October	November	December
$1.50	11 000	10 500	13 000
1.75	10 000	9 500	12 000
2.00	9 000	8 500	11 000
2.25	8 000	7 500	10 000
2.50	7 000	6 500	9 000
2.75	6 000	5 500	8 000
3.00	5 000	4 500	7 000
3.25	4 000	3 500	6 000
3.50	3 000	2 500	5 000

   a. When the price of sugar rises from $2.50 to $3.00 in the month of October there is a(n) (*increase/decrease*) in (*demand for/quantity demanded of*) sugar of 2000 kg.
   b. We can say that the demand curve for sugar in December shifted (*to the right/to the left*) of November's demand curve. This represents a(n) (*increase/decrease*) in demand for sugar.
   c. An increase in the demand for sugar means that quantity demanded at each price has (*increased/decreased*), while a decrease in demand for sugar means that quantity demanded at each price has (*increased/decreased*).
   d. In the month of December, a price change for sugar from $3.50 to $2.75 per kilogram would mean a change in (*demand for/quantity demanded of*) sugar of 3000 kg.
   e. Plot the three demand schedules on a graph and label each demand curve to indicate whether it is the demand for October, November, or December.

2. myeconlab For each of the following statements, determine whether there has been a change in supply or a change in quantity supplied. Draw a demand and supply diagram for each situation to show either a movement along the supply curve or a shift of the supply curve.
   a. The price of Canadian-grown peaches skyrockets during an unusually cold summer that reduces the size of the peach harvest.
   b. An increase in income leads to an increase in the price of beef and also to an increase in beef sales.
   c. Technological improvements in the microchip lead to price reductions for personal computers and an increase in computer sales.
   d. Greater awareness of the health risks from smoking lead to a reduction in the price of cigarettes and to fewer cigarettes being sold.

3. myeconlab The following diagram describes the hypothetical demand and supply for tuna in Canada in 2004.
   a. Suppose the price of a can of tuna is $4.00. What is the quantity demanded? What is the quantity supplied? At this price, is there a shortage or a surplus? By what amount?
   b. Suppose the price of a can of tuna is $1.50. What is the quantity demanded? What is the quantity supplied? At this price, is there a shortage or a surplus? By what amount?
   c. What is the equilibrium price and quantity in this market?

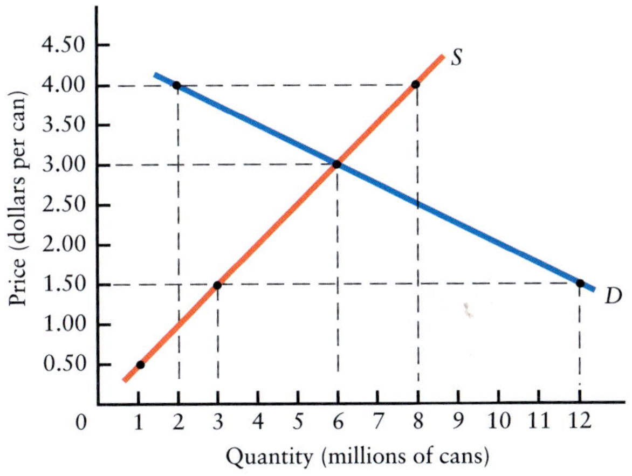

4. Consider households' demand for chicken meat. For each of the events listed below, state and explain the likely effect on the demand for chicken. How would each event be illustrated in a diagram?

   a. A medical study reports that eating chicken reduces the likelihood of suffering from particular types of heart problems.
   b. A widespread bovine disease leads to an increase in the price of beef.
   c. An increase in average household income.

5. myeconlab Consider the world market for a particular quality of coffee beans. The following table shows the demand and supply schedules for this market.

Price (per kilogram)	Quantity Demanded (millions of kilograms per year)	Quantity Supplied (millions of kilograms per year)
\$2.00	28	10
\$2.40	26	12
\$3.10	22	13.5
\$3.50	19.5	19.5
\$3.90	17	22
\$4.30	14.5	23.5

   a. Plot the demand and supply schedules on a diagram.
   b. Identify the amount of excess demand or supply associated with each price.
   c. Identify the equilibrium price in this market.
   d. Suppose that a collection of national governments were somehow able to set a minimum price for coffee equal to \$3.90 per kilogram. Explain the outcome in the world coffee market.

6. Consider the supply for Grade A beef. As the price of beef rises, ranchers will tend to sell more cattle to the slaughterhouses. Yet a central prediction from the supply-and-demand model of this chapter is that an increase in the supply of beef reduces the equilibrium price. Reconcile the apparent contradiction. Use a diagram to do so.

7. Consider the world market for wheat. Suppose there is a major failure in Russia's wheat crop due to a severe drought. Explain the likely effect on the equilibrium price and quantity in the world wheat market. Also explain why Canadian wheat farmers certainly benefit from Russia's drought. The diagrams below provide a starting point for your analysis.

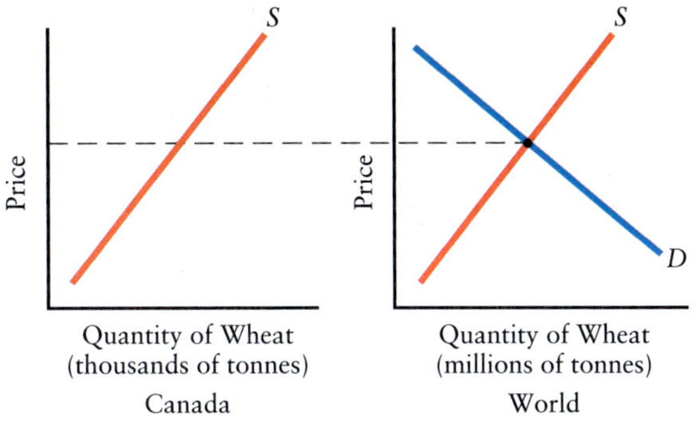

8. The *New York Times* recently stated:

   > *While the world's appetite for chocolate grows more voracious each year, cocoa farms around the globe are failing, under siege from fungal and viral diseases and insects . . . .Researchers predict a shortfall in beans from the cacao tree, the raw material from which chocolate is made, in as little as five to ten years.*

   Describe in terms of the supply-and-demand apparatus what is described in the quote. What is the implied prediction for the equilibrium price of chocolate? What is the implied prediction for the equilibrium quantity of chocolate?

9. This is a challenging question and is similar to the example shown in *Extensions in Theory 3-2*. It requires you to solve a supply-and-demand model as a system of *simultaneous equations* (meaning simply that both equations apply at the same time). Letting p be the price of the product, suppose the demand and supply functions for some product are given by

$$Q^D = 100 - 3p$$

$$Q^S = 10 + 2p$$

   a. Plot both the demand curve and the supply curve.
   b. What is the condition for equilibrium in this market?
   c. By imposing the condition for equilibrium, solve for the equilibrium price.
   d. Substitute the equilibrium price into either the demand or supply function to solve for the equilibrium quantity. Check to make sure you get the

same answer whether you use the demand function or the supply function.

e. Now suppose there is an increase in demand so that the new demand function is given by

$$Q^D = 180 - 3p.$$

Compute the new equilibrium price and quantity. Is your result consistent with the "law" of demand?

f. Now suppose that, with the new demand curve in place, there is an increase in supply so that the new supply function is given by $Q^S = 90 + 2p$. Compute the new equilibrium price and quantity. Is your result consistent with the "law" of supply?

DISCUSSION QUESTIONS

1. Recently, a government economist predicted that this spring's excellent weather would result in larger crops of wheat and canola than farmers had expected. But the economist warned consumers not to expect prices to decrease because the cost of production was rising and foreign demand for Canadian crops was increasing. "The classic pattern of supply and demand won't work this time," the economist said. Discuss his observation.

2. What do you think would be the effect on the equilibrium price and quantity of marijuana if its sale and consumption were legalized?

3. Classify the effect of each of the following as (i) a decrease in the demand for fish or (ii) a decrease in the quantity of fish demanded. Illustrate each diagrammatically.
   a. The government of Canada closes the Atlantic cod fishery.
   b. People buy less fish because of a rise in fish prices.
   c. The Catholic Church relaxes its ban on eating meat on Fridays.
   d. The price of beef falls and, as a result, consumers buy more beef and less fish.
   e. Fears of mercury pollution lead locals to shun fish caught in nearby lakes.
   f. It is generally alleged that eating fish is better for one's health than eating meat.

4. Predict the effect on the price of at least one product of each of the following events:
   a. Winter snowfall is at a record high in the interior of British Columbia, but drought continues in Quebec ski areas.
   b. A recession decreases employment in Oshawa automobile factories.
   c. The French grape harvest is the smallest in 20 years.
   d. The province of Ontario cancels permission for campers to cut firewood in provincial campgrounds.

5. Are the following two observations inconsistent?
   a. Rising demand for housing causes prices of new homes to soar.
   b. Many families refuse to buy homes as prices become prohibitive for them.

6. Look back at the supply-and-demand figure inside *Extensions in Theory 3-2*. Notice that the supply curve has a positive horizontal intercept, suggesting that producers will wish to produce and sell a positive amount of this product when the price is zero. Is this reasonable? Under what conditions might this occur?

CHAPTER 4

Elasticity

LO LEARNING OBJECTIVES

In this chapter you will learn

1. the meaning of price elasticity of demand and how it is measured.
2. about the relationship between demand elasticity and total expenditure.
3. the meaning of price elasticity of supply and how it is measured.
4. why the effect of an excise tax on equilibrium price and quantity depends on demand and supply elasticity.
5. about normal and inferior goods, and how to measure the income elasticity of demand.
6. how to measure cross elasticity of demand, and the meaning of substitute and complement goods.

The laws of demand and supply predict the *direction* of changes in equilibrium price and quantity in response to various shifts in demand and supply. However, it usually is not enough to know merely whether price and quantity rise or fall; it is also important to know by *how much* each changes.

For example, in the previous chapter we described the effect of Hurricane Katrina on the world price of oil in 2005. The hurricane caused a temporary reduction in the supply of crude oil which led to a 20-percent increase in the world price. How can we explain why the increase in price was 20 percent rather than 50 percent or only 5 percent? As we will see in this chapter, the extent of price changes in response to shifts in demand or supply is largely determined by the *shapes* of the demand and supply curves. Specifically, it is the *elasticity* of demand and supply that we examine in this chapter.

4.1 PRICE ELASTICITY OF DEMAND

Suppose there is a decrease in the supply of some farm crop—that is, a leftward shift in the supply curve. We saw in Figure 3-8 when we examined the laws of supply and demand that such a decrease in supply will cause the equilibrium price to rise and the equilibrium quantity to fall. But by how much will each change? The answer depends on what is called the *price elasticity of demand*.

Loosely speaking, demand is said to be *elastic* when quantity demanded is quite responsive to changes in price. When quantity demanded is relatively unresponsive to changes in price, demand is said to be *inelastic*.

The importance of elasticity is illustrated in Figure 4-1. The two parts of the figure have the same initial equilibrium, and that equilibrium is disturbed by the same leftward shift in the supply curve. But the demand curves are different in the two parts of the figure, and so the sizes of the changes in equilibrium price and quantity are also different.

Part (i) of Figure 4-1 illustrates a case in which the quantity that consumers demand is relatively responsive to price changes—that is, demand is relatively *elastic.* The reduction in supply pushes up the price, but, because the quantity demanded is quite responsive, only a small change in price is necessary to restore equilibrium.

Part (ii) of Figure 4-1 shows a case in which the quantity demanded is relatively unresponsive to price changes—that is, demand is relatively *inelastic.* As in part (i), the decrease in supply at the original price causes a shortage that increases the price. However, in this case the quantity demanded by consumers does not fall much in response to the rise in price. The result is that equilibrium price rises more, and equilibrium quantity falls less, than in the first case.

In both cases shown in Figure 4-1, the shifts of the supply curve are identical. The sizes of the effects on the equilibrium price and quantity are different only because of the different elasticities of demand.

FIGURE 4-1 The Effects of a Supply Shift with Two Different Demand Curves

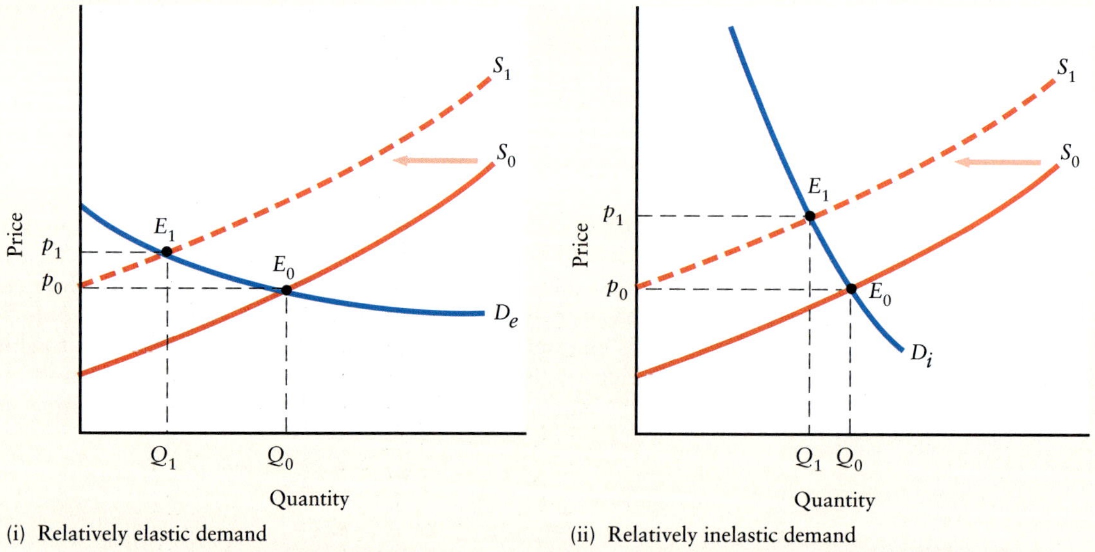

The more responsive the quantity demanded is to changes in price, the less the change in equilibrium price and the greater the change in equilibrium quantity resulting from any given shift in the supply curve. Both parts of the figure are drawn to the same scale. They show the same initial equilibrium, E_0, and the same shift in the supply curve, from S_0 to S_1. In each part, initial equilibrium is at price p_0 and output Q_0 and the new equilibrium, E_1, is at p_1 and Q_1. In part (i), the effect of the reduction in supply is a slight rise in the price and a large decrease in quantity. In part (ii), the effect of the identical reduction in supply is a large increase in the price and a relatively small decrease in quantity.

The Measurement of Price Elasticity

In Figure 4-1, we were able to say that the demand curve in part (i) showed more responsiveness to price changes than the demand curve in part (ii) because two conditions were fulfilled. First, both curves were drawn on the same scale. Second, the initial equilibrium prices and quantities were the same in both parts of the figure. Let's see why these conditions matter.

First, by drawing both figures on the same scale, we saw that the demand curve that *looked* steeper actually did have the larger absolute slope. (The slope of a demand curve tells us the amount by which price must change to cause a unit change in quantity demanded.) If we had drawn the two curves on different scales, we could have concluded nothing about which demand curve actually had the greater slope.

Second, because we started from the same price–quantity equilibrium in both parts of the figure, we did not need to distinguish between *percentage* changes and *absolute* changes. If the initial prices and quantities are the same in both cases, the larger absolute change is also the larger percentage change. However, when we wish to deal with different initial price–quantity equilibria, we need to decide whether we are interested in absolute or percentage changes.

To see why the difference between absolute and percentage change matters, consider the changes in price and quantity demanded for three different products: cheese, T-shirts, and CD players. The information is shown in Table 4-1. Should we conclude that the demand for CD players is not as responsive to price changes as the demand for cheese? After all, price cuts of $2 cause quite a large increase in the quantity of cheese demanded, but only a small increase in the quantity demanded of CD players. It should be obvious that a $2 price reduction is a large price cut for a low-priced product and an insignificant price cut for a high-priced product. In Table 4-1, each price reduction is $2, but they are clearly different proportions of the respective prices. It is usually more revealing to know the *percentage* change in the prices of the various products.

price elasticity of demand (η) A measure of the responsiveness of quantity demanded to a change in the commodity's own price.

For similar reasons, knowing the quantity by which demand changes is not very revealing unless the initial level of demand is also known. An increase of 7500 kilograms is quite a significant change if the quantity formerly bought was 15 000 kilograms, but it is insignificant if the quantity formerly bought was 10 million kilograms.

Table 4-2 shows the original and new levels of price and quantity. Note that it also shows the *average* price and *average* quantity. These averages will be necessary for our computation of elasticity.

The **price elasticity of demand,** the measure of responsiveness of the quantity of a product demanded to a change in that product's price, is symbolized by the Greek letter eta, η. It is defined as follows:

$$\eta = \frac{\text{Percentage change in quantity demanded}}{\text{Percentage change in price}}$$

This measure is called the price elasticity of demand, or simply *demand elasticity.* Because the variable causing the change in quantity demanded is the product's own price, the term *own-price elasticity of demand* is also used.

TABLE 4-1 Price Reductions and Corresponding Increases in Quantity Demanded for Three Products

Commodity	Reduction in Price	Increase in Quantity Demanded (per month)
Cheese	$2 per kilogram	7 500 kilograms
T-shirts	$2 per shirt	25 000 shirts
CD players	$2 per CD player	500 CD players

For each of the three products, the data show the change in quantity demanded resulting from the same absolute fall in price. The data are fairly uninformative about the responsiveness of quantity demanded to price because they do not tell us either the original price or the original quantity demanded.

TABLE 4-2 Price and Quantity Information Underlying Data of Table 4-1

Product	Unit	Original Price ($)	New Price ($)	Average Price ($)	Original Quantity	New Quantity	Average Quantity
Cheese	kilogram	5.00	3.00	4.00	116 250	123 750	120 000
T-shirts	shirt	17.00	15.00	16.00	187 500	212 500	200 000
CD players	player	81.00	79.00	80.00	9 750	10 250	10 000

These data provide the appropriate context for the data given in Table 4-1. The table relates the $2-per-unit price reduction of each product to the actual prices and quantities demanded.

The Use of Average Price and Quantity in Computing Elasticity Table 4-3 shows the percentage changes for price and quantity using the data from Table 4-2. The caption in Table 4-3 stresses that the demand elasticities are computed using changes in price and quantity measured in terms of the *average* values of each. Averages are used to avoid the ambiguity caused by the fact that when a price or quantity changes, the change is a different percentage of the original value than it is of the new value. For example, the $2.00 change in the price of cheese shown in Table 4-2 represents a 40 percent change in the original price of $5.00 but a 66.7 percent change in the new price of $3.00.

Practise with Study Guide Chapter 4, Exercise 4.

Using average values for price and quantity means that the measured elasticity of demand between any two points on the demand curve, call them *A* and *B,* is independent of whether the movement is from *A* to *B* or from *B* to *A*. In the example of cheese in Tables 4-2 and 4-3, the $2.00 change in the price of cheese is unambiguously 50 percent of the average price of $4.00, and that percentage applies to a price increase from $3.00 to $5.00 or to a price decrease from $5.00 to $3.00.

Once we have computed the average prices and quantities as in Table 4-2, the algebraic formula for price elasticity is straightforward. Suppose we have an initial price of p_0 and an initial quantity of Q_0. We then consider a new price of p_1 and a new quantity of Q_1 (both price-quantity combinations lie on the demand curve for the product). The formula for price elasticity is then

$$\eta = \frac{\Delta Q/\overline{Q}}{\Delta p/\overline{p}} = \frac{(Q_1 - Q_0)/\overline{Q}}{(p_1 - p_0)/\overline{p}}$$

where $\overline{p}$ is the average price and $\overline{Q}$ is the average quantity. In the case of cheese from Table 4-2, we have

$$\eta = \frac{7500/120\,000}{2.0/4.0} = \frac{0.0625}{0.5} = 0.125$$

as shown in Table 4-3. Notice that elasticity is *unit free*—even though prices are measured in dollars and quantity of cheese is measured in kilograms, the elasticity of demand has no units.

We leave it to you to use this formula to confirm the price elasticities for T-shirts and CD players shown in Table 4-3. [7]

TABLE 4-3 Calculation of Demand Elasticities

Product	(1) Percentage Decrease in Price	(2) Percentage Increase in Quantity	(3) Elasticity of Demand (2) ÷ (1)
Cheese	50.0	6.25	0.125
T-shirts	12.5	12.5	1.0
CD players	2.5	5.0	2.0

Elasticity of demand is the percentage change in quantity demanded divided by the percentage change in price. The percentage changes are based on average prices and quantities shown in Table 4-2. For example, the $2.00-per-kilogram decrease in the price of cheese is 50 percent of $4.00. A $2.00 change in the price of CD players is only 2.5 percent of the average price per CD player of $80.00.

Interpreting Numerical Elasticities Because demand curves have negative slopes, an increase in price is associated with a decrease in quantity demanded, and vice versa. Because the percentage changes in price and quantity have opposite signs, demand elasticity is a negative number. However, we will follow the usual practice of ignoring the negative sign and speak of the measure as a positive number, as we have done in the illustrative calculations in Table 4-3. Thus, the more responsive the quantity demanded to a change in price, the greater the elasticity and the larger is η.

The numerical value of demand elasticity can vary from zero to infinity. First consider the extreme cases. Elasticity is zero when a change in price leads to *no change* in quantity demanded. This is the case of a vertical demand curve, and is quite rare because it indicates that consumers do not alter their consumption at all when price changes. At the other extreme, elasticity is very large when even a very small change in price leads to an enormous change in quantity demanded. In these situations, which are also rare in the case of demands for individual commodities, the demand curve is very flat, almost horizontal. (In the limiting case, the demand curve is perfectly horizontal and elasticity is infinite.) Most of reality lies between the extremes of vertical and horizontal demand curves. We divide this "realistic" range of elasticities into two regions.

Practise with Study Guide Chapter 4, Exercise 1.

When the percentage change in quantity demanded is less than the percentage change in price (elasticity less than 1), there is said to be **inelastic demand**. When the percentage change in quantity is greater than the percentage change in price (elasticity greater than 1), there is said to be **elastic demand**. The dividing line between these two cases occurs when the percentage change in quantity demanded is exactly equal to the percentage change in price and so elasticity is equal to 1. Here we say that demand is *unit elastic*. This important terminology is summarized in part A of *Extensions in Theory 4-2*, which is found toward the end of the chapter.

inelastic demand Following a given percentage change in price, there is a smaller percentage change in quantity demanded; elasticity less than 1.

elastic demand Following a given percentage change in price, there is a greater percentage change in quantity demanded; elasticity greater than 1.

A demand curve need not, and usually does not, have the same elasticity over its whole length. Figure 4-2 shows that a negatively sloped linear demand curve does not have a constant elasticity, even though it does have a constant slope. A linear demand curve has constant elasticity only when it is vertical or horizontal. Figure 4-3 illustrates these two cases, in addition to a third case of a particular *nonlinear* demand curve that also has a constant elasticity. (These are only three examples of many demand curves with constant elasticities.)

What Determines Elasticity of Demand?

One of the main determinants of demand elasticity is the availability of substitutes. Some products, such as margarine, broccoli, lamb, and Toyota cars, have quite close substitutes—butter, other green vegetables, beef, and Mazda cars. A change in the prices of these products, *with the prices of the substitutes remaining constant*, can be expected to cause much substitution. A fall in price leads consumers to buy more of

Practise with Study Guide Chapter 4, Exercises 3 and 6.

FIGURE 4-2 Elasticity Along a Linear Demand Curve

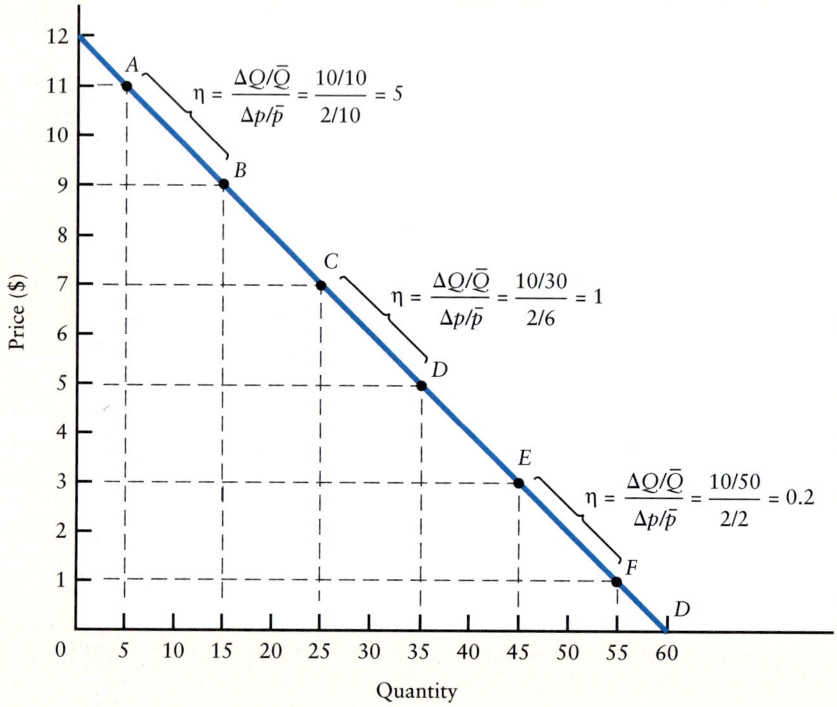

Moving down a linear demand curve, price elasticity falls continuously, even though the slope is constant. In the interval between points A and B, the percentage change in quantity is 100 ($\Delta Q = 10$ and $\bar{Q} = 10$) and the percentage change in price is 20 ($\Delta p = 2$ and $\bar{p} = 10$). The price elasticity over this interval of the demand curve is then 100/20 = 5.

The same *absolute* changes in price and quantity occur over the intervals CD and EF, but elasticity differs because these absolute changes represent different *percentage* changes. Between points C and D, price elasticity is equal to 1. Between points E and F, price elasticity is equal to 0.2. Note that elasticity approaches infinity as we get closer to where the demand curve intersects the vertical axis; elasticity approaches zero as we get closer to where the demand curve intersects the horizontal axis.

the product and less of the substitutes, and a rise in price leads consumers to buy less of the product and more of the substitutes. Products defined more broadly, such as *all* foods or *all* clothing or *all* methods of transportation, have many fewer satisfactory substitutes. A rise in their prices can be expected to cause a smaller fall in quantities demanded than would be the case if close substitutes were available.

Products with close substitutes tend to have elastic demands; products with no close substitutes tend to have inelastic demands.

Demand elasticity depends to a great extent on the availability of substitutes. The availability of substitutes, in turn, depends on how the product is defined and on the time period being considered. We explore these aspects next.

Definition of the Product For food taken as a whole, demand is inelastic over a large price range. It does not follow, however, that any specific food, such as white bread or peanut butter, also has inelastic demand. Individual foods can have quite elastic demands, and they frequently do.

Clothing provides a similar example. Clothing as a whole has a less elastic demand than do individual kinds of clothes. For example, when the price of wool sweaters rises, many households may substitute away from wool sweaters and buy cotton sweaters or fleece jackets instead. Thus, although purchases of wool sweaters fall, total purchases of clothing do not.

Any one of a group of related products will have a more elastic demand than the group as a whole.

FIGURE 4-3 Three Demand Curves with Constant Elasticity

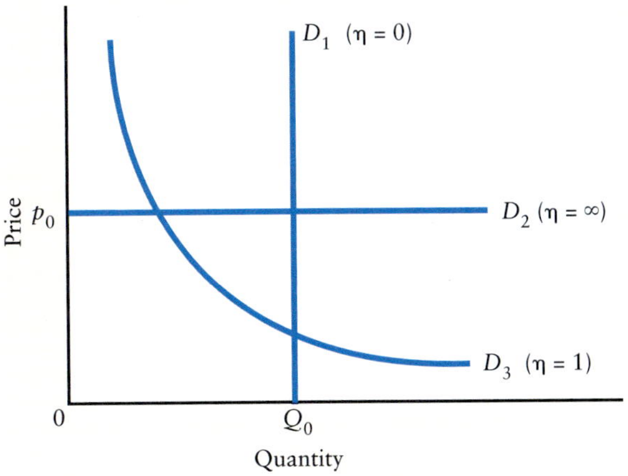

Each of these demand curves has a constant elasticity. D_1 has zero elasticity: The quantity demanded is equal to Q_0, independent of the price. D_2 has infinite elasticity at the price p_0: A small price increase from p_0 decreases quantity demanded from an indefinitely large amount to zero. D_3 has unit elasticity: A given percentage increase in price brings an equal percentage decrease in quantity demanded at all points on the curve; it is a rectangular hyperbola for which price times quantity demanded is a constant.

Short Run and Long Run Because it takes time to develop satisfactory substitutes, a demand that is inelastic in the short run may prove to be elastic when enough time has passed. A dramatic example of this principle occurred in 1973 when the Organization of Petroleum Exporting Countries (OPEC) shocked the world with its sudden and large increase in the price of oil. At that time, the short-run demand for oil proved to be highly inelastic. Large price increases were met in the short run by very small reductions in quantity demanded. In this case, the short run lasted for several years. Gradually, however, the high price of petroleum products led to such adjustments as the development of smaller, more fuel-efficient cars, economizing on heating oil by installing more efficient insulation, and replacement of fuel oil in many industrial processes with other power sources such as coal and hydroelectricity. The long-run elasticity of demand, relating the change in price to the change in quantity demanded after all adjustments were made, turned out to have an elasticity of well over 1, although the long-run adjustments took as much as a decade to work out.

The response to a price change, and thus the measured price elasticity of demand, will tend to be greater the longer the time span.

For such products as cornflakes and pillowcases, the full response to a price change occurs quickly, and there is little reason to make the distinction between short-run and long-run effects. But other products are typically used in connection with highly durable appliances or machines. A change in the price of, say, electricity and gasoline may not have its major effect until the stock of appliances and machines using these products has been adjusted. This adjustment may take several years to occur.

For products for which substitutes are developed over a period of time, it is helpful to identify two kinds of demand curves. A *short-run demand curve* shows the immediate response of quantity demanded to a change in price given the current stock of durable

Because most people cannot easily or quickly change the size of car they drive or their method of transportation, the demand for gasoline is much less elastic in the short run than in the long run.

FIGURE 4-4 Short-Run and Long-Run Equilibrium Following an Increase in Supply

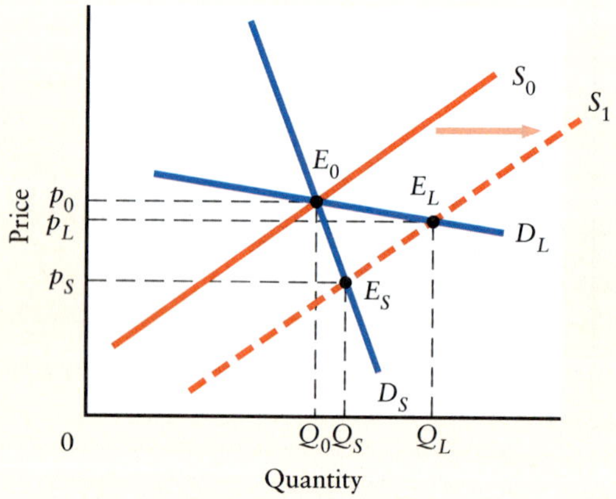

The magnitude of the changes in the equilibrium price and quantity following a shift in supply depends on the time allowed for demand to adjust. The initial equilibrium is at E_0, with price p_0 and quantity Q_0. Supply then increases and the supply curve shifts from S_0 to S_1.

Immediately following the increase in supply, the relevant demand curve is the short-run curve D_S, and the new equilibrium immediately following the supply shock is E_S. Price falls sharply to p_S, and quantity rises only to Q_S. In the long run, the demand curve is the more elastic one given by D_L, and equilibrium is at E_L. The long-run equilibrium price is p_L (greater than p_S), and quantity is Q_L (greater than Q_S).

goods. The *long-run demand curve* shows the response of quantity demanded to a change in price after enough time has passed to change the stock of durable goods.

The long-run demand for a product is more elastic than the short-run demand.

Figure 4-4 shows the short-run and long-run effects of an increase in supply. In the short run, the supply increase leads to a movement down the relatively inelastic short-run demand curve; it thus causes a large fall in price but only a small increase in quantity. In the long run, demand is more elastic; thus long-run equilibrium has price and quantity above those that prevailed in short-run equilibrium.

Elasticity and Total Expenditure

We know that quantity demanded increases as price falls, but what happens to the total expenditure on that product? It turns out that the response of total expenditure depends on the price elasticity of demand.

To see the relationship between the elasticity of demand and total expenditure, we begin by noting that total expenditure at any point on the demand curve is equal to price times quantity:

$$\text{Total expenditure} = \text{Price} \times \text{Quantity}$$

Because price and quantity move in opposite directions along a demand curve, one falling when the other rises, the change in total expenditure is ambiguous if all we know about the demand curve is that it has a negative slope. The change in total expenditure depends on the relative percentage changes in the price and quantity. If the percentage change in price exceeds the percentage change in quantity (elasticity less than 1), the price change will dominate, and total expenditure will change in the same direction as the price changes. If the percentage change in the price is less than the percentage change in the quantity demanded (elasticity greater than 1), the quantity change will dominate, and total expenditure will change in the same direction as quantity changes. If the two percentage changes are equal, total expenditure is unchanged—this is the case of unit elasticity.

Practise with Study Guide Chapter 4, Exercise 2 and Short-Answer Question 7.

Figure 4-5 illustrates the relationship between price elasticity and total expenditure; it is based on the linear demand curve in Figure 4-2. Total expenditure at each of a number of points on the demand curve is calculated in the table, and the general relationship between total expenditure and quantity demanded is shown by the plotted curve. In the figure we see that expenditure reaches its maximum when price elasticity is equal to 1. [8]

For information on OPEC and its activities, see **www.opec.org**.

Our earlier example of the 1973 OPEC-induced increase in the world price of oil can be used to illustrate this relationship between elasticity, price, and total expenditure. As the OPEC countries acted together to restrict supply and push up the world

FIGURE 4-5 Total Expenditure and Quantity Demanded

Price ($)	Quantity Demanded	Expenditure ($)
12	0	0
10	10	100
8	20	160
6	30	180
4	40	160
2	50	100
0	60	0

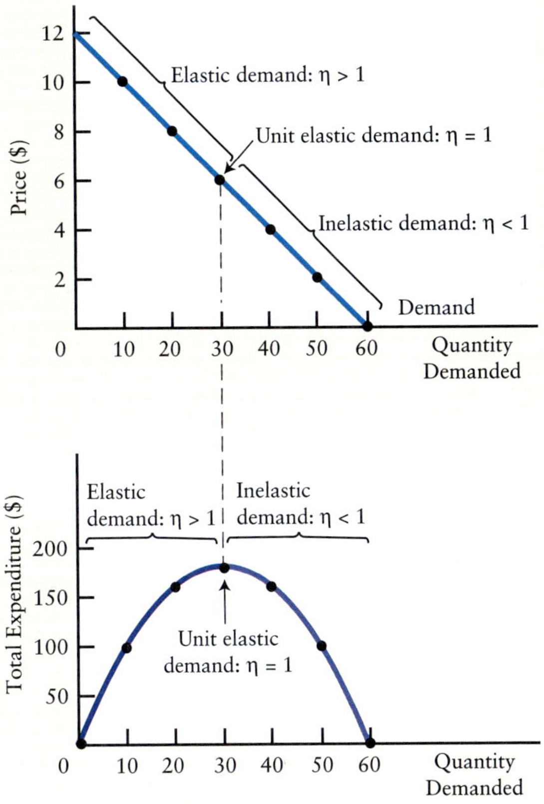

The change in total expenditure on a product in response to a change in price depends on the elasticity of demand. The table and graph are based on the demand curve shown in Figure 4-2. For quantities demanded that are less than 30, elasticity of demand is greater than 1, and hence any increase in quantity demanded will be proportionately larger than the fall in price that caused it. In that range, total expenditure increases as price falls. For quantities greater than 30, elasticity of demand is less than 1, and hence any increase in quantity demanded will be proportionately smaller than the fall in price that caused it. In that range, total expenditure decreases as price falls. The maximum of total expenditure occurs where the elasticity of demand equals 1.

price of oil, quantity demanded fell, but only by a small percentage—much smaller than the percentage increase in price. World demand for oil (at least in the short run) was very inelastic, and the result was that total expenditure on oil *increased* dramatically. The OPEC oil producers, therefore, experienced an enormous increase in income.

Another example relates to the world market for wheat, a market naturally influenced by weather conditions in the major wheat-producing countries. If one major wheat-producing country, like Russia, suffers a significant failure in its wheat crop, the world supply curve for wheat shifts to the left and the equilibrium world price rises. Because the world demand for wheat is inelastic, the world's total expenditure on wheat will rise. In this case, even though many individual Russian wheat producers will be worse off because their crop failed, the total income of the world's wheat producers will increase. One other observation is relevant: Wheat producers in other countries, like Canada, benefit by selling their (unchanged) crop at a higher world price. And the less elastic is the world demand for wheat, the more the price will rise as a result of the Russian crop failure, and thus the *more* Canadian wheat farmers will benefit.

4.2 PRICE ELASTICITY OF SUPPLY

price elasticity of supply (η_S) A measure of the responsiveness of quantity supplied to a change in the product's own price.

The concept of elasticity can be applied to supply as well as to demand. **Price elasticity of supply** measures the responsiveness of the quantity supplied to a change in the product's price. It is denoted η_s and defined as follows:

$$\eta_s = \frac{\text{Percentage change in quantity supplied}}{\text{Percentage change in price}}$$

This is often called *supply elasticity.* The supply curves considered in this chapter all have positive slopes: An increase in price causes an increase in quantity supplied. Such supply curves all have positive elasticities because price and quantity change in the same direction.

Practise with Study Guide Chapter 4, Exercise 7.

Figure 4-6 shows a simple linear supply curve to illustrate the measurement of supply elasticity. Between points *A* and *B*, the change in price is \$1.50 and the average price is \$4.25. Between the same two points, the change in quantity supplied is 20 units and the average quantity is 40 units. The value of supply elasticity between points *A* and *B* is therefore

$$\eta_s = \frac{\Delta Q/\overline{Q}}{\Delta p/\overline{p}} = \frac{20/40}{1.50/4.25} = \frac{0.5}{0.353} = 1.42$$

FIGURE 4-6 Computing Price Elasticity of Supply

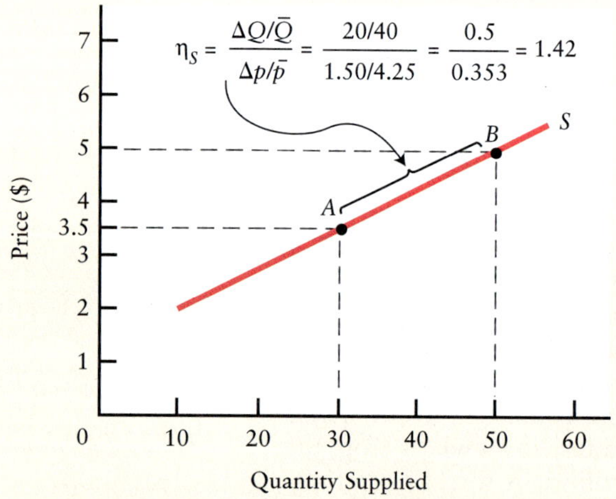

Supply elasticity is computed using average price and average quantity supplied. Between points *A* and *B*, the elasticity of supply is 1.42. The same approach shown here can be used to compute elasticity between any two points on the supply curve.

As was the case with demand, care must be taken when computing supply elasticity. Keep in mind that even though the supply curve may have a constant slope, the measure of supply elasticity may be different at different places on the curve.

There are also important special cases of supply curves that should be noted. If the supply curve is vertical—the quantity supplied does not change as price changes—then elasticity of supply is zero. A horizontal supply curve has an infinite elasticity of supply: A small drop in price will reduce the quantity that producers are willing to supply from an indefinitely large amount to zero. Between these two extremes, elasticity of supply varies with the shape of the supply curve. Loosely speaking, steeper supply curves imply a smaller quantity response for a given change in price, and thus a lower elasticity.[1]

Determinants of Supply Elasticity

Because much of the treatment of demand elasticity carries over to supply elasticity, we can cover the main points quickly.

---

[1] Here is another special case that is often puzzling at first glance. Consider a linear supply curve that begins at the origin. It is easy to show that the elasticity of supply along such a curve is always 1—no matter how steep the supply curve is! See Study Exercise #8 to explore this further.

Substitution and Production Costs The ease of substitution can vary in production as well as in consumption. If the price of a product rises, how much more can be produced profitably? This depends in part on how easy it is for producers to shift from the production of other products to the one whose price has risen. If agricultural land and labour can be readily shifted from one crop to another, the supply of any one crop will be more elastic than if they cannot. Or, if machines used to produce coats can be easily modified to produce pants (and vice versa), then the supply of both pants and coats will be more elastic than if the machines cannot be so easily modified.

Supply elasticity also depends on how costs behave as output is varied. If the costs of producing a unit of output rise rapidly as output rises, then the stimulus to expand production in response to a rise in price will quickly be choked off by increases in costs. In this case, supply will tend to be rather inelastic. If, however, the costs of producing a unit of output rise only slowly as production increases, a rise in price that raises profits will elicit a large increase in quantity supplied before the rise in costs puts a halt to the expansion in output. In this case, supply will tend to be rather elastic.

Short Run and Long Run As with demand, length of time for response is important. It may be difficult to change quantities supplied in response to a price increase in a matter of weeks or months, but easy to do so over a period of years. An obvious example is the planting cycle of crops. An increase in the price of wheat that occurs in mid-summer may lead wheat farmers to be more careful (and less wasteful) in their harvesting in the fall, but it occurs too late to influence how much wheat gets planted for this year's crop. If the high price persists, however, it will surely influence how much wheat gets planted the following spring. Another example relates to oil production. New oil fields can be discovered, wells drilled, and pipelines built over a period of years but not in just a few months. Thus, the elasticity of oil supply is much greater over five years than over one year.

As with demand, it is useful to make the distinction between the short-run and the long-run supply curves. The *short-run supply curve* shows the immediate response of quantity supplied to a change in price given producers' current capacity to produce the good. The *long-run supply curve* shows the response of quantity supplied to a change in price after enough time has passed to allow producers to adjust their productive capacity.

The long-run supply for a product is more elastic than the short-run supply.

Figure 4-7 illustrates the short-run and long-run effects of an increase in demand. The immediate effect of the shift in demand is a sharp increase in price (p_0 to p_S) and only a modest increase in quantity (Q_0 to Q_S). The inability of firms to change their output in the short run in response to the increase in demand means that the market-clearing response is mostly an increase in

FIGURE 4-7 Short-Run and Long-Run Equilibrium Following an Increase in Demand

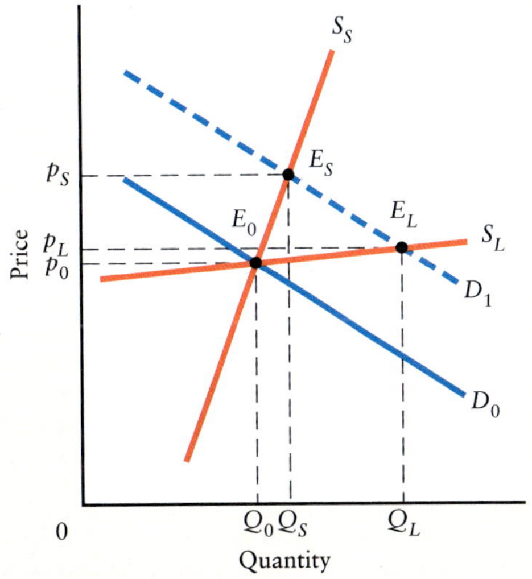

The size of the changes in the equilibrium price and quantity following a shift in demand depends on the time frame of the analysis. The initial equilibrium is at E_0, with price p_0 and quantity Q_0. Demand then increases such that the demand curve shifts from D_0 to D_1.

Immediately following the demand shift, the relevant supply curve is the short-run curve S_S, so that the new equilibrium immediately following the demand shock is at E_S. Price rises sharply to p_S, and quantity rises only to Q_S. In the long run, the supply curve is the more elastic one given by S_L. The long-run equilibrium is at E_L; price is p_L (less than p_S) and quantity is Q_L (greater than Q_S).

price. Over time, however, as firms are more able to increase their output of the product, the consequences of the demand shift fall more on quantity and less on price.

A recent example of this price and quantity behaviour is found in the world oil market in the years between 1998 and 2006. Due to relatively rapid rates of economic growth in many countries, and especially in the large emerging markets of China and India, the world demand for oil was growing significantly. During this period, however, most oil producers were at or close to their production limits: The number of oil-producing wells could only increase with costly new exploration and drilling, and each active well delivered a daily flow of oil that was difficult to increase. Producers' inability to easily expand oil production in the short term means that the short-run supply of oil is quite inelastic. As a result, the increase in demand led to sharp price increases—from about U.S.$15 per barrel in 1998 to over U.S.$75 per barrel in mid 2006 (well after the effects of the supply disruptions caused by Hurricane Katrina in the fall of 2005 had disappeared).

Over time, however, to the extent that oil producers are able to increase their exploration and drilling activities, the high price should induce a larger increase in quantity supplied. In other words, the long-run supply of oil can be expected to be more elastic than the short-run supply. If no other significant changes occur in the world oil market, the effect of this new oil production should be to reduce oil prices from the very high levels observed in 2006.

4.3 AN IMPORTANT EXAMPLE WHERE ELASTICITY MATTERS

So far, this chapter has been fairly tough going. We have spent much time examining price elasticity (of both demand and supply) and how to measure it. But why should we care about this? In this section, we explore the important concept of *tax incidence* and show that elasticity is crucial to determining whether consumers or producers (or both) end up bearing the burden of (or paying) excise taxes.

excise tax A tax on the sale of a particular commodity.

The federal and provincial governments levy special sales taxes called **excise taxes** on many goods such as cigarettes, alcohol, and gasoline. At the point of sale of the product, the sellers collect the tax on behalf of the government and then periodically remit the tax collections.

When the sellers write their cheques to the government, these firms feel that they are the ones paying the tax. Consumers, however, argue that *they* are the ones who are shouldering the burden of the tax because the tax causes the price of the product to rise. Who actually bears the burden of the tax?

tax incidence The location of the burden of a tax; that is, the identity of the ultimate bearer of the tax.

The question of who *bears the burden* of a tax is called the question of **tax incidence**. A straightforward application of demand-and-supply analysis will show that tax incidence has nothing to do with whether the government collects the tax directly from consumers or from firms.

The burden of an excise tax is distributed between consumers and sellers in a manner that depends on the relative elasticities of supply and demand.

Let's consider a case where the government imposes an excise tax on cigarettes. The analysis begins in Figure 4-8. To simplify the problem, we analyze the case where there is initially no tax. The equilibrium without taxes is illustrated by the solid supply and demand curves. What happens when a tax of $\$t$ per pack of cigarettes is introduced? With an excise tax, the price paid by the consumer, called the *consumer price,* and the price received by the seller, called the *seller price,* must differ by the amount of the tax, t.

In terms of the figure, we can analyze the effect of the tax by considering a new supply curve S' that is above the original supply curve S by the amount of the tax, t. To understand this new curve, consider the situation faced by firms at the original equilibrium quantity Q_0. To supply that quantity, producers must receive p_0 per pack of cigarettes sold. However, for producers to receive p_0 when there is a tax on cigarettes, the consumer must pay a total price of $p_0 + t$: whether the consumer "pays the tax directly" by giving p_0 to the firm and t to the government, or whether the consumer pays the total $p_0 + t$ to the firm and the firm then remits the tax t to the government. Either way, the total amount that consumers must pay to obtain a given quantity from firms has increased by the amount of the tax, t.

This upward shift in the supply curve for cigarettes is depicted in Figure 4-8 as the dashed curve, S'. This shift in the supply curve, caused by the imposition of the excise tax, will cause a movement *along* the demand curve, reducing the equilibrium quantity. At this new equilibrium, E_1, the consumer price rises to p_c (greater than p_0), the seller price falls to p_s (less than p_0), and the equilibrium quantity falls to Q_1.

Note that the quantity demanded *at the consumer price* is equal to the quantity supplied *at the seller price,* a condition that is required for equilibrium. As shown in the figure, compared to the original equilibrium, the consumer price is higher and the seller price is lower, although in each case the change in price is less than the full extent of the excise tax. The difference between p_0 and p_c is the amount of the tax that the consumer ends up paying; the difference between p_0 and p_s is the amount of the tax the seller ends up paying. The burden of the excise tax is shared between consumers and sellers in proportion to the rise in price to consumers relative to the fall in price received by sellers.

FIGURE 4-8 The Effect of a Cigarette Excise Tax

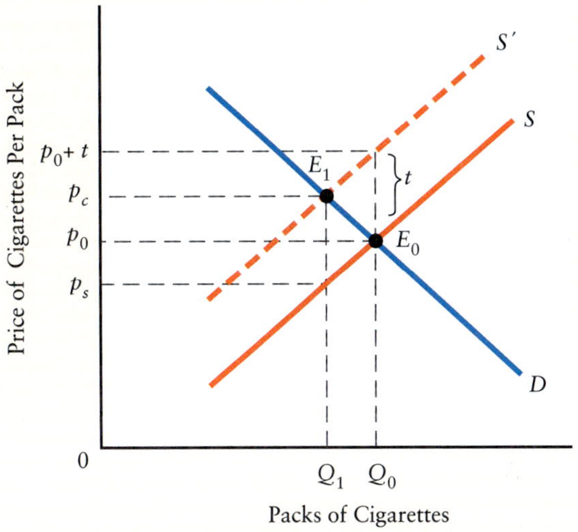

The burden of an excise tax is shared by consumers and producers. The original supply and demand curves for cigarettes are given by the solid lines S and D; equilibrium is at E_0 with price p_0 and quantity Q_0. When an excise tax of t per pack is imposed, the supply curve shifts up to the dashed line S', which lies above the original supply curve by the amount of the tax t. The new equilibrium is at E_1. The tax increases the consumer price, but by less than the full amount of the tax, and reduces the seller price, also by less than the full amount of the tax. It also reduces the equilibrium quantity exchanged.

After the imposition of an excise tax, the difference between the consumer and seller prices is equal to the tax. In the new equilibrium, the quantity exchanged is less than that exchanged prior to the imposition of the tax.

The role of the relative elasticities of supply and demand in determining the incidence of the excise tax is illustrated in Figure 4-9. In part (i), demand is inelastic relative to supply; as a result, the fall in quantity is quite small, whereas the price paid by consumers rises by almost the full extent of the tax. Because neither the price received by sellers nor the quantity sold changes very much, sellers bear little of the burden of the tax. In part (ii), supply is inelastic relative to demand; in this case, consumers can more easily substitute away from cigarettes. There is little change in the price, and hence they bear little of the burden of the tax, which falls mostly on suppliers. Notice in Figure 4-9 that the size of the upward shift in supply is the same in the two cases, indicating the same tax in both cases.

FIGURE 4-9 Elasticity and the Incidence of an Excise Tax

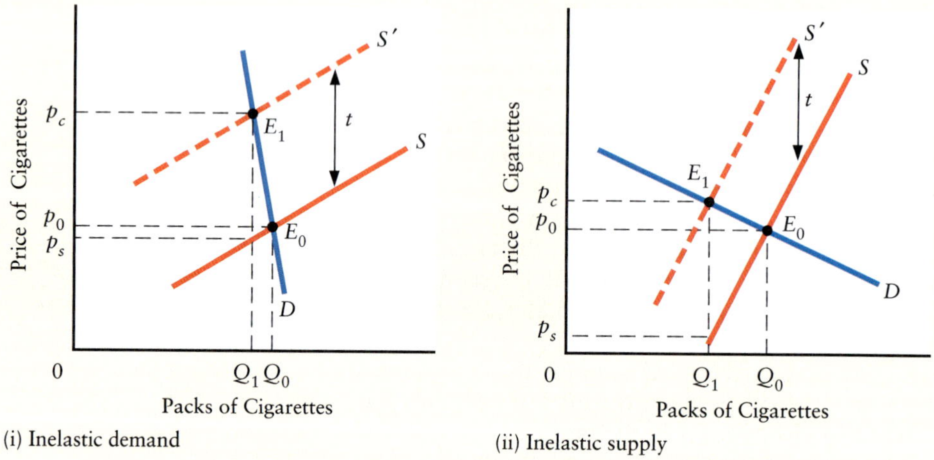

The distribution of the burden of an excise tax between consumers and producers depends on the relative elasticities of supply and demand. In both parts of the figure, the initial supply and demand curves are given by S and D; the initial equilibrium is at E_0 with equilibrium price p_0 and quantity Q_0. A tax of t per pack of cigarettes is imposed, causing the supply curve to shift up by the amount of the tax to S'. The new equilibrium is at E_1. The consumer price rises to p_c, the seller price falls to p_s, and the quantity falls to Q_1. Sellers bear little of the burden of the tax in the first case (and consumers bear a lot), whereas consumers bear little of the burden in the second case (and sellers bear a lot).

Practise with Study Guide Chapter 4, Exercise 8.

When demand is inelastic relative to supply, consumers bear most of the burden of excise taxes. When supply is inelastic relative to demand, producers bear most of the burden.

Now we can examine who really pays for cigarette tax increases (or tax increases on gasoline and alcohol). The demand for cigarettes is inelastic both overall and relative to supply, suggesting that the burden of a cigarette tax is borne more by consumers than by producers. The demand for gasoline is also inelastic, but much more so in the short run than in the long run. (In the long run, drivers can change their driving habits and improve the efficiency of their vehicles, but in the short run such changes are very costly.) The supply of gasoline, given world trade in petroleum and petroleum products, is elastic relative to demand. The relatively inelastic demand and elastic supply imply that the burden of gasoline taxes falls mostly on consumers.

Extensions in Theory 4-1 shows how to work through the algebra of demand and supply in the presence of an excise tax.

myeconlab

Another application of the concept of tax incidence relates to payroll taxes such as premiums that workers and firms pay for employment insurance and the Canada Pension Plan. For more information on this application of tax incidence, look for "Who Really Pays for Payroll Taxes?" in the *Additional Topics* section of this book's MyEconLab.

www.myeconlab.com

EXTENSIONS IN THEORY 4-1

The Algebra of Tax Incidence

It is straightforward to show the burden of an excise tax using algebra to solve for the equilibrium price and quantity. Suppose the demand-and-supply model of the market is given by the following two linear equations.

(1) $Q^D = a - bp_c$ Demand curve

(2) $Q^S = c + dp_s$ Supply curve

where Q^D is quantity demanded at the consumer price, p_c, and Q^S is quantity supplied at the seller price, p_s. The presence of an excise tax of t dollars per unit implies that the price received by the seller, p_s, must be t dollars less than the price paid by the consumer, p_c:

$$(3) \quad p_s = p_c - t$$

We can substitute equation (3) into (2) to express the supply curve in terms of the consumer price:

$$(4) \quad Q^S = c + d(p_c - t)$$

or

$$(5) \quad Q^S = c - dt + dp_c$$

When the market is in equilibrium, $Q^D = Q^S$, and so we can equate Q^D from equation (1) with Q^S from equation (5). This gives us

$$a - bp_c = c - dt + dp_c$$

This equation allows us to solve for the equilibrium consumer price, p_c*.

$$p_c^* = \frac{a - c}{b + d} + \frac{d}{b + d}t$$

This solution for p_c* can now be substituted back into the demand curve, equation (1), to solve for the equilibrium quantity, Q*.

$$Q^* = a - bp_c^* = a - \frac{b(a - c + dt)}{b + d}$$

Now consider these solutions for p_c* and Q* in the case where there is no tax, $t = 0$. This exercise reveals what we already know from Figures 4-8 and 4-9—that the excise tax increases the equilibrium consumer price and reduces the equilibrium quantity from the levels that we would observe in the absence of the excise tax.

Who bears the burden of the excise tax? To answer this question, we must examine both the equilibrium consumer and seller prices, p_c* and p_s*. We saw above that

$$(6) \quad p_c^* = \frac{a - c}{b + d} + \frac{d}{b + d}t$$

and we also know that $p_c^* - t = p_s^*$. It follows that

$$(7) \quad p_s^* = \frac{a - c}{b + d} + \frac{d}{b + d}t - t$$

$$= \frac{a - c}{b + d} - \frac{b}{b + d}t$$

Note that when $t = 0$, the equilibrium price in this model, for both consumers and sellers, is

$$p^* = \frac{a - c}{b + d}$$

We can therefore express the equilibrium consumer and seller prices in the presence of an excise tax in terms of p*:

$$(8) \quad p_c^* = p^* + \frac{d}{b + d}t$$

$$(9) \quad p_s^* = p^* - \frac{b}{b + d}t$$

These solutions for p_c* and p_s* show how the burden of the excise tax depends on the slopes of the demand and supply curves. For example, consider a small value of d which reflects a relatively steep supply curve. The small value of d means that p_c* is only a little above p*, whereas p_s* is considerably below p*; thus, when the supply curve is relatively steep, sellers bear more of the burden of the tax. In contrast, consider a small value of b, which reflects a relatively steep demand curve. The small value of b means that p_s* is only a little below p*, but p_c* is considerably above p*; thus, consumers bear more of the burden of the tax when the demand curve is relatively steep.

STUDY GUIDE

Practise with Study Guide Chapter 4, Extension Exercise E3.

4.4 OTHER DEMAND ELASTICITIES

The price of the product is not the only important variable determining demand for that product. Changes in income and changes in the prices of other products also lead to changes in demand, and elasticity is a useful concept in measuring their effects.

Income Elasticity of Demand

income elasticity of demand (η_Y) A measure of the responsiveness of quantity demanded to a change in income.

One important determinant of demand is the income of the customers. The responsiveness of demand to changes in income is termed the **income elasticity of demand** and is symbolized η_Y.

$$\eta_Y = \frac{\text{Percentage change in quantity demanded}}{\text{Percentage change in income}}$$

normal good A good for which quantity demanded rises as income rises—its income elasticity is positive.

inferior good A good for which quantity demanded falls as income rises—its income elasticity is negative.

For most goods, increases in income lead to increases in demand—their income elasticity is positive. These are called **normal goods.** Goods for which demand decreases in response to a rise in income have negative income elasticities and are called **inferior goods.**

The income elasticity of normal goods can be greater than 1 (elastic) or less than 1 (inelastic), depending on whether the percentage change in quantity demanded is greater or less than the percentage change in income that brought it about. It is also common to use the terms *income-elastic* and *income-inelastic* to refer to income elasticities of greater or less than 1. (See *Extensions in Theory* 4-2 for a summary of the different elasticity concepts.)

How the demand for goods and services reacts to changes in income has important economic effects. In most Western countries during the twentieth century, economic growth caused the level of income to double every 20 to 30 years. This rise in income was shared to some extent by almost all citizens. As they found their incomes increasing, they increased their demands for most products. In the first part of that century, however, the demands for some products (such as food and basic clothing) were income-inelastic whereas the demands for other products (such as durable goods) were income-elastic. As a result, the demand for food and clothing grew less rapidly than did the demand for durable goods. Later in the century, as incomes rose still further, the income elasticity of demand for manufactured durables (such as cars, TV sets, and refrigerators) fell while that for services (such as restaurant meals and movies) increased. During this period the ongoing income growth led the demand for services to grow more rapidly than the demand for durable goods.

In some developing countries today, where per capita incomes are close to those of the Western nations at the beginning of the twentieth century, it is the demands for durable manufactured goods that are increasing most rapidly as income rises. In future years (assuming that the current growth of income continues) these same countries will likely experience the same shift in demand toward services that was experienced by the Western countries in the last part of the twentieth century.

The uneven impact of the growth of income on the demands for different products has important effects on the pattern of employment. For example, in Western countries, employment in agriculture fell during the first part of the twentieth century, while employment in manufacturing rose. In the last half of the century, employment in manufacturing fell gradually whereas employment in services increased rapidly (and employment in agriculture continued its gradual decline). We shall see many other consequences of these demand shifts later in this book.

Luxuries Versus Necessities Different products typically have different income elasticities of demand. For example, empirical studies find that basic food items—such as vegetables, bread, and cereals—usually have positive income elasticities less than 1 (so an increase in income of 10 percent leads to an increase in quantity demanded of less than 10 percent). Such goods are often called *necessities*. In contrast, more expensive foods—such as high-quality cuts of meat, prepared meals, and wine—usually have positive income elasticities greater than 1 (so an increase in income of 10 percent leads to an increase in quantity demanded of more than 10 percent). These products are often called *luxuries*.

The more necessary is an item in the consumption pattern of consumers, the lower is its income elasticity.

Income elasticities for any one product also vary with the level of a consumer's income. When incomes are low, consumers may eat almost no green vegetables and consume lots of starchy foods such as bread and potatoes; when incomes are higher, they may eat cheap cuts of meat and more green vegetables along with their bread and potatoes; when incomes are higher still, they are likely to eat higher quality and prepared foods of a wide variety.

The distinction between luxuries and necessities helps to explain differences in income elasticities. The case of restaurant meals is one example. Such meals are almost always more expensive, calorie for calorie, than meals prepared at home. It would thus be expected that at lower incomes, restaurant meals would be regarded as an expensive luxury but that the demand for them would expand substantially as consumers became richer. This is actually what happens.

Cross Elasticity of Demand

The responsiveness of demand to changes in the price of *another* product is called the **cross elasticity of demand**. It is denoted η_{XY} and defined as follows:

cross elasticity of demand (η_{XY}) A measure of the responsiveness of the quantity of one commodity demanded to changes in the price of another commodity.

$$\eta_{XY} = \frac{\text{Percentage change in quantity demanded of good } X}{\text{Percentage change in price of good } Y}$$

The change in the price of good *Y* causes the *demand curve* for good *X* to shift. If *X* and *Y* are substitutes, an increase in the price of *Y* leads to an increase in the demand for *X*. If *X* and *Y* are complements, an increase in the price of *Y* leads to a reduction in demand for *X*. In either case, we are holding the price of *X* constant. We therefore measure the change in the quantity demanded of *X* (at its unchanged price) by measuring the shift of the demand curve for *X*.

Practise with Study Guide Chapter 4, Extension Exercise E1.

Cross elasticity can vary from minus infinity to plus infinity. Complementary products, such as cars and gasoline, have negative cross elasticities. A large rise in the price of gasoline will lead to a decline in the demand for cars, as some people decide to do without a car and others decide not to buy an additional car. Substitute products, such as cars and public transport, have positive cross elasticities. A large rise in the price of cars (relative to public transport) will lead to a rise in the demand for public transport as some people shift from cars to public transport. (See *Extensions in Theory 4-2* for a summary of elasticity terminology.)

EXTENSIONS IN THEORY 4-2

The Terminology of Elasticity

Term	Numerical Measure of Elasticity	Verbal Description
A. Price elasticity of demand (supply)		
Perfectly or completely inelastic	Zero	Quantity demanded (supplied) does not change as price changes.
Inelastic	Between zero and 1	Quantity demanded (supplied) changes by a smaller percentage than does price.
Unit elastic	One	Quantity demanded (supplied) changes by exactly the same percentage as does price.
Elastic	Greater than 1, but less than infinity	Quantity demanded (supplied) changes by a larger percentage than does price.
Perfectly, completely, or infinitely elastic	Infinity	Purchasers (sellers) are prepared to buy (sell) all they can at some price and none at all at a higher (lower) price.
B. Income elasticity of demand		
Inferior good	Negative	Quantity demanded decreases as income increases.
Normal good	Positive	Quantity demanded increases as income increases:
Income-inelastic	Less than 1	Less than in proportion to income increase
Income-elastic	Greater than 1	More than in proportion to income increase
C. Cross elasticity of demand		
Substitute	Positive	Price increase of a substitute leads to an increase in quantity demanded of this good.
Complement	Negative	Price increase of a complement leads to a decrease in quantity demanded of this good.

Substitute products have a positive cross elasticity; an increase in the price of one leads to an increase in demand for the other.

The positive or negative signs of cross elasticities tell us whether goods are substitutes or complements.

Measures of cross elasticity sometimes prove helpful in defining whether producers of similar products are in competition with each other. For example, glass bottles and tin cans have a high cross elasticity of demand. The producer of bottles is thus in competition with the producer of cans. If the bottle company raises its price, it will lose substantial sales to the can producer. In contrast, men's shoes and women's shoes have a low cross elasticity and thus a producer of men's shoes is not in close competition with a producer of women's shoes. If the former raises its price, it will not lose many sales to the latter. Knowledge of cross elasticity can be important in matters of *competition policy* in which the issue is whether a firm in one industry is or is not competing with firms in another industry. We discuss competition policy in more detail in Chapter 12.

SUMMARY

4.1 PRICE ELASTICITY OF DEMAND

LO 1 2

- *Price elasticity of demand* is a measure of the extent to which the quantity demanded of a product responds to a change in its price. Represented by the symbol η, it is defined as

$$\eta = \frac{\text{Percentage change in quantity demanded}}{\text{Percentage change in price}}$$

- The percentage changes are usually calculated as the change divided by the *average* value. Elasticity is defined to be a positive number, and it can vary from zero to infinity.
- When elasticity is less than 1, demand is *inelastic*—the percentage change in quantity demanded is less than the percentage change in price. When elasticity exceeds 1, demand is *elastic*—the percentage change in quantity demanded is greater than the percentage change in price.
- The main determinant of price elasticity of demand is the availability of substitutes for the product. Any one of a group of close substitutes will have a more elastic demand than will the group as a whole.
- Items that have few substitutes in the short run tend to develop many substitutes when consumers and producers have time to adapt. Therefore, demand is more elastic in the long run than in the short run.
- Elasticity and total expenditure are related in the following way: If elasticity is less than 1, total expenditure is positively related with price; if elasticity is greater than 1, total expenditure is negatively related with price; and if elasticity is 1, total expenditure does not change as price changes.

4.2 PRICE ELASTICITY OF SUPPLY

LO 3

- *Elasticity of supply* measures the extent to which the quantity supplied of some product changes when the price of that product changes. Represented by the symbol η_S, it is defined as

$$\eta_S = \frac{\text{Percentage change in quantity supplied}}{\text{Percentage change in price}}$$

- Supply tends to be more elastic in the long run than in the short run because it usually takes time for producers to alter their productive capacity in response to price changes.

4.3 AN IMPORTANT EXAMPLE WHERE ELASTICITY MATTERS

LO 4

- The distribution of the burden of an excise tax between consumers and producers depends on the relative elasticities of supply and demand for the product.
- The less elastic demand is relative to supply, the more of the burden of an excise tax falls on the consumers. The more elastic demand is relative to supply, the more of the burden of an excise tax falls on producers.

4.4 OTHER DEMAND ELASTICITIES

LO 5 6

- *Income elasticity of demand* is a measure of the extent to which the quantity demanded of some product changes as income changes. Represented by the symbol η_Y, it is defined as

$$\eta_Y = \frac{\text{Percentage change in quantity demanded}}{\text{Percentage change in income}}$$

- The income elasticity of demand for a product will usually change as income varies. A product that has a high income elasticity at a low income may have a low or negative income elasticity at higher incomes.
- *Cross elasticity of demand* is a measure of the extent to which the quantity demanded of one product changes when the price of a different product changes. Represented by the symbol η_{XY}, it is defined as

$$\eta_{XY} = \frac{\text{Percentage change in quantity demanded of good } X}{\text{Percentage change in price of good } Y}$$

It is used to define products that are substitutes for one another (positive cross elasticity) and products that are complements for one another (negative cross elasticity).

KEY CONCEPTS

Price elasticity of demand
Inelastic and perfectly inelastic demand
Elastic and infinitely elastic demand
Relationship between demand elasticity and total expenditure
Elasticity of supply
Short-run and long-run responses to shifts in demand and supply
The burden of an excise tax
Consumer price and seller price
Income elasticity of demand
Income-elastic and income-inelastic demands
Normal goods and inferior goods
Cross elasticity of demand
Substitutes and complements

STUDY EXERCISES

1. Fill in the blanks to make the following statements correct.
   a. When a 10-percent change in the price of a good brings about a 20-percent change in its quantity demanded, the price elasticity of demand is __________. We can say that demand for this good is __________.
   b. When a 10-percent change in the price of a good brings about a 4-percent change in its quantity demanded, the price elasticity of demand is __________. We can say that demand for this good is __________.
   c. When a 10-percent change in the price of a good brings about a 10-percent change in its quantity demanded, the price elasticity of demand is __________. We can say that demand for this good is __________.

2. A hypothetical demand schedule for comic books in a small town is provided below.

Demand Schedule for Comic Books

Price	Quantity Demanded	Total Expenditure	Percent Change in Price	Percent Change in Quantity Demanded	Elasticity of Demand
$11	1	____			
9	3	____	____	____	____
7	5	____	____	____	____
5	7	____	____	____	____
3	9	____	____	____	____
1	11	____	____	____	____

   a. Fill in the table and calculate the price elasticity of demand over each price range. Be sure to use *average* prices and quantities when computing the percentage changes.
   b. Plot the demand curve and show the elasticities over the different ranges of the curve.
   c. Explain why demand is more elastic at the higher prices.

3. Suppose the market for frozen orange juice is in equilibrium at a price of $1.00 per can and a quantity of 4200 cans per month. Now suppose that at a price of $1.50 per can, quantity demanded falls to 3000 cans per month and quantity supplied increases to 4500 cans per month.
   a. Draw the appropriate diagram for this market.
   b. Calculate the price elasticity of demand for frozen orange juice between the prices of $1.00 and $1.50. Is the demand elastic or inelastic?
   c. Calculate the elasticity of supply for frozen orange juice between the prices of $1.00 and $1.50. Is the supply elastic or inelastic?
   d. Explain in general what factors would affect the elasticity of demand for frozen orange juice.
   e. Explain in general what factors would affect the elasticity of supply of frozen orange juice.

4. What would you predict about the *relative* price elasticity of demand for each of the following items? Explain your reasoning.
   a. food
   b. vegetables
   c. leafy vegetables
   d. leafy vegetables sold at your local supermarket
   e. leafy vegetables sold at your local supermarket on Wednesdays

5. Suppose a stamp dealer buys the only two existing copies of a stamp at an auction. After the purchase, the dealer goes to the front of the room and burns one of the stamps in front of the shocked audience. What must the dealer believe in order for this to be a wealth-maximizing action? Explain with a demand-and-supply diagram.

6. myeconlab For each of the following events, state the relevant elasticity concept. Then compute the measure of elasticity, using average prices and quantities in your calculations. In all cases, assume that these are *ceteris paribus* changes.

a. When the price of theatre tickets is reduced from \$14.00 to \$11.00, ticket sales increase from 1200 to 1350.
b. As average household income in Canada increases by 10 percent, annual sales of Toyota Camrys increase from 56 000 to 67 000.
c. After a major failure of Brazil's coffee crop sent coffee prices up from \$3.00 per kilogram to \$4.80 per kilogram, sales of tea in Canada increased from 7500 kg per month to 8000 kg per month.
d. An increase in the world demand for pulp (used in producing newsprint) increases the price by 14 percent. Annual Canadian production increases from 8 million tonnes to 11 million tonnes.

7. myeconlab The following table shows the demand schedule for denim jeans.

	Price (per unit)	Quantity Demanded (per year)	Total Expenditure
A	\$30	400 000	
B	35	380 000	
C	40	350 000	
D	45	320 000	
E	50	300 000	
F	55	260 000	
G	60	230 000	
H	65	190 000	

a. Compute total expenditure for each row in the table.
b. Plot the demand curve and the total expenditure curve.
c. Compute the price elasticities of demand between points *A* and *B*, *B* and *C*, *C* and *D*, and so on.
d. Over what range of prices is the demand for denim jeans elastic? Explain.
e. Over what range of prices is the demand for denim jeans inelastic? Explain.

8. Consider the following straight-line supply curves. In each case, p is the price (measured in dollars per unit) and Q^S is the quantity supplied of the product (measured in thousands of units per month).

i) $p = 2Q^S$
ii) $p = 4Q^S$
iii) $p = 5Q^S$
iv) $p = 10Q^S$

a. Plot each supply curve on a scale diagram. In each case, plot point *A* (which corresponds to price equal to \$20) and point *B* (which corresponds to price equal to \$40).
b. For each supply curve, compute the price elasticity of supply between points *A* and *B*.
c. Explain why the *slope* of a supply curve is not the same as the *elasticity* of supply.

9. myeconlab This is a challenging question intended for those students who like mathematics. It will help you work through the issue of tax incidence. (See *Extensions in Theory 4-1* if you get stuck!)

Consider the market for gasoline. Suppose the market demand and supply curves are as given below. In each case, quantity refers to millions of litres of gasoline per month; price is the price per litre (in cents).

$$\text{Demand: } p = 80 - 5Q^D$$
$$\text{Supply: } p = 24 + 2Q^S$$

a. Plot the demand and supply curves on a scale diagram.
b. Compute the equilibrium price and quantity.
c. Now suppose the government imposes a tax of 14 cents per litre. Show how this affects the market equilibrium. What is the new "consumer price" and what is the new "producer price"?
d. Compute the total revenue raised by the gasoline tax. What share of this tax revenue is "paid" by consumers, and what share is "paid" by producers? (Hint: if the consumer price were unchanged from the pre-tax equilibrium, we would say that consumers pay none of the tax.)

DISCUSSION QUESTIONS

1. From the following quotations, what, if anything, can you conclude about elasticity of demand?
   a. "Good weather resulted in record wheat harvests and sent wheat prices tumbling. The result has been disastrous for many wheat farmers."
   b. "Ridership always went up when bus fares came down, but the increased patronage never was enough to prevent a decrease in overall revenue."
   c. "As the price of CD players fell, producers found their revenues soaring."
   d. "Coffee to me is an essential good—I've just gotta have it no matter what the price."
   e. "The soaring price of condominiums does little to curb the strong demand in Vancouver."
2. Home computers were a leader in sales appeal through much of the 1990s. But per capita sales are much lower in Mexico than in Canada, and lower in Newfoundland and Labrador than in Alberta. Manufacturers are puzzled by the big differences. Can you offer an explanation in terms of elasticity?
3. What elasticity measure or measures would be useful in answering the following questions?
   a. Will cheaper transport into the central city help to keep downtown shopping centres profitable?
   b. Will raising the bulk postage rate increase or decrease the revenues for Canada Post?
   c. Are producers of toothpaste and mouthwash in competition with each other?
   d. What effect will rising gasoline prices have on the sale of cars that use propane gas?
4. Interpret the following statements in terms of the relevant elasticity concept.
   a. "As fuel for tractors has become more expensive, many farmers have shifted from plowing their fields to no-till farming. No-till acreage increased dramatically in the past 20 years."
   b. "Fertilizer makers brace for dismal year as fertilizer prices soar."
   c. "When farmers are hurting, small towns feel the pain."
   d. "The development of the Hibernia oil field may bring temporary prosperity to Newfoundland and Labrador merchants."
5. When the New York City Opera faced a growing deficit, it cut its ticket prices by 20 percent, hoping to attract more customers. At the same time, the New York Transit Authority raised subway fares to reduce its growing deficit. Was one of these two opposite approaches to reducing a deficit necessarily wrong?

CHAPTER 5

Markets in Action

LEARNING OBJECTIVES

In this chapter you will learn

1. that individual markets do not exist in isolation, and that changes in one market typically have repercussions in other markets.
2. how a market works in the presence of price ceilings or price floors.
3. about the different short-run and long-run effects of legislated rent controls.
4. why government interventions that cause prices to deviate from their market-clearing levels are inefficient for society as a whole.

Over the past two chapters, we have developed the model of demand and supply that you can now use to analyze individual markets. A full understanding of the basic theory, however, comes only with practice. This chapter will provide some practice by analyzing several examples including minimum wages and rent controls.

Before examining these cases, however, we begin the chapter by discussing how various markets are related to each other. In Chapters 3 and 4, we used the simple demand-and-supply model to describe a single market, ignoring what was going on in other markets. For example, when we examined the market for carrots, we made no mention of the markets for broccoli, milk, or labour services. In other words, we viewed the market for carrots in isolation from all other markets. But this was only a simplification. In this chapter's opening section we note that the economy should *not* be viewed as a series of isolated markets. Rather, the economy is a complex system of inter-related markets. The implication of this complex structure is that events that lead to changes in one market typically lead to changes in other markets as well.

5.1 THE INTERACTION AMONG MARKETS

Suppose an advance is made that reduces the cost of extracting natural gas. This technological improvement would be represented as a rightward shift in the supply curve for natural gas. The equilibrium price of natural gas would fall and there would be an increase in the equilibrium quantity exchanged.

How would other markets be affected? As natural-gas firms expanded their production, they would increase their demand for the entire range of goods and services used for the extraction, processing, pumping, and distribution of natural gas. This increase in demand would raise the prices of those items, and lead the producers of those goods to devote more resources to their production. The natural-gas firms would also increase their demand for labour, since more workers would be required to drill for and extract more natural gas. The increase in demand for labour would tend to push wages up. Firms that hire similar workers in other industries would have to pay higher wages to retain their workers. The profits of those firms would fall and they would employ fewer workers, thus freeing up the extra workers needed in the natural-gas industry.

There would also be a direct effect on consumers. The reduction in the equilibrium price of natural gas would generate some substitution away from other fuels, such as oil or propane, and toward the now-lower-priced natural gas. Such reductions in demand would tend to push down the price of oil and propane, and producers of those fuels would devote fewer resources to their production.

In short, a technological improvement in the natural-gas industry would have effects in many other markets. But there is nothing special about the natural-gas industry. The same would be true about a change in almost any market you can think of.

No market or industry exists in isolation from the economy's many other markets.

Practise with Study Guide Chapter 5, Exercise 1.

A change in one market will lead to changes in many other markets. The induced changes in these other markets will, in turn, lead to changes in the first market. This is what economists call *feedback*. In the example of the natural-gas industry, the reduction in the price of natural gas leads consumers to reduce their demand for oil and propane, thus driving down the prices of these other fuels. But when we consider the demand and supply curves for natural gas, we assume that the *prices of all other goods are constant*. So, when the prices of oil and propane fall, the feedback effect on the natural-gas market is to shift the demand curve for natural gas to the left (because natural gas is a substitute for both oil and propane).

Predicting the precise size of this feedback effect is difficult, and the analysis of the natural-gas industry—or any other industry—would certainly be much easier if we could ignore it. But we cannot always ignore such feedback effects. Economists make a distinction between cases where the feedback effects are small enough that they can safely be ignored, and cases where the feedback effects are large enough that ignoring them would significantly change the analysis.

partial-equilibrium analysis The analysis of a single market in isolation, ignoring any feedbacks that may come from induced changes in other markets.

Partial-equilibrium analysis is the analysis of a single market in situations where the feedback effects from other markets are ignored. This is the type of analysis that we have used so far in this book, and it is the most common type of analysis in microeconomics. For example, when we examined the market for cigarettes at the end of Chapter 4, we ignored any potential feedback effects that could have come from the market for alcohol, coffee, or many other goods or services. In this case, we used partial-equilibrium analysis, focusing only on the market for cigarettes, because we assumed that the changes in the cigarette market would produce small enough changes on the other markets that the feedback effects from the other markets would, in turn, be sufficiently diffused that we could safely ignore them. This suggests the general rule telling us when partial-equilibrium analysis is a legitimate method of analysis.

If a specific market is quite small relative to the entire economy, changes in the market will have relatively small effects on other markets. The feedback effects on the original market will, in turn, be even smaller. In such cases, partial-equilibrium analysis can successfully be used to analyze the original market.

general-equilibrium analysis The analysis of all the economy's markets simultaneously, recognizing the interactions among the various markets.

When economists study all markets together, rather than a single market in isolation, they use what is called **general-equilibrium analysis**. This is more complicated than partial-equilibrium analysis because the economist not only must consider what is happening in each individual market but also must take into account how events in each market affect all the other markets.

General-equilibrium analysis is the study of how all markets function together, taking into account the various relationships and feedback effects between individual markets.

myeconlab

For a detailed discussion and several examples of the various ways that seemingly unrelated markets may be linked, look for "Linkages Between Markets" in the *Additional Topics* section of this book's MyEconLab.

www.myeconlab.com

As you go on to learn more microeconomics in this and later chapters, you will encounter mostly partial-equilibrium analysis. The book is written this way intentionally—it is easier to learn about the basic ideas of monopoly, competition policy, labour unions, and environmental policy (as well as many other topics) by restricting our attention to single markets. But keep in mind that there are always many other markets "behind the scenes" that are linked to the individual markets we choose to study.

We now go on to examine the effects of government-controlled prices. These appear prominently in labour markets and rental housing markets.

5.2 GOVERNMENT-CONTROLLED PRICES

In a number of important cases, governments fix the price at which a product must be bought and sold in the domestic market. Here we examine the general consequences of such policies. Later, we look at some specific examples.

In a free market the equilibrium price equates the quantity demanded with the quantity supplied. Government *price controls* are policies that attempt to hold the price at some disequilibrium value. Some controls hold the market price below its equilibrium value, thus creating a shortage at the controlled price. Other controls hold price above its equilibrium value, thus creating a surplus at the controlled price.

Disequilibrium Prices

When controls hold price at some disequilibrium value, what determines the quantity *actually traded* on the market? This is not a question we have to ask when examining a free market because the price adjusts to equate quantity demanded with quantity supplied. But this adjustment cannot take place if the government is controlling the price. So, in this case, what determines the quantity actually exchanged?

The key to the answer is the fact that any *voluntary* market transaction requires both a willing buyer and a willing seller. So, if quantity demanded is less than quantity supplied, demand will determine the amount actually exchanged, while the rest of the quantity supplied will remain in the hands of the unsuccessful sellers. Conversely, if quantity demanded exceeds quantity supplied, supply will determine the amount actually exchanged, while the rest of the quantity demanded will represent unsatisfied demand of would-be buyers. Figure 5-1 illustrates the general conclusion:

At any disequilibrium price, quantity exchanged is determined by the *lesser* of quantity demanded or quantity supplied.

FIGURE 5-1 The Determination of Quantity Exchanged in Disequilibrium

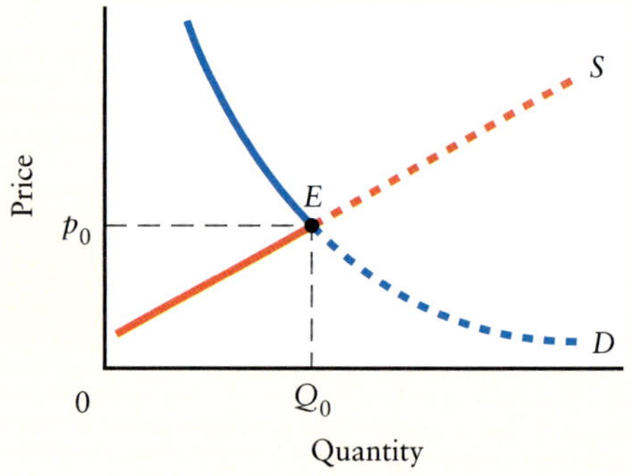

In disequilibrium, quantity exchanged is determined by the lesser of quantity demanded and quantity supplied. At *E,* the market is in equilibrium, with quantity demanded equal to quantity supplied. For any price below p_0, the quantity exchanged will be determined by the supply curve. For any price above p_0, the quantity exchanged will be determined by the demand curve. Thus, the solid portions of the *S* and *D* curves show the actual quantities exchanged at different disequilibrium prices.

FIGURE 5-2 A Binding Price Floor

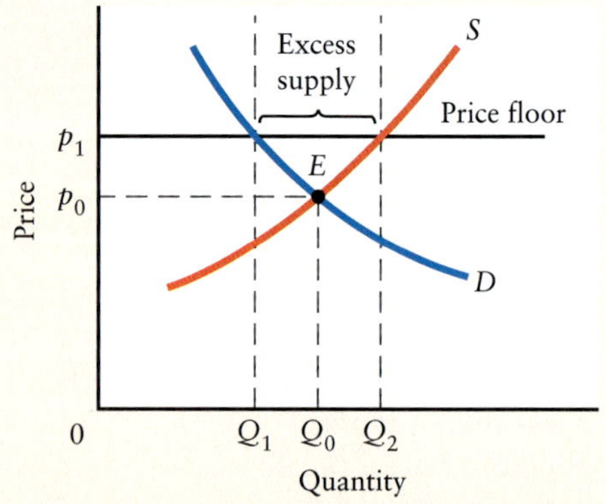

A binding price floor leads to excess supply. The free-market equilibrium is at *E,* with price p_0 and quantity Q_0. The government now establishes a binding price floor at p_1. The result is excess supply equal to Q_1Q_2.

Price Floors

Governments sometimes establish a *price floor,* which is the minimum permissible price that can be charged for a particular good or service. A price floor that is set at or below the equilibrium price has no effect because the free-market equilibrium remains attainable. If, however, the price floor is set above the equilibrium, it will raise the price, in which case it is said to be *binding.*

Price floors may be established by rules that make it illegal to sell the product below the prescribed price, as in the case of a legislated minimum wage. Or the government may establish a price floor by announcing that it will guarantee a certain price by buying any excess supply. Such guarantees are a feature of many agricultural support policies.

The effects of a binding price floor are illustrated in Figure 5-2, which establishes the following key result:

Binding price floors lead to excess supply. Either an unsold surplus will exist, or someone (usually the government) must enter the market and buy the excess supply.

The consequences of excess supply differ from product to product. If the product is labour, subject to a minimum wage, excess supply translates into people without jobs (unemployment). If the product is wheat, and more is produced than can be sold to consumers, the surplus wheat will accumulate in grain elevators or government warehouses. These consequences may or may not be worthwhile in terms of the other goals achieved. But worthwhile or not, these consequences are inevitable in a competitive market whenever a price floor is set above the market-clearing equilibrium price.

Why might the government wish to incur these consequences? One reason is that the people who succeed in selling their products at the price floor are better off than if they had to accept the lower equilibrium price. Workers and farmers are among the politically active, organized groups who have gained much by persuading the government to establish price floors that enable them to sell their goods or services at prices above free-market levels. If the demand is inelastic, as it often is for agricultural products, producers sell a lower quantity than they would at the equilibrium price (even though their total income is raised by the price floor). The losses are spread across the large and diverse set of purchasers, each of whom suffers only a small loss (although the *total* loss can be considerable).

Applying Economic Concepts 5-1 examines the case of a legislated minimum wage in more detail, and explains the basis of the often-heard claim that minimum wages increase unemployment. We discuss the effects of minimum wages in greater detail in Chapter 14 when we examine various labour-market issues.

For information on various labour-market policies in Canada, see HRSDC's website: **www.hrsdc.gc.ca**. Then click on "Labour and Workplace."

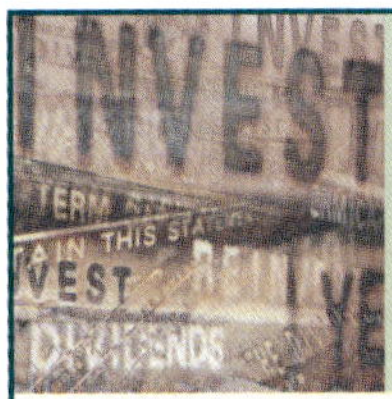

APPLYING ECONOMIC CONCEPTS 5-1

Minimum Wages and Unemployment

All Canadian governments, provincial and federal, have legislated minimum wages. For those industries covered by provincial legislation (which includes most industries except banking, airlines, trucking, and railways), the minimum wage in 2006 ranged from a low of $6.50 per hour in New Brunswick to a high of $8.50 per hour in Nunavut. This box examines the effects of implementing a minimum wage in a competitive labour market, and provides a basis for understanding the often-heard claim that minimum wages lead to an increase in unemployment.

The accompanying figure shows the demand and supply curves for labour services, with "Employment" on the horizontal axis and "Hourly Wage Rate" on the vertical axis. In the absence of any legislated minimum wage, the equilibrium in the labour market would be a wage equal to w_0 and a level of employment equal to E_0.

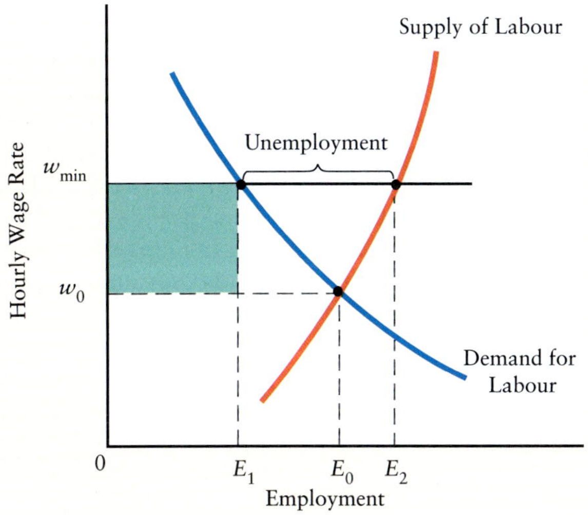

Now suppose the government introduces a minimum wage equal to w_{min} that is greater than w_0. The increased wage has two effects. First, by increasing the cost of labour services to firms, the minimum wage reduces the level of employment to E_1. The second effect is to increase the quantity supplied of labour services to E_2. Thus, the clear effect of the binding minimum wage, as seen in the figure, is to generate unemployment—workers that want a job but are unable to get one—equal to the amount E_1E_2.

Whom does this policy benefit? And whom does it harm? Firms are clearly made worse off since they are now required to pay a higher wage than before the minimum wage was imposed. They respond to this increase in costs by reducing their use of labour. Some (but not all) workers are made better off. The workers who are lucky enough to keep their jobs—E_1 workers in the figure—get a higher wage than before. The shaded area shows the redistribution of income away from firms and toward these fortunate workers. Some workers are harmed by the policy—the ones who lose their jobs as a result of the wage increase, shown in the figure as the quantity E_1E_0.

We have discussed here the effects of minimum wages in a *competitive* labour market—one in which there are many firms and many workers, none of whom have the power to influence the market wage. In Chapter 14 we will examine non-competitive labour markets and we will then see that minimum wages may have a different effect on the market. This different behaviour of competitive and non-competitive markets in the presence of minimum wages probably accounts for the disagreements among economists and policymakers regarding the desirability of minimum-wage legislation. Until we proceed to that more advanced discussion, however, the analysis of a competitive labour market in this box provides an excellent example of the economic effects of a binding price floor in specific circumstances.

FIGURE 5-3 A Price Ceiling and Black-Market Pricing

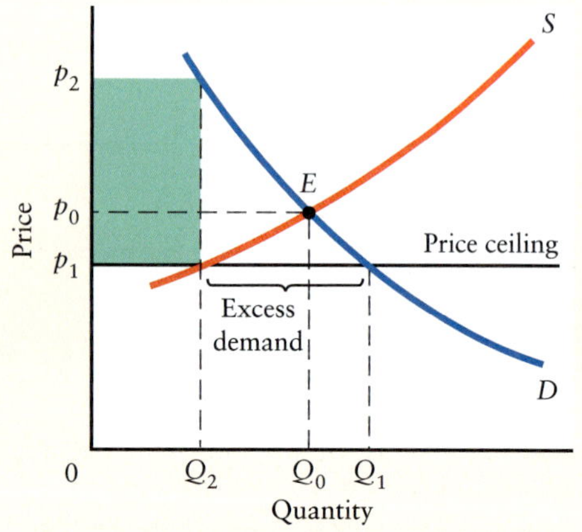

A binding price ceiling causes excess demand and invites a black market. The equilibrium point, E, is at a price of p_0 and a quantity of Q_0. If a price ceiling is set at p_1, the quantity demanded will rise to Q_1 and the quantity supplied will fall to Q_2. Quantity actually exchanged will be Q_2. But if all the available supply of Q_2 were sold on a black market, the price to consumers would rise to p_2. Because black marketeers buy at the ceiling price of p_1 and sell at the black-market price of p_2, their profits are represented by the shaded area.

Price Ceilings

A *price ceiling* is the maximum price at which certain goods and services may be exchanged. Price controls on oil, natural gas, and rental housing have been frequently imposed by federal and provincial governments. If the price ceiling is set above the equilibrium price, it has no effect because the free-market equilibrium remains attainable. If, however, the price ceiling is set below the free-market equilibrium price, the price ceiling lowers the price and is said to be *binding*. The effects of binding price ceilings are shown in Figure 5-3, which establishes the following conclusion:

Binding price ceilings lead to excess demand, with the quantity exchanged being less than in the free-market equilibrium.

Allocating a Product in Excess Demand

Free markets eliminate excess demand by allowing prices to rise, thereby allocating the available supply among would-be purchasers. Because this adjustment cannot happen in the presence of a binding price ceiling, some other method of allocation must be adopted. Experience suggests what we can expect.

If stores sell their available supplies on a *first-come, first-served* basis, people will rush to stores that are said to have stocks of the product. Buyers may wait hours to get into the store, only to find that supplies are exhausted before they can be served. This is why standing in lines became a way of life in the centrally planned economies of the Soviet Union and Eastern Europe in which price controls were pervasive.

In market economies, "first-come, first-served" is often the basis for allocating tickets to concerts and sporting events when promoters set a price at which demand exceeds the supply of available seats. In these cases, an illegal market often develops, in which ticket "scalpers" resell tickets at market-clearing prices. Storekeepers (and some ticket sellers) often respond to excess demand by keeping goods "under the counter" and selling only to customers of their own choosing. When sellers decide to whom they will and will not sell their scarce supplies, allocation is said to be by **sellers' preferences.**

sellers' preferences Allocation of commodities in excess demand by decisions of the sellers.

If the government dislikes the allocation of products by long line-ups or by sellers' preferences, it can choose to *ration* the product. To do so, it prints only enough ration coupons to match the quantity supplied at the price ceiling and then distributes the coupons to would-be purchasers, who then need both money and coupons to buy the product. The coupons may be distributed equally among the population or on the basis of some criterion such as age, family status, or occupation. Rationing of this sort was used by Canada and many other countries during both the First and Second World Wars.

Black Markets

Price ceilings usually give rise to black markets. A **black market** is any market in which goods are sold illegally at prices that violate a legal price control.

black market A situation in which goods are sold illegally at prices that violate a legal price control.

Binding price ceilings always create the potential for a black market because a profit can be made by buying at the controlled price and selling at the black-market price.

Figure 5-3 illustrates the extreme case in which all the available supply is sold on a black market. We say this case is extreme because there are law-abiding people in every society and because governments ordinarily have at least *some* power to enforce their price ceilings. Although some units of a product subject to a binding price ceiling will be sold on the black market, it is unlikely that all of that product will be.

Does the existence of a black market mean that the goals sought by imposing price ceilings have been thwarted? The answer depends on what the goals are. A government might have three main goals for imposing a price ceiling.

1. To restrict production (perhaps to release resources for other uses, such as wartime military production)
2. To keep specific prices down
3. To satisfy notions of equity in the consumption of a product that is temporarily in short supply

When price ceilings are accompanied by a black market, it is not clear that any of these objectives are achieved. First, if producers are willing to sell (illegally) at prices above the price ceiling, there is nothing restricting them to the level of output of Q_2 in Figure 5-3. As long as they can receive more than a price of p_1, they have an incentive to increase their production. Second, black markets clearly frustrate the second objective since the *actual* prices are not kept down; if quantity supplied remains below Q_0, then the black-market price will be *higher* than the free-market equilibrium price, p_0. The third objective may also be thwarted since with an active black market it is likely that much of the product will be sold only to those who can afford the black-market price, which will often be well above the free-market equilibrium price.

To the extent that binding price ceilings give rise to a black market, it is likely that the government's objectives motivating the imposition of the price ceiling will be thwarted.

5.3 RENT CONTROLS: A CASE STUDY OF PRICE CEILINGS

For long periods over the past hundred years, rent controls existed in London, Paris, New York, and many other large cities. In Sweden and Britain, where rent controls on apartments existed for decades, shortages of rental accommodations were chronic. When rent controls were initiated in Toronto and Rome, severe housing shortages developed, especially in those areas where demand was rising.

Rent controls provide a vivid illustration of the short- and long-term effects of this type of market intervention. Note, however, that the specifics of rent-control laws vary greatly and have changed significantly since they were first imposed many decades ago. In particular, current laws often permit exemptions for new buildings and allowances for maintenance costs and inflation. Moreover, in many countries rent controls have evolved into a "second generation" of legislation that focuses more on *regulating* the rental housing market than simply *controlling the price* of rental accommodation.

In this section, we confine ourselves to an analysis of rent controls that are aimed primarily at holding the price of rental housing below the free-market equilibrium value. It is this "first generation" of rent controls that produced dramatic results in cities like London, Paris, New York, and Toronto.

The Predicted Effects of Rent Controls

Binding rent controls are a specific case of price ceilings and therefore Figure 5-3 can be used to predict some of their effects:

Practise with Study Guide Chapter 5, Exercise 3.

1. There will be a housing shortage in the sense that quantity demanded will exceed quantity supplied. Since rents are held below their free-market levels, the available quantity of rental housing will be less than if free-market rents had been charged.
2. The shortage will lead to alternative allocation schemes. Landlords may allocate by sellers' preferences, or the government may intervene, often through security-of-tenure laws, which protect tenants from eviction and thereby give them priority over prospective new tenants.
3. Black markets will appear. For example, landlords may (illegally) require tenants to pay "key money" equal to the difference in value between the free-market and the controlled rents. In the absence of security-of-tenure laws, landlords may force tenants out when their leases expire in order to extract a large entrance fee from new tenants.

FIGURE 5-4 The Short-Run and Long-Run Effects of Rent Controls

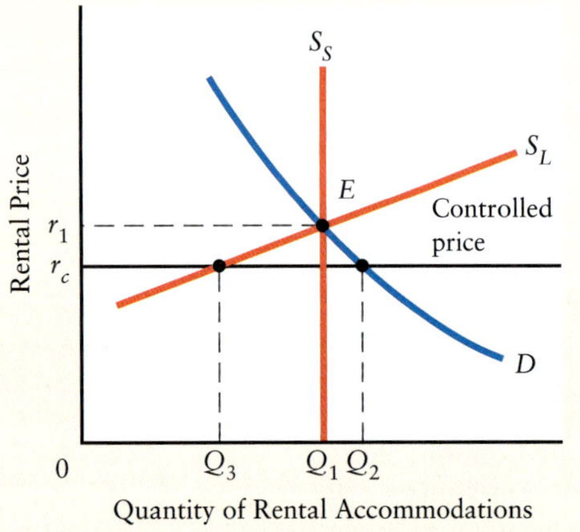

Rent control causes housing shortages that worsen as time passes. The free-market equilibrium is at point E. The controlled rent of r_c forces rents below their free-market equilibrium value of r_1. The short-run supply of housing is shown by the perfectly inelastic curve S_S. Thus quantity supplied remains at Q_1 in the short run, and the housing shortage is Q_1Q_2. Over time, the quantity supplied shrinks, as shown by the long-run supply curve S_L. In the long run, there are only Q_3 units of rental accommodations supplied, fewer than when controls were instituted. The long-run housing shortage of Q_3Q_2 is larger than the initial shortage of Q_1Q_2.

The unique feature of rent controls, however, as compared to price controls in general, is that they are applied to a highly *durable good* that provides services to consumers for long periods of time. Once built, an apartment can be used for decades. As a result, the immediate effects of rent control are typically quite different from the long-term effects.

The short-run supply response to the imposition of rent controls is usually quite limited. Some conversions of apartment units to condominiums (that are not covered by the rent-control legislation) may occur but the quantity of apartments does not change much. The short-run supply curve for rental housing is quite *inelastic*.

In the long run, however, the supply response to rent controls can be quite dramatic. If the expected rate of return from building new rental housing falls significantly below what can be earned on comparable investments, funds will go elsewhere. New construction will be halted, and old buildings will be converted to other uses, or will simply be left to deteriorate. The long-run supply curve of rental accommodations is highly *elastic*.

Figure 5-4 illustrates the housing shortage that worsens as time passes under rent control. Because the short-run supply of housing is inelastic, the controlled rent causes only a moderate housing shortage in the short run. Indeed, most of the shortage comes from an increase in the quantity demanded rather than from a reduction in quantity supplied. As time passes, however, fewer new apartments are built, more conversions take place, and older buildings are not replaced (and not repaired) as they wear out. As a result, the quantity supplied shrinks steadily and the extent of the housing shortage worsens.

Along with the growing housing shortage comes an increasingly inefficient use of rental accommodation space. Existing tenants will have an incentive to stay where they are even though their family size, location of employment, or economic circumstances may change. Since they cannot move without giving up their low-rent accommodation, some may accept lower-paying jobs nearby to avoid the necessity of moving. Thus, a situation will arise in which existing tenants will hang on to accommodation even if it is poorly suited to their needs while individuals and families who are newly entering the housing market will be unable to find any rental accommodation except at black-market prices.

The province of Ontario instituted rent controls in 1975 and tightened them on at least two subsequent occasions. The controls permitted significant increases in rents only where these were needed to pass cost increases on. As a result, the restrictive effects of rent controls were felt mainly in areas where demand was increasing rapidly (as opposed to areas where only costs were increasing rapidly).

During the mid- and late-1990s, the population of Ontario grew substantially but the stock of rental housing did not keep pace. A shortage developed in the rental-housing market, and was especially acute in Metro Toronto. This growing housing shortage led the Conservative Ontario government in 1997 to loosen rent controls, in particular by allowing landlords to increase the rent as much as they saw fit *but only as tenants vacated the apartment*. Not surprisingly, this policy had both critics and supporters. Supporters argued that a loosening of controls would encourage the construction of apartments and thus help to reduce the housing shortage. Critics argued that landlords would harass existing tenants, forcing them to move out so that rents could be increased for incoming tenants. (Indeed, this exact behaviour happened in rent-controlled New York City, where a landlord pleaded guilty in January 1999 to hiring a "hit man" to kill tenants and set fires to scare them out so that rents could be increased!)

In 2004, the newly elected Liberal government in Ontario revised the 1997 rent-control legislation and reduced the maximum rate of increase for rents on occupied apartments. The 2005 maximum was set at 1.5 percent, down from 3.9 percent three years earlier. Not surprisingly, the policy was heralded by tenants who saw the policy as increasing the affordability of rental housing, but decried by landlords who argued that a 1.5 percent increase was insufficient to cover their rising costs.

Who Gains and Who Loses?

Existing tenants in rent-controlled accommodations are the principal gainers from a policy of rent control. As the gap between the controlled and the free-market rents grows, and as the stock of available housing falls, those who are still lucky enough to live in rent-controlled housing gain more and more.

Landlords suffer because they do not get the rate of return they expected on their investments. Some landlords are large companies, and others are wealthy individuals. Neither of these groups attracts great public sympathy, even though the rental companies' shareholders are not all rich. But some landlords are people of modest means who may have put their retirement savings into a small apartment block or a house or two. They find that the value of their savings is diminished, and sometimes they find themselves in the ironic position of subsidizing tenants who are far better off than they are.

Perhaps the most striking effect of rent control is the long-term decline in the amount and quality of rental housing.

The other important group of people who suffer from rent controls are *potential future* tenants. The housing shortage hurts them because the rental housing they will require will not exist in the future. These people, who wind up living elsewhere, farther from their places of employment and study, are invisible in debates over rent control because they cannot obtain housing in the rent-controlled jurisdiction. Thus, rent control is often stable politically even when it causes a long-run housing shortage. The current tenants benefit, and they outnumber the current landlords, while the potential tenants, who are harmed, are nowhere to be seen or heard.

myeconlab

In some situations, legislated rent controls may impose relatively small costs. For a fuller explanation, look for "When Rent Controls Work and When They Don't" in the *Additional Topics* section of this book's MyEconLab.

www.myeconlab.com

Policy Alternatives

Most rent controls today are meant to protect lower-income tenants, not only against "profiteering" by landlords in the face of severe local shortages but also against the steadily rising cost of housing. The market solution is to let rents rise sufficiently to cover the rising costs. If people decide that they cannot afford the market price of apartments and will not rent them, construction will cease. Given what we know about consumer behaviour, however, it is more likely that people will make agonizing choices, both to economize on housing and to spend a higher proportion of total income on it, which mean consuming less housing and less of other things as well.

If governments do not wish to accept this market solution, there are many things they can do, but they cannot avoid the fundamental fact that the opportunity cost of good housing is high. Binding rent controls create housing shortages. The shortages can be removed only if the government, at taxpayer expense, either subsidizes housing production or produces public housing directly.

Alternatively, the government can make housing more affordable to lower-income households by providing income assistance to these households, allowing them access to higher-quality housing than they could otherwise afford. Whatever policy is adopted, it is important to recognize that providing greater access to rental accommodations has a resource cost. The costs of providing additional housing cannot be voted out of existence; all that can be done is to transfer the costs from one set of persons to another.

5.4 AN INTRODUCTION TO MARKET EFFICIENCY

In this chapter we have seen the effects of government intervening in competitive markets by setting price floors and price ceilings. In both cases, we noted that the imposition of a controlled price generates benefits for some individuals and costs for others. For example, in the case of the legislated minimum wage (a price floor), firms are made worse off by the minimum wage, but workers who retain their jobs are made better off. Other workers, those unable to retain their jobs at the higher wage, are made worse off. In the example of legislated rent controls (a price ceiling), landlords are made worse off by the rent controls, but some tenants are made better off. Those tenants who are no longer able to find an apartment when rents fall are made worse off.

Is it possible to determine the *overall* effects of such policies, rather than just the effects on specific groups? For example, can we say that a policy of legislated minimum wages, while harming firms, nonetheless makes *society as a whole* better off because it helps workers more than it harms firms? Or can we conclude that the imposition of rent controls makes society as a whole better off because it helps tenants more than it harms landlords?

To answer such questions, economists use the concept of *market efficiency*. We will explore this concept in more detail in later chapters, but for now we simply introduce the idea and see how it helps us understand the overall effects of price controls. We begin by taking a slightly different look at market demand and supply curves.

Demand as "Value" and Supply as "Cost"

In Chapter 3 we saw that the market demand curve for any product shows, for each possible price, how much of that product consumers want to purchase. Similarly, we saw that the market supply curve shows how much producers want to sell at each possible price. But we can turn things around and view these curves in a slightly different way—by starting with any given quantity and asking about the price. Specifically, we can consider the highest price that consumers are *willing to pay* and the lowest price that producers are *willing to accept* for any given unit of the product. As we will see, viewing demand and supply curves in this manner helps us think about how society as a whole benefits by producing and consuming any given amount of some product.

Let's begin by considering the market demand curve for pizza, as shown in part (i) of Figure 5-5. Each point on the demand curve shows the highest price consumers are willing to pay for a given pizza. At point *A* we see that consumers are willing to pay up to $20 for the 100th pizza, and at point *B* consumers are willing to pay up to $15 for the 200th pizza. In both cases, these maximum prices reflect the *value* consumers place on that particular pizza. If consumers valued the 100th pizza by more than $20, they would be willing to pay more to get that pizza, and the price as shown on the demand curve would be higher than $20. If they valued the 100th pizza less than $20, they would not be willing to pay as much as $20, and the price as shown on the demand curve would then be less than $20. Thus, for each pizza, the price on the demand curve shows the value to consumers from consuming that pizza.

There is nothing special about pizza, however. What is true for the demand for pizza is true for the demand for any other product.

For each unit of a product, the price on the market demand curve shows the value to consumers from consuming that unit.

Now let's consider the market supply curve for pizza, shown in part (ii) of Figure 5-5. Each point on the market supply curve shows the lowest price firms are willing to accept to produce and sell a given pizza. At point *E* firms are willing to accept a price no lower than $5 for the 100th pizza, and at point *F* firms are willing to accept a price no lower than $10 for the 200th pizza. The lowest acceptable price as shown on the supply curve reflects the *additional cost* firms incur to produce each given pizza. To see this, consider the production of the 200th pizza at point *F*. If the firm's total costs increase by $10 when this pizza is produced, the firm will be able to increase its profits as long as it can sell that pizza at a price greater than $10. If it sells the pizza at any price below $10, its profits will decline. If it sells the pizza at a price

FIGURE 5-5 Reinterpreting the Demand and Supply Curves in the Pizza Market

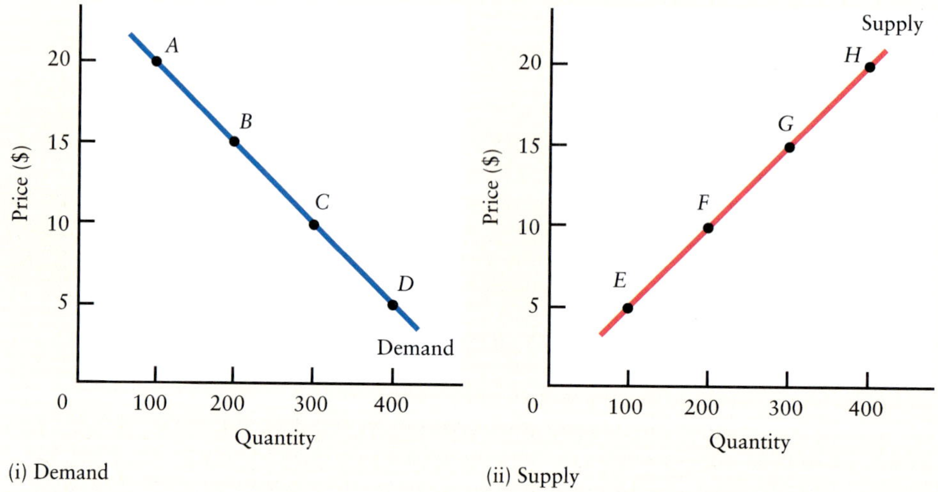

For each pizza, the price on the demand curve shows the value consumers receive from consuming that pizza; the price on the supply curve shows the additional cost to firms of producing that pizza. Each point on the demand curve shows the maximum price consumers are willing to pay to consume that unit. This maximum price reflects the value that consumers get from that unit of the product. Each point on the supply curve shows the minimum price firms are willing to accept for producing and selling that unit. This minimum price reflects the additional costs incurred by producing that unit.

of exactly $10, its profits will neither rise nor fall. Thus, for a profit-maximizing firm, the *lowest acceptable price* for the 200th pizza is $10.

Again, what is true for the supply of pizza is true for the supply of other products.

For each unit of a product, the price on the market supply curve shows the lowest acceptable price to firms for selling that unit. This lowest acceptable price reflects the additional cost to firms from producing that unit.

Economic Surplus and Market Efficiency

Practise with Study Guide Chapter 5, Short-Answer Question 3.

Once the demand and supply curves are put together, the equilibrium price and quantity can be determined. This brings us to the important concept of *economic surplus.* We continue with our pizza example in Figure 5-6, which shows the demand and supply curves together. Consider a quantity of 100 pizzas. For each one of those 100 pizzas, the value to consumers is given by the price on the demand curve. The additional cost to firms from producing each of these 100 pizzas is shown by the price on the supply curve. For the entire 100 pizzas, the difference between the value to consumers and the additional costs to firms is called *economic surplus* and is shown by the shaded area ① in the figure.

For any given quantity of a product, the area below the demand curve and above the supply curve shows the economic surplus associated with the production and consumption of that product.

What does this "economic surplus" represent? The economic surplus is the net value that *society as a whole* receives by producing and consuming these 100 pizzas. It arises because firms and consumers have taken resources that have a lower value (as shown by the height of the supply curve) and transformed them into something valued more highly (as shown by the height of the demand curve). To put it differently, the value from consuming the 100 pizzas is greater than the cost of the resources necessary to produce those 100 pizzas—flour, yeast, tomato sauce, cheese, and labour. Thus, the act of producing and consuming those 100 pizzas "adds value" and thus generates benefits for society as a whole.

We are now ready to introduce the concept of market efficiency. In later chapters, after we have explored consumer and firm behaviour in greater detail, we will have a more detailed discussion of efficiency. For now, we simply introduce the concept and see how it relates to the imposition of government price controls. Loosely speaking, a market for a specific product is said to be efficient if the quantity of the product produced and consumed is such that the *economic surplus* in the market is maximized.

Let's continue with the pizza example in Figure 5-6 and ask: What level of pizza production and consumption is efficient? Consider the quantity of 100 pizzas. At this quantity, the shaded area ① shows the total economic surplus that society receives from producing and consuming 100 pizzas. But if output were to increase beyond 100 pizzas, more economic surplus would be generated because the value placed by consumers on additional pizzas is greater than the additional costs associated with their production. Specifically, if production and consumption were to increase to 200 pizzas, additional economic surplus would be generated, as shown by shaded area ②. Continuing this logic, we see that the amount of economic surplus is maximized when the quantity is 250 units, and at that quantity the total economic surplus is equal to the sum of areas ①, ②, and ③.

What would happen if the quantity of pizzas were to rise further, say to 300 units? For any pizzas beyond 250, the value placed on these pizzas by consumers is *less than* the additional costs associated with their production. In this case, producing the last 50 pizzas would actually *decrease* the amount of economic surplus in this market because society would be taking highly valued resources (flour, cheese, etc.) and transforming them into pizzas which are valued less.

In our example of the pizza market, as long as the price is free to adjust to excess demands or supplies, the equilibrium price and quantity will be determined where the

FIGURE 5-6 Economic Surplus in the Pizza Market

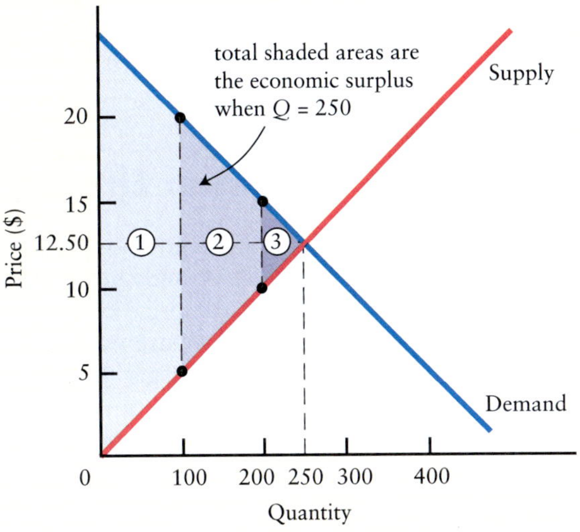

For any quantity of pizzas, the area below the demand curve and above the supply curve shows the economic surplus generated by the production and consumption of those pizzas. The demand curve shows the value consumers place on each additional pizza; the supply curve shows the additional cost associated with producing each pizza. For example, consumers value the 100th pizza at $20, whereas the additional cost to firms of producing that 100th pizza is $5. The economic surplus generated by producing and consuming this 100th pizza is therefore $15 ($20 – $5). For any range of quantity, the shaded area between the curves over that range shows the economic surplus generated by producing and consuming those pizzas.

Economic surplus in the pizza market is maximized—and thus market efficiency is achieved—at the free-market equilibrium quantity of 250 pizzas and price of $12.50. At this point, total economic surplus is the sum of the three shaded areas.

demand and supply curves for pizza intersect. In Figure 5-6, the equilibrium quantity is 250 pizzas, the quantity that maximizes the amount of economic surplus in the pizza market. In other words, the free interaction of demand and supply will result in market efficiency. This result in the pizza market suggests a more general rule:

A competitive market will maximize economic surplus and therefore be efficient when price is free to achieve its market-clearing equilibrium level.[1]

Market Efficiency and Price Controls

Practise with Study Guide Chapter 5, Exercise 4.

At the beginning of this section we asked whether we could determine if *society as a whole* is made better off or worse off as a result of the government's imposition of price floors or price ceilings. With an understanding of economic surplus and market efficiency, we are now ready to answer these questions.

Let's begin with the case of a price floor, as shown in part (i) of Figure 5-7. The free-market equilibrium is shown by point *E*, with price p_0 and quantity Q_0. When the government imposes a price floor at p_1, the quantity exchanged falls to Q_1. In the free-market case, each of the units of output between Q_0 and Q_1 generate some economic surplus. But when the price floor is put in place, these units of the good are no longer produced or consumed, and thus they no longer generate any economic surplus. The purple shaded area is called the *deadweight loss* caused by the binding price floor and

FIGURE 5-7 Market Inefficiency with Price Controls

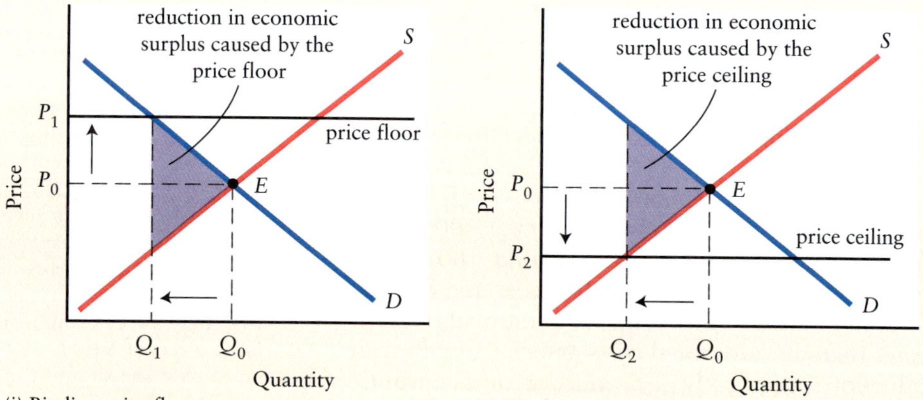

(i) Binding price floor

(ii) Binding price ceiling

Binding price floors and price ceilings in competitive markets lead to a reduction in overall economic surplus and thus to market inefficiency. In both parts of the figure, the free-market equilibrium is at point *E* with price p_0 and quantity Q_0. In part (i), the introduction of a price floor at p_1 reduces quantity to Q_1. In part (ii), the introduction of a price ceiling at p_2 reduces quantity to Q_2. In both parts, the purple shaded area shows the reduction in overall economic surplus—the deadweight loss—created by the price floor (or ceiling). Both outcomes display market inefficiency.

[1] In Part 6 of this book, we will see some important exceptions to this rule when we discuss "market failures."

it represents the overall loss of economic surplus to society. The size of the deadweight loss reflects the extent of market *inefficiency*.

The imposition of a binding price floor in an otherwise free and competitive market leads to a loss of economic surplus, and thus to market inefficiency.

A price floor does more than make sellers better off at the expense of buyers. It also leads to an overall reduction in economic surplus. Society as a whole therefore suffers by having less economic surplus generated in this market than could be achieved when price is free to achieve its market-clearing level.

Now let's consider the case of a price ceiling, as shown in part (ii) of Figure 5-7. The free-market equilibrium is again shown by point *E*, with price p_0 and quantity Q_0. When the government imposes a price ceiling at p_2, the quantity exchanged falls to Q_2. In the free-market case, each of the units of output between Q_0 and Q_2 generate some economic surplus. But when the price ceiling is imposed, these units of the good are no longer produced or consumed and so they no longer generate any economic surplus. The purple shaded area is the *deadweight loss* and represents the overall loss to society caused by the policy. The size of the deadweight loss reflects the extent of market *inefficiency*.

The imposition of a binding price ceiling in an otherwise free and competitive market leads to a loss of economic surplus, and thus to market inefficiency.

As with the case of the binding price floor, a binding price ceiling leads to an overall reduction in economic surplus. Society as a whole therefore suffers by having less economic surplus generated in this market than would be the case if the price were free to achieve its market-clearing level.

One Final Application: Output Quotas

Before ending this chapter, it is useful to consider one final application of government intervention in a competitive market, and to examine the effects on overall economic surplus and market efficiency. Figure 5-8 illustrates the effects of introducing a system of *output quotas* in a competitive market. Output quotas are commonly used in Canadian agriculture, especially in the markets for milk, butter, and cheese. Output quotas are sometimes used in other industries as well; for example, they are often used in large cities to regulate the number of taxi drivers.

The equilibrium in the free-market case is at point *E*, with price p_0 and quantity Q_0. When the government introduces an output quota, it restricts total output of this product to Q_1 units and then distributes quotas—"licences to produce"—among the producers. With output restricted to Q_1 units, the market price rises to p_1, the price that consumers are willing to pay for this quantity of the product. The purple shaded area—the deadweight loss of the

FIGURE 5-8 The Inefficiency of Output Quotas

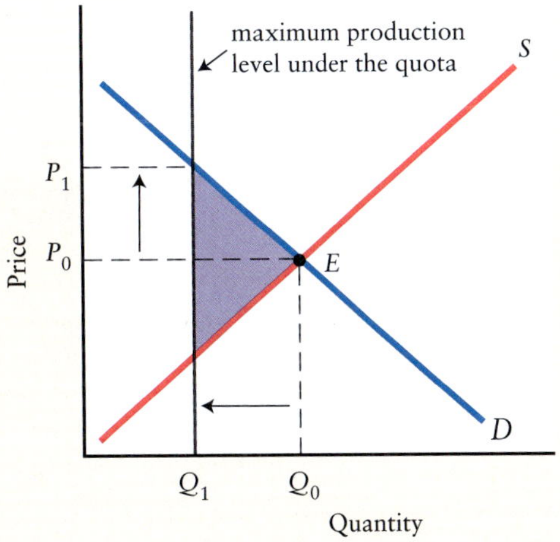

Binding output quotas lead to a reduction in output and a reduction in overall economic surplus. The free-market equilibrium is at point *E* with price p_0 and quantity Q_0. Suppose the government then restricts total quantity to Q_1 by issuing output quotas to firms. The market price rises to p_1. The purple shaded area shows the reduction in overall economic surplus—the deadweight loss—created by the quota system.

output quota—shows the overall loss of economic surplus as a result of the quota-induced output restriction.

One interesting consequence of the use of output quotas relates to the market value of the quotas themselves. When quota systems are used, firms initially issued quotas by the government are usually permitted to buy or sell quotas to each other or to new firms interested in entering the industry. The quota itself simply provides the holder permission to produce and sell in that industry, but the market value of the quota reflects the profitability of that production.

As you can see from Figure 5-8, the output restriction created by the quota leads to an increase in the product's price. If demand for the product is inelastic, as is the case in the dairy markets where quotas are commonly used, total income to producers rises as a result of the reduction in output. But since their output falls, firms' production costs also are reduced. The introduction of a quota system therefore leads to a rise in revenues and a fall in production costs—a clear benefit for producers! Not surprisingly, producers are often prepared to pay a high price to purchase new quota because having more quota gives them the ability to produce more output.

There is a catch, however: Producers must incur a very high cost in order to purchase the quotas. For example, an average dairy farm in Manitoba has about 90 cows and produces about 2300 litres of milk per day. The market value of the quota required to produce this amount of milk is approximately $1.8 million. The ownership of quota therefore represents a considerable asset for those producers who were lucky enough to receive it (for free) when it was initially issued by the government. But for new producers wanting to get into the industry, the need to purchase expensive quota represents a considerable obstacle. These large costs from purchasing the quota offset the benefits from selling the product at the (quota-induced) high price.

myeconlab

The agricultural sector offers an excellent setting in which to analyze the effects of government policies designed to support and stabilize producers' incomes. For more details about the challenges faced by farmers and the government's policy responses, look for "Agriculture and the Farm Problem" in the *Additional Topics* section of this book's MyEconLab.

www.myeconlab.com

A Cautionary Word

In this chapter we have examined the effects of government policies to control prices in otherwise free and competitive markets, and we have shown that such policies usually have two results. First, there is a redistribution between buyers and sellers; one group is made better off while the other group is made worse off—at least as far as the economic value of production is concerned. Second, there is a reduction in the overall amount of economic surplus generated in the market; the result is that the outcome is inefficient and society as a whole is made worse off.

The finding that government intervention in otherwise free markets leads to inefficiency should lead one to ask why government would ever intervene in such ways. The answer in many situations is that the government policy is motivated largely by the desire to help a specific group of people, and that the overall costs to society are deemed to be a worthwhile price to pay in order to achieve the desired effect. For example, legislated minimum wages are often viewed by politicians as an effective means of reducing poverty—by increasing the wages received by low-wage workers.

The costs such a policy imposes on firms, and on society overall, may be viewed as costs worth incurring in order to redistribute economic surplus toward low-wage workers. Similarly, the use of output quotas in certain agricultural markets is sometimes viewed by politicians as an effective means of increasing income to specific farmers. The costs that such quota systems impose on consumers, and on society as a whole, may be viewed as acceptable costs in achieving a redistribution of economic surplus toward these farmers.

In advocating these kinds of policies, ones that redistribute economic surplus but also reduce the total amount of economic surplus available, policy-makers are making *normative* judgements regarding which groups in society deserve to be helped at the expense of others. These judgements may be informed by a careful study of which groups are most genuinely in need, and they may also be driven by political considerations that the current government deems important to its prospects for re-election. In either case, there is nothing necessarily "wrong" about the government's decision to intervene in these markets, even if these interventions lead to inefficiency.

The job of the economist is to carefully analyze the effects of such policies, taking care to identify both the distributional effects as well as the implications for the overall amount of economic surplus generated in the market. This is *positive* analysis, emphasizing the *actual* effects of the policy rather than what might be *desirable*. These analytical results can then be used as "inputs" to the decision-making process, where they will be combined with normative and political considerations before a final policy decision is reached. In many parts of this textbook, we will encounter policies that governments implement (or consider implementing) to alter market outcomes, and we will examine the effects of those policies. A full understanding of why specific policies are implemented requires paying attention to the effects of such policies on both the overall amount of economic surplus and the distribution of that surplus.

SUMMARY

5.1 THE INTERACTION AMONG MARKETS

LO 1

- Partial-equilibrium analysis is appropriate when the market being examined is small relative to the entire economy.
- Partial-equilibrium analysis is the study of a single market in isolation, ignoring events in other markets. General-equilibrium analysis is the study of all markets together.

5.2 GOVERNMENT-CONTROLLED PRICES

LO 2

- Government price controls are policies that attempt to hold the price of some good or service at some disequilibrium value—a value that could not be maintained in the absence of the government's intervention.
- A binding price floor is set above the equilibrium price; a binding price ceiling is set below the equilibrium price.
- Binding price floors lead to excess supply. Either the potential seller is left with quantities that cannot be sold, or the government must step in and buy the surplus.
- Binding price ceilings lead to excess demand and provide a strong incentive for black marketeers to buy at the controlled price and sell at the higher free-market (illegal) price.

5.3 RENT CONTROLS: A CASE STUDY OF PRICE CEILINGS

LO 3

- Rent controls are a widespread form of price ceiling. The major consequence of binding rent controls is a shortage of rental accommodations and the allocation of rental housing by sellers' preferences.
- Because the supply of rental housing is much more elastic in the long run than in the short run, the extent of the housing shortage caused by rent controls worsens over time.

5.4 AN INTRODUCTION TO MARKET EFFICIENCY

LO 4

- Demand curves show consumers' willingness to pay for each unit of the product. For any given quantity, the area below the demand curve shows the overall value that consumers place on that quantity of the product.
- Supply curves show the lowest price producers are prepared to accept in order to produce and sell each unit of the product. This lowest acceptable price for each additional unit reflects the firm's costs required to produce each additional unit.
- For any given quantity exchanged of a product, the area below the demand curve and above the supply curve (up to that quantity) shows the economic surplus generated by the production and consumption of those units.
- Economic surplus in a market is maximized when the quantity exchanged is determined by the intersection of the demand and supply curves. This outcome is said to be efficient.
- Policies that intervene in otherwise free and competitive markets—such as price floors, price ceilings, and production quotas—generally lead to a reduction in the total amount of economic surplus generated in the market. For this reason such policies are inefficient for society overall.

KEY CONCEPTS

Partial-equilibrium analysis
General-equilibrium analysis
Price controls: floors and ceilings
Allocation by sellers' preferences and by black markets
Rent controls
Short-run and long-run supply curves of rental accommodations
Economic surplus
Market efficiency
Inefficiency of price controls and production quotas

STUDY EXERCISES

1. Consider the market for straw hats on a tropical island. The demand and supply schedules are given below.

Price ($)	Quantity Demanded	Quantity Supplied
1	1000	200
2	900	300
3	800	400
4	700	500
5	600	600
6	500	700
7	400	800
8	300	900

a. The equilibrium price for straw hats is __________. The equilibrium quantity demanded and quantity supplied is __________.

b. Suppose the government believes that no islander should have to pay more than $3 for a hat. The government can achieve this by imposing a __________.

c. At the government-controlled price of $3 there will be a __________ of __________ hats.

d. Suppose now that the government believes the island's hat makers are not paid enough for their hats and that islanders should pay no less than $6 for a hat. They can achieve this by imposing a __________.

e. At the new government-controlled price of $6 there will be a __________ of __________ hats.

2. The following questions are about resource allocation in the presence of price ceilings and price floors.
   a. A binding price ceiling leads to excess demand. What are some methods, other than price, of allocating the available supply?
   b. A binding price floor leads to excess supply. How might the government deal with this excess supply?
   c. Why might the government choose to implement a price ceiling?
   d. Why might the government choose to implement a price floor?

3. myeconlab Consider the market for some product X that is represented below in the demand-and-supply diagram.

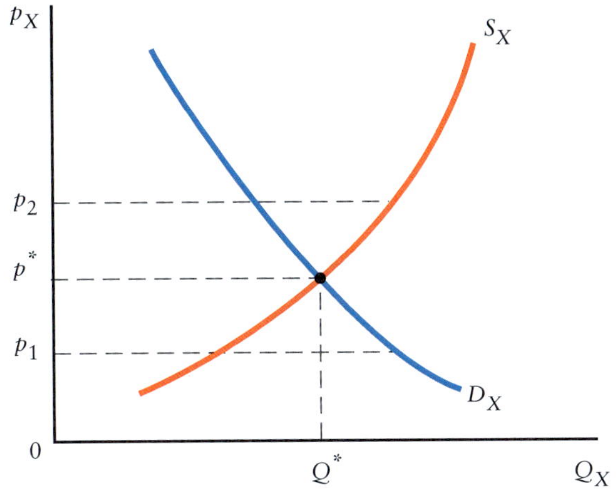

   a. Suppose the government decides to impose a price floor at p_1. Describe how this affects price, quantity, and market efficiency.
   b. Suppose the government decides to impose a price floor at p_2. Describe how this affects price, quantity, and market efficiency.
   c. Suppose the government decides to impose a price ceiling at p_1. Describe how this affects price, quantity, and market efficiency.
   d. Suppose the government decides to impose a price ceiling at p_2. Describe how this affects price, quantity, and market efficiency.

4. Consider the market for rental housing in Yourtown. The demand and supply schedules for rental housing are given in the table.

Price ($ per month)	Quantity Demanded (thousands of units)	Quantity Supplied (thousands of units)
1100	40	80
1000	50	77
900	60	73
800	70	70
700	80	67
600	90	65
500	100	60

   a. In a free market for rental housing, what is the equilibrium price and quantity?
   b. Now suppose the government in Yourtown decides to impose a ceiling on the monthly rental price. What is the highest level at which such a ceiling could be set, in order to have any effect on the market? Explain your answer.
   c. Suppose the maximum rental price is set equal to $500 per month. Describe the effect on the rental-housing market.
   d. Suppose a black market develops in the presence of the rent controls in (c). What is the black-market price that would exist if all of the quantity supplied were sold on the black market?

5. Explain and show in a diagram why the short-run effects of rent control are likely to be less significant than the long-run effects.

6. Consider the situation of Canadian barley farmers, who face weather conditions largely independent of those faced by barley growers in other countries. The incomes earned by the Canadian farmers, however, are affected by what happens to barley farmers in other countries. The key point is that Canadian barley farmers sell their barley on the same *world market* as all other barley farmers.
   a. Show in a diagram of the world barley market how a bumper crop of European barley will push down the world barley price.
   b. Show in a diagram of Canadian barley supply how a reduction in the world price of barley, *ceteris paribus*, will reduce the incomes of Canadian barley farmers.
   c. Explain why Canadian barley farmers are made better off when there are crop failures in other parts of the world.

7. Consider the market for burritos in a hypothetical Canadian city, blessed with thousands of students and dozens of small burrito stands. The demand and supply schedules are shown below.

Price ($)	Quantity Demanded (thousands of burritos per day)	Quantity Supplied (thousands of burritos per day)
0	500	125
1.00	400	175
1.50	350	200
2.00	300	225
2.50	250	250
3.00	200	275
3.50	150	300
4.00	100	325
5.00	0	375

a. Graph the demand and supply curves. What is the free-market equilibrium in this market?
b. What is the total economic surplus in this market in the free-market equilibrium? What area in the diagram represents this economic surplus?
c. Suppose the local government, out of concern for the students' welfare, enforces a price ceiling on burritos at a price of $1.50. Show in your diagram the effect on price and quantity exchanged.
d. Are students better off as a result of this policy? Explain.
e. What happens to overall economic surplus in this market as a result of the price ceiling? Show this in the diagram.

8. myeconlab Consider the market for milk in Saskatchewan. If p is the price of milk (cents per litre) and Q is the quantity of litres (in millions per month), suppose that the demand and supply curves for milk are given by:

Demand: $p = 225 - 15Q^D$
Supply: $p = 25 + 35Q^S$

a. Assuming there is no government intervention in this market, what is the equilibrium price and quantity?
b. Now suppose the government guarantees milk producers a price of $2 per litre and promises to buy any amount of milk that the producers cannot sell. What are the quantity demanded and quantity supplied at this guaranteed price?
c. How much milk would the government be buying (per month) with this system of price supports?
d. Who pays for the milk that the government buys? Who is helped by this policy and who is harmed?

9. myeconlab This question is related to the use of output quotas in the milk market in the previous question. Suppose the government used a quota system instead of direct price supports to assist milk producers. In particular, it issued quotas to existing milk producers for 1.67 million litres of milk per month.

a. If milk production is exactly equal to the amount of quotas issued, what price do consumers pay for milk?
b. Compared to the direct price controls in the previous question, whose income is higher under the quota system? Whose is lower?

10. This question relates to the section *Linkages Between Markets* found on the MyEconLab (www.myeconlab.com). In 1994, the Quebec and Ontario governments significantly reduced their excise taxes on cigarettes, but Manitoba and Saskatchewan left theirs in place. This led to cigarette smuggling between provinces that linked the provincial markets.

a. Draw a simple demand-and-supply diagram for the "Eastern" market and a separate one for the "Western" market.
b. Suppose that cigarette taxes are reduced in the Eastern market. Show the immediate effects.
c. Now suppose that the supply of cigarettes is (illegally) mobile. Explain and show what happens.
d. What limits the extent of smuggling that will take place in this situation?

DISCUSSION QUESTIONS

1. "When an item is vital to everyone, it is easier to start controlling the price than to stop controlling it. Such controls are popular with consumers, regardless of their harmful consequences." Explain why it may be inefficient to have such controls, why they may be popular, and why, if they are popular, the government might nevertheless choose to decontrol these prices.

2. It is sometimes asserted that the rising costs of construction are putting housing out of the reach of ordinary citizens. Who bears the heaviest cost when rentals are kept down by (a) rent controls, (b) a subsidy to tenants equal to some fraction of their rent payments, and (c) low-cost public housing?

3. "This year the weather smiled on us, and we made a crop," says a wheat farmer near Minnedosa in Manitoba. "But just as we made a crop, the economic situation changed." This quotation brings to mind the old saying, "If you are a farmer, the weather is always bad." Discuss the sense in which this saying might be true.

4. During the summer of 1993, severe floods swept through the American Midwest. Although many homes that flooded that year do not typically flood, for many people this was only one in a long string of floods. However, after the waters receded, most people rebuilt their homes, generally with low-interest loans and disaster relief grants from the federal government. Discuss how the policy of subsidizing the reconstruction of property following floods affects the market for real estate in flood-prone areas. Is the outcome more or less efficient in the long run with such government intervention?

5. Gary Storey, a professor of agricultural economics at the University of Saskatchewan, made the following statement: "One of the sad truths of the agricultural policies in Europe and the United States is that they do very little for the future generations of farmers. Most of the subsidies get capitalized into higher land prices, creating windfall gains for current landowners (i.e., gains that they did not expect). It creates a situation where the next generation of farmers require, and ask for, increased government support."
   a. Explain why subsidies to farmers increase land values and generate windfall gains to current landowners.
   b. Some Canadian agricultural policies are based on the use of production quotas. Do such quota systems avoid the problem described by Professor Storey?

6. This question relates to the section *Linkages Between Markets* found on the MyEconLab (www.myeconlab.com). Soon after the Liberal government was elected in 1993, an "infrastructure" program was implemented that involved spending several billion dollars on bridges, highways, sewer systems, and so on. One of the alleged benefits of this program was to create thousands of jobs, not only in the construction industry but also elsewhere in the economy as construction workers spent their now-higher income on cars, clothing, entertainment, and so on. Discuss how such spending would create jobs in the construction industry. Why would you expect some jobs to be *lost* in other industries as a result of this program?

CHAPTER 6

Consumer Behaviour

LEARNING OBJECTIVES

In this chapter you will learn

1. the difference between marginal and total utility.
2. that utility-maximizing consumers adjust their expenditure until the marginal utility per dollar spent is equalized across products.
3. how any change in price generates both an income and a substitution effect on quantity demanded.
4. that consumer surplus is the "bargain" the consumer gets by paying less for the product than the maximum price he or she is willing to pay.
5. the difference between total value and marginal value.

Imagine that you are walking down the aisle of a supermarket looking for a late-night snack to have while you are studying. With only a $5 bill in your pocket, you must choose how to divide this $5 between frozen burritos and cans of Coke. How do you make this decision? In this chapter we look at how economists think about such problems—the theory of consumer behaviour. Not surprisingly, economists (being consumers themselves) think about consumers as caring both about the prices of the goods and the satisfaction they get from the goods.

The first two sections of the chapter explore the underpinnings of consumer behaviour and explain in some detail why demand curves are negatively sloped—and also discuss the rare situations in which demand curves might be positively sloped. The third and final section examines an important implication of having negatively sloped demand curves and introduces the concept of *consumer surplus,* which is part of the economic surplus that we discussed in Chapter 5. As you will see in later chapters, consumer surplus is useful in showing that free and competitive markets often generate socially efficient outcomes.

6.1 MARGINAL UTILITY AND CONSUMER CHOICE

utility The satisfaction or well-being that a consumer receives from consuming some good or service.

Consumers make all kinds of decisions—they choose to drink coffee or tea (or neither), to go to the movies, to dine out, and to buy excellent (or not so good) computer equipment. As we discussed in Chapter 1, economists assume that in making their choices, consumers are motivated to maximize their **utility**, the total satisfaction that they derive from the goods and services that they consume.

Utility cannot be measured directly. But our inability to measure it does not mean it is not a useful concept. You know that you derive satisfaction—or utility—from a good meal, listening to a CD, or taking a walk through a park. And we need some way to think about how you as a consumer make your decisions. As we will see in this chapter, it is possible to construct a useful theory of consumer behaviour based on the idea of *utility maximization*.

In developing our theory of consumer behaviour, we begin by considering the consumption of a single product. It is useful to distinguish between the consumer's **total utility**, which is the full satisfaction resulting from the consumption of that product by a consumer, and the consumer's **marginal utility**, which is the *additional* satisfaction resulting from consuming one more unit of that product. For example, the total utility of consuming five Cokes per day is the total satisfaction that those five Cokes provide. The marginal utility of the fifth Coke consumed is the additional satisfaction provided by the consumption of that Coke.[1]

total utility The total satisfaction resulting from the consumption of a given commodity by a consumer.

marginal utility The additional satisfaction obtained by a consumer from consuming one additional unit of a commodity.

Diminishing Marginal Utility

The central hypothesis of utility theory, often called the *law of diminishing marginal utility*, is as follows:

The utility that any consumer derives from *successive* units of a particular product consumed over some period of time diminishes as total consumption of the product increases (if the consumption of all other products is unchanged).

Consider your utility from using clean water, either for drinking, bathing, washing your dishes or clothes, or some other purpose. Some minimum quantity is very important and you would, if necessary, give up a considerable sum of money to obtain that quantity of water. Thus, your marginal utility of that basic quantity of water is very high. You will, of course, consume more than this bare minimum, but your marginal utility of successive litres of water used over a period of time will decline steadily.

We will consider evidence for this hypothesis later, but you can convince yourself that it is at least reasonable by asking a few questions. How much money would be needed to induce you to reduce your consumption of water by one litre per week? The answer is: very little. How much would induce you to reduce it by a second litre? By a third litre? To only one litre consumed per week? The answer to the last question is: quite a bit. The fewer litres you are already using, the higher the marginal utility of one more litre of water.

Utility Schedules and Graphs

In Figure 6-1 we make the assumption that utility can be measured, and thus the different amount of utility received from consuming different units can be compared. Although this is an unrealistic assumption, it is a very helpful one in allowing us to see the important difference between total and marginal utility. The figure illustrates the assumptions that have been made about utility, using Alison's daily consumption of Coke as an example. The table shows that Alison's total utility rises as she drinks more

1 Technically, *incremental* utility is measured over a discrete interval, such as from four Cokes to five Cokes, whereas *marginal* utility is a rate of change measured over an infinitesimal interval. However, common usage applies the word *marginal* when the last unit is involved, even if a one-unit change is not infinitesimal. [9]

FIGURE 6-1 Alison's Total and Marginal Utility from Drinking Coke

Number of Cokes Alison Drinks Per Day	Alison's Total Utility	Alison's Marginal Utility
0	0	
		30
1	30	
		20
2	50	
		15
3	65	
		10
4	75	
		8
5	83	
		6
6	89	
		4
7	93	
		3
8	96	
		2
9	98	
		1
10	99	

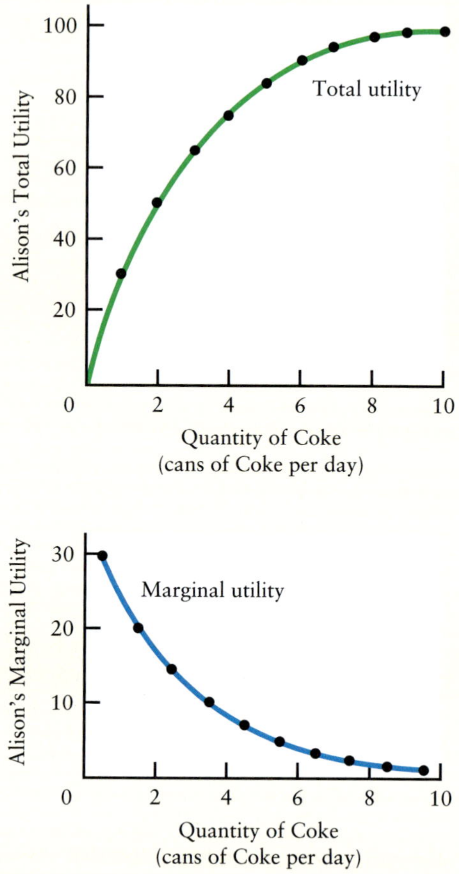

Total utility rises, but marginal utility declines, as consumption increases. The marginal utility of 20, shown as the second entry in the third column, arises because Alison's total utility increases from 30 to 50—a difference of 20—with consumption of the second Coke. To indicate that the marginal utility is associated with the *change* from one level of consumption to another, the figures in the third column are recorded between the rows of the figures in the second column.

Coke per day. However, the utility that she gets from each *additional* Coke per day is less than that of the previous one—that is, her marginal utility declines as the quantity she consumes rises. [10] The data are graphed in the two parts of Figure 6-1.

Maximizing Utility

Economists assume that consumers try to make themselves as well off as they possibly can in the circumstances in which they find themselves. In other words, consumers seek to maximize their total utility subject to the constraints they face—in particular, their income and the market prices of various products.

The Consumer's Decision Now that we have examined the concepts of total utility and marginal utility, we are ready to answer the question posed at the beginning of the chapter: How should consumers decide to allocate their consumption of Cokes and burritos in such a way as to maximize their utility? Of course, we could ask the same question about any two goods, or any number of goods, but we will focus on Cokes and burritos to keep the example simple.

A simple answer to the question is that any utility-maximizing consumer should consume Cokes and burritos until the marginal utility from the last Coke consumed is equal to the marginal utility from the last burrito consumed. But this would be sensible only if the price of a Coke and the price of a burrito were the same. The correct answer is that the consumer should consume Cokes and burritos to the point where the marginal utility *per dollar spent* on the last Coke is just equal to the marginal utility *per dollar spent* on the last burrito. In this way, the consumer's utility will be maximized.

Let's consider a specific example. Suppose Alison is buying burritos for $3 each and Cokes for $1 each. Buying burritos represents a poor use of her money if the marginal utility from the last burrito equals the marginal utility from the last Coke. Why? Because Alison would be spending $3 on a burrito to get additional utility equal to what she could have acquired for only $1 by buying a Coke.

A utility-maximizing consumer allocates expenditures so that the utility obtained from the last dollar spent on each product is equal.

Imagine that Alison's utility from the last dollar spent on Coke is three times her utility from the last dollar spent on burritos. In this case, Alison can increase her total utility by switching a dollar of expenditure from burritos to Coke and by gaining the difference between the utilities of a dollar spent on each.

Alison will continue to switch her expenditure from burritos to Coke as long as her last dollar spent on Coke yields more utility than her last dollar spent on burritos. This switching, however, reduces the quantity of burritos consumed and, given the law of diminishing marginal utility, raises the marginal utility of burritos. At the same time, switching increases the quantity of Coke consumed and thereby lowers the marginal utility of Coke.

Eventually, the marginal utilities will have changed enough so that the utility received from the last dollar spent on Coke is just equal to the utility received from the last dollar spent on burritos. At this point, Alison gains nothing from further switches. (In fact, switching further would *reduce* her total utility.)

So much for the simple example. What can we say more generally about utility maximization? Suppose we denote the marginal utility of the last unit of product X by MU_X and its price by p_X. Let MU_Y and p_Y refer, respectively, to the marginal utility of a second product Y and its price. The marginal utility per dollar spent on X will be MU_X/p_X. For example, if the last unit of X increases utility by 30 and costs $3, its marginal utility per dollar is 30/3 = 10. If the last unit of Y increases utility by 10 and costs $1, its marginal utility per dollar is 10/1 = 10. With these numbers, the marginal utilities from the last dollar spent on X and Y are equal.

The condition required for a consumer to be maximizing utility, for any pair of products, is

$$\frac{MU_X}{p_X} = \frac{MU_Y}{p_Y} \tag{6-1}$$

Practise with Study Guide Chapter 6, Exercise 1 and Short-Answer Question 1.

This equation says that a utility-maximizing consumer will allocate expenditure so that the utility gained from the last dollar spent on one product is equal to the utility gained from the last dollar spent on any other product.

This is the fundamental equation of marginal utility theory. A consumer demands each good up to the point at which the marginal utility per dollar spent on it is the same as the marginal utility per dollar spent on every other good. When this condition is met for all goods, the consumer cannot increase utility further by reallocating expenditure. That is, utility will be maximized.

Notice from our example that when Alison is deciding how much of a given product to purchase, she compares the utility from that product to the utility she could derive from spending the same money on other things. Thus, the idea of *opportunity cost* is central to our theory of consumer behaviour.

When expenditure is adjusted to maximize utility, the value to the consumer of consuming the marginal unit of some good is just equal to the opportunity cost—the value to the consumer of the money used to make the purchase.

An Alternative Interpretation If we rearrange the terms in Equation 6-1, we can gain additional insight into consumer behaviour.

$$\frac{MU_X}{MU_Y} = \frac{p_X}{p_Y} \qquad (6\text{-}2)$$

The right side of this equation is the *relative* price of the two goods. It is determined by the market and is beyond Alison's control. She reacts to these market prices but is powerless to change them. The left side is the *relative* ability of the two goods to add to Alison's utility. This is within her control because in determining the quantities of different goods to buy, she also determines their marginal utilities. (If you have difficulty seeing why, look again at Figure 6-1.)

If the two sides of Equation 6-2 are not equal, Alison can increase her total utility by rearranging her purchases of X and Y. Suppose that the price of X is \$4 and the price of Y is \$2. The right-hand side of Equation 6-2 is then $p_X/p_Y = 4/2 = 2$. Remember that Alison can do nothing to change the right-hand side of this equation—the prices are determined in the market and are beyond her control. Suppose also that Alison is currently purchasing X and Y such that the marginal utility for X is 12 and the marginal utility for Y is 4. The left-hand side of Equation 6-2 is then $MU_X/MU_Y = 12/4 = 3$. In this case $MU_X/MU_Y > p_X/p_Y$. Alison can increase her total utility by increasing her purchases of X and reducing her purchases of Y until the ratio MU_X/MU_Y is equal to 2, the same as the ratio of the prices. If she reduces her purchases of Y by 2 units (at \$2 each) she frees up \$4 and is able to buy one more unit of X (at \$4 each). Because that one extra unit of X had a marginal utility of 12, whereas the two units of Y that she gave up had a marginal utility of only 4 each, Alison's total utility has increased as a result of this switch. In this case, she will continue to switch until the ratio of MU_X/MU_Y is equal to p_X/p_Y. At this point Alison cannot increase her total utility any further by rearranging her purchases between the two products.

Consider what Alison is doing. She is faced with a set of prices that she cannot change. She responds to these prices and maximizes her utility by adjusting the things that she *can* change—the quantities of the various goods that she purchases—until Equation 6-2 is satisfied for all pairs of products.

It may seem unrealistic to argue that consumers maximize utility in the precise way we have described. After all, who stands in the grocery store and computes ratios of marginal utilities and prices? Keep in mind, though, that utility theory is used by economists to predict how consumers will behave when faced with such events as changing prices and incomes. As long as consumers seek to do the best they can for themselves with their limited resources, the consumer's actual thought process does not concern us. The theory is not meant to be a description of *how* they reach their decisions but is rather a convenient way of discovering the *implications* of their maximizing behaviour. Like many theories, utility-maximization theory leads to predictions that can be tested empirically. Economists continue to use the theory of utility maximization because its predictions are rarely rejected by the data. One of the most important of these predictions is that consumers who act as if they are following a rule like Equation 6-2 have negatively sloped demand curves for goods and services. In the next section we derive this result.

The Consumer's Demand Curve

To derive the consumer's demand curve for a product, we need to ask what happens when there is a change in the price of that product. As an example, let us derive Alison's demand curve for Coke. Consider Equation 6-2 and let X represent Coke and Y represent *all other products taken together.* In this case, the price of Y is interpreted as the average price of all other products. What will Alison do if, with all other prices remaining constant, there is an increase in the price of Coke? When the price of Coke rises, the right side of Equation 6-2 increases. But, until Alison adjusts consumption, the left side is unchanged. Thus, after the price changes but before Alison reacts, she will be in a position in which the following circumstance prevails:

$$\frac{MU \text{ of Coke}}{MU \text{ of } Y} < \frac{\text{price of Coke}}{\text{price of } Y}$$

What does Alison do to restore the equality? The hypothesis of diminishing marginal utility tells us that as she buys fewer Cokes, the *marginal* utility of Coke will rise and thereby increase the ratio on the left side. Thus, in response to an increase in the price of Coke, with all other prices constant, Alison reduces her consumption of Coke until the marginal utility of Coke rises sufficiently that Equation 6-2 is restored.

This analysis leads to the basic prediction of demand theory:

A rise in the price of a product (with all other determinants of demand held constant) leads each consumer to reduce the quantity demanded of the product.

Practise with Study Guide Chapter 6, Exercise 2.

If this is what each consumer does, it is also what all consumers taken together do. Thus, the theory of consumer behaviour that we have considered here predicts a negatively sloped market demand curve in addition to a negatively sloped demand curve for each individual consumer. *Extensions in Theory 6-1* shows how we can obtain a market demand curve by adding up the demand curves of individual consumers.

myeconlab

We said above that utility cannot be measured directly. However, some very new research in the social sciences has attempted to do just that—by simply asking people how happy they are and then examining how their reported level of happiness changes when they are in different circumstances. For a closer look at happiness and where it comes from, look for "What Makes People Happy?" in the *Additional Topics* section of this book's MyEconLab.

www.myeconlab.com

6.2 INCOME AND SUBSTITUTION EFFECTS OF PRICE CHANGES

We have just seen the relationship between the *law of diminishing marginal utility* and the slope of the consumer's demand curve for some product. Here we consider an alternative method for thinking about the slope of an individual's demand curve. From the discussion in *Extensions in Theory 6-1,* this alternative method can also be used to think about the slope of a market demand curve.

Let's consider Tony, a student who loves to eat—and especially loves to eat ice cream. A fall in the price of ice cream affects Tony in two ways. First, it provides an incentive to buy more ice cream (and less of other things) because eating ice cream is now a cheaper way to satisfy some of his cravings. Thus, a reduction in the price of ice cream—which, with all other prices constant means a fall in the *relative* price of ice cream—leads Tony to *substitute* away from other products toward ice cream.

EXTENSIONS IN THEORY 6-1

Market and Individual Demand Curves

Market demand curves show how much is demanded by all purchasers. For example, in Figure 3-1, the market demand for carrots is 85 tonnes when the price is $40 per tonne. This 85 tonnes is the sum of the quantities demanded by millions of different consumers. The demand curve in Figure 3-1 also tells us that when the price rises to $60, the total quantity demanded falls to 65 tonnes per year. This quantity, too, can be traced back to individual consumers.

The market demand curve is the horizontal sum of the demand curves of individual consumers. It is the horizontal sum because we wish to add quantities demanded at a given price, and quantities are measured in the horizontal direction on a conventional demand curve.

The figure below illustrates a market made up of only two consumers, Alison and Brenda. At a price of $3, Alison purchases 2 units and Brenda purchases 4 units; thus together they purchase 6 units, yielding one point on the market demand curve. No matter how many consumers are involved, the process is the same: Add the quantities demanded by all consumers at each price, and the result is the market demand curve.

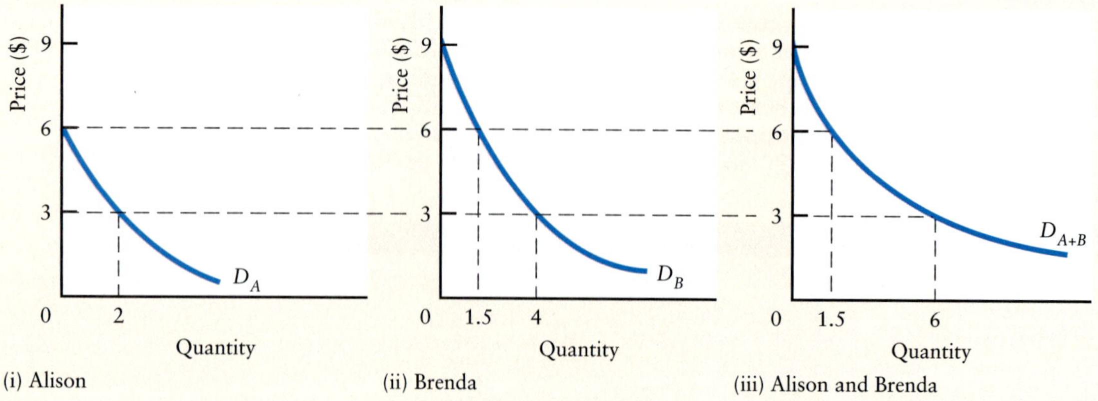

Second, because the price of ice cream has fallen, Tony has more *purchasing power* or **real income** available to spend on all products. Suppose the price of premium ice cream fell from $5.00 to $4.00 per litre and Tony was in the habit of eating half a litre of ice cream a day. In the course of a 30-day month, Tony could keep his ice cream habit unchanged but save $15.00, money that would be available for any purpose—more ice cream, video rentals, or photocopies of your economics notes.

Let's now explore these two separate effects in a little more detail.

real income Income expressed in terms of the purchasing power of money income, that is, the quantity of goods and services that can be purchased with the money income.

The Substitution Effect

To isolate the effect of the change in relative price when the price of ice cream falls, we can consider what would happen if we also reduce Tony's money income to restore the original purchasing power. Suppose Tony's uncle sends him a monthly allowance for ice cream, and when the price of ice cream falls, the allowance is reduced so that Tony can buy just as much ice cream—and everything else—as he could before. Tony's purchasing power will be unchanged. If his behaviour remains unchanged, however, he will no longer be maximizing his utility. Recall that utility maximization requires that the ratio of marginal utility to price be the same for all goods. In our example, with no change in behaviour, the quantities (and hence marginal utilities) and the prices of all goods other than ice cream are unchanged. The quantity of ice cream is also unchanged, but the price has fallen. To maximize his utility after the price of ice cream falls, Tony must therefore increase his consumption (reduce his marginal utility) of ice cream and reduce his consumption of other goods.

When purchasing power is held constant, the change in the quantity demanded of a good whose relative price has changed is called the **substitution effect** of the price change.[2]

substitution effect The change in the quantity of a good demanded resulting from a change in its relative price (holding real income constant).

The substitution effect increases the quantity demanded of a good whose price has fallen and reduces the quantity demanded of a good whose price has risen.

The Income Effect

To examine the substitution effect, we reduced Tony's *money* income following the price reduction so that we could see the effect of the relative price change, holding purchasing power constant. Now we want to see the effect of the change in purchasing power, *holding relative prices constant at their new value.* To do this, suppose that after Tony has adjusted his purchases to the new price and his reduced income, he then calls his uncle and pleads to have his allowance restored to its original (higher) amount. Tony's uncle agrees, and Tony's money income is returned to its original level. If we assume that ice cream is a normal good, Tony will increase his consumption of ice cream (even beyond the increase we have already seen as a result of the substitution effect). The change in the quantity of ice cream demanded as a result of Tony's reaction to increased real income is called the **income effect.**

income effect The change in the quantity of a good demanded resulting from a change in real income (holding relative prices constant).

The income effect leads consumers to buy more of a product whose price has fallen, provided that the product is a normal good.

[2] This measure, which isolates the substitution effect by holding the consumer's purchasing power constant, is known as the *Slutsky Effect.* A related but slightly different measure that holds the consumer's level of utility constant is discussed in the appendix to this chapter.

Notice that the size of the income effect depends on the amount of income spent on the good whose price changes and on the amount by which the price changes. In our example, if Tony were initially spending half of his income on ice cream, a reduction in the price of ice cream from $5 to $4 would be equivalent to a 10-percent increase in real income (20 percent of 50 percent). Now consider a different case: The price of gasoline falls by 20 percent. For a consumer who was spending only 5 percent of income on gas, this is equivalent to only a 1-percent increase in real income (20 percent of 5 percent).

The Slope of the Demand Curve

We have now divided Tony's reaction to a change in the price of ice cream into a substitution effect and an income effect. Of course, when the price changes, Tony moves directly from the initial consumption pattern to the final one; we do not observe any "halfway" consumption pattern. However, by breaking this movement into two parts for analytical purposes, we are able to study Tony's total change in quantity demanded as a response to a change in relative prices plus a response to a change in real income.

What is true for Tony is also true, in general terms, for all consumers. The substitution effect leads consumers to increase their demand for goods whose prices fall. The income effect leads consumers to buy more of all normal goods whose prices fall.

Putting the income and substitution effects together gives the following statement of the law of demand:

Practise with Study Guide Chapter 6, Exercise 3.

Because of the combined operation of the income and substitution effects, the demand curve for any normal commodity will be negatively sloped. Thus, a fall in price will increase the quantity demanded.

Figure 6-2 illustrates how the combination of the substitution effect and the income effect determines the slope of any demand curve. In each part of the figure, we begin at point *A* with the price p_0. We then consider a reduction in the price to p_1. In each case, the substitution effect (shown by the green arrow) increases the quantity demanded. In each case there is also an income effect (the red arrow), but the size and sign of the income effect differs in each case. The sum of the income and substitution effects determines how overall quantity demanded responds to the price reduction. Note that all normal goods have negatively shaped demand curves. The same is true for *most* inferior goods. The figure illustrates why in the case of an inferior good the income effect must be very strong in order to generate a positively sloped demand curve. This is a very rare case in economics, but there is some interesting history behind it.

Giffen Goods Great interest was generated by the apparent refutation of the law of demand by the English economist Sir Robert Giffen (1837–1910). He is alleged to have observed that when a rise in the price of imported wheat led to an increase in the price of bread, members of the British working class *increased* their consumption of bread, suggesting that their demand curve for bread was positively sloped.

Giffen good An inferior good for which the income effect outweighs the substitution effect so that the demand curve is positively sloped.

As is clear in Figure 6-2, two things must be true in order for a good to have a positively sloped demand curve—a so-called **Giffen good.** First, the good must be an inferior good, meaning that a reduction in real income leads households to purchase *more* of that good. Second, the good must take a large proportion of total household expenditure and therefore have a large income effect. Bread was indeed a dietary staple of the British working classes during the nineteenth century. A rise in the price of bread would therefore cause a large reduction in people's real income. This could lead people to eat more bread (and less meat) in order to consume enough calories to stay alive.

FIGURE 6-2 Income and Substitution Effects of a Price Change

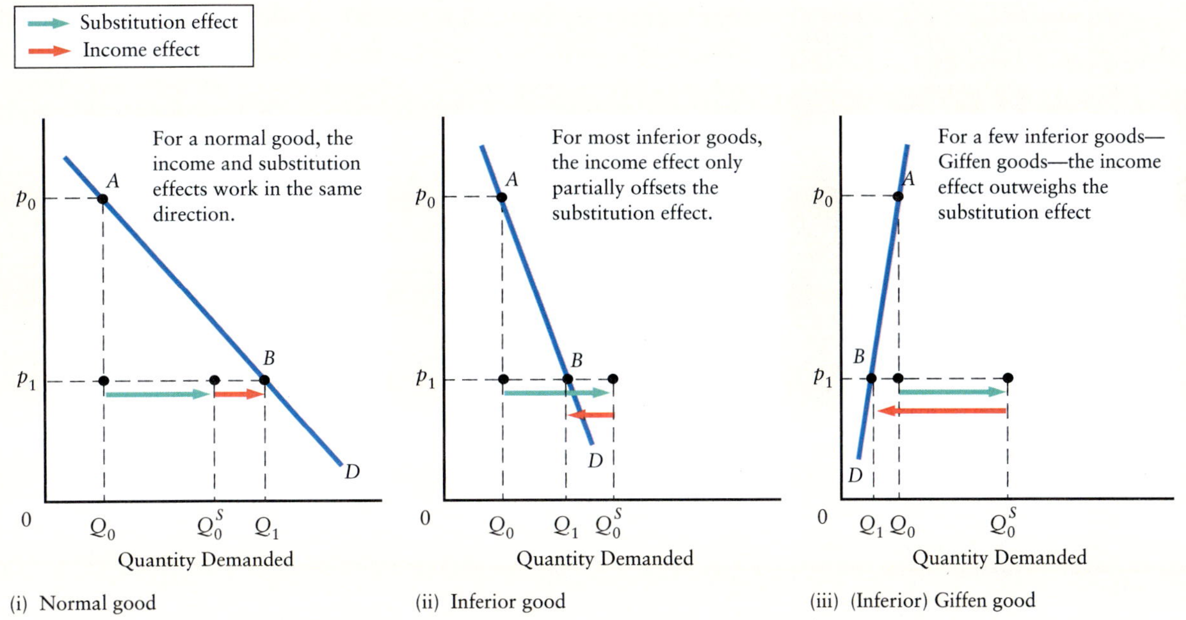

Demand curves for inferior goods are negatively sloped unless the income effect outweighs the substitution effect. In each of the diagrams, the initial price is p_0 and the initial quantity demanded is Q_0. Thus, *A* is a point on all three demand curves. For all three goods, a price reduction to p_1 creates a substitution effect that increases quantity demanded to Q_0^S.

For normal goods in part (i), the reduction in price increases real income and leads to a further increase in quantity demanded. The income effect is shown as the increase from Q_0^S to Q_1. The total increase in quantity demanded is therefore from Q_0 *to* Q_1, and point *B* is on the negatively sloped demand curve.

For inferior goods, the price reduction causes an increase in real income that leads to a *reduction* in quantity demanded. If the good makes up a small fraction of the consumer's total expenditure, which is the case for most goods, then this income effect will be small. In part (ii), the income effect reduces quantity demanded from Q_0^S to Q_1 and the overall change is therefore from Q_0 to Q_1. In this case, the income effect does not fully offset the substitution effect and so the demand curve is still negatively sloped through point *B*. In part (iii), the income effect is very large, reducing quantity demanded from Q_0^S to Q_1 and the overall change is therefore a *reduction* in quantity demanded from Q_0 to Q_1. In this case the demand curve is positively sloped through point *B*. This is the case of a Giffen good.

Though possible, such cases are all but unknown in the modern world, for in all but the poorest societies, typical households do not spend large proportions of their incomes on any single inferior good.

Conspicuous Consumption Goods Thorstein Veblen (1857–1929), in *The Theory of the Leisure Class,* noted that some products were consumed not for their intrinsic qualities but because they had "snob appeal." He suggested that the more expensive such a commodity became, the greater might be its ability to confer status on its purchaser.

Consumers might value diamonds, for example, precisely because everyone knows they are expensive. Thus, a fall in price might lead them to stop buying diamonds and to switch to a more satisfactory object of conspicuous consumption. They may behave in the same way with respect to luxury cars, buying them *because* they are expensive. Does this sort of behaviour violate our basic theory of utility maximization?

Some people are attracted to very expensive products because their extreme prices confer status on the purchaser. But holding the amount of this status constant, people would still probably buy more at lower prices, suggesting a downward-sloping demand curve.

Two comments are in order. First, in a case where individuals appear to buy more goods at a higher price *because of the high price*, there is actually something else going on that explains the apparent violation of the law of demand. What really appeals to such individuals is that *other people think* they paid a high price—this is the basis for the "snob appeal." But such snobs would still buy more at a lower price (and hence still have negatively sloped demand curves) as long as they were absolutely sure that other people *thought* they had paid the high price. As one advertising slogan for a discount department store puts it: "Only you know how little you paid."

Second, even if such conspicuous consumers do exist, it is still unlikely that the *market* demand curve is positively sloped. The reason is easy to discover. The fact that countless lower-income consumers would be glad to buy diamonds or Cadillacs only if these commodities were sufficiently inexpensive suggests that positively sloped demand curves for a few individual wealthy households are much more likely than a positively sloped *market* demand curve for the same commodity.

An Interesting Application to Taxation

Finally, note that the logic of breaking down a price change into the separate income and substitution effects is not limited to the analysis of demand. The same logic applies to two things that most individuals supply—their work effort (to labour markets) and their saving (to financial markets). For example, for a given pre-tax wage, a change in the income-tax rate will change the after-tax wage that workers earn. It will also change the after-tax interest rate that savers (lenders) receive. Using the same analysis as we used above with Tony and the change in the price of ice cream, we can analyze the effects of tax changes on the supply of work effort and the supply of saving. In both cases, in order to understand the overall effect of the change in tax rates, we need to make the important distinction between the income effects and the substitution effects.

myeconlab

For a detailed discussion of the income and substitution effects of tax changes, on both the supply of work effort and the supply of saving, look for "Do Taxes Discourage Work Effort and Saving?" in the *Additional Topics* section of this book's MyEconLab.

www.myeconlab.com

6.3 CONSUMER SURPLUS

Our discussion of consumer behaviour has led us to a better understanding of demand curves and how they are derived. At the heart of our discussion has been the concept of utility, and the law of diminishing marginal utility.

In this section we introduce the important concept of *consumer surplus,* which requires that we make a clear distinction between *marginal* and *total* utility. Understanding this difference will help us to resolve a famous paradox in the history of economic theory.

The Concept

Imagine yourself facing an either/or choice concerning some particular product, say, ice cream: You can have the amount you are now consuming, or you can have none of it. Suppose you would be willing to pay as much as $100 per month for the eight litres of gourmet ice cream that you now consume, rather than do without it. Further suppose you actually buy those eight litres for only $40 instead of $100. What a bargain! You have paid $60 less than the most you were willing to pay. Actually this sort of bargain occurs every day in the economy. Indeed, it is so common that the $60 "saved" in this example has been given a name: *consumer surplus.* **Consumer surplus** is the difference between the total value that consumers place on all the units consumed of some product and the payment they actually make to purchase that amount of the product.

consumer surplus The difference between the total value that consumers place on all units consumed of a commodity and the payment that they actually make to purchase that amount of the commodity.

Consumer surplus is a direct consequence of negatively sloped demand curves. This is easiest to understand if you think of an individual's demand curve as showing his or her willingness to pay for successive units of the product. (You may recall our discussion of this point in the final section of Chapter 5.) To illustrate the concept, suppose we have interviewed your classmate Moira and displayed the information from the interview in the table in Figure 6-3. Our first question to Moira is, "If you were drinking no milk at all, how much would you be willing to pay for one litre per week?" With no hesitation she replies, "$6.00." We then ask, "If you had already consumed that one litre, how much would you be willing to pay for a second litre per week?" After a bit of thought, she answers, "$3.00." Adding one litre per week with each question, we discover that she would be willing to pay $2.00 to get a third litre per week and $1.60, $1.20, $1.00, $0.80, $0.60, $0.50, and $0.40 for successive litres from the fourth to the tenth litre per week.

The sum of the values that she places on each litre of milk gives us the *total value* that she places on all ten litres. In this case, Moira values the ten litres of milk per week at $17.10. This is the amount that she would be willing to pay if she faced the either/or choice of 10 litres or none. This is also the amount she would be willing to pay if she were offered the milk one litre at a time and charged the maximum she was willing to pay for each litre.

Practise with Study Guide Chapter 6, Short-Answer Question 5.

However, Moira does not have to pay a different price for each litre of milk she consumes each week; she can buy all she wants at the prevailing market price. Suppose the price is $1.00 per litre. She will buy six litres per week because she values the sixth litre just at the market price but all earlier litres at higher amounts. She does not buy a seventh litre because she values it at less than the market price.

Because Moira values the first litre at $6.00 but gets it for $1.00, she makes a "profit" of $5.00 on that litre. Between her $3.00 valuation of the second litre and what she has to pay for it, she clears a "profit" of $2.00. She clears a "profit" of $1.00 on the third litre and so on. This "profit," which is shown in the third column of the table, is Moira's consumer surplus on each litre of milk.

We can calculate Moira's total consumer surplus of $8.80 per week by summing her surplus on each litre; we can calculate the same total by first summing what she would be willing to pay for all six litres, which is $14.80, and then subtracting the $6.00 that she actually does pay.

FIGURE 6-3 Moira's Consumer Surplus on Milk Consumption

Litres of Milk Moira Consumes Per Week	Amount Moira Is Willing to Pay to Obtain This Litre	Moira's Consumer Surplus on Each Litre If Milk Costs $1.00 Per Litre
First	$6.00	$5.00
Second	3.00	2.00
Third	2.00	1.00
Fourth	1.60	0.60
Fifth	1.20	0.20
Sixth	1.00	0.00
Seventh	0.80	—
Eighth	0.60	—
Ninth	0.50	—
Tenth	0.40	—

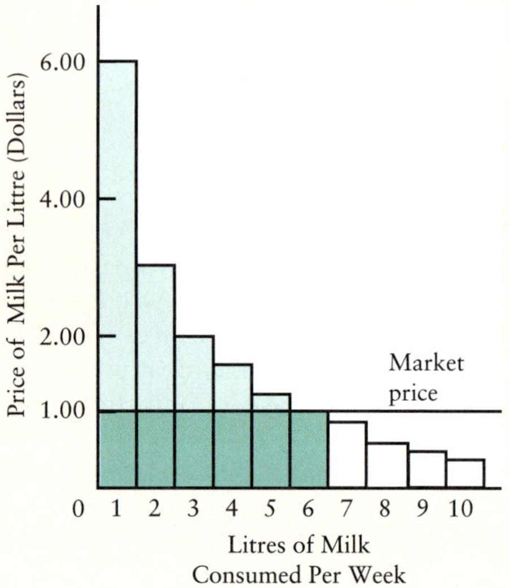

Consumer surplus on each unit consumed is the difference between the market price and the maximum price that the consumer is willing to pay to obtain that unit. The table shows the value that Moira puts on successive litres of milk consumed each week. Her negatively sloped demand curve shows that she would be willing to pay progressively smaller amounts for each additional unit consumed. If the market price is $1.00 per litre, Moira will buy six litres of milk per week and pay the amount in the dark shaded area. The total value she places on these six litres is the entire shaded area. Her consumer surplus is the light shaded area.

For any unit consumed, consumer surplus is the difference between the maximum amount the consumer is prepared to pay for that unit and the price the consumer actually pays.

Practise with Study Guide Chapter 6, Exercises 4 and 5.

For each unit of a product consumed, consumer surplus is the difference between what the consumer is willing to pay for that unit and what the consumer actually pays.

The data in the first two columns of the table give Moira's demand curve for milk. It is her demand curve because she will go on buying litres of milk as long as she values each litre at least as much as the market price she must pay for it. When the market price is $6.00 per litre, she will buy only one litre; when it is $3.00, she will buy two litres; and so on. The total valuation is the area below her demand curve, and consumer surplus is the part of the area that lies above the price line. These areas are shown in Figure 6-3.

Figure 6-4 shows that the same relationship holds for the smooth market demand curve that indicates the total amount that all consumers would buy at each price. Figure 6-3 is a bar chart because we only allowed Moira to vary her consumption in discrete units of one litre at a time. Had we allowed her to vary her consumption of milk one drop at a time, we could have traced out a continuous curve similar to the one shown in Figure 6-4.

The market demand curve shows the valuation that consumers place on each unit of the product. For any given quantity, the area under the demand curve and above the price line shows the consumer surplus received from consuming those units.

FIGURE 6-4 Consumer Surplus for the Market

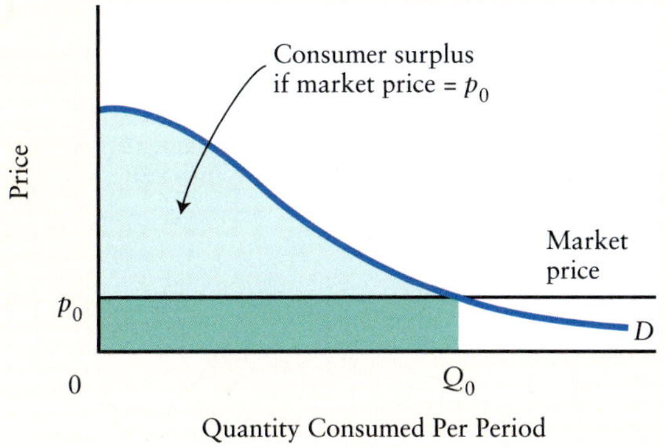

Total consumer surplus is the area under the demand curve and above the price line. The area under the demand curve shows the total valuation that consumers place on all units consumed. For example, the total value that consumers place on Q_0 units is the entire shaded area under the demand curve up to Q_0. At a market price of p_0, the amount paid for Q_0 units is the dark shaded area. Hence consumer surplus is the light shaded area.

Applications

Consumer surplus is an important concept. It will prove useful in later chapters when we evaluate the performance of the market system.[3] For now, however, we discuss two examples where the concept of consumer surplus helps us to understand apparently paradoxical market outcomes. Central to both examples is the distinction between total value and marginal value.

The Paradox of Value Early economists, struggling with the problem of what determines the relative prices of products, encountered what they called the *paradox of value*. Many necessary products, such as water, have prices that are low compared to the prices of luxury products, such as diamonds. Water is necessary to our existence, whereas diamonds are used mostly for luxury purposes and are not in any way essential to life. Does it not seem odd, then, that water is so cheap and diamonds are so expensive? As it took a long time to resolve this apparent paradox, it is not surprising that even today, similar confusions cloud many policy discussions.

The first step in resolving this paradox is to use the distinction between the total and marginal values of any product. We have seen already that the area under the demand curve is a measure of the *total value* placed on all of the units that the consumer consumes. For example, for all consumers together, the total value of consuming Q_0 units is the entire shaded area (light and dark) under the demand curve in Figure 6-4.

What about the *marginal value* that consumers place on one additional unit? This is given by the product's market price, which is p_0 in Figure 6-4. Facing a market price of p_0, each consumer buys all the units that he or she values at p_0 or greater but does not purchase any units valued at less than p_0. Therefore, each consumer values the last unit consumed of any product at that product's price.

The second step in resolving the paradox is to recognize that supply plays just as important a role in determining market price as does demand. Early economists thought the price or "value" of a product depended only on its use by consumers—that is, by demand. But we now know that supply aspects are just as important—including the costs of production, the number of producers, and so on.

Given this joint importance of supply and demand, it is easy to imagine a situation in which two products, such as water and diamonds, have very different market prices (and hence *marginal* values) even if their respective prices do not reflect the *total* value consumers place on the two goods. Figure 6-5 resolves the diamond–water paradox.

[3] Indeed, consumer surplus is part of what in Chapter 5 we called *economic surplus* when we discussed market efficiency. We will return to a discussion of market efficiency in Chapter 12.

FIGURE 6-5 Resolving the Paradox of Value

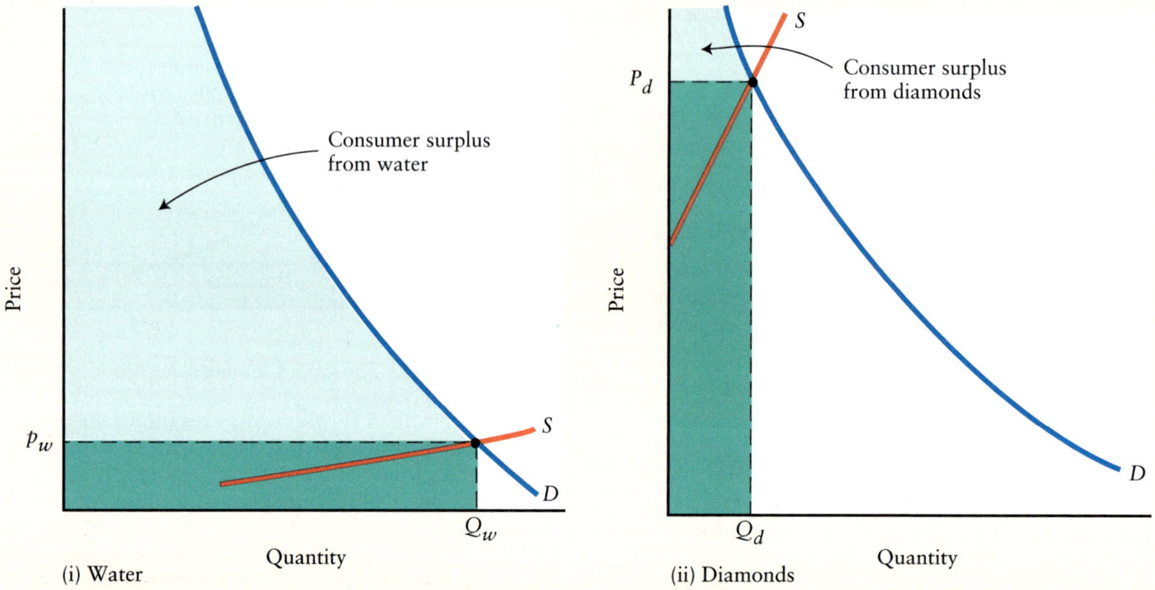

The market price of a product bears no necessary relationship to the total value that consumers place on that amount. The graph presents hypothetical demand curves for water and diamonds. The total value that consumers place on Q_w units of water, as shown by the total shaded area under the demand curve, is great. The total value that consumers place on Q_d units of diamonds is shown by the total shaded area under the demand curve for diamonds. This is clearly less than the total value placed on water.

The large supply of water makes water plentiful and makes water low in price, as shown by p_w in part (i) of the figure. The relatively low supply of diamonds makes diamonds scarce and keeps diamonds high in price, as shown by p_d in part (ii) of the figure. The high total value for water, combined with its low price, leads to a large consumer surplus for water. For diamonds, the low total value and high price lead to a small consumer surplus.

The resolution of the paradox of value is that a good that is very plentiful, such as water, will have a low price and will thus be consumed to the point where all consumers place a low value on the last unit consumed, whether or not they place a high value on their *total* consumption of the product. By contrast, a product that is relatively scarce in the marketplace will have a high market price, and consumption will therefore stop at a point where consumers place a high value on the last unit consumed, regardless of the value that they place on their total consumption of the good.

Because the market price of a product depends on both demand and supply, there is nothing paradoxical in there being a product on which consumers place a high *total* value (such as water) selling for a low price and hence having a low *marginal* value.

Attitude Surveys Attitude surveys often ask people which of several alternatives they prefer. Such questions reveal *total* rather than *marginal* utilities. Where the behaviour being predicted involves an either/or decision, such as whether to vote for the Liberal or Conservative or NDP or any other candidate, the total utility that is attached to each party or candidate will indeed be what matters, because the voter must choose one and reject the others. However, where the decision is a marginal one regarding a little more or a little less, total utility is not what will determine behaviour. If one attempts to predict behaviour in these cases from knowledge of total utilities, even if the information is correct, one will make serious errors.

Here are two examples of how surveys can be misinterpreted. A Canadian market research survey recently asked people to name the household device they thought was most important. Though many appliances ranked highly, vacuum cleaners were judged by the most households as being the most important device. Suppliers of a new version of vacuum cleaner used the survey to predict demand but subsequently found that it had failed to do so accurately. A post-mortem revealed that most people did not respond to the sales promotion because they already had a vacuum cleaner and were unwilling to pay the advertised price for a second one. In other words, although the *total* utility they got from their vacuum cleaner was high, the utility they would get from an additional one—their *marginal* utility—was low.

For a second example, a political party in the United Kingdom conducted a survey to determine what types of public expenditure people thought most valuable. Unemployment benefits rated very highly. The party was subsequently surprised when it aroused great voter hostility by advocating an increase in unemployment benefits. Although the party was surprised, there was nothing inconsistent or irrational in the voters' feeling that protection of the unemployed was a very good thing, providing a high total utility, but that *additional* payments were unnecessary, and therefore had a low marginal utility.

SUMMARY

6.1 MARGINAL UTILITY AND CONSUMER CHOICE

LO 1 2

- Marginal utility theory distinguishes between the total utility from the consumption of *all units* of some product and the incremental (or marginal) utility derived from consuming *one more unit* of the product.
- The basic assumption in marginal utility theory is that the utility consumers derive (over some given time period) from the consumption of successive units of a product diminishes as the number of units consumed increases.
- Consumers are assumed to make their decisions in a way that maximizes their utility. Utility-maximizing consumers make their choices such that the utilities derived from the last dollar spent on each product are equal. For two goods *X* and *Y*, utility will be maximized when

$$\frac{MU_X}{p_X} = \frac{MU_Y}{p_Y}$$

- Demand curves have negative slopes because when the price of one product falls, each consumer responds by increasing purchases of that product sufficiently to restore the ratio of that product's marginal utility to its now lower price (MU/p) to the same level achieved for all other products.

6.2 INCOME AND SUBSTITUTION EFFECTS OF PRICE CHANGES

LO 3

- A change in the price of a product generates both an income effect and a substitution effect. The substitution effect is the reaction of the consumer to the change in relative prices, with purchasing power (real income) held constant. The substitution effect leads the consumer to increase purchases of the product whose relative price has fallen.
- The income effect is the reaction of the consumer to the change in purchasing power (real income) that is caused by the price change, holding relative prices constant at their new level. A fall in one price will lead to an increase in the consumer's real income and thus to an increase in purchases of all normal goods.
- The combined income and substitution effects ensure that the quantity demanded of any normal good will increase when its price falls, other things being equal. Normal goods, therefore, have negatively sloped demand curves.
- An inferior good will have a negatively sloped demand curve unless the income effect is strong enough to outweigh the substitution effect. This situation is very rare and is called a Giffen good.

6.3 CONSUMER SURPLUS

LO 4 5

- For each unit of a product, consumer surplus is the difference between what consumers would be *willing to pay* for that unit and what consumers *actually pay* for that unit.
- Consumer surplus arises because demand curves are negatively sloped and consumers purchase units of a product up to the point where the value of the marginal unit consumed—the *marginal value*—equals the market price. On all units before the marginal unit, consumers value the product more than the price and hence they earn consumer surplus.
- It is important to distinguish between total and marginal values because choices concerning a bit more and a bit less cannot be predicted from a knowledge of total values. The paradox of value involves a confusion between total value and marginal value.
- Price is related to the *marginal* value that consumers place on having a bit more or a bit less of some product; it bears no necessary relationship to the *total* value that consumers place on all of the units consumed of that product.

KEY CONCEPTS

Total utility and marginal utility
Utility maximization
Equality of MU/p across different goods
Slope of the demand curve
Income effect and substitution effect
Giffen goods and conspicuous consumption goods
Consumer surplus
The paradox of value

STUDY EXERCISES

1. Fill in the blanks to make the following statements correct.
   a. Utility theory is based on the hypothesis that the ______________ received from each additional unit of the good ______________ as total consumption of the good increases.
   b. A utility-maximizing consumer will allocate expenditure such that the ______________ per dollar spent on each product is ______________ for all products.
   c. An equation that represents a utility-maximizing pattern of consumption of two goods, A and B, is ____________________.
   d. Marginal utility analysis tells us that a rise in the price of a good, *ceteris paribus*, leads each consumer to reduce the ______________ of the good. This, in turn, predicts a ______________ demand curve.
2. myeconlab The table below shows how Brett's utility increases as the number of avocados he consumes (per month) increases. Brett's utility is measured in *utils*, a name that economists invented to describe units of utility.

Avocados	Total Utility (in utils)	Marginal Utility (in utils)
Zero	0	
		___
First	100	
		___
Second	185	
		___
Third	245	
		___
Fourth	285	
		___
Fifth	315	
		___
Sixth	335	
		___
Seventh	345	
		___
Eighth	350	

   a. Plot Brett's total utility on a scale diagram, with utils on the vertical axis and the number of avocados (per month) on the horizontal axis.
   b. Compute the marginal utility for each avocado and fill in the table.
   c. Plot the marginal utility on a scale diagram, with utils on the vertical axis and the number of avocados (per month) on the horizontal axis. (Make sure to plot marginal utility at the midpoints between units.)
   d. Explain why it is reasonable that Brett's utility increases by smaller and smaller amounts for each successive avocado consumed.

3. myeconlab In each of the cases listed below, identify whether Claudia's expenditure on each product should rise or fall in order to maximize her utility.

Case	Price of X ($)	Marginal Utility of X (units of utility)	Price of Y ($)	Marginal Utility of Y (units of utility)
A	10	2	5	3
B	12	4	4	2
C	3	1	6	2
D	4	2	4	2
E	8	4	4	3

4. myeconlab Rupert really loves pizza, but he eventually tires of it. The table below shows the highest price that Rupert is willing to pay for each successive pizza per week.

Pizza	Rupert's Willingness to Pay
First	$18
Second	$16
Third	$13
Fourth	$9
Fifth	$4
Sixth	$0

a. Suppose Rupert were to eat five pizzas per week. What is the total value Rupert would place on his five weekly pizzas?
b. If the market price is $10 per pizza, how many pizzas will Rupert eat per week?
c. If the market price is $10 per pizza, what is the weekly consumer surplus that Rupert gets from eating pizza?

5. Suppose there is a 10-percent increase in the prices of the following products. Explain whether you think the income effect in each case would be small or large, and why.

a. salt
b. blue jeans
c. canned vegetables
d. gasoline
e. mini-vans
f. rental apartments
g. luxury cars

6. Use the following diagram of a market for potted plants to answer the questions below about consumer surplus.

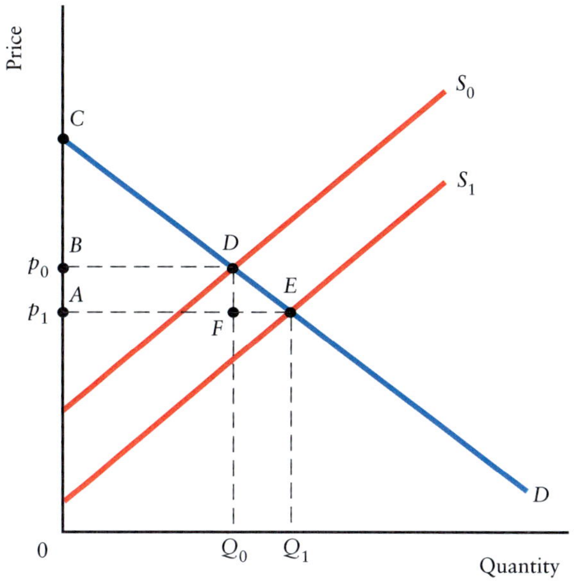

a. With demand curve D and supply curve S_0 the equilibrium price and quantity in this market are p_0 and Q_0. At the price p_0, what is the area that represents total consumer surplus in this market? (Use the letter point labels to describe the area.)
b. Now suppose supply increases to S_1. Determine the new equilibrium price and quantity. What is the area that now represents total consumer surplus?
c. At the new lower price, what is the area that represents the *increased* consumer surplus earned on the *original* units purchased?
d. At the new lower price, what is the area that represents consumer surplus earned on the *new* units purchased?

7. In what situations do the substitution effect and the income effect each predict a downward sloping demand curve? In what situations do they have opposing effects?

8. Consider the following supply-and-demand diagrams depicting the markets for X and Y, respectively. In the market for good X, supply is perfectly elastic, indicating that producers are prepared to supply any amount of X at price p_0.

a. In the market for X, demand increases from D_0 to D_1. Explain what happens to the *total* value that consumers place on X.
b. Explain how the increase in demand for X alters the *marginal* value that consumers place on X.
c. In the market for Y, a technological improvement causes supply to increase from S_0 to S_1, causing price to fall from p_0 to p_1. Explain what happens to the total value that consumers place *on a given quantity* of Y.

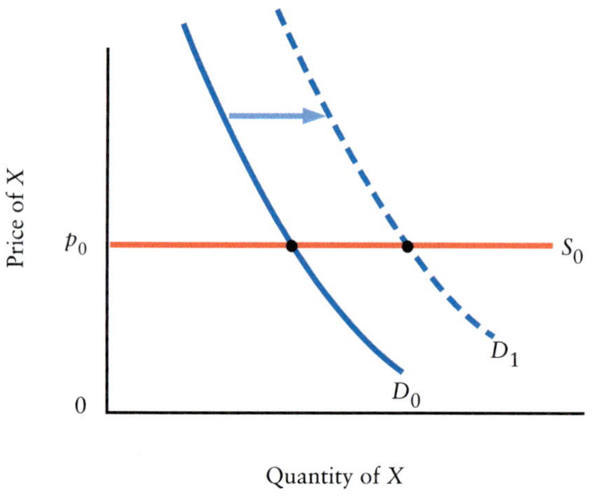

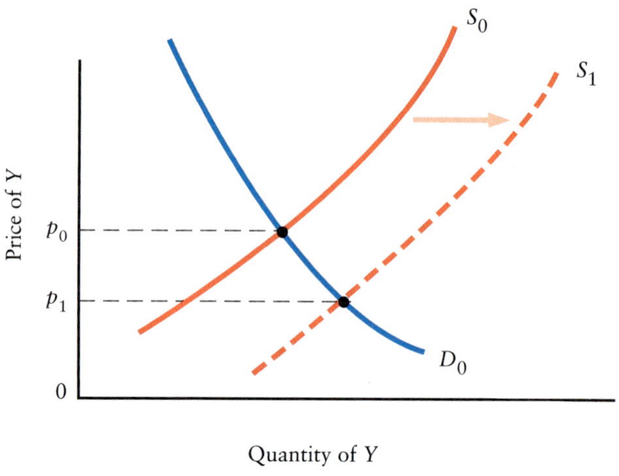

d. Explain why the increase in supply leads consumers to reduce their *marginal* value of Y even though there has been no change in their preferences regarding Y (and thus no shift in the demand curve).

9. Consider the market for some product. The demand and supply curves are given by:

Demand: $p = 30 - 4Q^D$
Supply: $p = 6 + 2Q^S$

a. Plot the demand and supply curves on a scale diagram. Compute the equilibrium price (p^*) and quantity (Q^*).

b. Show in the diagram the total value that consumers place on Q^* units of the good.

c. What is the value that consumers place on an *additional* unit of the good?

d. Now suppose that production costs fall and so the market supply curve shifts to a new position given by $p = 2 + 2Q^S$. How do consumers now value an additional unit of the good?

e. Explain why consumers' marginal value has fallen even though there has been no change in their preferences (and thus no change in the demand curve).

DISCUSSION QUESTIONS

1. Describe the difference in behaviour at a party at which drinks are free between someone who imbibes up to the point where the *marginal* value of more alcohol consumed is zero and someone who imbibes up to the point where the *average* value of alcohol consumed is zero.

2. Compare the consequences of the income effect of a drastic fall in food prices with the consequences of a rise in incomes when prices are constant.

3. Two U.S. economics professors, Jeff Biddle and Daniel Hamermesh, recently estimated that a 25-percent increase in wages will cause the average individual to reduce the time that he or she spends sleeping by about 1 percent. Interpret this finding in terms of the income and substitution effects of a wage change.

4. Consider the following common scenario. An economist is attending a conference in an unfamiliar city. She is in the mood for a high-quality dinner and wanders through the centre of the city looking for a restaurant. After narrowing her search to two establishments, she ultimately selects the restaurant with the higher prices. What might account for this behaviour?

5. Many medical and hospital services in Canada are provided at zero cost to all Canadians and are financed out of general government revenues. What would be the *marginal value* of such services consumed by each Canadian if the government provided the necessary resources to satisfy *all* demand? How does this relate to the *total* value that Canadians probably place on medical services?

APPENDIX TO CHAPTER 6

Indifference Curves

In Chapter 6, we covered some basic material concerning the theory of demand; here we extend the treatment of demand theory by considering in more detail the assumptions about consumer behaviour that underlie the theory of demand.

The history of demand theory has seen two major breakthroughs. The first was *marginal utility theory,* which we used in Chapter 6. By distinguishing total and marginal values, this theory helped to explain the so-called paradox of value. The second breakthrough came with *indifference theory,* which showed that the stringent assumption of measurable utility (required for marginal utility theory) could be dispensed with. Indifference theory is based on the much weaker assumption that consumers can always say which of two consumption bundles they prefer without having to say *by how much* they prefer it.

6A.1 INDIFFERENCE CURVES

Suppose Hugh currently has available some specific bundle of goods, say, 18 units of clothing and 10 units of food. Now offer him an alternative bundle of, say, 13 units of clothing and 15 units of food. This alternative combination of goods has 5 fewer units of clothing and 5 more units of food than the first one. Whether Hugh prefers this new bundle depends on the relative valuation that he places on 5 more units of food and 5 fewer units of clothing. If he values the extra food more than the forgone clothing, he will prefer the new bundle to the original one. If he values the extra food less than the forgone clothing, he will prefer the original bundle. If Hugh values the extra food the same as the forgone clothing, he is said to be *indifferent* between the two bundles.

Suppose that after much trial and error, we have identified several bundles between which Hugh is indifferent. In other words, all bundles give him equal satisfaction or utility. They are shown in the table in Figure 6A-1.

Of course, there are combinations of the two products other than those enumerated in the table that will give Hugh the same level of utility. All of these combinations are shown in Figure 6A-1 by the smooth curve that passes through the points plotted from the table. This curve, called an *indifference curve,* shows all combinations of products that yield Hugh the same utility.

The consumer is indifferent between the combinations indicated by any two points on one indifference curve.

Any points above the curve show combinations of food and clothing that Hugh prefers to points on the curve. Consider, for example, the combination of 20 units of food and 18 units of clothing, represented by point *g* in Figure 6A-1. Although it may not be obvious that this bundle must be preferred to bundle *a* (which has more clothing but less food), it is obvious that it will be preferred to bundle *c* because both less clothing and less food are represented at *c* than at *g*. Inspection of the graph shows that any point above the curve will be superior to some points on the curve in the sense that it will contain both more food and more clothing than those points on the curve. However, because all points on the curve are equal in Hugh's eyes, any point above the curve must be superior to all points on the curve. By a similar argument, all points below and to the left of the curve represent bundles that are inferior to bundles represented by points on the curve.

Any point above an indifference curve is preferred to any point along that same indifference curve; any point on the curve is preferred to any point below it.

Diminishing Marginal Rate of Substitution

How much clothing would Hugh be willing to give up to get one more unit of food but to keep his utility unchanged? The answer to this question measures what is called Hugh's marginal rate of substitution of

FIGURE 6A-1 Hugh's Indifference Curve

Alternative Bundles Giving Hugh Equal Utility

Bundle	Clothing	Food
a	30	5
b	18	10
c	13	15
d	10	20
e	8	25
f	7	30

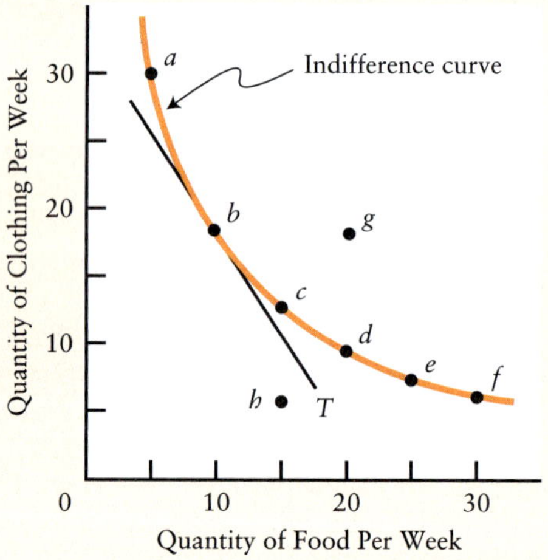

This indifference curve shows combinations of food and clothing that yield equal utility and between which Hugh is indifferent. The smooth curve through the points is an indifference curve; all combinations on it give Hugh equal utility. Point *g* above the line is a preferred combination to any point on the line; point *h* below the line is an inferior combination to any point on the line. The slope of the line *T* gives the marginal rate of substitution at point *b*. Moving down the indifference curve from *b* to *f*, the slope flattens, showing that the more food and the less clothing Hugh has, the less willing he is to sacrifice further clothing to get more food.

clothing for food. The *marginal rate of substitution (MRS)* is the amount of one product that a consumer is willing to give up to get one more unit of another product.

The first basic assumption of indifference theory is that the algebraic value of the *MRS* between two goods is always negative.

A negative *MRS* means that to increase consumption of one product, Hugh is prepared to decrease consumption of a second product. The negative value of the marginal rate of substitution is indicated graphically by the negative slope of indifference curves.

Consider a case in which Hugh has a lot of clothing and only a little food. Common sense suggests that he might be willing to give up quite a bit of plentiful clothing to get one more unit of scarce food. It suggests as well that if Hugh had little clothing and a lot of food he would be willing to give up only a little scarce clothing to get one more unit of already plentiful food.

This example illustrates the hypothesis of *diminishing marginal rate of substitution.* The less of one product, *A*, and the more of a second product, *B*, that the consumer has already, the smaller the amount of *A* that the consumer will be willing to give up to get one additional unit of *B*. The hypothesis says that the marginal rate of substitution changes when the amounts of two products consumed change. The graphical expression of this hypothesis is that any indifference curve becomes flatter as the consumer moves downward and to the right along the curve. In Figure 6A-1, a movement downward and to the right means that Hugh is consuming less clothing and more food. The decreasing steepness of the curve means that Hugh is willing to sacrifice less and less clothing to get each additional unit of food. **[11]**

Diminishing marginal rate of substitution (MRS) is the second basic assumption of indifference theory.

The hypothesis of diminishing marginal rate of substitution is illustrated in Table 6A-1, which is based on the example in Figure 6A-1. The last column of the table shows the rate at which Hugh is prepared to sacrifice units of clothing per unit of food obtained. At first, Hugh will sacrifice 2.4 units of clothing to get 1 unit more of food, but as his consumption of clothing diminishes and his consump-

TABLE 6A-1 Hugh's Marginal Rate of Substitution Between Clothing and Food

Movement	(1) Change in Clothing	(2) Change in Food	(3) Marginal Rate of Substitution (1) ÷ (2)
From *a* to *b*	−12	5	−2.4
From *b* to *c*	−5	5	−1.0
From *c* to *d*	−3	5	−0.6
From *d* to *e*	−2	5	−0.4
From *e* to *f*	−1	5	−0.2

The marginal rate of substitution of clothing for food declines (in absolute value) as the quantity of food increases. This table is based on Figure 6A-1. When Hugh moves from *a* to *b*, he gives up 12 units of clothing and gains 5 units of food; he remains at the same level of overall utility. At point *a*, Hugh is prepared to sacrifice 12 units of clothing for 5 units of food (i.e., 12/5 = 2.4 units of clothing per unit of food obtained). When he moves from *b* to *c*, he sacrifices 5 units of clothing for 5 units of food (a rate of substitution of 1 unit of clothing for each unit of food).

FIGURE 6A-2 Hugh's Indifference Map

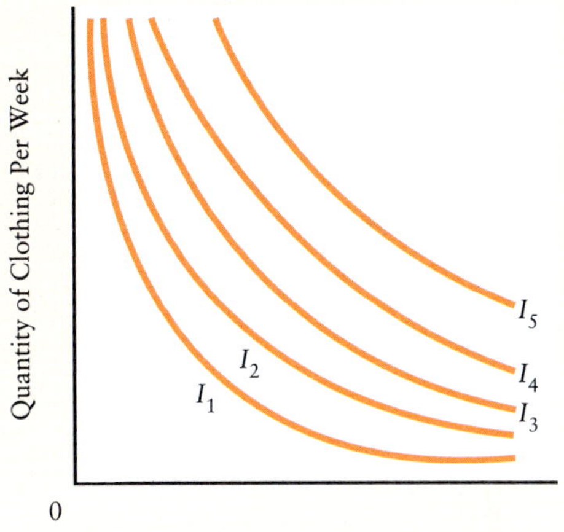

An indifference map consists of a set of indifference curves. All points on a particular curve indicate alternative combinations of food and clothing that give Hugh equal utility. The farther the curve is from the origin, the higher is the level of utility it represents. For example, I_5 is a higher indifference curve than I_4, which means that all the points on I_5 give Hugh a higher level of utility than do the points on I_4.

tion of food increases, Hugh becomes less and less willing to sacrifice further clothing for more food.

The Indifference Map

So far, we have constructed only a single indifference curve for Hugh. However, starting at any other point in Figure 6A-1, such as *g*, there will be other combinations that will give Hugh equal utility. If the points indicating all of these combinations are connected, they will form another indifference curve. This exercise can be repeated many times, and we can thereby generate many indifference curves for Hugh. The farther any indifference curve is from the origin, the higher will be the level of Hugh's utility given by any of the points on the curve.

A set of indifference curves is called an *indifference map*, an example of which is shown in Figure 6A-2. It specifies the consumer's tastes by showing his rate of substitution between the two products for every possible level of current consumption of these products.

When economists say that a consumer's tastes are given, they do not mean that the consumer's current consumption pattern is given; rather, they mean that the consumer's entire indifference map is given.

6A.2 THE BUDGET LINE

Indifference curves illustrate consumers' tastes. To develop a complete theory of their choices, we must also illustrate the available alternatives. These are shown as the solid line *ab* in Figure 6A-3. That line, called a *budget line*, shows all the combinations of food and clothing that Hugh can buy if he spends a fixed amount of money, in this case his entire money income of $720 per week, at fixed prices of the products (in this case, $12 per unit for clothing and $24 per unit for food).

FIGURE 6A-3 Hugh's Budget Line

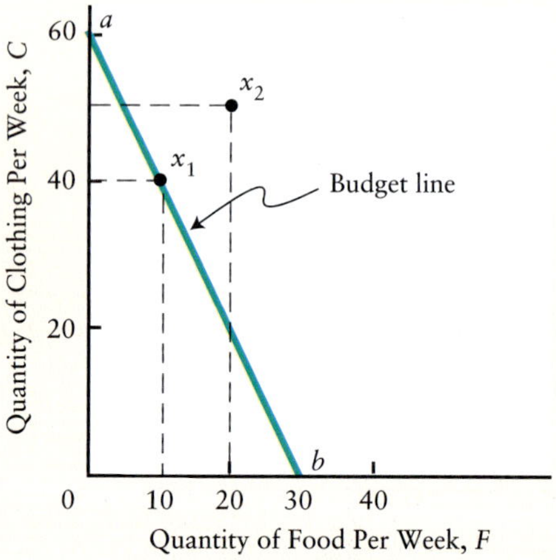

The budget line shows the quantities of goods available to a consumer given money income and the prices of goods. Any point in this diagram indicates a combination (or bundle) of so much food and so much clothing. Point x_1, for example, indicates 40 units of clothing and 10 units of food per week.

With an income of $720 a week and prices of $24 per unit for food and $12 per unit for clothing, Hugh's budget line is *ab*. This line shows all the combinations of *F* and *C* available to him if he spends the entire $720 per week. He could spend all of this money income on clothing and obtain 60 units of clothing and zero food each week. Or he could go to the other extreme and purchase only food, buying 30 units of *F* and zero units of *C*. Hugh could also choose an intermediate position and consume some of both goods—for example, spending $240 to buy 10 units of *F* and $480 to buy 40 units of *C* (point x_1). Points above the budget line, such as x_2, are not attainable.

Properties of the Budget Line

The budget line has several important properties:

1. Points on the budget line indicate bundles of products that use up the consumer's entire income. (Try, for example, the point 20*C*, 20*F*.)
2. Points between the budget line and the origin indicate bundles of products that cost less than the consumer's income. (Try, for example, the point 20*C*, 10*F*.)
3. Points above the budget line indicate combinations of products that cost more than the consumer's income. (Try, for example, the point 30*C*, 40*F*.)

The budget line shows all combinations of products that are available to the consumer given his money income and the prices of the goods that he purchases.

We can also show Hugh's alternatives with an equation that uses symbols to express the information contained in the budget line. Let *E* stand for Hugh's money income, which must be equal to his total expenditure on food and clothing. If p_F and p_C represent the money prices of food and clothing, respectively, and *F* and *C* represent the quantities of food and clothing that Hugh chooses, then his spending on food is equal to p_F times *F*, and his spending on clothing is equal to p_C times *C*. Thus the equation for the budget line is

$$E = p_F \times F + p_C \times C$$

The Slope of the Budget Line

Look again at Hugh's budget line in Figure 6A-3. The vertical intercept is 60 units of clothing, and the horizontal intercept is 30 units of food. Thus the slope is equal to −2. The minus sign means that increases in Hugh's purchases of one of the goods must be accompanied by decreases in his purchases of the other. The numerical value of the slope indicates how much of one good must be given up to obtain an additional unit of the other; in our example, the slope of −2 means that Hugh must forgo the purchase of 2 units of clothing to acquire 1 extra unit of food.

Recall that in Chapter 3 we contrasted the *absolute*, or *money*, price of a product with its *relative* price, which is the ratio of its absolute price to that of some other product or group of products. One important point is that the relative price determines the slope of the budget line. In terms of our example of food and clothing, the slope of the budget line is determined by the relative price of food in terms of clothing, p_F/p_C; with the price of food (p_F) at $24 per unit and the price of clothing (p_C) at $12 per unit, the slope of the budget line (in absolute value) is 2. **[12]**

The significance of the slope of Hugh's budget line for food and clothing is that it reflects his *oppor-*

tunity cost of food in terms of clothing. To increase food consumption while maintaining expenditure constant, Hugh must move along the budget line and therefore consume less clothing; the slope of the budget line determines how much clothing he must give up to obtain an additional unit of food.

The opportunity cost of food in terms of clothing is measured by the (absolute value of the) slope of the budget line, which is equal to the relative price ratio, p_F/p_C.

In the example, with fixed income and with the relative price of food in terms of clothing (p_F/p_C) equal to 2, Hugh must forgo the purchase of 2 units of clothing to acquire 1 extra unit of food. The opportunity cost of a unit of food is thus 2 units of clothing. Notice that the relative price (in our example, $p_F/p_C = 2$) is consistent with an infinite number of absolute prices. If $p_F = \$40$ and $p_C = \$20$, it is still necessary to sacrifice 2 units of clothing to acquire 1 unit of food.[4] Thus relative, not absolute, prices determine opportunity cost.

6A.3 THE CONSUMER'S UTILITY-MAXIMIZING CHOICES

An indifference map describes the preferences of a consumer, and a budget line describes the possibilities available to a consumer. To predict what a consumer will actually do, both sets of information must be combined, as is done in Figure 6A-4. Hugh's budget line is shown by the straight line, and the curves from the indifference map are also shown. Any point on the budget line is attainable, but which point will Hugh actually choose?

Because Hugh wishes to maximize utility, he wishes to reach the highest attainable indifference curve. Inspection of Figure 6A-4 shows that if Hugh purchases any bundle on the budget line at a point cut by an indifference curve, he can reach a higher indifference curve. Only when the bundle purchased is such that the indifference curve is tangent to the budget line is it impossible for Hugh to reach a higher curve by altering his purchases.

[4] Of course, with a given income, Hugh can afford much less of each at these higher money prices, but the opportunity cost of food in terms of clothing remains unchanged.

FIGURE 6A-4 Hugh's Utility-Maximizing Choice

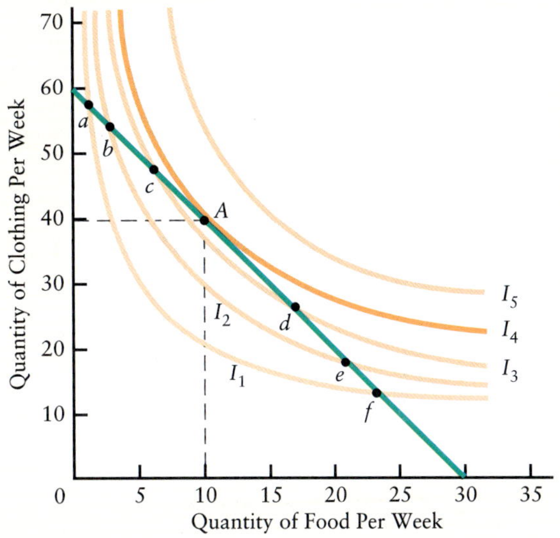

The consumer's utility is maximized at *A*, where an indifference curve is tangent to the budget line. Hugh has a money income of \$720 per week and faces money prices of \$12 per unit for clothing and \$24 per unit for food. A combination of units of clothing and food indicated by point *a* on I_1 is attainable but, by moving along the budget line, Hugh can reach higher indifference curves. The same is true at *b* on I_2 and at *c* on I_3. At *A*, however, where an indifference curve (I_4) is tangent to the budget line, Hugh cannot reach a higher curve by moving along the budget line.

The consumer's utility is maximized at the point where an indifference curve is tangent to the budget line. At that point, the consumer's marginal rate of substitution for the two goods is equal to the relative prices of the two goods.

The intuitive explanation for this result is that if Hugh values goods differently from the way the market does, there is room for profitable exchange. Hugh can give up some of the good that he values relatively less than the market does and take in return some of the good that he values relatively more than the market does. When he is prepared to exchange goods at the same rate as they can be traded on the market, there is no further opportunity for him to raise utility by substituting one product for the other.

The theory thus proceeds by supposing that Hugh is presented with market prices that he cannot change and then analyzing how he adjusts to these prices by choosing a bundle of goods such that, at the margin, his own subjective evaluation of the goods coincides with the valuations given by market prices.

We will now use this theory to predict the typical consumer's response to a change in income and in prices.

The Consumer's Reaction to a Change in Income

A change in Hugh's money income will, *ceteris paribus*, shift his budget line. For example, if Hugh's income doubles, he will be able to buy twice as much of both food and clothing compared with any combination on his previous budget line. His budget line will therefore shift out parallel to itself to indicate this expansion in his consumption possibilities. (The fact that it will be a parallel shift is established by the previous demonstration that the slope of the budget line depends only on the relative prices of the two products.)

For each level of Hugh's income, there will be a utility-maximizing point at which an indifference curve is tangent to the relevant budget line. Each such utility-maximizing position means that Hugh is doing as well as possible at that level of income. If we move the budget line through all possible levels of income and if we join up all the utility-maximizing points, we will trace out what is called an *income–consumption line*, an example of which is shown in Figure 6A-5. This line shows how Hugh's consumption bundle changes as his income changes, with relative prices being held constant.

FIGURE 6A-5 Hugh's Income–Consumption Line

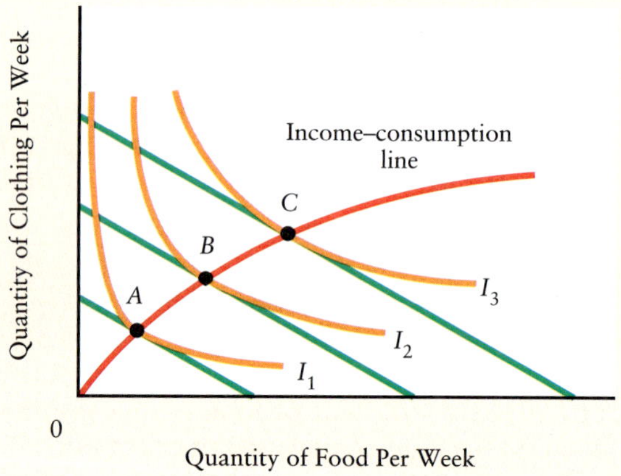

The income–consumption line shows how the consumer's purchases react to a change in money income with relative prices being held constant. Increases in Hugh's money income cause a parallel outward shift of his budget line, moving his utility-maximizing point from *A* to *B* to *C*. By joining all the utility-maximizing points, Hugh's income–consumption line is traced out.

The Consumer's Reaction to a Change in Price

We already know that a change in the relative prices of the two goods changes the slope of the budget line. Given the price of clothing, for each possible price of food there is a different utility-maximizing consumption bundle for Hugh. If we connect these bundles, at a given money income, we will trace out a *price–consumption line*, as shown in Figure 6A-6. Notice that in this example, as the relative prices of food and clothing change, the quantities of food and clothing that Hugh purchases also change. In particular, as the price of food falls, Hugh buys more food and less clothing.

6A.4 DERIVING THE DEMAND CURVE

What happens to the consumer's demand for some product, say, gasoline, as the price of that product changes, *holding constant the prices of all other goods?*

If there were only two products purchased by consumers, we could derive a demand curve for one of the products from the price–consumption line like the one we showed for Hugh in Figure 6A-6. When there are many products, however, a change in the price of one product generally causes substitution toward (or away from) *all other goods.* Thus we would like to have a simple way of representing the individual's tastes in a world of many products.

In part (i) of Figure 6A-7, a new type of indifference map is plotted in which litres of gasoline per

FIGURE 6A-6 Hugh's Price–Consumption Line

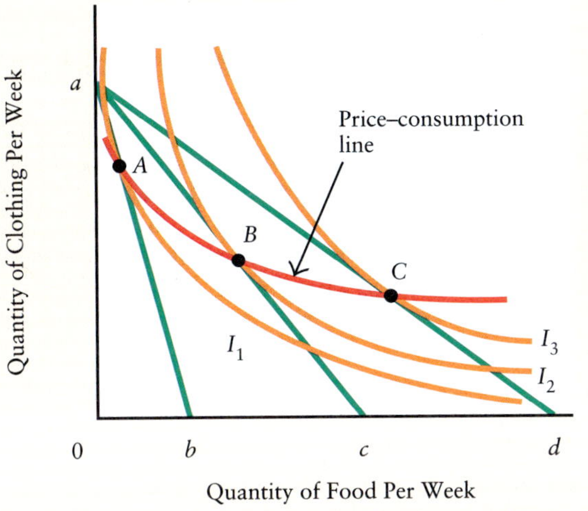

The price–consumption line shows how the consumer's purchases react to a change in one price with money income and other prices being held constant. Decreases in the price of food (with money income and the price of clothing held constant) pivot Hugh's budget line from *ab* to *ac* to *ad*. Hugh's utility-maximizing bundle moves from *A* to *B* to *C*. By joining all the utility-maximizing points, a price–consumption line is traced out, showing that Hugh purchases more food and less clothing as the price of food falls.

month are measured on the horizontal axis and the *value* of all other goods consumed per month is plotted on the vertical axis. We have in effect used "everything but gasoline" as the second product. The indifference curves in this figure then show the rate at which the consumer is prepared to substitute gasoline for money (which allows him to buy all other goods) at each level of consumption of gasoline and of all other goods.

To illustrate the derivation of demand curves, we use the numerical example shown in Figure 6A-7. The consumer is assumed to have an after-tax money income of $4000 per month. This level of money income is plotted on the vertical axis, showing that if the consumer consumes no gasoline, he can consume $4000 worth of other goods each month. When gasoline costs $1.50 per litre, the consumer could buy a maximum of 2667 litres per month. This set of choices gives rise to the innermost budget line. Given the consumer's tastes, utility is maximized at point *A*,

FIGURE 6A-7 Derivation of a Consumer's Demand Curve

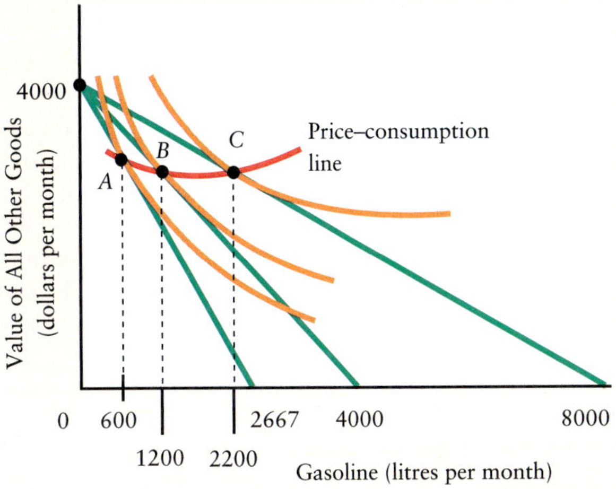

(i) Price–consumption line

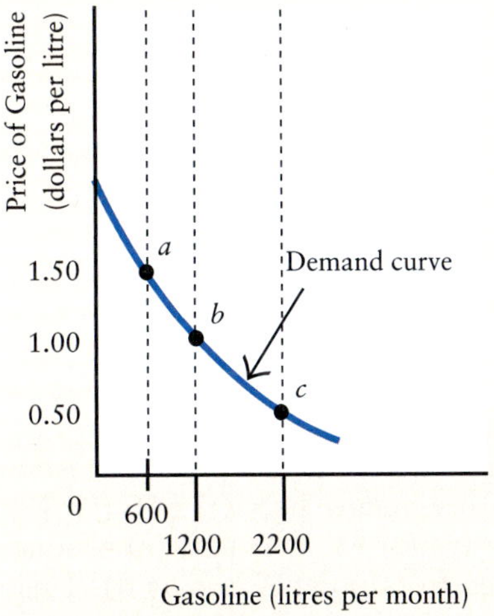

(ii) Demand curve

Every point on the price–consumption line corresponds to both a price of the product and a quantity demanded; this is the information required for a demand curve. In part (i), the consumer has a money income of $4000 and alternatively faces prices of $1.50, $1.00, and $0.50 per litre of gasoline, choosing positions *A*, *B*, and *C* at each price. The information for litres of gasoline demanded at each price is then plotted in part (ii) to yield the consumer's demand curve. The three points *a*, *b*, and *c* in part (ii) correspond to the points *A*, *B*, and *C* in part (i).

consuming 600 litres of gasoline and $3100 worth of other products.

Next, let the price of gasoline fall to $1.00 per litre. Now the maximum possible consumption of gasoline is 4000 litres per month, giving rise to the middle budget line in the figure. The consumer's utility is maximized, as always, at the point where the new budget line is tangent to an indifference curve. At this point, *B*, the consumer is consuming 1200 litres of gasoline per month and spending $2800 on all other goods. Finally, let the price fall to 50 cents per litre. The consumer can now buy a maximum of 8000 litres per month, giving rise to the outermost of the three budget lines. The consumer maximizes utility by consuming 2200 litres of gasoline per month and spending $2900 on other products.

If we let the price vary over all possible amounts, we will trace out a complete price–consumption line, as shown in Figure 6A-7. The points derived in the preceding paragraph are merely three points on this line.

We have now derived all that we need to plot the consumer's demand curve for gasoline, now that we know how much the consumer will purchase at each price. To draw the curve, we merely replot the data from part (i) of Figure 6A-7 onto a demand graph, as shown in part (ii) of Figure 6A-7.

Like part (i), part (ii) has quantity of gasoline on the horizontal axis. By placing one graph under the other, we can directly transcribe the quantity determined on the upper graph to the lower one. We first do this for the 600 litres consumed on the innermost budget line. We now note that the price of gasoline that gives rise to that budget line is $1.50 per litre. Plotting 600 litres against $1.50 in part (ii) produces the point *a*, derived from point *A* in part (i). This is one point on the consumer's demand curve. Next we consider the middle budget line, which occurs when the price of gasoline is $1.00 per litre. We take the figure of 1200 litres from point *B* in part (i) and transfer it to part (ii). We then plot this quantity against the price of $1.00 to get the point *b* on the demand curve. Doing the same thing for point C yields the point *c* in part (ii): price 50 cents, quantity 2200 litres.

Repeating the operation for all prices yields the demand curve in part (ii). Note that the two parts of Figure 6A-7 describe the same behaviour. Both parts measure the quantity of gasoline on the horizontal axes; the only difference is that in part (i) the price of gasoline determines the slope of the budget line, whereas in part (ii) the price of gasoline is plotted explicitly on the vertical axis.

Income and Substitution Effects

The price–consumption line in part (i) of Figure 6A-7 indicates that as price decreases, the quantity of gasoline demanded increases, thus giving rise to the negatively sloped demand curve in part (ii). As we saw in Chapter 6, the key to understanding the negative slope of the demand curve is to distinguish between the income effect and the substitution effect of a change in price. We can make this distinction more precisely, and somewhat differently, using indifference curves.

In Chapter 6, we examined the substitution effect of a reduction in price by eliminating the income effect. We did this by reducing money income until the consumer could just purchase the original bundle of goods. We then examined how the change in relative prices affected the consumer's choices. In indifference theory, however, the income effect is removed by changing money income until the *original level of utility*—the original indifference curve—can just be achieved. This method results in a slightly different measure of the income effect, but the principle involved in separating the total change into an income effect and a substitution effect is exactly the same as in Chapter 6.

The separation of the two effects according to indifference theory is shown in Figure 6A-8. The figure shows in greater detail part of the price–consumption line first drawn in Figure 6A-7. Points A_0 and A_2 are on the price–consumption line for gasoline; A_0 is the consumer's utility-maximizing point at the initial price, whereas A_2 is the consumer's utility-maximizing point at the new price.

We can think of the separation of the income and substitution effects as occurring in the following way. After the price of the good has fallen, we reduce money income *until the original indifference curve can just be obtained*. The consumer moves from point A_0 to an intermediate point A_1, and this response is defined as the substitution effect. Then, to measure the income effect, we restore money income. The consumer moves from the point A_1 to the final point A_2, and this response is defined as the income effect.

FIGURE 6A-8 The Income and Substitution Effects of a Price Change

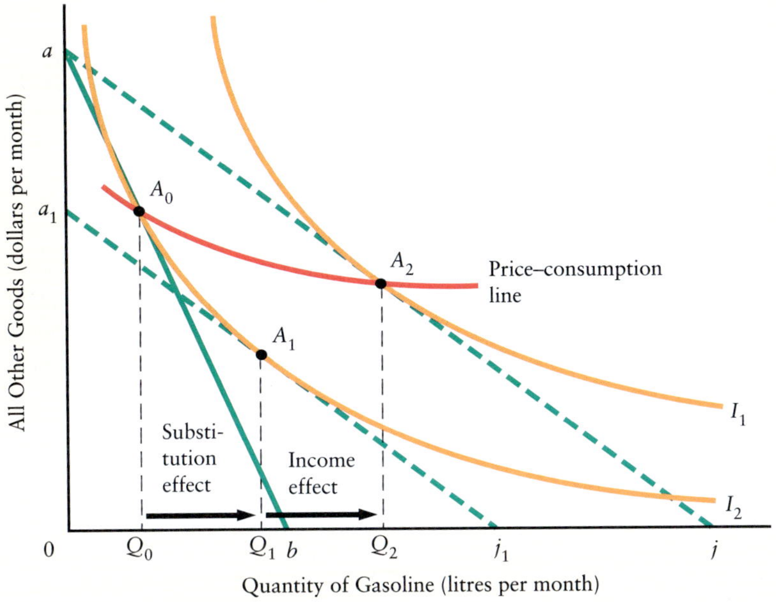

The substitution effect is defined by sliding the budget line around a fixed indifference curve; the income effect is defined by a parallel shift of the budget line. The original budget line is at *ab*, and a fall in the price of gasoline takes it to *aj*. The original utility-maximizing point is at A_0 with Q_0 of gasoline being consumed, and the new utility-maximizing point is at A_2 with Q_2 of gasoline being consumed. To remove the income effect, imagine reducing the consumer's money income until the original indifference curve is just attainable. We do this by shifting the line *aj* to a parallel line nearer the origin a_1j_1 that just touches the indifference curve that passes through A_0. The intermediate point A_1 divides the quantity change into a substitution effect Q_0Q_1 and an income effect Q_1Q_2.

STUDY EXERCISES

1. Consider Katie's preferences for videos and ice cream cones. Several "consumption bundles" are shown in the table below.

Bundle	Ice Cream Cones	Videos
a	9	0
b	7	2
c	6	2
d	5	3
e	4	4
f	4	3
g	3	4
h	2	6
i	0	6

   a. On a scale diagram with the quantity of ice cream cones on the vertical axis and the quantity of videos on the horizontal axis, plot the various bundles.
   b. Suppose that Katie is indifferent between bundles *c* and *i*. She is also indifferent between bundles *d*, *g*, and *h*, but all three of these are preferred to *c* or *i*. Finally, suppose that, of the bundles shown in the table, bundle *e* is Katie's favourite. Draw three indifference curves showing this information.
   c. Consider bundles *e*, *f*, and *g*. What can you conclude about how Katie would rank these bundles?

2. Continue with Katie from the previous question. Katie has a monthly allowance of $18 that she chooses to divide between video rentals and ice cream cones. Videos rent for $3 each and ice cream cones cost $2 each.

   a. For each of the consumption bundles shown in the table, compute the total expenditure. Which ones can Katie afford, and which ones can't she afford?
   b. Draw Katie's budget line. What is the slope of the line?
   c. Given Katie's monthly budget constraint, which bundle does she choose to maximize her utility?

3. Debra travels to Mexico and enjoys both burritos and Coronas. The diagram shows her utility-maximizing choices.

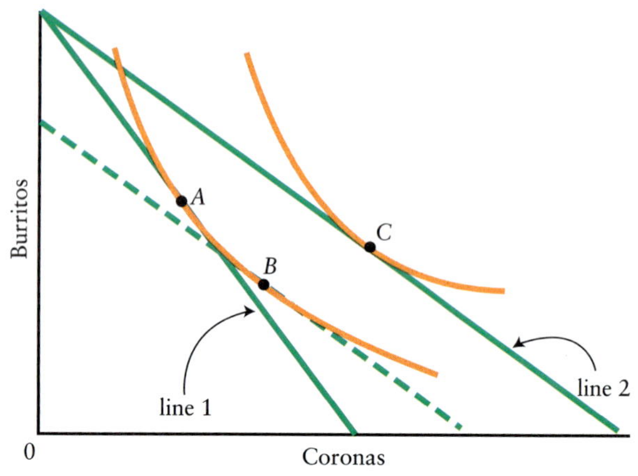

a. If the budget line is line 1, describe why point *A* is Debra's utility-maximizing choice.
b. What event can explain why the budget line moves to line 2?
c. What is the meaning of point *B* in the figure?
d. Suppose Coronas are a normal good for Debra. What does this restriction imply about the location of point *C*? Is this restriction satisfied in the diagram?
e. Suppose Coronas were an inferior good for Debra. How would this information be reflected in her choice following the move of the budget line to line 2?

4. Consider your sets of indifference curves for

   i) Coke and chips
   ii) Coke and Pepsi

   Explain why these sets of indifference curves are likely to look different. Illustrate with a diagram. What does this difference imply about the magnitude of the substitution effects in response to changes in the price of Coke?

CHAPTER 7

Producers in the Short Run

LEARNING OBJECTIVES

In this chapter you will learn

1. the various forms of business organization and the different ways that firms can be financed.
2. the difference between accounting profits and economic profits.
3. about the relationships between total product, average product, and marginal product, and the law of diminishing marginal returns.
4. the difference between fixed and variable costs, and the relationships between total costs, average costs, and marginal costs.

In Chapter 6, we went behind the demand curve to understand how it is determined by the behaviour of consumers. In this chapter and the next, we go behind the supply curve to understand how it is determined by the behaviour of firms.

We begin by comparing the firms that we see in the real world with those that appear in economic theory. Next we introduce the concepts of costs, revenues, and profits and outline the key role that profits play in determining the allocation of the nation's resources. To determine the most profitable quantity for a firm to produce and supply to the market, we need to see how its costs vary with its output.

When examining the relationship between output and cost, *time* plays an important role. In this chapter, we focus on the short run, where a firm can change only some of its inputs, and output is governed by the famous "law of diminishing returns." In the next chapter we examine the firm's behaviour in the long run—when all the firm's factors are variable—and in the very long run—when the state of technology changes. There we encounter scale economies and firms' incentives for research and development.

7.1 WHAT ARE FIRMS?

We start by taking a brief look at the basic unit of production, the firm. How are firms organized? How are firms financed? What are their goals?

Organization of Firms

A firm can be organized in any one of six different ways.

single proprietorship A firm which has one owner who is personally responsible for the firm's actions and debts.

ordinary partnership A firm which has two or more joint owners, each of whom is personally responsible for the firm's actions and debts.

limited partnership A firm which has two classes of owners: general partners, who take part in managing the firm and are personally liable for the firm's actions and debts, and limited partners, who take no part in the management of the firm and risk only the money that they have invested.

corporation A firm which has a legal existence separate from that of the owners.

state-owned enterprise A firm that is owned by the government. In Canada, these are called *Crown corporations*.

non-profit organizations Firms that provide goods and services with the objective of just covering their costs.

multinational enterprises (MNEs) Firms that have operations in more than one country.

1. A **single proprietorship** has one owner–manager who is personally responsible for all aspects of the business, including its debts.
2. An **ordinary partnership** has two or more joint owners, each of whom is personally responsible for all of the parternship's debts.
3. The **limited partnership**, which is less common than ordinary partnerships, provides for two types of partners. *General partners* take part in the running of the business and are liable for all the firm's debts. *Limited partners* take no part in the running of the business, and their liability is limited to the amount they actually invest in the enterprise.
4. A **corporation** is a firm regarded in law as having an identity of its own; its owners are not personally responsible for anything that is done in the name of the firm, though its directors may be. The shares of a *private* corporation are not traded on any stock exchange (such as the Toronto or New York Stock Exchanges) whereas the shares of a *public* corporation are.
5. A **state-owned enterprise** is owned by the government but is usually under the direction of a more or less independent, state-appointed board. Although its ownership differs, the organization and legal status of a state-owned enterprise are similar to those of a corporation. In Canada, such state-owned enterprises are called *Crown corporations.*
6. **Non-profit organizations** are established with the explicit objective of providing goods or services to customers, but any profits that are generated remain with the organization and are not claimed by individuals. In many cases, some goods or services are sold to consumers while others are provided free of charge. Non-profit firms therefore earn their revenues from a combination of sales and donations. An example is your local YMCA—it sells memberships to consumers for use of the health facilities, but it also provides free services to needy individuals in the community.

Not all production in the economy takes place within firms. Many government agencies provide goods and services, such as defence, roads, primary and secondary education, and health-care services. In most of these cases, goods and services are provided to citizens without charging directly for their use; costs are financed through the government's general tax revenues.

Firms that have locations in more than one country are often called **multinational enterprises (MNEs)**. Their numbers and importance have increased greatly over the last few decades. A large amount of international trade represents business transactions of MNEs—between different corporations as well as between different regional operations of the same corporation. The growing number of MNEs thus reveals an increasing role for these corporations in the ongoing process of globalization.

myeconlab

For a more detailed discussion of multinational enterprises, and especially their role in determining flows of foreign investment, look for "Multinational Enterprises and Foreign Direct Investment" in the *Additional Topics* section of this book's MyEconLab.

www.myeconlab.com

Financing of Firms

The money a firm raises for carrying on its business is sometimes called its financial capital, as distinct from its real capital, which is the firm's physical assets such as factories, machinery, offices, and stocks of materials and finished goods. Although the use of the term "capital" to refer to both an amount of money and a quantity of goods can be confusing, it will usually be clear from the context which sense is being used.

The basic types of financial capital used by firms are *equity* and *debt*. Equity is the funds provided by the owners of the firm. Debt is the funds borrowed from creditors outside the firm.

Equity In individual proprietorships and partnerships, one or more owners provide much of the required funds. A corporation acquires funds from its owners in return for stocks, shares, or equities (as they are variously called). These are basically ownership certificates. The money goes to the company and the shareholders become owners of the firm, risking the loss of their money, and gaining the right to share in the firm's profits. Profits that are paid out to shareholders are called **dividends.**

dividends Profits paid out to shareholders of a corporation. Sometimes called distributed profits.

One easy way for an established firm to raise money is to retain current profits rather than paying them out to shareholders. Financing investment from such *undistributed profits* has become an important source of funding in modern times. Reinvested profits add to the value of the firm, and hence raise the market value of existing shares; they are funds provided by owners.

Debt The firm's creditors are not owners; they have lent money in return for some form of loan agreement, or IOU. There is a bewildering array of such agreements, which are collectively called *debt instruments* in the business world and **bonds** in economic theory. Each has its own set of characteristics and its own name. Two characteristics are, however, common to all debt instruments issued by firms. First, they carry an obligation to repay the amount borrowed, called the *principal* of the loan. Second, they carry an obligation to make some form of payment to the lender called *interest.* The time at which the principal is to be repaid is called the *redemption date* of the debt. The amount of time between the issue of the debt and its redemption date is called its *term.* See *Applying Economic Concepts 7-1* for more details about debt instruments.

bond A debt instrument carrying a specified amount and schedule of interest payments and (usually) a date for redemption of its face value.

Goals of Firms

The theory of the firm that we study in this book is based on two key assumptions. First, all firms are assumed to be profit-maximizers, seeking to make as much profit for their owners as possible. Second, each firm is assumed to be a single, consistent decision-making unit.

The desire to maximize profits is assumed to motivate all decisions made within a firm, and such decisions are assumed to be unaffected by the peculiarities of the persons making the decisions and by the organizational structure in which they work.

To see what the Canadian Council of Chief Executives thinks about "corporate citizenship," go to **www.ceocouncil.ca** and click on "Corporate and Public Governance."

These assumptions allow the theory to ignore the firm's internal organization and its financial structure. Using these assumptions, economists can predict the behaviour of firms. To do this, they first study the choices open to the firm, establishing the effect that each choice would have on the firm's profits. They then predict that the firm will select the alternative that produces the largest profits.

Is maximizing profit the only thing firms should care about? In recent years there has been much public discussion of the need for firms to be "socially responsible" in

APPLYING ECONOMIC CONCEPTS 7-1

Kinds of Debt Instruments

Most debt instruments can be grouped into three broad classes. First, some debt is in the form of *loans* from financial institutions such as chartered banks. These are private agreements between the firm and the bank usually calling for the periodic payment of interest and repayment of the principal, either at a stipulated future date or "on demand," meaning whenever the bank requests repayment.

Second, *bills* and *notes* are commonly used for short-term loans of up to a year. They carry no fixed interest payments, only a principal value and a redemption date. Interest arises because the borrowing firm sells the new bills that it issues at a price below their redemption value. If, for example, a bill promising to pay $1000 in one year's time is sold to a lender for $950, this gives the lender an interest payment of $50 in one year's time when the bill that he bought for $950 is redeemed for $1000. This makes an interest rate of 5.26 percent per year ((50/950) × 100). Bills are *negotiable,* which means they can be bought and sold in financial markets. So if you buy a 90-day bill from some firm and want your money back 30 days later, you can sell the bill on the open market. The purchaser must be prepared to assume the loan to the firm for the 60 days that it still has to run.

The third type of instrument carries a fixed redemption date, as does a bill, and the obligation to make periodic interest payments, as do most loans. These instruments have many different details and correspondingly many different names, such as *bonds* and *debentures.* They are commonly used for long-term loans—up to 20 or 30 years. A firm that issues a 7-percent 30-year bond of this sort with redemption value of $1000 is borrowing money now and promising to pay $70 a year for 30 years and then to pay $1000 on the redemption date. All such bonds are negotiable. This is important, because few people would be willing to lend money for such long periods of time if there were no way to get it back before the redemption date.

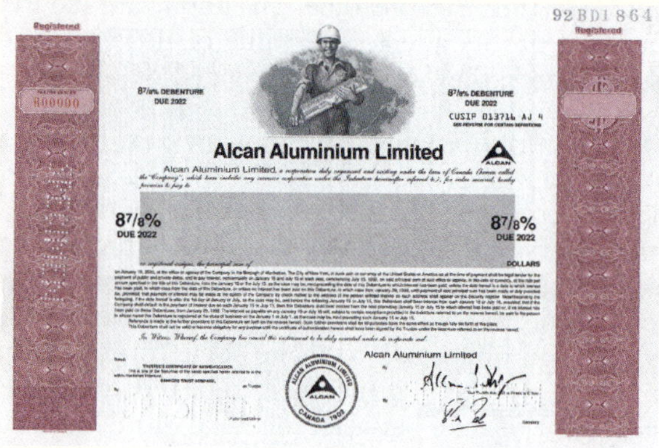

Many large firms borrow money by issuing long-term bonds, like this one issued by Alcan Aluminium Limited.

A relatively new Canadian magazine is devoted entirely to discussing and identifying socially responsible corporate behaviour. See **www.corporateknights.ca**.

addition to being motivated by the pursuit of profits. Some people argue that every firm has a responsibility to society that goes well beyond the responsibility to its shareholders. Others disagree, and argue that by maximizing profits, firms *are* providing a valuable service to society. For a discussion of both sides of this interesting debate, see *Applying Economic Concepts 7-2.*

myeconlab

Firms that choose objectives other than maximizing profits may become a "takeover" target in the market for corporate control. For a more detailed discussion of whether firms actually maximize profits, and the possible consequences of not doing so, look for "Do Firms Really Maximize Profits?" in the *Additional Topics* section of this book's MyEconLab.

www.myeconlab.com

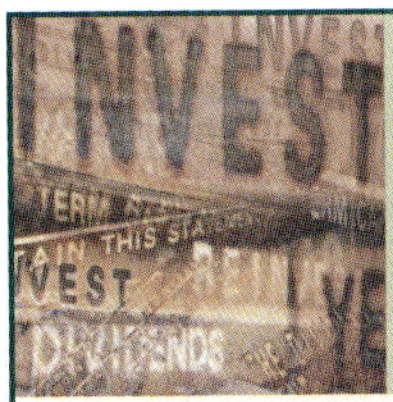

APPLYING ECONOMIC CONCEPTS 7-2

Is It Socially Responsible to Maximize Profits?

In recent years there has been growing public discussion of the need for firms, especially large ones, to behave in a socially responsible manner. Advocates of this view start from the position that unadorned capitalism, and the associated goal of profit maximization, does not serve the broader public interest: Corporate profits clearly help firms' shareholders, but the public interest is not being served. In this view, corporate social responsibility must involve more than simply maximizing profits.

Others argue that firms should indeed focus on the goal of maximizing profits and that, by doing so, they are providing significant benefits to their customers and their employees, not just their shareholders. In addition, it is the pursuit of profits that leads firms to develop new products and production methods, innovations which lie at the heart of ongoing improvements in overall living standards. This opposing view is grounded in the same insight of Adam Smith's that we saw in Chapter 1—that the pursuit of private gain creates benefits for society as a whole.

But what about corporate profits generated through a production process that damages the environment? Surely there are costs imposed on society when firms, through their profit-maximizing decisions, are led to emit poisonous effluents into the air or into local waterways. Or how about firms making unethical business decisions and thereby earning profits at the expense of other parties? Isn't simple profit maximization in these cases socially irresponsible?

One response to these arguments is that it is the duty of governments to set rules in the public interest and then leave firms free to maximize their profits within the constraints set by those rules. For example, the government can design and enforce environmental, labour, accounting, and tax regulations deemed to be in the public interest. Faced with these laws and regulations, private firms are then free to take whatever action is expected to maximize their profits; violations of the established laws or regulations will be met with appropriate penalties. Such a division of responsibilities—the government setting the rules and the firms maximizing profits within the implied constraints—recognizes that although private firms are usually not good judges of the public interest, they are quite good at making decisions about how best to use scarce resources in order to satisfy consumers' desires. Government policymakers, through a process that involves consultation with various groups in society, and the trading off of competing demands, are usually better placed to judge what is and is not in the public interest.

The adoption of this position still recognizes two methods for modifying corporate behaviour. Those who believe that certain corporate actions are not in the public interest can try to convince policymakers to design new rules that will make it costly for firms to continue such actions. Various non-governmental organizations (NGOs), ranging from environmental organizations to consumer-advocacy groups, can play an important role in identifying and publicizing poor corporate behaviour, and also in lobbying the government for change. If the case is persuasive, and sufficient public pressure can be brought to bear on the policymakers, policies will eventually be changed. An example is the relatively recent design of environmental protection policies. Many years ago, Canadian firms could pollute the environment with impunity, whereas today many types of pollution are illegal and some emissions are closely monitored by government agencies.

A second way that firms can be encouraged to change their behaviour is by the expression of consumers' preferences in the marketplace. If enough consumers dislike a certain activity by a specific firm, and these views can be expressed clearly enough in terms of consumers' demand for the firm's products, the firm may be convinced to change its behaviour. In this case, new laws or regulations may not be required; the firm decides, on the basis of the possible decline in sales it will suffer if it continues its unpopular activities, that a change in its behaviour is required for profit maximization. An example occurred in the mid-1990s when Nike was heavily criticized for contracting its production to Asian "sweatshops" where workers were treated poorly and paid very low wages. A widespread boycott of Nike products began and Nike eventually responded by raising wages, improving working conditions, and allowing independent monitors into its factories. The threat of a loss of sales was so powerful that competing companies Reebok and Adidas, who had not yet attracted any negative publicity, began making improvements in their factories just to prevent being tarred by the Nike brush.

What is the bottom line? Corporations *do* change their behaviour over time—in response to changes in laws and regulations, and also in response to changes in consumer attitudes. If governments can be relied upon to establish and enforce rules and regulations in the public interest, and consumers continue to actively express their preferences through their decisions in the marketplace, then firms may be able to be socially responsible and profit-maximizing at the same time.

7.2 PRODUCTION, COSTS, AND PROFITS

We must now specify a little more precisely the concepts of production, costs, and profits that are used by economists.

Production

In order to produce the goods or services that it sells, each firm needs inputs. Hundreds of inputs enter into the production of any specific output. Among the many inputs entering into car production, for example, are steel, rubber, spark plugs, electricity, the site of the factory, machinists, accountants, spray-painting machines, forklift trucks, painters, and managers. These can be grouped into four broad categories:

- inputs to the car firm that are outputs from some other firm, such as spark plugs, electricity, and steel;
- inputs that are provided directly by nature, such as land;
- inputs that are provided directly by people, such as the services of workers and managers; and
- inputs that are provided by the factories and machines used for manufacturing cars.

intermediate products All outputs that are used as inputs by other producers in a further stage of production.

The items that make up the first group of inputs are called **intermediate products.** For example, one firm mines iron ore and sells it to a steel manufacturer. Iron ore is an intermediate product: an output of the mining firm and an input for the steel plant. These appear as inputs only because the stages of production are divided among different firms. If these intermediate products are traced back to their sources, all production can be accounted for by the services of the other three kinds of input, which we first discussed in Chapter 1 and which are called *factors of production.* These are: the gifts of nature, such as soil and raw materials called *land;* physical and mental efforts provided by people, called *labour;* and factories, machines, and other man-made aids to production, called *capital.*

production function A functional relation showing the maximum output that can be produced by each and every combination of inputs.

The **production function** describes the technological relationship between the inputs that a firm uses and the output that it produces. In terms of functional notation, a simplified production function (in which we ignore the role of land) is written as

$$Q = f(L,K)$$

where Q is the flow of output, K is the flow of capital services, and L is the flow of labour services.[1] "f" is the production function itself. Changes in the firm's technology, which alter the relationship between inputs and output, are reflected by changes in the function f.

Costs and Profits

The production function specifies the amount of output that can be obtained from any given amounts of inputs. Firms arrive at what they call profits by taking the revenues

---

[1] Remember that production is a flow: It is so many units per period of time. For example, when we say that production rises from 100 to 101 units, we mean that the rate of production has risen from 100 units each period to 101 units each period.

they obtain from selling their output and deducting all the costs associated with their inputs. When all costs have been correctly deducted, the resulting profits are the return to the owners' capital.

Economic Versus Accounting Profits Compared with accountants, economists use somewhat different concepts of costs and profits. When accountants measure profits, they begin with the firm's revenues and then subtract all of the *explicit* costs incurred by the firm. By explicit costs, we mean the costs that actually involve a purchase of goods or services by the firm. The obvious explicit costs include the hiring of workers, the rental of equipment, interest payments on debt, and the purchase of intermediate inputs.[2]

Practise with Study Guide Chapter 7, Exercise 2 and Short-Answer Question 2.

$$\text{Accounting profits} = \text{Revenues} - \text{Explicit costs}$$

Like accountants, economists subtract from revenues all explicit costs, but they also subtract some *implicit* costs that accountants ignore. These are items for which there is no market transaction but for which there is still an opportunity cost for the firm that should be included in the complete measure of costs. The two most important implicit costs are the opportunity cost of the owner's time (over and above his or her salary) and the opportunity cost of the owner's capital (including a possible risk premium). When this more complete set of costs is subtracted from the firm's revenues, the result is called **economic profit** and is sometimes called *pure profit.*

economic profits The difference between the revenues received from the sale of output and the opportunity cost of the inputs used to make the output. Negative economic profits are called economic losses.

$$\begin{aligned}\text{Economic profits} &= \text{Revenues} - (\text{Explicit costs} + \text{Implicit costs})\\ &= \text{Accounting profits} - \text{Implicit costs}\end{aligned}$$

Opportunity Cost of Owner's Time. Especially in small and relatively new firms, owners spend a tremendous amount of their time developing the business. Often they pay themselves far less than they could earn if they were instead to offer their labour services to other firms. For example, an entrepreneur who opens a restaurant may pay herself only $1000 per month while she is building her business, even though she could earn $4000 per month in her next best alternative job. In this case, there is an *implicit* cost to her firm of $3000 per month that would be missed by the accountant who measures only the explicit cost of her wage at $1000 per month.[3]

Opportunity Cost of Owner's Capital. What is the opportunity cost of the financial capital that the owner has tied up in a firm? The answer is best broken into two parts. First, ask what could be earned by lending this amount to someone else in a *riskless* loan. The owners could have purchased a government bond, which has no significant risk of default. Suppose the return on this is 6 percent per year. This amount is the risk-free rate of return on capital. It is clearly an opportunity cost, since the firm could close down operations, lend out its money, and earn a 6-percent return. Next, ask what the firm could earn in addition to this amount by lending its money to another firm where risk of default was equal to the firm's own risk of loss. Suppose this is an additional 4 percent. This is the risk premium and it is clearly also a cost. If the firm does not expect to earn this much in its own operations, it could close down and lend its money out to some equally risky firm and earn 10 percent (6-percent pure return plus 4-percent risk premium).

[2] *Depreciation* is also among the firm's explicit costs, even though it does not involve a market transaction. Depreciation is a cost to the firm that arises due to the wearing out of its physical capital.

[3] For larger firms that are not operated by their owners, this element of implicit costs is not relevant because the owners usually do not work at the firm. In these cases, the salaries to the firm's managers appear in the firm's accounts as explicit costs.

TABLE 7-1 Accounting Versus Economic Profit for Ruthie's Gourmet Soup Company

Total Revenues ($)		2000
Explicit Costs ($)		
Wages and Salaries	500	
Intermediate Inputs	400	
Rent	80	
Interest on Loan	100	
Depreciation	80	
Total Explicit Costs	1160	
Accounting Profit		840
Implicit Costs ($)		
Opportunity Cost of Owner's Time	160	
Opportunity Cost of Owner's $1500 Capital		
(a) risk-free return of 6%	90	
(b) risk premium of 4%	60	
Total Implicit Costs	310	
Economic Profit		530

Economic profits are less than accounting profits because of implicit costs. The table shows a simplified version of a real profit-and-loss statement. Accounting profits are computed as revenues minus explicit costs (including depreciation), and in the table are equal to $840 for the period being examined. When the correct opportunity cost of the owner's time (in excess of what is recorded in wages and salaries) and capital are recognized as implicit costs, the firm appears less profitable. Economic profits are still positive but equal only $530.

Implicit costs are just as important as explicit costs. Economists include both implicit and explicit costs in their measurement of profits, whereas accounting profits include only explicit costs. Economic profits are therefore less than accounting profits.

Table 7-1 compares economic and accounting profits for a hypothetical owner-operated firm that produces gourmet soups. In that example, both accounting profits and economic profits are positive (though accounting profits are larger). Another possibility, however, is that a firm has positive *accounting* profits even though it has zero *economic* profits. If a firm's accounting profits represent a return just equal to what is available if the owner's capital and time were used elsewhere, then opportunity costs are just being covered. In this case, there are zero *economic* profits, even though the firm's accountant will record positive profits.

Is one of these concepts better than the other? No. Firms are interested in the return to their owners, which is what they call profits. They must also conform with tax laws which define profits in the same way. In contrast, economists are interested in how profits affect resource allocation and their definition is best for that purpose and is the definition used throughout this book. Let's see why economic profit is a useful concept when thinking about resource allocation.

Profits and Resource Allocation When resources are valued by the opportunity-cost principle, their costs show how much these resources would earn if used in their best alternative uses. If the revenues of all the firms in some industry exceed opportunity cost, the firms in that industry will be earning pure or economic profits. Hence, the owners of factors of production will want to move resources into the industry, because the earnings potentially available to them are greater there than in alternative uses. If, in some other industry, firms are incurring economic losses, some or all of this industry's resources are more highly valued in other uses, and owners of the resources will want to move them to those other uses.

Economic profits and losses play a crucial signalling role in the workings of a free-market system.

Economic profits in an industry are the signal that resources can profitably be moved into the industry. Losses are the signal that the resources can profitably be moved elsewhere. Only if there are zero economic profits is there no incentive for resources to move into or out of an industry.

Profit-Maximizing Output

To develop a theory of supply, we need to determine the level of output that will maximize a firm's profit, to which we give the symbol π (the lowercase Greek letter pi). This is the difference between the total revenue (*TR*) each firm derives from the sale of its output and the total cost (*TC*) of producing that output:

$$\pi = TR - TC$$

Thus, what happens to profits as output varies depends on what happens to both revenues and costs.[4] In the rest of this chapter, we develop a theory of how costs vary with output when the firm has some inputs that are fixed. In the next chapter, we allow all inputs to be variable. The theory that we develop about costs and output is common to all firms. In the chapters that follow, we consider how revenue varies with output. Costs and revenues are then combined to determine the profit-maximizing choices for firms in various market situations. The resulting theory can then be used to predict the outcome of changes in such things as demand, costs, taxes, and subsidies. This may seem like quite a long route to get to a theory of supply, and it is, but the payoff when we get there is in being able to understand and evaluate a great deal of economic behaviour.

We start with inputs. Suppose that a firm wishes to increase its rate of output. To do so, it must increase the inputs of one or more factors of production. For the rest of this chapter, we consider a very simple example relating to the production of some industrial product such as newsprint or aluminum. We can best focus on essentials by dealing with only two inputs. The first is labour, to which we give the symbol L. The second is capital, to which we give the symbol K. Thus, we are ignoring land and all intermediate inputs and dealing with the simplified production function introduced earlier in this chapter:

$$Q = f(L,K)$$

where Q is quantity of output per period of time, L is the flow of labour services employed in production, and K is the flow of capital services used. The letter f again stands for the relation that links the inputs to the output.

Time Horizons for Decision Making

Economists classify the decisions that firms make into three types: (1) how best to use existing plant and equipment—the *short run;* (2) what new plant and equipment and production processes to select, given known technical possibilities—the *long run;* and (3) how to encourage, or adapt to, the development of new techniques—the *very long run.*

The Short Run The **short run** is a time period in which the quantity of some inputs, called **fixed factors,** cannot be changed. A fixed factor is usually an element of capital (such as plant and equipment), but it might be land, the services of management, or even the supply of skilled labour. Inputs that are not fixed but instead can be varied in the short run are called **variable factors.**

short run A period of time in which the quantity of some inputs cannot be increased beyond the fixed amount that is available.

fixed factor An input whose quantity cannot be changed in the short run.

variable factor An input whose quantity can be changed over the time period under consideration.

The short run does not correspond to a specific number of months or years. In some industries, it may extend over many years; in others, it may be a matter of months or even weeks. In the electric power industry, for example, it takes three or more years to acquire and install a steam turbine generator. An unforeseen increase in demand will involve a long period during which the extra demand must be met with

[4] From this point on, all costs include both explicit and implicit costs, and thus profits are economic rather than accounting profits.

the existing capital equipment. In contrast, a machine shop can acquire new equipment in a few weeks. An increase in demand will have to be met with the existing stock of capital for only a brief time, after which it can be adjusted to the level made desirable by the higher demand.

The short run is the length of time over which some of the firm's factors of production are fixed.

long run A period of time in which all inputs may be varied, but the existing technology of production cannot be changed.

The Long Run The **long run** is a time period in which all inputs may be varied but in which the basic technology of production cannot be changed. Like the short run, the long run does not correspond to a specific length of time.

The long run corresponds to the situation the firm faces when it is planning to go into business, to expand the scale of its operations, to branch out into new products or new areas, or to change its method of production. The firm's *planning decisions* are long-run decisions because they are made from given technological possibilities but with freedom to choose from a variety of production processes that will use factor inputs in different proportions.

The long run is the length of time over which all of the firm's factors of production can be varied, but its technology is fixed.

very long run A period of time that is long enough for the technological possibilities available to a firm to change.

The Very Long Run Unlike the short run and the long run, the **very long run** is a period of time in which the technological possibilities available to a firm will change. Modern industrial societies are characterized by continuously changing technologies that lead to new and improved products and production methods.

The very long run is the length of time over which all the firm's factors of production and its technology can be varied.

For the remainder of this chapter, we consider costs and production in the short run. We continue with our simplified situation in which there are only two factors of production—labour and capital. We will assume that capital is the fixed factor whereas labour is the variable factor. In the next chapter, we explore the firm's decisions in the long run and the very long run.

7.3 PRODUCTION IN THE SHORT RUN

Consider a Winnipeg-based company producing hockey sticks. The firm owns a small factory with the necessary machinery and equipment—this is the firm's stock of capital, and we will assume that it is fixed in quantity. We call these the *fixed* factors of production. The firm also purchases intermediate inputs such as wood, glue, and electricity and, of course, hires workers. The intermediate inputs and the labour services are the firm's *variable* inputs.

In the following discussion, we will focus on the relationship between the firm's use of labour and the firm's production of output. In particular, we want to know—with a fixed amount of capital—how output changes as the firm varies its amount of labour. The table in Figure 7-1 shows three different ways of looking at how output varies with the quantity of labour services.

FIGURE 7-1 Total, Average, and Marginal Products in the Short Run

Quantity of Labour (L) (1)	Total Product (TP) (2)	Average Product $\left(AP = \frac{TP}{L}\right)$ (3)	Marginal Product $\left(MP = \frac{\Delta TP}{\Delta L}\right)$ (4)
0	0		
1	3	3	3
2	7	3.5	4
3	13	4.3	6
4	22	5.5	9
5	35	7.0	13
6	55	9.2	20
7	80	11.4	25
8	98	12.3	18
9	107	11.9	9
10	113	11.3	6
11	117	10.6	4
12	119	9.9	2
13	120	9.2	1

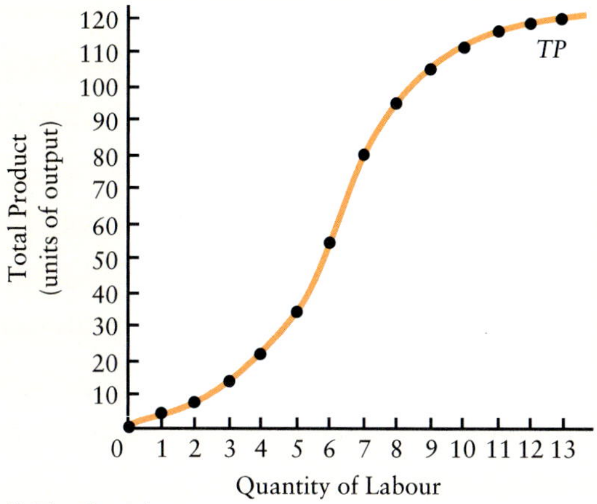

(i) Total product

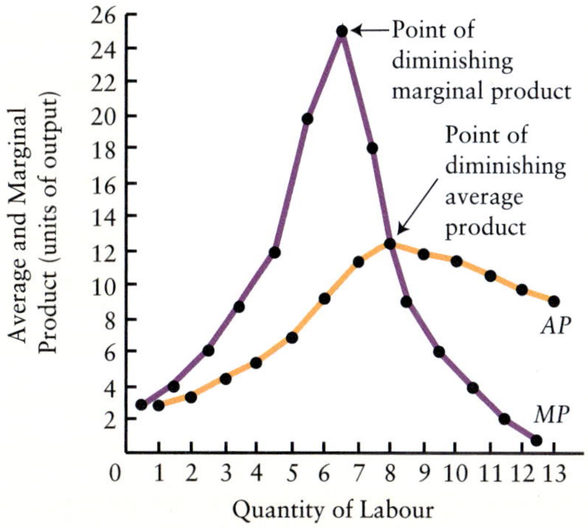

(ii) Average and marginal product

The relation of output to changes in the quantity of the variable factor can be looked at in three different ways. As the quantity of labour increases, total output increases, as shown in column 2. The average product in column 3 is found by dividing the total product in column 2 by the quantity of labour shown in the corresponding row of column 1. The marginal product is shown between the rows because it refers to the change in output from one level of labour input to another. The curves are plotted from the data in the table. In part (i), the *TP* curve shows the total product steadily rising, first at an increasing rate, then at a decreasing rate. This causes both the average and the marginal product curves in part (ii) to rise at first and then decline. Where *AP* reaches its maximum, *MP* = *AP*.

Total, Average, and Marginal Products

Total product (*TP*) is the total amount that is produced during a given period of time. Total product will change as more or less of the variable factor is used in conjunction with the given amount of the fixed factor. This variation is shown in columns 1 and 2 of the table in Figure 7-1. Part (i) of Figure 7-1 plots the schedule from the table. (The shape of the curve will be discussed shortly.)

total product (*TP*) Total amount produced by a firm during some time period.

Average product (*AP*) is the total product divided by the number of units of the variable factor used to produce it. If we let the number of units of labour be denoted by L, the average product is given by

average product (*AP*) Total product divided by the number of units of the variable factor used in its production.

$$AP = \frac{TP}{L}$$

Notice in column 3 of the table that as more labour is used, average product first rises and then falls. The level of labour input at which average product reaches a maximum (8 units of labour in the example) is called the *point of diminishing average productivity.* Up to that point, average product is increasing; beyond that point, average product is decreasing.

marginal product (*MP*) The change in total output that results from using one more unit of a variable factor.

Marginal product (*MP*) is the change in total product resulting from the use of one additional unit of labour. [13] Recalling that the Greek letter Δ (delta) means "the change in," marginal product is given by:

$$MP = \frac{\Delta TP}{\Delta L}$$

Practise with Study Guide Chapter 7, Exercise 3.

Computed values of marginal product are shown in column 4 of the table in Figure 7-1. The values in this column are placed between the other rows of the table to stress that the concept refers to the *change* in output caused by the *change* in quantity of the variable factor. For example, the increase in labour from 3 to 4 units ($\Delta L = 1$) increases output from 13 to 22 ($\Delta TP = 9$). Thus the *MP* equals 9, and it is recorded between 3 and 4 units of labour. Note that *MP* in the table first rises and then falls as output increases. The level of labour input at which marginal product reaches a maximum (between 6 and 7 units of labour in this example) is called the *point of diminishing marginal productivity.*

Part (ii) of Figure 7-1 plots the average product and marginal product curves from the table. Although three different curves are shown in Figure 7-1, they are all aspects of the same single relationship described by the production function. As we vary the quantity of labour, with capital being fixed, output changes. Sometimes it is interesting to look at total product, sometimes at average product, and sometimes at the marginal product.

We will see later in this chapter that understanding firms' costs requires understanding how total, average, and marginal products are related to each other. We now turn to examining two aspects of this relationship.

Diminishing Marginal Product

The variations in output that result from applying more or less of a variable factor to a given quantity of a fixed factor are the subject of a famous economic hypothesis, referred to as the **law of diminishing returns.**

law of diminishing returns The hypothesis that if increasing quantities of a variable factor are applied to a given quantity of fixed factors, the marginal product of the variable factor will eventually decrease.

The law of diminishing returns states that if increasing amounts of a variable factor are applied to a given quantity of a fixed factor (holding the level of technology constant), eventually a situation will be reached in which the marginal product of the variable factor declines.

Notice in Figure 7-1 that the marginal product curve rises at first and then begins to fall with each successive increase in the quantity of labour.

The common sense explanation of the law of diminishing returns is that as output is increased in the short run, more and more of the variable factor is combined with a given amount of the fixed factor. As a result, each unit of the variable factor has less and less of the fixed factor to work with. When the fixed factor is capital and the variable factor is labour, each unit of labour gets a declining amount of capital to assist it as the total output grows. It is not surprising, therefore, that sooner or later, equal increases in labour eventually begin to add less and less to total output.

To illustrate the concept, consider the number of workers in our hockey-stick manufacturing firm. If there is only one worker, that worker must do all the tasks, shifting from one to another and becoming competent at each. As a second, third, and subsequent workers are added, each can specialize in one task, becoming expert at it. One can cut the wood into the required pieces, the second can glue the pieces together, and the third worker can do the necessary planing and sanding. This process, as we noted in Chapter 1, is called the *division of labour.* If additional workers allow more efficient divisions of labour, marginal product will rise: Each newly hired worker will add more to total output than each previous worker did. However, according to the law of diminishing returns, the scope for such increases must eventually disappear, and sooner or later the marginal products of additional workers must decline. When the decline takes place, each additional worker will increase total output by less than did the previous worker.

Eventually, as more and more of the variable factor is employed, marginal product may reach zero and even become negative. It is not hard to see why if you consider the extreme case, in which there would be so many workers in a limited space that additional workers would simply get in the way, thus reducing the total output.

Empirical confirmation of diminishing marginal returns occurs frequently. Some examples are illustrated in *Applying Economic Concepts 7-3*. But one might wish that it were not so. There would then be no reason to fear a food crisis caused by the population explosion in developing countries. If the marginal product of additional workers applied to a fixed quantity of land were constant, food production could be expanded in proportion to population growth merely by keeping a constant fraction of the population on farms. With fixed techniques, however, diminishing returns dictate an inexorable decline in the marginal product of each additional worker because an expanding population must work with a fixed supply of agricultural land.

Thus, except where it is offset by sufficiently powerful improvements in the techniques of production, continuous population growth would bring with it, according to the law of diminishing returns, declining living standards and eventually widespread famine. Because he did not appreciate the extent to which agricultural technologies would be improved over time, the English economist Thomas Malthus (1766–1834) predicted that the increase in the world's population would be accompanied by such a fall in living standards. His gloomy (and incorrect) forecast is discussed further in the next chapter.

The Average–Marginal Relationship

We have so far examined the concept of diminishing *marginal* returns; but *average* returns are also expected to diminish. If increasing quantities of a variable factor are applied to a given quantity of fixed factors, the average product of the variable factor will eventually decrease. **[14]**

Notice that in part (ii) of Figure 7-1, the *MP* curve cuts the *AP* curve at the *AP*'s maximum point. This is not a matter of luck or the way the artist just happened to draw the figure. Rather, it illustrates a fundamental property of the relationship between average and marginal product curves, one that is important to understand.

If you have a portfolio of financial assets that earns 10 percent per year, adding a new asset will only increase the portfolio's average rate of return if the return on the new (marginal) asset exceeds 10 percent.

APPLYING ECONOMIC CONCEPTS 7-3

Three Examples of Diminishing Returns

Sport Fishing

British Columbia's Campbell River, a noted sport-fishing area, has long been the centre of a thriving, well-promoted tourist trade. As sport fishing has increased over the years, the total number of fish caught has steadily increased, but the number of fish *per person fishing* has decreased and the average hours fished for each fish caught has increased.*

Pollution Control

When Southern California Edison was required to modify its Mojave power plant to reduce the amount of pollutants emitted into the atmosphere, it discovered that a series of filters applied to the smokestacks could do the job. A single filter eliminated one-half of the discharge. Five filters in series reduced the discharge to the 3 percent allowed by law. When a state senator proposed a new standard that would permit no more than 1 percent of the pollutant to be emitted, the company brought in experts who testified that this would require at least 15 filters per stack and would triple the cost. In other words, increasing the number of filters leads to diminishing marginal returns in pollution reduction.

Wartime Protection

During the early days of the Second World War, so few naval ships were available that each North Atlantic convoy had only a few escort vessels to protect it from German submarines. The inadequate number of escorts sank very few submarines. As the construction program made more ships available, the escorts could protect the whole convoy more effectively: Some could close in on the various flanks; others could hunt farther afield. Not only did the total number of submarines sunk per convoy rise, but also the number of submarines sunk per escort vessel rose. Still later in the war, as each successive convoy was provided with more and more escort vessels, the number of submarines sunk per convoy continued to rise, but the number of submarines sunk *per escort vessel* began to fall sharply. Total output (submarines sunk) increased, but marginal output per escort vessel fell.

*For a *given stock of fish* and increasing numbers of boats, this example is a good illustration of the law of diminishing returns. But in recent years the story has become more complicated as overfishing has depleted the stock of fish. We examine the reasons for overfishing in Chapter 16.

The average product curve slopes upward as long as the marginal product curve is *above* it; whether the marginal product curve is itself sloping upward or downward is irrelevant. For example, if an additional worker is to raise the average product of all workers, that additional worker's output must be greater than the average output of the other workers. In other words, in order for the average product to rise, the marginal product must exceed the average product. [15]

The relationship between marginal and average measures is very general. If the marginal is greater than the average, the average must be rising; if the marginal is less than the average, the average must be falling. For example, if you had a 3.6 cumulative grade point average (GPA) through last semester and in this (marginal) semester you get only a 3.0 GPA, your cumulative GPA will fall. To increase your cumulative GPA, you must score better in this (marginal) semester than you have on average in the past—that is, to increase the average, the marginal must be greater than the average.

7.4 COSTS IN THE SHORT RUN

We now shift our attention from production to costs. The majority of firms cannot influence the prices of the inputs that they employ; instead they must pay the going market price for their inputs. For example, a shoe factory in Montreal, a metals manufacturer in Sarnia, a rancher in Red Deer, and a boat builder in Prince Rupert are each too small a part of the total demand for the factors that they use to be able to influence their prices significantly. The firms must pay the going rent for the land that they need, the going wage rate for the labour that they employ, and the going interest rate that banks charge for loans; so it is with most other firms. Given these prices and the physical returns summarized by the product curves, the costs of different levels of output can be calculated.

Defining Short-Run Costs

There are several different types of costs that are relevant in the short run, and we must be careful to get them straight. They are all related to the product concepts that we have just discussed.

Total Cost (TC). Total costs are the sum of all costs that the firm incurs to produce a given level of output. **Total cost** is divided into two parts: total fixed cost and total variable cost.

total cost (*TC*) The total cost of producing any given level of output; it can be divided into *total fixed cost* and *total variable cost.*

$$TC = TFC + TVC$$

Total Fixed Cost (TFC). Total fixed cost is the cost of the fixed factor(s). This does not vary with the level of output; it is the same whether output is one unit or 1000 units. **Total fixed cost** is also referred to as *overhead cost.* An example of a fixed cost is the annual cost associated with renting a factory (or servicing the debt incurred to build a factory). Whether the level of output increases or decreases, this annual cost does not change.

total fixed cost (*TFC*) All costs of production that do not vary with the level of output.

Total Variable Cost (TVC). **Total variable cost** is the cost of the variable factors. It varies directly with the level of output—that is, it rises when output rises and it falls when output falls. Examples of variable costs are the cost of labour and intermediate inputs that are used to produce output. As the level of output increases or decreases, the amount of labour and intermediate inputs required for production will typically change in the same direction.

total variable cost (*TVC*) Total costs of production that vary directly with the level of output.

Average Total Cost (ATC). The total cost of producing any given number of units of output divided by that number of units tells us the **average total cost** per unit of output. We let Q be the total units of output (what we earlier referred to as total product, TP). Since total cost is divided into fixed and variable costs, we can also divide average total cost into its fixed and variable components:

average total cost (*ATC*) Total cost of producing a given output divided by the number of units of output; it can also be calculated as the sum of average fixed costs and average variable costs. Also called *unit cost* or *average cost.*

$$ATC = TC/Q$$

$$ATC = AFC + AVC$$

Average Fixed Cost (AFC). Total fixed cost divided by the number of units of output tells us the average fixed cost per unit of output. **Average fixed cost** declines continuously as output increases because the amount of the fixed cost attributed to each unit of output falls. This is known as *spreading overhead.*

average fixed cost (*AFC*) Total fixed costs divided by the number of units of output.

$$AFC = TFC/Q$$

average variable cost (*AVC*) Total variable costs divided by the number of units of output.

marginal cost (*MC*) The increase in total cost resulting from increasing output by one unit.

Average Variable Cost (AVC). Total variable cost divided by the number of units of output tells us the average variable cost per unit of output. For reasons that we will soon see, **average variable cost** first declines as output rises, reaches a minimum, and then increases as output continues to rise.

$$AVC = TVC/Q$$

Marginal Cost (MC). The increase in total cost resulting from a one-unit increase in the level of output is called **marginal cost.** (Marginal costs are always marginal *variable* costs because fixed costs do not change as output varies.) Marginal cost is calculated as the change in total cost divided by the change in output that brought it about: [16]

$$MC = \Delta TC/\Delta Q$$

Short-Run Cost Curves

Practise with Study Guide Chapter 7, Exercise 6.

Using the firm's production relationships from Figure 7-1, suppose the price of labour is $20 per unit and the price of capital is $10 per unit. Also suppose the firm has 10 units of capital (the fixed factor). The firm's resulting costs are shown in Table 7-2.

Columns 4 through 6 in Table 7-2 show the firm's total costs. *TFC* is simply $10 per unit of capital times 10 units of capital. *TVC* is $20 per unit of labour times the increasing amount of labour shown in column 2. *TC* is the sum of *TFC* and *TVC*. Columns 7 through 9 show the average costs. For each average cost concept, the number is computed as the total cost from columns 4, 5, or 6 divided by the number of units of output shown in column 3.

TABLE 7-2 Short-Run Costs: Fixed Capital and Variable Labour

Inputs		Output	Total Costs			Average Costs			Marginal Cost
Capital (*K*) (1)	Labour (*L*) (2)	(*Q*) (3)	Fixed (*TFC*) (4)	Variable (*TVC*) (5)	Total (*TC*) (6)	Fixed (*AFC*) (7)	Variable (*AVC*) (8)	Total (*ATC*) (9)	(*MC*) (10)
10	0	0	$100	$0	$100	—	—	—	
10	1	3	100	20	120	$33.33	$6.67	$40.00	$6.67
10	2	7	100	40	140	14.29	5.71	20.00	5.00
10	3	13	100	60	160	7.69	4.62	12.31	3.33
10	4	22	100	80	180	4.55	3.64	8.18	2.22
10	5	35	100	100	200	2.86	2.86	5.71	1.54
10	6	55	100	120	220	1.82	2.18	4.00	1.00
10	7	80	100	140	240	1.25	1.75	3.00	0.80
10	8	98	100	160	260	1.02	1.63	2.65	1.11
10	9	107	100	180	280	0.93	1.68	2.62	2.22
10	10	113	100	200	300	0.88	1.77	2.65	3.33
10	11	117	100	220	320	0.85	1.88	2.74	5.00
10	12	119	100	240	340	0.84	2.02	2.86	10.00
10	13	120	100	260	360	0.83	2.17	3.00	20.00

These cost schedules are computed from the product curves of Figure 7-1, given the price of capital of $10 per unit and the price of labour of $20 per unit.

Column 10 shows the marginal cost. For each *change* in the level of output, *MC* is equal to the change in *TC* divided by the change in output. For example, as output increases from 22 to 35 units, total costs rise from \$180 to \$200. Thus, marginal cost over this range of output is equal to \$20/13 = \$1.54.

The graphs in Figure 7-2 plot the cost curves from the data in Table 7-2. Part (i) plots the various total cost curves and shows that *TVC* rises at a decreasing rate until output is approximately 60 units. For output levels above 60, *TVC* rises at an increasing rate. Total fixed costs (*TFC*), of course, do not vary as the level of output changes. Since *TFC* is horizontal, the shape of *TC* comes from the shape of *TVC*.

Part (ii) of Figure 7-2 plots the average cost curves and the marginal cost curve. Notice that the *MC* curve cuts the *ATC* curve and the *AVC* curve at their lowest points. This is another example of the relationship between a marginal and an average curve. The *ATC* curve slopes downward whenever the *MC* curve is below it; it slopes upward whenever the *MC* curve is above it. Now let's consider the various curves in a little more detail.

The *AFC*, *AVC*, and *ATC* Curves In part (ii) of Figure 7-2, the average fixed cost (*AFC*) curve is steadily declining as output rises. Since there is a given amount of capital with a total fixed cost of \$100, increases in the level of output lead to a steadily declining fixed cost per unit of output. This is the phenomenon of *spreading overhead*.

The average variable cost (*AVC*) curve shows the variable cost per unit of output. It declines as output rises, reaching a minimum at approximately 100 units of output. As output increases above this level, *AVC* rises.

Since average total cost (*ATC*) is simply the sum of *AFC* and *AVC*, it follows that the *ATC* curve is derived geometrically by vertically adding the *AFC* and *AVC* curves. That is, for each level of output, the point on the *ATC* curve is derived by adding together the values of *AFC* and *AVC*. The result is an *ATC* curve that declines initially as output increases, reaches a minimum, and then rises as output increases further. Economists usually refer to this as a "U-shaped" *ATC* curve.

The *MC* Curve Figure 7-2 also shows the marginal cost (*MC*) curve. Notice that the points on the curve are plotted at the *midpoint* of the output interval shown in the table (because marginal cost refers to the *change* in cost as output rises from one level to another). For example, when we plot the marginal cost of \$1.54 as output increases from 22 to 35 units, the point is plotted at an output level of 28.5 units (the midpoint between 22 and 35). The *MC* curve declines steadily as output initially increases, reaches a minimum somewhere near 70 units of output, and then rises as output increases further.

Why U-Shaped Cost Curves? It is clear from Figure 7-2 that the *AVC*, *ATC*, and *MC* curves are all U-shaped. What explains this shape?

Recall that the *MP* and *AP* curves in Figure 7-1 are both "hill-shaped" (an inverted "U") whereas the *AVC* and *MC* curves are both U-shaped. Is this just a coincidence, or is there some relationship between the two sets of curves? The answer is that this is no coincidence. Since labour input adds directly to cost, it should not surprise you that the relationship between labour input and output—the *AP* and *MP* curves—is closely linked to the relationship between output and cost—the *AVC* and *MC* curves.

Consider first the relationship between the *AP* and *AVC* curves. The *AP* curve shows that as the amount of labour input increases, the average product of labour rises, reaches a maximum, and then eventually falls. But each unit of labour adds the same amount to total variable cost (\$20 in this example). Thus, each additional worker adds the same amount to cost but a different amount to output. When output per worker (*AP*) is rising, the variable cost per unit of output (*AVC*) is falling, and when

Practise with Study Guide Chapter 7, Exercises 4 and 5.

FIGURE 7-2 Total, Average, and Marginal Cost Curves

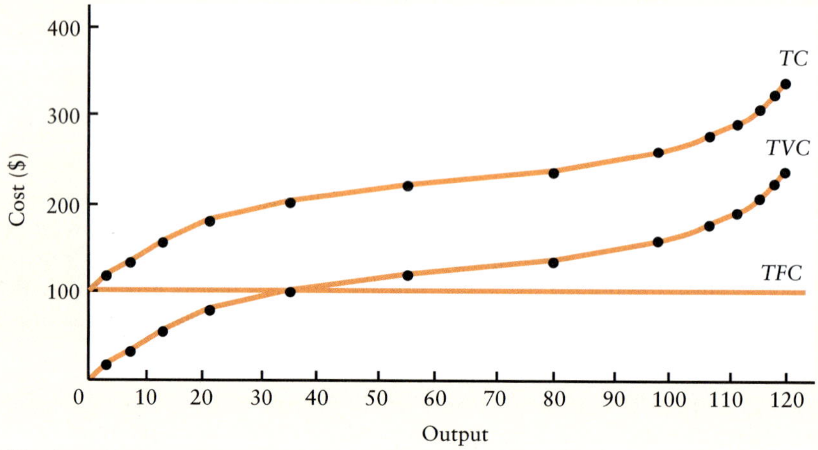

(i) Total cost curves

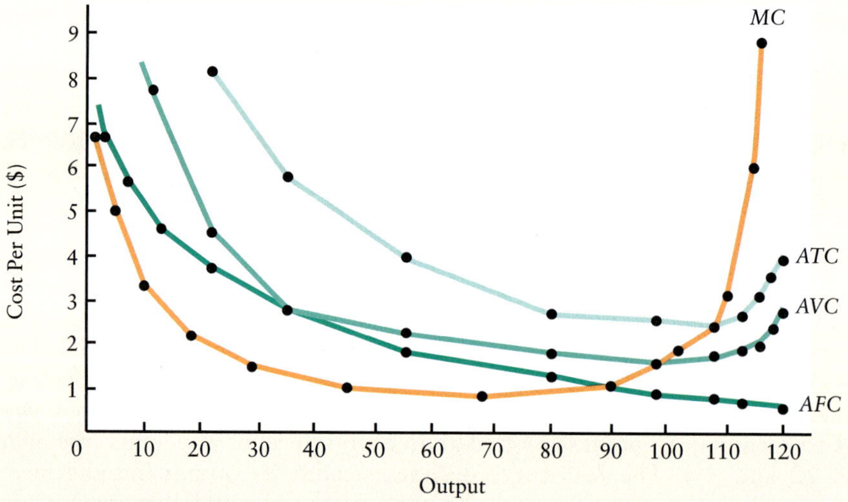

(ii) Marginal and average cost curves

These curves are plotted from the data in Table 7-2. Total fixed cost does not vary with output. Total variable cost and the total of all costs ($TC = TVC + TFC$) rise with output, first at a decreasing rate, then at an increasing rate. The total cost curves in (i) give rise to the average and marginal curves in (ii). Average fixed cost (*AFC*) declines as output increases. Average variable cost (*AVC*) and average total cost (*ATC*) fall and then rise as output increases. Marginal cost (*MC*) does the same, intersecting the *ATC* and *AVC* curves at their minimum points. Capacity output is at the minimum point of the *ATC* curve, which is an output of about 105 in this example.

output per worker (*AP*) is falling, average variable cost (*AVC*) is rising. *AVC* is at its minimum when *AP* reaches its maximum. [17]

Eventually diminishing average product of the variable factor implies eventually increasing average variable cost.

Exactly the same logic applies to the relationship between the *MP* and *MC* curves. Since each unit of labour adds the same amount to cost but has a different marginal product, it follows that when *MP* is rising *MC* is falling, and when *MP* is falling *MC* is rising. The *MC* curve reaches its minimum when the *MP* curve reaches its maximum. [18]

Eventually diminishing marginal product of the variable factor implies eventually increasing marginal costs.

Finally, we can return to the *ATC* curve to consider its shape. Since *ATC* = *AFC* + *AVC*, the *ATC* curve gets its shape from both the *AFC* and *AVC* curves. The *AFC* curve is steadily declining as a given amount of overhead (fixed factor) is spread over an increasing number of units of output. And the *AVC* curve is U-shaped for the reasons we have just seen regarding the relationship between *AP* and *AVC*. It follows that the *ATC* curve only begins to rise (after reaching its minimum) when the effect of the increasing *AVC* dominates the effect of the declining *AFC*. We therefore see the *ATC* curve reaching its minimum at a level of output above where *AVC* reaches its minimum.

Capacity

The level of output that corresponds to the minimum short-run average total cost is often called the *capacity* of the firm. In this sense, capacity is the largest output that can be produced without encountering rising average costs per unit. In part (ii) of Figure 7-2, capacity output is about 105 units, but higher outputs can be achieved, provided that the firm is willing to accept the higher per-unit costs that accompany any level of output that is "above capacity." A firm that is producing at an output less than the point of minimum average total cost is said to have *excess capacity*.

The technical definition gives the word *capacity* a meaning that is different from the one used in everyday speech, in which it often means an upper limit that cannot be exceeded. The technical definition is, however, a useful concept in economic and business discussions.

Shifts in Short-Run Cost Curves

Remember that a firm's short-run cost curves are drawn holding two things constant. First, the amount of the fixed factor used by the firm is held constant (indeed, it is the existence of such a fixed factor that ensures we are in the short run). Second, factor prices—the price per unit of labour and the price per unit of capital—are held constant. How would changes in factor prices and in the amount of the fixed factor affect the firm's short-run cost curves?

Changes in Factor Prices Factor prices change frequently, sometimes dramatically, and such changes naturally affect firms' costs. Consider a change in the wage, the price of a unit of labour services. An increase in the wage increases variable costs, leaves fixed costs unaffected, and therefore increases the firm's total costs. Since marginal costs are always marginal *variable* costs, such a change will also increase the firm's marginal costs. An increase in the price of the variable factor will therefore cause an upward shift in the firm's *ATC* and *MC* curves, as shown in Figure 7-3.

Now consider an increase in the price of a unit of the fixed factor. The firm's total *fixed* costs will rise, but its variable costs will be unaffected. Thus, in a diagram like Figure 7-3, the *ATC* curve will shift up but the *MC* curve will not move.

FIGURE 7-3 An Increase in Variable Input Prices

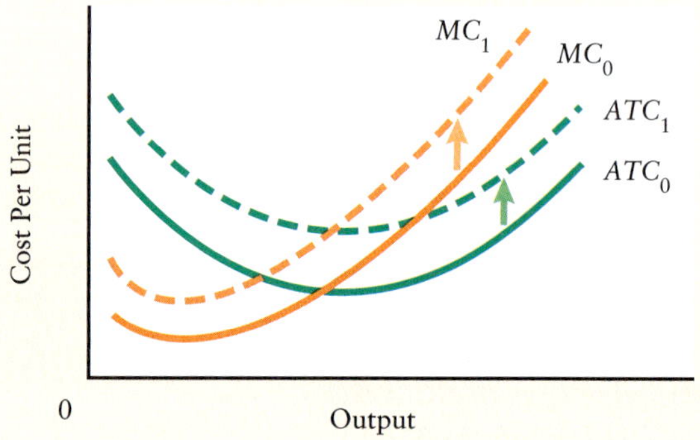

A change in the price of a variable input shifts the average total cost curve and the marginal cost curve. The original average total cost and marginal cost curves are shown by ATC_0 and MC_0. A rise in the price of a variable input—for example, the wage rate—raises the cost of producing each level of output. As a result, the average total cost curve and the marginal cost curve shift upward to ATC_1 and MC_1.

Changes in the Amount of the Fixed Factor In the short run, the firm has a fixed amount of some factor of production. Economists usually think of physical capital as the fixed factor in the short run, especially the physical capital embodied in a plant or factory. What happens to the firm's production costs if it increases the size of its factory?

There are two effects from such a change. First, once the larger factory is in place, the firm's total fixed costs have increased. Second, the increase in the size of the factory means that labour and other variable factors now have more physical capital with which to work, and this generally increases their average and marginal product, and thus reduces marginal and average costs (at any given level of output). What is the combined effect of these two forces?

The overall effect on the *ATC* curve is difficult to predict without having more information about the firm's technology. It depends on how much the firm's output rises when it increases its use of *all* factors. In other words, we need to have more detailed information about the firm's production function before we know how a change in the firm's plant size will affect its *ATC* curve.

Changing from one plant size to another is considered by economists to be a long-run decision by the firm. This brings us to the next chapter, in which we explore how firms make decisions in a setting in which all factors of production are variable.

SUMMARY

7.1 WHAT ARE FIRMS? LO 1

- Production is organized either by private-sector firms, which take four main forms—single proprietorships, ordinary partnerships, limited partnerships, and corporations—or by state-owned enterprises and non-profit organizations.
- Modern firms finance themselves by selling shares, reinvesting their profits, or borrowing from lenders such as banks.
- A firm's profit is the difference between its total revenue and its total costs.
- Economists usually assume that firms attempt to maximize profits.

7.2 PRODUCTION, COSTS, AND PROFITS LO 2

- The production function relates inputs of factor services to output.
- Accounting profit is the difference between the firm's revenues and its explicit costs, including labour costs, capital costs, and the costs of intermediate inputs.

- Economic profit is the difference between the firm's revenues and total costs, including both explicit and implicit costs. Implicit costs include the opportunity cost of the owner's time (for owner-managed firms) and capital.
- Economic profits play a key role in resource allocation. Positive economic profits attract resources into an industry; negative economic profits induce resources to move elsewhere.
- Economists divide the firm's production decisions into three time frames. The short run involves decisions in which one or more factors of production are fixed. The long run involves decisions in which all factors are variable but technology is unchanging. The very long run involves decisions in which technology can change.

7.3 PRODUCTION IN THE SHORT RUN

LO 3

- The theory of short-run costs is concerned with how output varies as different amounts of the variable factors are combined with given amounts of the fixed factors. Total, average, and marginal product describe relationships between output and the quantity of the variable factors of production.
- The law of diminishing returns asserts that if increasing quantities of a variable factor are combined with given quantities of fixed factors, the marginal and the average products of the variable factor will eventually decrease. For given factor prices, this hypothesis implies that marginal and average costs will eventually rise.

7.4 COSTS IN THE SHORT RUN

LO 4

- Short-run average total cost curves are often U-shaped because average productivity increases at low levels of outputs but eventually declines sufficiently to offset advantages of spreading overheads. The output corresponding to the minimum point of a short-run average total cost curve is called the plant's capacity.
- Changes in factor prices shift the short-run cost curves—upward when prices rise and downward when prices fall.

KEY CONCEPTS

Forms of business organization
Methods of financing modern firms
Profit maximization
Inputs and factors of production
Accounting versus economic profits
Economic profits and resource allocation
Short run, long run, and very long run
Total product, average product, and marginal product
The law of diminishing returns
Total cost, marginal cost, and average cost
The relationship between productivity and cost
Short-run cost curves
Capacity

STUDY EXERCISES

1. Fill in the blanks to make the following statements correct.
   a. The relationship between the inputs of factor services and output is called the _______________.
   b. A firm earning positive accounting profits could have zero _______________ if the owner's capital is earning exactly its _______________.
   c. A firm's planning decisions made when some inputs are variable but others are fixed are made in the time period known as the _______________. The time period over which all factors are variable but technology is fixed is known as the _______________.

2. Fill in the blanks to make the following statements correct.

   a. The _______________ tells us that as more of a variable factor is used in combination with given quantities of fixed factors, the marginal product of the variable factor will eventually decrease.
   b. The _______________ is the change in total output resulting from the use of one additional unit of the variable factor.
   c. If average product and marginal product curves are plotted on a graph, the *AP* curve is rising as long as the *MP* curve lies _______________ the *AP* curve. The *AP* curve is falling when the *MP* curve lies _______________ the *AP* curve.

3. Fill in the blanks to make the following statements correct.

   a. For given factor prices, when average product per worker is at a maximum, average variable cost is at a _______________.
   b. If marginal costs are above average costs, then producing one more unit of output will _______________ the average cost.
   c. The level of output that corresponds to a firm's minimum short-run average total cost is called the _______________ of the firm.

4. Wacky Wintersports Inc. can produce snowboards according to the following schedule. Complete the table by calculating the marginal and average products.

Inputs of Labour (per week)	Number of Snowboards (per week)	Average Product	Marginal Product
0	0	—	
			—
1	2	—	
			—
2	5	—	
			—
3	9	—	
			—
4	14	—	
			—
5	18	—	
			—
6	21	—	
			—
7	23	—	
			—
8	24	—	

5. Consider the revenues and costs in 2007 for Spruce Decor Inc., an Alberta-based furniture company entirely owned by Mr. Harold Buford.

Furniture Sales	$645 000
Catalogue Sales	$ 12 000
Labour Costs	$325 000
Materials Costs	$157 000
Advertising Costs	$ 28 000
Debt-Service Costs	$ 32 000

   a. What would accountants determine Spruce Decor's profits to be in 2007?
   b. Suppose Mr. Buford has $400 000 of capital invested in Spruce Decor. Also suppose that equally risky enterprises earn a 16-percent rate of return on capital. What is the opportunity cost for Mr. Buford's capital?
   c. What are the *economic* profits for Spruce Decor in 2007?
   d. If Spruce Decor's economic profits were typical of furniture makers in 2007, what would you expect to happen in this industry? Explain.

6. Consider an example of a production function that relates the monthly production of widgets to the monthly use of capital and labour services. Suppose the production function takes the following specific algebraic form:

$$Q = KL - (0.1)\,L^2$$

where Q is the output of widgets, K is the input of capital services, and L is the input of labour services.

   a. Suppose that, in the short run, K is constant and equal to 10. Fill in the following table.

K	*L*	*Q*
10	5	—
10	10	—
10	15	—
10	20	—
10	25	—
10	30	—
10	40	—
10	50	—

   b. Using the values from the table, plot the values of Q and L on a scale diagram, with Q on the vertical axis and L on the horizontal axis.
   c. Now suppose that K increases to 20 because the firm increases the size of its widget factory. Recompute the value of Q for each of the alternative values of L. Plot the values of Q and L on the same diagram as in (b).
   d. Explain why an increase in K increases the level of Q (for any given level of L).

7. The following table shows how the total output of skates (per month) changes when the quantity of the variable input (labour) changes. The firm's amount of capital is fixed.

Hours of Labour (per month)	Pairs of Skates (per month)	Average Product	Marginal Product
100	200	—	
120	260	—	—
140	350	—	—
160	580	—	—
180	720	—	—
200	780	—	—
220	800	—	—
240	810	—	—

a. Compute the average product of labour for each level of output and fill in the table. Plot the *AP* curve on a scale diagram.

b. Compute the marginal product of labour for each interval (that is, between 100 and 120 hours, between 120 and 140 hours, and so on). Fill in the table and plot the *MP* curve on the same diagram. Remember to plot the value for *MP* at the midpoint of the intervals.

c. Is the "law of diminishing marginal returns" satisfied?

d. Explain the relationship between the marginal product of labour and the average product of labour.

8. Consider the table below, which shows the total fixed costs (*TFC*) and total variable costs (*TVC*) for producing specialty bicycles in a small factory with a fixed amount of capital.

Output Per Year (thousands of bicycles)	*TFC*	*TVC*	*AFC*	*AVC*	*ATC*
	(thousands of dollars)				
1	200	40	—	—	—
2	200	70	—	—	—
3	200	105	—	—	—
4	200	120	—	—	—
5	200	135	—	—	—
6	200	155	—	—	—
7	200	185	—	—	—
8	200	230	—	—	—
9	200	290	—	—	—
10	200	350	—	—	—
11	200	425	—	—	—

a. Compute average fixed costs (*AFC*) for each level of output.

b. Compute average variable costs (*AVC*) for each level of output.

c. Compute average total cost (*ATC*) for each level of output. What level of output (per year) is the firm's "capacity"?

d. Plot the *AFC*, *AVC*, and *ATC* curves on a scale diagram with dollars on the vertical axis and the level of output on the horizontal axis.

9. myeconlab This question requires you to understand the relationship between total product, average product, and marginal product. Each of the diagrams below shows how total product (*TP*) changes as the quantity of the variable input (which we call *L*) changes. These reflect four *different* production functions.

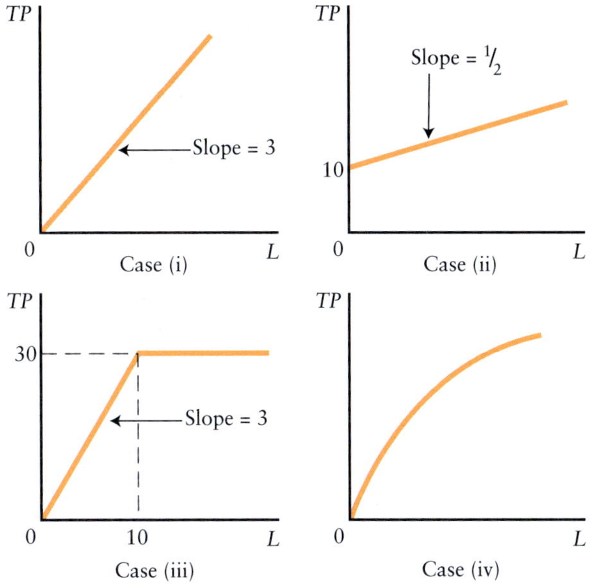

a. In each case, describe in words how total output depends on the amount of variable input.

b. For each production function, draw a diagram showing the average product (*AP*) curve. (Recall that *AP* is given by total output divided by total variable input. The value of *AP* is also equal to the slope of a straight line from the origin to the *TP* curve.)

c. On the same diagram, draw the marginal product (*MP*) curve. (Recall that *MP* is given by the *change* in total output divided by the *change* in the variable input. The value of *MP* is also equal to the slope of a tangent line to the *TP* curve.)

d. Is the relationship between *AP* and *MP* discussed in the text satisfied by each of the production functions?

10. In 1921, a classic set of experiments with chemical fertilizers was performed at the Rothampsted Experimental Station, an agricultural research institute in Hertfordshire, England. Researchers applied different amounts of a particular fertilizer to 10 apparently identical plots of land. The results for one test, using identical seed grain, are listed in the following table. Compute the average and marginal product of fertilizer, and identify the (approximate) points of diminishing average and marginal productivity.

Plot	Fertilizer Dose	Yield Index*
1	15	104.2
2	30	110.4
3	45	118.0
4	60	125.3
5	75	130.2
6	90	131.4
7	105	131.9
8	120	132.3
9	135	132.5
10	150	132.8

* Yield without fertilizer = 100.

DISCUSSION QUESTIONS

1. Which concept of profits—accounting or economic—is implied in the following quotations?
   a. "Profits are necessary if firms are to stay in business."
   b. "Profits are signals for firms to expand production and investment."
   c. "Accelerated depreciation allowances reduce profits and thus benefit the company's owners."
2. Does the short run consist of the same number of months for increasing output as for decreasing it? Must the short run in an industry be the same length for all firms in the industry? Under what circumstances might the short run actually involve a longer time span than the very long run for one particular firm?
3. Indicate whether each of the following conforms to the hypothesis of diminishing returns and, if so, whether it refers to marginal returns, average returns, or both.
   a. "The bigger they are, the harder they fall."
   b. "As more and more of the population receives chicken pox vaccinations, the reduction in the chicken pox disease rate for each additional 100 000 vaccinations becomes smaller."
   c. "Five workers produce twice as much today as 10 workers did 40 years ago."
   d. "Diminishing returns set in last year when the rising rural population actually caused agricultural output to fall."
4. Consider the education of a person as a process of production. Regard years of schooling as one variable factor of production. What are the other factors? What factors are fixed? At what point would you expect diminishing returns to set in? For an Einstein, would diminishing returns set in during his lifetime?
5. A carpenter quits his job at a furniture factory to open his own cabinetmaking business. In his first two years of operation, his sales average $100 000 and his operating costs for wood, workshop and tool rental, utilities, and miscellaneous expenses average $70 000. Now his old job at the furniture factory is again available. Should he take it or remain in business for himself? How would you make this decision?
6. The point of minimum average cost is referred to as the capacity of the firm. Yet we draw the average cost curve extending both to the left and to the right of this point. Obviously, a firm can operate below capacity, but how can a firm operate above capacity? Are there any types of firms for which it may be desirable to have a capacity below the level at which the firm may have to produce occasionally or even relatively frequently? Explain.

CHAPTER 8

Producers in the Long Run

LEARNING OBJECTIVES

In this chapter you will learn

1. why profit maximization requires firms to equate the marginal product per dollar spent for all factors.
2. why profit-maximizing firms will use more of the factors whose prices have fallen, and less of the factors whose prices have increased.
3. about the relationship between short-run and long-run cost curves.
4. the importance of technological change and why firms are often motivated to improve their production methods.

In the first part of this chapter, we look at the long run, in which firms are free to vary all factors of production. Recall from the last chapter that different amounts of the fixed factor lead to different short-run cost curves. The choice faced by a firm in the long run is to determine how much of the fixed factor to use—that is, to decide *which* of the several short-run cost curves to be using. Some firms use a great deal of capital and only a small amount of labour. Others use less capital and more labour. Here we examine the effects these choices have on firms' costs, and we look at the conditions that influence these choices.

In the second part of the chapter, we examine the very long run, a period of analysis over which technology changes. The discussion concerns the improvements in technology and productivity that have dramatically increased output and incomes in all industrial countries over centuries. Firms are among the most important economic actors that cause technological advances to take place. Evidence shows that the hypothesis of profit maximization can help us to understand technological changes. Here, as in the short and long run, firms respond to events such as changes in factor prices. But in the very long run, firms often respond by innovating—that is, by developing *new* technologies.

Throughout this chapter, we should remember that the lengths of the various "runs" under consideration are defined by the kinds of changes that can take place, not by calendar time. Thus, we would expect actual firms in any given time period: to be on their short-run cost curves, as described in Chapter 7; to choose among alternative short-run cost curves in the long run, as described in the first part of this chapter; and to change technologies in the very long run as described in the latter part of this chapter.

8.1 THE LONG RUN: NO FIXED FACTORS

In the short run, in which at least one factor is fixed, the only way to produce a given output is to adjust the input of the variable factors. In the long run, in which all factors can be varied, there are numerous ways to produce any given output. For example, the firm could use many machines and few workers, or few machines and many workers. Thus, firms in the long run must choose the type and amount of plant and equipment and the size of their labour force.

technical efficiency When a given number of inputs are combined in such a way as to maximize the level of output.

In making these choices, the profit-maximizing firm will try to be **technically efficient** by using no more of all inputs than necessary—that is, the firm does not want to waste any of its valuable inputs. For example, consider the situation faced by a crate-manufacturing firm. If the firm is *able* to produce 100 crates per day using two machines and eight workers, the firm would be technically *inefficient* if it decided instead to produce only 90 crates while still employing the same amount of (expensive) labour and capital. If the firm decided that it wished to produce only 90 crates per day, technical efficiency requires that it use fewer workers, fewer machines, or both.

Practise with Study Guide Chapter 8, Exercise 1 and Short-Answer Question 1.

Technical efficiency is not enough, however. In order to maximize its profit, the firm must choose from among the many technically efficient options the one that produces a given level of output at the lowest cost. For example, if the firm decides to produce 100 crates per day, it still must decide whether to use two machines and eight workers, or perhaps three machines and six workers. It should choose the combination that minimizes its total costs.

Such choices about how much capital and labour to use are *long-run* choices because all factors of production are assumed to be variable. These long-run planning decisions are important. A firm that decides to build a new steel mill and invest in the required machinery will choose among many alternatives. Once installed, that equipment is fixed for a long time. If the firm makes a wrong choice, its survival may be threatened; if it estimates correctly, it may be rewarded with large profits.

myeconlab

Concepts of efficiency used by economists differ from those used by other professionals, especially engineers. For a detailed explanation of the differences, look for "Explaining Different Concepts of Efficiency" in the *Additional Topics* section of this book's MyEconLab.

www.myeconlab.com

Profit Maximization and Cost Minimization

Any firm that is trying to maximize its profits in the long run should select the production method that produces its output at the lowest possible cost. This implication of the hypothesis of profit maximization is called **cost minimization**: From among the many technically efficient methods of production available to it, the profit-maximizing firm will choose the least costly means of producing whatever level of output it chooses.

cost minimization An implication of profit maximization that firms choose the production method that produces any given level of output at the lowest possible cost.

Long-Run Cost Minimization If it is possible to substitute one factor for another to keep output constant while reducing total cost, the firm is currently not minimizing its costs. In such a situation, the firm should substitute one factor for another factor as long as the marginal product of the one factor *per dollar spent on it* is greater than the marginal product of the other factor *per dollar spent on it*. The firm is not minimizing its costs whenever these two magnitudes are unequal. For example, if an extra dollar spent on labour produces more output than an extra dollar spent on capital, the firm can reduce costs by spending less on capital and more on labour.

Suppose we use K to represent capital, L to represent labour, and p_L and p_K to represent the prices per unit of the two factors. The necessary condition for cost minimization is then:

$$\frac{MP_K}{p_K} = \frac{MP_L}{p_L} \tag{8-1}$$

Whenever the ratio of the marginal product of each factor to its price is not equal for all factors, there are possibilities for factor substitutions that will reduce costs (for a given level of output).

To see why Equation 8-1 must be satisfied when costs are being minimized, consider an example where the equation is *not* satisfied. Suppose the marginal product of capital is 40 units of output and the price of one unit of capital is \$10. Also suppose the marginal product of labour is 20 units of output and the price of one unit of labour is \$2. Then we have:

$$\frac{MP_K}{p_K} = \frac{40}{10} = 4 < \frac{MP_L}{p_L} = \frac{20}{2} = 10$$

Thus, the last dollar spent on capital adds only 4 units to output, whereas the last dollar spent on labour adds 10 units to output. In this case, the firm can reduce the cost of producing its current level of output by using more labour and less capital. Specifically, suppose the firm used two more units of labour and one fewer unit of capital. The two more units of labour would cause output to rise by 40 units and costs to increase by \$4; the one fewer unit of capital would cause output to fall back by 40 units and costs to decline by \$10. After this substitution of labour for capital, output would be unchanged but costs would be lower by \$6. Thus, the original combination of factors was not a cost-minimizing one.

Oil is a very important input in many industries. Increases in the price of oil will lead profit-maximizing firms to substitute away from oil toward other factors of production, whenever that is technically possible.

Of course, as the firm substitutes between labour and capital, the marginal products of both factors, MP_L and MP_K, will change. Specifically, the law of diminishing marginal returns says that, with other inputs held constant, an increase in the amount of one factor used will decrease that factor's marginal product. So as the firm in the previous example reduces its use of K and increases its use of L, MP_K will rise and MP_L will fall. These changes help to restore the equality in Equation 8-1.

By rearranging the terms in Equation 8-1, we can look at the cost-minimizing condition a bit differently.

$$\frac{MP_K}{MP_L} = \frac{p_K}{p_L} \tag{8-2}$$

Practise with Study Guide Chapter 8, Exercise 1 and Short-Answer Question 2.

The ratio of the marginal products on the left side compares the contribution to output of the last unit of capital and the last unit of labour. The right side shows how the cost of an additional unit of capital compares to the cost of an additional unit of labour. If the two sides of Equation 8-2 are the same, then the firm cannot make any substitutions between labour and capital to reduce costs (if output is held constant). However, with the marginal products and factor prices used in the example above, the left side of the equation equals 2 but the right side equals 5; the last unit of capital is twice as productive as the last unit of labour but it is five times as expensive. It will thus pay the firm to switch to a method of production that uses less capital and more labour. If, however, the ratio on the right side were less than the ratio on the left, then it would pay the firm to switch to a method of production that used less labour and more capital. Only when the ratio of marginal products is exactly equal to the ratio of factor prices is the firm using the cost-minimizing production method.[1]

Profit-maximizing firms adjust the quantities of factors they use to the prices of the factors given by the market.

The Principle of Substitution The preceding discussion suggests that profit-maximizing (and therefore cost-minimizing) firms will react to changes in factor prices by changing their methods of production. This is referred to as the **principle of substitution.**

principle of substitution The principle that methods of production will change if relative prices of inputs change, with relatively more of the cheaper input and relatively less of the more expensive input being used.

Suppose the firm's use of capital and labour currently satisfies Equation 8-1. Then consider a decrease in the price of capital while the price of labour remains unchanged. The least-cost method of producing any output will now use less labour and more capital than was required to produce the same output before the factor prices changed.

Methods of production will change if the relative prices of factors change. Relatively more of the cheaper factor and relatively less of the more expensive factor will be used.

The principle of substitution plays a central role in resource allocation because it relates to the way in which individual firms respond to changes in relative factor prices that are caused by the changing relative scarcities of factors in the economy as a whole. Individual firms are motivated to use less of factors that become scarcer to the economy and more of factors that become more plentiful. Here are two examples of the principle of substitution in action.

In many developing countries, labour is used much more intensively in agriculture than is the case in richer, developed countries. This does not mean methods are somehow "backward" in the developing countries; the intensive use of labour simply reflects a cost-minimizing response to low wages.

Over the past three decades, the improvements in computing equipment have led to many changes in everyday life. One change involves customers' transactions with their commercial banks—especially cash deposits and withdrawals. Banks used to employ large numbers of tellers to deal with the hundreds of customers that needed to be serviced each day. Now most retail banking transactions are facilitated with computers and are dealt with either by automated teller machines (ATMs), automated telephone banking, or Internet banking. The dramatic reduction in the price of computers over the past three decades (and also the more modest increase in wages) has encouraged banks to make this substitution of capital for labour.

The principle of substitution can also explain why methods of producing the same product often differ across countries. In Canada, where labour is generally highly skilled and expensive, farmers use elaborate machinery to economize on labour. In China, however, where labour is abundant and

[1] The appendix to this chapter provides a graphical analysis of this condition, which is similar to the analysis of consumer behaviour that we developed in the appendix to Chapter 6.

capital is scarce, a much less mechanized method of production is appropriate. The Western engineer who believes that the Chinese are inefficient because they are using methods long ago discarded in the West is missing the truth about efficiency in the use of resources: Where factor scarcities differ across nations, so will the cost-minimizing methods of production.

Long-Run Cost Curves

We have been discussing a typical firm's cost-minimizing choices between capital and labour. Remember that these are *long-run* decisions because we are assuming that the firm is free to alter the amounts of all factors of production. As we have seen, when all factors can be varied, there exists a least-cost method of producing any given level of output. Thus, with given factor prices, there is a minimum achievable cost for each level of output; if this cost is expressed in terms of dollars per unit of output, we obtain the long-run average cost of producing each level of output. When this minimum cost of producing each level of output is plotted on a graph, the result is called a **long-run average cost (*LRAC*) curve**. Figure 8-1 shows one such curve.

long-run average cost (*LRAC*) curve The curve showing the lowest possible cost of producing each level of output when all inputs can be varied.

The *LRAC* curve is determined by the firm's current technology and by the prices of the factors of production. It is a "boundary" in the sense that points below it are unattainable; points on the curve, however, are attainable if sufficient time elapses for all inputs to be adjusted. To move from one point on the *LRAC* curve to another requires an adjustment in *all* factor inputs, which may, for example, require building a larger, more elaborate factory.

The *LRAC* curve is the boundary between cost levels that are attainable, with known technology and given factor prices, and those that are unattainable.

Just as the short-run cost curves discussed in Chapter 7 relate to the production function describing the physical relationship between factor inputs and output, so does the *LRAC* curve. The difference is that in deriving the *LRAC* curve, there are no fixed factors of production. Thus, since all costs are variable in the long run, we do not need to distinguish between *AVC*, *AFC*, and *ATC*, as we did in the short run; in the long run, there is only one *LRAC* for any given set of input prices.

The Shape of the Long-Run Average Cost Curve The *LRAC* curve shown in Figure 8-1 first falls and then rises. Like the short-run cost curves we saw in Chapter 7, this curve is often described as U-shaped, although empirical studies suggest it is often "saucer-shaped." Consider the three portions of any such saucer-shaped *LRAC* curve.

Decreasing Costs. Over the range of output from zero to Q_m, the firm has falling long-run average costs: An expansion of output permits a reduction of average costs. When long-run average costs fall as output rises, the firm is said to have **economies of scale**. Because the *LRAC* curve is drawn under the assumption of constant factor prices, the decline in long-run average cost occurs because output is increasing *more than* in proportion to inputs as the scale of the firm's production expands. Over this range of output, the decreasing-cost firm is often said to enjoy long-run **increasing returns.**[2]

economies of scale Reduction of long-run average costs resulting from an expansion in the scale of a firm's operations so that more of all inputs is being used.

increasing returns (to scale) A situation in which output increases more than in proportion to inputs as the scale of a firm's production increases. A firm in this situation is a decreasing-cost firm.

Increasing returns may occur as a result of increased opportunities for specialization of tasks made possible by the division of labour. Even the most casual observation of the differences in production techniques used in large and small plants shows that

2 Economists shift back and forth between speaking in physical terms ("increasing returns") and cost terms ("decreasing costs"). As the text explains, the same relationship can be expressed either way.

FIGURE 8-1 A "Saucer-Shaped" Long-Run Average Cost Curve

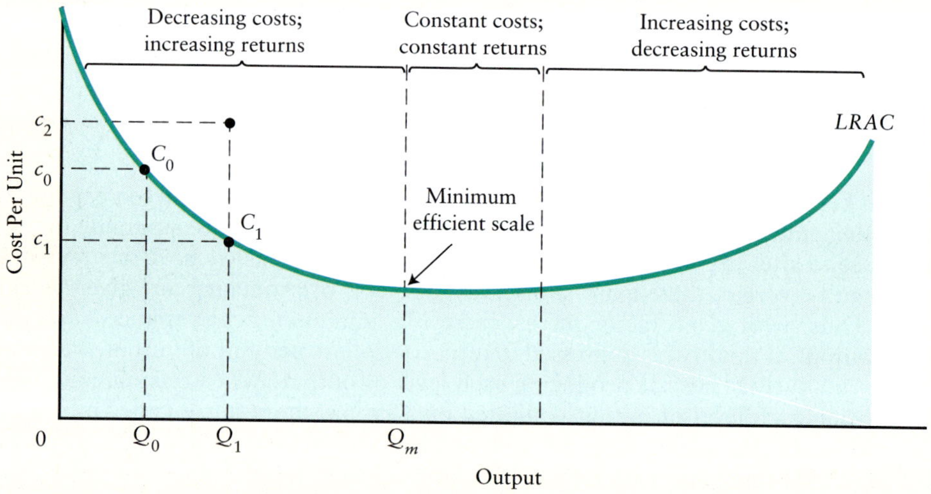

The long-run average cost (*LRAC*) curve is the boundary between attainable and unattainable levels of costs. If the firm wishes to produce output Q_0, the lowest attainable cost is c_0 per unit. Thus, point C_0 is on the *LRAC* curve. At point C_1, the firm has achieved the lowest possible average cost of producing Q_1. Suppose a firm is producing at Q_0 and desires to increase output to Q_1. In the long run, a larger plant can be built and the average cost of c_1 can be attained. However, in the short run, it will not be able to vary all factors, and thus costs per unit will be above c_1, say, c_2. For a range of output beginning at Q_m, the firm attains its lowest possible average cost of production for the given technology and factor prices.

larger plants use greater specialization. These differences arise because large, specialized equipment is useful only when the volume of output that the firm can sell justifies employment of that equipment. For example, assembly lines and body-stamping machinery are cost-minimizing techniques for automobile production only when individual operations are repeated thousands of times. Use of elaborate and very expensive harvesting equipment provides the least-cost method of production on a big farm but not on one of only a few acres.

minimum efficient scale (MES) The smallest output at which *LRAC* reaches its minimum. All available economies of scale have been realized at this point.

constant returns (to scale) A situation in which output increases in proportion to inputs as the scale of production is increased. A firm in this situation is a constant-cost firm.

Constant Costs. In Figure 8-1, the firm's long-run average costs fall until output reaches Q_m, which is known as the firm's **minimum efficient scale.** It is the smallest level of output at which *LRAC* reaches its minimum. The *LRAC* curve is then flat over some range of output. With such a flat portion, the firm would be encountering constant costs over the relevant range of output, meaning that the firm's long-run average costs do not change as its output changes. Because factor prices are assumed to be fixed, the firm's output must be increasing *exactly in proportion to* the increase in inputs. When this happens, the constant-cost firm is said to be exhibiting **constant returns.**

Increasing Costs. When the *LRAC* curve is rising, a long-run expansion in production is accompanied by a rise in average costs. If factor prices are constant, the firm's output must be increasing *less than* in proportion to the increase in inputs. When this happens, the increasing-cost firm is said to encounter long-run **decreasing returns**. Decreasing returns imply that the firm suffers some *diseconomies of scale*.

decreasing returns (to scale) A situation in which output increases less than in proportion to inputs as the scale of a firm's production increases. A firm in this situation is an increasing-cost firm.

Such diseconomies may be associated with the difficulties of managing and controlling an enterprise as its size increases. For example, planning problems do not necessarily vary in direct proportion to size. At first, there may be scale economies as the firm grows and benefits from greater specialization. But, sooner or later, planning and coordination problems may multiply more than in proportion to the growth in size. If so, management costs per unit of output will rise.

Other diseconomies are the possible alienation of the labour force as size increases; it becomes more difficult to provide appropriate supervision as more layers of supervisors and middle managers come between the person at the top and the workers on the shop floor. Control of middle-range managers may also become more difficult. As the firm becomes larger, managers may begin to pursue their own goals rather than devote all of their efforts to making profits for the firm. Much of the "re-engineering" of large firms in the 1990s has been aimed at reducing the extent to which management difficulties increase with firm size, but the problem has not been, and probably cannot be, eliminated entirely.

Practise with Study Guide Chapter 8, Exercise 3.

Note that long-run decreasing returns differ from short-run diminishing returns. In the short run, at least one factor is fixed, and the law of diminishing returns ensures that returns to the variable factor will eventually diminish. In the long run, all factors are variable, and it is possible that physically diminishing returns will never be encountered—at least as long as it is genuinely possible to increase inputs of all factors.

The Relationship Between Long-Run and Short-Run Costs The short-run cost curves from the previous chapter and the long-run cost curve studied in this chapter are all derived from the same production function. Each curve assumes given prices for all factor inputs. The long-run average cost (*LRAC*) curve shows the lowest cost of producing any output when all factors are variable. Each short-run average total cost (*SRATC*) curve shows the lowest cost of producing any output when one or more factors are fixed.

No short-run cost curve can fall below the long-run cost curve because the *LRAC* curve represents the lowest attainable cost for each possible output.

As the level of output is changed, a different-size plant is normally required to achieve the lowest attainable cost. Figure 8-2 shows the *SRATC* curve above the *LRAC* curve at all levels of output except Q_0.

As we saw in the last chapter, any individual *SRATC* curve is just one of many such curves. The *SRATC* curve in Figure 8-2 shows how costs vary as output is varied, holding the plant size constant. Figure 8-3 shows a family of *SRATC* curves, along with a single *LRAC* curve. The *LRAC* curve is sometimes called an *envelope curve* because it encloses a series of *SRATC* cost curves by being tangent to them.

Each *SRATC* curve is tangent to the *LRAC* curve at the level of output for which the quantity of the fixed factor is optimal and lies above it for all other levels of output.

FIGURE 8-2 *LRAC* and *SRATC* Curves

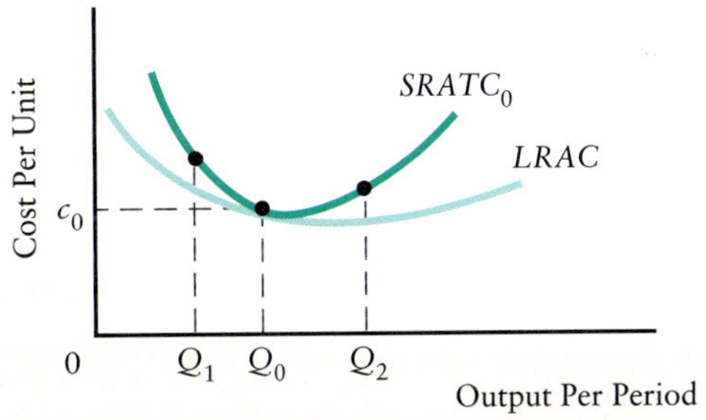

Each *SRATC* curve is tangent at some point to the *LRAC* curve. With given technology, each plant size gives rise to a different *SRATC* curve. The *SRATC* curve shown corresponds to the optimal plant size for producing Q_0 units of output because the average cost, c_0, is the lowest attainable. For output levels less than or greater than Q_0, such as Q_1 or Q_2, the plant size embodied in $SRATC_0$ is not optimal because the cost given by the $SRATC_0$ curve is greater than the minimum possible cost, given by the *LRAC* curve.

FIGURE 8-3 The Relationship Between the *LRAC* Curve and the *SRATC* Curves

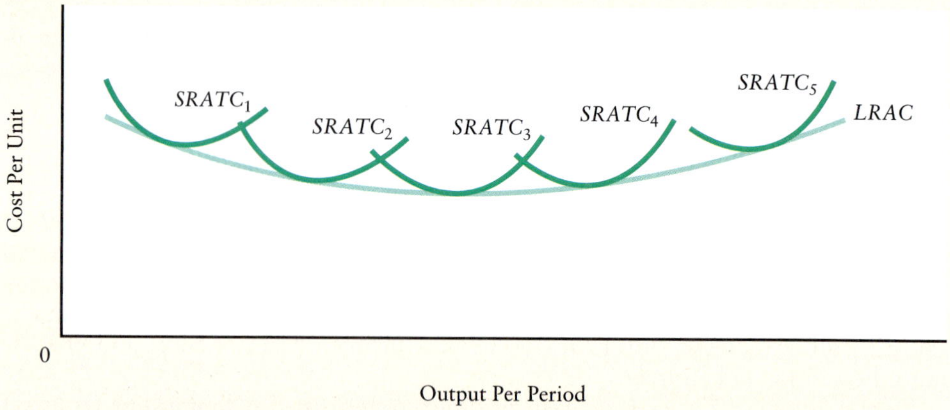

To every point on the *LRAC* curve, there is an associated *SRATC* curve tangent at that point. Each short-run curve is drawn for a given plant size, and shows how costs vary if output varies (holding constant the size of the plant). The level of output at the tangency between each *SRATC* curve and the *LRAC* curve shows the level of output for which the plant size is optimal.

The relationship between the *LRAC* curve and the many different *SRATC* curves has a famous history in economics. The economist who is credited with first working out this relationship, Jacob Viner, initially made a serious mistake that ended up being published; *Lessons From History 8-1* explains his mistake and shows how it illustrates an important difference between short-run and long-run costs.

Shifts in *LRAC* Curves

We saw in Chapter 7 how changes in either technological knowledge or factor prices will cause the entire family of short-run cost curves to shift. The same is true for long-run cost curves. Because loss of existing technological knowledge is rare, we focus on the effects of technological improvement. Improved ways of producing existing products make lower-cost methods of production available, thereby shifting *LRAC* curves downward.

Changes in factor prices can exert an influence in either direction. If a firm has to pay more for any factor that it uses, the cost of producing each level of output will rise; if the firm has to pay less for any factor that it uses, the cost of producing each level of output will fall.

A rise in factor prices shifts *LRAC* curves upward. A fall in factor prices or a technological improvement shifts *LRAC* curves downward.

LESSONS FROM HISTORY 8-1

Jacob Viner and the Clever Draftsman

Jacob Viner (1892–1970) was born in Montreal and studied economics at McGill University under Stephen Leacock (1869–1944). Viner was clearly an outstanding student and, according to some of his McGill classmates, knew much more about economics than did Leacock, who was actually better known as a humorist than an economist. Viner was such a good economist that he was the first person to work out the relationship between a firm's long-run average costs and its short-run average costs. He went on to teach economics at the University of Chicago and at Princeton University and became one of the world's leading economic theorists.

The student who finds the relationship between *SRATC* and *LRAC* hard to understand may take some comfort from the fact that when Jacob Viner first worked out this relationship, and published it in 1931, he made a crucial mistake. In preparing a diagram like Figure 8-3, he instructed his draftsman to draw the *LRAC* curve through the *minimum points* of all the *SRATC* curves, "but so as to never lie above" the *SRATC* curves. Viner later said of the draftsman: "He is a mathematician, however, not an economist, and he saw some mathematical objection to this procedure which I could not succeed in understanding. I could not persuade him to disregard his scruples as a craftsman and to follow my instructions, absurd though they might be."

Viner's mistake was to require that the draftsman connect all of the *minimum* points of the *SRATC* curves rather than to construct the curve that would be the *lower envelope* of all the *SRATC* curves. The former curve can of course be drawn, but it *is not* the *LRAC* curve. The latter curve *is* the *LRAC* curve, and is tangent to each *SRATC* curve.

Since Viner's article was published in 1931, generations of economics students have experienced great satisfaction when they finally figured out his crucial mistake. Viner's famous article was often reprinted, for its fame was justly deserved, despite the importance of the mistake. But Viner always rejected suggestions that he correct the error because he did not wish to deprive other students of the pleasure of feeling one up on him.

The economic sense of the fact that tangency is *not* at the minimum points of *SRATC* rests on the subtle distinction between the least-cost method of utilizing *a given plant* and the least-cost method of producing *a given level of output*. The first concept defines the minimum of any given *SRATC* curve, whereas the second defines a point on the *LRAC* curve for any given level of output. It is the second concept that interests us in the long run. If bigger plants can achieve lower average costs, there will be a gain in building a bigger plant *and underutilizing it* whenever the gains from using the bigger plant are enough to offset the costs of being inefficient in the use of the plant. If there are gains from building bigger plants (i.e., if *LRAC* is declining), some underutilization is always justified.

Montreal-born Jacob Viner taught at Princeton and Chicago and was one of the world's leading economic theorists.

8.2 THE VERY LONG RUN: CHANGES IN TECHNOLOGY

In the long run, profit-maximizing firms faced with given technologies choose the cost-minimizing mix of factors to produce their desired level of output. Firms are therefore on, rather than above, their long-run cost curves. In the very long run, however, there are changes in the available techniques and resources. Such changes cause *shifts* in long-run cost curves.

The decrease in costs that can be achieved by choosing from among available factors of production, known techniques, and alternative levels of output is necessarily limited by the existing state of knowledge. Improvements by invention and innovation are potentially limitless, however, and hence sustained growth in living standards is critically linked to technological change.

technological change Any change in the available techniques of production.

productivity Output produced per unit of some input; frequently used to refer to labour productivity, measured by total output divided by the amount of labour used.

Technological change refers to all changes in the available techniques of production. To measure its extent, economists usually use the notion of **productivity**, defined as a measure of output produced per unit of input used. Two widely used measures of productivity are output per worker and output per hour of work. The rate of increase in productivity provides one measure of technological change. The significance of productivity growth is explored in *Applying Economic Concepts 8-1*.

myeconlab

In recent years, many economists and policymakers have expressed concern about Canada's low rate of productivity growth, especially as compared with that in the United States. But there is little agreement on how best to address the issue. For more details, look for "Understanding and Addressing Canada's Productivity Challenges" in the *Additional Topics* section of this book's MyEconLab.

www.myeconlab.com

Technological Change

Practise with Study Guide Chapter 8, Exercise 4.

Technological change was once thought to be mainly a random process, brought about by inventions made by crackpots and eccentric scientists working in garages and scientific laboratories. As a result of recent research by economists, we now know better.

Changes in technology are often *endogenous responses* to changing economic signals; that is, they result from responses by firms to the same things that induce the substitution of one factor for another within the confines of a given technology.

In our discussion of long-run demand curves in Chapter 4, we looked at just such technological changes in response to rising relative prices when we spoke of the development, in the 1970s, of smaller, more fuel-efficient cars in the wake of dramatic increases in the price of gasoline. From the mid-1980s to the mid-1990s, declines in the price of gasoline led to the re-emergence of large cars and the development of fuel-inefficient "sport utility vehicles," or SUVs. More recently, however, we have once again seen consumers respond to higher gasoline prices by reducing their demand for such large vehicles, returning to smaller, more fuel-efficient cars.

Production methods in many parts of the economy have responded to changes in relative factor prices. For example, much of the move to substitute capital for labour in manufacturing, transportation, communications, mining, and agriculture in

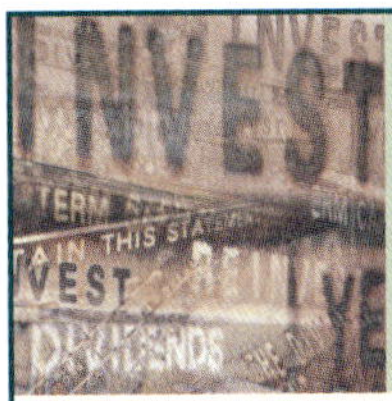

APPLYING ECONOMIC CONCEPTS 8-1

The Significance of Productivity Growth

Economics used to be known as the "dismal science" because some of its predictions were grim. Thomas Malthus (1766–1834) and other Classical economists predicted that the pressure of more and more people on the world's limited resources would cause a decline in output per person due to the law of diminishing returns. Human history would see more and more people living less and less well and the surplus population, which could not be supported, dying off from hunger and disease.

This prediction has proven wrong for industrialized countries for two main reasons. First, their populations have not expanded as rapidly as predicted by early economists, who were writing before birth-control techniques were widely used. Second, technological advances have been so important during the past 150 years that output has increased much faster than the population. We have experienced sustained growth in productivity that has permitted significant increases in output per person. As the accompanying figure shows, real output per worker in Canada increased by 318 percent between 1926 and 2005, an average annually compounded growth rate of 1.8 percent.

Even such small annual productivity increases are a powerful force for increasing living standards over many years. Our great-grandparents would have regarded today's standard of living in most industrialized countries as unattainable. An apparently modest rate of increase in productivity of 2 percent per year leads to a doubling of per capita output every 35 years.

Due to the importance of productivity growth in raising long-run living standards, it is not surprising that explaining the sources of technological progress has become a very active area of research, among both academic and government economists.

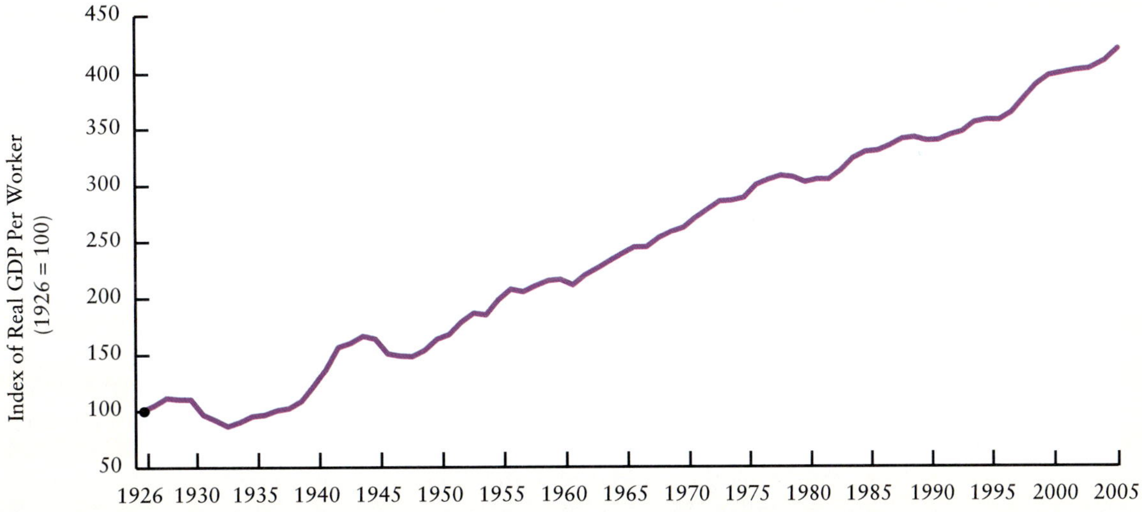

(*Source:* Statistics Canada, CANSIM database (Real GDP: Series V3862685. Employment: Series V2091072) and authors' calculations.)

response to rising wage rates has taken the form of inventing new labour-saving methods of production.

Consider three kinds of change that influence production and cost in the very long run—*new techniques, improved inputs,* and *new products.*

New Techniques Throughout the nineteenth and twentieth centuries, changes in the techniques available for producing existing products have been dramatic; this is called *process innovation.* A century ago, roads and railways were built by gangs of workers who used buckets, shovels, and draft horses. Today, bulldozers, giant trucks, and other specialized equipment have banished the workhorse completely from construction sites and to a great extent have displaced the pick-and-shovel worker. Prior to the Second World War, electricity was generated either by burning fossil fuels or by harnessing the power of flowing water. With the rise of the atomic age immediately following the war, many countries developed large-scale nuclear generating capacity. Economies of scale in electricity production were significant. In recent years, however, the development of small-scale, gas-combustion and wind-powered turbines has permitted inexpensive construction of small generating stations that can produce electricity at a lower average cost than the much larger nuclear, hydro, or fossil fuel-burning generating stations. The product—electricity—is absolutely unchanged, but the techniques of production have changed markedly over the past several decades.

Improved Inputs Improvements in health and education raise the quality of labour services. Today's workers and managers are healthier and better educated than their grandparents. Many of today's unskilled workers are literate and competent in arithmetic, and their managers are apt to be trained in methods of business management and computer science.

Similarly, improvements in material inputs are constantly occurring. For example, the type and quality of metals have changed. Steel has replaced iron, and aluminum substitutes for steel in a process of change that makes a statistical category such as "primary metals" seem unsatisfactory. Even for a given category, say, steel, today's product is lighter, stronger, and more flexible than the "same" product manufactured only 20 years ago. Furthermore, the modern "materials revolution" allows new materials to be tailor-made for the specific purposes for which they are required.

The invention of new production techniques and the development of new and better inputs are important aspects of technological improvement. They lead to reductions in firms' costs and a downward shift in *LRAC* curves.

New Products New goods and services are constantly being invented and marketed; this is called *product innovation.* VCRs, personal computers, Palm Pilots, CD players, DVDs, cellular phones, and many other current consumer products did not exist thirty years ago. Other products have changed so dramatically that the only connection they have with the "same" product from the past is the name. Today's Ford automobile is very different from a 1920 Ford, and it is even different from a 1980 Ford in size, safety, and gasoline consumption. Modern jet airliners are revolutionary compared with the first passenger jet aircraft, which were in turn many times larger and faster than the DC–3, the workhorse of the airlines during the 1930s and 1940s. Beyond having wings and engines, the DC–3 itself bore little resemblance to the Wright brothers' original flying machine.

The development of new products is a crucial part of the steady increase in living standards.

Applying Economic Concepts 8-2 discusses an everyday example of technological change in banking: the creation and adoption of the automated teller machine (ATM). The adoption of ATMs by commercial banks involves both long-run decisions—substitutions between capital and labour—and very-long-run decisions involving innovation and the creation of new products.

APPLYING ECONOMIC CONCEPTS 8-2

Substitution and Innovation with Automated Teller Machines (ATMs)

Before the relatively recent invention of automated teller machines (ATMs), all personal banking required a visit to the bank. For many working individuals, banking could only take place on the lunch hour with the result that long line-ups were commonplace. Banks were then faced with a difficult choice: Have unhappy customers in long line-ups, or hire more tellers.

The development of ATMs, made possible by the declining cost and increasing efficiency of computing equipment, revolutionized banking and presented banks with a new set of choices. As you know, ATMs are now located on street corners, in shopping malls and universities, and inside many large stores and even some small ones. As a result, individuals do not have to go to a bank to gain access to their money. And ATMs are very efficient: They take no time at all to "learn" their job and they can handle thousands of transactions per week—all with no direct labour cost per transaction. There is, of course, a significant capital cost for each ATM as well as some labour cost for servicing the equipment.

Since the early 1980s, the use of ATMs has skyrocketed in Canada. Whereas in 1982 there were only a handful in the downtown core of even the major Canadian cities, today it is virtually impossible to walk even a few blocks anywhere in any Canadian city without seeing one. Over the same period, there has been a decline in the number of bank tellers (although because of ATMs we typically go to the bank so seldom that we don't notice this!). In the language of this chapter, the rise of ATMs and decline of bank tellers has been a long-run substitution of capital for labour.

There are also some very-long-run changes involved in this story. The creation of ATMs—and the related developments in telephone and online banking—has truly revolutionized personal banking. Not only are traditional types of transactions made easier, but new banking services have been created. One example is the creation of online accounts for buying and selling stocks and bonds in the global financial markets. Whereas even a few years ago individuals could only make such transactions by employing the services of a registered stock broker (at considerable expense), it is now very simple to create a trading account at your bank—linked to your other accounts and accessible by the ATMs—and make trades whenever you want and at a much lower cost per transaction. In the language of this chapter, such creation of new banking services is an example of very-long-run innovation.

The development and widespread provision of ATMs by commercial banks represents both a long-run substitution of capital for labour and a very-long-run innovation.

Firms' Choices in the Very Long Run

Firms respond to signals that indicate changes in the economic environment. For example, consider the situation faced by Stelco—a major Canadian steel producer—when the price of coal (a major input) increases and is expected to remain at the higher level for some time. How can Stelco respond to this change in the economic environment?

One option for Stelco is to make a long-run response by substituting away from the use of coal by changing its production techniques within the confines of existing technology. This might involve switching to other fuels (whose prices have not increased) to operate Stelco's enormous blast furnaces. Another option is to invest in research in order to develop new production techniques that innovate away from coal (and other fuels as well), such as the design of blast furnaces that require less fuel to process each unit of iron ore.

Faced with increases in the price of an input, firms may either *substitute away* or *innovate away* from the input—or do both over different time horizons.

It is important to recognize that the two options can involve quite different actions and can ultimately have quite different implications for productivity.

For example, consider three different responses to an increase in Canadian labour costs. One firm reallocates its production activities to Mexico or Southeast Asia, where labour costs are relatively low and hence labour-intensive production techniques remain quite profitable. A second firm chooses to reduce its use of labour but increase its use of capital equipment. These two firms have, in different ways, chosen to *substitute away* from the higher-priced Canadian labour. A third firm devotes resources to developing new production techniques, perhaps using robotics or other new equipment. This firm has *innovated away* from higher-priced Canadian labour.

All three are possible reactions to the changed circumstances. The first two are largely well understood in advance and will lead to reduced costs relative to continued reliance on the original production methods. The third response, depending on the often unpredictable results of the innovation, may reduce costs sufficiently to warrant the investment in research and development and may even lead to substantially more effective production techniques that allow the firm to maintain an advantage over its competitors for a number of years.

SUMMARY

8.1 THE LONG RUN: NO FIXED FACTORS

LO 1 2 3

- There are no fixed factors in the long run. Profit-maximizing firms choose from the available alternatives the least-cost method of producing any specific output. A long-run cost curve represents the boundary between attainable and unattainable costs for the given technology and given factor prices.
- The principle of substitution states that, in response to changes in factor prices, profit-maximizing firms will substitute toward the cheaper factors and substitute away from the more expensive factors.
- The shape of the *LRAC* curve depends on the relationship of inputs to outputs as the whole scale of a firm's operations changes. Increasing, constant, and decreasing returns lead, respectively, to decreasing, constant, and increasing long-run average costs.
- The *LRAC* and *SRATC* curves are related. Each *SRATC* curve represents a specific plant size and is tangent to the *LRAC* curve at the level of output for which that plant size is optimal.
- *LRAC* curves shift upward or downward in response to changes in the prices of factors or changes in technology. Increases in factor prices shift *LRAC* curves upward. Decreases in factor prices and technological advances shift *LRAC* curves downward.

8.2 THE VERY LONG RUN: CHANGES IN TECHNOLOGY

LO 4

- Over the very long run, the most important influence on costs of production and on standards of living has been increases in output made possible by technological improvements.
- Changes in technology are often *endogenous responses* to changing economic signals; that is, they result from the firms' responses to changes in the economic environment.
- There are three important kinds of technological change—developments of new production techniques, improved inputs, and new products. All three play an important role in increasing living standards.
- To understand any industry's response to changes in its operating environment, it is important to consider the effects of endogenous innovations in technology as well as substitution based on changes in the use of existing technologies.

KEY CONCEPTS

The implication of cost minimization
The interpretation of $MP_K/MP_L = p_K/p_L$
The principle of substitution
Increasing, constant, and decreasing returns
Economies of scale
LRAC curve as an envelope of *SRATC* curves
Technological change and productivity growth
Changes in technology as endogenous responses

STUDY EXERCISES

1. Explain why a profit-maximizing firm must also minimize costs.

2. myeconlab Industrial Footwear Inc. uses capital and labour to produce workboots. Suppose this firm is using capital and labour such that the MP_K is equal to 80 and the MP_L is equal to 20.

   a. If the prices per unit of capital and labour are $2 and $10, respectively, is this firm minimizing its costs? If not, what factor substitution should be made to minimize costs?
   b. If the prices per unit of capital and labour are $20 and $5, respectively, is this firm minimizing its costs? If not, what factor substitution should be made to minimize costs?
   c. If the prices per unit of capital and labour are $40 and $5, respectively, is this firm minimizing its costs? What factor substitution should be made to minimize costs?

3. Use the principle of substitution to predict the effect in each of the following situations.

   a. During the past 10 years, technological advances in the computer industry have led to dramatic reductions in the prices of personal and business computers. At the same time, real wages have increased slowly.
   b. The ratio of land costs to building costs is much higher in big cities than in small cities.
   c. Wages of textile workers and shoe machinery operators are higher in Canada than in the Southern United States, but the price of capital equipment is approximately the same.
   d. A new collective agreement results in a significant increase in wages for pulp and paper workers.

4. The following table shows the marginal product of capital and labour for each of several methods of producing 1000 kilograms of flour per day.

Production Method	MP_K	MP_L
A	14	3
B	12	6
C	10	9
D	8	12
E	6	15
F	4	18
G	2	21

   a. As we move from *A* to *G*, are the production methods becoming more or less *capital intensive*? Explain.
   b. If capital costs $8 per unit and labour costs $4 per unit, which production method minimizes the cost of producing 1000 kg of flour?

c. For each of the methods that are not cost minimizing (with the factor prices from part (b), describe how the firm would have to adjust its use of capital and labour to minimize costs.
d. Now suppose the price of capital falls to $4 per unit and the price of labour rises to $6 per unit. Which method now minimizes costs?

5. Consider the following diagram of *SRATC* and *LRAC* curves.

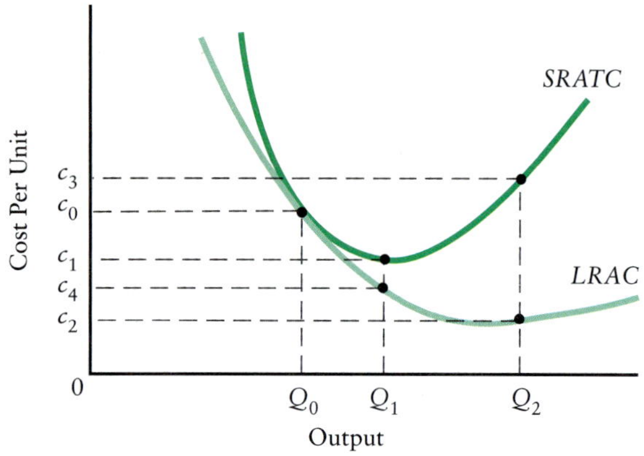

a. The *SRATC* curve is drawn for a given plant size. Given this plant size, what is the level of output that minimizes short-run average costs? What are unit costs in the short run at this level of output?
b. What is the level of output for which this plant size is optimal in the long run? What are unit costs in the short run at this level of output?
c. Explain the economics of why c_1 is greater than c_4.
d. Suppose the firm wants to increase output to Q_2 in the short run. How is this accomplished, and what would unit costs be?
e. Suppose the firm wants to increase output to Q_2 in the long run. How is this accomplished, and what would unit costs be?

6. The following diagram shows three possible *SRATC* curves and an *LRAC* curve for a single firm producing light bulbs, where each *SRATC* curve is associated with a different-sized plant.

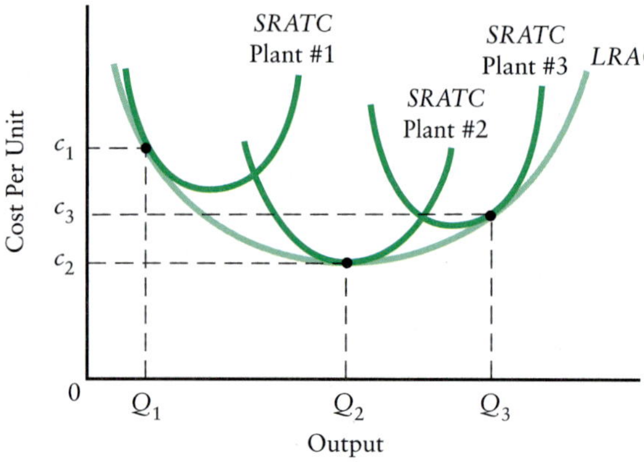

a. If the firm is producing Q_1 light bulbs with Plant #1, what are the firm's average costs?
b. At Q_1, does the firm display decreasing, constant, or increasing costs?
c. How does your answer in (b) relate to the concept of *economies of scale*?
d. Repeat parts (a), (b), and (c) for output level Q_2 with Plant #2 and output level Q_3 with Plant #3.

7. In the text, we stated that the *LRAC* curve eventually slopes upward because of *diseconomies of scale*. In the previous chapter we saw that the *SRATC* curve eventually slopes upward because of *diminishing marginal product of the variable factor.*

a. Explain the difference between *diseconomies of scale* and *diminishing marginal product of the variable factor.* Why is one a short-run concept and the other a long-run concept?
b. Draw a diagram with short-run and long-run average cost curves that illustrates *for the same level of output* both diseconomies of scale and diminishing marginal product of the variable factor.

8. In the text, we stated that the *LRAC* curve initially slopes downward because of *economies of scale*. In the previous chapter we saw that the *SRATC* curve can initially slope downward because of *spreading overhead.*

a. Explain the difference between *economies of scale* and *spreading overhead.* Why is one a short-run concept and the other a long-run concept?
b. Draw a diagram with short-run and long-run average cost curves that illustrates *for the same level of output* both economies of scale and spreading overhead.

9. This question combines the various concepts from Questions 7 and 8.

a. Draw a diagram with short-run and long-run average cost curves that illustrates *for the same level of output* economies of scale in the long run but diminishing marginal product for the variable factor in the short run.
b. Draw a diagram with short-run and long-run average cost curves that illustrates *for the same level of output* diseconomies of scale in the long run but falling average total costs in the short run.

10. This question relates to the material in the Appendix. The following table shows several methods of producing 500 rubber tires per day. There are two factors, labour and capital, with prices per unit of $3 and $6, respectively.

Production Method	Units of Labour	Units of Capital	Total Cost
A	110	20	—
B	90	25	—
C	70	33	—
D	50	43	—
E	30	55	—
F	10	70	—

a. Compute the total cost for each production method and fill in the table.
b. Which production method minimizes costs for producing 500 tires?
c. Plot the isoquant for 500 tires.
d. Given the factor prices, draw the isocost line that corresponds to the cost-minimizing production method.
e. Now suppose the price of labour rises to $5 per unit but the firm still wants to produce 500 tires per day. Explain how a cost-minimizing firm adjusts to this change (with no change in technology).

DISCUSSION QUESTIONS

1. In *The Competitive Advantage of Nations*, Michael Porter of Harvard University claimed: "Faced with high relative labor cost,... American consumer electronics firms moved to locate labor-intensive activities in ... Asian countries, leaving the product and production process essentially the same.... Japanese rivals ... set out instead to eliminate labor through automation. Doing so involved reducing the number of components which further lowered cost and improved quality. Japanese firms were soon building assembly plants in the United States, the place American firms had sought to avoid." Discuss these reactions in terms of changes over the long run and the very long run.

2. Why must a profit-maximizing firm choose the least-cost method of producing any given output? Might a non-profit-maximizing organization such as a university, church, or government intentionally choose a method of production other than the least-cost one?

3. What is the interpretation of a move from one point on a long-run average cost curve to another point on the same curve? Contrast this with a movement along a short-run average total cost curve.

4. Each of the following is a means of increasing productivity. Discuss which groups in a society might oppose each one.

   a. A labour-saving invention that permits all goods to be manufactured with less labour than before
   b. The removal of all government production safety rules
   c. A reduction in corporate income taxes

5. Policymakers and commentators often argue that the Canadian health-care system is "more efficient" than the U.S. health-care system. What do they mean by "more efficient"?

6. In December 1998, after a year in which Asian demand for B.C. lumber had fallen dramatically, an article in *The Globe and Mail* had the following headline: "Drastic Cost Reductions Needed to Save 13 B.C. Sawmills."

   a. Does the headline suggest that the B.C. lumber companies are not profit maximizers?
   b. If long-run unit costs are "too high," what is stopping the lumber companies from simply moving down their *LRAC* curves?

7. "Necessity is the mother of invention." Explain why this statement captures the essence of the view that firms often innovate their way around unfavourable changes in their economic environment.

APPENDIX TO CHAPTER 8

Isoquant Analysis

The production function gives the relationship between the factor inputs that the firm uses and the output that it obtains. In the long run, the firm can choose among many different combinations of inputs that yield the same output. The production function and the long-run choices open to the firm can be represented graphically by using *isoquants*.

8A.1 ISOQUANTS

The table in Figure 8A-1 illustrates a hypothetical example in which several combinations of two inputs, labour and capital, can produce a given quantity of output. The data from the table are plotted graphically in Figure 8A-1. A smooth curve is drawn through the points to indicate that there are additional ways, which are not listed in the table, of producing the same output.

This curve is called an *isoquant.* It shows the whole set of technically efficient factor combinations for producing a given level of output. This is an example of graphing a relationship among three variables in two dimensions. It is analogous to the contour line on a map, which shows all points of equal altitude, and to an indifference curve (discussed in the Appendix to Chapter 6), which shows all combinations of products that yield the consumer equal utility.

As we move from one point on an isoquant to another, we are *substituting one factor for another* while holding output constant. If we move from point *b* to point *c,* we are substituting 1 unit of labour for 3 units of capital.

The marginal rate of substitution measures the rate at which one factor is substituted for another with output being held constant.

Sometimes the term *marginal rate of technical substitution* is used to distinguish this concept from the analogous one for consumer theory (the marginal rate of substitution) that we examined in Chapter 6.

Graphically, the marginal rate of substitution is measured by the slope of the isoquant at a particular point. We adopt the standard practice of defining the marginal rate of substitution as the negative of the slope of the isoquant so that it is a positive number. The table in Figure 8A-1 shows the calculation of some marginal rates of substitution between various points on an isoquant. **[19]**

The marginal rate of substitution is related to the marginal products of the factors of production. To see how, consider an example. Suppose at the present level of inputs of labour and capital, the marginal product of labour is 2 units of output and the marginal product of capital is 1 unit of output. If the firm reduces its use of capital and increases its use of labour to keep output constant, it needs to add only one-half unit of labour for 1 unit of capital given up. If, at another point on the isoquant with more labour and less capital, the marginal products are 2 for capital and 1 for labour, the firm will have to add 2 units of labour for every unit of capital it gives up. The general proposition is this:

The marginal rate of (technical) substitution between two factors of production is equal to the ratio of their marginal products.

Economists assume that isoquants satisfy two important conditions: They are downward sloping, and they are convex when viewed from the origin. What is the economic meaning of these conditions?

The downward slope indicates that each factor input has a positive marginal product. If the input of one factor is reduced and that of the other is held constant, output will be reduced. Thus, if one input is decreased, production can be held constant only if the other factor input is increased.

To understand the convexity of the isoquant, consider what happens as the firm moves along the isoquant of Figure 8A-1 downward and to the right. Labour is being added and capital reduced to keep output constant. If labour is added in increments of exactly 1 unit, how much capital can be dispensed with each time? The key to the answer is that both factors are assumed to be subject to the law of diminishing returns. Thus, the gain in output associated

FIGURE 8A-1 An Isoquant

Alternative Methods of Producing a Given Level of Output

Method	K	L	ΔK	ΔL	Marginal Rate of Substitution (absolute value of $\Delta K/\Delta L$)
a	18	2			
			−6	1	6.00
b	12	3			
			−3	1	3.00
c	9	4			
			−3	2	1.50
d	6	6			
			−2	3	0.67
e	4	9			
			−1	3	0.33
f	3	12			
			−1	6	0.17
g	2	18			

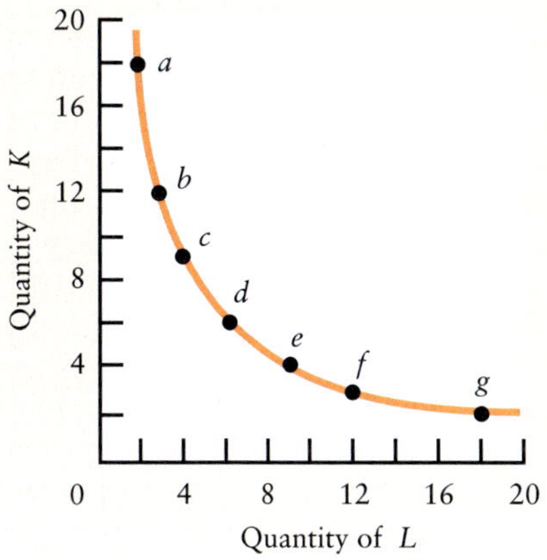

An isoquant describes the firm's alternative methods for producing a given level of output. Method *a* uses a great deal of capital (K) and very little labour (L). As we move down the table, labour is substituted for capital in such a way as to keep output constant. Finally, at the bottom, most of the capital has been replaced by labour. The marginal rate of substitution between the two factors is calculated in the last three columns of the table. Note that as we move down the table, the marginal rate of substitution declines.

When the isoquant is plotted it is downward sloping and convex. The downward slope reflects the requirement of technical efficiency: Keeping the level of output constant, a reduction in the use of one factor requires an increase in the use of the other factor. The convex shape of the isoquant reflects a diminishing marginal rate of (technical) substitution.

with each additional unit of labour added is *diminishing,* whereas the loss of output associated with each additional unit of capital forgone is *increasing.* Therefore, it takes ever-smaller reductions in capital to compensate for equal increases in labour. Viewed from the origin, therefore, the isoquant is convex.

An Isoquant Map

The isoquant of Figure 8A-1 is for a given level of output. Suppose it is for 6 units. In this case, there is another isoquant for 7 units, another for 7000 units, and a different one for every other level of output. Each isoquant refers to a specific level of output and connects combinations of factors that are technically efficient methods of producing that output. If we plot a representative set of these isoquants from the same production function on a single graph, we get an *isoquant map* like that in Figure 8A-2. The higher the level of output along a particular isoquant, the farther the isoquant is from the origin.

FIGURE 8A-2 An Isoquant Map

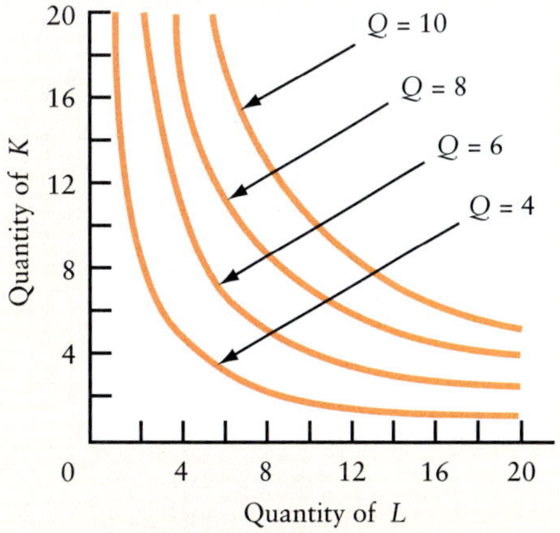

An isoquant map shows a set of isoquants, one for each level of output. Each isoquant corresponds to a specific level of output and shows factor combinations that are technically efficient methods of producing that output.

8A.2 **COST MINIMIZATION**

Finding the cost-minimizing method of producing any output requires knowledge of the factor prices. Suppose capital is priced at $4 per unit and labour at $1 per unit. An *isocost line* shows alternative combinations of factors that a firm can buy for a given total cost. Four different isocost lines appear in Figure 8A-3. The slope of each isocost line reflects *relative* factor prices. For given factor prices, a series of parallel isocost lines will reflect the alternative levels of expenditure on factor purchases that are available to the firm. The higher the level of expenditure, the farther the isocost line is from the origin.

In Figure 8A-4, the isoquant and isocost maps are brought together. The cost-minimizing method of production must be a point on an isoquant that just touches (is tangent to) an isocost line. If the isoquant cuts the isocost line, it is possible to move along the isoquant and reach a lower level of cost. Only at a point of tangency is a movement in either direction along the isoquant a movement to a higher cost level.

As shown in Figure 8A-4, the lowest attainable cost of producing 6 units is $24 and this requires using 12 units of labour and 3 units of capital.

FIGURE 8A-3 Isocost Lines

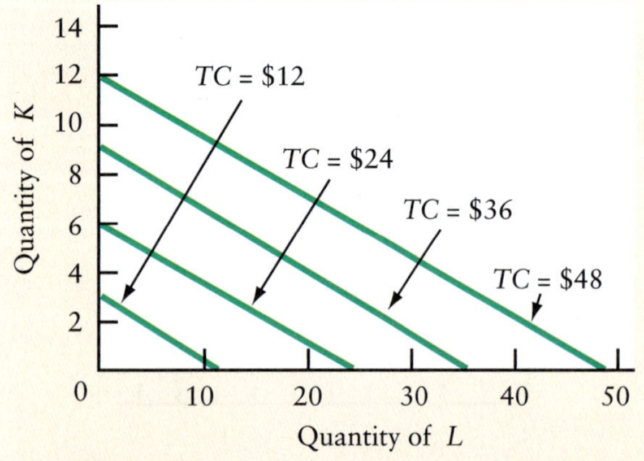

Each isocost line shows alternative factor combinations that require the same expenditure. The graph shows the four isocost lines that result when labour costs $1 per unit and capital $4 per unit and when expenditure (total cost, *TC*) is held constant at $12, $24, $36, and $48, respectively.

The least-cost position is given graphically by the tangency point between the isoquant and the isocost lines.

The slope of the isocost line is given by the ratio of the prices of the two factors of production. The slope of the isoquant is given by the ratio of their marginal products. When the firm reaches its cost-minimizing position, it has equated the price ratio (which is given to it by the market) with the ratio of the marginal products (which it can adjust by changing its usage of the factors). In symbols,

$$\frac{MP_L}{MP_K} = \frac{p_L}{p_K}$$

This is the same condition that we derived in the text (see Equation 8-2), but here we have derived it by using the isoquant analysis of the firm's decisions. [20]

Note the similarity of this condition for a cost-minimizing firm to Equation 6-2 where we saw how utility maximization for a consumer requires that the ratio of marginal utilities of consuming two products must equal the ratio of the two product prices. Both conditions reveal the basic principle that the decision makers (consumers or producers) face market prices beyond their control and so adjust quantities (consumption or factor inputs) until they are achieving their objective (utility maximization or cost minimization).

The Principle of Substitution

Suppose with technology unchanged (that is, for a given isoquant map), the price of one factor changes. In particular, suppose with the price of capital unchanged at $4 per unit, the price of labour rises from $1 to $4 per unit. Originally, the cost-minimizing factor combination for producing 6 units of output was 12 units of labour and 3 units of capital. Total cost was $24. To produce that same output in the same way would now cost $60 at the new factor prices. Figure 8A-5 shows why this production method is no longer the cost-minimizing one. The slope of the isocost line has changed, which makes it efficient to substitute the now relatively cheaper capital for the relatively more expensive labour. The change in slope of the isocost line illustrates the principle of substitution.

FIGURE 8A-4 Cost Minimization

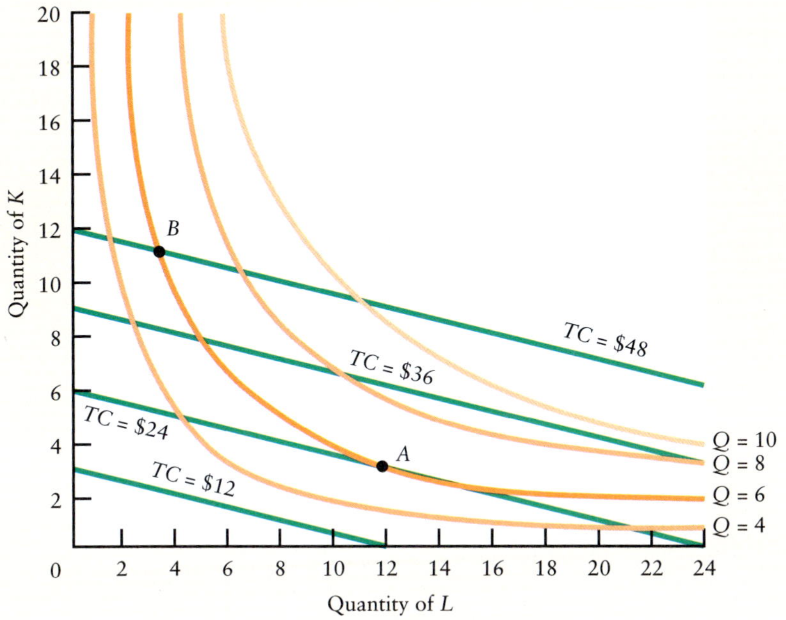

Cost minimization occurs at points of tangency between isoquant and isocost lines. The isoquant map of Figure 8A-2 and the isocost lines of Figure 8A-3 are brought together. Consider point *A*. It is on the 6-unit isoquant and the $24 isocost line. Thus, it is possible to achieve the output *Q* = 6 for a total cost of $24. There are other ways to achieve this output, for example, at point *B*, where *TC* = $48. Moving along the isoquant from point *A* in either direction increases cost. Similarly, moving along the isocost line from point *A* in either direction lowers output. Thus, either move would raise cost per unit.

Changes in relative factor prices will cause a partial replacement of factors that have become relatively more expensive by factors that have become relatively cheaper.

Of course, substitution of capital for labour cannot fully offset the effects of a rise in the cost of labour, as Figure 8A-5(i) shows. Consider the output attainable for $24. In the figure, there are two isocost lines representing $24 of outlay—at the old and new prices of labour. The new isocost line for $24 lies inside the old one (except where no labour is used). The $24 isocost line must therefore be tangent to a lower isoquant. Thus, if production is to be held constant, higher costs must be accepted. However, because of substitution, it is not necessary to accept costs as high as those that would accompany an unchanged factor proportion. In the example, 6 units can be produced for $48 rather than the $60 that would be required if no change in factor proportions were made.

This analysis leads to the following predictions:

A rise in the price of one factor with all other factor prices held constant will (1) shift the cost curves of products that use that factor upward and (2) lead to a substitution of factors that are now relatively cheaper for the factor whose price has risen.

Both of these predictions were stated in Chapter 8; now they have been derived formally by the use of isoquants and isocost lines.

FIGURE 8A-5 The Effects of a Change in Factor Prices on Costs and Factor Proportions

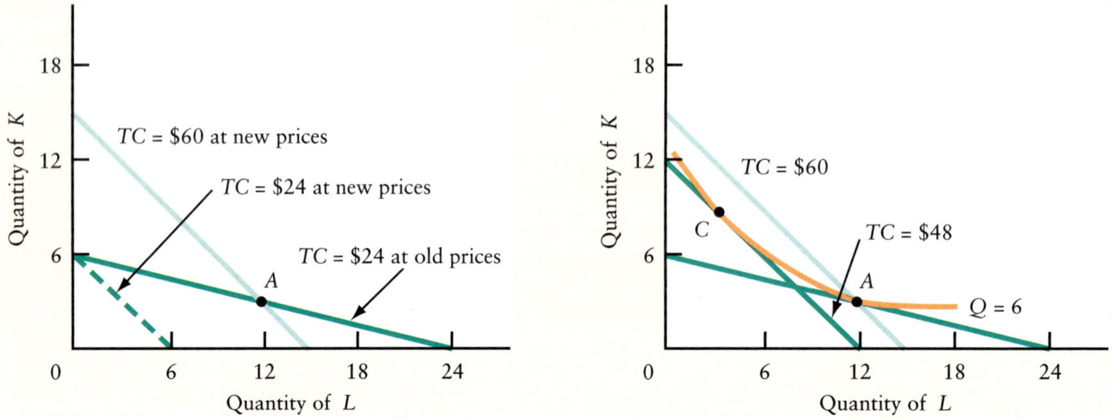

(i) The effect on the isocost line of an increase in the price of labour

(ii) Substitution of capital for labour resulting from an increase in the price of labour

An increase in the price of labour pivots the isocost line inward, increasing its slope. This changes the cost-minimizing method of producing any level of output. In part (i), the rise in the price of *L* from $1 to $4 per unit (with the price of *K* being held constant at $4) pivots the $24 isocost line inward to the dashed line. Any output previously produced for $24 will cost more at the new prices if it uses any labour. The new cost of using the factor combination at *A* rises from $24 to $60. In part (ii), the steeper isocost line is tangent to the *Q* = 6 isoquant at *C*, not *A*, so that more capital and less labour is used. Costs at *C* are $48, higher than they were before the price increase but not as high as they would be if the factor substitution had not occurred.

PART 4: MARKET STRUCTURE AND EFFICIENCY

CHAPTER 9

Competitive Markets

LO LEARNING OBJECTIVES

In this chapter you will learn

1. the key assumptions of the theory of perfect competition.
2. how to derive a competitive firm's supply curve.
3. to determine whether competitive firms are making profits or losses in the short run.
4. the role played by profits, entry, and exit in a competitive industry's long-run equilibrium.

Does American Express compete with Visa? Does a wheat farmer from Biggar, Saskatchewan, compete with a wheat farmer from Brandon, Manitoba? If we use the ordinary meaning of the word compete, the answer to the first question is plainly yes, and the answer to the second question is no.

American Express and Visa both advertise extensively to persuade consumers to use their credit cards. A host of world travellers in various tight spots attest on television or in magazines to the virtues of American Express, while other happy faces advise us that only with a Visa card can their pleasures be ours.

When we shift our attention to wheat farmers, however, we see the Saskatchewan farmer can do nothing to affect either the sales or the profits of the Manitoba farmer. Even if the Saskatchewan farmer could do something to influence the profits of the Manitoba farmer, there would be no point in doing so, since changes in the profits of the Manitoba farmer would not affect the Saskatchewan farmer.

To sort out the questions of who is competing with whom and in what sense, it is useful to distinguish between the behaviour of individual firms and the type of market in which they operate. Economists are interested in two different concepts—*competitive market structure* and *competitive behaviour.*

market structure All features of a market that affect the behaviour and performance of firms in that market, such as the number and size of sellers, the extent of knowledge about one another's actions, the degree of freedom of entry, and the degree of product differentiation.

9.1 MARKET STRUCTURE AND FIRM BEHAVIOUR

The term **market structure** refers to all the features that may affect the behaviour and performance of the firms in a market, such as the number of firms in the market or the type of product that they sell. In this chapter, we focus on a *competitive* market structure.

Competitive Market Structure

market power The ability of a firm to influence the price of a product or the terms under which it is sold.

Economists say that firms have **market power** when they can influence the price of their product or the terms under which their product is sold. The *competitiveness* of the market is the extent to which individual firms *lack* such market power.

A market is said to have a competitive structure when its firms have little or no market power. The more market power the firms have, the less competitive is the market structure.

The extreme form of competitive market structure occurs when each firm has zero market power. In such a case, there are so many firms in the market that each must accept the price set by the forces of market demand and market supply. The firms perceive themselves as being able to sell as much as they choose at the prevailing market price and as having no power to influence that price. If the firm charged a higher price, it would make no sales; so many other firms would be selling at the market price that buyers would take their business elsewhere.

This extreme is called a *perfectly competitive market structure* or, more simply, a *perfectly competitive market.* In such a market there is no need for individual firms to compete actively with one another because none has any power over the market. One firm's ability to sell its product does not depend on the behaviour of any other firm. For example, the Saskatchewan and Manitoba wheat farms operate in a perfectly competitive market over which they have no power. Neither can change the market price for its wheat by altering its own behaviour.

American Express and VISA "compete" very actively against each other in the credit-card market, but economists nonetheless refer to the structure of this market as imperfectly competitive.

Competitive Behaviour

In everyday language, the term *competitive behaviour* refers to the degree to which individual firms actively vie with one another for business. For example, American Express and Visa clearly engage in competitive behaviour. It is also true, however, that both companies have some real power over their market. Each has the power to decide the fees that people will pay for the use of their credit cards, within limits set by buyers' tastes and the fees of competing cards. Either firm could raise its fees and still continue to attract some customers. Even though they actively compete with each other, they do so in a market that does not have a perfectly competitive structure.

In contrast, the Saskatchewan and Manitoba wheat farmers do not engage in competitive behaviour because the only way they can affect their profits is by changing their own outputs of wheat or their own production costs.

The distinction that we have just made between behaviour and structure explains why firms in perfectly competitive markets (e.g., the Saskatchewan and Manitoba wheat producers) do not compete actively with each other, whereas firms that do compete actively with each other (e.g., American Express and Visa) do not operate in perfectly competitive markets.

The Significance of Market Structure

When a firm decides how much output to produce in order to maximize its profit, it needs to know the demand for its product and also the costs of production. We examined the various costs in detail in Chapters 7 and 8. Now we need to think about the demand for the firm's product. This is where market structure enters the picture because the details of market structure determine how we get from the *industry* demand curve to the demand curve facing any individual *firm* in that industry.

We will see in the next few chapters that market structure plays a central role in determining the behaviour of individual firms and also in the overall *efficiency* of the market outcomes. In this chapter, we focus only on *competitive* market structures. In later chapters, we explore non-competitive market structures.

A wheat farmer in Saskatchewan does not "compete" in any real way with a wheat farmer elsewhere in the world. However, both exist in what economists call a highly "competitive" market.

9.2 THE THEORY OF PERFECT COMPETITION

The perfectly competitive market structure—usually referred to simply as **perfect competition**—applies directly to a number of markets, especially many agricultural and raw-materials markets. It also provides an important benchmark for comparison with other market structures.

perfect competition A market structure in which all firms in an industry are price takers and in which there is freedom of entry into and exit from the industry.

The Assumptions of Perfect Competition

In addition to the fundamental assumption that firms seek to maximize their profits, the theory of perfect competition is built on a number of assumptions relating to each firm and to the industry as a whole.

1. All the firms in the industry sell an identical product. Economists say that the firms sell a **homogeneous product.**
2. Consumers know the nature of the product being sold and the prices charged by each firm.
3. The level of a firm's output at which its long-run average cost reaches a minimum is small relative to the *industry's* total output. (This is a precise way of saying that the firm is small relative to the size of the industry.)
4. The industry is characterized by *freedom of entry and exit*; that is, any new firm is free to enter the industry and start producing if it so wishes, and any existing firm is free to cease production and leave the industry. Existing firms cannot block the entry of new firms, and there are no legal prohibitions or other barriers to entering or exiting the industry.

homogeneous product In the eyes of purchasers, every unit of the product is identical to every other unit.

The first three assumptions imply that each firm in a perfectly competitive industry is a **price taker**, meaning that the firm can alter its rate of production and sales

price taker A firm that can alter its rate of production and sales without affecting the market price of its product.

without affecting the market price of its product. Thus, a firm operating in a perfectly competitive market has no market power. It must passively accept whatever happens to be the market price, but it can sell as much as it wants at that price.

The Saskatchewan and Manitoba wheat farmers we considered earlier provide us with good illustrations of firms that are operating in a perfectly competitive market. Because each individual wheat farmer is just one of a very large number of producers who are all growing the same product, one firm's contribution to the industry's total production is a tiny drop in an extremely large bucket. Each firm will correctly assume that variations in its output have no effect on the price of wheat. Thus, each firm, knowing that it can sell as much or as little as it chooses at that price, adapts its behaviour to a given market price of wheat. Furthermore, there is nothing that any one farmer can do to stop another farmer from growing wheat, and there are no legal deterrents to becoming a wheat farmer. Anyone who has enough money to buy or rent the necessary land, labour, and equipment can become a wheat farmer.

The difference between the wheat farmers and American Express is the *degree of market power.* Each firm that is producing wheat is an insignificant part of the whole market and thus has no power to influence the price of wheat. American Express does have power to influence the credit-card market because its own sales represent a significant part of the total sales of credit-card services.

The Demand Curve for a Perfectly Competitive Firm

Practise with Study Guide Chapter 9, Short-Answer Question 4.

A major distinction between firms in perfectly competitive markets and firms in any other type of market is the shape of the demand curve facing the firm.

Even though the demand curve for the entire industry may be negatively sloped, each firm in a perfectly competitive market faces a horizontal demand curve because variations in the firm's output have no effect on price.

The horizontal (perfectly elastic) demand curve does not indicate that the firm could actually sell an infinite amount at the going price. It indicates, rather, that the variations in production *that it will normally be possible for the firm to make* will leave price unchanged because their effect on total industry output will be negligible.

Figure 9-1 contrasts the market demand curve for the product of a competitive industry with the demand curve that a single firm in that industry faces. *Applying Economic Concepts 9-1* provides an example of the important difference between the firm's demand curve and the market demand curve. It uses a numerical example to show why the demand curve facing any individual wheat farmer is very nearly perfectly elastic, even though the *market* demand for wheat is quite inelastic.

Total, Average, and Marginal Revenue

To study the revenues that firms receive from the sale of their products, economists define three concepts called *total, average,* and *marginal revenue.*

total revenue (*TR*) Total receipts from the sale of a product; price times quantity.

Total revenue (*TR*) is the total amount received by the firm from the sale of a product. If Q units are sold at p dollars each:

$$TR = p \times Q$$

FIGURE 9-1 The Demand Curve for a Competitive Industry and for One Firm in the Industry

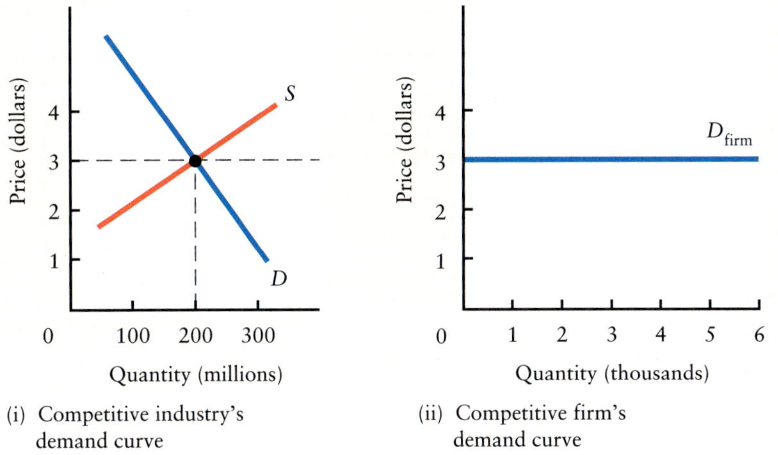

The industry's demand curve is negatively sloped; the competitive firm's demand curve is horizontal. Notice the difference in the quantities shown on the horizontal scale in each part of the figure. The competitive industry has an output of 200 million units when the price is \$3. The individual firm takes that market price as given and considers producing up to, say, 6000 units. The firm's demand curve in part (ii) is horizontal because any change in output that this single firm could manage would leave price virtually unchanged at \$3. The firm's output variation has an imperceptible effect on industry output.

average revenue (*AR*) Total revenue divided by quantity sold; this is the market price when all units are sold at the same price.

Average revenue (***AR***) is the amount of revenue per unit sold. It is equal to total revenue divided by the number of units sold, and is thus equal to the price at which the product is sold:

$$AR = \frac{TR}{Q} = \frac{(p \times Q)}{Q} = p$$

marginal revenue (*MR*) The change in a firm's total revenue resulting from a change in its sales by one unit.

Marginal revenue (***MR***) is the change in a firm's total revenue resulting from a change in its sales by 1 unit. Whenever output changes by more than 1 unit, the change in revenue must be divided by the change in output to calculate marginal revenue. For example, if an increase in output of 3 units is accompanied by an increase in revenue of \$1500, the marginal revenue is \$1500/3, or \$500. **[21]**

$$MR = \frac{\Delta TR}{\Delta Q}$$

To illustrate each of these revenue concepts, consider a farmer who is selling barley in a perfectly competitive market at a price of \$3 per bushel. Total revenue rises by \$3 for every bushel sold. Because every bushel brings in \$3, the average revenue per bushel sold is clearly \$3. Furthermore, because each *additional* bushel sold brings in \$3, the marginal revenue of an extra bushel sold is also \$3. The table in Figure 9-2 shows calculations of these revenue concepts for a range of outputs between 10 and 13 bushels. The figure plots the various revenue curves.

The important point illustrated in the table is that as long as the firm's own level of output cannot affect the price of the product it sells, then the firm's marginal revenue is equal to its average revenue. Thus, for a price-taking firm, $AR = MR =$ price. Graphically, as shown in part (i) of Figure 9-2, average revenue and marginal revenue are the same horizontal line drawn at the level of market price. Because the firm can sell any quantity it chooses at this price, the horizontal line is also the firm's demand curve; it shows that any quantity the firm chooses to sell will be associated with this same market price.

APPLYING ECONOMIC CONCEPTS 9-1

Demand Under Perfect Competition: Firm and Industry

Consider an individual wheat farmer and the world market for wheat. Since products have negatively sloped market demand curves, any increase in the industry's output (caused by a shift in supply) will cause some fall in the market price. However, as the calculations here show, any conceivable increase that one wheat farm could make in its output has such a negligible effect on the industry's price that the farmer correctly ignores it—the individual wheat farmer is thus a price taker.

The *market* elasticity of demand for wheat is approximately 0.25. (Recall from Chapter 4 that an elasticity of 0.25 means that a 10 percent decline in market price is associated with only a 2.5 percent increase in quantity demanded.) Thus, if the quantity of wheat supplied in the world were to increase by 1 percent, the price of wheat would have to fall by roughly 4 percent to induce the world's wheat buyers to purchase the extra wheat.

The total world production of wheat in 2003 was approximately 550 million tonnes, of which 23.5 million tonnes were produced in Canada. In that year there were approximately 20 000 wheat farms in Canada. Thus, the average crop size for a Canadian wheat farmer in 2003 was about 1175 tonnes (= 23.5 million/20 000), only 0.0002 percent of the world wheat crop.

As a result of being such a small fraction of the overall market, individual wheat farmers face a horizontal demand curve. To see this, suppose an individual farmer on an average-sized farm decided in one year to produce nothing and in another year managed to produce twice the average output of 1175 tonnes. This is an extremely large variation in one farm's output. The increase in output from zero to 2350 tonnes represents a 200-percent variation measured around the farm's average output. Yet the percentage increase in world output is only $(2350 / 550 \text{ million}) \times 100 = 0.0004$ percent. Given the demand elasticity of 0.25, this increase in output would lead to a decrease in the world price of 0.0016 percent.

This very small decline in price, together with the 200-percent increase in the farm's *own* output, implies that the farm's own demand curve has an elasticity of 125 000 (= 200 / 0.0016). This enormous elasticity of demand means that the farm would have to increase its output by 125 000 percent to bring about a 1-percent decrease in the world price of wheat. Because the farm's output cannot be varied this much, it is not surprising that the farmer regards the price of wheat as unaffected by any change in output that he or she could conceivably make. For all intents and purposes, the individual farmer faces a perfectly elastic—horizontal—demand curve for the product and is thus a *price taker.*

If the market price is unaffected by variations in the firm's output, the firm's demand curve, its average revenue curve, and its marginal revenue curve all coincide in the same horizontal line.

This result can be stated in a slightly different way that turns out to be important for our later study:

For a firm in perfect competition, price equals marginal revenue.

FIGURE 9-2 Revenues for a Price-Taking Firm

Revenue Concepts

Price p	Output Q	$TR = p \times Q$	$AR = TR/Q$	$MR = \Delta TR/\Delta Q$
$3	10	$30	$3	
				$3
3	11	33	3	
				3
3	12	36	3	
				3
3	13	39	3	

Revenue Curves

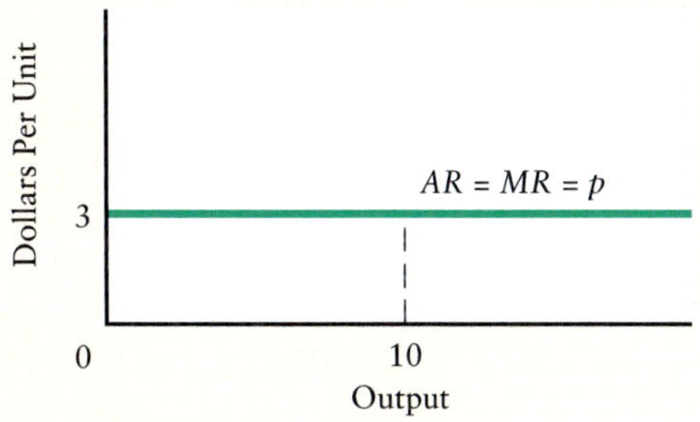

(i) Average and marginal revenue

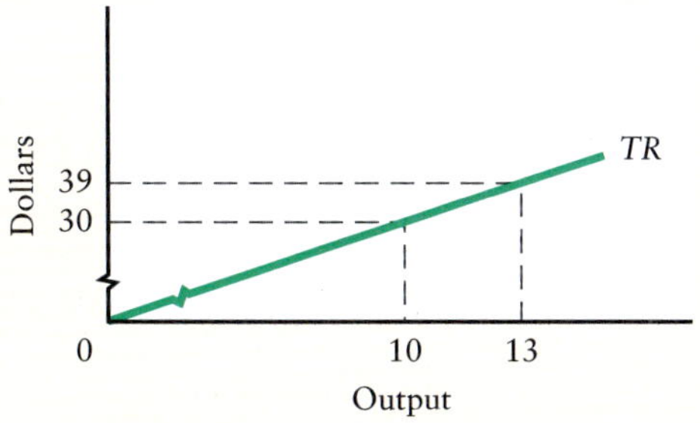

(ii) Total revenue

When the firm is a price taker, $AR = MR = p$. Because price does not change as a result of the firm changing its output, neither marginal revenue nor average revenue varies with output. In the table, marginal revenue is shown between the rows because it represents the *change* in total revenues in response to a *change* in quantity. When price is constant, total revenue (which is price times quantity) is an upward-sloping straight line starting from the origin.

9.3 SHORT-RUN DECISIONS

We learned in Chapter 7 how each firm's costs vary with its output in the short run. Recall that in the short run, the firm has one or more fixed factors, and the only way it can change its output is by changing the amount of its variable factor inputs. In this chapter, we have seen how the firm's total, average, and marginal revenues vary as the firm changes its level of output. The next step is to put the cost and revenue information together to determine the level of output that will maximize the firm's profits.

Rules for All Profit-Maximizing Firms

Two rules apply to *all* profit-maximizing firms, whether or not they operate in perfectly competitive markets. The first rule determines whether the firm should produce at all, and the second determines how much it should produce.

Should the Firm Produce at All? The firm always has the option of producing nothing. If it produces nothing, it will have an operating loss that is equal to its fixed costs. If it decides to produce, it will add the variable cost of production to its costs and the receipts from the sale of its product to its revenue. Therefore, since it must pay its fixed costs in any event, it will be worthwhile for the firm to produce as long as it can find some level of output for which revenue exceeds *variable* cost. However, if its revenue is less than its variable cost at every level of output, the firm will actually lose more by producing any level of output than by not producing at all.

Table 9-1 shows an example of a profit-maximizing firm that decides to produce no output when facing a low market price. The table shows the firm's variable and fixed costs for each level of output. (If you were to graph the *TVC*, *TFC*, and *TC* curves from this table, you would find that they look very much like the curves we studied in Chapter 7.) The table also shows the firm's total revenues and profits at each level of output. When the market price is $2 per unit, the firm's profits are negative *at any level of output*—the firm's revenues *never* cover its costs. At this low market price, the firm's revenues don't even cover its variable costs and, in fact, the negative profits (losses) only grow larger as output increases. In this situation, the firm is better off to shut down and produce no output at all. (The table also presents a situation where the price is $5 per unit; for reasons that we will soon see, the firm's best option is then to produce output even though its profits are negative.)

Rule 1: A firm should not produce at all if, for all levels of output, the total variable cost of producing that output exceeds the total revenue derived from selling it. Equivalently, the firm should not produce at all if, for all levels of output, the average variable cost of producing the output exceeds the price at which it can be sold. [22]

TABLE 9-1 Negative Profits and the Firm's Shut-Down Decision

				Price = $2		Price = $5	
Q	*TVC*	*TFC*	*TC*	*TR*	Profit	*TR*	Profit
0	0	200	200	0	−200	0	−200
10	50	200	250	20	−230	50	−200
20	80	200	280	40	−240	100	−180
30	100	200	300	60	−240	150	−150
40	110	200	310	80	−230	200	−110
50	130	200	330	100	−230	250	−80
60	160	200	360	120	−240	300	−60
70	200	200	400	140	−260	350	−50
80	260	200	460	160	−300	400	−60
90	320	200	520	180	−340	450	−70
100	380	200	580	200	−380	500	−80

A competitive firm may maximize its profits (or minimize its losses) by shutting down and producing zero output. The data in the table show costs and revenues at various levels of output. The firm must pay its fixed costs even if it shuts down and earns no revenue. At a price of $2, there is *no* level of output at which the firm's revenues cover its variable costs. In this situation, the firm can minimize its losses by shutting down and producing zero output.

At a higher price of $5, the profit-maximizing firm should choose to produce 70 units of output even though its profits are negative. At this level of output, the firm's revenues more than cover its variable costs and help to pay some portion of the fixed costs. Since the firm must pay its fixed costs no matter what level of output is produced, it would be worse off if it chose to produce zero output.

The price at which the firm can just cover its average variable cost, and so is indifferent between producing and not producing, is called the **shut-down price**. Such a price is shown in part (i) of Figure 9-4. (We will return in a moment to Figure 9-3.) At the price of $20, the firm can just cover its average variable cost by producing Q_0 units. For any price below $20, there is no output at which variable costs can be covered, and thus the firm will shut down. The price of $20 in part (i) is therefore the shut-down price.

shut-down price The price that is equal to the minimum of a firm's average variable costs. At prices below this, a profit-maximizing firm will shut down and produce no output.

How Much Should the Firm Produce? If a firm decides that, according to Rule 1, production is worth undertaking, it must then decide *how much* to produce. The key to understanding how much the firm should produce is to think about it on a unit-by-unit basis. If any unit of production adds more to revenue than it does to cost, producing and selling that unit will increase profits. According to the terminology introduced earlier, a unit of production raises profits if the *marginal* revenue obtained from selling it exceeds the *marginal* cost of producing it. The reverse is also true: An extra unit of production will reduce profits if the marginal revenue is less than the marginal cost.

Now let a firm with some existing rate of output consider increasing or decreasing that output. If a further unit of production will increase the firm's revenues by *more* than it increases costs ($MR > MC$), the firm should expand its output. However, if the last unit produced increases revenues by *less* than it increases costs ($MR < MC$), the firm should reduce its output. From this it follows that the only time the firm should leave its output unaltered is when the last unit produced adds the same amount to revenues as it does to costs ($MR = MC$).[1]

Rule 2: If it is worthwhile for the firm to produce at all, the firm should produce the output at which marginal revenue equals marginal cost. [23]

The two rules that we have stated refer to each firm's own costs and revenues, and they apply to all profit-maximizing firms, whatever the market structure in which they operate.

Rule 2 Applied to Price-Taking Firms Rule 2 tells us that any profit-maximizing firm that produces at all will produce at the point where marginal cost equals marginal revenue. However, we have already seen that for price-taking firms, marginal revenue is equal to the market price. Combining these two results gives us an important conclusion:

A firm that is operating in a perfectly competitive market will produce the output that equates its marginal cost of production with the market price of its product (as long as price exceeds average variable cost).

In a perfectly competitive industry, the market determines the price at which the firm sells its product. The firm then picks the quantity of output that maximizes its profits. We have seen that this is the output for which price equals marginal cost. When the firm has reached a position where its profits are maximized, it has no incentive to change its output. Therefore, unless prices or costs change, the firm will continue to produce this output because it is doing as well as it can do, given the market situation. This profit-maximizing behaviour is illustrated in Figure 9-3.

Practise with Study Guide Chapter 9, Exercise 1.

The perfectly competitive firm adjusts its level of output in response to changes in the market-determined price.

[1] The equality of MR and MC is a *necessary* condition for profit maximization but it is not *sufficient*. If the MC curve cuts the MR curve from above, as it might if MC were *falling* as output increased, then the level of output where MR equals MC would actually *minimize* profits. Here, we restrict ourselves to the more realistic settings in which the MC curve is upward sloping over the relevant range of output. In such cases, the equality of MR and MC is both necessary and sufficient for profit maximization.

FIGURE 9-3 Profit Maximization for a Competitive Firm

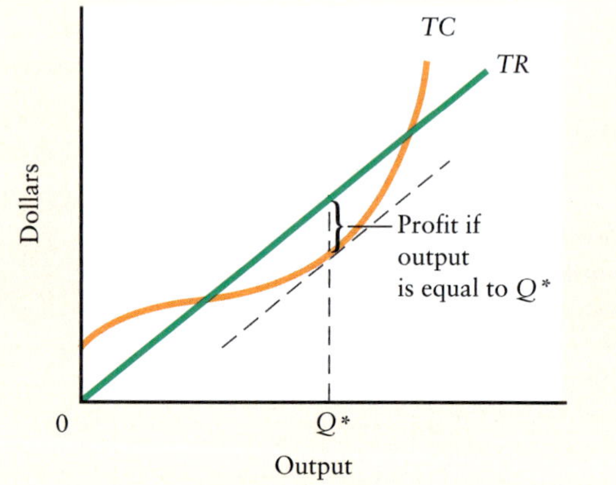

(i) Total costs and total revenues

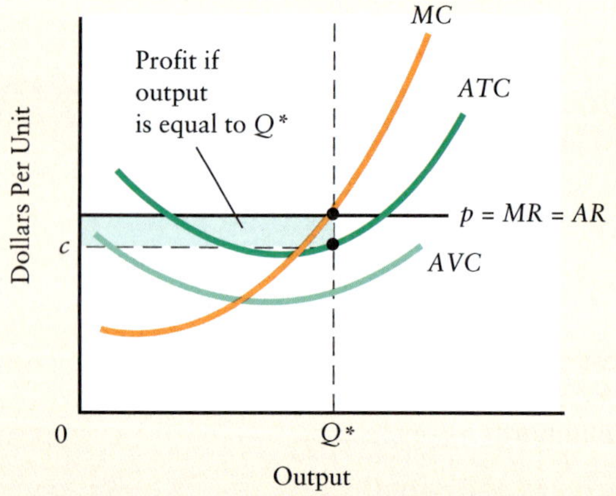

(ii) Marginal cost and marginal revenue

The firm chooses the level of output at which profits are maximized. If it is profitable to produce at all (so that price exceeds the minimum of average variable cost), the firm chooses the level of output where marginal revenue equals marginal cost. In part (i), this is shown as the level of output where the vertical distance between *TR* and *TC* is largest (and thus where the slopes of the *TR* and *TC* curves are the same). In part (ii), price is equal to marginal revenue since the firm is a price taker, and so the profit-maximizing level of output is where price (marginal revenue) equals marginal cost. For each of the Q^* units sold, the firm earns revenue of p and the average total cost is c; therefore, total profit is $(p - c)Q^*$, which is the shaded area.

Figure 9-3 shows the profit-maximizing choice of the firm in two different ways. In part (i), the firm's total cost and total revenue curves are shown, and the profit-maximizing level of output, Q^*, is the level that shows the largest positive gap between total revenues and total costs. In part (ii), the firm's average and marginal cost curves are shown together with the market price (which for a price-taking firm equals average and marginal revenue) and the profit-maximizing level of output, Q^*, is the level at which price equals marginal cost. These are two different ways of viewing the same profit-maximization problem; the value of Q^* in part (i) must be the same as the value of Q^* in part (ii).

Short-Run Supply Curves

Now that we know how the perfectly competitive firm determines its profit-maximizing level of output, we can derive its supply curve that reflects these decisions. Once we have derived the individual firm's supply curve, we can derive the supply curve for the entire market.

The Supply Curve for One Firm The competitive firm's supply curve is derived in part (i) of Figure 9-4, which shows a firm's marginal cost curve and four alternative prices. The horizontal line at each price is the firm's demand curve when the market price is at that level. The firm's marginal cost curve gives the marginal cost corresponding to each level of output. What we are trying to derive is a supply curve that shows the quantity of output that the firm will supply at each price. For prices below average variable cost, the firm will supply zero units (Rule 1). For prices above average variable cost, the competitive firm will choose its level of output to equate price and marginal cost (Rule 2). This behaviour leads to the following conclusion:

A competitive firm's supply curve is given by the portion of its marginal cost curve that is above its average variable cost curve.

The Supply Curve for an Industry Figure 9-5 shows the derivation of an industry supply curve for an industry containing only two firms. The general result is as follows:

In perfect competition, the industry supply curve is the horizontal sum of the marginal cost curves (above the level of average variable cost) of all firms in the industry.

FIGURE 9-4 The Derivation of the Supply Curve for a Competitive Firm

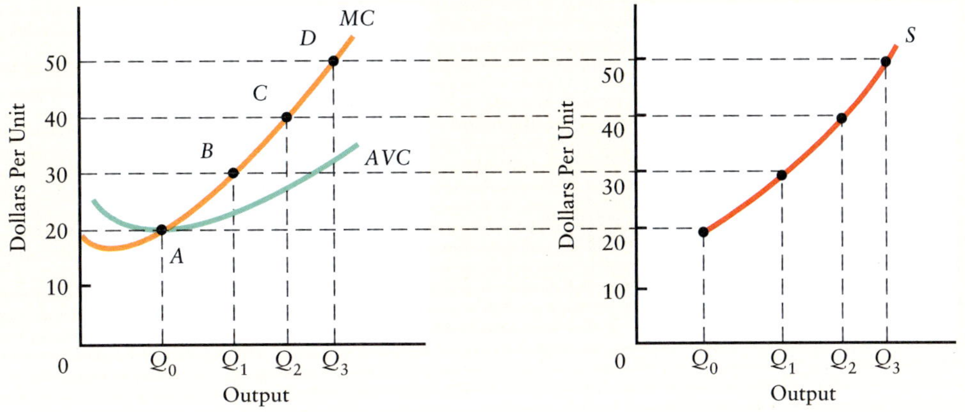

(i) Marginal cost and average variable cost curves

(ii) Firm's supply curve

The supply curve of the competitive firm is the portion of its *MC* curve above the *AVC* curve. For prices below \$20, output is zero because there is no output at which *AVC* can be covered. The point *A*, where the price of \$20 is just equal to *AVC*, is the point at which the firm will shut down. As price rises to \$30, \$40, and \$50, the profit-maximizing point changes to *B*, *C*, and *D*, taking output to Q_1, Q_2, and Q_3. At any of these prices, the firm's revenue exceeds its variable costs of production and thus can help to cover some part of its fixed costs.

FIGURE 9-5 The Derivation of a Competitive Industry's Supply Curve

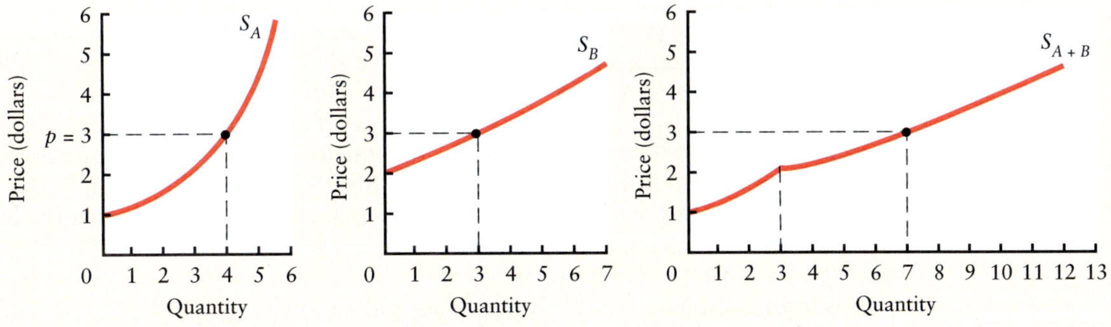

(i) Firm A's supply curve

(ii) Firm B's supply curve

(iii) Industry supply curve

The industry's supply curve is the horizontal sum of the supply curves of each of the firms in the industry. At a price of \$3, Firm A would supply 4 units and Firm B would supply 3 units. Together, as shown in part (iii), they would supply 7 units. If there are hundreds of firms, the process is the same. In this example, because Firm B does not enter the market at prices below \$2, the supply curve S_{A+B} is identical to S_A up to price \$2 and is the horizontal sum of S_A and S_B above \$2.

Each firm's marginal cost curve shows how much that firm will supply at each given market price, and the industry supply curve is the sum of what each firm will supply.

This supply curve, based on the short-run marginal cost curves of all the firms in the industry, is the industry's supply curve that we first encountered in Chapter 3. We have now established the profit-maximizing behaviour of individual firms that lies behind that curve. It is sometimes called a *short-run supply curve* because it is based on the short-run, profit-maximizing behaviour of all the firms in the industry.

Short-Run Equilibrium in a Competitive Market

The price of a product sold in a perfectly competitive market is determined by the interaction of the industry's supply curve and the market demand curve. Although no single firm can influence the market price significantly, the collective actions of all firms in the industry (as shown by the industry supply curve) and the collective actions of households (as shown by the market demand curve) together determine the equilibrium price. This occurs at the point where the market demand and supply curves intersect.

short-run equilibrium For a competitive industry, the price and output at which industry demand equals short-run industry supply, and all firms are maximizing their profits. Either profits or losses for individual firms are possible.

When a perfectly competitive industry is in **short-run equilibrium**, each firm is producing and selling a quantity for which its marginal cost equals the market price. No firm is motivated to change its output in the short run. Because total quantity demanded equals total quantity supplied, there is no reason for market price to change in the short run.

When an industry is in short-run equilibrium, quantity demanded equals quantity supplied, and each firm is maximizing its profits given the market price.

Practise with Study Guide Chapter 9, Exercise 2.

Figure 9-6 shows the relationship between the market equilibrium, determined by the intersection of demand and supply, and a typical profit-maximizing firm within that market. The individual firm is shown to have positive (economic) profits in the short-run equilibrium. We know the firm's profits are positive because the market price exceeds average total costs when the firm is producing its profit-maximizing level of output, q^*. But such positive profits need not always be the case in the short run. In general, we do not know whether firms in the short-run competitive equilibrium will be earning positive, zero, or negative profits. We *do* know that each firm is maximizing its profits; we just don't know how large those profits are.

Figure 9-7 shows three possible positions for a firm when the industry is in short-run equilibrium. In all cases, the firm is maximizing its profits by producing where price equals marginal cost, but in part (i) the firm is suffering losses, in part (ii) it is just covering all of its costs (breaking even), and in part (iii) it is making profits because price exceeds average total cost. In all three cases, the firm is doing as well as it can, given its costs and the market price.

It is worth emphasizing that some firms will continue producing even though they are making losses. The firm shown in part (i) of Figure 9-7 is incurring losses every period that it remains in business, but it is still better for it to carry on producing than to temporarily halt production. If the firm produces nothing this period it still must pay its fixed costs, so it makes sense to continue producing as long as its revenues more than cover its variable costs or, equivalently, as long as price exceeds *AVC*. Any amount of money left over after the variable costs have been paid can then go toward paying some of the fixed costs. This is more than the firm would have if it simply produced nothing and hence earned no revenue whatsoever. (Look back to Table 9-1 to see an example of this situation, in the case where market price is $5 per unit.) *Applying*

FIGURE 9-6 A Typical Firm When the Competitive Market Is in Short-Run Equilibrium

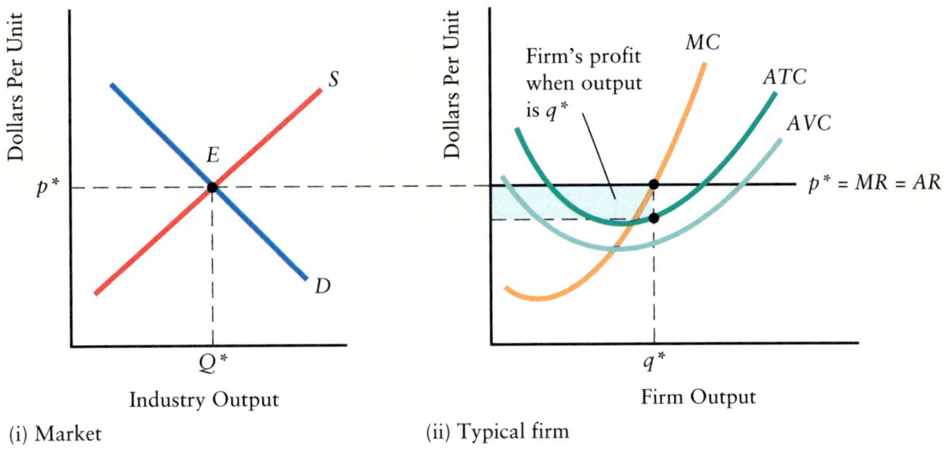

Short-run equilibrium in a competitive market has a market-clearing price and each firm is maximizing its profits. Part (i) shows the overall market. The equilibrium price and quantity (p^*, Q^*) are determined at the intersection of the market demand and supply curves at point *E*. Part (ii) shows a typical firm in the market. Notice that the horizontal scales are different in the two parts of the figure—total market output is designated by *Q*, whereas firm-level output is designated by *q*. The equilibrium price in part (i) becomes the *MR* curve for each firm in the market. Given its *MC* curve, the firm's profit-maximizing level of output is q^*. In the case shown, the firm is making positive profits equal to the shaded area.

Economic Concepts 9-2 on page 206 discusses an interesting example of a firm that remains in operation even though it is making losses. You have probably seen many firms like this one as you drive through small towns in any part of Canada.

myeconlab

A firm that is maximizing its profit but still making losses is actually *minimizing* its losses. To see a detailed numerical example of a firm in such a situation, look for "An Example of Loss Minimization as Profit Maximization" in the *Additional Topics* section of this book's MyEconLab.

www.myeconlab.com

9.4 LONG-RUN DECISIONS

In Chapters 7 and 8, we described the short run as the span of time for which individual firms have a fixed factor of production (typically capital), and the long run as the span of time for which individual firms have no fixed factors. When we look at the entire industry, the distinction is very similar. In the short run, there is a given number of firms and each has a given plant size. In the long run, both the number of firms and the size of each firm's plant are variable.

FIGURE 9-7 Alternative Short-Run Profits of a Competitive Firm

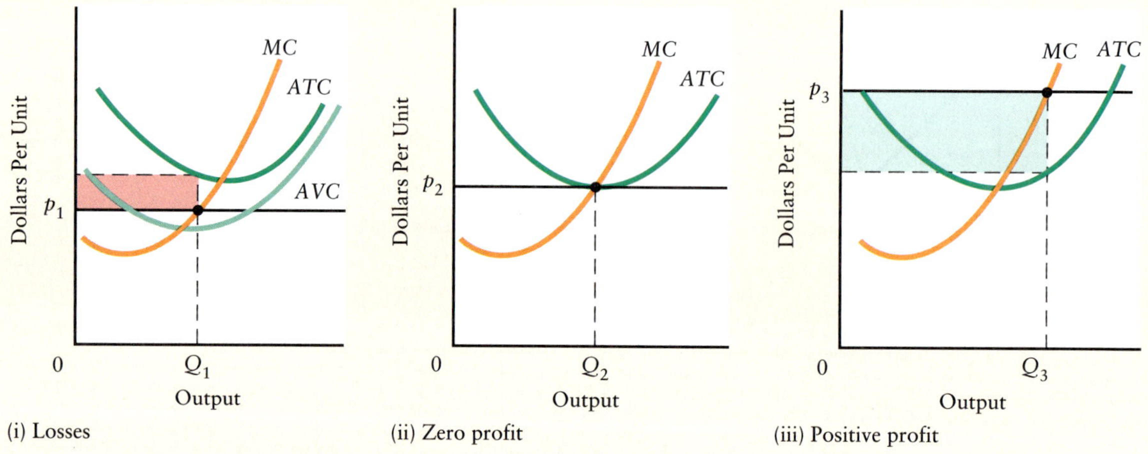

When the industry is in short-run equilibrium, a competitive firm may be suffering losses, breaking even, or making profits. The diagrams show a firm with given costs that faces three alternative short-run equilibrium market prices: p_1, p_2, and p_3. In each part of the figure, $MC = MR =$ price. Because in all three cases price exceeds *AVC,* the firm produces positive output in each case.

In part (i), price is p_1 and the firm is suffering losses, shown by the red shaded area, because price is below average total cost. Because price exceeds average variable cost, it is worthwhile for the firm to keep producing, but it is not worthwhile for it to replace its capital equipment as it wears out. In part (ii), price is p_2 and the firm is just covering its total costs. It is worthwhile for the firm to replace its capital as it wears out, since it is covering the full opportunity cost of its capital. In part (iii), price is p_3 and the firm is earning profits, shown by the green shaded area.

We begin our discussion of the long run by assuming that all firms in the industry have the same technology and therefore have the same set of cost curves. Thus, the short-run equilibrium in the industry will have *all* firms in the industry being equally profitable (or making equal losses). Toward the end of the chapter we relax this assumption when we allow new firms to have better technologies and thus lower costs than older firms already in the industry.

Entry and Exit

The key difference between a perfectly competitive industry in the short run and in the long run is the entry or exit of firms. We have seen that all the firms in the industry may be making profits, suffering losses, or just breaking even when the industry is in short-run equilibrium. Because costs include the opportunity cost of capital, if the firms are just breaking even they are doing as well as they could do by investing their capital elsewhere. Hence, there will be no incentive for firms to leave the industry if profits are zero. Similarly, if new entrants expect just to break even, there will be no incentive for firms to enter the industry because capital can earn the same return elsewhere in the economy. If, however, the existing firms are earning revenues in excess of all costs, including the opportunity cost of capital, new capital will eventually enter the industry to share in these profits. Conversely, if the existing firms are suffering losses, capital will eventually leave the industry because a better return can be obtained elsewhere in the economy. Let us now consider this process in a little more detail.

An Entry-Attracting Price First, suppose there are 100 firms in a competitive industry, all making positive profits like the firm shown in part (iii) of Figure 9-7. New firms, attracted by the profitability of existing firms, will enter the industry. Suppose that in response to the high profits, 20 new firms enter. The market supply curve that formerly added up the outputs of 100 firms must now add up the outputs of 120 firms. At any price, more will be supplied because there are more producers. This entry of new firms into the industry causes a rightward shift in the industry supply curve.

With an unchanged market demand curve, this rightward shift in the industry supply curve will reduce the equilibrium price. Both new and old firms will have to adjust their output to this new price. New firms will continue to enter, and the equilibrium price will continue to fall, until all firms in the industry are just covering their total costs. The industry has now reached what is called a *zero-profit equilibrium.* The entry of new firms then ceases. The effect of entry is shown in Figure 9-8.

Profits in a competitive industry are a signal for the entry of new firms; the industry will expand, pushing price down until profits fall to zero.

An Exit-Inducing Price We saw in Figure 9-4 that the firm's supply curve is the section of its marginal cost curve above the average variable cost curve. If the market price falls below the minimum of average variable cost, the firm will simply shut down its

FIGURE 9-8 The Effect of New Entrants Attracted by Positive Profits

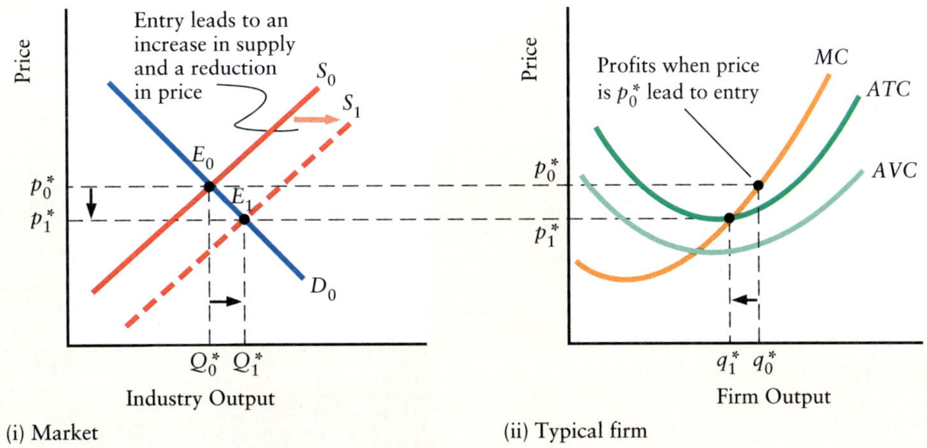

Positive profits lead to the entry of new firms; this entry reduces the equilibrium market price and reduces the profits of all firms. The initial short-run equilibrium is E_0 in part (i) with equilibrium price p_0*. At this price, a typical firm in the industry is producing q_0* units of output and is earning positive profits (since p_0* >*ATC* at q_0*). These positive profits attract other firms who then enter the industry, causing the supply curve to shift to the right and reducing the market price. The process of entry will continue until profits are driven to zero. S_1 is the final supply curve and the equilibrium market price has fallen to p_1*. At the new market price, firms have each reduced their output to q_1* and are now just covering their total costs. Notice that each of the original firms is producing less than before, but because of the new entrants total industry output has increased from Q_0* to Q_1*.

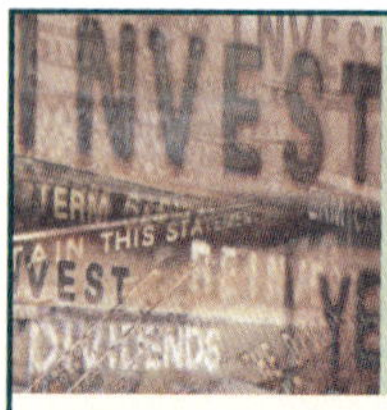

APPLYING ECONOMIC CONCEPTS 9-2

The Parable of the Seaside Inn

Why do some resort hotels stay open during the off-season, even though to do so they must offer bargain rates that do not even cover their "full costs"? Why do the managers of other hotels allow them to fall into disrepair even though they are able to attract enough customers to stay in business? Are the former being overly generous, and are the latter being irrational penny-pinchers?

To illustrate what is involved, consider an imaginary resort hotel called the Seaside Inn. Its revenues and costs of operating during the four months of the high-season and during the eight months of the off-season are shown in the accompanying table. When the profit-maximizing price for its rooms is charged in the high-season, the hotel earns revenues of \$58 000 and incurs variable costs equal to \$36 000. Thus, there is an "operating profit" of \$22 000 during the high-season. This surplus goes toward meeting the hotel's annual fixed costs of \$24 000. Thus, \$2000 of the fixed costs are not yet paid.

If the Seaside Inn were to charge the same rates during the off-season, it could not attract enough customers even to cover its costs of maids, bellhops, and managers. However, the hotel discovers that by charging lower rates during the off-season, it can rent some of its rooms and earn revenues of \$20 000. Its costs of operating (variable costs) during the off-season are \$18 000. So, by operating at reduced rates in the off-season, the hotel is able to contribute another \$2000 toward its annual fixed costs, thereby eliminating the shortfall.

Therefore, the hotel stays open during the whole year by offering off-season bargain rates to grateful guests. Indeed, if it were to close during the off-season, it would not be able to cover its total fixed and variable costs solely through its high-season operations.

The Seaside Inn: Total Costs and Revenues (\$)

Season	Total Revenue (*TR*)	Total Variable Cost (*TVC*)	Contribution to Fixed Costs (*TR-TVC*)	Total Fixed Costs
High-Season	58 000	36 000	22 000	
Off-Season	20 000	18 000	2 000	
Total	78 000	54 000	24 000	24 000

We have not yet discussed firms' long-run decisions in the chapter, but you can get a feel for the issues by considering the following situation. Suppose the off-season revenues fall to \$19 000 (everything else remaining the same). The short-run condition for staying open, that total revenue (*TR*) must exceed total variable cost (*TVC*), is met both for the high-season and for the off-season. However, since the *TR* over the whole year of \$77 000 is less than the total costs of \$78 000, the hotel is now making losses for the year as a whole. The hotel will remain open as long as it can do so with its present capital—it will produce in the short run. However, it will not be worthwhile for the owners to replace the capital as it wears out.

If the reduction in revenues persists, the hotel will become one of those run-down hotels about which guests ask, "Why don't they do something about this place?"—but the owners are behaving quite sensibly. They are operating the hotel as long as it covers its variable costs, but they are not putting any more investment into it because it cannot cover its fixed costs. Sooner or later, the fixed capital will become too old to be run, or at least to attract customers, and the hotel will be closed.

Hotels and other resorts often charge low prices in the off-season, low enough that they do not cover their total costs. But as long as the price more than covers the variable costs, it is better than shutting down during the off-season.

production. Indeed, the firm's *shut-down price* is defined to be the minimum of the firm's average variable costs because, at any price lower than this, the firm is better off producing nothing than producing any positive amount.

If market price declines below the minimum of a competitive firm's *AVC* curve, the firm will shut down immediately and exit the industry.

If firms are making losses but the market price is *above* the shut-down point, there will still be exit from the industry, but it will be more gradual. Suppose the firms in a competitive industry are making losses, like the firm shown in part (i) of Figure 9-7. Although the firms are covering their variable costs, the return on their capital is less than the opportunity cost of capital. They are not covering their total costs. This is a signal for the gradual exit of firms. Old plants and equipment will not be replaced as they wear out. As a result, the industry's supply curve eventually shifts leftward, and the market price rises. Firms will continue to exit, and the market price will continue to rise, until the remaining firms can cover their total costs. Once again the market reaches a zero-profit equilibrium. The exit of firms then ceases. This gradual process of exit is shown in Figure 9-9.

Losses in a competitive industry are a signal for the exit of firms; the industry will contract, driving the market price up until the remaining firms are just covering their total costs.

FIGURE 9-9 The Effect of Exit Caused by Losses

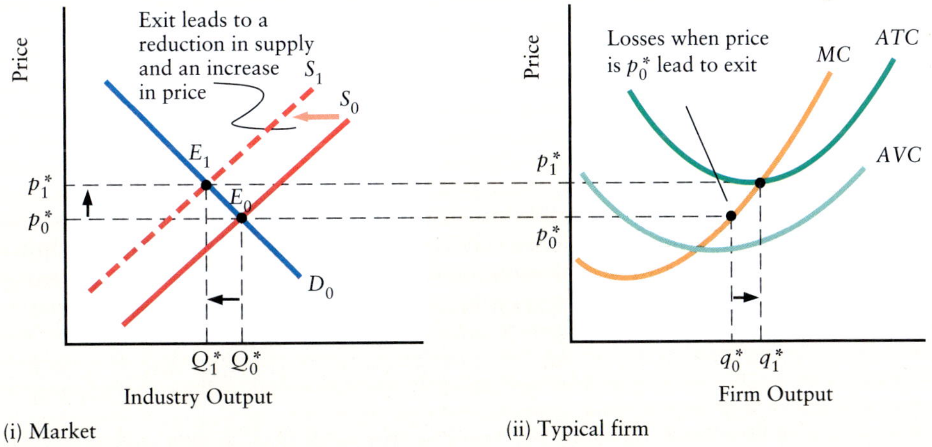

Negative profits lead to the eventual exit of some firms as their capital becomes obsolete or becomes too costly to operate; this exit increases the equilibrium price and increases profits for those firms remaining in the market. The initial market equilibrium is E_0 in part (i), with equilibrium price p_0*. At this market price, a typical firm is producing q_0* units and is making *negative* profits but, because price exceeds *AVC*, the firm remains in business. Since firms are earning less than the opportunity cost on their capital, they do not replace their capital as it becomes obsolete. Eventually, some firms close down. As firms exit the industry, the industry supply curve shifts to the left and the market price increases to p_1*. For the remaining firms, this price increase leads them to increase their output from q_0* to q_1*, the level of output at which they are just covering their total costs. Notice that the remaining firms are producing more than before, but because of the exit of firms total industry output has fallen from Q_0* to Q_1*.

Sunk Costs and the Speed of Exit The process of exit is not always quick and is sometimes painfully slow for the loss-making firms in the industry. The rate at which firms leave unprofitable industries depends on how quickly their capital becomes obsolete or becomes too costly to operate due to rising maintenance costs as it ages. In many professional service industries, such as graphic design or consulting, the physical capital is mostly office equipment such as computers, printers, and so on. This equipment becomes obsolete in just a few years, and thus loss-making firms will tend to exit the industry very quickly. In other industries, such as railways or shipping, the physical capital takes much longer to become obsolete. The result is that loss-making firms in these industries will remain in operation for many years.

The longer it takes for firms' capital to become obsolete or too costly to operate, the longer firms will remain in the industry while they are earning economic losses.

Another important factor in the speed of exit from an industry is the nature of firms' fixed costs. Economists divide a firm's fixed costs into *sunk costs*—costs that could never be recovered—and *non-sunk costs*—costs that could be recovered by the firm selling its capital or terminating its rental agreement.

As an example, consider a competitive firm in the machine-tools industry. It builds a factory and equips it for a total cost of $30 million. This $30 million is an important fixed cost for the firm. If the factory and machines are useful only for producing in this industry, it might be very difficult to sell the factory if the firm ever wanted to exit the industry. If the firm is unable to sell the plant at all, the $30 million is a sunk cost. On the other hand, if the factory and equipment can be used to produce other products, as is often the case, then the firm could sell the factory if it ever wanted to exit the industry. If the firm could sell its factory for the full $30 million, the factory would be a fixed, but non-sunk, cost.

Not all fixed costs are associated with the capital cost of building or renting a factory. Other costs that are fixed while the firm is operating include the rental or leasing costs of office equipment and furniture. Such fixed costs are often non-sunk costs for the firm, however, because if the firm shuts down it can terminate these rental or lease agreements, thus avoiding the costs altogether.

This distinction between sunk and non-sunk costs affects the speed of exit for loss-making firms. To see why, suppose our machine-tools firm is making losses in the short-run market equilibrium (as in Figure 9-9). If the $30 million factory is a sunk cost, then the firm cannot recover the cost by selling the factory. In this case, the firm will remain in business as long as the market price of its product exceeds its *AVC*; the alternative of closing down and earning no revenue is less profitable. If all firms are like this, the adjustment shown in Figure 9-9 will be slow and gradual. On the other hand, if the firm is able to sell the factory, it can shut down its production and *avoid* paying the fixed costs. In this case, it makes no sense to remain in business making losses just because price is greater than average variable cost. It would be better to sell the factory, recover the fixed costs, and exit the industry. If all firms are like this, the adjustment shown in Figure 9-9 will be relatively quick.

If firms' fixed costs are mostly sunk costs, the process of exit in loss-making industries will be slow. If firms' fixed costs are mostly non-sunk costs, the process of exit will be faster.

Long-Run Equilibrium

Practise with Study Guide Chapter 9, Exercises 3 and 4.

Because sooner or later firms exit when they are making losses and enter in pursuit of profits, we get the following conclusion:

The long-run equilibrium of a competitive industry occurs when firms are earning zero profits.

When a perfectly competitive industry is in long-run equilibrium, each firm will be like the firm in part (ii) of Figure 9-7, earning zero economic profit. For such firms, the price p_2 is sometimes called the **break-even price.** It is the price at which all costs, including the opportunity cost of capital, are being covered. Any firm that is just breaking even is willing to stay in the industry. It has no incentive to leave, nor do other firms have an incentive to enter.

break-even price The price at which a firm is just able to cover all of its costs, including the opportunity cost of capital.

Conditions for Long-Run Equilibrium The previous discussion suggests four conditions for a competitive industry to be in long-run equilibrium.

1. Existing firms must be maximizing their profits, given their existing capital. Thus, short-run marginal costs of production must be equal to market price.
2. Existing firms must not be suffering losses. If they are suffering losses, they will not replace their capital and the size of the industry will decline over time.
3. Existing firms must not be earning profits. If they are earning profits, then new firms will enter the industry and the size of the industry will increase over time.
4. Existing firms must not be able to increase their profits by changing the size of their production facilities. Thus, each existing firm must be at the minimum point of its *long-run* average cost (*LRAC*) curve.

This last condition is new to our discussion. Figure 9-10 shows that if the condition does not hold—that is, if the firm is *not* at the minimum of its *LRAC* curve—a firm can increase its profits. In the case shown, although the firm is maximizing its profits with its existing production facilities, there are unexploited economies of scale. By building a larger plant, the firm can move down its *LRAC* curve and reduce its average cost. Alternatively, if the firm were producing at an output that put it beyond the lowest point on its *LRAC* curve, it could raise its profits by reducing its plant size. Because in either situation average cost is just equal to the market price, any reduction in average cost must yield profits.

FIGURE 9-10 Short-Run Versus Long-Run Profit Maximization for a Competitive Firm

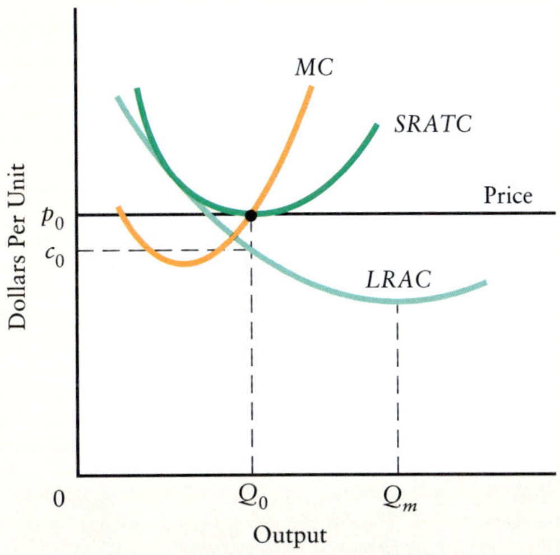

A competitive firm that is not at the minimum point on its *LRAC* curve is not maximizing its long-run profits. A competitive firm with short-run cost curves *SRATC* and *MC* faces a market price of p_0. The firm produces Q_0, where *MC* equals price and total costs are just being covered. However, the firm's long-run average cost curve lies below its short-run curve at output Q_0. The firm could produce output Q_0 at cost c_0 by building a larger plant so as to take advantage of economies of scale. Profits would rise, because average total costs of c_0 would then be less than price p_0. The firm cannot be maximizing its long-run profits at any output below Q_m because, with any such output, average total costs can be reduced by building a larger plant. The output Q_m is the *minimum efficient scale* of the firm.

FIGURE 9-11 A Typical Competitive Firm When the Industry Is in Long-Run Equilibrium

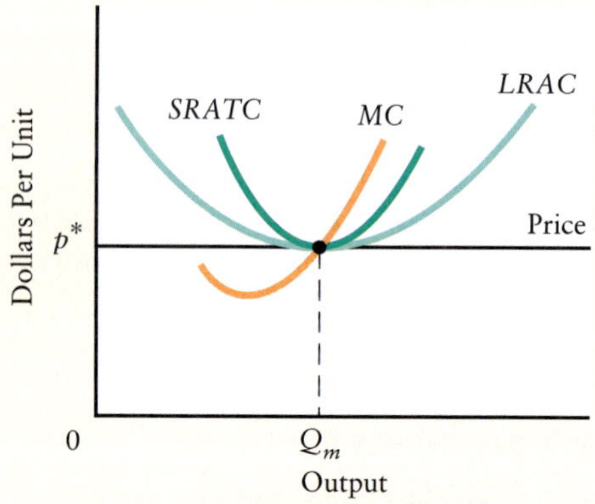

In long-run competitive equilibrium, each firm is operating at the minimum point on its *LRAC* curve. In long-run equilibrium, each firm must be (1) maximizing short-run profits, $MC = p$; (2) earning profits of zero on its existing plant, $SRATC = p$; and (3) unable to increase its profits by altering the scale of its operations. These three conditions can be met only when the firm is at the minimum point on its *LRAC* curve, with price p^* and output Q_m.

For a competitive firm to be maximizing its long-run profits, it must be producing at the minimum point on its *LRAC* curve.

As we saw in Chapter 8, the level of output at which *LRAC* reaches a minimum is known as the firm's *minimum efficient scale (MES)*.

When each firm in the industry is producing at the minimum point of its long-run average cost curve and just covering its costs, as in Figure 9-11, the industry is in long-run equilibrium. Because marginal cost equals price, no firm can improve its profits by varying its output in the short run. Because each firm is at the minimum point on its *LRAC* curve, there is no incentive for any existing firm to alter the scale of its operations. Because there are neither profits nor losses, there is no incentive for entry into or exit from the industry.

In long-run competitive equilibrium, each firm's average cost of production is the lowest attainable, given the limits of known technology and factor prices.

Changes in Technology

Our discussion of firms' long-run decisions has assumed that all firms in the industry have the same technology and thus the same cost curves. We now relax that assumption and consider how a competitive industry responds to technological improvements *by new firms.*

Consider a competitive industry in long-run equilibrium. Because the industry is in long-run equilibrium, each firm must be earning zero profits. Now suppose that some technological development lowers the cost curves of *newly built plants.* Because price is just equal to the average total cost for the *existing plants,* new plants will be able to earn profits, and some of them will now be built. The resulting expansion in capacity shifts the short-run supply curve to the right and drives price down.

The expansion in industry output and the fall in price will continue until price is equal to the short-run average total cost of the *new* plants. At this price, old plants will not be covering their long-run costs. As long as price exceeds their average variable cost, however, such plants will continue in production. As the outmoded plants wear out or become too costly to operate, they will gradually be closed. Eventually, a new long-run equilibrium will be established in which all plants will use the new technology; market price will be lower and output higher than under the old technology.

New plants are usually built with the latest technology. This often results in new plants having lower unit costs (and thus higher profits) than the existing plants built with older technology.

What happens in a competitive industry in which technological change does not occur as a single isolated event but instead happens more or less continuously? Plants built in any one year will tend to have lower costs than plants built in any previous year. This common occurrence is illustrated in Figure 9-12.

Industries that are subject to continuous technological change have three common characteristics. The first is that plants of different ages and with different costs exist side by side. In the steel and newsprint industries, for example, there are ongoing and gradual technological improvements, and thus it is common for new plants to have considerably lower costs than the plants built several years earlier. Most of us do not see these differences, however, because we rarely if ever visit production facilities in these industries. But the same characteristic is dramatically displayed in an industry that most of us observe casually through our car windows—agriculture. You will probably have noticed different farms with different vintages of agricultural machinery; some farms have much newer and better equipment than others. Indeed, even any individual farm that has been in operation for a long time will have various vintages of equipment, all of which are in use. Older models are not discarded as soon as a better model comes on the market.

Critics who observe the continued use of older, higher-cost plants and equipment often urge that something be done to "eliminate these wasteful practices." These critics miss an important aspect of profit maximization. If the plant or piece of equipment is already there, it can be profitably operated as long as its revenues more than cover its *variable* costs. As long as a plant or some equipment can produce goods that are valued by consumers at an amount above the value of the resources currently used up for their production (variable costs), the value of society's total output is increased by using it.

FIGURE 9-12 Plants of Different Vintages in an Industry with Continuous Technological Progress

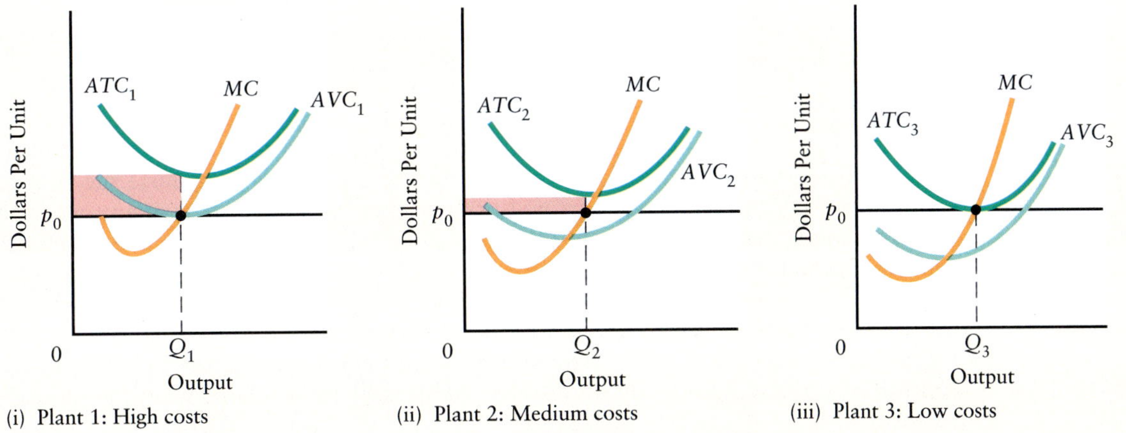

Entry of progressively lower-cost firms forces price down, but older plants with higher costs remain in the industry as long as price covers their average variable costs. Plant 3 is the newest plant with the lowest costs. Long-run equilibrium price will be determined by the average total costs of plants of this type because entry will continue as long as the owners of the newest plants expect to earn profits from them. Plant 1 is the oldest plant in operation. It is just covering its *AVC*, and if the price falls any further, it will be closed down. Plant 2 is a plant of intermediate age. It is covering its variable costs and earning some contribution toward its fixed costs. Losses at all but the newest plants, in parts (i) and (ii), are shown by the shaded areas.

Practise with Study Guide Chapter 9, Exercise 5.

In industries with continuous technological improvement, low-cost firms will exist side by side with older high-cost firms. The older firms will continue operating as long as their revenues cover their variable costs.

A second characteristic of a competitive industry that is subject to continuous technological improvement is that price is eventually governed by the minimum *ATC* of the *lowest-cost* plants. New firms using the latest technologies will enter the industry until their plants are just expected to earn normal profits over their lifetimes. The benefits of the new technology are passed on to consumers because all of the units of the product, whether produced by new or old plants, are sold at a price that is related solely to the *ATC*s of the new plants. Owners of older plants find that their returns over variable costs fall steadily as newer plants drive the price of the product down.

A third characteristic is that old plants are discarded (or "mothballed") when the price falls below their *AVC*s. This may occur well before the plants are physically worn out. In industries with continuous technological progress, capital is usually discarded because it is *economically obsolete,* not because it is physically worn out. Old capital is obsolete when the market price of output does not even cover its average variable cost of production. Thus, a steel mill that is still fully capable of producing top-quality steel may be shut down for perfectly sensible reasons; if the price of steel cannot cover the average variable cost of the steel produced, then profit-maximizing firms will shut down the plant.

Declining Industries

What happens when a competitive industry in long-run equilibrium experiences a continual decrease in the demand for its product? One example of this might be a long-term change in tastes that leads households to substitute away from red meat and toward fish and poultry. Another example is the ongoing substitution away from glass beverage containers to plastic ones. As market demand for these products declines, market price falls, and firms that were previously covering average total costs are no longer able to do so. They find themselves suffering losses instead of breaking even; the signal for the exit of capital is given, but exit takes time.

The Response of Firms The profit-maximizing response to a steadily declining demand is to continue to operate with existing equipment as long as its variable costs of production can be covered. As equipment becomes obsolete because the firm cannot cover even its variable cost, it will not be replaced unless the new equipment can cover its total cost. As a result, the capacity of the industry will shrink. If demand keeps declining, capacity will continue shrinking.

Declining industries typically present a sorry sight to the observer. Revenues are below long-run total costs and, as a result, new equipment is not brought in to replace old equipment as it wears out. The average age of equipment in use rises steadily. The untrained observer, seeing the industry's plight, is likely to blame it on the old equipment.

The antiquated equipment in a declining industry is often the effect rather than the cause of the industry's decline.

The Response of Governments Governments are often tempted to support declining industries because they are worried about the resulting job losses. Experience suggests, however, that propping up genuinely declining industries only delays their demise—at significant national cost. When the government finally withdraws its support, the decline is usually more abrupt and, hence, the required adjustment is more difficult than it would have been had the industry been allowed to decline gradually under the natural market forces.

Once governments recognize the decay of certain industries and the collapse of certain firms as an inevitable aspect of a changing and evolving economy, a more effective response is to provide retraining and income-support schemes that cushion the impacts of change. These can moderate the effects on the incomes of workers who lose their jobs and make it easier for them to transfer to expanding industries. Intervention that is intended to increase mobility while reducing the social and personal costs of mobility is a viable long-run policy; trying to freeze the existing industrial structure by shoring up an inevitably declining industry is not.

myeconlab

Demand shocks in competitive industries naturally lead to price changes. As prices change, firms' profits rise or fall, and these adjustments cause entry to or exit from the industry. After a new long-run equilibrium is reached, will the market price be at its initial level? The answer depends on the nature of costs within the industry. For more details, look for "The Long-Run Industry Supply Curve" in the *Additional Topics* section of this book's MyEconLab.

www.myeconlab.com

SUMMARY

9.1 MARKET STRUCTURE AND FIRM BEHAVIOUR

- A competitive market structure is one in which individual firms have no market power—that is, they have no power to influence the market in which they sell their product.
- Competitive behaviour exists when firms actively compete against one another, responding directly to other firms' actions.
- Perfectly competitive firms *do not* have competitive behaviour because the actions of any one firm would have no effect on any other firm.

9.2 THE THEORY OF PERFECT COMPETITION

LO 1

- Four key assumptions of the theory of perfect competition are as follows:
    1. All firms produce a homogeneous product.
    2. Consumers know the nature of the product and the price charged for it.
    3. Each firm's minimum efficient scale occurs at a level of output that is small relative to the industry's total output.
    4. The industry displays freedom of entry and exit.
- Each firm in perfect competition is a price taker. It follows that each firm faces a horizontal demand curve at the market price (even though the market demand curve is downward sloping).

9.3 SHORT-RUN DECISIONS

LO 2 3

- Any profit-maximizing firm will produce at a level of output at which (a) price is at least as great as average variable cost and (b) marginal cost equals marginal revenue. In perfect competition, firms are price takers, so marginal revenue is equal to price. Thus, a profit-maximizing competitive firm chooses its output so that its marginal cost equals the market price.
- Under perfect competition, each firm's short-run supply curve is identical to its marginal cost curve above average variable cost. The perfectly competitive industry's short-run supply curve is the horizontal sum of the supply curves of the individual firms.
- In short-run equilibrium, each firm is maximizing its profits. However, any firm may be suffering losses (price is less than average total cost), making profits (price is greater than average total cost), or just breaking even (price is equal to average total cost).

9.4 LONG-RUN DECISIONS

LO 4

- In the long run, profits or losses will lead to firms' entry into or exit out of the industry. This pushes any competitive industry to a long-run, zero-profit equilibrium and moves production to the level that minimizes average cost.
- The long-run response of an industry to steadily changing technology is the gradual replacement of less efficient plants by more efficient ones. Older plants will be discarded and replaced by more modern ones only when price falls below average variable cost.
- The long-run response of a declining industry will be to continue to satisfy demand by employing its existing plants as long as price exceeds short-run average variable cost.

KEY CONCEPTS

Competitive behaviour and competitive market structure
Perfect competition
Price taking and a horizontal demand curve
Average revenue, marginal revenue, and price under perfect competition
Rules for maximizing profits
The relationship of supply curves to marginal cost curves
Short-run and long-run equilibrium of competitive industries
Entry and exit in achieving long-run equilibrium

STUDY EXERCISES

1. Fill in the blanks to make the following statements correct.
   a. The demand curve faced by a single firm in a perfectly competitive market is ____________.
   b. The demand curve faced by a single firm in a perfectly competitive industry coincides with the firm's ____________ curve and its ____________ curve.
   c. Total revenue is calculated by multiplying ____________ and ____________. Average revenue is calculated by dividing ____________ by ____________. Marginal revenue is calculated by dividing ____________ by ____________.
   d. A firm's loss when it produces *no* output is equal to its ____________.

2. Fill in the blanks to make the following statements correct.
   a. The shut-down price is the price at which the firm can just cover its ____________.
   b. If the average variable cost of producing any given level of output exceeds the price at which it can be sold, then the firm should ____________.
   c. If a firm is producing a level of output such that $MC > MR$, that firm should ____________ output.
   d. The profit-maximizing level of output for a price-taking firm is the output at which MR and MC are ____________ and the gap between TR and TC is ____________.
   e. If a perfectly competitive firm is producing its profit-maximizing level of output and the price of its output rises, then MR will be ____________ MC and the firm should ____________ output.

3. Fill in the blanks to make the following statements correct.

   a. The short-run supply curve for a perfectly competitive firm is that firm's marginal cost curve for levels of output where marginal cost exceeds ____________.
   b. If a firm is producing a level of output where $MR = MC$ but is suffering losses, we know that price is below ____________. This firm should continue to produce as long as price exceeds ____________.
   c. If a firm is earning profits, we know that price is above its ____________. There is an incentive for other firms to ____________ this industry.

4. In Figure 9-1 in the chapter, we explain the difference between the demand curve for a competitive industry and the demand curve facing an individual firm in that industry. Review that figure and answer the following questions.

   a. Explain what would happen if the individual firm tried to charge a higher price for its product.
   b. Explain why the individual firm has no incentive to charge a lower price for its product.
   c. Explain why the demand curve for an individual firm is horizontal at the current market price.

5. myeconlab Consider the following table showing the various revenue concepts for DairyTreat Inc., a perfectly competitive firm that sells milk by the litre. Suppose the firm faces a constant market price of $2 per litre.

Price (p)	Quantity	Total Revenue (TR)	Average Revenue (AR)	Marginal Revenue (MR)
$2	150	—	—	
2	175	—	—	—
2	200	—	—	—
2	225	—	—	—
2	250	—	—	—

   a. Compute total revenue for each level of output. Fill in the table.
   b. Compute average and marginal revenue for each level of output. Fill in the table. (Remember to compute marginal revenue *between* successive levels of output.)
   c. Explain why for a perfectly competitive firm, $AR = MR = p$.
   d. Plot the TR, MR, and AR curves on a scale diagram. What is the slope of the TR curve?

6. The diagram below shows the various short-run cost curves for a perfectly competitive firm.

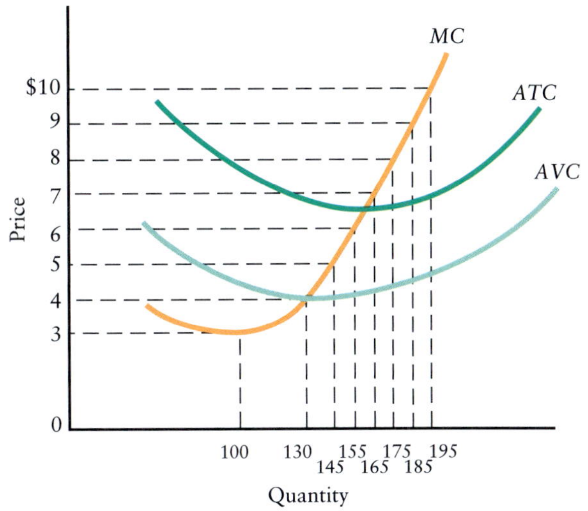

   a. Based on the diagram above, and the assumption that the firm is maximizing its profit, fill in the following table. The last three columns require only a "yes" or "no."

Market Price ($)	Firm's Output	Is price $>ATC$?	Is price $>AVC$?	Are Profits Positive?
$3	—	—	—	—
4	—	—	—	—
5	—	—	—	—
6	—	—	—	—
7	—	—	—	—
8	—	—	—	—
9	—	—	—	—
10	—	—	—	—

   b. What is this firm's shut-down price? Explain.
   c. What is this firm's supply curve? Explain.

7. myeconlab Consider the table below showing the supply schedules for three competitive firms, each producing honey. These three firms make up the entire industry.

Market Price ($/kg)	Output (kg) Firm A	Firm B	Firm C	Industry
2.50	100	0	0	—
3.00	125	0	0	—
3.50	150	100	0	—
4.00	175	150	0	—
4.50	200	200	100	—
5.00	225	250	175	—
5.50	250	300	250	—
6.00	275	350	325	—

a. Compute the total industry supply at each price and fill in the table.
b. On a scale diagram similar to Figure 9-5, plot the supply curve for each firm and for the industry as a whole.
c. Explain why Firm B produces no output at prices $3 and lower, and why Firm C produces no output at prices $4 and lower.

8. Consider the perfectly competitive barley industry. It is initially in long-run equilibrium at quantity Q_0 and price p_0.

a. Draw a supply-and-demand diagram for the barley market, showing the initial long-run equilibrium.
b. Draw a diagram for a typical firm when the industry is in its initial long-run equilibrium, showing its *MC*, *ATC*, and *LRAC* curves. Are any profits being earned by the typical barley farmer?
c. Now suppose there is an increase in demand (caused by an increase in demand for beer, which uses barley as an input). Price rises to p_1. In your diagram, show the typical firm's response to the increase in market price from p_0 to p_1. Show the typical firm's profits at this new price.
d. Explain how this industry adjusts to its new long-run equilibrium. Illustrate this adjustment both in the demand-and-supply diagram and in the diagram of the typical firm. (You may assume that costs for barley firms are unaffected by this change.)

9. This question is based on the section "The Long-Run Industry Supply Curve" found on this book's MyEconLab (www.myeconlab.com). A major theme of this chapter is the role that *free entry and exit* play in determining a competitive industry's long-run equilibrium. Keeping this theme in mind, think of the following statement:

In Industry X, demand and supply do determine price in the short run, but in the long run, only supply matters.

a. Assuming that Industry X is a constant-cost industry, use a demand-and-supply diagram to illustrate why the statement is exactly correct.
b. Now, assuming that Industry X is an increasing-cost industry, show in a demand-and-supply diagram why the statement is not quite correct.

DISCUSSION QUESTIONS

1. Discuss the common allegation that when all firms in an industry are charging the same price, this indicates the absence of competition and the presence of some form of price-setting agreement.

2. Which of the following observed facts about an industry are inconsistent with its being a perfectly competitive industry?

a. Different firms use different methods of production.
b. The industry's product is extensively advertised by a trade association.
c. Individual firms devote a large fraction of their sales receipts to advertising their own product brands.
d. There are 24 firms in the industry.
e. The largest firm in the industry makes 40 percent of the sales, and the next largest firm makes 20 percent of the sales, but the products are identical, and there are 61 other firms.
f. All firms made large profits last year.

3. In which of the following sectors of the Canadian economy might you expect to find competitive *behaviour*? In which might you expect to find industries that are classified as operating under perfectly competitive market *structures*?

a. Manufacturing
b. Agriculture
c. Transportation and public utilities
d. Wholesale and retail trade
e. Illegal drugs

4. Today's typical office contains personal computers of various vintages, with the newest machines having the largest output per unit of cost. There are also old machines that, though still able to function, are not in use at all. What determines the secondhand price of the older machines? What is the economic value of the machines that are no longer used?

5. What, if anything, does each one of the following tell you about ease of entry into or exit from an industry?

   a. Profits have been very high for two decades.
   b. No new firms have entered the industry for 20 years.
   c. The average age of the firms in the 40-year-old industry is less than 7 years.
   d. Most existing firms are using old-technology equipment alongside newer, more modern equipment.
   e. Profits are low or negative; many firms are still producing, but from steadily aging equipment.

6. This question refers to "The Long-Run Industry Supply Curve" in the *Additional Topics* section of the MyEconLab. Explain why perfectly competitive agricultural industries may have external economies of scale—and thus may be declining-cost industries—arising from the behaviour of the farm machinery industry. Is it relevant that the farm machinery industry is dominated by a small number of very large firms?

CHAPTER 10

Monopoly, Cartels, and Price Discrimination

LEARNING OBJECTIVES

In this chapter you will learn

1. why marginal revenue is less than price for a profit-maximizing monopolist.
2. how entry barriers allow monopolists to maintain positive profits in the long run.
3. how firms can form a cartel to restrict industry output and increase their profits.
4. why firms can increase their profits through price discrimination.

monopoly A market containing a single firm.

monopolist A firm that is the only seller in a market.

Perfect competition is at one end of the spectrum of market structures. At the other end is **monopoly**. Economists say that a monopoly occurs when the output of an entire industry is produced and sold by a single firm, called a **monopolist** or a *monopoly firm*. Examples of monopoly are rare at the national level but are more common for smaller geographical areas. The company that supplies electric power to your home is almost certainly a monopoly, as are the firms that provide local (but not long-distance) telephone service and cable television. Because monopoly is the market structure that allows for the maximum possible exercise of market power on the part of the firm, monopoly markets and perfectly competitive markets provide two extremes of behaviour that are useful for economists in their study of market structure.

In this chapter we examine how a profit-maximizing monopolist determines its price and quantity. We begin by considering a monopolist that sells all of its output at a single price. We then consider *cartels* that are formed when several firms band together in order to behave more like a monopolist. We end the chapter by examining situations in which firms with market power are able to charge different prices to different customers—something you have probably observed with airlines, movie theatres, and even your local grocery store.

10.1 A SINGLE-PRICE MONOPOLIST

We look first at a monopolist that charges a single price for its product. This firm's profits, like those of all firms, will depend on the relationship between its costs and its revenues.

Cost and Revenue in the Short Run

We saw in Chapter 7 that U-shaped short-run cost curves are a consequence of the law of diminishing returns. Because this law applies to the conditions under which goods are produced rather than to the market structure in which they are sold, monopolists have U-shaped short-run cost curves for the same reasons as do perfectly competitive firms. Therefore we do not need to introduce any new cost concepts to analyze a monopoly firm—everything that we saw in Chapter 7 applies equally to firms in *all* market structures. We can therefore focus our attention on a monopolist's revenues.

Because a monopolist is the sole producer of the product that it sells, the demand curve it faces is simply the market demand curve for that product. The market demand curve, which shows the total quantity that buyers want to purchase at each price, also shows the quantity that the monopolist will be able to sell at each price.

Unlike a perfectly competitive firm, a monopolist faces a negatively sloped demand curve.

A monopolist therefore faces a tradeoff between the price it charges and the quantity it can sell at that price. For a monopolist, sales can be increased only if price is reduced, and price can be increased only if sales are reduced.

Average Revenue Starting with the market demand curve, we can readily derive the monopolist's average and marginal revenue curves. When the monopolist charges the same price for all units sold, its total revenue (TR) is simply equal to the single price times the quantity sold,

$$TR = p \times Q$$

Since average revenue is total revenue divided by quantity, it follows that average revenue is equal to the price,

$$AR = \frac{TR}{Q} = \frac{p \times Q}{Q} = p$$

And since the price is given by the position of the demand curve, it follows that the demand curve is also the monopolist's average revenue curve.

Marginal Revenue Now let's consider the monopolist's *marginal revenue*—the revenue resulting from the sale of one more unit of the product. Because its demand curve is negatively sloped, the monopolist must reduce the price that it charges on *all* units in order to sell an extra unit. But this implies that the price received for the extra unit sold is *not* the firm's marginal revenue because, by reducing the price on all previous units, the firm lost some revenue. Marginal revenue is therefore equal to the price *minus* this lost revenue. It follows that the marginal revenue resulting from the sale of an extra unit is less than the price that the monopolist receives for that unit.

The monopolist's marginal revenue is less than the price at which it sells its output. Thus the monopolist's *MR* curve is below its demand curve. [24]

The relationship between marginal revenue and price for an example is shown in detail in Figure 10-1. Consider the table first. Notice that the numbers in columns 4 and 5 are plotted between the rows that refer to specific prices, because the numbers refer to what happens when the price changes from one row to the next. As price declines and quantity sold increases, marginal revenue is calculated as the change in total revenue divided by the change in quantity:

$$MR = \frac{\Delta TR}{\Delta Q}$$

FIGURE 10-1 A Monopolist's Average and Marginal Revenue

Computing Average and Marginal Revenue

Price (Average Revenue) (1)	Quantity Sold Q (2)	Total Revenue ($p \times Q$) (3)	Change in Total Revenue (ΔTR) (4)	Marginal Revenue ($\Delta TR/\Delta Q$) (5)
10	0	0		
			90	9
9	10	90		
			70	7
8	20	160		
			50	5
7	30	210		
			30	3
6	40	240		
			10	1
5	50	250		
			−10	−1
4	60	240		
			−30	−3
3	70	210		
			−50	−5
2	80	160		
			−70	−7
1	90	90		
			−90	−9
0	100	0		

Average and Marginal Revenue Curves

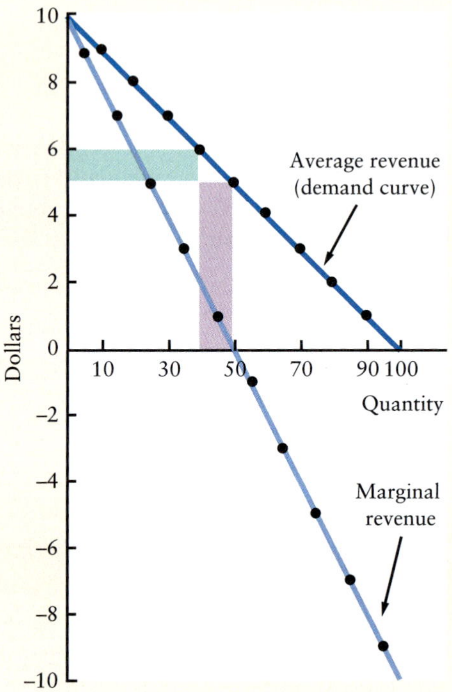

Marginal revenue is less than price because the price must be reduced in order to sell more units. The data show that every time the firm lowers its price by $1, its sales increase by 10 units. At a price of $6, the firm sells 40 units for a total revenue of $240. If it lowers its price to $5 *on all units,* total sales rise to 50 units and total revenue rises to $250. The purple rectangle shows the $50 gain in revenue associated with the 10 extra units sold at $5 each. The green rectangle shows the $40 *loss* in revenue associated with reducing the price by $1 on the original 40 units sold. Thus, the firm's marginal revenue when it reduces its price from $6 to $5 is the change in total revenue ($250 – $240 = $10) divided by the change in quantity (50 – 40 = 10). MR = $10/10 = $1.

Now look at the figure. It plots the demand curve described by the price and quantity values shown in the table. It also plots the marginal revenue curve and locates the specific points on it that were calculated in the table. For purposes of illustration, a straight-line demand curve has been chosen.[1]

Notice that marginal revenue is positive up to 50 units of sales, indicating that reductions in price between $10 and $5 increase total revenue. Notice also that marginal revenue is *negative* for sales greater than 50 units, indicating that reductions in price below $5 cause total revenue to fall.

---

1 When drawing these curves, note that if the demand curve is a negatively sloped straight line, the MR curve is also a negatively sloped straight line but is exactly twice as steep as the demand curve. The MR curve's price intercept (where $Q = 0$) is the same as that of the demand curve, and its quantity intercept (where $p = 0$) is one-half that of the demand curve. [25]

The figure also illustrates the two opposing forces that are present whenever the price is changed. As an example, consider the reduction in price from \$6 to \$5. First, the 40 units that the firm was already selling bring in less money at the new lower price than at the original higher price. This loss in revenue is the amount of the price reduction multiplied by the number of units already being sold (40 units × \$1 per unit = \$40). This is shown as the green shaded area in the figure. The second force, operating in the opposite direction, is that new units are sold, which adds to revenue. This gain in revenue is given by the number of new units sold multiplied by the price at which they are sold (10 units × \$5 = \$50). This is shown as the purple shaded area. The *net change* in total revenue is the *difference* between these two amounts. In the example shown in the figure, the increase resulting from the sale of new units exceeds the decrease resulting from existing sales now being made at a lower price. Marginal revenue is thus positive. Furthermore, the change in total revenue is \$10, whereas the change in the number of units sold is 10 units. Thus, marginal revenue, given by $\Delta TR/\Delta Q$, is equal to \$10/10 = \$1.

The proposition that marginal revenue is always less than price for a monopolist provides an important contrast with perfect competition. Recall that in perfect competition, the firm's marginal revenue from selling an extra unit of output is equal to the price at which that unit is sold. The reason for the difference is not difficult to understand. The perfectly competitive firm is a price taker; it can sell all it wants at the given market price. In contrast, the monopolist faces a negatively sloped demand curve; it must reduce the market price to increase its sales.

If you plot the data on *TR* from Figure 10-1, you will notice that *TR* rises (*MR* is positive) as price falls, reaching a maximum where p = \$5 and $MR = 0$. Then, as price continues to fall, *TR* falls (*MR* is negative). Using the relationship between elasticity and total revenue that we first saw in Chapter 4, it follows that demand is elastic ($\eta > 1$) when *MR* is positive and demand is inelastic ($\eta < 1$) when *MR* is negative. The value of η declines steadily as we move down the demand curve. As we will see shortly, a profit-maximizing monopolist will always produce on the elastic portion of its demand curve (that is, where *MR* is positive).

Short-Run Profit Maximization

We began this chapter by noting that the cost concepts from Chapter 7 apply equally to a monopolist as to a competitive firm. We have now examined a monopolist's average and marginal revenues and are therefore ready to combine the cost and revenue information to determine the monopolist's profit-maximizing price and level of output.

Practise with Study Guide Chapter 10, Exercises 1 and 2.

Recall the two general rules about profit maximization from Chapter 9:

Rule 1: The firm should not produce at all unless its average revenue exceeds its average variable cost.

Rule 2: If the firm does produce, it should produce a level of output such that its marginal revenue equals its marginal cost.

Figure 10-2 illustrates a monopolist's choice of output to equate its marginal cost with its marginal revenue. At this profit-maximizing level of output, the monopolist's price is then read off the demand curve. With the firm's costs given by the *ATC* curve shown in the figure, the monopolist is making positive profits, as shown by the red shaded area.

FIGURE 10-2 Short-Run Profit Maximization for a Monopolist

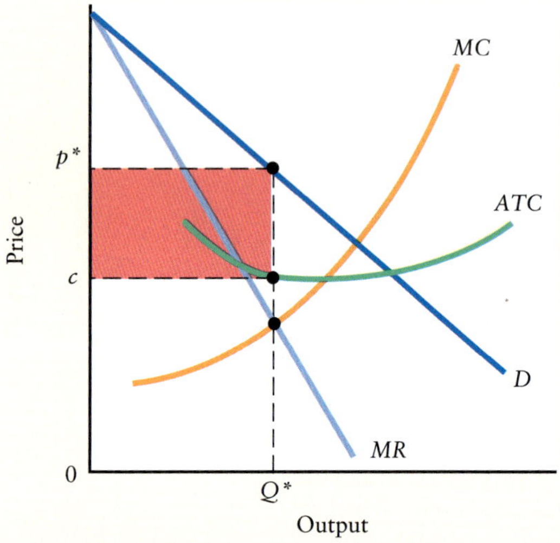

The profit-maximizing output is Q^*, where $MR = MC$; price is p^*. The rules for profit maximization require $MR = MC$ and $p > AVC$. (AVC is not shown in the graph, but it must be below ATC.) With average costs given by ATC, unit costs at Q^* are given by c and the monopolist makes positive profits shown by the red shaded area.

In general, however, a profit-maximizing monopolist need not be making *positive* profits. Even when the firm is choosing its quantity to maximize its profits, the *size* of those profits depends on the position of the *ATC* curve. In Figure 10-2 the monopolist is earning positive profits. But you can easily imagine other possibilities. If the firm's *ATC* curve was higher (perhaps because of higher fixed costs) the firm with the same level of output and charging the same price could be breaking even (zero profits) or even making negative profits (losses). (Readers can create their own diagrams like Figure 10-2 and draw in the appropriate *ATC* curves to illustrate these two possibilities.)

Nothing guarantees that a monopolist will make positive profits in the short run, but if it suffers persistent losses, it will eventually go out of business.

No Supply Curve for a Monopolist In describing the monopolist's profit-maximizing behaviour, we did not introduce the concept of a supply curve, as we did in the discussion of perfect competition. In perfect competition, each firm's supply curve is given by its own *MC* curve. It follows that in perfect competition there is a unique relationship between market price and quantity supplied by any single firm: An increase in the market price leads to an increase in quantity supplied. But there is no such unique relationship in monopoly.

For a monopolist, there is no unique relationship between market price and the quantity of output supplied. A monopolist therefore does not have a supply curve.

The simple explanation is that the price set by a monopolist depends on the *shape* of the demand curve, and therefore the monopolist's profit-maximizing quantity is not necessarily higher when it sets its price higher.

To prove this point to yourself, draw a monopolist's marginal cost curve and any marginal revenue curve to intersect the *MC* curve at some output that you call Q^*. Now draw as many other different *MR* curves as you like, all of which intersect *MC* at Q^*. All of these curves give rise to profit-maximizing output of Q^*, but because each *MR* curve is different, each must be associated with a different demand curve and hence a different price at which Q^* is sold. This exercise shows that a given quantity may be associated with many different prices, depending on the slope of the demand curve that the monopolist faces.

Firm and Industry Because the monopolist is the only producer in an industry, there is no need for a separate discussion about the firm and the industry, as is necessary with perfect competition. The monopolist *is* the industry. Thus, the short-run, profit-maximizing position of the firm, as shown in Figure 10-2, is also the short-run equilibrium of the industry.

Competition and Monopoly Compared The comparison of monopoly with perfect competition is important. For a perfectly competitive industry, the equilibrium is determined by the intersection of the industry demand and supply curves. Since the industry supply curve is simply the sum of the individual firms' marginal cost curves, the equilibrium output in a perfectly competitive industry is such that price equals marginal cost. For the monopolist, in contrast, equilibrium output is such that price is greater than marginal cost. And since demand curves are downward sloping and *MC* curves are typically upward sloping, the gap between price and marginal cost implies one thing: The level of output in a monopolized industry is less than the level of output that would be produced if the industry were instead made up of many price-taking firms. This comparison is illustrated in Figure 10-3.

A perfectly competitive industry produces a level of output such that price equals marginal cost. A monopolist produces a lower level of output, with price exceeding marginal cost.

FIGURE 10-3 The Inefficiency of Monopoly

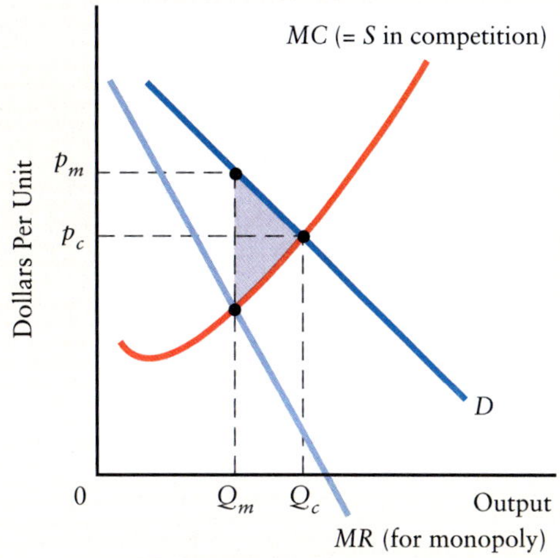

The level of output in a monopolized industry is less than the level of output that would be produced if the industry were perfectly competitive. If the industry is made up of many price-taking firms, the industry supply curve *S* is the horizontal sum of the many individual marginal cost curves. Given the market demand curve *D*, the competitive equilibrium quantity is Q_c and the price is p_c. Now suppose the industry has a monopolist with marginal costs given by the *MC* curve shown. In this case, *MR* is the monopolist's marginal revenue curve. The profit-maximizing monopolist produces Q_m units of output and charges a price of p_m.

Notice in the monopoly outcome that for the units of output between Q_m and Q_c, the marginal value to society of extra units of the good (as shown by the demand curve) exceeds the marginal cost of producing extra units, and thus society would benefit from having these units produced. The monopolist's restriction of output below Q_c creates a deadweight loss for society shown by the purple area. The monopoly outcome is *inefficient.*

In Chapter 5 we briefly discussed the meaning of *market efficiency* and how it relates to the amount of *economic surplus* generated in the market. We will examine these concepts in more detail in Chapter 12. For now we can observe why the decisions of the monopolist—though perhaps very profitable for the firm—lead to an inefficient outcome for society as a whole.

Since price exceeds marginal cost for a monopolist, society as a whole would benefit if more units of the good were produced—because the marginal value to society of extra units, as reflected by the price, exceeds the marginal cost of producing the extra units. In the terminology we introduced in Chapter 5, more *economic surplus* would be generated for society if the monopolist increased its level of output. The monopolist's profit-maximizing decision to restrict output below the competitive level creates a loss of economic surplus for society—a deadweight loss—and thus leads to market *inefficiency.*

A monopolist restricts output below the competitive level and thus reduces the amount of economic surplus generated in the market. The monopolist therefore creates an inefficient market outcome.

Entry Barriers and Long-Run Equilibrium

In a monopolized industry, as in a perfectly competitive one, losses and profits provide incentives for exit and entry. If the monopoly is suffering losses in the short run, it will continue to operate as long as it can cover its variable costs. In the long run, however, it will leave the industry unless it can find a scale of operations at which its full opportunity costs can be covered.

If the monopoly is making profits, other firms will wish to enter the industry in order to earn more than the opportunity cost of their capital. If such entry occurs, the firm will cease to be a monopoly. Instead of facing the entire market demand curve, the (former) monopolist will have to compete with the new firms and thus will capture only part of the overall market demand.

If monopoly profits are to persist in the long run, the entry of new firms into the industry must be prevented.

entry barrier Any barrier to the entry of new firms into an industry. An entry barrier may be natural or created.

Anything that prevents the entry of new firms is called an **entry barrier**. They may be natural or created.

Natural Entry Barriers Natural barriers most commonly arise as a result of economies of scale. When the long-run average cost curve is negatively sloped over a large range of output, big firms have significantly lower average total costs than small firms. Recall from Chapter 8 that the *minimum efficient scale (MES)* is the smallest-size firm that can reap all of the economies of large-scale production. It occurs at the level of output where the firm's long-run average cost curve reaches a minimum.

Practise with Study Guide Chapter 10, Exercise 3.

To see how economies of scale can act as an entry barrier, consider the production of hockey sticks. Suppose the technology of hockey-stick production is such that a firm's *MES* is 10 000 sticks per week at an average total cost of $20 per stick. Further suppose that at a price of $20, the quantity demanded in the entire market is 11 000 sticks per week. Under these circumstances, only one firm can operate at or near its *MES*. Any potential entrant would have unit costs higher than those of the existing firm and so could not compete successfully.

natural monopoly An industry characterized by economies of scale sufficiently large that only one firm can cover its costs while producing at its minimum efficient scale.

A **natural monopoly** occurs when the industry's demand conditions allow no more than one firm to cover its costs while producing at its minimum efficient scale. Electrical power transmission is a natural monopoly—with current technology it is cheaper to have only one set of power lines (rather than two or more) serving a given region.

Another type of natural entry barrier is *setup cost.* If a firm could be catapulted fully grown into the market, it might be able to compete effectively with the existing monopolist. However, the cost to the new firm of entering the market, developing its products, and establishing such things as its brand image and its dealer network may be so large that entry would be unprofitable.

Many industries have considerable economies of scale. These scale economies can provide an entry barrier and allow existing firms to sustain high profits.

Created Entry Barriers Many entry barriers are created by conscious government action. Patent laws, for instance, may prevent entry by conferring on the patent holder the sole legal right to produce a particular product for a specific period of time. A firm may also be granted a charter or a franchise that prohibits competition by law. Canada Post, for example, has a government-sanctioned monopoly on the delivery of first-class mail. In other cases the regulation and/or licensing of firms severely restricts entry. Professional organizations for dentists or engineers, for example, might restrict the number of places in accredited dental or engineering schools, and thus restrict entry into those industries.

Other barriers can be created by the firm or firms already in the market. In extreme cases, the threat of force or sabotage can deter entry. The most obvious entry barriers of this type are encountered in organized crime, where operation outside the law makes available an array of illegal but potent barriers to new entrants. But law-abiding firms must use legal tactics in an attempt to increase a new entrant's setup costs. Such tactics range from the threat of price cutting—designed to impose unsustainable losses on a new entrant—to heavy brand-name advertising. (These and other created entry barriers will be discussed in more detail in Chapter 11.)

The Significance of Entry Barriers Because there is freedom of entry and exit in perfect competition, and thus no entry barriers, profits cannot persist in the long run. In monopolized industries, however, profits can persist in the long run whenever there are effective barriers to entry.

In competitive industries, profits attract entry, and entry erodes profits. In monopolized industries, positive profits can persist as long as there are effective entry barriers.

Applying Economic Concepts 10-1 discusses an interesting example from Ireland where government regulations, by restricting entry, have led local pubs to have considerable monopoly power. At a time when Irish pubs are becoming a popular trend in many countries, it is ironic to see how a booming Irish economy combined with government regulation has caused a shortage of Irish pubs in Ireland itself!

The Very Long Run and Creative Destruction

In the very long run, technology changes. New ways of producing old products are invented, and new products are created to satisfy both familiar and new wants. These are related to the concept of entry barriers; a monopoly that succeeds in preventing the entry of new firms capable of producing its product will sooner or later find its barriers circumvented by innovations. Here are three examples.

First, a firm may be able to develop a new production process that avoids a patent upon which a monopolist relies to bar the entry of competing firms.

Second, a firm may compete by producing a somewhat different product satisfying the same need as the monopolist's product. An example is the courier services provided by United Parcel Service or Federal Express that compete with the package delivery of Canada Post. Canada Post still has a government-granted monopoly on the delivery of first-class mail, but it has no monopoly on the delivery of "packages," whatever their size.

Finally, a firm may get around a natural monopoly by inventing a technology that produces at a low minimum efficient scale (*MES*) and allows it to enter the industry and still cover its full costs. The creation of cellular-phone technology, for example, allows the provider of cell-phone services to compete with the provider of local "land line" telephone services without having to establish an expensive network of wires, thus allowing successful competition at a much smaller scale of operations.

A monopolist's entry barriers are often circumvented by the innovation of production processes and the development of new goods and services. Such innovation explains why monopolies rarely persist, except those that are protected through government charter or regulation.

APPLYING ECONOMIC CONCEPTS 10-1

Entry Barriers for Irish Pubs

In recent years, the Irish economy has been booming—so much so that many economists refer to it as the "Celtic Tiger," putting it in the same category as the Asian tigers of Taiwan, Singapore, Hong Kong, and South Korea. As the Irish economy has boomed, however, line-ups and prices in many Irish pubs have skyrocketed. The shortage of pubs has been so severe that some pub operators have implemented their own rationing schemes by turning away young people, bachelor parties, and sloppy dressers. In some cases, publicans have even threatened to expel anyone who starts to sing, a long-standing tradition in Irish pubs.

So what is going on in the pub industry in Ireland? Ordinarily, as demand increases and profits rise, new pubs would be established. This entry of new pubs would keep the existing pubs from earning high profits.

The problem in Ireland is that the issuance of pub licences is governed by a 1902 law that froze the number of licences at the level in place at that time. As incomes grew over time and the demand for pubs increased, the entry of new pubs was prevented. It is therefore no surprise that prices in pubs have been rising and that existing pubs are extremely profitable. This profitability is reflected in the high purchase prices of the pub licences, which are freely tradable (although in fixed total supply). If pubs earned zero economic profit, these licences would have no market value. The Irish Competition Authority estimated the total value of existing licences at between 1 billion and 2 billion euros. The market value of these licences is a rough measure of the cost imposed on society by the regulations limiting the entry of new pubs.

Another aspect of the 1902 legislation that has caused local pub shortages is that pub owners are prevented from transferring licences across county lines. As the population has increasingly moved from small towns to larger cities over the past several decades, small towns are left with too many pubs while neighbourhoods in the larger cities have far too few. This distortion is seen clearly in Dublin, where approximately 35 percent of the Irish population is served by only 12 percent of the country's pubs. Though new pubs cannot be built in urban areas, the legislation does allow existing urban pubs to expand. This enables more consumers to be served, but some complain that it has led to the rise of the "super pubs"—larger establishments that lack the social atmosphere that made Irish pubs famous the world over.

Who gains from this legislation, and who loses? The clear losers are the pubs' customers (especially in growing towns and cities) who are faced with higher prices and longer line-ups. The clear gainers are the current owners of the pubs in areas where demand is strong. It is no surprise, therefore, that Ireland's powerful pub lobby continues to fight efforts by the government to review pub legislation.

Government legislation in Ireland has restricted the entry of new pubs and has therefore permitted existing pubs to earn high profits without the threat of competition.

(For the Irish Competition Authority's submission to the Liquor Licensing Commission (October 2001), see www.tca.ie and click on "Authority Documents.")

The distinguished economist Joseph Schumpeter (1883–1950) took the view that entry barriers were not a serious problem in the very long run. He argued that the short-run profits of a monopoly provide a strong incentive for others, through their own innovations and product development, to try to usurp some of these profits for themselves. If a frontal attack on the monopolist's entry barriers is not possible, the barriers will be circumvented by such means as the development of similar products against which the monopolist will not have entry protection.

LESSONS FROM HISTORY 10-1

Creative Destruction Through History

Creative destruction, the elimination of one product by a superior product, is a major characteristic of all advanced countries. It eliminates the strong market position of the firms and workers who make the threatened product.

The steel-nibbed pen eliminated the quill pen with its sharpened bird's feather nib. The fountain pen eliminated the steel pen and its accompanying inkwell. The ballpoint pen virtually eliminated the fountain pen. Who knows what will come next in writing implements?

The silent films eliminated vaudeville. The talkies eliminated silent films and colour films have all but eliminated black and white. Television seriously reduced the demand for films (and radio) while not eliminating either of them. Cable greatly reduced the demand for direct TV reception by offering a better picture and a more varied selection. Satellite TV is now threatening to eliminate cable by offering much more selection, and access to programs on the Internet is now challenging the dominance of television networks.

For long-distance passenger travel by sea, the steamship eliminated the sailing vessel around the beginning of the twentieth century. The airplane eliminated the ocean liner in the 1950s and 1960s. For passenger travel on land, the train eliminated the stage coach while the bus competed with the train without eliminating it. The airplane wiped out the passenger train in most of North America while leaving the bus still in a low-cost niche used mainly for short and medium distances.

These examples all involve the elimination of a product by the development of a new, preferred product. But creative destruction also occurs with the development of better *processes*. The laborious hand-setting of metal type for printing was replaced by the linotype that allowed the type to be set by a keyboard operator, but that still involved a costly procedure for making corrections. The linotype was swept away by computer typesetting and much of the established printing shop operations have now been replaced by desktop publishing.

A century ago, automobiles were produced with skilled craftsmen operating relatively unsophisticated equipment. When Henry Ford perfected the techniques of mass production in the early 1920s, masses of less-skilled workers operated specialized and inflexible equipment. Now, far fewer workers, but more highly skilled ones, operate even more sophisticated robotics equipment to produce today's vehicles.

These cases all illustrate the same general message. Technological change transforms the products we consume, how we make those products, and how we work. It continually sweeps away positions of high income and economic power established by firms that were in the previous wave of technological change and by those who work for them. It is an agent of dynamism in our economy, an agent of change and economic growth, but it is not without its dark side in terms of the periodic loss of privileged positions on the part of the replaced firms and their workers.

Schumpeter called the replacement of one product by another the *process of creative destruction.* "Creative" referred to the rise of new products; "destruction" referred to the demise of the existing products and perhaps the firms that produced them. Some examples of creative destruction are presented in *Lessons From History 10-1.*

Schumpeter argued that this process of creative destruction reflects new firms' abilities to circumvent entry barriers that would otherwise permit monopolists to earn profits in the long run. He also argued that because creative destruction thrives on innovation, the existence of monopoly profits is a major incentive to economic growth. Schumpeter was writing at a time when the two dominant market structures studied by economists were perfect competition and monopoly. His argument easily extends, however, to any market structure that allows profits to exist in the long run. Today, pure monopolies are few, but there are many industries in which profits can be earned for long periods of time. Such industries, which are called *oligopolies,* are candidates for the operation of the process of creative destruction. We study these industries in detail in Chapter 11.

10.2 CARTELS AS MONOPOLIES

So far in our discussion, a monopoly has meant that there is only one firm in an industry. A second way a monopoly can arise is for many firms in an industry to agree to cooperate with one another, eliminating competition among themselves. In this case, they would band together and behave as if they were a single seller with the objective of maximizing their *joint profits*. Such a group of firms is called a **cartel**. The firms can agree among themselves to restrict their total output to the level that maximizes their *joint profits*.

cartel An organization of producers who agree to act as a single seller in order to maximize joint profits.

Some of the best examples of cartels come from history. In the United States in the last half of the nineteenth century, cartels existed in the steel and oil industries. These cartels were so successful in restricting output and elevating prices that much of current U.S. anti-trust policy dates from that time. As we will see in Chapter 12, U.S. and Canadian policy has been quite effective at preventing the creation of large cartels that would otherwise possess considerable market power.

As a result of successful policies aimed at preventing the creation of *domestic* cartels, the best current examples of cartels are ones that operate in global markets and are supported by national governments. The Organization of Petroleum Exporting Countries (OPEC) is perhaps the best-known cartel in the world. This cartel first came to prominence when, in 1973, its members collectively agreed to restrict their output of crude oil and thereby increased the world price of oil by nearly 200 percent. In 1979, further output restrictions led the price to increase by another 120 percent. During the 1980s and 1990s, as oil production by non-OPEC countries increased significantly, OPEC found it difficult to maintain such a controlling influence on the oil market. OPEC also ran into problems enforcing the agreements among its members. As we will see in this section, these are typical challenges that all cartels face.

To learn more about OPEC, see its website at **www.opec.org**.

A less well-known example, but one that has been successful over many years, is the diamond cartel, controlled by the South African company DeBeers. DeBeers produces roughly 40 percent of the world's annual production of rough diamonds but also purchases diamonds from smaller producers worldwide. The result is that about half of the world's annual diamond supply is marketed through the DeBeers-controlled Diamond Trading Company (DTC). In years when demand is slack, DeBeers restricts the output of diamonds through the DTC to keep prices from falling.

DeBeers controls approximately half of the world's supply of diamonds through its Diamond Trading Company.

Notice in both examples that there are firms *outside* the cartel. There are many oil producers (including Canada) that are not part of OPEC; similarly, there are many diamond mines that are not owned or controlled by DeBeers (two of which are the Ekati and Diavik mines in the Northwest Territories that together make up approximately 14 percent of total world diamond production). Indeed, this type of cartel is much more common than one in which *all* firms in the industry successfully band together.

In this chapter, however, we simplify the analysis by considering the case in which *all* firms in the industry form a cartel. This is the easiest setting in which to see the central point—that cartels are inherently unstable.

The Effects of Cartelization

If all firms in a competitive industry come together to form a cartel, they must recognize the effect their *joint* output has on price. That is, like a monopolist they must recognize that an increase in the volume of their sales requires a reduction in price. They can agree to restrict industry output to the level that maximizes their joint profits (where the industry's marginal cost is equal to the industry's marginal revenue). The incentive for firms to form a cartel lies in the cartel's ability to restrict output, thereby raising price and increasing profits. This is shown in Figure 10-4.

The profit-maximizing cartelization of a competitive industry will reduce output and raise price from the perfectly competitive levels.

FIGURE 10-4 The Effect of Cartelizing a Competitive Industry

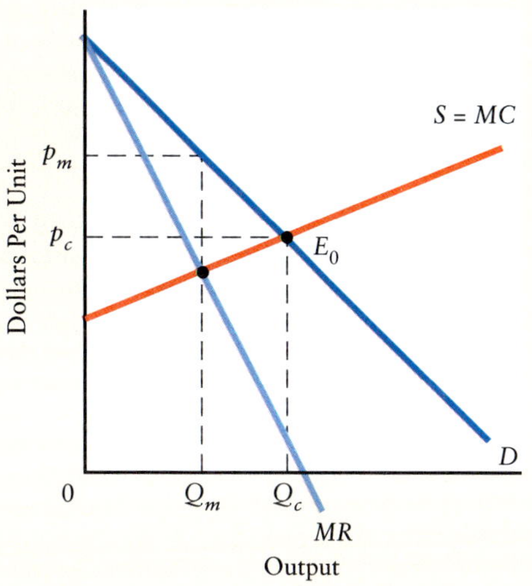

Cartelization of a competitive industry can always increase that industry's profits. Equilibrium for a competitive industry occurs at E_0. Equilibrium price and output are p_c and Q_c.

If the industry is cartelized, profits can be increased by reducing output. All units between Q_m and Q_c add less to revenue than to cost—the *MR* curve lies below the *MC* curve—and therefore will not be produced by a profit-maximizing cartel. The cartel maximizes its joint profits by producing output of Q_m and setting price equal to p_m.

Problems That Cartels Face

Cartels encounter two characteristic problems. The first is ensuring that members follow the behaviour that will maximize the cartel members' *joint* profits. The second is preventing these profits from being eroded by the entry of new firms.

Enforcement of Output Restrictions The managers of any cartel want the industry to produce its profit-maximizing output. Their job is made more difficult if individual firms either stay out of the cartel or join the cartel and then "cheat" by producing too much output. Any one firm, however, has an incentive to do just this—to be either the one that stays out of the organization or the one that enters and then cheats. For the sake of simplicity, assume that all firms enter the cartel; thus enforcement problems are concerned strictly with cheating by its members.

If Firm X is the only firm to cheat, it is then in the best of all possible situations. All other firms restrict output and hold the industry price up near its monopoly level. They earn profits but only by restricting output. Firm X can then reap the full benefit of the other firms' output restraint and sell some additional output at the high price that has been set by the cartel's actions. However, if all of the firms cheat, the price will be pushed back to the competitive level, and all of the firms will return to their competitive position.

This conflict between the interests of the group as a whole and the interests of each individual firm is the cartel's main dilemma. Provided that enough firms cooperate in restricting output, all firms are better off than they would be if the industry remained perfectly competitive. Any one firm, however, is even better off if it remains outside or if it enters and cheats. However, if all firms act on this incentive, all will be worse off than if they had joined the cartel and restricted output.

Cartels tend to be unstable because of the incentives for individual firms to violate the output restrictions needed to sustain the joint-profit-maximizing (monopoly) price.

Practise with Study Guide Chapter 10, Exercise 4.

The conflict between the motives for cooperation and for independent action is analyzed in more detail in Figure 10-5. In Chapter 11, we will consider an explicit theory, called *game theory*, that economists use to analyze conflicts of this kind.

The predicted instability of cartels is evident in the data. After the tremendous successes in 1973 and 1979 in restricting the output of crude oil and elevating its world price, the members of the OPEC cartel began to encounter difficulties in enforcing their agreements. After several years of sluggish world demand for oil, the cartel almost collapsed in 1986 as several OPEC members increased their output in efforts to generate more income. Throughout the 1990s, however, OPEC members learned the important lesson that their attempts to push oil prices very high attract alternative oil supplies and undermine their output restrictions. As a result, OPEC members avoided the large output restrictions and price increases of the 1970s, instead trying to keep oil prices relatively stable at more moderate levels.

In the last few years, however, OPEC's market power has increased. The world price of oil increased from about U.S.$15 per barrel in 1998 to over U.S.$75 per barrel in 2006. The main cause of the price increase (in addition to some geopolitical tensions, especially during 2006) was growing world demand in a market in which most

FIGURE 10-5 A Cartel Member's Incentive to Cheat

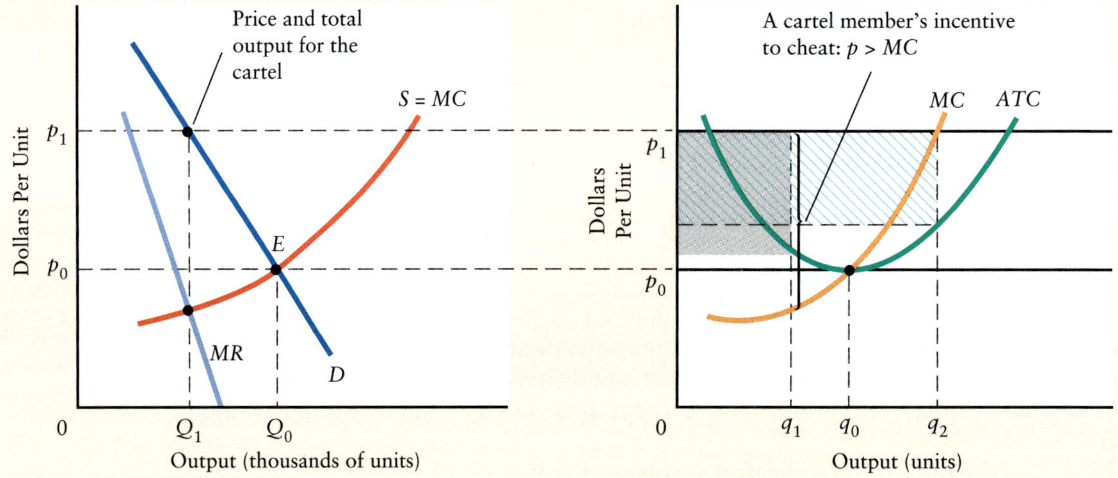

(i) Market equilibrium

(ii) Firm incentives

Cooperation leads to the monopoly price, but individual self-interest leads to production in excess of the monopoly output. Market conditions are shown in part (i), and the situation of a typical firm is shown in part (ii). (The change of scale between the two graphs is reflected by the upper case Q in part (i) and the lower case q in part (ii).) Initially, the market is in competitive equilibrium with price p_0 and quantity Q_0. The individual firm is producing output q_0 and is just covering its total costs.

A successful cartel reduces total output to Q_1 and elevates price to p_1. Q_1 is the joint profit-maximizing level of output because industry *MR* equals industry *MC*. A typical firm in the cartel then produces output of q_1 in part (ii). The firm's profits rise from zero to the amount shown by the grey shaded area in part (ii). Once price is raised to p_1, however, the individual firm would like to increase output to q_2, where marginal cost is equal to the price set by the cartel. This would allow the firm to earn much larger profits, shown by the diagonally striped area. However, if all firms increase their output, industry output will increase beyond Q_1, and the resulting fall in price will reduce the joint profits of the cartel.

producers had a limited ability to increase production. In other words, the world demand curve was shifting to the right while the world supply curve was quite steep. In this environment, a decision by OPEC to considerably restrict output, even though OPEC represents only about a third of total world production, would have a significant effect on the market price.

Another example of a cartel's instability involves the world coffee market. In 2000, the Association of Coffee Producing Countries (ACPC), a cartel of 15 countries that produced approximately 75 percent of the world's coffee, agreed to restrict coffee output to keep coffee prices between U.S.$0.95 and U.S.$1.05 per pound. Within two years, however, a bumper crop in Brazil, the world's largest coffee producer, led to the inevitable pressure to cheat. Brazil had the incentive to sell its new production rather than incur storage costs. Other countries, facing low prices, had the incentive to increase their sales to bolster their incomes. By January of 2003, the ACPC planned to close down its operations. Perhaps the cartel will be re-established at some point in the future when it has improved its ability to enforce its members' behaviour.

For interesting information about coffee and the world coffee market, go to **www.ico.org**.

Restricting Entry A successful cartel not only must police the behaviour of its members but also must be able to prevent the entry of new producers. An industry that is able to support a number of individual firms presumably has no overriding natural entry barriers. Thus, if it is to maintain its profits in the long run, a cartel of many separate firms must create barriers that prevent the entry of new firms that are attracted by the cartel's profits. Successful cartels are often able to license the firms in the industry and to control entry by restricting the number of licences. This practice is often used by professionals, from physicians to beauticians. At other times, the government has operated a quota system and has given it the force of law. If no one can produce without a quota and the quotas are allocated among existing producers, entry is successfully prevented. This approach is used to limit the number of taxicabs in many cities.

As we mentioned earlier, for many years DeBeers was successful at preventing the entry of new diamond producers and was able to control a large fraction of the world's annual sales of rough diamonds. But recently, restricting entry into the diamond industry has been more challenging. In the diamond industry, of course, "entry" means the development of new diamond mines. In 2004, two new mines in the Northwest Territories reached full-scale production. The combined annual output of rough diamonds from the Ekati and Diavik mines is about U.S.$1.65 billion, roughly 14 percent of total world production. The owners of the Ekati and Diavik mines, however, will market the diamonds independently rather than going through DeBeers. With entries such as this, combined with some Russian and Australian producers also choosing to sell their diamonds independently, DeBeers is faced with the challenge of keeping diamond prices supported above competitive levels. Time and further developments will determine how successful DeBeers will be in maintaining its dominant position in the industry.

For more information on the diamond industry in the Northwest Territories, see **www.iti.gov.nt.ca/diamond/development.htm**.

10.3 PRICE DISCRIMINATION

So far in this chapter, we have assumed that the monopolist charges the same price for every unit of its product, no matter where or to whom it sells that product. But as we shall soon see, a monopolist always finds it profitable to sell different units of the same product at different prices whenever it gets the opportunity. Because this practice is prevalent both for monopoly and for markets in which there are a few large sellers, the range of examples we will discuss covers both types of market structure.

Airlines often charge less to people who stay over a Saturday night than to those who come and go within the week. In countries where medical services are provided by the market, physicians in private practice often charge for their services according to the incomes of their patients. Movie theatres often have lower admission prices for seniors. Electric companies sell electricity at one rate to homes and at a different rate to firms.

price discrimination The sale by one firm of different units of a commodity at two or more different prices for reasons not associated with differences in cost.

Price discrimination occurs when a producer charges different prices for different units of the same product *for reasons not associated with differences in cost.* Not all price differences represent price discrimination. Quantity discounts, differences between wholesale and retail prices, and prices that vary with the time of day or the season of the year may not represent price discrimination because the same product sold at a different time, in a different place, or in different quantities may have different costs. An excellent example is electricity. If an electric power company has unused capacity at certain times of the day, it may cost less for the company to provide service at those hours than at peak demand hours.

If price differences reflect cost differences, they are not discriminatory. When a price difference is based on different buyers' valuations of the same product, it is discriminatory.

It does not cost a movie-theatre operator less to fill seats with senior citizens than with non-seniors, but it is worthwhile for the movie theatre to let the seniors in at a discriminatory low price if few of them would attend at the full adult fare and if they take up seats that would otherwise be empty. Similarly, it does not cost an airline any less to sell a ticket to a student than to a non-student. But since few students may be inclined to buy airline tickets at the full price, it is profitable for the airline to attract more students with a lower price and, in that manner, fill up seats that would otherwise be empty.

Why do firms price discriminate? It may seem odd that they sell some units of output at a low price and other units at a high price. The simple answer is that firms price discriminate because they find it profitable to do so. As we will see shortly, price discrimination is profitable for two reasons. First, even if firms do not alter their level of output, price discrimination allows them to "capture" some consumer surplus that would otherwise go to the buyer. Second, price discrimination allows firms to sell extra units of output without reducing the price on their existing sales.

Any firm that faces a downward-sloping demand curve can increase its profits if it is able to charge different prices for different units of its product.

Practise with Study Guide Chapter 10, Exercise 5.

Note two important points. First, only firms facing downward-sloping demand curves—that is, firms with market power—are able to price discriminate. Perfectly competitive firms are price takers and therefore have no ability to set one price, let alone set multiple prices. Second, firms will price discriminate *if they are able* to. Before we explore the various types of price discrimination, let's lay out the conditions under which it is possible.

When Price Discrimination Is Possible

Three conditions must be satisfied before a firm can successfully price discriminate.

1. Market Power As we said above, any firm that is a price taker cannot discriminate because it has no power to influence the price at which it sells its product. Our entire discussion about price discrimination therefore applies only to firms with some amount of market power. For simplicity, we will consider the case of a monopoly firm, although *any* firm with market power will, in general, be interested in the greater profits that are possible through price discrimination.

2. Consumers with Different Valuations of the Product Price discrimination is only possible when consumers value different units of the product differently. This could occur in two situations. First, the same consumer might be prepared to pay a different price for each unit of the good. Second, consumers of one particular type (or in one geographic region) may be prepared to pay more for the good than consumers of a different type (or in a different region). We will see some examples shortly.

In the situation where price discrimination occurs between groups of consumers, the firm must somehow be able to determine which group of consumers is prepared to pay a high price and which group is prepared to pay only a low price. This is referred to as *segmenting* the market. Sometimes this market segmentation is relatively easy, as when the market is divided into geographic regions. Other times the firm must create innovative pricing strategies that will lead consumers to segment themselves. We will see examples of both below.

3. No Arbitrage Whenever the same product is being sold at different prices, there is an incentive for buyers to purchase the product at the lower price and re-sell it at the higher price, thereby making a profit on the transaction. This is called *arbitrage*. A price-discriminating firm must be able to prevent people from conducting such transactions. Otherwise the firm will end up selling only at the low price and all of the profits that the strategy of price discrimination was designed to produce will accrue to those who do the arbitrage. As we will soon see, the successful prevention of this arbitrage depends crucially on the nature of the product being sold.

Different Forms of Price Discrimination

Now that we have seen the conditions that make price discrimination possible, let's examine the two general forms that it can take: price discrimination among *units of output* and price discrimination among *market segments*.

Price Discrimination Among Units of Output Recall our discussion in Chapter 6 where we noted that the demand curve can be viewed as a *willingness to pay* curve. We also discussed the concept of *consumer surplus*, the difference between the price the consumer is *willing* to pay and the price that the consumer *actually* pays.

A firm that charges different prices for different units of a product is trying to capture this consumer surplus. Figure 10-6 shows a monopolist's profits in two situations. In the first, the monopolist is only able to charge a single price per unit. In the second, the monopolist is able to charge different prices on different units of output and it increases its profits by doing so. Notice that even in the case where the firm charges several prices, consumers still earn some consumer surplus. In principle, however, a firm could charge a different price for each different unit of the product and thereby extract all of the consumer surplus. This situation is referred to as *perfect price discrimination* and is very rare because it is very difficult for the firm to ascertain the consumers' willingness to pay for each individual unit. However, in some countries where local doctors know their patients very well and thus can make informed judgements about the consumers' willingness to pay, this type of price discrimination is observed.

Practise with Study Guide Chapter 10, Exercise 6.

Price discrimination among units of output sold to the same consumer requires that the firm be able to keep track of the units that a buyer consumes in each period. Thus, the tenth unit purchased by a given consumer in a given month can be sold at a

FIGURE 10-6 Price Discrimination Among Units of Output

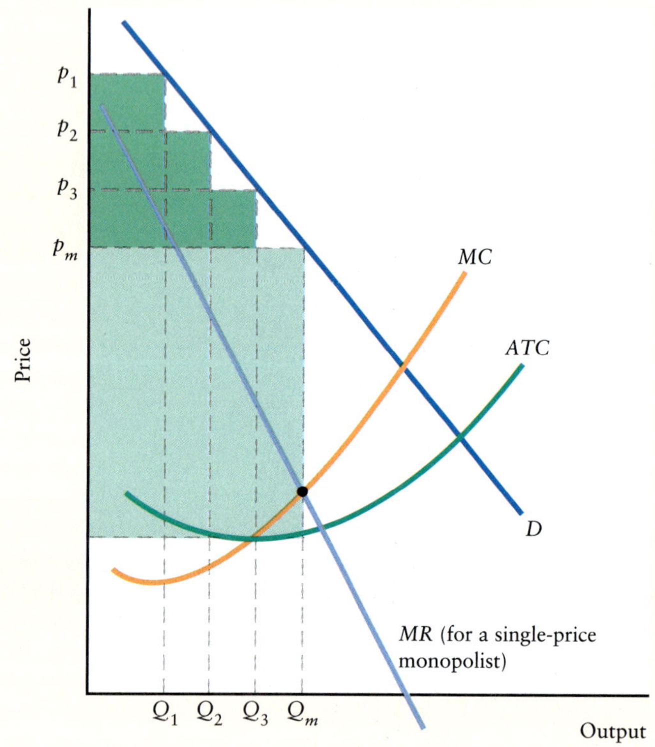

Profits can be increased by price discriminating. A single-price monopolist produces where $MR = MC$; output is Q_m and price is p_m. In this case, profits are the light shaded area, and consumers receive consumer surplus given by the entire area above p_m and below the demand curve.

Price discrimination is designed to transfer some of this consumer surplus to the firm. Suppose the firm keeps output constant at Q_m but is able to charge different prices for different blocks of units. For example, it might charge p_1 for the first Q_1 units, p_2 for the next block of units up to Q_2, p_3 for the next block of units up to Q_3, and p_m for the remaining units up to Q_m. (The firm would expand output beyond Q_m if it could offer even more prices, but we simplify here to focus on the transfer of surplus with unchanged output.) In this case, the firm's costs have not changed but its revenues have increased by the dark shaded area. Since costs have not changed, the increase in revenue earned by price discrimination also represents an increase in profits for the firm. Consumer surplus has been reduced to the unshaded triangles just below the demand curve.

price that is different from the fifth unit *only* if the firm can keep track of that consumer's purchases. This can be done, for example, by an electric company through its meter readings or by a magazine publisher by distinguishing between renewals and new subscriptions. Another way in which some sellers keep track of the consumer's purchases is to offer quantity discounts that take the form "buy two and get the third at half-price."

Price Discrimination Among Market Segments It is often easier for firms to distinguish between different groups of consumers of a product—different market segments—than it is to detect an individual consumer's willingness to pay for different units of that product. As a result, price discrimination among market segments is more common than price discrimination among units.

Suppose a monopolist faces a market demand curve that is made up of distinct market segments. These market segments may correspond to the age of consumers, such as children, adults, and seniors. Or the segments may correspond to different regions in which the consumers live, such as the North American automobile market being segmented into the Canadian and U.S. market segments. Whatever the nature of the market segmentation, suppose the monopolist recognizes the distinct market segments and is able to prevent any purchase-and-resale between them. What is the firm's profit-maximizing pricing policy?

The answer is for the firm to charge a higher price in the market segment with the *less elastic demand,* as shown in the numerical example in Figure 10-7. To understand this result, recall our discussion from Chapter 4 regarding elasticity. The elasticity of demand reflects consumers' ability or willingness to substitute between this product and other products. The market segment with less elastic demand therefore contains consumers that are more "committed" to this product than are the consumers in the market segment with more elastic demand. To put it differently, the consumers with less elastic demand represent a more "captive" market for the firm. It should not be surprising, therefore, that the profit-maximizing firm will charge a higher price to the more captive consumers and a lower price to those consumers who can more easily substitute away to other products.

Practise with Study Guide Chapter 10, Exercise 7.

A firm with market power that can identify distinct market segments will maximize its profits by charging higher prices in those segments with less elastic demand.

Price discrimination among market segments is very common. When the different segments occur in different regions or countries, distance and transport costs or government regulation help to keep the markets separate. For example, Levi Strauss, the manufacturer of jeans, actively discriminates in its pricing of Levi's 501s (and other products). The price in France is more than twice that in the United States. Ordinarily we would expect importers in France to import inexpensive 501s from the United States and sell them in France, thus pushing down the price. In this case, however, the price discrimination is made possible by European Union legislation barring the import of less expensive brand-name goods from outside the European Union. French consumers understandably don't like this price discrimination, but their less elastic demand combined with the EU legal barriers leads Levi Strauss to maximize its profits by charging much more in France than in the United States.

A more familiar example of price discrimination among market segments is the different prices charged by movie theatres for adults and seniors. The cost to the theatre of providing a seat to any customer is independent of the customer's age. But the two market segments contain consumers who are thought to have different elasticities of demand, the adults with the less elastic demand than seniors. The profit-maximizing pricing policy by the theatre is therefore to charge a higher price to adults than to seniors. This same logic applies to many goods and services for which there are "seniors' discounts."

The example of seniors' discounts at theatres also illustrates an important point about how the firm prevents arbitrage when price discriminating. When you buy a ticket to see a movie, you are buying a *service* rather than a tangible good. You don't take anything away with you after the movie—you are really just paying for the right to see the movie. This aspect of the product makes price discrimination easier to enforce. A young adult trying to circumvent the price discrimination could buy a senior's ticket, but upon entry to the theatre that person would be stopped and easily recognized as ineligible for the seniors' discount.

Price discrimination is easier for services than for tangible goods because for most services the firms transact directly with the customer, and thus can more easily prevent arbitrage.

That price discrimination is easier to sustain with services than with goods explains another familiar observation. As we noted above, seniors' discounts are quite common, even for tangible goods such as groceries. What prevents entrepreneurial seniors in these situations from buying a large number of units at the special price and reselling them to non-seniors at a higher price? The answer is that firms usually place quantity limits on special deals, thus preventing any large-scale arbitrage that would undermine their pricing policy.

FIGURE 10-7 A Numerical Example of Profitable Price Discrimination

Market Segment A

Demand: $Q_A^D = 48 - 2p_A$

Marginal Cost: $MC_A = 4$

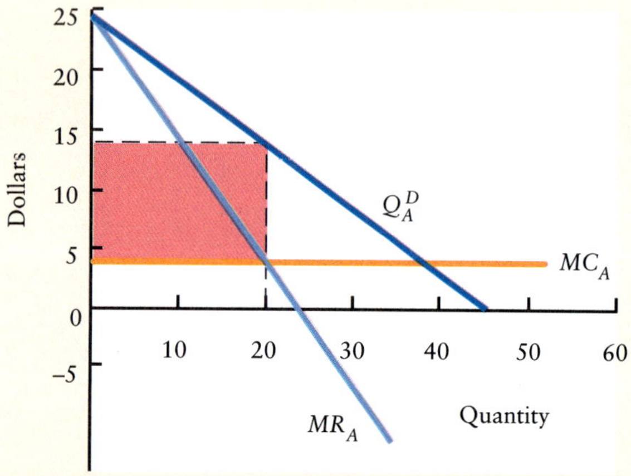

Market Segment B

Demand: $Q_B^D = 96 - 6p_B$

Marginal Cost: $MC_B = 4$

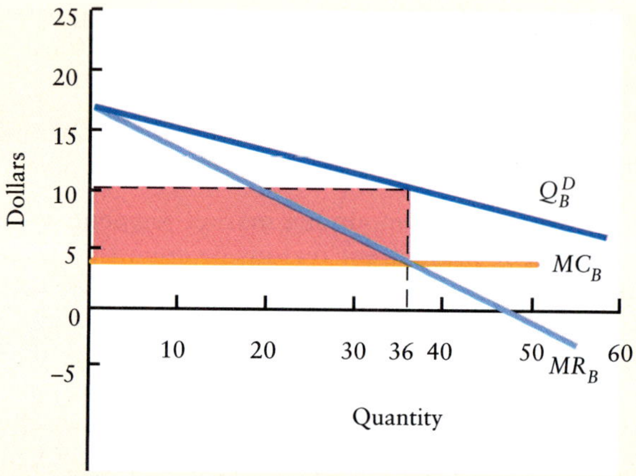

p_A	Q_A	TR_A	TC_A	Profits
9	30	270	120	150
10	28	280	112	168
11	26	286	104	182
12	24	288	96	192
13	22	286	88	198
14	20	280	80	200
15	18	270	72	198

p_B	Q_B	TR_B	TC_B	Profits
9	42	378	168	210
10	36	360	144	216
11	30	330	120	210
12	24	288	96	192
13	18	234	72	162
14	12	168	48	120
15	6	90	24	66

Profit-maximizing price discrimination results in higher prices in those market segments with less elastic demand. The figure shows two market segments, each with a different demand curve. At any given price, demand in segment A is less elastic than demand in segment B. Profit-maximizing price discrimination requires that $MC = MR$ in each market segment.

For each market segment, the table shows different possible prices, and the associated quantities, revenues, costs, and profits. Marginal costs are assumed to be \$4 for each unit produced. If the firm is unable to price discriminate, and therefore must charge the same price in both market segments, the single profit-maximizing price is \$11, total output is 56 units, and the resulting total profit is \$392, as shown by the green shaded row. The firm can increase its profits, however, if it can price discriminate across the two market segments. By charging \$14 in segment A and only \$10 in segment B, the firm's total output is unchanged at 56 units, but the allocation of that output across the market segments is changed, and the firm's total profit increases to \$416, as shown by the two red shaded rows.

In recent years, Canadian entrepreneurs have taken advantage of international price discrimination in prescription drugs by creating on-line businesses to sell inexpensive drugs from Canada to U.S. consumers. For a detailed discussion, look for "The Growing Battle Over On-line Prescription Drugs" in the *Additional Topics* section of this book's MyEconLab.

Hurdle Pricing Often there are market segments that are well defined but very difficult to detect by the firm. For example, we all know people who are sufficiently impatient that they *must* buy new electronic equipment—such as personal DVD players or cellular phones—when they first come out, whereas many other people are prepared to wait several months until they are no longer such hot items and buy them at considerably lower prices. This pricing strategy is intentional and is referred to as *hurdle pricing*. The firms producing these goods know that some people are patient and others are impatient. By setting a high initial price and a lower price only after several months, the firms are setting a "hurdle" that consumers must "jump over" in order to get the low price. In this case, the hurdle is that consumers must wait a few months. This same type of hurdle exists in the pricing of high-priced hardcover books and lower-priced paperback books that are released a few months later. In this case, the slightly altered products do have different costs, although the cost differences are considerably smaller than the differences in prices.

Hurdle pricing exists when firms create an obstacle that consumers must overcome in order to get a lower price. Consumers then assign themselves to the various market segments—those who don't want to jump the hurdle and are willing to pay the high price, and those who choose to jump the hurdle in order to benefit from the low price.

Another familiar example of hurdle pricing involves coupons for discounts at grocery stores. Most of us receive grocery-store flyers in the mail every week. Many people ignore them because they can't be bothered to look through them. Others carefully scan the coupons and clip the ones they will use, and it is common to see someone in a grocery-store line-up with a dozen or more coupons to apply to the purchase. In this case, the price discrimination is between those people who can't be bothered to deal with the coupons, and those people who care enough about the discounts to clip the coupons. Everyone is presented with the option between higher prices and lower prices, and the hurdle of clipping coupons is designed to have people assign themselves to the two market segments.

The Consequences of Price Discrimination

What are the consequences of price discrimination? We can examine the consequences for firm profits, output, and consumer welfare.

Price Discrimination and Firm Profits Our first proposition is about the consequences of price discrimination for firm profits:

For any given level of output, the most profitable system of discriminatory prices will always provide higher profits to the firm than the profit-maximizing single price.

This proposition, which was illustrated in Figure 10-6, requires only that the demand curve have a negative slope. To see that the proposition is correct, remember that a monopolist with the power to discriminate could produce exactly the same quantity as a single-price monopolist and charge everyone the same price. Therefore, it need never receive less revenue, and it can do better if it can raise the price on even one unit sold, so long as the price need not be reduced on any other.

Price Discrimination and Output Our second proposition relates to how price discrimination affects the level of output.

A monopolist that price discriminates among units will produce more output than will a single-price monopolist.

To understand this second proposition, remember that a single-price monopolist will produce less than would all the firms in a perfectly competitive industry (recall Figure 10-3). It produces less because it knows that selling more depresses the price. Price discrimination allows it to reduce this disincentive. To the extent that the firm can sell its output in separate blocks, it can sell another block without spoiling the market for blocks that are already sold. In the case of perfect price discrimination, in which every unit of output is sold at a different price, the profit-maximizing monopolist will produce every unit for which the price charged is greater than or equal to its marginal cost. A perfect-price-discriminating monopolist will therefore produce the same quantity of output as would all firms combined in a perfectly competitive industry.

This second proposition has implications for *market efficiency*, a concept we introduced in Chapter 5 and reviewed earlier in this chapter. Recall that a single-price monopolist produces at a level of output where price exceeds marginal cost. Thus, society would benefit from having more of the good produced because the marginal value of the good to society (as reflected by its price) exceeds the marginal cost of the good. Put differently, a higher level of output would lead to more economic surplus being generated in the market, and thus a more efficient outcome for society as a whole.

For a monopolist that price discriminates among units, however, there are several prices rather than just a single price. As you can see in Figure 10-6, if the firm sold another block of output beyond Q_m at a price below p_m it would increase its profits further (because the new price would still be above MC). And the more output it produces, the more economic surplus is generated in the market.

If price discrimination leads the firm to increase total output, the total economic surplus generated in the market will increase, and the outcome will be more efficient.

Price Discrimination and Consumer Welfare The final aspect of price discrimination is its effect on consumers, and here is where we often witness strong emotional reactions to price discrimination. But one's view will depend on who benefits and who loses.

For instance, when railways discriminate against small farmers, the results arouse public anger. It seems acceptable to many people, however, that doctors practise price discrimination in countries where medical services are provided by the market, charging lower prices to poor patients than to wealthy ones. Not everyone disapproves when airlines discriminate by giving senior citizens and vacationers lower fares than business travellers.

By increasing the seller's profits, price discrimination transfers income from buyers to sellers. When buyers are poor and sellers are rich, this transfer may seem undesirable. However, as in the case of doctor's fees and senior citizens' discounts, discrimination sometimes allows lower-income people to buy a product that they would otherwise be unable to afford if it were sold at the single price that maximized the producer's profits. In this case some consumers are made better off by the firm's decision to price discriminate.

There is no general relationship between price discrimination and consumer welfare. Price discrimination makes some consumers better off and other consumers worse off.

SUMMARY

10.1 A SINGLE-PRICE MONOPOLIST

LO 1 2

- Monopoly is a market structure in which an entire industry is supplied by a single firm. The monopolist's own demand curve is identical to the market demand curve for the product. The market demand curve is the monopolist's average revenue curve, and its marginal revenue curve always lies below its demand curve.
- A single-price monopolist is maximizing its profits when its marginal revenue is equal to marginal costs. Since marginal costs are positive, profit maximization means that marginal revenue is positive. Thus, in turn, elasticity of demand is greater than 1 at the monopolist's profit-maximizing level of output.
- A monopolist produces such that price exceeds marginal cost, whereas in a perfectly competitive industry price equals marginal cost. By restricting output below the competitive level, the monopolist imposes a deadweight loss on society; this is the inefficiency of monopoly.
- The profits that a monopoly earns may be positive, zero, or negative in the short run, depending on the relationship between demand and cost.
- For monopoly profits to persist in the long run, there must be effective barriers to the entry of other firms. Entry barriers can be natural or created.
- Monopoly power is limited by the presence of substitute products, the development of new products, and the entry of new firms. In the very long run, it is difficult to maintain entry barriers in the face of the process of creative destruction—the invention of new processes and new products to attack the entrenched position of existing firms.

10.2 CARTELS AS MONOPOLIES

LO 3

- A group of firms may form a cartel by agreeing to restrict their joint output to the monopoly level. Cartels tend to be unstable because of the strong incentives for each individual firm to cheat by producing more than its agreed-upon level of output.

10.3 PRICE DISCRIMINATION

LO 4

- A price-discriminating monopolist can capture some of the consumer surplus that exists when all of the units of a product are sold at a single price.
- Successful price discrimination requires that the firm be able to control the supply of the product offered to particular buyers and to prevent the resale of the product.
- A firm that price discriminates among units will produce more output than if it sets only a single price. Price discrimination of this type is possible only if it can monitor use of the product by consumers.
- A firm that discriminates between different market segments will equate *MC* and *MR* in each market. The market with the less elastic demand will have the higher price.
- Hurdle pricing is a common form of price discrimination that requires customers to overcome some obstacle in order to benefit from a lower price. This method of price discrimination leads customers to reveal which market segment they are in.
- If price discrimination leads the firm to increase output, market efficiency is improved. In general, some consumers will benefit and others will be made worse off by the firm's ability to price discriminate.

KEY CONCEPTS

The relationship between price and marginal revenue for a monopolist
Short-run monopoly profits
Natural and created entry barriers
The process of creative destruction
Cartels as monopolies
The instability of cartels
Arbitrage
Price discrimination among units
Perfect price discrimination
Price discrimination among market segments
Hurdle pricing

STUDY EXERCISES

1. Fill in the blanks to make the following statements correct.

   a. A perfectly competitive firm faces a __________ demand curve, whereas a single-price monopolist faces a __________ demand curve.

   b. A single-price monopolist that maximizes profits will produce at the output where __________ equals __________. A perfectly competitive firm (and industry) produces a level of output such that price __________ marginal cost. The monopolist produces a level of output such that price __________ marginal cost.

   c. A monopolist will be earning profits as long as price is __________ average total cost.

   d. At its profit-maximizing level of output, marginal cost for a single-price monopolist is always __________ the price it charges for its output.

2. myeconlab The following table shows data for a monopolist. The first two columns provide all the data necessary to plot the monopolist's demand curve.

Price	Quantity Demanded	Total Revenue (*TR*)	Average Revenue (*AR*)	Marginal Revenue (*MR*)
$20	100	—	—	
18	125	—	—	—
16	150	—	—	—
14	175	—	—	—
12	200	—	—	—
10	225	—	—	—
8	250	—	—	—
6	275	—	—	—
4	300	—	—	—

   a. Compute total and average revenue for each level of output and fill in the third and fourth columns in the table. Explain why average revenue is equal to price.

   b. Compute marginal revenue for each successive *change* in output and fill in the last column. Explain why *MR* is less than price.

   c. On a scale diagram, plot the demand (average revenue) curve and the marginal revenue curve.

   d. On a second scale diagram, with dollars on the vertical axis and output on the horizontal axis, plot the *TR* curve. What is the value of *MR* when *TR* reaches its maximum?

3. myeconlab The diagram below shows the demand curve, marginal revenue curve, and cost curves for a monopolist that owns all the golf courses on Golf Island. The monopolist's product is 18-hole golf games.

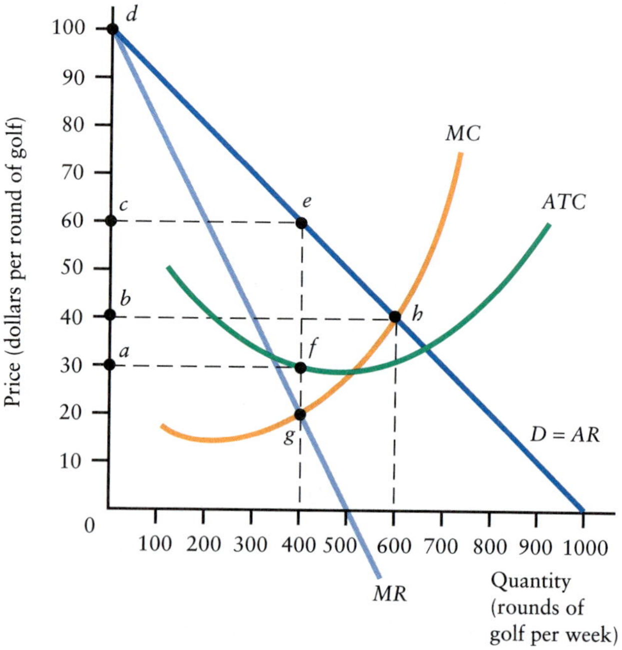

   a. What is the profit-maximizing price and output (number of rounds of golf per week) for the monopolist on Golf Island?

   b. What is the average total cost per round of golf at the profit-maximizing level of output?

   c. Calculate the profit, in dollars per week, to this monopolist.

4. The diagram below shows a monopolist's *MC* and *ATC* curves as well as the industry demand and *MR* curves.

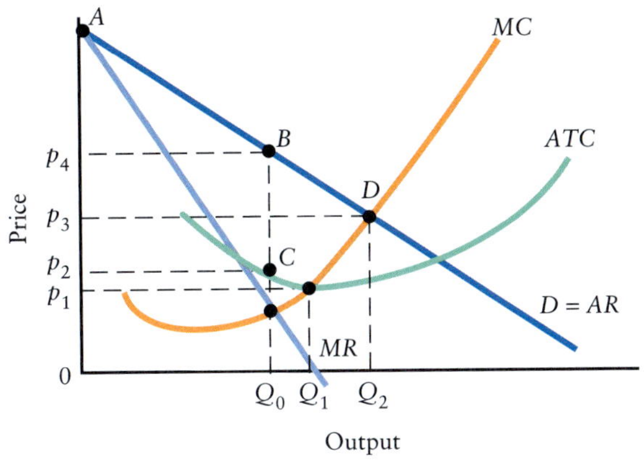

a. What is the profit-maximizing price and level of output for the monopolist?
b. What area in the figure shows the level of profits for the monopolist? Are profits positive or negative?
c. What area shows the deadweight loss to society resulting from the monopolist's output decision?
d. Now suppose the industry is made up of many small, price-taking firms (with the same technology). What are the equilibrium price and level of output in this case?

5. Imagine a monopolist that has fixed costs but no variable costs (thus there are no marginal costs, so $MC = 0$). For example, consider a firm that owns a spring of water that can produce indefinitely once it installs certain pipes, in an area where no other source of water is available.

a. Draw a downward-sloping demand curve for water, its associated *MR* curve, and the monopolist's *MC* curve.
b. On your diagram, show the monopolist's profit-maximizing price and level of output.
c. What is the marginal value of this good to society, and how does it compare to the marginal cost?

6. Consider the market for corn. Suppose this is a competitive industry, made up of many price-taking farmers. We begin in a situation where market price is p_0, industry output is Q_0, and the typical farm is earning zero profit.

a. Draw two diagrams like the ones at the bottom of this page.
b. Now suppose that the farmers in this industry form a cartel and collectively agree to restrict the industry output of corn to the level that a monopolist would produce. Call this level of output Q^m and call the new price p^m. Each firm now produces output of $q^m < q_0$. Show this outcome in the two diagrams.
c. Show how the cartel raises the profits for the typical farmer.
d. Now consider the incentives for an individual farm to cheat on its fellow cartel members. Would it be profitable to produce an extra unit and sell it at the cartel price? How is this incentive illustrated in your diagram?
e. Show how the typical farm's profits would rise if it were the only farm to cheat. What level of output would the cheating farm produce?
f. Explain what would happen if *all* farms tried to cheat in this way.

7. Consider each of the following examples where a firm sells the same product to different customers at different prices. Identify in each case whether price discrimination is likely to be taking place. If there is unlikely

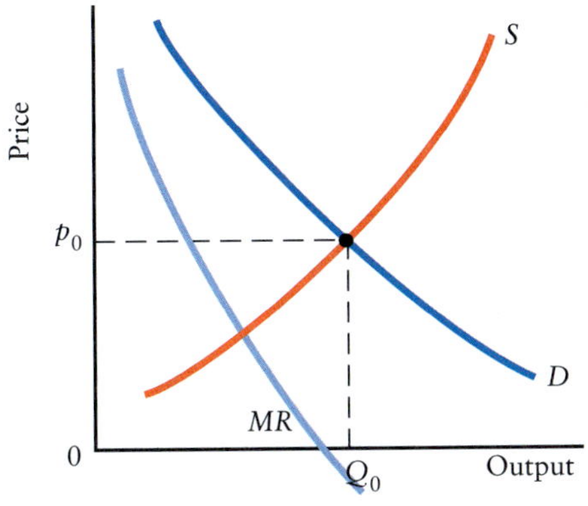

Corn Industry

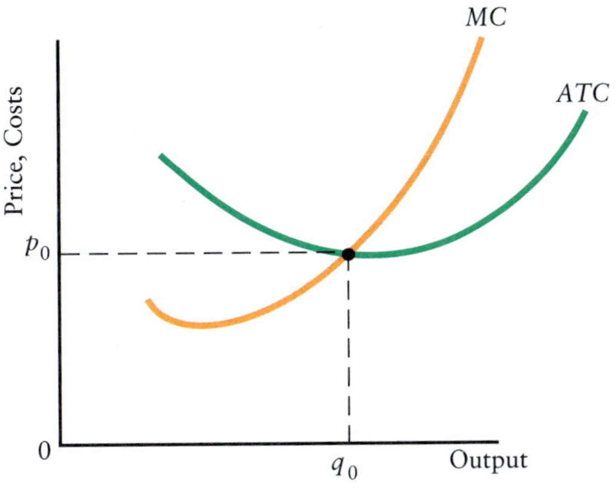

Typical Corn Farmer

to be price discrimination occurring, what explains the different prices?

a. Weekend airline fares that are less than mid-week fares.
b. Business-class airline fares that are 50% higher than economy-class fares. (Recognize that two business-class seats take the same space inside the plane as three economy-class seats.)
c. Discounts on furniture negotiated from "suggested retail price" for which sales personnel are authorized to bargain and to get as much in each transaction as the customer is prepared to pay.
d. Higher tuition for law students than for graduate students in economics.

8. Look back to the diagram of the monopolist on Golf Island in Question 3.

a. Suppose the monopolist is able to practise *perfect* price discrimination. What would be the total number of rounds of golf sold per week? What would be the price on the last round sold?
b. What is the area representing consumer surplus in the absence of any price discrimination?
c. What is the area representing consumer surplus when the monopolist is practising perfect price discrimination?
d. Could this monopolist realistically engage in perfect price discrimination? Describe a more likely form of price discrimination that this monopolist could achieve on Golf Island.

9. In the text we mentioned how Levi Strauss price discriminates between the European and American markets. This question is designed to help you analyze this situation. The following equations are hypothetical demand curves for Levi's 501s in Europe and in America. We have expressed the price in dollars in both markets, and quantity is thousands of units per year.

European Demand: $Q^D_E = 150 - p$
American Demand: $Q^D_A = 250 - 4p$

a. On two separate scale diagrams, one for Europe and one for America, plot the two demand curves.
b. Recalling that a straight-line demand curve has an associated *MR* curve that has twice its slope, plot the two *MR* curves.
c. Suppose Levi Strauss has a constant marginal cost of $15 per unit. Plot the *MC* curve in both diagrams.
d. What is the profit-maximizing price in each market? Explain why profit maximization requires that *MC* be equated to *MR in each market segment.*
e. Compute the price elasticity of demand (at the profit-maximizing points) in each market segment. (You may want to review Chapter 4 on elasticity at this point.) Does the market segment with less elastic demand have the higher price?

10. Consider each of the following examples of price discrimination. For each case, explain how the price discrimination works. Also explain which consumers would be worse off and which consumers would be better off if the firm were *unable* to price discriminate in this way.

a. Seniors pay lower prices for theatre tickets than do other adults.
b. Consumers pay less for paperback books than for hardcover books, but must wait six to twelve months before the paperbacks are made available.
c. Customers at garage sales often pay a lower price if they ask for one—that is, if they reveal that they are prepared to haggle.
d. Airline customers get a discount fare if they are prepared to stay over a Saturday night at their destination.

DISCUSSION QUESTIONS

1. Suppose only one professor teaches economics at your university. Would you say that this professor is a monopolist who can exact any "price" from students in the form of readings assigned, tests given, and material covered? Suppose now that two additional professors have been hired. Has the original professor's market power been decreased? What if the three professors form a cartel agreeing on common reading lists, workloads, and the like?

2. Which of these industries—licorice candy, copper wire, outboard motors, coal, or the local newspaper—would it be most profitable to monopolize? Why? Does your answer depend on several factors or on just one or two? Which would you as a consumer least like to have monopolized by someone else? If your answers to the two questions are different, explain why.

3. Aristotle Murphy owns movie theatres in two towns of roughly the same size, 100 kilometres apart. In Monopolia, he owns the only chain of theatres; in Competitia, there is no theatre chain, and he is only one of a number of independent theatre operators. Would you expect movie prices to be higher in Monopolia or in Competitia in the short run? In the

long run? If differences occur in his prices, would Murphy be discriminating in price?

4. Airline fares to Europe are higher in summer than in winter. Some railways charge lower fares during the week than on weekends. Electric companies charge consumers lower rates the more electricity they use. Are these all examples of price discrimination? What additional information would you like to have before answering this question?

5. Acme Department Store has a sale on luggage. It is offering $30 off any new set of luggage to customers who trade in an old suitcase. Acme has no use for the old luggage and throws it away at the end of each day. Is this price discrimination? Why or why not? Which of the conditions necessary for price discrimination are or are not met?

6. The world price of coffee has declined in real terms over the past 40 years. In 1950, coffee was priced at just under U.S.$3 per pound (in 1994 dollars), whereas by 1995 the world price had fallen to just over U.S.$1 per pound. On July 29, 1995, *The Economist* magazine reported that

   > *On July 26 the Association of Coffee Producing Countries agreed in New York to limit exports to 60m bags for 12 months. The current level is 70m bags.... Coffee prices rallied a bit on the news, but few expect the pact to last: some big coffee producers such as Mexico have not signed up, and even those who have will probably cheat.*

   a. Explain why "few expect the pact to last" in situations like this when producers form a cartel.
   b. Early in 2006, the price of coffee was approximately U.S.$1.25 per pound. Was the cartel successful?

CHAPTER 11

Imperfect Competition and Strategic Behaviour

LEARNING OBJECTIVES

In this chapter you will learn

1. that most industries in Canada have either a large number of small firms or a small number of large firms.
2. why imperfectly competitive firms have differentiated products and often engage in non-price competition.
3. the key elements of the theory of monopolistic competition.
4. that strategic behaviour is a key feature of oligopoly.
5. how to use game theory to explain the difference between cooperative and non-cooperative outcomes amongst oligopolists.

The two market structures that we have studied so far—perfect competition and monopoly—are polar cases; they define the two extremes of a firm's market power within an industry. Under perfect competition, firms are price takers, price is equal to marginal cost, and economic profits in the long run are zero. Under monopoly, the firm is a price setter, it sets price above marginal cost, and it can earn positive profits in the long run if there are sufficient entry barriers.

Although they provide important insights, these two polar cases are insufficient for understanding the behaviour of *all* firms. Indeed, most of the products that we easily recognize—computers, breakfast cereals, automobiles, cameras, and fast food, to name a few—are produced by firms that have some market power yet are not monopolists.

This chapter discusses market structures that lie between these two polar cases of perfect competition and monopoly. Before discussing the theory, however, we turn to a brief discussion of the prevalence of these "intermediate" market structures in the Canadian economy.

11.1 THE STRUCTURE OF THE CANADIAN ECONOMY

We can divide Canadian industries into two broad groups—those with a large number of relatively small firms and those with a small number of relatively large firms.

Industries with Many Small Firms

About two-thirds of Canada's total annual output is produced by industries made up of firms that are small relative to the size of the market in which they sell.

The perfectly competitive model does quite well in explaining the behaviour of some of these industries. These are the ones in which individual firms produce more-or-less identical products and so are price takers. Forest and fish products are two broad examples. Agriculture also fits fairly well in most ways since individual farmers are clearly price takers. Many basic raw materials, such as iron ore, tin, and copper, are sold on world markets where most individual firms lack significant market power.

Other industries, however, are not well described by the perfectly competitive model, even though they contain many small firms. In retail trade and in services, for example, most firms have some influence over prices. Your local grocery stores, clothing shops, night clubs, and restaurants spend a good deal of money advertising on television and in newspapers—something they would not have to do if they were price takers. Moreover, each store in these industries has a unique location that may give it some local market power over nearby customers.

The theory of *monopolistic competition,* which we will examine in this chapter, was originally developed to help explain economic behaviour and outcomes in industries in which there are many small firms, each with some market power.

Industries with a Few Large Firms

About one-third of Canada's total annual output is produced by industries that are dominated by either a single firm or a few large ones.

The most striking cases of monopolies in today's economy are the electric utilities (which are typically owned by provincial governments) and the firms that provide local telephone and cable or digital TV and Internet services (which are subject to government regulation and which we examine in Chapter 12). Other than these and a few other similar cases in which government ownership or regulation play an important role, cases of monopoly are rare in Canada today. However, there are some notable examples of monopoly (or near monopoly) from many years ago. For example, the Eddy Match Company was virtually the sole producer of wooden matches in Canada between 1927 and 1940, and Canada Cement Limited produced nearly all of the output of cement until the 1950s.

This type of market dominance by a single large firm is now a thing of the past. Today, most modern industries that are dominated by large firms contain several firms. Their names are part of the average Canadian's vocabulary: Canadian National and Canadian Pacific; Bank of Montreal, Royal Bank, and Scotiabank; Imperial Oil, Petro-Canada, and Irving; Stelco, Dofasco, and Algoma; Alcan, Barrick, and Teck Cominco; Loblaws, Safeway, and Sobey's; Ford, Toyota, and GM; Sony, Mitsubishi, and Toshiba; Great West Life, Sun Life, and Manulife; and General Foods, Nabisco, and Kellogg. Many service industries that used to be dominated by small independent producers have in recent decades seen the development of large firms operating on a world-wide basis. SNC-Lavalin and Acres are two examples of very large engineering firms that have business contracts all over the world. In management consulting, McKinsey & Co., Boston Consulting Group, and Monitor are also very large firms with market power.

The theory of *oligopoly,* which we will examine later in this chapter, helps us understand industries in which there are small numbers of large firms, each with market power, that compete actively with each other.

Industrial Concentration

For data on many aspects of Canadian industries, see Industry Canada's website: **www.strategis.ic.gc.ca**.

An industry with a small number of relatively large firms is said to be highly *concentrated*. An industry with a large number of relatively small firms is less concentrated. A formal measure of such industrial concentration is given by the *concentration ratio*.

concentration ratio The fraction of total market sales (or some other measure of market activity) controlled by a specified number of the industry's largest firms.

Concentration Ratios When we measure whether an industry has power concentrated in the hands of only a few firms or dispersed over many, it is not sufficient to count the firms. For example, an industry with one enormous firm and 29 very small ones is more concentrated in any meaningful sense than an industry with only five equal-sized firms. One approach to this problem is to calculate what is called a **concentration ratio**, which shows the fraction of total market sales controlled by the largest sellers. Common types of concentration ratios cite the share of total market sales made by the largest four or eight firms.

Figure 11-1 shows the four-firm concentration ratios in several Canadian manufacturing industries. As is clear, the degree of concentration is quite varied across these industries. In the tobacco industry, for example, the largest four firms account for almost 100 percent of total sales, and in the petroleum and transportation equipment industries the largest four firms account for over 70 percent of sales. At the other extreme, the largest four firms in the furniture and clothing industries account for less than 10 percent of sales. These largest firms may be large in some absolute sense, but the low concentration ratios suggest that they have quite limited market power.

FIGURE 11-1 Concentration Ratios in Selected Canadian Industries

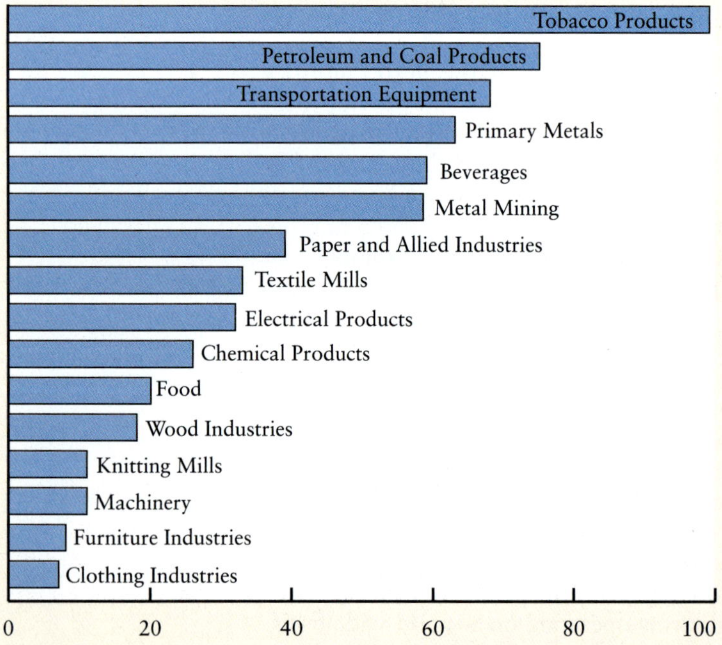

Concentration ratios vary greatly among manufacturing industries. These data show the share of total annual shipments (in dollar terms) accounted for by the four largest firms in the industry.

(*Source:* Based on Douglas West, *Modern Canadian Industrial Organization,* HarperCollins 1994, p. 37.)

Defining the Market The main problem associated with using concentration ratios is to *define the market* with reasonable accuracy. On the one hand, the market may be much smaller than the whole country. For example, concentration ratios in national cement sales are low, but they understate the market power of cement companies because high transportation costs divide the cement *industry* into a series of regional *markets,* with each having relatively few firms. On the other hand, the market may be larger than one country, as is the case for most internationally traded commodities. This is particularly important for Canada.

The globalization of competition brought about by the falling costs of transportation and communication has been one of the most significant developments in the world economy in recent decades. As the world has "become smaller" through the advances in transportation and communication technologies, the nature of domestic markets has changed dramatically. For example, the presence of only a single firm in one industry in Canada in no way implies monopoly power when it is in competition with several foreign firms that can easily sell in the Canadian market. This is the situation faced by many Canadian companies producing raw materials, such as Petro-Canada, Canfor, Alcan, and Barrick. These companies may be large relative to the *Canadian* market, but the relevant market in each case (oil, forest products, aluminum, and gold) is the *global* one in which these firms have no significant market power.

However, concentration ratios, adjusted to define the relevant market correctly, can still be used to provide valuable information about the degree to which production in a given market is concentrated in the hands of a few firms.

myeconlab

The ongoing forces of globalization have been changing the world economy for centuries. For more information on how relatively recent advances in transportation and communications technologies have led to changes in the location of production and the nature of competition, look for "The Nature of Globalization" in the *Additional Topics* section of this book's MyEconLab.

www.myeconlab.com

11.2 WHAT IS IMPERFECT COMPETITION?

We have identified two types of industries that are not well described by the theories of perfect competition or monopoly. In one type, there is a large number of small firms, but the theory of perfect competition is not appropriate because each of the many firms has some market power. In the other type, there is a small number of large firms, each with considerable market power. That these industries have more than a single firm makes the theory of monopoly inappropriate. We need theories to understand these market structures *between* the polar cases of perfect competition and monopoly.

The market structures that we are now going to study are called *imperfectly competitive*. The word *competitive* emphasizes that we are not dealing with monopoly, and the word *imperfect* emphasizes that we are not dealing with perfect competition (in which firms are price takers). Let's begin by noting a number of characteristics that are typical of imperfectly competitive firms. To help organize our thoughts, we classify these under two main headings. First, firms choose the *variety* of the product that they produce and sell. Second, firms choose the *price* at which they will sell that product.

Firms Choose Their Products

If a new farmer enters the wheat industry, the full range of products that the farmer can produce is already in existence. In contrast, if a new firm enters the snack food industry, that firm must decide on the characteristics of the new snacks that it is to produce. It will not produce snacks that are identical to those already in production. Rather, it will develop variations on existing snack foods or even a totally new food. Each of these will have its own distinctive characteristics. As a result, firms in the snack food industry sell an array of differentiated products, no two of which are identical.

differentiated product A group of commodities that are similar enough to be called the same product but dissimilar enough that all of them do not have to be sold at the same price.

The term **differentiated product** refers to a group of commodities that are similar enough to be called the same product but dissimilar enough that they can be sold at different prices. For example, although one brand of shampoo is similar to most others, shampoos differ from each other in chemical composition, colour, smell, brand name, packaging, reputation, and a host of other characteristics that matter to customers. All shampoos taken together can be regarded as one differentiated product.

Most firms in imperfectly competitive markets sell differentiated products. In such industries, the firm itself must choose which characteristics to give the products that it will sell.

Firms Choose Their Prices

Because firms in perfect competition sell an identical product, they face a market price that they are unable to influence. In all other market structures, firms face negatively sloped demand curves and thus face a tradeoff between the price that they charge and the quantity that they sell.

Whenever different firms' products are not identical, each firm must decide on a price to set. For example, no market sets a single price for cars or TVs or jeans by equating overall demand with overall supply. What is true for cars and TVs is true for virtually all consumer goods. Any one manufacturer will typically have several product lines that differ from each other and from the competing product lines of other firms. Each product has a price that must be set by its producer.

administered price A price set by the conscious decision of the seller rather than by impersonal market forces.

price setter A firm that faces a downward sloping demand curve for its product. It chooses which price to set.

In such circumstances, economists say that firms *administer* their price. An **administered price** is a price set by the conscious decision of an individual firm rather than by impersonal market forces. Firms that administer their prices are said to be **price setters.** Each firm has expectations about the quantity it can sell at each price that it might set. Unexpected demand fluctuations then cause unexpected variations in the quantities that are sold at the administered prices.

In market structures other than perfect competition, firms set their prices and then let demand determine sales. Changes in market conditions are signalled to the firm by changes in the firm's sales.

One striking contrast between perfectly competitive markets and markets for differentiated products concerns the behaviour of prices. In perfect competition, prices change continually in response to changes in demand and supply. In markets where differentiated products are sold, prices change less frequently.

These breakfast cereals are different enough that each can have its own price, but they are similar enough to be called the same product—they are a differentiated product.

Modern firms that sell differentiated products typically have hundreds of distinct products on their price lists. Changing such a long list of administered prices is often costly enough that it is done only infrequently—although improved computer technology has made rapid price changes increasingly possible, as when airlines post prices on their websites that change hourly. The costs of changing the prices include the costs of printing new list prices and notifying all customers, the difficulty of keeping track of frequently changing prices for purposes of accounting and billing, and the loss of customer and retailer goodwill due to the uncertainty caused by frequent changes in prices. As a result, imperfectly competitive firms often respond to fluctuations in demand by changing output and holding prices constant. Only after changes in demand are expected to persist will firms incur the expense of adjusting their entire list of prices.

Non-Price Competition

Firms in imperfect competition behave in other ways that are not observed under either perfect competition or monopoly.

First, many firms spend large sums of money on advertising. They do so in an attempt both to shift the demand curves for the industry's products and to attract customers from competing firms. A firm in a perfectly competitive market would not engage in advertising because the firm faces a perfectly elastic (horizontal) demand curve at the market price and so advertising would involve costs but would not increase the firm's revenues. A monopolist has no competitors in the industry and so will not advertise to attract customers away from other brands. However, in some cases a monopolist will still advertise in an attempt to convince consumers to shift their spending away from other types of products and toward the monopolist's product.

Second, many firms engage in a variety of other forms of non-price competition, such as offering competing standards of quality and product guarantees. In the automobile industry, for example, Toyota and GM compete actively in terms of the duration of their "bumper-to-bumper" warranties. Many firms also compete through the services they offer along with their products. The automobile industry is again a good example, with manufacturers and dealers competing in their "after-sales" services provided to the customer, ranging from oil changes and car washes to emergency on-road assistance.

Third, firms in many industries engage in activities that appear to be designed to hinder the entry of new firms, thereby preventing existing pure profits from being eroded by entry. For example, the public commitment to match any price offered by a competitor may convince potential entrants not to enter the industry.

Two Market Structures

Our discussion in this section has been a general one concerning firms in imperfectly competitive market structures. We now go into a little more detail, and make a distinction between industries with a large number of small firms and industries with a small number of large firms.

Behaviour in the first group of industries can be understood with the theory of *monopolistic competition.* To understand behaviour in the second group we use the theory of *oligopoly,* in which *game theory* plays a central role. As you will see in the remainder of this chapter, a key difference between these two market structures is the amount of *strategic behaviour* displayed by firms.

11.3 MONOPOLISTIC COMPETITION

The theory of **monopolistic competition** was originally developed to deal with the phenomenon of product differentiation. This theory was first developed by the U.S. economist Edward Chamberlin in his pioneering 1933 book, *The Theory of Monopolistic Competition.*

monopolistic competition Market structure of an industry in which there are many firms and freedom of entry and exit but in which each firm has a product somewhat differentiated from the others, giving it some control over its price.

This market structure is similar to perfect competition in that the industry contains many firms and exhibits freedom of entry and exit. It differs, however, in one important respect: Whereas firms in perfect competition sell an identical product and are price takers, firms in monopolistic competition sell a differentiated product and thus have some power over setting price.

Familiar retail stores like these ones compete in industries in which there are many firms. Such industries are said to be monopolistically competitive.

Product differentiation leads to the establishment of brand names and advertising, and it gives each firm a degree of market power over its own product. Each firm can raise its price, even if its competitors do not, without losing all its sales. This is the *monopolistic* part of the theory. However, each firm's market power is severely restricted in both the short run and the long run. The short-run restriction comes from the presence of similar products sold by many competing firms; this causes the demand curve faced by each firm to be very elastic. The long-run restriction comes from free entry into the industry, which permits new firms to compete away the profits being earned by existing firms. These restrictions comprise the *competition* part of the theory.

The Assumptions of Monopolistic Competition

The theory of monopolistic competition is based on three key simplifying assumptions.

1. Each firm produces one specific brand of the industry's differentiated product. Each firm thus faces a demand curve that, although negatively sloped, is highly elastic because competing firms produce many close substitutes.
2. The industry contains so many firms that each one ignores the possible reactions of its many competitors when it makes its own price and output decisions. In this respect, firms in monopolistic competition are similar to firms in perfect competition.
3. There is freedom of entry and exit in the industry. If profits are being earned by existing firms, new firms have an incentive to enter. When they do, the demand for the industry's product must be shared among more brands.

Predictions of the Theory

Product differentiation, which is the *only* thing that makes monopolistic competition different from perfect competition, has important consequences for behaviour in both the short and the long run.

The Short-Run Decision of the Firm In the short run, a firm that is operating in a monopolistically competitive market structure is similar to a monopoly. It faces a negatively sloped demand curve and maximizes its profits by equating marginal cost with marginal revenue. The firm shown in part (i) of Figure 11-2 makes positive profits.

The Long-Run Equilibrium of the Industry Profits, as shown in part (i) of Figure 11-2, provide an incentive for new firms to enter the industry. As they do so, the total demand for the industry's product must be shared among this larger number of firms; thus, each firm gets a smaller share of the total market. Such entry shifts the demand curve for each existing firm's product to the left. Entry continues until profits are eliminated. When this has occurred, each firm is in the position shown in part (ii) of Figure 11-2. Its demand curve has shifted to the left until the curve is *tangent* to the

Practise with Study Guide Chapter 11, Exercises 1 and 2.

FIGURE 11-2 Profit Maximization for a Firm in Monopolistic Competition

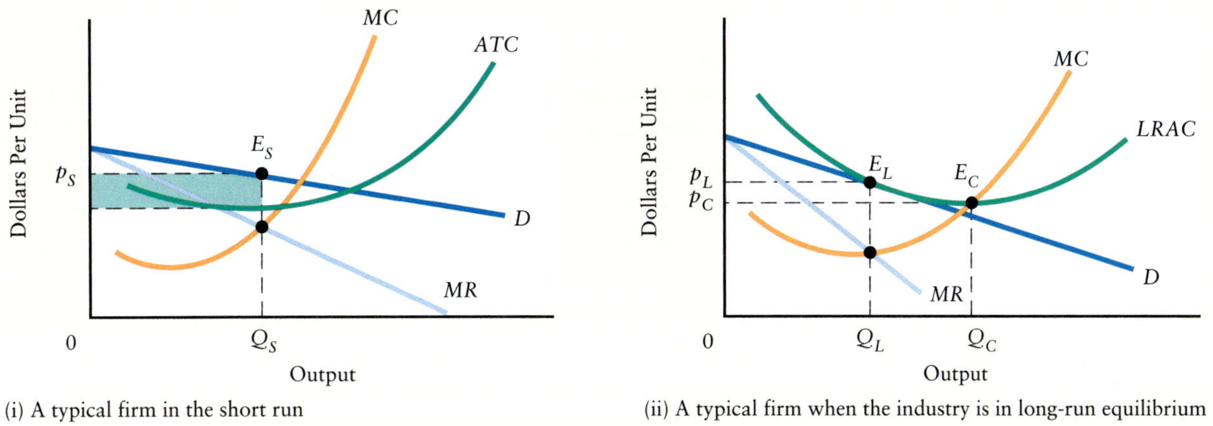

The short-run position for a monopolistically competitive firm is similar to that of a monopolist. In the long run, firms in a monopolistically competitive industry have zero profits and excess capacity. Note the very elastic demand curve—this reflects the fact that each firm produces a good for which there are many close (but not perfect) substitutes. Short-run profit maximization occurs in part (i) at E_s, the output for which $MR = MC$. Price is p_S and quantity is Q_S. Profits may exist; in this example they are shown by the shaded area. Starting from the short-run position shown in part (i), entry of new firms shifts each firm's demand curve to the left and eliminates profits. In part (ii), point E_L, where demand is tangent to *LRAC*, is the position of each firm when the industry is in long-run equilibrium. Price is p_L and quantity is Q_L. Price is greater and quantity is less than would exist in the long run if the industry were perfectly competitive (p_C and Q_C). When the industry is in long-run equilibrium, each monopolistically competitive firm has excess capacity of Q_LQ_C.

long-run average cost (*LRAC*) curve. Each firm is maximizing its profit, but its profit is equal to zero.[1]

To see why this "tangency solution" provides the only possible long-run equilibrium for an industry that fulfills all of the theory's assumptions, consider the two possible alternatives. First, suppose the firm's demand curve *nowhere touched* the *LRAC* curve. There would then be no output at which costs could be covered, and exit would occur. The exit of firms from the industry would then lead each *remaining* firm's demand curve to shift to the right, until it eventually touched the *LRAC* curve. Second, suppose the demand curve *cut* the *LRAC* curve. There would then be a range of output over which profits could be earned. These profits would lead firms to enter the industry, and this entry would shift each *remaining* firm's demand curve to the left until it was just tangent to the *LRAC* curve.

The Excess-Capacity Theorem Part (ii) of Figure 11-2 makes it clear that monopolistic competition results in a long-run equilibrium of zero profits, even though each individual firm faces a negatively sloped demand curve. It does this by forcing each

1 A standard assumption in this theory is that the industry is *symmetric* in the sense that when a new firm enters the industry, it takes demand away *equally* from all existing firms, thus ensuring that all industry profits are eliminated in the long run. The asymmetric case, in which long-run profits are possible, is discussed in advanced courses in industrial organization.

firm into a position in which it has *excess capacity;* that is, each firm is producing an output less than that corresponding to the lowest point on its long-run average cost (*LRAC*) curve. If the firm were to increase its output, it would reduce its cost per unit, but it does not do so because selling more would reduce revenue by more than it would reduce cost. This result is often called the **excess-capacity theorem.**

excess-capacity theorem The property of long-run equilibrium in monopolistic competition that firms produce on the falling portion of their long-run average cost curves. This results in excess capacity, measured by the gap between present output and the output that coincides with minimum average cost.

In long-run equilibrium in monopolistic competition, goods are produced at a point where average total costs are not at their minimum, in contrast to perfect competition, where they are produced at their lowest possible cost.

The excess-capacity theorem once aroused passionate debate among economists because it seemed to show that all industries selling differentiated products would produce them at a higher cost than was necessary. Because product differentiation is a characteristic of virtually all modern consumer goods industries, this theorem suggested that modern market economies were systematically inefficient.

Subsequent analysis by economists has shown that the charge of inefficiency has not been proven. The excess capacity of monopolistic competition does not necessarily indicate a waste of resources because some benefits accrue to consumers from the greater choice and variety of products.

Saying that consumers value variety is not saying that *each* consumer necessarily values variety. You might like only one of the many brands of toothpaste and be better off if only that one brand were produced and the price were lower. But other consumers would prefer one of the other brands. Thus, it is the differences in tastes *across many consumers* that gives rise to the social value of variety, and the price of that greater variety is the higher price per unit.

From society's point of view, there is a tradeoff between producing more brands to satisfy diverse tastes and producing fewer brands at a lower cost per unit.

Monopolistic competition produces a wider range of products but at a somewhat higher cost per unit than perfect competition. As consumers clearly value variety, the benefits of variety must be matched against the extra cost that variety imposes in order to find the *socially optimal* amount of product differentiation. Product differentiation is wasteful only if the costs of providing variety exceed the benefits conferred by providing that variety. Depending on consumers' tastes and firms' costs, monopolistic competition may result in too much, too little, or the optimal amount of product variety.

The Canadian wine-making industry contains many firms producing similar but differentiated products. It is a monopolistically competitive industry.

Empirical Relevance of Monopolistic Competition

A controversy raged for several decades as to the empirical relevance of monopolistic competition. Of course, product differentiation is pervasive in many industries. Nonetheless, many economists maintained that the monopolistically competitive market structure was almost never found in practice.

To see why, we need to distinguish between products and firms. Single-product firms are extremely rare in manufacturing industries. Typically, a vast array of differentiated products is produced by each of the few firms in the industry. Most of the vast variety of breakfast cereals, for example, is produced by only three firms

(Kellogg, Nabisco, and General Foods). Similar circumstances exist in soap, chemicals, cigarettes, and numerous other industries where many competing products are produced by a few very large firms. These industries are clearly not perfectly competitive and neither are they monopolies. Are they monopolistically competitive? The answer is no because they contain few enough firms for each to take account of the others' reactions when determining its own behaviour. Furthermore, these firms often earn large profits without attracting new entry (thereby violating the third assumption of monopolistic competition). In fact, they operate under the market structure called *oligopoly,* which we consider in the next section.

Although monopolistic competition is not applicable to differentiated products produced in industries with high concentration, many economists think that the theory is useful for analyzing industries where concentration ratios are low and products are differentiated, as in the cases of restaurants, clothing and furniture stores, gas stations, dry cleaners, hair salons, and landscaping services. Indeed, many of the small stores and services that are located in or near your neighbourhood are monopolistically competitive firms.

11.4 OLIGOPOLY AND GAME THEORY

Industries that are made up of a small number of large firms have a market structure called *oligopoly,* from the Greek words *oligos polein,* meaning "few to sell." An **oligopoly** is an industry that contains two or more firms, at least one of which produces a significant portion of the industry's total output. Whenever there is a high concentration ratio for the firms that are serving one particular market, that market is oligopolistic. The market structures of oligopoly, monopoly, and monopolistic competition are similar in that firms in all of these markets face negatively sloped demand curves.

oligopoly An industry that contains two or more firms, at least one of which produces a significant portion of the industry's total output.

In contrast to a monopoly (which has no competitors) and to a monopolistically competitive firm (which has many competitors), an oligopolistic firm faces only a few competitors. The number of competitors is small enough for each firm to realize that its competitors may respond to anything that it does and that it should take such possible responses into account. In other words, *oligopolists are aware of the interdependence among the decisions made by the various firms in the industry.*

Economists say that oligopolists exhibit **strategic behaviour**, which means that they take explicit account of the impact of their decisions on competing firms and of the reactions they expect competing firms to make. In contrast, firms in perfect competition or monopolistic competition are assumed to engage in *non-strategic behaviour,* which means they make decisions based on their own costs and their own demand curves without considering any possible reactions from their large number of competitors. Monopolists also do not engage in strategic behaviour—simply because they have no competitors to worry about.

strategic behaviour Behaviour designed to take account of the reactions of one's rivals to one's own behaviour.

The Basic Dilemma of Oligopoly

The basic dilemma faced by oligopolistic firms is very similar to the dilemma faced by the members of a cartel, which we studied in Chapter 10. There we saw that the cartel as a whole had an incentive to form an agreement to restrict total output, but each individual member of the cartel had the incentive to cheat on the agreement and increase its own level of output.

For the small number of firms in an oligopoly, the incentives are the same. We say that firms can either *cooperate* (or *collude*) in an attempt to maximize joint profits, or they can *compete* in an effort to maximize their individual profits. Not surprisingly, the decision by one firm to cooperate or to compete will depend on how it thinks its rivals will respond to its decision.

Oligopolistic firms often make strategic choices; they consider how their rivals are likely to respond to their own actions.

cooperative (collusive) outcome A situation in which existing firms cooperate to maximize their joint profits.

When thinking about how firm behaviour leads to market outcomes, we distinguish between *cooperative* and *non-cooperative* behaviour. If the firms cooperate to produce among themselves the monopoly output, they can maximize their joint profits. If they do this, they will reach what is called a **cooperative (or collusive) outcome**, which is the position that a single monopoly firm would reach if it owned all the firms in the industry.

non-cooperative outcome An industry outcome reached when firms maximize their own profit without cooperating with other firms.

If the firms are at the cooperative outcome, it will usually be worthwhile for any one of them to cut its price or to raise its output, so long as the others do not do so. However, if every firm does the same thing, they will be worse off as a group and may all be worse off individually. An industry outcome that is reached when firms proceed by calculating only their own gains without cooperating with other firms is called a **non-cooperative outcome.**

The behaviour of firms in an oligopoly is complex, and studying it requires much attention to detail. As in other market structures, it is necessary to think about how individual firm behaviour affects the overall market outcome. Unlike other market structures, however, in oligopoly each firm typically thinks about how the other firms in the industry will react to its own decisions. Then, of course, the other firms may respond to what the first firm does, and so on. To help us keep our thoughts organized, we will use *game theory.*

Some Simple Game Theory

game theory The theory that studies decision making in situations in which one player anticipates the reactions of other players to its own actions.

Game theory is used to study decision making in situations in which there are a number of players, each knowing that others may react to their actions and each taking account of others' expected reactions when making moves. For example, suppose a firm is deciding whether to raise, lower, or maintain its price. Before arriving at an answer, it asks: "What will the other firms do in each of these cases, and how will their actions affect the profitability of whatever decision I make?"

When game theory is applied to oligopoly, the players are firms, their game is played in the market, their strategies are their price or output decisions, and the payoffs are their profits.

duopoly An industry that contains only two firms.

Practise with Study Guide Chapter 11, Exercises 3 and 5.

An illustration of the basic dilemma of oligopolists, to cooperate or to compete, is shown in Figure 11-3 for the case of a two-firm oligopoly, called a **duopoly**. In this simplified game, we assume that both firms are producing the same product, and so there is a single market price. The only choice for each firm is how much output to produce. If the two firms "cooperate" to jointly act as a monopolist, each firm produces one-half of the monopoly output and each earns large profits. If the two firms "compete," they each produce more than half (say two-thirds) of the monopoly output, and in this case both firms earn low profits. As we will see, even this very simple example is sufficient to illustrate several key ideas in the modern theory of oligopoly.

A Payoff Matrix Figure 11-3 shows a *payoff matrix* for this simple game. It shows the profits that each firm earns in each possible combination of the two firms' actions. The upper-left cell in this example shows that if each firm produces one-half of the monopoly output, each firm will earn profits of 20. The lower-right cell shows that if each firm produces two-thirds of the monopoly output, each firm will earn a profit of 17. Since *joint* profits must be maximized at the monopoly output, the total profit in the upper-left cell (40) is greater than the total profit in the lower-right cell (34).

The upper-right and lower-left cells show the profits in the case where one firm produces one-half of the monopoly output and the other firm produces two-thirds of the monopoly output. Note that in these cells, the firm that produces more earns the greater profit. The firm that produces one-half of the monopoly output is helping to restrict output and keep prices high. The firm that produces two-thirds of the monopoly output then benefits from the first firm's output restrictions.

FIGURE 11-3 The Oligopolist's Dilemma: To Cooperate or to Compete?

		Firm A's output	
		One-half monopoly output	Two-thirds monopoly output
Firm B's output	One-half monopoly output	20 20	15 22
	Two-thirds monopoly output	22 15	17 17

Cooperation to determine the overall level of output can maximize joint profits, but it leaves each firm with an incentive to cheat. The figure shows a payoff matrix for a two-firm game. Firm A's production is indicated across the top, and its payoffs (profits in millions of dollars) are shown in the green circles within each cell. Firm B's production is indicated down the left side, and its payoffs are shown in the red circles within each cell.

If A and B cooperate, each produces one-half the monopoly output and receives a payoff of 20, as shown in the upper-left cell. But at this position, each firm has an incentive to cheat and produce the larger amount, so the cooperative outcome is only achievable if the firms can somehow enforce their agreement.

Now suppose that A and B make their decisions non-cooperatively. A reasons that whether B produces either one-half or two-thirds of the monopoly output, A's best output is two-thirds. B reasons similarly. In this case, they reach the non-cooperative outcome, where each produces two-thirds of the monopoly output, and each makes less than it would if the two firms cooperated. In this example, the non-cooperative outcome is a Nash equilibrium.

Strategic Behaviour The payoff matrix shows the profit each player earns with each combination of the two players' moves. But what will actually happen? To answer this question, we must first know what type of game is being played. Specifically, can the players *cooperate* or is the game a *non-cooperative* one?

Cooperative Outcome. If the two firms in this duopoly can cooperate, the payoff matrix shows that their highest *joint* profits will be earned if each firm produces one-half of the monopoly output. This is the cooperative outcome. The payoff matrix also shows, however, that if each firm thinks the other will cooperate (by producing half of the monopoly output), then it has an incentive to cheat and produce two-thirds of the monopoly output. Thus, the cooperative outcome can only be achieved if the firms have some effective way to enforce their output-restricting agreement. As we will see in Chapter 12, overt output-restricting agreements are usually illegal.

Non-Cooperative Outcome. Now suppose that firms believe that cooperation is not possible because they have no way of enforcing an agreement. What will be the non-cooperative outcome in this duopoly game? To answer this question, we must examine each player's incentives, given the possible actions of the other player.

Firm A reasons as follows: "If B produces one-half of the monopoly output (upper row of the matrix), then my profit will be higher if I produce two-thirds of the monopoly output. Moreover, if B produces two-thirds of the monopoly output (bottom row of the matrix), my profit will be higher if I also produce two-thirds of the monopoly output. Therefore, no matter what B does, I will earn more profit if I produce two-thirds of the monopoly output." A quick look at the payoff matrix in Figure 11-3 reveals that this game is *symmetric,* and so Firm B's reasoning will be identical to A's: it will conclude that its profit will be higher if it produces two-thirds of the monopoly output no matter what A does.

The final result is clear. Each firm will end up producing two-thirds of the monopoly output and each firm will receive a profit of 17. This is the non-cooperative outcome. Note that each firm will be worse off than it would have been had they been able to achieve the cooperative outcome. This type of game, in which the non-cooperative outcome makes *both* players worse off than if they had been able to cooperate, is called a *prisoners' dilemma*. The reason for this curious name is discussed in *Extensions in Theory 11-1*.

myeconlab

Our discussion of game theory has used examples of *simultaneous* games in which both players make their decisions at the same time. But often one firm is in a position to make its decision before its competitors. To see an example of a *sequential* game, look for "A Sequential Game in Fibre Optics" in the *Additional Topics* section of this book's MyEconLab.

www.myeconlab.com

Nash equilibrium An equilibrium that results when each firm in an industry is currently doing the best that it can, given the current behaviour of the other firms in the industry.

Nash Equilibrium The non-cooperative outcome shown in Figure 11-3 is called a **Nash equilibrium**, after the U.S. mathematician John Nash, who developed the concept in the 1950s and received the Nobel Prize in Economics in 1994 for this work. (The 2002 movie *A Beautiful Mind* is about John Nash's life and contains a few fascinating bits of game theory!) In a Nash equilibrium, each player's best strategy is to maintain its present behaviour *given the present behaviour of the other players.*

It is easy to see that there is only one Nash equilibrium in Figure 11-3. In the bottom-right cell, the best decision for each firm, given that the other firm is producing two-thirds of the monopoly output, is to produce two-thirds of the monopoly output itself. Between them, they produce a joint output of 1⅓ times the monopoly output. Neither firm has an incentive to depart from this position (except through enforceable cooperation with the other). In any other cell, each firm has an incentive to change its output *given the output of the other firm.*

The basis of a Nash equilibrium is rational decision making in the absence of co-operation. Its particular importance in oligopoly theory is that it is the only type of self-policing equilibrium. It is self-policing in the sense that there is no need for group behaviour to enforce it. Each firm has a self-interest to maintain it because no move will improve its profits, given what other firms are currently doing.

If a Nash equilibrium is established by any means whatsoever, no firm has an incentive to depart from it by altering its own behaviour.

11.5 OLIGOPOLY IN PRACTICE

We have examined the incentives for firms in an oligopoly to cooperate, and also the incentives for firms to cheat on any cooperative agreement. We can now look at the behaviour that we actually observe among oligopolists. How do they cooperate? How do they compete?

EXTENSIONS IN THEORY 11-1

The Prisoners' Dilemma

The game shown in Figure 11-3 is often known as a prisoners' dilemma game. This is the story that lies behind the name:

> *Two men, John and William, are arrested for jointly committing a crime and are interrogated separately. They know that if they both plead innocence, they will get only a light sentence, and if they both admit guilt they will both receive a medium sentence. Each is told, however, that if either protests innocence while the other admits guilt, the one who claims innocence will get a severe sentence while the other will be released with no sentence at all.*

Here is the payoff matrix for that game:

William's Plea	John's Plea: Innocent	John's Plea: Guilty
Innocent	J: light sentence; W: light sentence	J: no sentence; W: severe sentence
Guilty	J: severe sentence; W: no sentence	J: medium sentence; W: medium sentence

John reasons as follows: William will plead either guilty or innocent. If he pleads innocent, I will get a light sentence if I also plead innocent but no sentence at all if I plead guilty, so guilty is my better plea. If he pleads guilty, I will get a severe sentence if I plead innocent and a medium sentence if I plead guilty. So once again guilty is my preferred plea. William reasons in the same way and, as a result, they both plead guilty and get a medium sentence. Note, however, that if they had been able to communicate and coordinate their pleas, they could both have agreed to plead innocent and get off with a light sentence.

The prisoners' dilemma arises in many economic situations. We have already seen an example of a two-firm oligopoly. Economists use the basic structure of this simple game to think about how firms compete in their decisions to build new factories, launch advertising campaigns, and adjust the prices of their differentiated products.

Simple game theory and the prisoner's dilemma also figure prominently in the study of political science. Robert Axelrod's 1984 book *The Evolution of Cooperation* discusses how the key insights from the prisoners' dilemma have been used in the analysis of elections (where candidates' choices are their electoral platforms) and the nuclear arms race (in which national governments' choices are their decisions to build and stockpile weapons).*

* For those interested in a very readable treatment of game theory applied to many aspects of life, see *Thinking Strategically* (Norton, 1993), written by Avinash Dixit and Barry Nalebuff, two leading economists.

Types of Cooperative Behaviour

When firms agree to cooperate in order to restrict output and raise prices, their behaviour is called **collusion**. Collusive behaviour may occur with or without an explicit agreement to collude. Where explicit agreement occurs, economists speak of *overt* or *covert collusion,* depending on whether the agreement is open or secret. Where no explicit agreement actually occurs, economists speak of *tacit collusion*. In this case, all firms behave cooperatively without an explicit agreement to do so. They merely understand that it is in their mutual interest to restrict output and to raise prices.

collusion An agreement among sellers to act jointly in their common interest. Collusion may be overt or covert, explicit or tacit.

Explicit Collusion The easiest way for firms to ensure that they will all maintain their joint profit-maximizing output is to make an explicit agreement to do so. Such collusive agreements have occurred in the past, although they have been illegal among privately owned firms in Canada for a long time. When they are discovered today, they are rigorously prosecuted. We shall see, however, that such agreements are not illegal everywhere in the world, particularly when they are supported by national governments.

Practise with Study Guide Chapter 11, Exercise 4.

We saw in Chapter 10 that when several firms get together to act in this way, they create a *cartel.* Cartels show in stark form the basic conflict between cooperation and competition that we just discussed. Cooperation among cartel members allows them to restrict output and raise prices, thereby increasing the cartel members' profits. But it also presents each cartel member with the incentive to cheat. The larger the number of firms, the greater the temptation for any one of them to cheat. After all, cheating by one small firm may not be noticed because it will have a small effect on price. Conversely, a cartel made up of a small number of firms is more likely to persist because cheating by any one member is more difficult to conceal from the other members.

As we mentioned in Chapter 10, DeBeers is an example of a firm that has been able to assemble a cartel in the world's diamond industry. Through its own Diamond Trading Company (DTC), DeBeers markets almost 50 percent of the world's annual diamond production. With such influence over the market, it is able to manage the flow of output, in response to changes in world demand, to keep prices high. In recent years, however, the discovery of large diamond mines by firms that wished to remain independent of DeBeers has led to a reduction in DeBeers' ability to set the market price. In fact, the independent producers—in particular, Canadian—have been successful at establishing their own "brand" of diamonds. This has led DeBeers to reduce its efforts through the DTC to manage market prices and instead focus more of its efforts on creating its own brand of diamonds and other luxury products. Only time will tell how this brand competition in the diamond industry will develop.

For more information on OPEC, check out its website: **www.opec.org**.

The most famous example of a cartel—and the one that has had the most dramatic effect on the world economy—is the Organization of Petroleum Exporting Countries (OPEC). OPEC's explicit cooperation over the past three decades is discussed in *Lessons From History 11-1.*

Tacit Collusion Although collusive behaviour that affects prices is illegal, a small group of firms that recognize the influence that each has on the others may act without any explicit agreement to achieve the cooperative outcome. In such tacit agreements, the two forces that push toward cooperation and competition are still evident. First, firms have a common interest in cooperating to maximize their joint profits at the cooperative solution. Second, each firm is interested in its own profits, and any one of them can usually increase its profits by behaving competitively.

In many industries there is suggestive evidence of tacit collusion, although it is very difficult to prove rigorously. For example, when one large steel company announces that it is raising its price for a specific quality of steel, other steel producers will often announce similar price increases within a day or two. This seemingly coordinated price increase may be the result of a secret explicit agreement or of tacit collusion. On the other hand, the firms that followed the first firm's price increase could easily argue (and usually do in such cases) that with their competitor raising prices, and driving some customers toward them, the natural response is to raise their own prices.

Types of Competitive Behaviour

Although the most obvious way for a firm to violate the cooperative solution is to produce more than its share of the joint profit-maximizing output, there are other ways in which rivalrous behaviour can occur.

Competition for Market Share Even if *joint* profits are maximized, there is still a question of how the profit-maximizing level of sales is to be divided among the colluding firms. Competition for market share may upset the tacit agreement to hold to joint profit-maximizing behaviour. Firms often compete for market share through various forms of non-price competition, such as advertising and variations in the quality of their product. Such costly competition may be largely a zero-sum activity among the firms, and thus may reduce industry profits.

In an industry with many differentiated products and in which sales are often by contract between buyers and sellers, covert rather than overt cheating may seem attractive. Secret discounts and rebates can allow a firm to increase its sales at the expense of its competitors while appearing to hold to the tacitly agreed price.

Innovation A firm may find that by innovating it can behave competitively, keeping ahead of its rivals, and thereby maintain a larger market share. In this way, it will earn larger profits than it would if it cooperated with the other firms in the industry, even though all the firms' joint profits are lower. As Joseph Schumpeter argued about the process of "creative destruction," such competition through innovation contributes to the long-run growth of living standards and may provide social benefits over time that outweigh any losses due to the restriction of output at any one point in time.

Oligopolistic firms typically compete by innovating. A firm can rectify a mistake in its price-setting decisions easily, but falling behind its competitors in developing new products and new production processes can spell disaster. A reading of the business pages of any newspaper shows firms in continuous competition to outdo each other in innovations.

Oligopolistic firms producing differentiated products often compete very little through prices. Sometimes the most aggressive competition takes place through their continual processes of innovation, as well as the introduction of new products.

There are strong incentives for oligopolistic firms to compete rather than to maintain the cooperative outcome, even when they understand the inherent risks to their joint profits.

A good example is the continuous process of innovation by the relatively small number of firms producing cellular phones, such as Nokia, Ericsson, NEC, and Panasonic. As one firm introduces a new feature, such as text messaging, video screens, or full audio/video capability, the competing firms quickly follow suit. In this market, the introduction of new product features is an important part of competitive behaviour.

The Importance of Entry Barriers

Suppose firms in an oligopolistic industry succeed in raising prices above long-run average costs and earn substantial profits that are not completely eliminated by non-price competition. In the absence of significant entry barriers, new firms will enter the

LESSONS FROM HISTORY 11-1

Explicit Cooperation in OPEC

The experience of the Organization of Petroleum Exporting Countries (OPEC) in the 1970s and 1980s illustrates the power of cooperative behaviour to create short-run profits, as well as the problems of trying to exercise long-run market power in an industry without substantial entry barriers.

OPEC did not attract worldwide attention until 1973, when its members voluntarily restricted their output by negotiating quotas among themselves. In that year, OPEC countries accounted for about 70 percent of the world's supply of crude oil. Although it was not a complete monopoly, the cartel came close to being one. By reducing output, the OPEC countries were able to reduce the world supply of oil and thereby increase its world price by almost 300 percent. Their actions resulted in massive profits both for themselves and for non-OPEC producers, who obtained the high prices without having to limit their output. After several years of success, however, OPEC began to experience the typical problems of cartels.

Entry

Entry became a problem for the OPEC countries. The high price of oil encouraged the development of new supplies, and within a few years, new productive capacity was coming into use at a rapid rate in non-OPEC countries. The development of North Sea oil by the United Kingdom and the development of the Athabasca Tar Sands in Alberta are two examples of this new productive capacity.

Long-Run Adjustment of Demand

The short-run demand for oil proved to be highly inelastic. Over time, however, adaptations to reduce the demand for oil were made within the confines of existing technology. Homes and offices were insulated more efficiently, and smaller, more fuel-efficient cars became popular. This is an example of the distinction between the short-run and long-run demand for a commodity first introduced in Chapter 4.

Innovation further reduced the demand for oil in the very long run. Over time, technologies that were more efficient in their use of oil were developed, as were alternative energy sources. Had the oil prices stayed up longer than they did, major breakthroughs in solar and geothermal energy would surely have occurred in the 1970s or early 1980s.

This experience in both the long run and the very long run shows the price system at work, signalling the need for adaptation and providing the incentives for that adaptation. It also provides an illustration of Joseph Schumpeter's concept of creative destruction, which we first discussed in Chapter 10. To share in the profits generated by high energy prices, new technologies and new substitute products were developed, and these reduced much of the market power of the original cartel.

Cheating

At first, there was little incentive for OPEC countries to violate quotas. Member countries found themselves with such undreamed-of increases in incomes that they found it difficult to use all of their money productively. As the output of non-OPEC oil grew, however, OPEC's output had to be reduced to maintain the high prices. Furthermore, as the long-run adjustments in demand occurred, even larger output restrictions by OPEC were required to prop up the price of oil. Incomes in OPEC countries declined as a result.

Many OPEC countries had become used to their enormous incomes, and their attempts to maintain them in the face of falling output quotas brought to the surface the instabilities inherent in all cartels. In 1981, oil prices reached U.S.$35 per barrel. In real terms, this was about five times as high as the 1972 price, but production quotas were less than one-half of OPEC's capacity. Eager to increase their oil revenues, many individual OPEC members gave in to the pressure to cheat and produced in excess of their production quotas. In 1984, Saudi Arabia indicated that it would not tolerate further cheating by its partners and demanded that others share equally in reducing their quotas yet further. However, agreement proved impossible. In December 1985, OPEC decided to eliminate production quotas and let each member make its own decisions about output.

After the Collapse

OPEC's collapse as an output-restricting cartel led to a major reduction in world oil prices. Early in 1986, the downward slide took the price to U.S.$20 per barrel, and it fell to U.S.$11 per barrel later in the year. Allowing for inflation, this was still double the price that had prevailed just before OPEC introduced its output restrictions in 1973. Following the 1986 collapse, and for the next decade or so, the world price of oil fluctuated between U.S.$15 per barrel and U.S.$25 per barrel. With the continuing expansion of output from non-OPEC producers, OPEC's share of world output steadily fell, reaching approximately 35 percent by the mid-1990s, where it remains today.

Beginning in the late 1990s, the world price of oil began to rise again, as the accompanying figure shows. Measured in 2001 dollars, the price increased sharply from a low of about U.S.$13 per barrel in 1998 to over U.S.$55 per barrel in 2006. This price increase was *not* caused by OPEC output restrictions. In addition to some growing political tensions in the Middle East, especially in 2006, the main cause of the price increase was a steadily growing world demand for oil, driven by relatively rapid economic growth, especially in the large emerging markets of China and India. The sharp price increase reflected an increase in demand at a time when the world supply curve was relatively inelastic. This supply inelasticity, in turn, reflected the fact that most oil producers—both inside and outside OPEC—were producing at or close to their capacity, and thus were unable to easily respond to higher prices by increasing their output. In this setting of low global excess capacity, OPEC's ability to increase prices through output restrictions was partially restored, even though their share of world output was much less than in the 1970s. By late in 2006, however, the OPEC producers had not appeared to take advantage of their renewed market power.

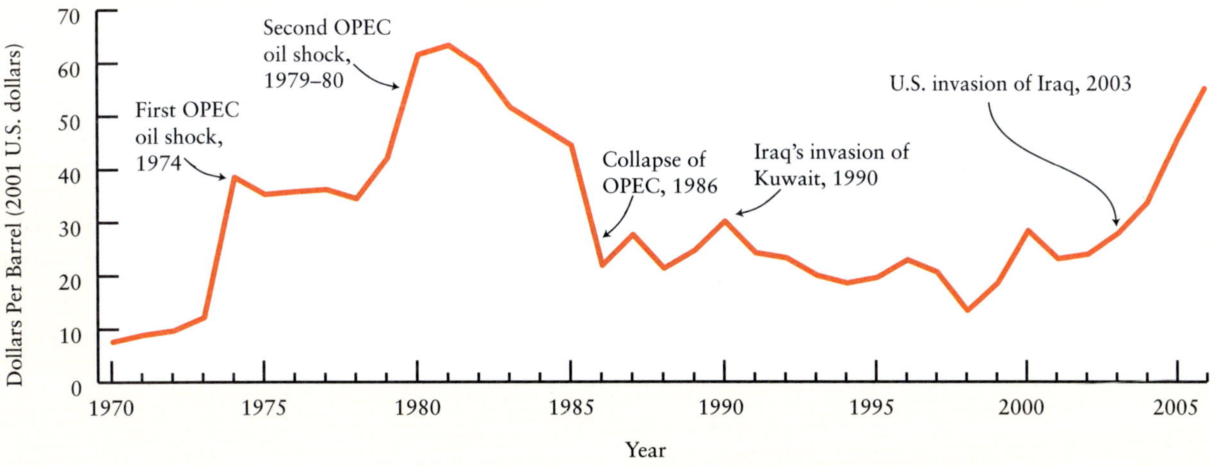

(*Source:* Nominal U.S.-dollar price of OPEC's reference basket: www.opec.org. U.S. CPI (all items): www.bls.gov.)

Many beer-producing firms produce several brands. Such brand proliferation by individual firms is an effective way to deter other firms from entering the market.

industry and erode the profits of existing firms, as they do in monopolistic competition. Natural barriers to entry were discussed in Chapter 10. They are an important part of the explanation of the persistence of profits in many oligopolistic industries.

Where such natural entry barriers do not exist, however, oligopolistic firms can earn profits in the long run only if they can *create* entry barriers. To the extent this is done, existing firms can move toward joint profit maximization without fear that new firms will enter the industry. We now discuss some types of *firm-created* entry barriers.

Brand Proliferation as an Entry Barrier By altering the characteristics of a differentiated product, it is possible to produce a vast array of variations on the general theme of that product, each with its unique identifying brand. Think, for example, of the many different brands of soap or shampoo, breakfast cereals or cookies, and even automobiles or motorcycles. In these cases, each firm in the industry produces *several* brands of the differentiated product.

Although such brand proliferation is no doubt partly a response to consumers' tastes, it can have the effect of discouraging the entry of new firms. To see why, suppose the product is the type for which there is a substantial amount of brand switching by consumers. In this case, the larger the number of brands sold by existing firms, the smaller the expected sales of a new entrant.

Suppose, for example, that an industry contains three large firms, each selling one brand of beer, and say that 30 percent of all beer drinkers change brands in a random fashion each year. If a new firm enters the industry, it can expect to pick up one-third of the customers who change brands (a customer who switches brands now has three *other* brands among which to choose). The new firm would get 10 percent (one-third of 30 percent) of the total market the first year merely as a result of picking up its share of the random switchers, and it would keep increasing its share for some time thereafter. If, however, the existing three firms have five brands each, there would be 15 brands already available, and a new firm selling one new brand could expect to pick up only one-fifteenth of the brand switchers, giving it only 2 percent of the total market the first year, with smaller gains also in subsequent years. This is an extreme case, but it illustrates a general result.

The larger the number of differentiated products that are sold by existing oligopolists, the smaller the market share available to a new firm that is entering with a single new product. Brand proliferation therefore can be an effective entry barrier.

Advertising as an Entry Barrier Advertising is one means by which existing firms can impose heavy costs on new entrants. Advertising, of course, serves purposes other than that of creating barriers to entry. Among them, it performs the useful function of informing buyers about their alternatives. Indeed, a new firm may find that advertising is essential, even when existing firms do not advertise at all, simply to call attention to its entry into an industry in which it is currently unknown.

Nonetheless, advertising can also operate as a potent entry barrier by increasing the costs of new entrants. Where heavy advertising has established strong brand images for existing products, a new firm may have to spend heavily on advertising to create its own brand images in consumers' minds. If the firm's sales are small, advertising costs *per unit* will be large, and price will have to be correspondingly high to cover those costs. Consider Nike, Reebok, and their competitors. They advertise not so much the quality of their athletic shoes as images that they wish consumers to associate with the shoes. The same is true for cosmetics, beer, cars, hamburgers, and many more consumer goods. The ads are lavishly produced and photographed. They constitute a formidable entry barrier for a new producer.

A new entrant with small sales but large required advertising costs finds itself at a substantial cost disadvantage relative to its established rivals.

Advertising can be very informative for consumers. But by raising the costs of new entrants, advertising can also act as a potent entry barrier.

The combined use of brand proliferation and advertising as an entry barrier helps to explain one apparent paradox of everyday life—that one firm often sells multiple brands of the same product, which compete actively against one another as well as against the products of other firms. The soap and beer industries provide classic examples of this behaviour. Because all available scale economies can be realized by quite small plants, both industries have few natural barriers to entry. Both contain a few large firms, each of which produces an array of heavily advertised products. The numerous existing products make it harder for a new entrant to obtain a large market niche with a single new product. The heavy advertising, although directed against existing products, creates an entry barrier by increasing the average costs of a new product that seeks to gain the attention of consumers and to establish its own brand image.

Predatory Pricing as an Entry Barrier A firm will not enter a market if it expects continued losses after entry. An existing firm can create such an expectation by cutting prices below costs whenever entry occurs and keeping them there until the entrant goes bankrupt. The existing firm sacrifices profits while doing this, but it sends a discouraging message to potential future rivals, as well as to present ones. Even if this strategy is costly in terms of lost profits in the short run, it may pay for itself in the long run by creating *reputation effects* that deter the entry of new firms at other times or in other markets that the firm controls.

Predatory pricing is controversial. Some economists argue that pricing policies that appear to be predatory can be explained by other motives and that existing firms only hurt themselves when they engage in such practices instead of accommodating new entrants. Others argue that predatory pricing has been observed and that it is in the long-run interests of existing firms to punish the occasional new entrant even when it is costly to do so in the short run.

Canadian courts have taken the position that predatory pricing does indeed occur and a number of firms have been convicted of using it as a method of restricting entry. The airline industry provides an interesting example.

See Industry Canada's website at **www.strategis.gc.ca** for a discussion of predatory pricing in Canada.

Soon after Air Canada merged with Canadian Airlines in 1999, it was accused of charging prices below its average costs in an attempt to drive its young competitors out of the market. Air Canada argued that it was simply responding to the competitive pressures introduced by WestJet and other small, but growing, airlines that had recently entered the industry. The federal government argued that the short-term benefits to consumers from low airfares were unlikely to offset the long-term costs from much higher airfares that would occur if Air Canada was successful at driving WestJet and others out of business.

Over the next few years, it was Air Canada that experienced severe financial difficulties. In 2004, Air Canada emerged from bankruptcy protection as a restructured company with a modified corporate strategy. It increased its use of small regional jets and introduced several different categories to its pricing of airline tickets. Meanwhile, WestJet expanded out of its base in Western Canada and began servicing all major cities across the country. As both firms appear to become more firmly established, the main strategic decisions—for both firms—will likely be whether they choose to co-operate or compete.

myeconlab

We have been discussing how the entry of firms to an industry can reduce oligopoly profits toward the competitive level. But sometimes it is only the *threat* of entry that is necessary to achieve this outcome. For a detailed discussion of this point, look for "Oligopoly and Contestable Markets" in the *Additional Topics* section of this book's MyEconLab.

www.myeconlab.com

Oligopoly and the Economy

Oligopoly is found in many industries and in all advanced economies. It typically occurs in industries where both perfect and monopolistic competition are made impossible by the existence of major economies of scale. In such industries, there is simply not enough room for a large number of firms all operating at or near their minimum efficient scales.

Three questions are important for the evaluation of oligopoly. First, do oligopolistic firms respond to changes in market conditions very differently than perfectly competitive firms? Second, in their short-run and long-run outcomes, where do oligopolistic firms typically settle between the extreme outcomes of earning zero profits and earning monopoly profits? Third, how much do oligopolists contribute to economic growth by encouraging innovative activity in the very long run? We consider each of these questions in turn.

Market Adjustment Under Oligopoly We have seen that under perfect competition, prices are set by the impersonal forces of demand and supply, whereas firms in oligopolistic markets administer their prices. The market signalling system works slightly differently when prices are administered rather than being determined by the market. Changes in market conditions are signalled to the perfectly competitive firm by changes in the price of its product. For example, an increase in demand will lead to an increase in market price; as the market price rises, the competitive firm will choose to increase its output.

For an oligopolist, however, the order of events is a little different. An increase in demand will cause the sales of oligopolistic firms to rise. Firms will then respond by increasing output. Only after the increase in demand is expected to persist will oligopolistic firms increase their prices.

Temporary changes in demand lead to more price volatility in perfectly competitive markets than in oligopoly markets. Permanent changes in demand, however, lead to similar adjustments in both market structures.

Profits Under Oligopoly Some firms in some oligopolistic industries succeed in coming close to joint profit maximization in the short run. In other oligopolistic industries, firms compete so intensely among themselves that they come close to achieving competitive prices and outputs.

In the long run, those profits that do survive competitive behaviour among existing firms will tend to attract entry. Profits will persist only insofar as entry is restricted either by natural barriers, such as large minimum efficient scales for potential entrants, or by barriers created, and successfully defended, by the existing firms.

Innovation Which market structure—oligopoly or perfect competition—is most conducive to innovation? As we discussed in Chapter 8, innovation and productivity improvements are the driving force of the economic growth that has so greatly raised living standards over the past two centuries. They are intimately related to Schumpeter's concept of creative destruction, which we first encountered in our discussion of entry barriers in Chapter 10.

Examples of creative destruction abound. In the nineteenth century, railways began to compete with wagons and barges for the carriage of freight. In the twentieth century, trucks operating on newly constructed highways began competing with trains. During the 1950s and 1960s, airplanes began to compete seriously with both trucks and trains. In recent years, fax machines and e-mail have eliminated the monopoly of the postal service in delivering hard-copy (printed) communications. Cellular phones have significantly weakened the monopoly power that telephone companies had for the provision of local phone service. And the Internet has allowed consumers to download music easily, thereby reducing the market power of the music production companies that sell CDs.

An important defence of oligopoly is based on Schumpeter's idea of creative destruction. Some economists argue that oligopoly leads to more innovation than would occur in either perfect competition or monopoly. They argue that the oligopolist faces strong competition from existing rivals and cannot afford the more relaxed life of the monopolist. Moreover, oligopolistic firms expect to keep a good share of the profits that they earn from their innovative activity and thus have considerable incentive to innovate.

Everyday observation provides support for this view. Leading North American firms that operate in highly concentrated industries, such as Abitibi-Consolidated, DuPont, Kodak, General Electric, Alcan, Canadian National, Xerox, and Boeing, have been highly innovative over many years.

This observation is not meant to suggest that *only* oligopolistic industries are innovative. Much innovation is also done by very small new firms (although most of these are in monopolistically competitive rather than perfectly competitive markets). If today's small firms are successful in their innovation, they may become tomorrow's corporate giants. For example, Hewlett-Packard, Microsoft, and Intel, which are enormous firms today, barely existed 30 years ago; their rise from new start-up firms to corporate giants reflects their powers of innovation.

Oligopoly is an important market structure in modern economies because there are many industries in which the minimum efficient scale is simply too large to support many competing firms. The challenge to public policy is to keep oligopolists competing, rather than colluding, and using their competitive energies to improve products and to reduce costs, rather than merely to erect entry barriers.

SUMMARY

11.1 THE STRUCTURE OF THE CANADIAN ECONOMY

LO 1

- Most industries in the Canadian economy lie between the two extremes of monopoly and perfect competition. Within this spectrum of market structure we can divide Canadian industries into two broad groups—those with a large number of relatively small firms and those with a small number of relatively large firms. Such intermediate market structures are called imperfectly competitive.
- When measuring whether an industry has power concentrated in the hands of only a few firms or dispersed over many, it is not sufficient to count the firms. Instead, economists consider the concentration ratio, which shows the fraction of total market sales controlled by a group of the largest sellers.
- One important problem associated with using concentration ratios is to define the market with reasonable accuracy. Since many goods produced in Canada compete with foreign-produced goods, the national concentration ratios overstate the degree of industrial concentration.

11.2 WHAT IS IMPERFECT COMPETITION?

LO 2

- Most firms operating in imperfectly competitive market structures sell differentiated products whose characteristics they choose themselves.
- Imperfectly competitive firms usually administer their prices and engage in non-price competition.

11.3 MONOPOLISTIC COMPETITION

LO 3

- Monopolistic competition is a market structure that has the same characteristics as perfect competition except that the many firms each sell a differentiated product rather than all selling a single homogeneous product. Firms face negatively sloped demand curves and may earn profits in the short run.
- As in a perfectly competitive industry, the long run in the theory of monopolistic competition sees new firms enter the industry whenever profits can be made. Long-run equilibrium in the industry requires that each firm earn zero profits.
- In long-run equilibrium in the theory of monopolistic competition, each firm produces less than its minimum-cost level of output. This is the excess-capacity theorem associated with monopolistic competition.
- Even though each firm produces at a cost that is higher than the minimum attainable cost, the resulting product choice is valued by consumers and so may be worth the extra cost.

11.4 OLIGOPOLY AND GAME THEORY

LO 4

- Oligopolies are dominated by a few large firms that usually sell differentiated products and have significant market power. They can maximize their joint profits if they cooperate to produce the monopoly output. By acting individually, each firm has an incentive to depart from this cooperative outcome.
- Oligopolists have difficulty cooperating to maximize joint profits unless they have a way of enforcing their output-restricting agreement.
- Economists use game theory to think about the strategic behaviour of oligopolists—that is, how each firm will behave when it recognizes that other firms may respond to its actions.
- A possible non-cooperative outcome is a Nash equilibrium in which each player is doing the best it can, given the actions of all other players.

11.5 OLIGOPOLY IN PRACTICE

LO 5

- Explicit collusion between oligopolists is illegal in domestic markets. But it can take place in situations where firms in global markets are supported by national governments, as is the case for OPEC.
- Tacit collusion is possible but may break down as firms struggle for market share, indulge in non-price competition, and seek advantages through the introduction of new technology.
- Oligopolistic industries will exhibit profits in the long run only if there are significant barriers to entry. Natural barriers relate to the economies of scale in production, finance, and marketing, and also to large entry costs. Firm-created barriers can be created by proliferation of competing brands, heavy brand-image advertising, and the threat of predatory pricing when new entry occurs.
- In the presence of major scale economies, oligopoly may be the best of the feasible alternative market structures. Evaluation of oligopoly depends on how much interfirm competition (a) drives the firms away from the cooperative, profit-maximizing solution and (b) leads to innovations in the very long run.

KEY CONCEPTS

Concentration ratios
Administered prices
Product differentiation
Monopolistic competition
The excess-capacity theorem
Oligopoly
Strategic behaviour
Game theory
Cooperative and non-cooperative outcomes
Nash equilibrium
Explicit and tacit collusion
Natural and firm-created entry barriers
Oligopoly and creative destruction

STUDY EXERCISES

1. Fill in the blanks to make the following statements correct.
   a. Suppose the four largest steel producers in Canada among them control 85 percent of total market sales. We would say that this industry is highly __________. We say that 85 percent is the __________ in this industry.
   b. A firm that has the ability to set prices faces a ________ demand curve.
   c. The theory of monopolistic competition helps explain industries with a __________ number of __________ firms. The theory of oligopoly helps explain industries with a _______ number of __________ firms.
   d. A firm operating in a monopolistically competitive market structure maximizes profits by equating __________ and __________. A firm that is operating in an oligopolistic market structure maximizes profit by equating __________ and __________.
   e. In long-run equilibrium, and in comparison to perfect competition, monopolistic competition produces a _________ range of products but at a _______ cost per unit.

2. Fill in the blanks to make the following statements correct.
   a. Economists say that oligopolistic firms exhibit __________ behaviour. These firms are aware of and take account of the decisions of __________.
   b. The firms in an oligopoly have a collective incentive to ________ in order to maximize joint ________; individually, each firm has an incentive to __________ in order to maximize individual ________.
   c. Oligopolistic firms exhibit profits in the long run only if there are significant __________.
   d. Three examples of non-competitive behaviour practised by firms with market power are: __________, __________, and __________.
   e. An important defence of oligopoly is the idea that it leads to more __________ than would occur in either perfect competition or monopoly. The oligopolistic firm has an incentive to __________ because it can expect to keep a good share of the resulting profit.

3. Each of the statements below describes a characteristic of the following market structures: perfect competition, monopolistic competition, oligopoly, and monopoly. Identify which market structure displays each of the characteristics. (There may be more than one.)

- each firm faces a downward-sloping demand curve
- price is greater than marginal revenue
- each firm produces at MES in long-run equilibrium
- firms earn profit in long-run equilibrium
- firms produce a homogeneous product
- firms advertise their product
- each firm produces output where $MC = MR$
- each firm produces output where $P = MC$
- there is free entry to the industry
- firms produce a differentiated product

4. myeconlab The following table provides annual sales for the four largest firms in four industries in Canada. Also provided are total Canadian and total world sales for the industry. (All figures are hypothetical and are in millions of dollars.)

	Firm 1	Firm 2	Firm 3	Firm 4	Total Sales (Canada)	Total Sales (World)
Forestry products	185	167	98	47	550	1368
Chemicals	27	24	9	4	172	2452
Women's clothing	6	5	4	2	94	3688
Pharmaceuticals	44	37	22	19	297	2135

a. Suppose Canada does not trade internationally any of the goods produced in these industries. Compute the four-firm Canadian concentration ratio for each industry.
b. Rank the industries in order from the most concentrated to the least concentrated.
c. Now suppose goods in these industries are freely traded around the world. Are the concentration ratios from (a) still relevant? Explain.

5. The table below provides price, revenue, and cost information for a monopolistically competitive firm selling drive-through car washes in a large city.

Quantity (number of car washes per month)	Price	Total Revenue	Marginal Revenue	Total Cost	Average Total Cost	Marginal Cost	Profit (per car wash)
1000	30	____		25 000	____		____
1100	29	____	____	26 000	____	____	____
1200	28	____	____	27 200	____	____	____
1300	27	____	____	28 500	____	____	____
1400	26	____	____	30 000	____	____	____
1500	25	____	____	32 200	____	____	____
1600	24	____	____	35 000	____	____	____
1700	23	____	____	38 500	____	____	____
1800	22	____	____	43 000	____	____	____

a. Complete the table.
b. Plot the demand, marginal revenue, marginal cost, and average cost curves for the firm. (Be sure to plot MR and MC at the midpoint of the output intervals.)
c. What is the profit-maximizing number of car washes (per month)?
d. What is the profit-maximizing price?
e. Calculate the total maximum profit (per month).
f. How can this firm differentiate its product from other car washes?

6. Draw two diagrams of a monopolistically competitive firm. In the first, show the firm earning profits in the short run. In the second, show the firm in long-run equilibrium earning zero profits. What changed for this firm between the short run and the long run?

7. The following figure shows the revenue and cost curves for a typical monopolistically competitive firm in the short run.

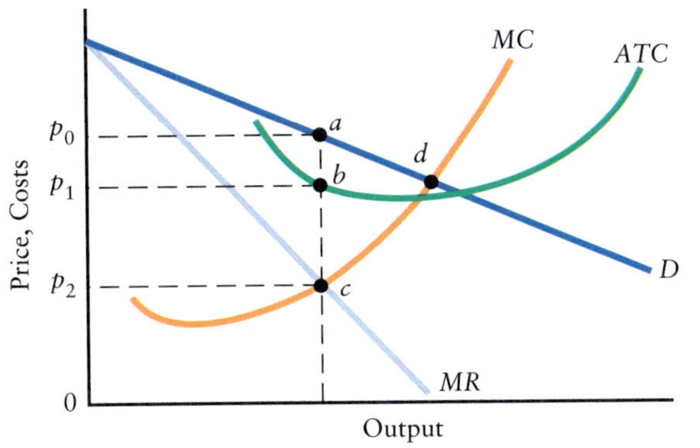

a. Note that the firm's demand curve is shown to be quite flat. Explain which assumption of monopolistic competition suggests a relatively elastic demand curve for each firm.
b. Show the profit-maximizing level of output for the firm on the diagram.
c. At the profit-maximizing level of output, are profits positive or negative? What area in the diagram represents the firm's profits?
d. Will firms enter or exit the industry? Explain.

8. The diagram below shows a typical monopolistically competitive firm when the industry is in long-run equilibrium.

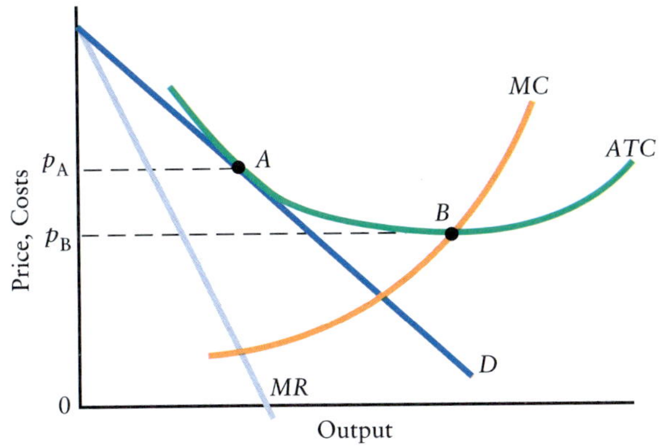

a. Explain why free entry and exit implies that the long-run equilibrium is at point *A*.
b. What is the significance of point *B* and price p_B?
c. Explain the sense in which long-run equilibrium in monopolistic competition is less efficient than in perfect competition.

9. In the text we argued that a key difference between monopolistic competition and oligopoly is that in the former firms do not behave *strategically* whereas in the latter they do. For each of the goods or services listed below, state whether the industries are likely to be best described by monopolistic competition or oligopoly. Explain your reasoning.
a. Car repair
b. Haircuts
c. Dry cleaning
d. Soft drinks
e. Breakfast cereals
f. Restaurant meals
g. Automobiles

10. myeconlab The table below is the payoff matrix for a simple two-firm game. Firms A and B are bidding on a government contract, and each firm's bid is not known by the other firm. Each firm can bid either $10 000 or $5000. The cost of completing the project for each firm is $4000. The low-bid firm will win the contract at its stated price; the high-bid firm will get nothing. If the two bids are equal, the two firms will split the price and costs evenly. The payoffs for each firm under each situation are shown in the matrix.

	A bids $10 000	**A bids $5000**
B bids $10 000	Firms share the contract Payoff to A = $3000 Payoff to B = $3000	A wins the contract Payoff to A = $1000 Payoff to B = $0
B bids $5000	B wins the contract Payoff to A = $0 Payoff to B = $1000	Firms share the contract Payoff to A = $500 Payoff to B = $500

a. Recall from the text that a Nash equilibrium is an outcome in which each player is maximizing his or her own payoff *given the actions of the other players*. Is there a Nash equilibrium in this game?
b. Is there more than one Nash equilibrium? Explain.
c. If the two firms could cooperate, what outcome would you predict in this game? Explain.

11. The table below shows the payoff matrix for a game between Toyota and Honda, each of which is contemplating building a factory in a new market. Each firm can either build a small factory (and produce a small number of cars) or build a large factory (and produce

a large number of cars). Suppose no other car manufacturers are selling in this market.

		Toyota's Decision	
		Small Factory	**Large Factory**
Honda's Decision	**Small Factory**	*High Industry Price* Honda profits: $20 million Toyota profits: $20 million	*Medium Industry Price* Honda profits: $12 million Toyota profits: $25 million
	Large Factory	*Medium Industry Price* Honda profits: $25 million Toyota profits: $12 million	*Low Industry Price* Honda profits: $14 million Toyota profits: $14 million

a. Assuming that the demand curve for cars in this new market is negatively sloped and unchanging, explain the economic reasoning behind the prices and profits shown in each cell in the payoff matrix.
b. What is the cooperative outcome in this game? Is it likely to be achievable? Explain.
c. What is Honda's best action? Does it depend on Toyota's action?
d. What is Toyota's best action? Does it depend on Honda's action?
e. What is the non-cooperative outcome in this game? Is it a Nash equilibrium?

DISCUSSION QUESTIONS

1. It is sometimes said that there are more drugstores and gasoline stations than are needed. In what sense might this be correct? Does the consumer gain anything from this plethora of retail outlets?
2. Do you think any of the following industries might be monopolistically competitive? Why or why not?
   a. Textbook publishing (more than 12 introductory economics textbooks are in use on campuses in Canada this year)
   b. Post-secondary education
   c. Cigarette manufacturing
   d. Restaurant operation
   e. Automobile retailing
3. "The periods following each of the major OPEC price shocks proved to the world that there were many available substitutes for gasoline, among them bicycles, car pools, moving closer to work, cable TV, and Japanese cars." Discuss how each of these may be a substitute for gasoline.
4. Evidence suggests that the profits earned by all the firms in many oligopolistic industries are less than the profits that would be earned if the industry were monopolized. What are some reasons why this might be so?
5. What is the key difference between monopolistic competition and oligopoly? Assume that you are in an industry that is monopolistically competitive. What actual steps might you take to transform your industry into a more oligopolistic form?
6. Consider the following industries in Canada that have traditionally been oligopolistic.
   - Brewing
   - Airlines
   - Railways
   - Banking

   a. What are the barriers to entry in each of these industries that might explain persistently high profits?
   b. Explain in each case how technology is changing in ways that circumvent these entry barriers.

CHAPTER 12

Economic Efficiency and Public Policy

LEARNING OBJECTIVES

In this chapter you will learn

1. the distinction between productive and allocative efficiency.
2. why perfect competition is allocatively efficient, whereas monopoly is allocatively inefficient.
3. alternative methods for regulating a natural monopoly.
4. some details about Canadian competition policy.

In the previous three chapters we examined various market structures, from perfect competition at one end of the spectrum to monopoly at the other end. In the middle were two forms of imperfect competition: monopolistic competition and oligopoly. We have considered how firms behave in these various market structures, and we are now able to evaluate the *efficiency* of the market structures. Then we will see why economists are suspicious of monopolistic practices and seek to encourage competitive behaviour. Table 12-1 provides a review of the four market structures and the industry characteristics relevant to each.

We begin our discussion in this chapter by examining the various concepts of efficiency used by economists. This discussion will develop more fully the concept of efficiency we first saw at the end of Chapter 5. We then discuss how public policy deals with the challenges of monopoly and oligopoly in an effort to improve the efficiency of the economy.

12.1 PRODUCTIVE AND ALLOCATIVE EFFICIENCY

Efficiency requires that factors of production are fully employed. However, full employment of resources is not enough to prevent the *waste* of resources. Even when resources are fully employed, they may be used inefficiently. Here are three examples of inefficiency in the use of fully employed resources.

1. If firms do not use the least-cost method of producing their chosen outputs, they are being inefficient. For example, a firm that produces 30 000 pairs of shoes at a resource cost of $400 000 when it could have been done at a cost of only $350 000 is using resources inefficiently. The lower-cost method would allow $50 000 worth of resources to be transferred to other productive uses.

TABLE 12-1 Review of Four Market Structures

Market Structure	Industry Characteristics
Perfect competition	• Many small firms • Firms sell identical products • All firms are price takers • Free entry and exit • Zero profits in long-run equilibrium • Price = *MC*
Monopolistic competition	• Many small firms • Firms sell differentiated products • Each firm has some power to set price • Free entry and exit • Zero profits in long-run equilibrium • Price > *MC*; less output than in perfect competition; excess capacity
Oligopoly	• Few firms, usually large • Strategic behaviour among firms • Firms usually sell differentiated products and are price setters • Often significant entry barriers • Usually economies of scale • Profits depend on the nature of firm rivalry and on entry barriers
Monopoly	• Single firm faces the entire market demand • Firm is a price setter • Profits persist if sufficient entry barriers • Price > *MC*; less output than in perfect competition

2. If the marginal cost of production is not the same for every firm in an industry, the industry is being inefficient. For example, if the cost of producing the last tonne of steel is higher for some firms than for others, the industry's overall cost of producing a given amount of steel is higher than necessary. The same amount of steel could be produced at lower total cost if the total output were distributed differently among the various producers.

3. If too much of one product and too little of another product are produced, the economy's resources are being used inefficiently. To take an extreme example, suppose so many shoes are produced that every consumer has all the shoes he or she could possibly want and thus places a zero value on obtaining an additional pair of shoes. Suppose also that so few coats are produced that consumers place a high value on obtaining an additional coat. In these circumstances, consumers can be made better off if resources are reallocated from shoe production, where the last shoe produced has a low value in the eyes of each consumer, to coat production, where one more coat produced would have a higher value to each consumer.

These three examples illustrate inefficiency in the use of resources. But the *type* of inefficiency is different in each case. The first example considers the cost for a single firm producing some level of output. The second example is closely related, but the focus is on the total cost for all of the firms in an industry. The third example relates to the level of output of one product compared to another. Let's explore these three types of efficiency in more detail.

Productive Efficiency

productive efficiency for the firm When the firm chooses among all available production methods to produce a given level of output at the lowest possible cost.

Productive efficiency has two aspects, one concerning production within each firm and one concerning the allocation of production among the firms in an industry. The first two examples above relate to these two different aspects of productive efficiency.

Productive efficiency for the firm requires that the firm produce any given level of output at the lowest possible cost. In the short run, with only one variable factor, the firm merely uses enough of the variable factor to produce the desired level of output. In the long run, however, more than one method of production is available. Productive efficiency requires that the firm use the least costly of the available methods of producing any given output—that is, firms are located on, rather than above, their long-run average cost curves.

Productive efficiency for the firm requires the firm to be producing its output at the lowest possible cost.

Any firm that is not being productively efficient is producing at a higher cost than is necessary and thus will have lower profits than it could have. It follows that any profit-maximizing firm will seek to be productively efficient no matter the market structure within which it operates—perfect competition, monopoly, oligopoly, or monopolistic competition.

Productive efficiency for the industry requires that the industry's total output be allocated among its individual firms in such a way that the total cost in the industry is minimized. If an industry is productively *inefficient,* it is possible to reduce the industry's total cost of producing any given output by reallocating production among the industry's firms.

Profit-maximizing firms will adopt the lowest-cost methods of production, and thus will be productively efficient. An industry will be productively efficient only when its firms all have the same marginal cost.

Productive efficiency for the industry requires that the marginal cost of production must be the same for each firm.

To see why marginal costs must be equated across firms, consider a simple example that is illustrated in Figure 12-1. Aslan Shoe Company has a marginal cost of $80 for the last shoe of some standard type it produces. Digory Shoes Inc. has a marginal cost of only $40 for its last shoe of the same type. If Aslan were to produce one fewer pair of shoes and Digory were to produce one more pair, total shoe production would be unchanged. Total industry costs, however, would be lower by $40.

productive efficiency for the industry When the industry is producing a given level of output at the lowest possible cost. This requires that marginal cost be equated across all firms in the industry.

FIGURE 12-1 Production Efficiency for the Industry

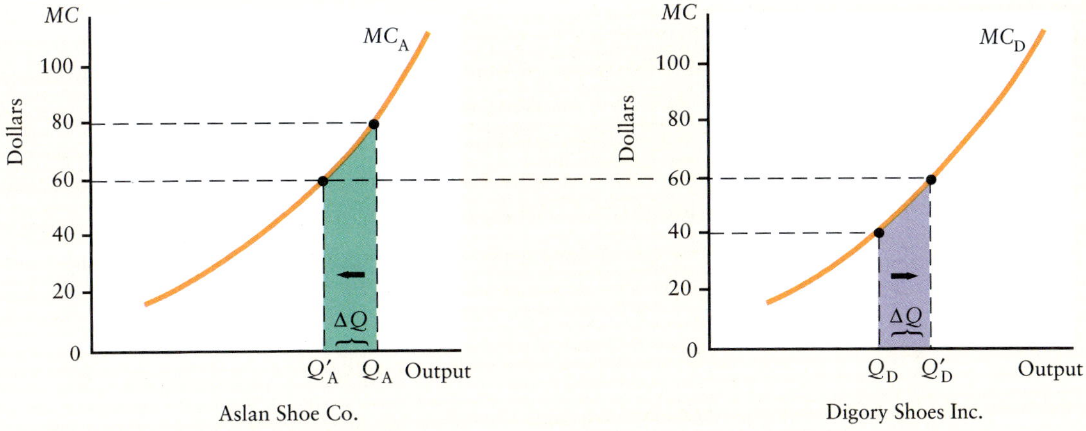

Productive efficiency for the industry requires that marginal costs be equated for all firms. At the initial levels of output, Q_A and Q_D, marginal costs are $80 for Aslan and $40 for Digory. If Digory increases output by ΔQ to Q'_D and Aslan reduces output by the same amount, ΔQ, to Q'_A, total output is unchanged. Aslan's total costs have fallen by the green shaded area, whereas Digory's total costs have increased by the smaller purple shaded area. Total industry costs are therefore reduced when output is reallocated between the firms. When marginal costs are equalized, at $60 in this example, no further reallocation of output can reduce costs—productive efficiency will have been achieved.

FIGURE 12-2 Production Efficiency and the Production Possibilities Boundary

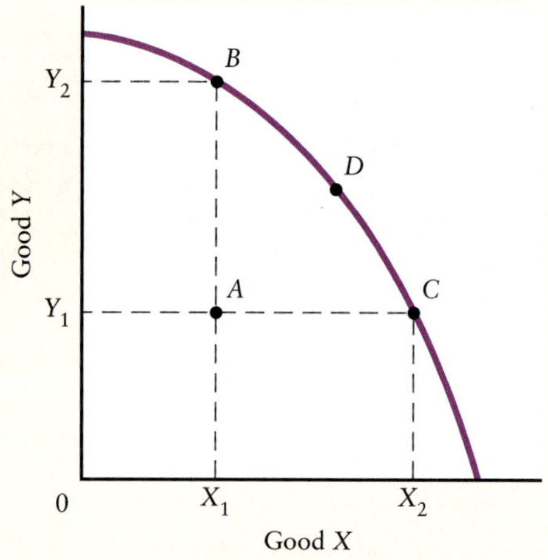

Any point on the production possibilities boundary is productively efficient. The boundary shows all combinations of two goods X and Y that can be produced when the economy's resources are fully employed and productively efficient.

Any point inside the curve, such as *A*, is productively inefficient. If the inefficiency exists in industry *X*, then either some producer of *X* is productively inefficient or industry *X* as a whole is productively inefficient. In either case, it is possible to increase total production of *X* without using more resources, and thus without reducing the output of *Y*. This would take the economy from point *A* to point *C*. Similarly, if the inefficiency exists in industry *Y*, production of *Y* could be increased, moving the economy from point *A* to point *B*.

Clearly, this cost saving can go on as long as the two firms have different marginal costs. However, as Aslan produces fewer shoes, its marginal cost falls, and as Digory produces more shoes, its marginal cost rises. Once marginal cost is equated across the two firms, at a marginal cost of \$60 in the figure, there are no further cost savings to be obtained by reallocating production.

Over the next few pages we will see *how* such an efficient allocation of output across firms is achieved, but for now the point is simply that if marginal costs are not equated across firms, then a reallocation of output is necessary in order for the industry to become productively efficient.

Productive Efficiency and the Production Possibilities Boundary If firms are productively efficient, they are minimizing their costs; there is no way for them to increase output without using more resources. If an industry is productively efficient, the industry as a whole is producing its output at the lowest possible cost; the industry could not increase its output without using more resources.

Now think about the economy's production possibilities boundary (PPB), which we first saw in Chapter 1 and which is shown again in Figure 12-2. The PPB shows the combinations of output of two products that are possible when the economy is using its resources *efficiently*. An economy that is producing at a point inside the PPB is being productively inefficient—it could produce more of one good without producing less of the other. This may occur because individual firms are not minimizing their costs or because, within an industry, marginal costs are not equalized across the various firms. Either situation would lead the economy to be inside its production possibilities boundary.

If firms and industries are productively efficient, the economy will be on, rather than inside, the production possibilities boundary.

In Figure 12-2, every point on the PPB is productively efficient. Is there one point on the PPB that is "better" in some way than the others? The answer is yes, and this brings us to the concept of *allocative efficiency*.

Allocative Efficiency

allocative efficiency A situation in which the market price for each good is equal to that good's marginal cost.

Allocative efficiency concerns the quantities of the various products to be produced. When the combination of goods produced is allocatively efficient, economists say that the economy is *Pareto efficient*, in honour of the nineteenth-century Italian economist Vilfredo Pareto (1843–1923), who developed this concept of efficiency.

How do we find the allocatively efficient point on the production possibilities boundary? The answer is as follows:

The economy is allocatively efficient when, for each good produced, its marginal cost of production is equal to its price.

To understand this answer, recall our discussion in Chapters 5 and 6 about the marginal value that consumers place on the next unit of some good. When consumers face the market price for some good, they adjust their consumption of the good until their marginal value is just equal to the price. Thus, the market price reflects consumers' marginal value of the good. Since price reflects the marginal value of the good to consumers, we can restate the condition for allocative efficiency to be that, for each good produced, marginal cost must equal marginal value.[1]

If the level of output of some product is such that marginal cost to producers exceeds marginal value to consumers, too much of that product is being produced, because the cost to society of the last unit produced exceeds the benefits of consuming it. Conversely, if the level of output of some good is such that the marginal cost is less than the marginal value, too little of that good is being produced, because the cost to society of producing the next unit is less than the benefits that would be gained from consuming it.

Allocative Efficiency and the Production Possibilities Boundary Figure 12-3 shows a production possibilities boundary in an economy that can produce wheat and steel, and also shows the individual supply-and-demand diagrams for the two markets. Notice that the vertical axis in each of the supply-and-demand diagrams shows the *relative* price of the appropriate good. For example, in the market for wheat, the relevant price is the price of wheat *relative to the price of steel.* This is consistent with our initial treatment of supply and demand in Chapter 3, in which we held constant all other prices and then examined how the price of any specific product was determined.

Figure 12-3 illustrates how the allocation of resources in the economy changes as we move along the production possibilities boundary. For example, as the economy moves from point *A* to point *B* to point *C* along the PPB, resources are being transferred from the steel sector to the wheat sector. Thus, steel output is falling and wheat output is rising.

What is the allocatively efficient combination of steel and wheat output? Allocative efficiency will be achieved when in each market the marginal cost of producing the good equals the marginal value of consuming the good. In Figure 12-3, allocative efficiency is achieved at point *B*, with S_B steel being produced and W_B wheat being produced.[2]

[1] Allocative efficiency is exactly the same concept as *market efficiency* that we discussed in Chapter 5. Now that we have introduced the distinction between productive and allocative efficiency, we will continue to use these two terms only.

[2] Note that allocative efficiency requires that price equal marginal cost in *all* industries simultaneously. Based on what economists call the "theory of the second best," there is no guarantee that achieving $p = MC$ in one industry will improve overall welfare when price does not equal marginal cost in all other industries. For the purposes of this introductory textbook, however, we assume that the concept of allocative efficiency is useful for examining welfare improvements within individual industries.

FIGURE 12-3 Allocative Efficiency and the Production Possibilities Boundary

Allocative efficiency requires that all goods be produced to the point where the marginal cost to producers equals the marginal value to consumers. The production possibilities boundary shows the combinations of wheat and steel that are possible if firms and industries are productively efficient. The lower diagrams show the marginal cost (supply) and marginal value (demand) curves in each industry.

At point *A*, steel output is S_A and wheat output is W_A. As the lower figures show, however, at W_A, the marginal value of wheat consumption exceeds its marginal cost of production. Thus, society would be better off if more wheat were produced. Similarly, at S_A, the marginal cost of steel production exceeds its marginal value to consumers, and thus society would be better off with less steel being produced.

Point *A* is therefore not allocatively efficient; there is too little wheat and too much steel being produced. Resources should be reallocated to move the economy toward point *B*. The argument is similar at point *C*, at which there is too much wheat and too little steel being produced. Only at point *B* is each good produced to the point where the marginal cost to producers is equal to the marginal value to consumers. Only point *B* is allocatively efficient.

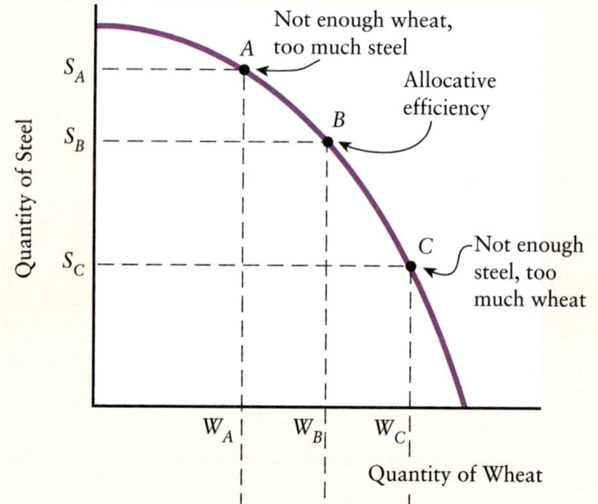

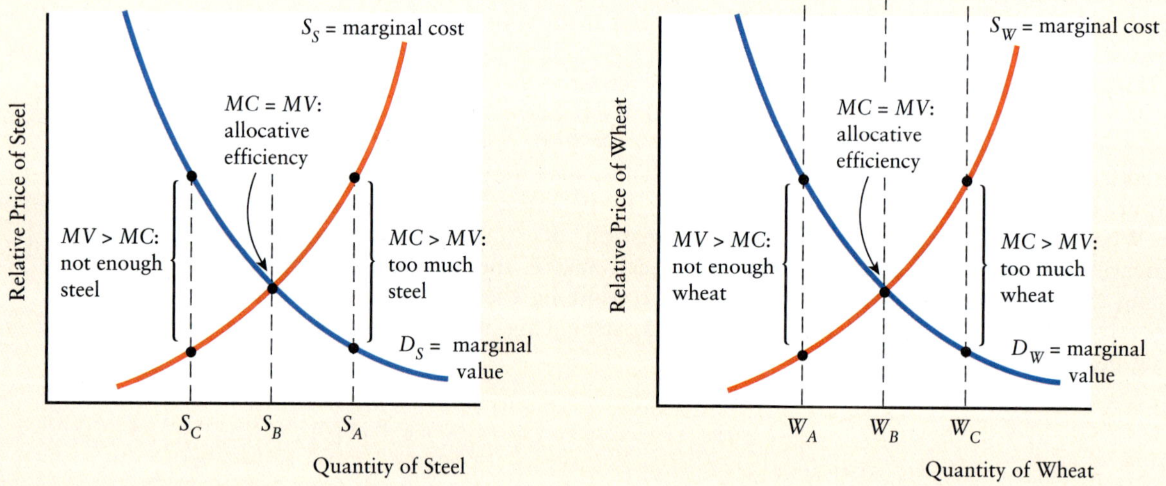

Which Market Structures Are Efficient?

We now know that for productive efficiency, all firms must be minimizing their costs and marginal cost should be the same for all firms in any one industry. For allocative efficiency, marginal cost should be equal to price in each industry. Do the market structures that we have studied in earlier chapters lead to productive and allocative efficiency?

Perfect Competition We saw in Chapter 9 that in the long run under perfect competition, each firm produces at the lowest point on its long-run average cost curve. Therefore, no one firm could reduce its costs by altering its own production. Every firm in perfect competition is therefore productively efficient.

We also know that in perfect competition, all firms in an industry face the same price of their product and they equate marginal cost to that price. It follows immediately that marginal cost will be the same for all firms. (Suppose, for example, that Aslan and Digory faced the same market price in Figure 12-1. Aslan would produce where $MC_A = p$ and Digory would produce where $MC_D = p$. It follows that $MC_A = MC_D$.) Thus, in perfectly competitive industries, the industry as a whole is productively efficient.

We have already seen that perfectly competitive firms maximize their profits by choosing an output level such that marginal cost equals market price. Thus, when perfect competition is the market structure for the whole economy, price is equal to marginal cost in each industry, resulting in allocative efficiency.

Perfectly competitive industries are productively efficient. If an economy could be made up entirely of perfectly competitive industries, the economy would be allocatively efficient.

Note, however, that perfect competition exists only in some industries in modern economies. So, while specific industries may be perfectly competitive and therefore allocatively efficient, entire modern economies are neither perfectly competitive nor allocatively efficient.

Monopoly Monopolists have an incentive to be productively efficient because their profits will be maximized when they adopt the lowest-cost production method. Hence, profit-maximizing monopolists will operate on their *LRAC* curves and thus be productively efficient.

Although a monopolist will be productively efficient, it will choose a level of output that is too low to achieve allocative efficiency. This result follows from what we saw in Chapter 10—that the monopolist chooses an output at which the price charged is *greater than* marginal cost. Such a choice violates the conditions for allocative efficiency because the price, and hence the marginal value to consumers, exceeds the marginal cost of production. From this result follows the classic efficiency-based preference for competition over monopoly:

Monopoly is not allocatively efficient because the monopolist's price always exceeds its marginal cost.

This result has important policy implications for economists and for policymakers, as we shall see later in this chapter.

Allocative efficiency is a property of the entire economy. The economy is allocatively efficient only when the quantity of each product is such that its marginal cost equals its price.

Other Market Structures The allocative inefficiency of monopoly extends to other imperfectly competitive market structures. Whenever a firm has any market power, in the sense that it faces a negatively sloped demand curve, its marginal revenue will be less than its price. When it equates marginal cost to marginal revenue, as

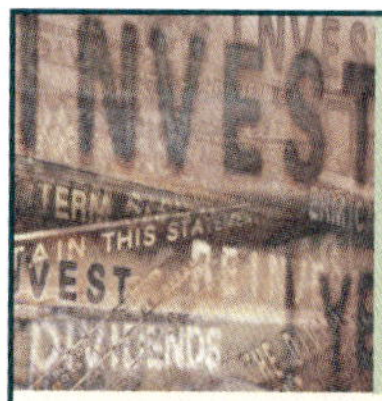

APPLYING ECONOMIC CONCEPTS 12-1

The Ongoing Debate Over Bank Mergers

As we said in the text, the 1986 *Competition Act* places considerable emphasis on the probable economic effects of proposed mergers. One challenge for the Competition Bureau is to weigh the possible benefits of a merger, resulting from cost reductions, against any lessening of competition when the merger reduces the number of actively competing firms.

A high-profile example is the possible mergers of some of Canada's largest chartered banks, an issue that has been debated on and off over the past decade. In the spring of 1998, the Royal Bank and the Bank of Montreal announced their intention to merge. Toronto Dominion and CIBC announced their intention to merge only a few days later. In the case of Canada's chartered banks, however, it is the federal Minister of Finance, and not the Competition Tribunal, that must ultimately approve the merger. Not surprisingly, the mergers became as much a political issue as an economic one. Considerable public hostility toward bank mergers created political pressure on the Minister of Finance, Paul Martin, and it did not take long before he disallowed the mergers. But the issue did not go away, and by 2006 the government was again being asked by the banks to re-open the issue and consider the possibility of bank mergers.

The Case Against Bank Mergers

When the four chartered banks first announced their intentions to merge in 1998, the Competition Bureau began to study the issue. After studying all relevant aspects of the financial-services industry, it concluded that bank mergers would substantially lessen competition in many local personal banking markets, especially in many of the small towns scattered across the Canadian landscape. The Competition Bureau predicted that many small towns would be left with only a single bank after the mergers and that the reduction in competition would result in higher fees and poorer service. The Bureau also predicted a lessening of competition to occur in many banking markets for small and medium-sized businesses, with the result that such firms would find it more difficult to secure loans and expand their operations.

The existence of considerable entry barriers is an important part of the case against bank mergers. The large chartered banks currently have extensive networks of bank branches that reach into all parts of the country. Any potential entrant to this industry, in order to compete effectively with the established banks, would need to build a competing branch network; but this would be extremely difficult, if not impossible, to do in a short period of time. The existence of such entry barriers suggests that if mergers among some of the existing banks lead to reduced competition and higher profits, new firms would not be able to easily enter the market and compete those profits away. In this case, there may be little to prevent the abuse of the banks' increased market power. The Competition Bureau argued that even if the existing legislation barring foreign firms from operating banks in Canada were amended, the established network of branch banking would give the existing banks a stranglehold on the Canadian banking industry.

The Case For Bank Mergers

Since their 1998 merger announcement, the four chartered banks have consistently argued that in order to compete effectively in the *world* market for financial

Looking Forward

The 1986 *Competition Act* will not be the end of the evolution of Canadian competition policy, but it appears to have marked the end of a major chapter. Canadian legislation has for a long time provided substantial protection to consumers against the misuse of market power by large firms. For the first time, it now also seems to provide some substantial protection against the creation, through mergers, of market power that is not justified by gains to efficiency or international competitiveness.

services, they needed to achieve larger scale. They argue that their current small scale prevents them from participating in the financing of many large international projects, and therefore a ban on mergers would preclude them from competing in the global financial market. In addition, they argue that mergers would allow them to spread some of their enormous fixed costs (such as computing systems) over a much larger customer base, thereby achieving reductions in their average costs. Indeed, some recent empirical research by the Bank of Canada suggests that a doubling of output by a Canadian chartered bank (roughly what would happen if two of the banks merged and consolidated these large fixed costs) would reduce average total costs by between 6 and 20 percent.*

The banks also argue that their large branch banking networks are *not* the entry barrier they once were. With the rise of the Internet and telephone banking, companies based elsewhere in the world can easily offer an entire range of financial services—deposits, mortgages, credit cards, and asset management—to Canadians without having to establish a *physical* presence in the Canadian market. As a result, the Canadian market for financial services is much more competitive than would be suggested by the simple observation that the six largest banks have over 90 percent of the established branches.

An Added Twist

By 2006, a new issue was added to the debate. In addition to bank mergers, the chartered banks were pushing to be permitted to sell insurance inside their bank branches—an additional financial product that would fit naturally within the suite of financial services that banks already provide to their customers. The banks argue that by allowing them to sell insurance, the level of competition in that market would rise and services to consumers would improve. Not surprisingly, independent insurance brokers are generally opposed to the possibility that firms as large and successful as Canadian chartered banks might suddenly appear as direct competitors. As of 2006, banks *can* own insurance companies but they are prohibited from selling insurance products inside their bank branches. In some cases, the chartered banks simply establish branches of their insurance companies right beside their bank branches, giving their banking customers easy access to the insurance products being sold next door. Many observers think this is merely the first step toward new legislation that will allow chartered banks to openly compete with the insurance companies.

A Resolution on the Merger Issue?

At the time this book went to print (late fall 2006), the issue of bank mergers had not yet been resolved. In 2006, the newly elected Conservative government under Prime Minister Stephen Harper was showing no sign that this issue was a priority. But many people think it is only a matter of time before the government again closely reviews the issue. When that time comes, the difficulty for the Minister of Finance (aside from the political issues involved) will be to determine the relative merits of the two arguments above. A final decision will require weighing the magnitude of the possible cost reductions against the importance of the potential lessening in competition.

*See J. Allen and Y. Liu, "Efficiency and Economies of Scale of Large Canadian Banks," Bank of Canada Working Paper 2005-13.

What type of reforms might we expect in the years ahead? The ongoing process of globalization poses two challenges for Canadian competition policy. First, as the flow of goods and services across national boundaries increases, it becomes more important to define markets on an international rather than a national basis. For example, consider the Canadian banking industry. With the continuing development of the Internet, it becomes possible for foreign-based banks to sell some financial services to Canadians without establishing a costly *physical* presence in Canada—such as a network of branches. In this case, the appropriate definition of the market (for the case of assessing the impact of a merger) is larger than just the one defined by Canada's borders.

The second challenge posed by globalization is the desirability of standardizing competition policy across countries. Firms that are mobile and have considerable market power may tend to locate their firms where competition policy is the most lax, exporting into other countries. To avoid such socially inefficient locational choices, countries have an incentive to standardize their competition policy—in this case, firms would choose their locations on the basis of economic rather than legal forces.

These are challenges for the near future. Time will tell how Canadian competition authorities respond.

SUMMARY

12.1 PRODUCTIVE AND ALLOCATIVE EFFICIENCY

LO 1 2

- Economists distinguish two main kinds of efficiency: productive and allocative.
- Productive efficiency for the firm requires that the firm be producing its output at the lowest possible cost. Productive efficiency for the industry requires that all firms in the industry have the same marginal cost.
- Allocative efficiency in an individual industry exists when the level of output is such that the marginal cost of production equals the market price. The overall economy is allocatively efficient when price equals marginal cost in all industries simultaneously.
- Productive efficiency and allocative efficiency are both achieved in perfect competition.
- Monopoly is allocatively inefficient because price exceeds marginal cost. Monopoly leads to a deadweight loss for the economy.

12.2 ECONOMIC REGULATION TO PROMOTE EFFICIENCY

LO 3

- Two broad types of policies are designed to promote allocative efficiency in imperfectly competitive markets. These can be divided into *economic regulations* and *competition policy.* Economic regulation is used both in the case of a natural monopoly and in the case of an oligopolistic industry. Competition policy applies more to the latter.
- Marginal-cost pricing is allocatively efficient but will lead the firm to make economic losses if it is on the declining portion of the *ATC* curve.
- Average-cost pricing allows the firm to break even but leads to allocative inefficiency (because price is not equal to marginal cost).
- Two-part tariffs can allow the firm with falling long-run costs to break even and also be consistent with allocative efficiency.
- The deregulation of oligopolistic industries has been based on the observations that: (1) oligopolistic industries are major engines of growth, and (2) direct control of such industries has produced disappointing results in the past.

12.3 CANADIAN COMPETITION POLICY

LO 4

- Canadian competition policy is designed to restrict mergers and trade practices that unduly lessen competition.
- In the past, mergers were criminal offences and difficult to prosecute. The current legislation allows civil cases to be brought against firms, making prosecution less difficult.
- The *Competition Act* of 1986 established a Competition Tribunal to adjudicate cases brought to it by the Competition Bureau.
- In the case of mergers, the Competition Bureau and Tribunal must consider whether the merger will generate cost reductions that will offset the effects of any lessening of competition.

KEY CONCEPTS

Productive and allocative efficiency
Consumer and producer surplus
The allocative efficiency of competition
The allocative inefficiency of monopoly
Regulation of natural monopolies
Marginal- and average-cost pricing
Two-part tariffs
Regulation of oligopolies
Deregulation and privatization
Canadian competition policy

STUDY EXERCISES

1. Summer Tees and Fancy Tees are two firms producing T-shirts. The table below shows the average cost of producing T-shirts for the two companies.

Summer Tees				Fancy Tees			
Quantity	*ATC*	*TC*	*MC*	Quantity	*ATC*	*TC*	*MC*
5	$ 8	—		5	$ 9	—	
10	7	—	—	10	7	—	—
15	6	—	—	15	6	—	—
20	6	—	—	20	5	—	—
25	7	—	—	25	5.50	—	—
30	9	—	—	30	6.50	—	—
35	11	—	—	35	8	—	—

a. Calculate *TC* and *MC* for both companies and fill in the table.
b. Draw, in two separate diagrams, the *ATC* and *MC* curves for each firm.
c. Summer Tees is initially producing 30 shirts; Fancy Tees is initially producing 15 shirts. What is the total industry production cost?
d. Now suppose that Summer Tees produces 10 fewer shirts. By how much do its costs fall?
e. Suppose that Fancy Tees produces 10 more shirts. By how much do its costs rise?
f. If the two firms are to produce 45 shirts in total, what is the cost-minimizing way to allocate production between the two firms? (Assume that production must be changed by increments of five shirts, as shown in the table.)

2. Fill in the blanks to make the following statements correct.

a. If the marginal cost of producing the last unit of a product is the same for all firms in an industry, we can say that the industry is _________ efficient, but we do not know enough to say that the industry is _________ efficient.
b. If the marginal cost of some product is $12, and the market price of that product is $15, then to achieve allocative efficiency, the economy should produce ______ of this product and therefore _______ of other products.
c. The market structure that leads to both productive and allocative efficiency is _________.
d. A monopolistic industry may be productively efficient but will not be allocatively efficient because _________.
e. The sum of consumer surplus and producer surplus is _________ at the competitive equilibrium.
f. At the monopolist's profit-maximizing output there is _________ total surplus than at the competitive output. Some surplus is transferred from _________ to _________. The surplus lost because the output is not produced is called _________.

3. Assume that the market for eggs is perfectly competitive. The diagram shows the demand and supply for eggs.

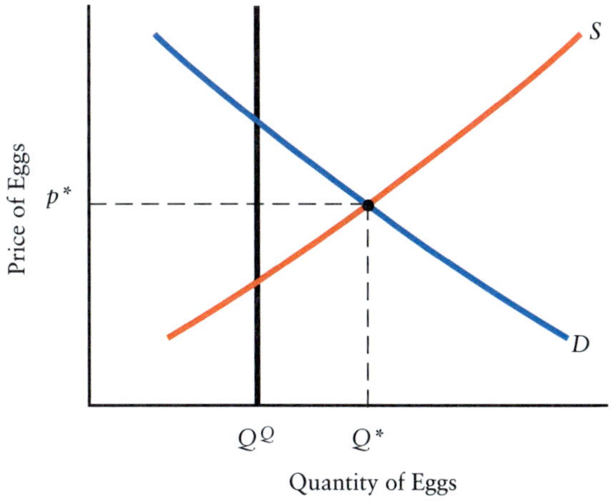

a. At the free-market equilibrium, p^* and Q^*, show what areas represent consumer and producer surplus.

b. Now suppose the egg producers organize themselves and establish a system of quotas. Each farmer's output is restricted by an amount to keep aggregate output at Q^Q. What happens to industry price?

c. In the quota system in part (b), what areas now represent consumer and producer surplus? Is the quota system allocatively efficient? Explain.

4. The diagram below shows supply and demand in the labour market.

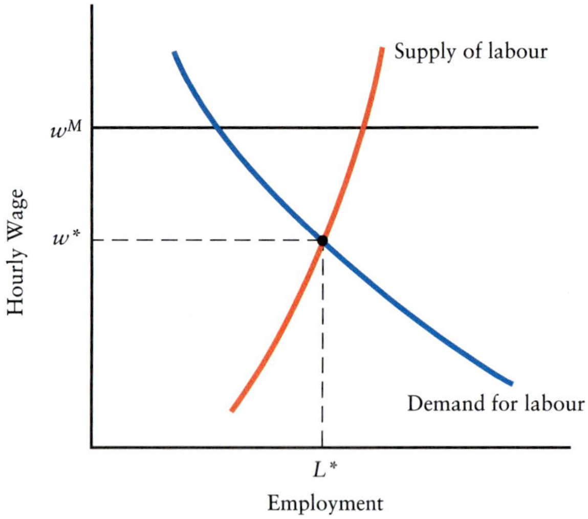

a. At the free-market equilibrium, w^* and L^*, show what areas represent consumer and producer surplus.

b. Now suppose the government establishes a minimum wage at w^M. What is the level of employment in this case?

c. In the situation of part (b), what areas now represent consumer and producer surplus? Is the outcome allocatively efficient? Explain.

5. The diagram below shows the demand, marginal cost, and marginal revenue curves for a monopolist. Redraw the diagram for yourself to be able to answer the following questions.

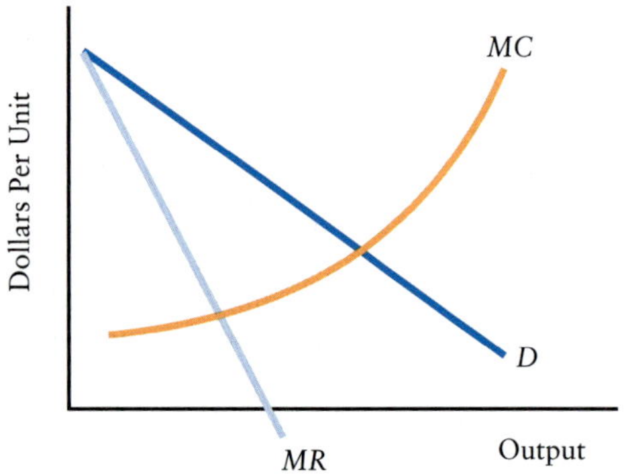

a. If the monopolist charges its single profit-maximizing price, show what areas are consumer surplus and producer surplus.

b. Now suppose the industry is perfectly competitive and the industry supply curve is given by the *MC* curve. What areas would be consumer and producer surplus in this case?

c. Use the concept of surplus to explain the economic argument against monopoly and in favour of competition.

d. Consider again the situation of monopoly, but now assume the firm can *perfectly* price discriminate—that is, it can charge a different price for every unit of the good. What areas now represent consumer and producer surplus?

e. Does the possibility of perfect price discrimination lead you to change your argument from part (c)? Are there considerations other than allocative efficiency that might be important here?

6. The diagram below shows the production possibilities boundary for a country that produces only two goods, limes and coconuts. Assume that resources are fully employed at points *A*, *B*, *C*, and *D*.

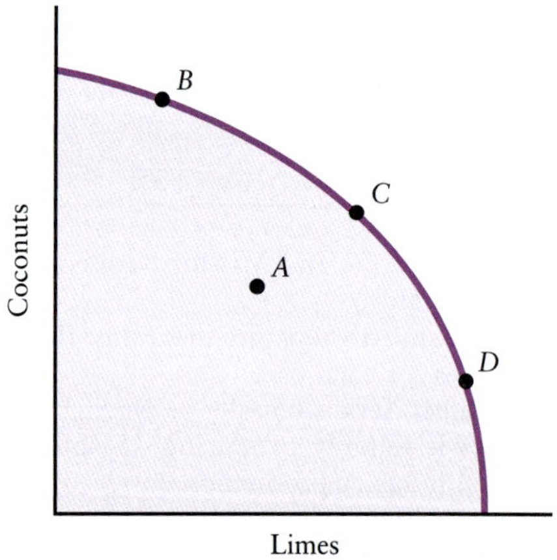

a. Suppose individual firms in the lime industry are not producing at their minimum possible cost. Which point(s) could represent this situation?

b. Suppose all firms and both industries are productively efficient. Which points could represent this situation?

c. Suppose point *B* occurs when the lime industry is monopolized but the coconut industry is perfectly competitive. Is point *B* allocatively efficient? Is it productively efficient?

d. Suppose point *D* occurs when the coconut industry is monopolized but the lime industry is perfectly competitive. Is point *D* allocatively efficient? Is it productively efficient?

e. Suppose point *C* is allocatively efficient. What do we know about each industry in this case?

7. Fill in the blanks to make the following statements correct.

   a. The term *natural monopoly* refers to an industry where only a single firm can operate at its __________.

   b. A regulated natural monopoly that is forced to set its price equal to marginal cost will earn ________ if its average costs are falling.

   c. A regulated natural monopoly that is subject to average-cost pricing and operating on the downward-sloping portion of its average cost curve will earn ________ profits. Since price ________ marginal cost, this outcome will not be allocatively efficient.

   d. Marginal-cost pricing for a natural monopoly is an efficient pricing system, but it leads to ________ for the firm if average costs are falling.

8. The following diagram shows the *ATC* and *MC* curves for a natural monopoly—average costs are falling over the entire range of the demand curve.

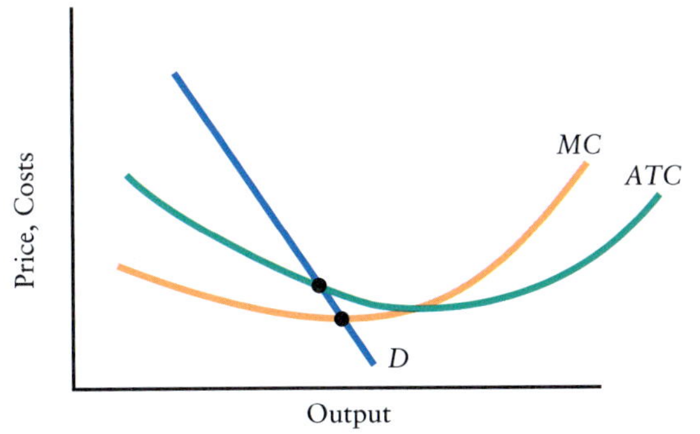

   a. Identify what price and quantity would exist if the firm were required by regulators to set price equal to average cost.

   b. In the diagram, show the profits (or losses) in this case.

   c. Would the outcome be allocatively efficient? Explain why or why not.

   d. Suppose now that the firm were required by regulators to set price equal to marginal cost. What would be the price and quantity in this case?

   e. In the diagram, show the profits (or losses) in this case.

   f. Would the outcome be allocatively efficient? Explain why or why not.

9. One important factor that the Canadian Competition Bureau must consider when assessing the likely effects of a merger is the definition of the market. Discuss how geography is likely to affect the definition of the market for the following products:

   a. Fresh-baked breads and cakes
   b. Cement
   c. Gold jewellery
   d. Computer hardware

DISCUSSION QUESTIONS

1. Suppose allocative inefficiency of some economy amounts to 5 percent of the value of production. What does this statement mean? If it is true, would consumers *as a whole* be better off if policy measures were successful in moving the economy to an allocatively efficient outcome? Would *every* consumer be better off if the economy moved to an allocatively efficient outcome?

2. Evaluate the wisdom of having the Competition Bureau use profits as a measure of monopoly power in deciding whether to prosecute a case. Would such a rule be expected to affect the behaviour of firms with high profits? In what ways might any changes induced by such a rule be socially beneficial, and in what ways might they be socially harmful?

3. It is often asserted that whenever a regulatory agency is established, ultimately it will become controlled by the people whom it was intended to regulate. (This argument raises the question of who regulates the regulators.) Can you identify why this phenomenon might happen? How might the integrity of regulatory boards be protected?

4. This chapter has identified several strategies for dealing with natural monopolies and their associated inefficiencies. Alternatively, assume that you are a regulator and that the monopoly you face is able to price discriminate—perhaps perfectly. Does this ability change the options you have for encouraging the efficient level of production? Would you choose to use this additional option? Why or why not?

5. "Canadian air travellers opting for U.S. carriers were [partly] responsible for Canadian airlines deregulation."

   —C. D. Howe Institute

"Canadian consumers crossing the border to buy cheap U.S. agricultural products may be responsible for the end of supply management in Canada."

—Canadian economist

What market forces lie behind each of these quotations? What difficulties do they reveal for the regulation of particular industries?

6. "Allocative efficiency is really about whether the economy 'has the quantities right'—it is not really about prices at all. Prices are important only in a discussion about allocative efficiency because *in a free market* changes in prices bring about the efficient allocation of resources."

   Comment.

PART 5: FACTOR MARKETS

CHAPTER 13

How Factor Markets Work

LEARNING OBJECTIVES

In this chapter you will learn

1. about the size and functional distributions of income in Canada.
2. what determines a profit-maximizing firm's demand for a factor.
3. about the role of factor mobility in determining factor supply.
4. how to distinguish between temporary and equilibrium factor-price differentials.
5. how economic rent is related to factor mobility.

What determines the wages that individuals earn? What explains why neurosurgeons usually are paid more than family doctors, or why movie stars are paid more than the "extras"? Labour is not the only factor of production, of course. Physical capital and land are also important. What determines the payments that these factors earn? Why does an acre of farm land in Northern Saskatchewan rent for much less than an acre of land in downtown Toronto? Not surprisingly, understanding why different factors of production earn different payments requires us to understand both demand-side and supply-side aspects of the relevant factor markets.

In this chapter we examine the issue of factor pricing and the closely related issue of factor mobility. Understanding what determines the payments to different factors of production will help us to understand the overall distribution of income in the economy, which is where we begin.

13.1 INCOME DISTRIBUTION

The founders of Classical economics, Adam Smith (1723–1790) and David Ricardo (1772–1823), were concerned with the distribution of income among what were then the three great social classes: workers, capitalists, and landowners. They defined three factors of production as labour, capital, and land. The payment to each factor was treated as the income of the respective social class.

Smith and Ricardo were interested in what determined the share of total income that each class received. Their theories predicted that as society progressed, landlords would become relatively better off and capitalists would become relatively worse off. Karl Marx (1818–1883) had a different theory, which predicted that as growth occurred, capitalists would become relatively better off and workers would become relatively worse off (until the whole capitalist system collapsed).

functional distribution of income The distribution of national income among the major factors of production: labour, capital, and land.

size distribution of income The distribution of income among individuals, without regard to source of income.

These nineteenth-century debates focused on what is now called the **functional distribution of income,** defined as the distribution of national income among the major factors of production. Modern economists, however, emphasize the **size distribution of income.** This refers to the distribution of income among different individuals without reference to the source of the income or the "social class" of the individual.

If we want to measure and understand the income inequality between individuals, the size distribution of income is a better indicator than is the functional distribution of income. The reason is that income classes no longer coincide closely with "social" classes. Many capitalists, such as the owners of small retail stores, are in the lower part of the income scale. Conversely, many wage earners, such as professional athletes, are in the upper income scale. Furthermore, it is becoming increasingly difficult to distinguish "workers" from "capitalists." Through employer-sponsored pension plans, workers now own much more of the country's capital than do the richer "non-working" capitalists.

Figure 13-1 shows that even among full-time, full-year workers, there was substantial inequality in the distribution of (pre-tax) income across individuals in 2000, the most recent year for which Census data are available. Another way to show the size

FIGURE 13-1 Earnings of Full-Time, Full-Year Workers

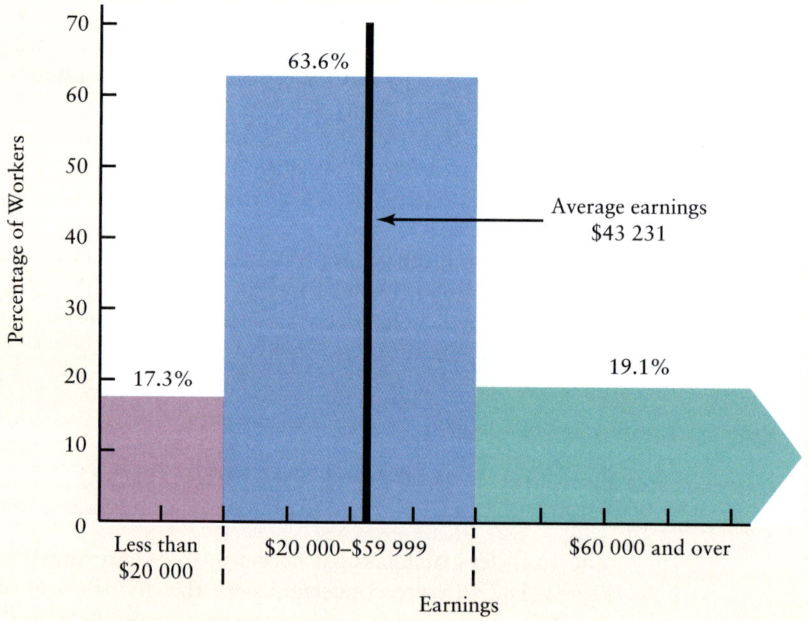

There is considerable inequality in the distribution of (pre-tax) earned income, even among full-time workers. At the time of Canada's most recent Census, just over 19 percent of full-time workers earned more than $60 000 per year; 17.3 percent earned less than $20 000. Nearly two-thirds of full-time workers earned between $20 000 and $60 000 per year. With perfect equality of income, all individuals would have the same earnings. In this case, the figure would show a single bar of height 100 percent at the average income level—$43 231 in the year 2000.

(*Source:* These data are from the 2001 Census and are available on Statistics Canada's website: www.statcan.ca. Click on "Census" and go to "Data and Analysis." Then click on "Search by Topic" and go to "Earnings of Canadians." Reprinted with permission of Statistics Canada.)

distribution of income is found in Figure 13-2. The curve in the figure is a **Lorenz curve**, showing how much of total income goes to different proportions of the nation's families. If every family had the same income, 20 percent of total income would go to 20 percent of families, 40 percent of total income would go to 40 percent of families, and so on. In this case, the Lorenz curve would lie exactly along the diagonal. The farther the curve bends away from the diagonal, the less equal the distribution of income. The curve in Figure 13-2 shows that at the time of Canada's most recent Census in 2001, the bottom 20 percent of all Canadian families received 5.2 percent of all pre-tax income, whereas the highest-income 20 percent of families received 43.6 percent of all pre-tax income.

Lorenz curve A graph showing the extent of inequality of income distribution.

To understand the size distribution of income, we must first study how individual incomes are determined. Superficial explanations of differences in income, such as "People earn according to their ability," are inadequate. Incomes are distributed much more unequally than any *measured* index of ability, be it IQ, physical strength, or typing skill. The best professional sports players may only score twice as many points as the average players, but their salary is many times more than the average salary. Something other than simple ability is at work here. However, if answers that are couched in terms of ability are easily refuted, so are answers such as "It's all a matter of luck" or "It's just the system." In this chapter, we look beyond such superficial explanations.

FIGURE 13-2 The Lorenz Curve for Family Income

	Families		Income	
	Percentage	Cumulative Percentage	Percentage	Cumulative Percentage
A	Lowest 20	20	5.2	5.2
B	Second-lowest 20	40	11.3	16.5
C	Middle 20	60	16.7	33.2
D	Second-highest 20	80	23.3	56.5
E	Highest 20	100	43.6	100.0

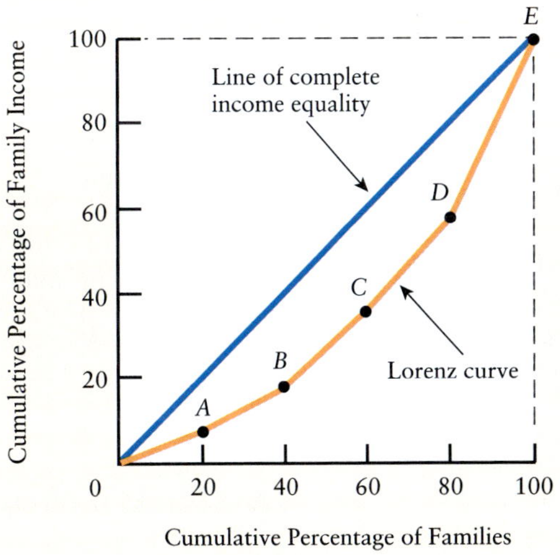

The size of the area between the Lorenz curve and the diagonal is a measure of the inequality of income distribution. If there were complete income equality, the bottom 20 percent of income receivers would receive 20 percent of total income, and so forth, and the Lorenz curve would coincide with the diagonal line.

(*Source:* These data are from the 2001 Census and are available on Statistics Canada's website: www.statcan.ca. Click on "Census" and go to "Analysis Series." Then go to "Income of Canadian Families." Reprinted with permission of Statistics Canada.)

A Glimpse of the Theory Ahead

In this chapter, we confine ourselves to factor markets that are perfectly competitive. As a result, the firms we study face a given price of each factor that they buy. Similarly, owners of factors face a given price for the factor services that they sell.

Dealing first with competitive factor markets allows us to study the principles of factor-price determination in the simplest context. Once these principles are understood, it is relatively easy to extend the theory to more complicated settings. This is done for labour markets in Chapter 14.

Goods markets and factor markets are closely related. Firms' production decisions imply specific demands for the various factors of production. These demands, together with the supplies of the factors of production (which are determined by the owners of the factors), come together in factor markets. Together they determine the quantities of the various factors of production that are employed, their prices, and the incomes earned by their owners. This relationship between goods markets and factor markets leads to one of the great insights about economics:

When demand and supply interact to determine the prices and quantities of various goods, they also determine the incomes of the factors that are used in producing the goods.

The rest of this chapter is an elaboration of this important theme. We first study the demand for factors, then their supply, and finally how demand and supply come together to determine equilibrium factor prices and quantities.

13.2 THE DEMAND FOR FACTORS

Firms require the services of land, labour, and capital to be used as inputs. Firms also use as inputs the products of other firms, such as steel, legal services, computer software, and electricity.

Firms require inputs not for their own sake but as a means to produce goods and services. For example, the demand for computer programmers and technicians is growing as more and more computers and software are produced. The demand for carpenters and building materials rises and falls as the amount of housing construction rises and falls. The demand for any input is therefore *derived from the demand* for the goods and services that it helps to produce; for this reason, the demand for a factor of production is said to be a **derived demand.**

derived demand The demand for a factor of production that results from the demand for the products that it is used to make.

The Firm's Marginal Decision on Factor Use

What determines whether an individual firm will choose to hire one extra worker, or whether the same firm will decide to use one extra machine, or an extra kilowatt-hour of electricity? Since we are considering whether the firm will use *one extra unit* of some factor, we refer to this as the firm's *marginal* decision on factor use.

As we have seen in earlier chapters, any profit-maximizing firm increases its output until its marginal cost equals its marginal revenue. Since producing more output requires hiring more factors of production, we can describe this decision another way—the firm will increase its use of any factor of production until the last unit of the factor adds as much to revenue as it does to costs.

A railway's demand for locomotives—a factor input—is derived from the demand for the product it provides—transportation services.

When a firm hires one more unit of a factor, the firm's total costs rise. This increase in total cost is the factor's marginal cost. For example, if the going wage in a competitive labour market is \$10 per hour, then labour's marginal cost is \$10.

Hiring an extra unit of the factor also leads to an increase in the firm's output and revenue. The increase in the firm's revenue attributed to this extra unit of the factor is called the factor's **marginal revenue product** (***MRP***). The factor's *MRP* has two components—a *physical* component and a *dollar* component. The physical component is how much one unit of the factor adds to total output. This is the factor's *marginal product,* a concept discussed in detail in Chapter 7. The dollar component is the amount that total revenue rises per extra unit of output. This is the firm's *marginal revenue,* a concept discussed in both Chapters 9 and 10.

The factor's marginal revenue product is simply the combination of this physical component and this dollar component—it is the marginal product (*MP*) times the firm's marginal revenue (*MR*). [26] For example, if the factor's marginal product is 2 units and the firm's marginal revenue is \$7.50, the factor's *MRP* is \$15 (\$7.50 × 2).

marginal revenue product (*MRP*) The extra revenue that results from using one unit more of a variable factor.

We can now restate the condition for a firm to be maximizing its profits:

$$\text{Marginal cost of the factor} = \text{Marginal revenue product of the factor} \qquad (13\text{-}1)$$

This condition applies to *any* firm and any factor, in any market structure. In the special case of competitive goods and factor markets, however, we can simplify the equation. In competitive factor markets the marginal cost of the factor is simply the factor's price, since the firm can hire any amount of the factor at a given price. Call this factor price w. Also, we know that in competitive goods markets, the firm's *MR* is just the market price of the product, p. It follows that *MRP* is equal to $MP \times p$. Thus, the condition for profit maximization becomes

$$w = MP \times p \qquad (13\text{-}2)$$

To check your understanding of Equation 13-2, consider an example. Suppose labour is available to the firm at a cost of \$10 per hour (w = \$10). Suppose also that employing another hour of labour adds 3 units to output ($MP = 3$). Suppose further that any amount of output can be sold for \$5 per unit (p = \$5). Thus, the additional hour of labour adds \$15 to the firm's revenue but only \$10 to its costs. In this case, the firm will increase profits by hiring more hours of labour.

Now suppose, however, that the last hour of labour hired by the firm has a marginal product of 1 unit of output and so adds only \$5 to revenue. In this case, the firm can increase profits by reducing its use of labour.

Finally, suppose another hour of labour adds to revenue by \$10. Now the firm cannot increase its profits by altering its use of labour in either direction.

To maximize its profits, any firm must hire each factor of production to the point where the factor's marginal revenue product equals the factor's price.

In Chapters 9 and 10, we saw the firm varying its output until the marginal cost of producing another unit was equal to the marginal revenue derived from selling that unit. Now we see the same profit-maximizing behaviour in terms of the firm's varying its inputs until the marginal cost of another unit of input is just equal to the extra revenue derived from selling that unit's marginal product.

The Firm's Demand Curve for a Factor

Practise with Study Guide Chapter 13, Exercise 1.

We now know what determines the quantity of a variable factor a profit-maximizing firm will buy when facing some specific price of the factor and some specific price of its output. Next, we wish to derive the firm's *entire* demand curve for a factor, which tells us how much of the factor the firm will buy at *each* price.

To derive a firm's demand curve for a factor, we start by considering the right-hand side of Equation 13-1, which tells us that the factor's marginal revenue product is composed of a physical component and a dollar component. We examine these two components in turn.

The Physical Component: *MP* As the quantity of the variable factor changes, output will change. The hypothesis of diminishing marginal returns, first discussed in Chapter 7, predicts what will happen: As the firm adds further units of the variable factor to a given quantity of the fixed factor, the additions to output will eventually get smaller and smaller. In other words, the factor's marginal product declines, as shown in part (i) of Figure 13-3.

The Dollar Component: *MR* To convert the marginal product curve of Figure 13-3(i) into a curve showing the marginal revenue product of the factor, we need to know the dollar value of the extra output. Part (ii) of Figure 13-3 shows a marginal revenue product curve in the case where the firm sells its product in a competitive market at a price (and *MR*) of $5 per unit. The *MRP* curve represents $MP \times MR$ for each additional unit of the factor. Since the *MR* for a firm in perfect competition is simply equal to the price of the product, the *MRP* curve has the same shape as the *MP* curve.

From *MRP* to the Demand Curve Equation 13-2 states that a profit-maximizing competitive firm will employ additional units of the factor up to the point at which the *MRP* equals the price of the factor. For example, in Figure 13-3, if the price of hiring one unit of the factor were $2000 per month, the profit-maximizing firm would employ 60 units of the factor. However, if hiring an extra unit of the factor cost $3000 per month, the firm would only choose to hire 45 units. It should be clear that since the *MRP* curve shows how many units of the factor will be hired at different factor prices, the factor's *MRP* curve is the firm's demand curve for the factor.

A competitive firm's demand curve for a factor is given by that factor's *MRP* curve.

This logic applies equally to any factor of production. A profit-maximizing farmer will rent land up to the point where the marginal revenue product from an extra acre of land is just equal to the rental price for that acre of land. A profit-maximizing machine-tools manufacturer will use extra machines (capital) until the marginal revenue product from an extra machine just equals the price of using that machine. And a profit-maximizing paper mill will hire workers up to the point where the marginal revenue product of an extra worker is just equal to that worker's wage.

FIGURE 13-3 From Marginal Product to Demand Curve

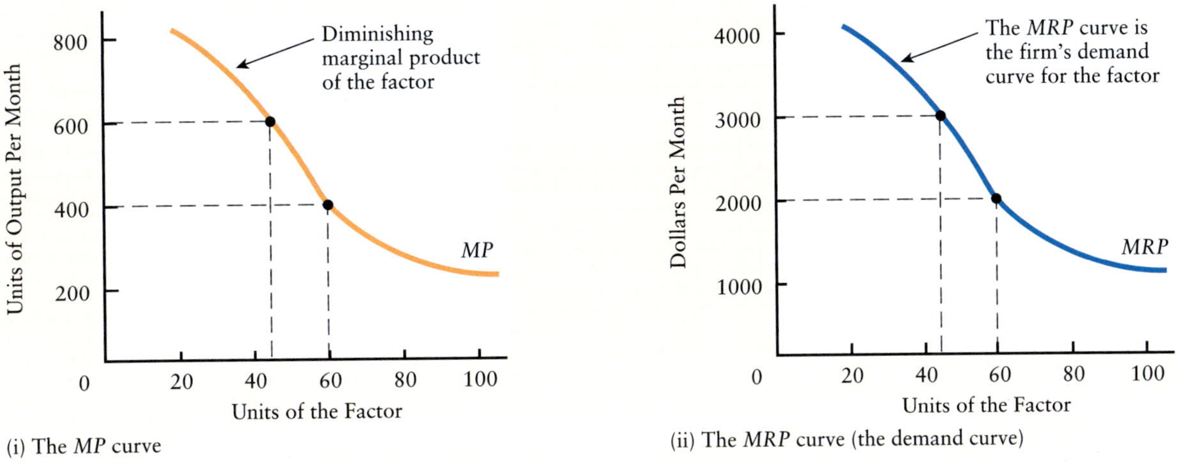

The law of diminishing marginal returns implies that firms have a negatively sloped demand curve for factors of production. In part (i), the *MP* curve for a factor is downward sloping because of the law of diminishing marginal returns. If the firm uses 60 units of the factor per month, the factor's *MP* will be 400 units of output per month. In part (ii), it is assumed that each unit of the firm's output can be sold at $5. If the firm uses 60 units of the factor per month, the factor's *MRP* is $2000 (400 units per month × $5 per unit). Since the *MRP* curve shows, for each separate factor price, how many units of the factor will be hired by a profit-maximizing firm, the *MRP* curve is the firm's demand curve for the factor.

Note that if the firm is not perfectly competitive in its product market, each additional unit of output produced leads to a decline in the product's price. In this case, the firm's *MR* decreases as output increases and so the factor's *MRP* curve is steeper than the one shown here.

Elasticity of Factor Demand

The elasticity of demand for a factor measures the *degree* of the response of the quantity demanded to a change in its price. The preceding sections have explained the *direction* of the response; that is, that quantity demanded is negatively related to price. But you should not be surprised to learn that the magnitude of the response depends on the strength of various effects. For example, the extent of diminishing returns to labour and the ability of the firm to substitute between labour and other factors of production will both affect the firm's elasticity of demand for labour.

Diminishing Returns The first influence on the slope of the demand curve for a factor is the diminishing marginal product of that factor. If marginal product declines rapidly as more of a factor is employed, a fall in the factor's price will not induce many more units to be employed. This is the case of a relatively steep *MP* curve, and thus *MRP* curve, in Figure 13-3. Conversely, if marginal product falls only slowly as more of a factor is employed, there will be a large increase in quantity demanded as price falls. This is the case of a relatively flat *MP* curve, and thus *MRP* curve, in Figure 13-3.

Substitution Between Factors In the long run, all factors are variable. If one factor's price rises, profit-maximizing firms will substitute relatively cheaper factors for it. (This is the *principle of substitution,* which we first encountered in Chapter 8.) For this reason, the slope of the demand curve for a factor is influenced by the ease with which other factors can be substituted for the factor whose price has changed.

The ease of substitution depends on the substitutes that are available and on the technical conditions of production. It is often possible to vary factor proportions in surprising ways. For example, in automobile manufacturing and in building construction, glass and steel can be substituted for each other simply by varying the dimensions of the windows.

Importance of the Factor Other things being equal, the more important is a factor in producing some good, the greater the elasticity of demand for that factor.

To see this, suppose that for some particular firm wages account for 50 percent of the marginal costs of producing a good and raw materials account for 10 percent. A 20-percent rise in the price of labour raises the firm's marginal costs by 10 percent (20 percent of 50 percent), but a 20-percent rise in the price of raw materials raises the firm's marginal costs by only 2 percent (20-percent of 10 percent). The larger the increase in marginal costs, the more the firm reduces its level of output and hence reduces its demand for factors of production. So, in this case, a 20-percent rise in the price of labour leads to a large decline in the amount of labour used; in contrast, the same 20-percent increase in the price of raw materials leads to only a small reduction in the amount of raw materials used. In other words, the firm's demand for labour (the more important factor) is more elastic than its demand for raw materials (the less important factor).

FIGURE 13-4 More Elastic Product Demand Leads to More Elastic Factor Demand

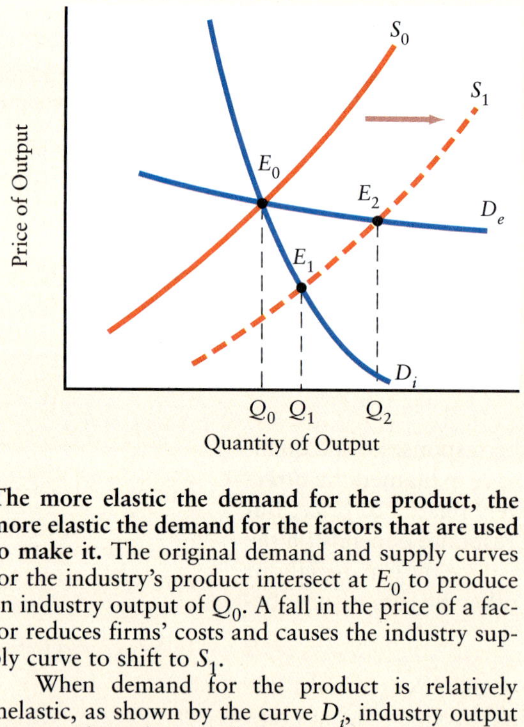

The more elastic the demand for the product, the more elastic the demand for the factors that are used to make it. The original demand and supply curves for the industry's product intersect at E_0 to produce an industry output of Q_0. A fall in the price of a factor reduces firms' costs and causes the industry supply curve to shift to S_1.

When demand for the product is relatively inelastic, as shown by the curve D_i, industry output increases by only a small amount, to Q_1. The quantity of the factor demanded increases by a correspondingly small amount.

When demand for the product is relatively elastic, as shown by the curve D_e, industry output increases by a large amount to Q_2. The quantity of the factor demanded then increases by a correspondingly large amount.

Elasticity of Demand for the Output Other things being equal, the more elastic is the demand for the product that the factor is used to produce, the more elastic is the demand for the factor.

If an increase in the price of the product causes a large decrease in the quantity demanded—that is, if the demand for the product is highly elastic—there will be a large decrease in the quantity of a factor needed to produce it in response to a rise in the factor's price. However, if an increase in the price of a product causes only a small decrease in the quantity demanded—that is, if the demand for the product is inelastic—there will be only a small decrease in the quantity of the factor required in response to a rise in its price. Figure 13-4 illustrates this principle in the case where the price of the factor falls and hence each firm's marginal cost curve—and thus the industry supply curve—shifts to the right.

We have discussed a firm's demand curve for any specific factor of production and have examined what influences the elasticity of demand for that factor. Two issues remain to be discussed. First, how do we get from a firm's demand for a factor to the overall market demand? Second, what causes a shift in the market demand curve for various factors of production?

The Market Demand Curve for a Factor

We saw in Chapter 6 that the market demand curve for any good or service is simply the horizontal summation of all the individual consumers' demand curves. With factor demand curves, the same basic logic applies except for one important complication. As all firms hire more of any specific factor of production, the supplies of the goods produced by that factor increase and the prices of these products fall. This decline in product prices leads firms to increase their hiring of the factors by less than would otherwise occur. The result is that the *market* demand curve for any specific factor of production is *less elastic* than would be the case if we took a simple horizontal summation of the individual firms' factor demand curves.

An example will clarify this point. Consider a competitive furniture-building industry and the individual firms' demand for carpenters. Any one firm's production of furniture will have no significant effect on the equilibrium price of furniture, and so its hiring of carpenters similarly has no effect on the market price of furniture. But all furniture-building firms taken together *do* have an effect on the equilibrium price of furniture. As *all* such firms increase their hiring of carpenters, the total supply of furniture increases and the equilibrium price of furniture declines. As the price falls, each firm will reduce its hiring of carpenters, offsetting to some extent the initial increase in hiring.

Practise with Study Guide Chapter 13, Short-Answer Question 2.

The market demand curve for any factor of production is less elastic than what would result from a simple horizontal summation of all the firms' demand curves for that factor.

Shifts of the Market Factor Demand Curve

Why might the market demand curve for a factor shift? To answer this question, let's go back and think about what is happening at the level of the individual firms. If we know why individual firms' factor demand curves shift, we will also know why the *market* factor demand curve shifts.

Practise with Study Guide Chapter 13, Short-Answer Question 3.

Figure 13-3 illustrated a firm's demand curve for a factor of production and showed that the factor's *MRP* curve was also the firm's demand curve for that factor. Since *MRP* is equal to *MP* times *MR*, there are two reasons why the demand curve for a factor can shift—because of a shift in the factor's *MP* curve or because of a change in firms' *MR*.

A Change in the Factor's Marginal Product Anything that changes the marginal product of a factor will change the *MP* curve and therefore the *MRP* curve in Figure 13-3. Improvements in technology often increase the marginal product of factors of production, and thus lead to a rightward shift of the *MP* curve. For example, if better education increases the marginal product of labour, the *MP* curve for labour will shift to the right, firms' demand for labour will increase, and firms will hire more labour at any given wage.

A second way in which the marginal product of a factor can increase is if there are more units of other factors with which to work. An increase in the amount of capital, for example, will generally increase the marginal product of any given amount of labour. Suppose that Figure 13-3 shows the marginal product (and *MRP*) for labour under the assumption that the firm has a given stock of capital. If the firm now expands its capital stock by building a larger factory, the marginal product of any given amount of labour will increase, thus shifting the *MP* curve in part (i) to the right. The result will be that the *MRP* curve in part (ii) also shifts to the right, thus increasing the firm's demand for labour.

Any increase in a factor's marginal product will lead to an increase in demand for that factor. Such an increase can come about through improvements in the quality of the factor or an increase in the amount of other factors of production.

A Change in Firms' Marginal Revenue Anything that increases firms' marginal revenue will increase the *MRP* of a factor and thus lead to an increase in demand for that factor. For firms that operate in a competitive product market, an increase in marginal revenue is simply an increase in the market price of the product. In Figure 13-3, if the product price rises from \$5 to \$10, the *MRP* curve shifts to the right (even though the *MP* curve does not move). For imperfectly competitive firms, an increase in *MR* occurs if the demand curve faced by those firms shifts to the right. In both cases, the increase in *MR* leads to an increase in the demand for the factor.

Anything that leads to an increase in demand for a product will lead to an increase in demand for the factors used to produce that product.

13.3 THE SUPPLY OF FACTORS

When we consider the supply of any factor of production, we can consider supply at three different levels of aggregation:

- the amount supplied to the economy as a whole
- the amount supplied to a particular industry
- the amount supplied to a particular firm

This individual seeking employment has decided to supply her labour services to the economy's labour market. But she must still decide to which industry and to which firm she will supply her services.

To illustrate, consider your decision to seek employment—to supply your labour services to the labour market. You must make three general decisions. First, you must decide whether to supply your labour services at all, the alternative being not to seek employment. Your decision will influence the overall supply of labour to the economy (though only by a tiny amount). Second, once you have decided to supply your labour services, you must choose an industry and occupation. Your decision to seek employment in the telecommunications industry rather than the automobile manufacturing industry influences the economy's allocation of labour across industries. Third, once you have decided to seek employment in a particular industry, you must choose which firms in that industry appeal to you. Your decision influences the allocation of labour across firms.

The elasticity of supply of a factor will normally be different at each of these levels of aggregation because the amount of *factor mobility* is different at these different levels of aggregation. A given factor of production is often very mobile between firms within a given industry, less mobile between different industries, and even less mobile from the perspective of the entire economy. For example, an electrician may be very mobile between industries within a given city, and reasonably mobile between provinces, but it may be very difficult for that electrician to move to another country to find a job. In this section, we examine the relationship between factor mobility and the supply of factors of production. We start with the highest level of aggregation, the supply of each factor to the economy as a whole.

The Supply of Factors to the Economy

At any one time, the total supply of each factor of production is given. For example, in each country, the labour force is of a certain size, so much arable land is available, and there is a given supply of discovered petroleum. However, these supplies can and do change. Sometimes the change is very gradual, as when climate change slowly turns arable land into desert or when medical advances reduce the rate of infant mortality and increase the rate of population growth, thereby eventually increasing the supply of adult labour. Sometimes the changes can be quite rapid, as when a boom in business activity brings retired persons back into the labour force.

Physical Capital The capital stock in a country is the existing machines, factories, and equipment. Capital is a manufactured factor of production, and its total supply changes only slowly. Each year, the stock of capital goods is diminished by the amount that becomes physically or economically obsolete and is increased by the amount that is newly produced. On balance, the trend has been for the capital stock to grow from decade to decade over the past few centuries. We will consider the determinants of investment in capital in Chapter 15.

Land The total area of dry land in a country is almost completely fixed, but the supply of *fertile* land is not. Considerable care and effort are required to sustain the productive power of land. If farmers earn low incomes, they may not provide the necessary care, and the land's fertility may be destroyed within a short time. In contrast, high earnings from farming may provide the incentive to increase the supply of arable land by irrigation and other forms of reclamation.

Labour The number of people willing to work is called the labour force; the total number of hours they are willing to work is called the *supply of labour.* The supply of labour depends on three influences: the size of the population, the proportion of the population willing to work, and the number of hours that each individual wishes to work. Each of these is partly influenced by economic forces.

Population. The population of a country varies over time, and these variations are influenced to some extent by economic forces. There is some evidence, for example, that the birthrate and the net immigration rate (immigration minus emigration) are higher in good times than in bad.

Labour-Force Participation. The proportion of the total population that is willing to work is called the *labour-force participation rate*. Economists also define participation rates for subgroups, such as women or youths. Participation rates vary in response to many influences, including changes in attitudes and tastes. The enormous rise in female participation rates in the past four decades, for example, has had a significant effect on the Canadian labour force.

The significant increase in female labour-force participation that occurred between the 1960s and the 1990s had a significant effect on the growth of Canada's aggregate labour supply.

Changes in real wages also play a role in determining the labour-force participation rate. A rise in the demand for labour, and an accompanying rise in the wage, will lead to an increase in the proportion of the population willing to work. For example, in Alberta in 2006, a booming economy driven by high energy prices increased wages up to the point that there was a notable increase in high-school drop-out rates as some students chose instead to pursue employment in the labour market.

Hours Per Person. The wage rate not only influences the number of people that want to work, but also the number of hours that each person wants to work. When workers sell their labour services to employers, they are giving up leisure in order to gain income with which to buy goods. They can therefore be thought of as trading leisure for goods. A rise in the wage implies a change in the relative price of goods and leisure. An increase in the wage means that leisure becomes more expensive relative to goods, because each hour of leisure consumed is at the cost of more goods forgone.

It is not necessarily the case, however, that an increase in the wage increases the amount of hours worked. In fact, an increase in the wage generates both income and substitution effects (see Chapter 6). As the wage rises, the substitution effect leads the individual to work more hours (consume less leisure) because leisure is now relatively more expensive. The income effect of a higher wage, however, leads the individual to work fewer hours (consume more leisure). Because the two effects work in the opposite direction we are, in general, unsure how a rise in the wage will affect the number of hours an individual chooses to work.

The total supplies of land, labour, and capital each respond to economic forces, but tend to change only gradually.

The Supply of Factors to a Particular Industry

Most factors have many uses. A given piece of land can be used to grow any one of several crops, or it can be subdivided for a housing development. A computer programmer living in the Ottawa Valley can work for one of many firms, for the government, or for Carleton University. A lathe can be used to make many different products, and it requires no adaptation when it is turned for one use or another.

One industry can attract a factor away from another industry, even though the economy's total supply of that factor may be fixed. Thus, a factor's elasticity of supply to a particular industry is larger than its elasticity of supply to the entire economy.

factor mobility The ease with which a factor of production can move between firms, industries, occupations, or regions.

When we consider the supply of a factor for a particular use, the most important concept is **factor mobility**. A factor that shifts easily between uses in response to small changes in incentives is said to be *mobile*. Its supply to any one use will be elastic because a small increase in the price offered will attract many units of the factor from other uses. A factor that does not shift easily from one use to another, even in response to large changes in remuneration, is said to be *immobile*. It will be in inelastic supply in any one use because even a large increase in the price offered will attract only a small inflow from other uses. Generally, a factor is less mobile in the short run than in the long run.

An important determinant of factor mobility is time: The longer the time interval, the easier it is for a factor to convert from one use to another.

Consider the factor mobility among particular uses of each of the three key factors of production.

The Mobility of Capital Some kinds of capital equipment—lathes, trucks, and computers, for example—can be shifted readily among firms, among industries, and even across different regions of the country. These are considered *mobile* capital. Other kinds of capital are quite immobile. For example, some plants and machinery are built for a specific purpose, and are difficult if not impossible to modify for other purposes. Equipment of this type is immobile across uses, although it might be mobile in the sense that one firm could sell it to another. Factories designed for a specific purpose are immobile both across uses and across regions, though they could still be transferred from one owner to another.

The Mobility of Land Land, which is physically the least mobile of factors, is one of the *most* mobile in an economic sense. Consider agricultural land. In a given year, one crop can be harvested and a totally different crop can be planted. A farm on the outskirts of a growing city can be sold for subdivision and development on short notice. Once land is built on, however, its mobility is much reduced.

Although land is highly mobile among alternative uses, it is completely immobile as far as location is concerned. There is only so much land within a given distance of the centre of any city, and no increase in the price paid can induce further land to be located within that distance. This locational immobility has important consequences, including high prices for desirable locations and the tendency to build tall buildings to economize on the use of scarce land. It is no accident that the downtown cores of New York, Hong Kong, Toronto, Chicago, and many other large cities are populated by so many tall buildings.

The Mobility of Labour The supply of labour services often requires the physical presence of the person who supplies it. Absentee landlords, while continuing to live in the place of their choice, can obtain income from land that is located in remote parts of the world. Similarly, investment can be shifted from iron mines in South Africa to mines in Labrador while the mine owners commute between Calgary and Hawaii. The same is true for some workers, such as designers or bookkeepers, who can work in one location and submit their work to clients in other locations. But almost all workers involved in manufacturing and most of those involved in serving the public in stores, restaurants, and so on, must actually be present to supply their labour services to an employer. When a worker who is employed by a firm producing men's ties in Montreal decides instead to supply his or her labour services to a firm producing women's shoes in Winnipeg, the worker must physically travel to Winnipeg. This has an important consequence.

Because of the need for labour's physical presence when its services are provided for the production of many goods, non-monetary considerations are much more important for the supply of labour than for other factors of production.

People may be satisfied with or frustrated by the kind of work that they do, where they do it, the people with whom they do it, and the social status of their occupations. Because these considerations influence their decisions about what they will do with their labour services, they will not always move just because they could earn a higher wage.

Nevertheless, labour is mobile among industries, occupations, and regions in response to changes in the signals provided by wages and opportunities for employment. The ease with which such mobility occurs depends on many forces. For example, it is not difficult for a secretary to shift from one company to another in order to

A cruise ship like this one is very mobile between firms, but almost completely immobile between industries—it is very difficult to convert a cruise ship into any other kind of capital equipment.

take a job in Edmonton instead of Regina, but it can be difficult for a secretary to become an editor, a model, a machinist, or a doctor within a short period of time. Workers who lack ability, training, or inclination find certain kinds of mobility difficult or impossible.

Some barriers to movement may be virtually insurmountable once a person's training has been completed. For example, it may be impossible for a farmer to become a surgeon or for a truck driver to become a professional athlete, even if the relative wage rates change greatly. However, the children of farmers, doctors, truck drivers, and athletes, when they are deciding how much education or training to obtain, are not nearly as limited in their choices as their parents, who have already completed their education and are settled in their occupations.

The labour force as a whole is mobile, even though many individual members in it are not.

myeconlab

One particular case of labour mobility has been actively debated in Canada over the past few years—Canada's alleged "brain drain" to the United States. For more details, look for "Is Canada Suffering a Brain Drain?" in the *Additional Topics* section of this book's MyEconLab.

www.myeconlab.com

The Supply of Factors to a Particular Firm

Most firms usually employ only a very small proportion of the economy's total supply of each factor. As a result, they can usually obtain their factors at the going market price. This is true for labour, capital, and land. For example, a commercial bank that is hoping to expand its economics department can hire an extra economist and it will need to pay the going wage (or salary) to attract that economist. An automotive manufacturer can purchase new robotics equipment and will pay the market price to get it. And a rancher can buy more land at the going market price. In each case the firm's actions will have no effect on the market price for the factors of production.

Individual firms generally face perfectly elastic supply curves for factors, even though the supply for the economy as a whole may be quite inelastic.

13.4 THE OPERATION OF FACTOR MARKETS

Once you have mastered the basic analysis of demand and supply in Chapters 3 through 5, the determination of the price, quantity, and income of a factor in a single market poses no new problems. Figure 13-5 shows a competitive market for a factor. In both parts of the figure, the intersection of the demand and supply curves determines

FIGURE 13-5 Demand and Supply Shifts in a Competitive Factor Market

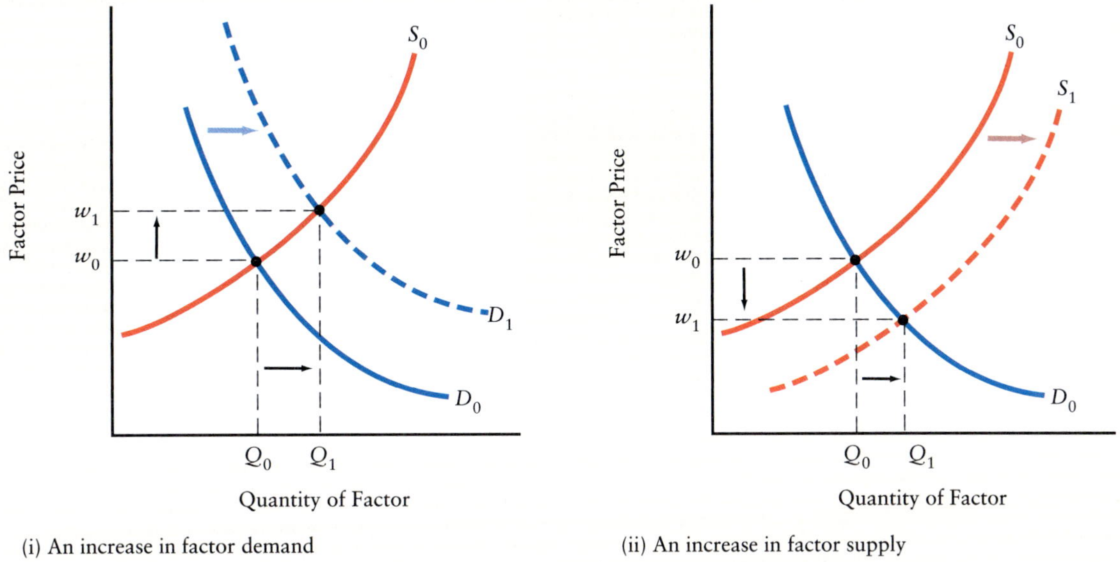

Equilibrium factor prices and quantities are determined by the demand for and supply of factors. In both parts of the figure, the initial equilibrium is determined by D_0 and S_0. The equilibrium factor price is w_0 and the equilibrium quantity of the factor is Q_0.

In part (i), an increase in demand for the factor shifts the demand curve to D_1. The equilibrium factor price rises to w_1 and quantity increases to Q_1. Since both price and quantity have increased, the total income earned by the factor clearly increases.

In part (ii), an increase in the supply of the factor shifts the supply curve to S_1. The equilibrium factor price falls to w_1 but the quantity increases to Q_1. Since price falls but quantity rises, the effect on total factor income is unclear. If demand for the factor is inelastic, total factor income will fall; if demand is elastic, total factor income will rise.

the factor's price and the quantity of the factor employed. The total income earned by the factor is given by the equilibrium price times the equilibrium quantity.

Changes in factor markets can occur either because of a change in demand for the factor or because of a change in the supply of the factor, or both. Part (i) of Figure 13-5 illustrates a case in which an increase in demand for a factor leads to a rise in that factor's price and an increase in total income earned by that factor. What could cause such a change? Recall that the market demand curve for any factor comes from the many firms' *MRP* curves for that factor. An increase in the productivity of that factor would lead to a rightward shift in the *MRP* curves and thus to an increase in the market demand for the factor. Indeed, increases in productivity account for a gradual but ongoing increase in the demand for most factors of production.

Part (ii) of Figure 13-5 shows that an increase in the supply of some factor of production leads to a decline in that factor's equilibrium price and an increase in the quantity of the factor employed. (The total income earned by the factor may rise or fall, depending on the elasticity of demand for the factor.) Though the supply of any factor to a specific firm may change suddenly, the supply to the economy as a whole tends to change very gradually. The labour force grows slowly, physical capital accumulates gradually as firms build more capital equipment, and the amount of arable land changes slowly as new land is cleared or reclaimed.

We now go on to explore three issues relating to factor pricing. First, what explains the differences in payments received by different units of the same factor? For example, why do some workers get paid more than others? Second, what is the effectiveness of government policies designed to reduce these differences? Finally, we explore the important concept of *economic rent*.

Differentials in Factor Prices

Airline pilots typically get paid more than auto mechanics. And a hectare of land in downtown Calgary rents for much more than a hectare of land 150 kilometres away in the Crowsnest Pass. Are such *factor-price differentials* to be expected in well-functioning factor markets?

If all workers were the same, if the attractiveness of all jobs were the same, and if workers moved freely among markets, all workers would earn the same wage. Imagine what would happen if wages were different across jobs that were very similar. Workers would move from low-wage to high-wage jobs. The supply of labour would fall in low-wage occupations and the resulting labour shortage would tend to force those wages up. Conversely, the supply of labour would increase in high-wage occupations and would force those wages down. The movement would continue until there were no further incentives to change occupations—that is, until wages were equalized in all uses.

In fact, however, wage differentials commonly occur, as is clear from even the most cursory examination of the help-wanted ads in any newspaper. As it is with labour, so it is with other factors of production. If all units of any factor of production were identical and moved freely among markets, all units would receive the same remuneration in equilibrium. In fact, however, different units of any one factor receive different payments.

Factor-price differentials can be divided into two types: those that exist only temporarily and those that exist in long-run equilibrium.

Temporary factor-price differentials lead to, and are eroded by, factor mobility. Equilibrium differentials in factor prices are not eliminated by factor mobility.

Temporary Differentials Some factor-price differentials reflect temporary disturbances such as the growth of one industry or the decline of another. The differentials themselves lead to the movement of factors, and such movements in turn act to eliminate the differentials.

Consider the effect on factor prices of a rise in the demand for air transport when there is no change in the demand for rail transport. The airline industry's demand for factors increases while there is no change in demand for factors in the railway industry. Factor prices will rise in the airline industry and create a factor-price differential. The differential in factor prices causes a net movement of factors away from the railway industry and toward the airline industry, and this movement causes the differentials to lessen and eventually to disappear. This adjustment process is illustrated in Figure 13-6. How long this process takes depends on how easily factors can be reallocated from one industry to the other—that is, on the degree of factor mobility.

The behaviour that causes the erosion of temporary differentials is summarized in the hypothesis of the *maximization of net advantage:* The owners of factors of production will allocate those factors to uses that maximize the net advantages to themselves, taking both monetary and non-monetary rewards into consideration. If net advantages were higher in occupation *A* than in occupation *B*, factors would move from *B* to *A*. The increased supply in *A* and the reduced supply in *B* would drive fac-

Practise with Study Guide Chapter 13, Exercise 6.

FIGURE 13-6 The Creation and Erosion of Temporary Factor-Price Differentials

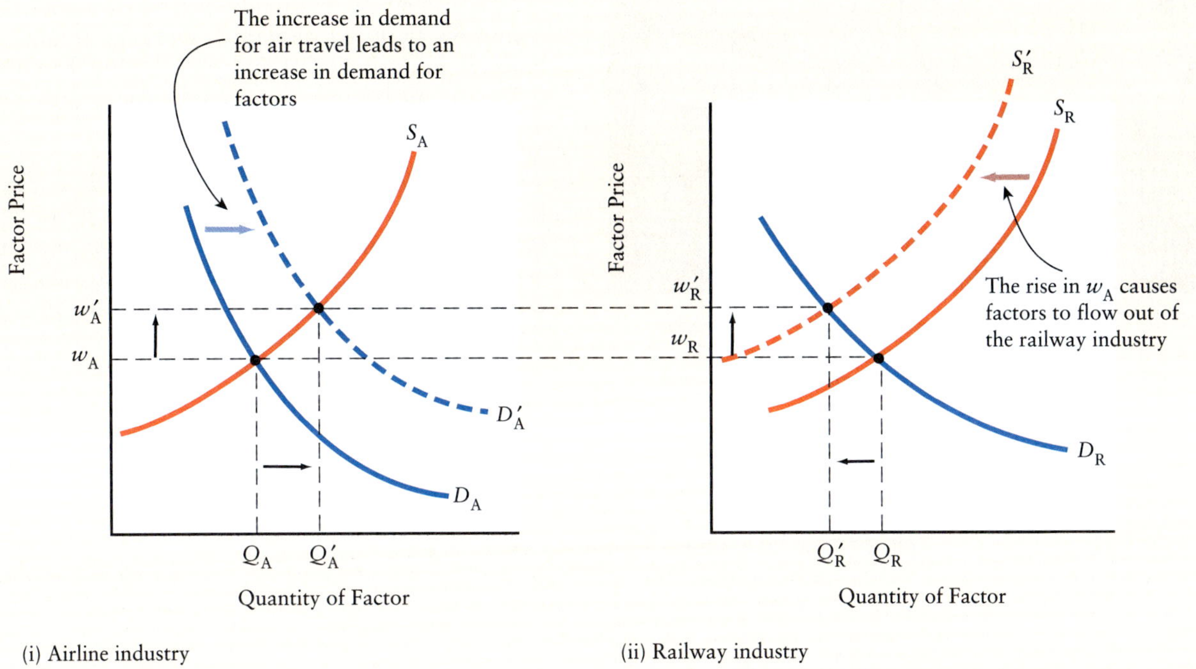

The mobility of factors leads to the erosion of temporary differentials in factor prices. The two figures show the markets for some factor of production (land, labour, or capital) in the airline and railway industries. Suppose the initial equilibrium has the factor receiving the same price in both industries ($w_A = w_R$). Q_A units are employed in the airline industry, and Q_R units are employed in the railway industry.

An increase in demand for air travel leads to an increase in demand for factors in the airline industry. The demand curve shifts to D_A' and factor prices in that industry rise to w'_A. As factor prices in the airline industry rise, factors leave the railway industry and enter the airline industry. This flow of factors is a leftward shift of S_R to S'_R and a movement upward along S_A. There is a reduction of factors employed in the railway industry and an increase in the airline industry. The flow of factors stops when factor prices are again equalized, $w'_A = w'_R$.

tor earnings down in *A* and up in *B* until net advantages would be equalized, after which no further movement would occur. This analysis gives rise to the prediction of *equal net advantage:* In equilibrium, units of each kind of factor of production will be allocated among alternative possible uses in such a way that the net advantages in all uses are equalized.

A change in the relative price of a factor between two uses will change the net advantages of the uses. It will lead to a shift of some units of that factor to the use for which relative price has increased.

Equilibrium Differentials Some factor-price differentials persist without generating any forces that eliminate them. These equilibrium differentials can be explained by intrinsic differences in the factors themselves and, for labour, by differences in the cost of acquiring skills and by different non-monetary advantages of different occupations.

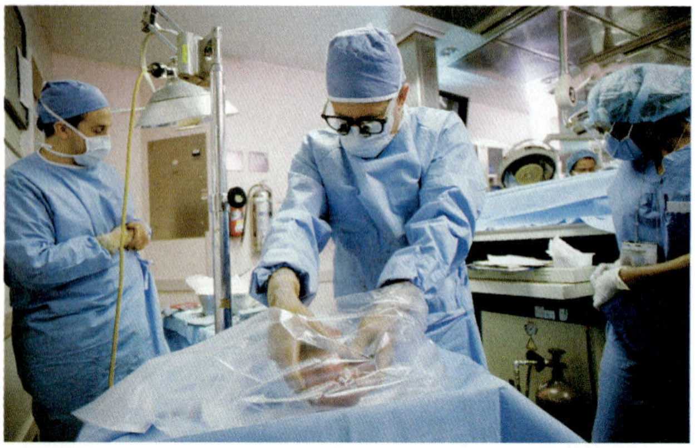

The long and costly training required to become a surgeon reduces the supply of surgeons relative to many other occupations. As a result, surgeons typically earn very high incomes. This is an equilibrium wage differential.

Intrinsic Differences. If various units of a factor have different characteristics, the price that is paid may differ among these units. If dexterity is required to accomplish a task, manually dexterous workers will earn more than less dexterous workers. If land is to be used for agricultural purposes, highly fertile land will earn more than poor land. These differences will persist even in long-run equilibrium.

Acquired Differences. If the fertility of land can be increased only by costly methods, then more fertile land must command a higher price than less fertile land. If it did not, landowners would not incur the costs of improving fertility. The same principle holds true for labour since it is costly to acquire most skills. For example, an engineer must train for some time, and unless the earnings of engineers remain sufficiently above what can be earned in less skilled occupations, people will not incur the cost of training.

compensating differential A difference in the financial payment to a factor of production (usually labour) across two jobs to compensate the factor for differences in non-monetary aspects of the two jobs.

Compensating Differentials. Whenever working conditions differ across jobs, workers will earn different equilibrium wages. The difference between a test pilot's wage and a chauffeur's wage is only partly a matter of skill; the rest is compensation to the worker for facing the higher risk of testing new planes as compared to driving a car. If both were paid the same, there would be an excess supply of chauffeurs and a shortage of test pilots. Because such factor-price differentials *compensate* for non-monetary aspects of the job, they are commonly called **compensating differentials**; they were introduced into economics more than 200 years ago by Adam Smith.

Academic researchers commonly earn less than they could earn in the world of commerce and industry because of the substantial non-monetary advantages of academic employment. If chemists were paid the same in both sectors, many chemists would prefer academic to industrial jobs. Excess demand for industrial chemists and excess supply of academic chemists would then force chemists' wages up in industry and down in academia until the two types of jobs seemed equally attractive on balance.

Compensating differentials also exist in the regional earnings of otherwise identical factors. People who work in remote logging or mining areas are paid more than are people who do jobs requiring similar skills in large cities. Without higher pay, not enough people would be willing to work at sometimes dangerous jobs in unattractive or remote locations.

Practise with Study Guide Chapter 13, Short-Answer Question 4.

Policies to Promote "Pay Equity"

The distinction between temporary and equilibrium factor-price differentials raises an important consideration for policy. Trade unions and governments often have explicit policies about earnings differentials, sometimes seeking to eliminate them in the name of equity. The success of such policies depends to a great extent on the kind of differential that is being attacked. An important general lesson from this experience is the following: Policies that attempt to eliminate *temporary* differentials may be successful in speeding up what may otherwise be a slow adjustment process. But policies aimed at eliminating *equilibrium* differentials will encounter several difficulties.

In recent years, Canadian governments have introduced legislation to redress male–female wage differentials that appear to exist *only* because of discrimination in the labour market. We will discuss labour-market discrimination in more detail in Chapter 14, but for now think of discrimination between men and women who have the same qualifications and are in the same jobs. As the social norms that sustain these discriminatory forces change, so too will the wage differentials. But the adjustment may be very gradual, as the norms themselves will change only gradually. Canadian *pay-equity* legislation has been designed to speed this adjustment and, in the process, reduce the underlying discriminatory forces. These policies have been successful in reducing male–female wage differentials in situations where the men and women concerned are equally qualified and are in the same jobs.

Jobs with unpleasant working conditions usually pay higher wages than more pleasant jobs requiring the same skills. Such differences in wages are called "compensating differentials." Any policy that attempts to eliminate these differentials is likely to be ineffective.

Other government pay-equity legislation is less successful because it attempts to reduce or eliminate *equilibrium* wage differentials. Some pay-equity legislation is based on the principle of *equal pay for work of equal value,* an idea that is very difficult to implement in practice. Such policy is designed to eliminate the wage differentials that exist between workers *in different jobs* but who are deemed to have approximately the same skills and responsibilities. For example, the policy might require that a nurse with 10 years of experience receive the same salary as a teacher with 10 years of experience. Whatever the social value of such laws, they run into trouble whenever they require equal pay for jobs that have different non-monetary advantages.

To illustrate the nature of the problem encountered by such legislation, consider the example of two types of construction workers—those who work mostly indoors doing home and building renovations, and those who work mostly outdoors on bridges or the exteriors of buildings. Suppose these two jobs demand equal skills, training, and everything else that is taken into account in a decision about what constitutes work of equal value. But in a city with a harsh climate, the outside construction job is less pleasant than the inside construction job. If legislation requires equal pay for both jobs, there will be a shortage of people who are willing to work outside and an excess of people who want to work inside. Employers will seek ways to attract outside workers. Higher pensions, shorter hours, and longer holidays may be offered. If these are allowed, they will achieve the desired result but will defeat the original purpose of equalizing the monetary benefits of the inside and outside jobs; they will also cut down on the number of outside workers that employers will hire because the total cost of an outside worker to an employer will have risen. If the jobs are unionized or if the government prevents such "cheating," the shortage of workers for outside jobs will remain.

In Chapter 14, we discuss the effects of race and sex discrimination on wage differentials. Although these effects can be important, it remains true that many factor-price differentials are a natural market consequence of supply and demand conditions that have nothing to do with inequitable treatment of different groups in the society.

Policies that seek to eliminate equilibrium factor-price differentials without consideration of what causes them or how they affect the supply of the factor often have perverse results.

Economic Rent

One of the most important concepts in economics is that of *economic rent.*

transfer earnings The minimum payment required by a factor in order to prevent it from leaving to other uses.

A factor must earn a certain amount in its present use to prevent it from moving to another use—the great nineteenth-century economist Alfred Marshall called this amount the factor's **transfer earnings**. If there were no non-monetary advantages in alternative uses, as is typically the case for land and capital, the factor would have to earn its opportunity cost (what it could earn elsewhere) to prevent it from moving elsewhere.

For labour, however, the non-monetary advantages of various jobs are very important. Labour must earn enough in each use to equate the total advantages—both monetary and non-monetary—among various jobs. For example, in order to remain in a job that is dirty or unsafe, workers will require a higher wage so that the total advantage of the unsafe job equals the total advantage of some alternative job.

economic rent The excess of total earnings over the minimum necessary to prevent a factor from moving to another use.

A factor's transfer earnings are the amount it needs in order to remain in its current use. Any amount that the factor earns *above* this is called **economic rent.** Economic rent is analogous to economic profit as a surplus over the opportunity cost of capital. Here are three examples:

1. Consider a farmer who grows wheat and earns $1000 per hectare. She has calculated that if her earnings fall to $900 per hectare, she will switch to growing barley instead, her next best alternative. In this case, each hectare of land growing wheat is earning $100 of economic rent.

2. A famous actor earns $15 million per year. He decides that his next best alternative to acting is to promote automobiles in television commercials, in which case he would earn $2.5 million per year. He is earning $12.5 million per year of economic rent.

3. An individual has invested $300 000 of capital into a restaurant, and currently earns a 20-percent annual return—investment income of $60 000 annually. The next best alternative investment (with similar risk) can earn a 15-percent return, or $45 000 annually. The $300 000 of capital is thus earning economic rent equal to $15 000 per year. In this case, rent is just another name for profit in the economist's sense of the term.

The concept of economic rent is crucial in predicting the effects that changes in earnings have on the movement of factors among alternative uses. However, the terminology is confusing because economic rent is often simply called *rent,* which can of course also mean the price paid to hire something, such as a machine, a piece of land, or an apartment. How the same term came to be used for these two different concepts is explained in *Lessons From History 13-1.*

Practise with Study Guide Chapter 13, Exercises 3 and 5.

How Much of Factor Earnings Is Rent? In most cases, as in the three previous examples, economic rent makes up part of the factor's total earnings. From the definitions above, however, note that total earnings for any factor are the sum of its transfer earnings and its economic rent.

A factor's transfer earnings plus its economic rent equals its total earnings.

But *how much* of total earnings is economic rent? A different but related question is: How much would the factor price have to fall before the factor left its current use?

The possibilities are illustrated in Figure 13-7. When supply is perfectly elastic, as in part (i), the factor is extremely mobile between various uses. In this case, all of the

LESSONS FROM HISTORY 13-1

David Ricardo and "Economic Rent"

In the early nineteenth century, there was a public debate about the high price of wheat in England. The high price was causing great hardship because bread was a primary source of food for the working class. Some people argued that wheat had a high price because landlords were charging high rents to tenant farmers. In short, it was argued that the price of wheat was high because the rents of agricultural land were high. Some of those who held this view advocated restricting the rents that landlords could charge.

David Ricardo (1772–1823), a great British economist who was one of the originators of Classical economics, argued that the situation was exactly the reverse. The price of wheat was high, he said, because there was a shortage, caused by the Napoleonic Wars. Because wheat was profitable to produce, there was keen competition among farmers to obtain land on which to grow wheat. This competition in turn forced up the rental price of wheat land. Ricardo advocated removing the existing tariff on wheat so that imported wheat could come into the country. The increase in imports would then increase the supply of wheat in England and lower its price. This would then reduce the rent on land.

The essentials of Ricardo's argument were these: The supply of land was fixed. Land was regarded as having only one use, the growing of wheat. Nothing had to be paid to prevent land from transferring to a use other than growing wheat because it had no other use. No landowner would leave land idle as long as some return could be obtained by renting it out. Therefore, all the payment to land, that is, rent in the ordinary sense of the word, was a surplus over and above what was necessary to keep it in its present use.

Given a fixed supply of land, the price of land depended on the demand for land, which depended in turn on the demand for wheat (i.e., the demand for land was *derived from* the demand for wheat). Rent, the term for the payment for the use of land, thus became the term for a surplus payment to a factor over and above what was necessary to keep it in its present use.

Later, two facts were realized. First, land often had alternative uses, and, from the point of view of any one use, part of the payment made to land would necessarily have to be paid to keep it in that use. Second, factors of production other than land also often earned a surplus over and above what was necessary to keep them in their present use. This surplus is now called *economic rent,* whether the factor is land, labour, or a piece of capital equipment.

factor's income is transfer earnings and so none of it is economic rent. If any lower price is offered, nothing whatsoever will be supplied since all units of the factor will transfer to some other use.

When supply is perfectly inelastic, as in part (iii), the same quantity is supplied whatever the price. Evidently, the quantity supplied does not decrease, no matter how low the price goes. This inelasticity indicates that the factor has no alternative use, and thus requires no minimum payment to keep it in its present use. In this case, there are no transfer earnings and so the whole of the payment is economic rent.

The more usual situation is that of an upward-sloping supply curve, as shown in part (ii) of Figure 13-7. A rise in the factor's price serves the allocative function of attracting more units of the factor into the market in question, but the same rise provides additional economic rent to all units of the factor that are *already employed.* We know that the extra pay that is going to the units

Increases in the price of oil that are not needed to increase the quantity supplied generate economic rents for producers. For example, if the owner of this well is only willing to operate it when the price of oil is $35 per barrel or higher, then any price above that level generates some economic rent for the producer.

FIGURE 13-7 The Determination of Rent in Factor Markets

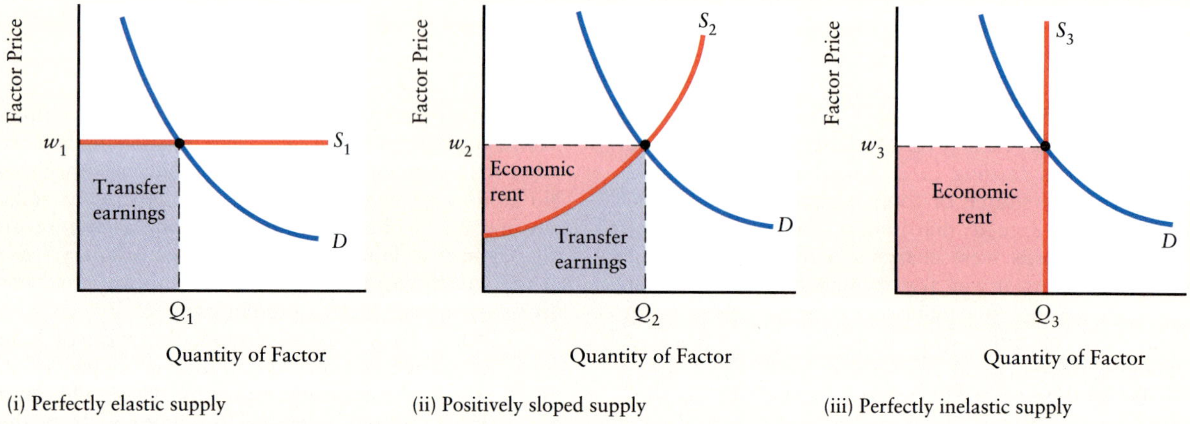

The amount of a factor's earnings that is economic rent depends on the mobility (and thus on the elasticity of supply) of the factor. In each case, the equilibrium is determined by the intersection of the demand and supply curves, and total factor earnings are given by factor price times quantity, wQ.

In part (i), supply is perfectly elastic, indicating that even a slightly lower factor price would cause the factor to leave. None of the earnings are economic rent; all are the factor's transfer earnings.

In part (ii), supply is positively sloped, indicating that more units of the factor will be supplied at a higher price. The area below the supply curve is the amount needed to keep Q_2 units of the factor in its current use—this area is the factor's transfer earnings. The red shaded area above the supply curve is economic rent.

In part (iii), supply is perfectly inelastic, indicating that the factor has no other uses. In this case, transfer earnings are zero and all of the factor's earnings are economic rent.

already employed is economic rent because the owners of these units were willing to supply them at the lower price.

The production and sale of oil (and natural gas) in Alberta in the past few years provides a good example of economic rent and market prices. In Canada, natural resources are owned by the province, and oil producers must pay a share of their revenues as *royalties* to the provincial government. Alberta's supply curve for oil is upward-sloping, as in part (ii) of Figure 13-7. As the market price for oil rises, production from wells that were not profitable at lower prices comes on-line and producers therefore increase the quantity of barrels supplied. For these *marginal* barrels of oil, the market price is just equal to the transfer earnings; there are no economic rents earned on these units. But the increase in market price does generate pure economic rent for those output levels that were already being produced at lower prices; these units were being produced anyway (at lower prices), and the rise in market price simply increases the rents earned by the producer. These economic rents in Alberta's oil industry account for a considerable fraction of that province's increase in income in recent years.

Various Perspectives on Economic Rent The proportion of a given factor payment that is economic rent varies from situation to situation. We cannot point to a factor of production and assert that some fixed fraction of its income is always its economic rent. The proportion of its earnings that is rent depends on its alternatives.

Consider first a narrowly defined use of a given factor—say, its use by a particular firm. From that firm's point of view, the factor will be highly mobile, as it could readily move to another firm in the same industry. The firm must pay the going wage or risk losing that factor. From the perspective of the single firm, a large proportion of the payment made to a factor is needed to prevent it from transferring to another use. Thus, only a small portion of its payment is rent.

Now consider a more broadly defined use—for example, the factor's use in an entire industry. From the industry's point of view, the factor is less mobile because it would be more difficult for it to gain employment quickly outside the industry. From the perspective of the particular *industry* (rather than the specific *firm* within the industry), a larger proportion of the payment to a factor is economic rent.

From the even more general perspective of a particular *occupation,* mobility is likely to be even less, and the proportion of the factor payment that is economic rent is likely to be more. It may be easier, for example, for a carpenter to move from the construction industry to the furniture industry than to retrain to be a computer programmer.

As the perspective moves from a narrowly defined use of a factor to a broadly defined use of a factor, the mobility of the factor decreases; as mobility decreases, the share of the factor payment that is economic rent increases.

Consider how this relationship applies to the often controversial large salaries that are received by some highly specialized types of labourers, such as movie stars and professional athletes. These performers have a unique style and a talent that cannot be duplicated, whatever the training. The earnings that they receive are mostly economic rent from the viewpoint of the occupation: These performers generally enjoy their occupations and would pursue them for much less than the high remuneration that they actually receive.

For example, Sidney Crosby would probably have chosen hockey over other alternatives even at a much lower salary. However, because of Crosby's amazing skills as a hockey player, most hockey teams would pay handsomely to have him on their rosters, and he is able to command a high salary from the team for which he does play. From the perspective of the individual firm, the Pittsburgh Penguins, most of Crosby's salary is required to keep him from switching to another team and hence is not economic rent. From the point of view of the hockey "industry," however, much of his salary is economic rent.

Notice also that Sidney Crosby's salary is largely determined by the demand for his services. The supply is perfectly inelastic—no one else has his particular combination of skills. So the market-clearing price is determined by the position of the demand curve.

Whether Sidney Crosby's salary with the Pittsburgh Penguins is economic rent depends on the perspective. From the perspective of the entire NHL, most of his salary is economic rent.

A Final Word

This chapter has examined the operation of factor markets. You should now be able to answer the questions that we posed in the opening paragraph. Here are some of the key points for two of those questions.

What explains why neurosurgoens usually get paid more than family doctors? Part of the answer surely lies in the fact that to be a neurosurgeon requires more years of costly specialized training than that needed to be a family doctor. Since that extra training is costly and time-consuming, it is not surprising that fewer people are willing to become neurosurgeons than family doctors. This lower supply for neurosurgeons, other things being equal, leads to a higher wage.

Why does a hectare of farm land in Northern Saskatchewan rent for far less than a hectare of land in downtown Toronto? To answer this, just think about the alternative uses for the farm land, and compare them to the alternative uses for the hectare in downtown Toronto. The hectare of farm land has very few alternative uses. Or, more correctly, it has many alternative uses, but there is little demand to use that particular piece of land to build a skyscraper, shopping mall, or baseball stadium. But one hectare of land in downtown Toronto has many alternative uses—there always seems to be demand for additional space for parking garages, office buildings, retail stores, and many other things. Since the piece of farm land in Saskatchewan must stay where it is, its rental price is determined by demand. Since there is little demand for the land, its rental price is low. Similarly, the land in downtown Toronto cannot move anywhere, and so its rental price is determined by demand. And since there is lots of demand for a hectare in downtown Toronto, its rental price is high.

Having learned about factor markets in general, we are now ready to examine some specific factor markets. In Chapter 14, we examine some details about labour markets, such as minimum wages, discrimination, and labour unions. In Chapter 15, we examine physical capital and the interest rate.

SUMMARY

13.1 INCOME DISTRIBUTION

LO 1

- The functional distribution of income refers to the shares of total national income going to each of the major factors of production; it focuses on sources of income. The size distribution of income refers to the shares of total national income going to various groups of households; it focuses only on the amount of income, not its source.
- Canada has considerable inequality in the distribution of income. The poorest fifth of families currently receives 5.2 percent of aggregate pre-tax income; the richest fifth receives 43.6 percent.

13.2 THE DEMAND FOR FACTORS

LO 2

- A firm's decisions on how much to produce and how to produce it imply demands for factors of production, which are said to be derived from the demand for goods they are used to produce.
- A profit-maximizing firm will hire units of a factor until the last unit adds as much to cost as it does to revenue. Thus, the marginal cost of the factor will be equated with that factor's marginal revenue product.
- When the firm is a price taker in factor markets, the marginal cost of the factor is its price per unit. When the firm sells its output in a competitive market, the marginal revenue product is the factor's marginal product multiplied by the market price of the output.
- A price-taking firm's demand for a factor is negatively sloped because the law of diminishing returns implies that the marginal product of a factor declines as more of that factor is employed (with other inputs held constant).
- The industry's demand for a factor will be more elastic (a) the less the marginal product of the factor declines as more of the factor is used, (b) the larger the proportion of costs accounted for by the factor in question, and (c) the more elastic the demand for the good that the factor is used to produce.

13.3 THE SUPPLY OF FACTORS

LO 3

- The total supply of each factor is fixed at any moment but varies over time. The supply of labour depends on the size of the population, the participation rate, and the number of hours that people want to work.
- A rise in the wage rate has a substitution effect, which tends to induce more work, and an income effect, which tends to induce less work (more leisure consumed).
- The supply of a factor to a particular industry or occupation is more elastic than its supply to the whole economy because one industry can bid units away from other industries. The elasticity of supply to a particular use depends on factor mobility, which tends to be greater the longer the time allowed for a reaction to take place.

13.4 THE OPERATION OF FACTOR MARKETS

LO 4 5

- Factor-price differentials often occur in competitive markets. Temporary differentials in the earnings of different units of factors of production induce factor movements that eventually remove the differentials. Equilibrium differentials reflect differences among units of factors as well as non-monetary benefits of different jobs; they can persist indefinitely.
- Factors will be allocated between uses to generate the greatest net advantage to their owners, allowing for both the monetary and non-monetary advantages of a particular employment.
- Some amount must be paid to a factor to prevent it from transferring to another use. This amount is the factor's transfer earnings. Economic rent is the difference between that amount and a factor's actual earnings.
- Whenever the supply curve is positively sloped, part of the total payment going to a factor is needed to prevent it from transferring to another use, and part of it is economic rent. The more narrowly defined the use, the larger the fraction that is transfer earnings and the smaller the fraction that is economic rent.

KEY CONCEPTS

Functional distribution and size distribution of income
Derived demand for a factor
Marginal product (*MP*)
Marginal revenue product (*MRP*)
The determinants of elasticity of factor demand
Factor mobility
Temporary versus equilibrium factor-price differentials
Equal net advantage
Transfer earnings
Economic rent

STUDY EXERCISES

1. myeconlab The table below shows the size distribution of income for Fantasyland.

Household Income Rank	Percentage of Aggregate Income	Cumulative Total
Lowest fifth	6.8	—
Second fifth	14.1	—
Third fifth	21.5	—
Fourth fifth	26.2	—
Highest fifth	31.4	—

   a. Compute the cumulative percentage of total income. Fill in the table.
   b. On a scale diagram, with the percentage of households on the vertical axis and the percentage of aggregate income on the horizontal axis, plot the Lorenz curve for Fantasyland.
   c. How does the diagram show the extent of income inequality in Fantasyland?
   d. Now suppose Fantasyland introduces a system that redistributes income from higher-income households to lower-income households. How would this affect the Lorenz curve?

2. Demands for the following goods and services are increasing rapidly. In each case, list two derived demands that you predict will be increasing as a result.
   a. Demand for natural gas
   b. Demand for medical services

c. Demand for international travel
d. Demand for children's computer games

3. Fill in the blanks to make the following statements correct.

   a. Marginal revenue product is calculated by multiplying __________ and __________.
   b. Marginal revenue product represents the addition to a firm's total revenue as a result of __________.
   c. To maximize its profits, a firm will hire all units of a factor that have an __________ greater than or equal to their __________.
   d. To maximize its profits, any firm will hire each factor of production to the point where the factor's __________ equals the __________.

4. Fill in the blanks to make the following statements correct.

   a. The *MRP* curve for a factor is the same as the firm's __________ for that factor.
   b. Demand for a factor will be relatively __________ if the marginal product declines rapidly as more of that factor is used.
   c. Other things being equal, if the demand for a product that a factor is used to produce is relatively inelastic, the demand for that factor will be relatively __________.
   d. An increase in the price at which a competitive firm sells its product leads the firm's demand curve for its factor to __________.
   e. If a technological improvement leads every unit of a given factor to produce 10 percent more output than previously, the __________ curve will __________ and thus the firm's demand curve for the factor will __________.

5. The Apple Pie Factory produces apple pies. The firm sells its product and hires its workers in competitive markets. The market price (p) for a pie is $4 and the wage rate ($w$) is $10 per hour. The table at the bottom of the page shows the total hourly production for varying amounts of workers. (Remember that for a price-taking firm, $p = MR$.)

   a. Fill in the p and w columns.
   b. Calculate the *MP* and the *MRP* for each amount of labour employed. Put the numbers *between* the rows.
   c. What is the logic of the firm's profit-maximizing condition for hiring labour?
   d. How many workers should this profit-maximizing firm hire?

6. Refer back to the production schedule for the Apple Pie Factory in Question 5. In this question we will derive the firm's demand curve for labour.

   a. On a diagram, with *MRP* on the vertical axis and the number of workers on the horizontal axis, plot the *MRP* curve.
   b. If the wage is $10 per hour, how many workers will be hired? Why?
   c. If the wage is $5 per hour, how many workers will be hired? Why?
   d. If the wage is $20 per hour, how many workers will be hired? Why?
   e. Explain why the *MRP* curve is the firm's factor demand curve.

Number of Workers	Output	Wage Rate (w) ($ per hour)	Price of a Pie (p)	*MP*	*MRP*
4	40	______	______		
5	48	______	______	______	______
6	55	______	______	______	______
7	61	______	______	______	______
8	66	______	______	______	______
9	70	______	______	______	______
10	73	______	______	______	______
11	75	______	______	______	______
12	76	______	______	______	______

7. The diagram below shows the market for fast-food workers in British Columbia.

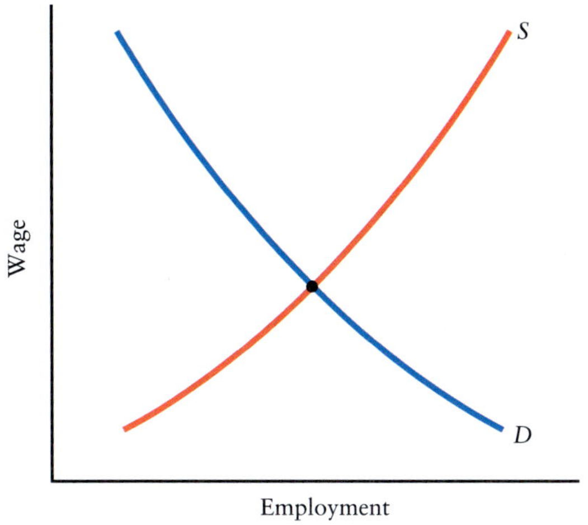

a. The supply curve is upward sloping. If the wage in this industry rises, from where do the extra workers come?
b. Suppose there is a significant decrease in demand for fast food. How is this likely to affect fast-food workers' earnings? Show this in the diagram.
c. Now suppose new legislation bans high school students from doing any homework. As a result, more students look for jobs in the fast-food industry. How will this affect the labour market for fast-food workers? Show this in the diagram.
d. What will be the effect on total earnings in the fast-food industry from the change in part (c)? On what does the answer depend?

8. The three following diagrams show the supply of luxury ocean liners at three different levels of aggregation—the entire world, a particular country, and a particular firm.

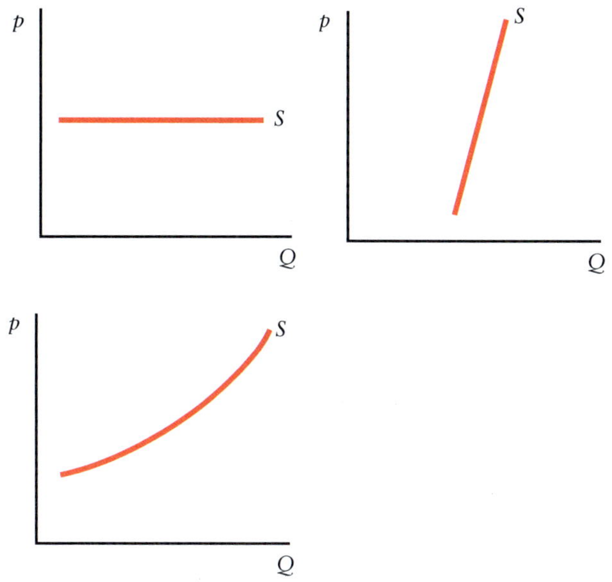

a. Which diagram shows the supply of ocean liners to the world as whole? Explain its elasticity.
b. Which diagram shows the supply of ocean liners to Canada? Explain its elasticity.
c. Which diagram shows the supply of ocean liners to an individual Canadian firm? Explain its elasticity.
d. What is the general relationship between factor mobility and the elasticity of factor supply?

9. In the text we argued that temporary factor-price differentials tend to be eroded by factor mobility. This question requires you to think about this process. Consider the two markets for sheet-iron workers and steel-pipe workers in the same region. Suppose both markets are competitive. We begin in a situation in which both sheet-iron workers and steel-pipe workers earn $20 per hour. Assume that workers can switch easily between the two jobs.

a. Draw diagrams showing the supply and demand for labour in each market.
b. Now suppose there is a sharp increase in the demand for steel pipe. Explain what happens in the market for steel-pipe workers.
c. If the employment of steel-pipe workers increased in part (b), explain where the extra workers came from.
d. What effect does the event in part (b) have on the market for sheet-iron workers?
e. What is the long-run effect of the shock on the relative wages in the two types of jobs?

10. How much of the following payments for factor services is likely to be economic rent?

a. The $750 per month that a landlord receives for an apartment rented to students
b. The salary of the Canadian prime minister
c. The annual income of Tiger Woods or Shania Twain
d. The salary of a window cleaner who says, "It's dangerous work, but it beats driving a truck."

DISCUSSION QUESTIONS

1. Other things being equal, how would you expect each of the following events to affect the size distribution of after-tax income?
   a. An increase in unemployment
   b. Rapid population growth in an already crowded city
   c. An increase in food prices relative to other prices
   d. An increase in social insurance benefits and taxes
   e. Elimination of the personal income-tax exemption for interest earned within an RRSP.
2. A labour dispute has broken out at a university between the faculty and the university's board of governors. One of the issues is the faculty's complaint that summer school teaching salaries are below the regional average and hence too low. The trustees argue that considering that they have more professors asking to teach summer school at the current pay than they have courses for these faculty to teach, the pay is adequate. Comment.
3. This chapter introduced the Lorenz curve, which gives a graphical representation of the equality of income distribution. Many observers criticize Canadian policy because Canada's Lorenz curve is bent significantly off the diagonal. Can you provide an economically valid defence of this criticism? If you could pick a shape for the nation's Lorenz curve, what would it be? Defend your choice using positive economic tools.
4. A recent *Wall Street Journal* article asks, "Why do baseball players earn millions of dollars a year for their negligible contribution to society while major contributors—such as schoolteachers, police officers, firefighters, and ambulance drivers—earn barely enough to survive?" Can you offer an answer based on what was discussed in this chapter?
5. For most of the years in the past two decades, the unemployment rate in the province of Quebec has been higher than the Canadian average. It has also been higher than the unemployment rate in next-door Ontario. Given that there are few legal restrictions on the flow of labour across Canadian provincial boundaries, provide an explanation for how such a gap in unemployment rates can persist for so long.
6. Using the concepts of transfer earnings and economic rent, can you derive a form of taxation—of the earnings by oil companies, for example—that would generate tax revenue but *not* influence the companies' supply decisions? Is your approach consistent with that followed by Canada's provincial governments when they collect royalties on natural-resource revenues?

CHAPTER 14

Labour Markets

LEARNING OBJECTIVES

In this chapter you will learn

1. how to explain wage differentials in both competitive and non-competitive labour markets.
2. the effects of legislated minimum wages.
3. about the tradeoff that unions face between wages and employment.
4. why the trend away from manufacturing jobs and toward service jobs is not necessarily a problem for the economy as a whole.

The competitive theory of factor-price determination, presented in Chapter 13, tells us a great deal about the determinants of factor prices, factor movements, and the distribution of income. In this chapter, we look specifically at labour markets. We begin by discussing why some workers get high wages and others get low wages. We then look beyond our theory of competitive labour markets to examine situations where either firms or workers have some market power. We also discuss the effects of legislated minimum wages, as well as the debate surrounding this contentious policy. The chapter then discusses labour unions, and the tradeoff they face between increasing their membership and increasing their members' wages. Finally, we examine an often-heard claim that Canada and other developed economies are gaining "bad jobs" in the service sector at the expense of "good jobs" in the manufacturing sector.

14.1 WAGE DIFFERENTIALS

We argued in the last chapter that if all workers were identical, all jobs had the same working conditions, and labour markets were perfectly competitive, all workers would earn the same wage. In reality, however, wages vary enormously across such dimensions as occupations, skills, amounts of education, and geographical areas. Generally, the more education and experience a worker has, the higher are his or her wages. Given equal education and experience, women on average earn less than men. Workers in highly unionized industries tend to get paid more than workers with similar skills and experience in non-unionized industries. Such differentials arise because workers are not all identical, jobs are not all identical, and because many important non-competitive forces operate in labour markets. We now look more systematically at some of the main reasons why different types of labour earn different wages.

Wage Differentials in Competitive Markets

Many jobs involve dangerous or unpleasant working conditions. Wages in such jobs are generally higher than in other jobs requiring comparable skills. These are called compensating wage differentials.

Where there are many employers (buyers) and many workers (sellers), there is a competitive labour market of the kind discussed in Chapter 13. Under competitive conditions, the wage rate and level of employment are set by supply and demand. No worker or group of workers, and no firm or group of firms, is able to affect the market wage. In practice, however, there are many kinds of workers and many kinds of jobs. We can therefore think of a series of related labour markets rather than a single national market. Among these various labour markets, there are several reasons for wage differentials.

Working Conditions Given identical skills, those working under relatively onerous or risky conditions earn more than those working in pleasant or safe conditions. For example, construction workers who work the "high iron," assembling the frames for skyscrapers, are paid more than workers who do similar work at ground level. The reason is simple: Risk and unpleasantness reduce the supply of labour, thus raising the wage above what it would otherwise be. Different working conditions in different jobs thus lead to *compensating differentials* as we discussed in Chapter 13. These wage differentials are not temporary—they are *equilibrium* wage differentials.

In competitive labour markets, supply and demand set the equilibrium wage, but the wage will differ according to the non-monetary aspects of the job.

Inherited Skills Large incomes will be earned by people who have scarce skills that cannot be taught and that are in high demand—for example, an NBA basketball player, an opera singer, or a movie star. In these cases, the combination of a small and inelastic supply and a large enough demand of the relevant kind of labour cause the market-clearing wage to be high. Wage differentials of this kind are also equilibrium wage differentials.

Inherited skills, which are mostly beyond the individual's control, can have important effects on wages.

Human Capital A machine is physical capital. It requires an investment of time and money to create it, and once created, it yields valuable services over a long time. In the same way, labour skills require an investment of time and money to acquire, and once acquired, they may yield an increased income to their owner over a long time. Since investment in labour skills is similar to investment in physical capital, acquired skills are called **human capital**. The more costly it is to acquire the skill required for a particular job, the higher its pay must be to attract people to train for it.

human capital The acquired skills that individuals have; usually from formal education or on-the-job training.

Investment in human capital is costly, and the return is usually in terms of higher future wages.

The two main ways in which human capital is acquired are through formal education and on-the-job training.

Formal Education. Compulsory primary and secondary education provides some minimum human capital for all citizens. People who decide to stay in school beyond the years of compulsory education, such as those of you who are reading this book, are deciding to invest voluntarily in acquiring further human capital. The opportunity cost is measured by the income that you could have earned if you had entered the labour force immediately, in addition to any out-of-pocket costs for such items as tuition fees and equipment. The return is measured by the higher income earned when a better job is obtained.

How large is the payoff to higher education? Figure 14-1 shows how average employment income varies with years of schooling. In 2001, the year of Canada's most recent Census, the average employment income for Canadians with a university degree was over $48 500; in contrast, someone who failed to complete high school had an average employment income of less than half this amount.

Evidence suggests that in recent years the demand for workers with more skills and education has been rising relative to the demand for those with less. As we would expect, this change in relative demand raises the relative wages of more-educated people, thereby increasing the payoff to their investment in education. Not surprisingly, students today find the further investment in human capital much more important than did students a generation ago.

Changes in demand and supply change the costs and benefits of acquiring human capital. Individuals respond according to their personal assessment of these costs and benefits.

FIGURE 14-1 Education and Employment Income

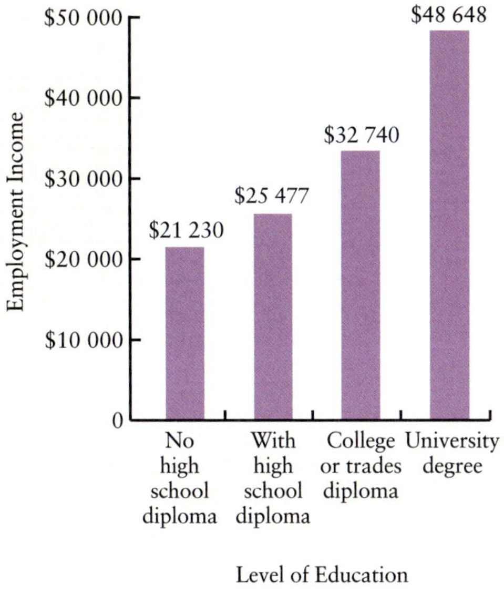

There is a financial payoff to formal education, especially a university degree. The increase in employment income that can be expected from extra education is modest for levels of education below a university degree. But the payoff for completing a university degree is very substantial.

(*Source:* These data are available on Statistics Canada's website, www.statcan.ca, by searching for "Earnings.")

On-the-Job Training. Wage differentials according to experience are readily observable in most firms and occupations. To a significant extent, these differentials are a response to human capital acquired on the job. For example, a civil engineer with 20 years' experience in bridge design will generally earn more than a newly graduated civil engineer, even though they both have the same formal education.

On-the-job training is important in creating rising wages for employees and for making firms competitive. Evidence suggests that people who miss on-the-job training early in life are handicapped relative to others throughout much of their later working careers.

Temporary or Equilibrium Differentials? Wage differentials due to differences in human capital are partly temporary and partly equilibrium differentials. If university graduates earn much more than high school graduates, more people will decide to attend university in pursuit of the higher earnings. This increase in the supply of university-trained individuals will reduce their wage relative to high school graduates, thus diminishing the observed differentials such as those shown in Figure 14-1. As long as it is costly to acquire human capital—and as you know, attending university *is* costly—then in equilibrium there will still be wage differentials in favour of university graduates. In equilibrium, the higher wages of university graduates will just compensate them for the higher costs associated with acquiring their greater stock of human capital.

Practise with Study Guide Chapter 14, Short-Answer Question 1.

Wage differentials due to differences in human capital acquisition lead to changes in the pattern of human-capital acquisition, and to an erosion of the differentials. As long as human capital is costly to acquire, however, some wage differentials will persist in equilibrium.

Discrimination Crude statistics show that incomes vary by race and gender. For example, in 2006 the average female worker in Canada earned about 83 percent of the wage of the average full-time male worker. More detailed studies suggest that a significant part of these differences can be explained by such considerations as the nature of the job and the amount of human capital acquired through both formal education and on-the-job experience. When all such explanations are taken into account, however, there still appears to be some discrimination on the basis of both gender and race.

To understand the effects of labour-market discrimination, we begin by building a simplified picture of a non-discriminating labour market and then introduce discrimination between two sets of equally qualified workers. The discussion here is phrased in terms of males and females but the analysis applies equally well to any situation in which workers are distinguished on grounds *other than* their ability, such as race or skin colour, citizenship, religion, sexual preference, or political beliefs.

Suppose half of the people in the labour force are male and the other half are female. Each group has the same proportion who are educated to various levels, identical distributions of talent, and so on. Suppose also that there are two occupations. Occupation E (*elite*) requires people of above-average education and skills, and occupation O (*ordinary*) can use anyone. Finally, suppose the non-monetary aspects of the two occupations are the same.

In the absence of discrimination, the theory of competitive factor markets that we have developed suggests that the wages in E occupations will be bid up above those in O occupations in order that the E jobs attract the workers of above-average skills. Men and women of above-average skill will take the E jobs, while the others, both men and women, will have no choice but to seek O jobs. Because skills are equally distributed between both sexes, each occupation will employ one-half men and one-half women.

Now suppose discrimination enters in an extreme form. All E occupations are hereafter open only to men, but O occupations are open to either men or women. The immediate effect is to reduce by 50 percent the supply of job candidates for E occupations; all previously qualified female candidates are no longer eligible because candidates must now be *both* men and above average. The discrimination also increases the supply of applicants for O jobs because the women who cannot be employed in E jobs move instead to get O jobs. The new group of O-job candidates now includes all women and the below-average men.

As shown in Figure 14-2, wages rise in E occupations and fall in O occupations.

Labour-market discrimination, by changing equilibrium supply, decreases the wages of a group that is discriminated against and increases the wages of the "favoured" group.

In the longer run, further changes may occur. Employers that continue to discriminate against women may find ways to attract the slightly-below-average male workers away from the O occupations. Although this will raise O wages slightly, it will also make these occupations increasingly "female occupations." If discrimination has been in place for a sufficient length of time, women will learn that it does not pay to acquire above-average skills. Regardless of ability, women are forced by discrimination to work in unskilled jobs.

The final point to address regarding labour-market discrimination is whether discriminatory wage differentials are equilibrium or temporary differentials. The simple

FIGURE 14-2 The Effect of Discrimination on Wages

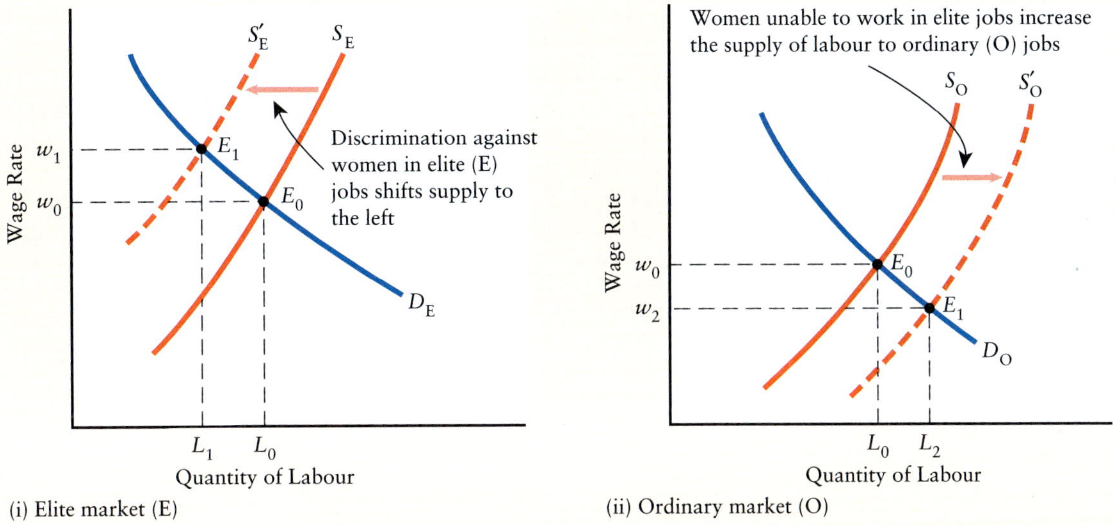

If market E discriminates against one group and market O does not, wages will rise in E and fall in O. Market E requires above-average skills, while market O requires only ordinary skills. When there is no discrimination, demand and supply are D_E and S_E in market E and D_O and S_O in market O. Initially, the wage rate is w_0 and employment is L_0 in each market. (w_0 in market E is higher than w_0 in market O because the workers in E have higher skills than those in O. This is an equilibrium wage differential.) When discrimination excludes women from E occupations, the supply curve shifts to S'_E, and the wage earned by the remaining workers, all of whom are men, rises to w_1. Women put out of work in the E occupations now seek work in the O occupations. The resulting shift in the supply curve to S'_O reduces the wage to w_2 in the O occupations. Because all women are in O occupations, they have a lower wage rate than many men. The average male wage in the economy is higher than the average female wage.

answer is that the differentials will persist as long as the discrimination itself persists. Consider three general cases.

In the first case, the discrimination is supported by government policy, as in the South African apartheid system in which blacks were prohibited by law from holding prestigious and high-paying jobs. In such cases, as long as the law remains in place, so too will the discriminating wage differentials. If political pressure forces a change in the law, as happened in South Africa in the 1980s and 1990s, the effects of the discrimination will be reversed, but it may take some time. In particular, it will take time for the once-discriminated-against individuals, who had little incentive to invest in their own human capital, to acquire the human capital necessary for them to qualify for the prestigious jobs. The effects of the legislated discrimination will linger beyond the policy itself.

In the second case, discrimination is not supported by official government policy but instead reflects the views of the firms' managers. In this case, there are economic pressures opposing the discrimination. For example, if some firms discriminate against even well-qualified women, our analysis in Figure 14-2 suggests there will be well-qualified women who can only find low-wage jobs. There is an incentive for other, non-discriminating, firms to hire these well-qualified women and thereby benefit from lower costs. If enough firms see this advantage, there will be an increase in demand for

The attitudes of many white customers were responsible for much discrimination against black people in the United States in the first few decades of the past century. As long as these attitudes persist, so will the discrimination, unless legislation forces a change.

well-qualified women, eventually reversing the effects of the initial discrimination.

In the third case, the cause of the discrimination is the preferences of the *customers*. Unlike the second case where the discrimination reflects the views of the firms' managers, there are no economic forces working to offset this customer-driven discrimination. As long as such discriminatory views persist, the discriminatory wage differentials will be sustained—only legislation or fundamental changes in customers' attitudes will reverse the situation. For many years, this was an important aspect of racial discrimination in the southern U.S. states, where many white customers were not prepared to have some services, such as haircuts, provided to them by blacks.

If discrimination is supported by governments or reflects the views of consumers, the discriminatory wage differentials will persist as long as the discrimination itself persists. If the discrimination only reflects the views of the firms' managers, the pursuit of profits generates economic forces that tend to reduce the discriminatory wage differentials.

myeconlab

Public officials often announce how their assistance to particular firms or industries will "create jobs." An understanding of wage differentials and the mobility of labour, however, suggests that governments may create fewer jobs than they think. For more details, look for "Do Government Job-Creation Programs Really Create Jobs?" in the *Additional Topics* section of this book's MyEconLab.

www.myeconlab.com

Wage Differentials in Non-Competitive Markets

We have examined several explanations for why wage differentials exist in competitive labour markets. Another explanation for wage differentials is that the labour market may *not* be competitive. In Chapters 9 through 11, we distinguished different *structures* for the markets in which firms sell their outputs. The inputs that firms use are also bought in markets that can have different structures. Although many factor markets are perfectly competitive, some show elements of market power on either the demand or the supply side.

To study the influence of different labour-market structures on wages, consider the case of an industry that employs identical workers for only one kind of job. In this way, we eliminate the possibility that any wage differentials are caused by differences between workers or differences between jobs—we thus highlight the role of market structure.

Let's examine two general cases. The first is one in which workers form a group and exercise some market power over setting the wage. This is a case in which a labour union acts as a monopoly seller of labour services. The second case is one in which a single firm is the only purchaser of labour—a *monopsony* firm in the labour market.

A Union in a Competitive Labour Market For the purposes of our discussion of labour markets, a **union** (or *labour union*) is an association that is authorized to represent workers in negotiations with their employers. We examine unions in greater detail later in this chapter. For now we take the simple view that when workers are represented by a labour union, there is only a single supplier of labour.

union An association authorized to represent workers in bargaining with employers. Also called a *labour union.*

As the single seller of labour for many buyers, the union is a monopolist, and it can establish a wage below which no one will work, thus changing the supply curve of labour. Firms can hire as many units of labour as are prepared to work at the union wage but no one at a lower wage. Thus, the industry as a whole (and each firm in the industry) faces a supply curve that is horizontal at the level of the union wage up to the maximum quantity of labour that is willing to work at that wage.

If the union uses its monopoly power, it will negotiate a wage above the competitive level. This situation is shown in Figure 14-3, in which the intersection of this horizontal supply curve and the demand curve establishes a higher wage rate and a lower level of employment than the competitive equilibrium. In this case, there will be some workers who would like to work in the unionized industry or occupation but cannot. A conflict of interest has been created between serving the interests of the union's employed and unemployed members.

monopsony A market structure in which there is a single buyer.

An alternative way to achieve the higher wage is to shift the supply curve to the left. The union may do this by restricting entry into the occupation by methods such as lengthening the required period of apprenticeship and reducing openings for trainees. The union could also shift the supply curve to the left by persuading the government to impose restrictive licensing or certification requirements on people who wish to work in certain occupations. The union might even lobby the government to implement restrictive immigration policies in an attempt to reduce the supply of labour to specific industries.

By restricting entry into the occupation or industry, unions can drive the wage above the competitive level. As a result, the level of employment will fall.

Raising wages by restricting entry is not limited to unions. It occurs, for example, with many professional groups, including doctors, architects, engineers, and lawyers. By limiting enrollments in professional programs at universities, the restricted supply of labour drives wages in these occupations higher than they would otherwise be.

A Monopsony Firm in the Labour Market A **monopsony** is a market in which there is only one buyer; monopsony is to the buying side of the market what monopoly is to the selling side. Although monopsony is not very common, it sometimes occurs in small towns that contain only one industry and often only one large plant or mine. For example, Iroquois Falls in Ontario and Pine Falls in Manitoba are small towns where the principal employer is a single firm that operates a newsprint plant. Although

FIGURE 14-3 A Union in a Competitive Labour Market

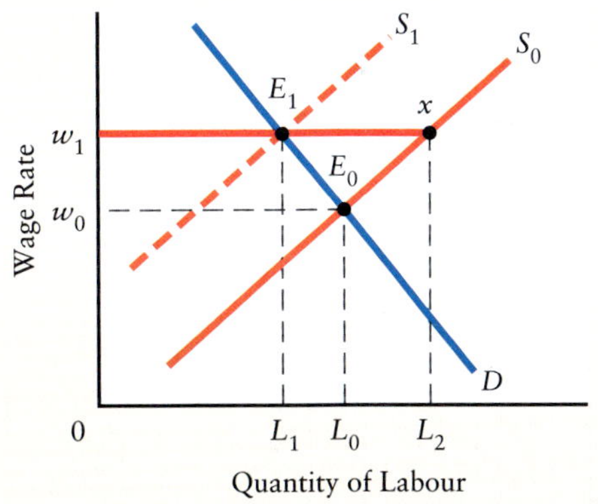

A union can raise the wages of people who continue to be employed but only by reducing the number of people employed. The competitive equilibrium is at E_0, the wage is w_0, and employment is L_0. If a monopoly union enters this market and sets a wage of w_1, a new equilibrium will be established at E_1. The supply curve has become w_1xS_0. At the new wage w_1, employment will be L_1, and there will be L_1L_2 workers who would like to work but whom the industry will not hire.

The wage w_1 can be achieved without generating a pool of unemployed persons. To do so, the union must restrict entry into the occupation and thus shift the supply curve to the left to S_1. Employment will again be L_1.

Practise with Study Guide Chapter 14, Exercise 2 and Extension Exercise E1.

both towns provide alternative sources of employment in retailing and service establishments, the large industrial employer has some monopsony power over the local labour market. In other cases, local labour markets may contain only a few large industrial employers. Individually, each has substantial market power, and if they act together, either explicitly or tacitly, they can behave as if they were a single monopsonist. Our analysis applies whenever employers have substantial monopsony power, but for concreteness, we consider a case in which the few firms operating in one labour market form an employers' hiring association in order to act as a single buying unit. We therefore refer to a single monopsonist.

Monopsony Without a Union. Suppose there are many potential workers and they are not members of a union. The monopsonist can offer any wage rate that it chooses, and the workers must either accept employment at that rate or find a different job.

Suppose the monopsonist decides to hire some specific quantity of labour. The labour supply curve shows the wage that it must offer. To the monopsonist, this wage is the *average cost* of labour. In deciding how much labour to hire, however, the monopsonist trying to maximize its profits is interested in the *marginal cost* of hiring additional workers. The monopsonist wants to know how much its total costs will increase as it takes on additional units of labour.

Whenever the supply curve of labour slopes upward, the marginal cost of employing extra units will exceed the average cost.

The marginal cost exceeds the wage paid (the average cost) because the increased wage rate necessary to attract an extra worker must also be paid to *everyone already employed.* [27] For example, assume that 100 workers are employed at $15.00 per hour and that to attract an extra worker, the wage must be raised to $15.25 per hour. The marginal cost of the 101st worker is not the $15.25 per hour paid to the worker but $40.25 per hour—made up of the extra 25 cents per hour paid to the 100 existing workers and $15.25 paid to the new worker. Thus, the marginal cost is $40.25, whereas the average cost is $15.25.

The profit-maximizing monopsonist will hire labour up to the point at which the marginal cost of labour just equals the amount that the firm is willing to pay for an additional unit of labour. That amount is determined by labour's marginal revenue product (*MRP*) and is shown by the demand curve illustrated in Figure 14-4.

FIGURE 14-4 Monopsony in a Labour Market

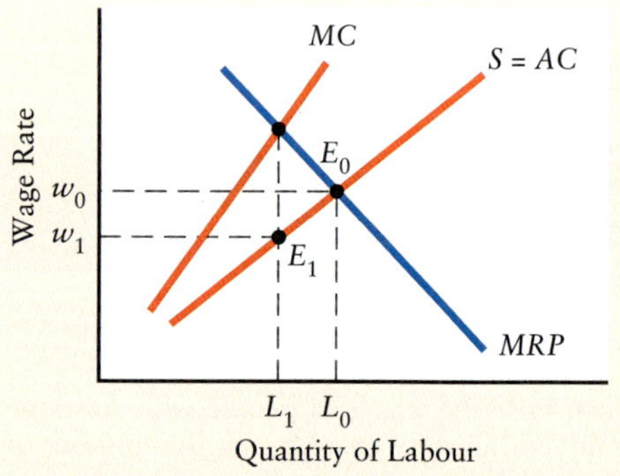

A profit-maximizing monopsonist lowers both the wage rate and employment below their competitive levels. *MRP* and *S* are the competitive demand and supply curves, respectively. The competitive equilibrium is E_0. The marginal cost of labour (*MC*) to the monopsonist is above the average cost. The monopsonistic firm maximizes profits at E_1. It hires only L_1 units of labour. At L_1, the marginal cost of the last worker is just equal to the amount that the worker adds to the firm's revenue, as shown by the demand curve. The wage that must be paid to get L_1 workers is only w_1.

The full exercise of monopsony power in a labour market will result in a lower level of employment and lower wages than would exist in a competitive labour market.

The intuitive explanation is that the monopsonistic employer is aware that by trying to purchase more, it is responsible for driving up the wage. If it wishes to maximize its profits it will therefore stop short of the point that is reached when workers are hired by many competitive firms, no one of which can exert a significant influence on the wage rate.

Monopsony with a Union. In situations where there is a single large firm in the labour market, workers often create or join a labour union so their collective market power can better match that of the firm. This situation is often referred to as *bilateral monopoly* since both sides of the market have considerable market power. In this case, the two sides will settle the wage through a process known as *collective bargaining*. The outcome of this bargaining process will depend on each side's objective and on the skill that each has in bargaining for its objective. We have seen that, left to itself, the profit-maximizing employer's organization will set the monopsonistic wage shown in Figure 14-4. To understand the possible outcomes for the wage after the monopoly union enters the market, let us ask what the union would do if it had the power to set the wage unilaterally. The result will give us insight into the union's objectives in the actual collective bargaining that does occur.

Practise with Study Guide Chapter 14, Exercise 3.

Suppose the union can set a wage below which its members will not work. Here, just as in the case of a wage-setting union in a competitive market, the union presents the employer with a horizontal supply curve (up to the maximum number of workers who will accept work at the union wage). As shown in Figure 14-5, if the union sets the wage above the monopsony wage but below the competitive wage, the union can raise *both* wages and employment above the monopsonistic level.

However, the union may not be content merely to neutralize the monopsonist's market power. It may choose to raise wages further above the competitive level. If it does, the outcome will be similar to that shown in Figure 14-3. If the wage is raised above the competitive level, the employer will no longer wish to hire all the labour that is offered at that wage. The amount of employment will fall, and unemployment will develop. These changes are also shown in Figure 14-5.

We now know that the profit-maximizing employer would like to set the monopsonistic wage (w_1) while the union would like a wage *no less than* the competitive wage (w_0). (Any wage below w_0 will reduce *both* wages and employment.) The union may target a still higher wage, depending on how it trades off employment losses against wage gains. If the union is content with an amount of employment as low as would occur at the monopsonistic wage, it could target a wage substantially higher than the competitive wage.

Simple demand and supply analysis can take us no further. The actual outcome will depend on such other things as what target wage the two sides actually set for themselves, their relative bargaining skills, and how each side assesses the costs of concessions. We discuss unions in more detail in the next section of this chapter.

FIGURE 14-5 Bilateral Monopoly in the Labour Market

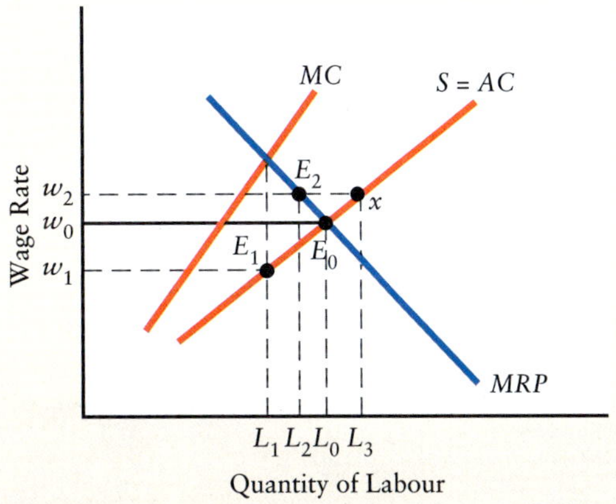

By presenting a monopsonistic employer with a fixed wage, the union can raise both wages and employment over the monopsonistic level. The monopsony position before the union enters is at E_1 (from Figure 14-4), with a wage rate of w_1 and L_1 workers hired. A union now enters and sets the wage at w_0. The supply curve of labour becomes w_0E_0S, and wages and employment rise to their competitive levels of w_0 and L_0 without creating a pool of unemployed workers. If the wage is raised further, say, to w_2, the supply curve will become w_2xS, the quantity of employment will fall below the competitive level to L_2, and a pool of unsuccessful job applicants of L_2L_3 will develop.

Legislated Minimum Wages

We have examined wage differentials arising in competitive and non-competitive labour markets. Government policy can also affect observed wage differentials by legislating minimum wages. Governments in Canada and many other countries legislate specific **minimum wages**, which define the lowest wage rates that may legally be paid. In 2006, minimum wages ranged from \$6.50 per hour in New Brunswick and Newfoundland and Labrador to \$8.50 per hour in Nunavut.

minimum wages Legally specified minimum rate of pay for labour.

For a large proportion of all employment covered by the law, the minimum wage is below the actual market wage, and thus in such cases the minimum wage is *not binding*. Some workers, however, are employed in industries in which the free-market wage would be below the legal minimum, and thus the legislated minimum wage is *binding*. It is only in these cases where the effects of minimum wages are of interest.

Although legislated minimum wages are now an accepted part of the labour scene in Canada and many other industrialized countries, many economists are skeptical about the benefits from such a policy. As our analysis in Chapter 5 indicated, a binding price floor in a competitive market leads to a market surplus of the product—in this case, an excess supply of labour, or unemployment. Thus, theory predicts that a policy that legislates minimum wages in an otherwise competitive market will benefit some workers only by hurting others. In the cases of non-competitive labour markets, however, the analysis is a little more complicated.

For interesting information on labour-market policies in Canada, see the website for Human Resources and Social Development: **www.hrsdc.gc.ca**. Click on "Labour Programs."

Theoretical Effects of a Minimum Wage Minimum-wage laws usually apply uniformly to almost all occupations, but they will be *binding* only in the lowest-paid occupations and industries, which often involve unskilled or semi-skilled workers. These workers are usually not members of labour unions. Thus, the situations in which minimum wages are likely to be binding include competitive labour markets and those in which employers exercise some monopsony power. The effects on employment are different in the two cases.

Practise with Study Guide Chapter 14, Exercise 1.

Competitive Labour Markets. The predicted consequences for employment of a binding minimum wage are unambiguous when the labour market is competitive. By raising the wage that employers must pay, minimum-wage legislation leads to a reduction in the quantity of labour that is demanded and an increase in the quantity of labour that is supplied. As a result, the actual level of employment falls, and unemployment rises. The excess supply of labour at the minimum wage also creates incentives for people to evade the law by working "under the table" at wages below the legal minimum wage. The predicted effect of a minimum wage in a competitive labour market is shown in part (i) of Figure 14-6.

Many workers in the fast-food industry are young and earn the legislated minimum wage. To the extent that the minimum wage is effective, they get more than they would in its absence, while there is mixed evidence regarding the effects on the overall level of employment.

Firms with Monopsony Power. Our theory predicts that the minimum-wage law can simultaneously increase both wages and employment in markets in which firms have monopsony power. In part (ii) of Figure 14-6, the monopsony wage is w_1. If the minimum wage pushes the wage up only slightly, to w_2, both employment and wages will rise. But beyond the competitive wage (w^*), further increases in the minimum wage will begin to decrease employment and create a pool of unemployed workers.

FIGURE 14-6 The Effects of Legislated Minimum Wages

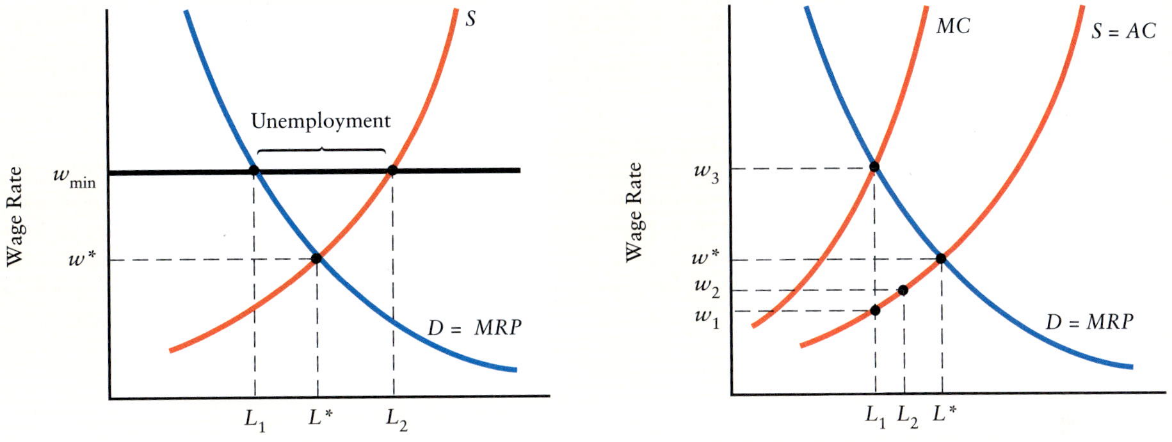

(i) Competitive labour market

(ii) Firms have monopsony power

Minimum wages are predicted to reduce employment in competitive labour markets; the predicted effects on employment in monopsonistic labour markets are less clear. Part (i) shows a competitive labour market with the competitive equilibrium at w^* and L^*. A binding minimum wage raises the wage to w_{min}. Firms respond by reducing employment to L_1. The quantity of labour supplied by workers increases to L_2. Unemployment is equal to L_1L_2 workers.

Part (ii) shows a labour market in which firms behave as a monopsonist. The monopsony equilibrium is w_1 and L_1. If the minimum wage is set at w_2, employment will rise to L_2. If the minimum wage is set as high as the competitive wage w^*, employment rises to the competitive level L^*. But if the minimum wage rises above w^*, employment will fall below L^*. If the minimum wage were set above w_3, employment would fall below the monopsony level, L_1.

Evidence on the Effects of Minimum Wages Empirical research on the effects of minimum-wage laws reflects these mixed theoretical predictions. There is some evidence that people who keep their jobs gain when the minimum wage is raised. There is some evidence that some groups suffer a decline in employment consistent with raising the wage in a fairly competitive market. At other times and places, there is evidence that both wages and employment rise when the minimum wage rises, consistent with labour markets in which employers have monopsony power.

Some widely discussed research in the United States has produced hotly debated results. David Card, from Berkeley, and Alan Krueger, from Princeton University, traced the effects of minimum-wage increases in California during 1988 and New Jersey during 1992 and found that substantial rises in these states' minimum wages not only increased wages but also were associated with small employment *gains* for teenagers. Card and Krueger argue that these findings are inconsistent with a competitive labour market and thus take the results as evidence in support of the view that firms have some monopsony power in the labour market.

The Card and Krueger results have been criticized by many economists in the last few years. One criticism is that some of the data used by Card and Krueger are faulty, and that their conclusions are therefore suspect. Another relates to the short span of time covered by their study. The argument is that firms will not immediately reduce the

APPLYING ECONOMIC CONCEPTS 14-1

The Puzzle of Interindustry Wage Differentials in Canada

Differences in wages across industries have been observed for as long as information on wages has been collected. But only recently have economists examined carefully whether they can be explained by differences in skills, jobs, or market structure. In Canada, a study published by Surendra Gera and Gilles Grenier shows the extent of these wage differentials in 1986.*

The table shows results from their study for selected industries; for each industry, the number in the table shows the industry's *wage premium*—that is, the amount by which wages in each industry exceed the average after controlling for such factors as the worker's education, age, gender, occupation, union status, and so on. The challenge is to explain such wage premia.

Competitive Wage Differentials?

Following our discussion in the text, three possible explanations of these wage differentials are consistent with the labour market being competitive.

The first possibility is that these observed wage differentials for 1986 may reflect temporary shifts in the pattern of labour demand or supply across industries. For example, a large increase in demand in the forestry industry that occurs together with a large decline in demand in the textiles industry could account for some of the data in the table. To address this possible explanation, Gera and Grenier examine Canadian Census data for 1970, 1980, and 1985. They find that the pattern of interindustry wage differentials is very similar across these three periods, suggesting that the observed wage differentials are not simply temporary phenomena.

The second possibility is that the wage differentials can be explained by differences in the quality of the workers that are not observable to economists when conducting such a study. For example, they are not able to observe whether a worker is "highly motivated," "innovative," or "a good problem solver." But many of these characteristics *are* observable to potential employers, either by watching the individual work for a short period of time or by asking previous employers who know the worker. To examine this explanation, Gera and Grenier examine the group of individuals in their sample that move from a job in one industry to a job in a different industry. For example, if high wages to a particular worker in the tobacco industry are due to that worker's unobserved skills, then when that worker switches to the clothing industry, the high wage should persist. But Gera and Grenier find the opposite. A worker who moves from a high-wage industry to a low-

Selected Industry Wage Premia in Canada (percentage above average wage)

Tobacco Products	33.4
Mineral Fuels	25.5
Forestry	18.9
Electric Power, Gas, and Water Utilities	14.4
Paper and Allied Products	12.0
Communications	10.5
Transportation Equipment	7.0
Wholesale Trade	3.8
Electrical Products	2.6
Education and Related Services	−1.0
Food and Beverages	−3.5
Insurance and Real Estate Agencies	−4.1
Clothing	−8.1
Fishing and Trapping	−9.5
Personal Services	−16.7
Retail Trade	−11.1
Textiles	−19.0
Accommodation and Food Services	−20.3

*S. Gera and G. Grenier, "Interindustry Wage Differentials and Efficiency Wages: Some Canadian Evidence," *Canadian Journal of Economics,* 1994. © 2002–2007 Canadian Economics Association.

wage industry tends to suffer a fall in wage; similarly, a worker who moves from a low-wage industry to a high-wage industry tends to experience a rise in the wage. This finding suggests that the observed wage differentials are not due mainly to unobserved labour quality.

The final possible explanation consistent with a competitive labour market is that the observed wage differentials reflect different characteristics of the *jobs*. Maybe the jobs in the high-wage industries are less pleasant jobs—longer hours, less job security, less safe—than those in the low-wage industries. Gera and Grenier offer two pieces of evidence against this explanation. First, they note that workers in *similar occupations* receive very different wages in different industries, and it is difficult to believe that working conditions for, say, a clerk are very different in the tobacco industry than in the textiles industry. Second, if the observed wage differentials reflect just different job characteristics, then in competitive equilibrium workers are indifferent between (pleasant) jobs in the low-wage industries and (unpleasant) jobs in the high-wage industries. Yet workers appear to quit jobs in the high-wage industries much less frequently than they quit jobs in the low-wage industries. In other words, workers *appear* to view the high-wage jobs as valuable relative to the low-wage jobs. This phenomenon suggests that the observed wage differentials are reflecting more than just differences in working conditions.

Other Explanations?

Maybe the explanation for these observed wage differentials lies in a non-competitive market structure. Perhaps unions have a large presence in some industries and little or no presence in others. When Gera and Grenier examine this possibility, they find that the interindustry wage differentials are just as marked among unionized workers as they are among non-unionized workers.

If the observed wage differentials across Canadian industries cannot be explained by considering different characteristics of the workers, jobs, or market structures, what is the explanation? One possible explanation is based on the theory of *efficiency wages*. According to this theory, firms in even a competitive labour market may find it profitable to pay *more* than the competitive wage to their workers. Firms do this because they perceive that a higher wage will make their workers more productive. Since workers are receiving more than is required to attract their services, they are earning *economic rents* (a concept that we examined in Chapter 13). The fact that workers are receiving rents, in turn, explains why they are reluctant to leave these good jobs—and thus their quit rates from such jobs are low.

Though the efficiency-wage theory offers one possible explanation for why some workers might earn rents, it does not directly offer an explanation for why these rents might be different across industries. In order for the efficiency-wage theory to explain the observed interindustry wage differentials, it must explain why firms' incentives to pay higher wages are greater in some industries than in others. So far, proponents of the theory have not come up with convincing reasons.

The efficiency-wage theory generates considerable disagreement among economists. But there is little debate that there exist significant wage differentials across industries, even after taking account of observable characteristics of workers and jobs. As more data become available, perhaps economists will find better explanations for the observed interindustry wage differentials.

Workers in the forestry industry receive wages roughly 20 percent higher than workers of similar ages and skills in the average industry.

level of employment in response to an increase in the minimum wage—they will instead choose *not to replace* workers who leave their jobs in the natural turnover process that occurs in labour markets. But workers who are receiving the minimum wage may be more reluctant to leave their job after an increase in their wage, thereby reducing this natural turnover. Thus, it is not surprising to see few employment losses (or slight gains) when one examines the labour market immediately before and immediately after the change in legislation. Proponents of this view argue that the total employment effects of minimum wages can be detected only by examining the data over longer periods of time.

Several Canadian studies have examined the relationship between minimum wages and employment (or unemployment). Though the studies differ in their approaches and data used, there is a broad consensus that minimum wages decrease the level of employment (and raise unemployment), particularly for low-skilled workers. Since workers with few skills often earn only low wages, a binding minimum wage has a larger impact on the employment prospects of these workers than it does for higher-skilled, higher-wage workers. In this sense, the Canadian results confirm the theoretical predictions of the effects of minimum wages in competitive labour markets. In these cases, the wage gains by the majority of workers who retain their jobs must be set against the loss of employment by a smaller group of workers.

A Final Word

We have examined several explanations for why some workers get paid more than others. The explanations include differences in workers' educations and skills, differences in job characteristics, discrimination, and differences in the structure of the various labour markets. But this apparent abundance of explanations should not lead you to believe that economists understand *all* wage differentials observed in the labour market. Recent studies, both in Canada and in the United States, have revealed significant differences in wages across industries that appear to defy explanations based on the sorts of arguments we have examined. *Applying Economic Concepts 14-1* discusses the continuing puzzle of interindustry wage differentials in Canada.

FIGURE 14-7 Union Membership in Canada, 1921–2002

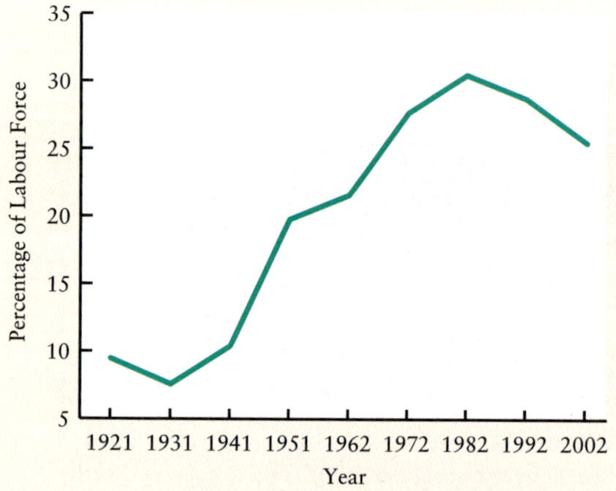

As a share of the labour force, the number of union members has increased significantly over the past century, but has declined since the 1980s. The large increases in Canadian unionization occurred during and after the Second World War, and during the 1960s.

(*Source:* Most recent data are available at the website for Human Resources and Social Development Canada: www.hrsdc.gc.ca. © Public Works and Government Services Canada.)

14.2 LABOUR UNIONS

Unions currently represent about 25 percent of the labour force in Canada. Of those workers employed in the public sector, however, approximately two-thirds are unionized. Figure 14-7 shows how union membership has changed in Canada over the past several decades. Table 14-1 shows unionization rates by industry. As is clear from the table, unionization is most common in the public and educational sectors and least common in agriculture, finance, and trade.

Despite the relatively low degree of unionization among Canada's private-sector workers, unions have a considerable influence in the private sector. One reason is the impact that union wage contracts have on other labour markets. When, for example, the Canadian Auto Workers negotiates a new contract with an automobile producer in Oshawa, its provisions set a pattern that directly or indirectly affects other labour markets, both in Ontario and in other provinces. A second reason is the major leadership role that unions have played in the past 50 years in the development of labour market practices and in lobbying for legislation that applies to all workers.

In this section, we discuss the process of *collective bargaining* and, in particular, examine the inherent conflict that unions face between striving for higher wages and for increasing employment. *Lessons From History 14-1* examines the historical development of labour unions in Canada.

TABLE 14-1 Unionization Rates by Industry, 2005

Industry	Union Density (membership as percentage of paid workers)	
Goods Producing		**29.6**
Agriculture	6.8	
Natural Resources	21.5	
Utilities	66.8	
Construction	29.9	
Manufacturing	29.6	
Services Producing		**30.1**
Trade	13.1	
Transportation and Warehousing	41.3	
Finance, Insurance, and Real Estate	8.3	
Management and Administrative	12.5	
Education	68.2	
Health Care	53.0	
Public Administration	68.1	
Total Canadian Economy		**30.0**

There is considerable variation across Canadian industries in the extent of unionization. The public sector and the educational services sector are the most unionized; agriculture, finance, and trade are the least unionized.

(*Source:* Statistics Canada, *Perspectives on Labour and Income,* Catalogue no. 75-001. Reprinted with permission of Statistics Canada.)

Collective Bargaining

The process by which unions and employers reach an agreement is known as **collective bargaining.** This process has an important difference from the theoretical models that we discussed in the previous section. In those models, we assumed that the union had the power to set the wage unilaterally; the employer then decided how much labour to hire. In actual collective bargaining, however, the firm and union typically bargain over the wage (as well as other aspects of the employment relationship such as fringe benefits, working conditions, overtime conditions, and flexibility in scheduling). There is usually a substantial range over which an agreement can be reached, and the actual result in particular cases will depend on the strengths of the two bargaining parties and on the skill of their negotiators.

collective bargaining The process by which unions and employers arrive at and enforce agreements.

To see the possible outcomes, refer back to Figure 14-5. It may be that the firm wants the wage to be w_1 and the union wants the wage to be w_2. Depending on each side's market power, and on their bargaining tactics, the final agreed-upon wage may be anywhere in between. Note that while actual collective bargaining has the firm and union bargaining over the wage, it is typically the case that the firm retains the "right to manage"—meaning that the firm can decide how much labour it wants to employ at the negotiated wage.

Wages Versus Employment Unions seek many goals when they bargain with management. They may push for higher wages, higher fringe benefits, or less onerous working conditions. Many unions in Canada also emphasize the importance of "job security," meaning a commitment by the firm not to lay workers off in the event of a downturn in business conditions. Firms, however, are understandably reluctant to promise such security since reducing their workforce is an effective way to reduce costs when business conditions deteriorate.

LESSONS FROM HISTORY 14-1

The Development of Unions in Canada

Early Canadian unionization was strongly dominated by the influence of international unions, which had their headquarters and an overwhelming proportion of their membership outside Canada. The creation of Canadian locals of American unions began in the 1860s. By 1911, 90 percent of Canadian workers who were union members belonged to international unions.

During the first half of the twentieth century, there was strong pressure: first, toward a single national federation; and second, to achieve autonomy from American unions. The issues became intertwined when conflicts in the United States arose between craft and industrial unions. Until the 1930s, *craft unions*—which cover persons in a particular occupation—were the characteristic form of collective action in the United States. In Canada, meanwhile, trade unionists were attracted to *industrial unions* that embraced unskilled workers as well as skilled craftsmen in one industry such as steel making, forest products, or railways.

Because of the impossibility of establishing bargaining strength by controlling the supply of unskilled workers, the rise of industrial unionism in Canada was associated with political action as an alternative means of improving the lot of the membership. In general, social and political reform were given much more emphasis by Canadian unionists than by their American counterparts. Political action here extended to the support for social democratic political parties: first, the Co-operative Commonwealth Federation (CCF), established in 1932, and later its successor, the New Democratic Party (NDP), formed in 1961.

The late senator Eugene Forsey, a former director of research for the Canadian Labour Congress (CLC), viewed the unification of the bulk of Canadian unions under the CLC in 1956 as the beginning of virtual autonomy for Canadian locals from their U.S. head offices. Throughout the postwar period, the percentage of total Canadian union membership represented by international unions fell: In the mid-1950s, it was about 70 percent, and by the mid-1990s, it was just over 30 percent.

One factor in the increased share of national unions is the growth of membership in the two unions representing government workers: the Canadian Union of Public Employees and the Public Service Alliance. Another major component of non-international union membership has arisen out of the distinct aspirations of French-Canadian workers. More recently, the formation of the Canadian Auto Workers, independent of the American Auto Workers, represented a significant further reduction of membership in international unions.

Rapid gains in union membership in Canada occurred in the years during the Second World War. This led to pressure for the rights of workers to organize and to elect an exclusive bargaining agent. These rights were established by provisions of the *Wartime Labour Relations Regulations Act* of 1944.

The Winnipeg General Strike of 1919 began a wave of increased unionism and militancy across Canada.

Whatever unions' specific goals, unless they face a monopsonist across the bargaining table, they must deal with a fundamental dilemma.

There is an inherent conflict between the level of wages and the size of the union itself.

The more successful a union is in raising wages, the more management will reduce the size of its workforce, substituting capital for labour. This will lead to lower union membership. However, if the union does not provide some wage improvement for its members, they will have little incentive to stay around.

The Union Wage Premium Despite the costs to unions (i.e., reduced membership) of pushing for higher wages, there is clear evidence in Canada of a *union wage premium*—that is, a higher wage attributed only to the union status of the job. It is not easy to measure this wage premium, however, because it is not appropriate simply to compare the average wage of unionized workers with the average wage of non-unionized workers. After all, unions may occur mainly in industries where workers have higher skills or where working conditions are less pleasant. And we know from the first section of this chapter that differences in skills or working conditions can lead to wage differentials. Economists have therefore been forced to use complicated statistical techniques to identify this union wage premium. The consensus appears to be that the union wage premium in Canada is somewhere between 10 and 15 percent—that is, unionized workers with a particular set of skills in particular types of jobs get paid 10 to 15 percent more than *otherwise identical workers* who are not members of unions.

For information on the Canadian labour movement, see the website for the Canadian Labour Congress: **www.clc.org**.

Unionized workers earn, on average, between 10 and 15 percent higher wages than non-unionized workers with similar characteristics.

There is also evidence that the size of this union wage premium differs across industries. Given that workers in different industries and with different occupations are often represented by different unions, this cross-industry difference in the union wage premium may simply reflect the differences in unions' preferences for higher wages versus higher employment.

Employment Effects of Unions We said earlier that unions face an inherent conflict between the level of wages and the level of employment. This conflict simply reflects the firm's profit-maximizing behaviour as embodied in its downward-sloping demand curve for labour. As the union pushes for higher wages, the firm naturally chooses to hire fewer workers.

What continues to puzzle economists, however, is how the clear evidence of a 10- to 15-percent union wage premium can be consistent with a second empirical result—the absence of any clear effect on employment. One possible explanation for the absence of an employment effect is that unions use the collective bargaining process to pressure firms to hire more workers than they otherwise would. This practice is known as *featherbedding*, and for years was infamous in the railways where union contracts required the railways to hire firemen (whose job was to keep the coal fires burning) long after the widespread adoption of diesel locomotives.

If such featherbedding is pervasive in unionized firms, it may be the explanation for the absence of an observable union effect on employment. The employment reduction caused by the higher wage may be offset by the employment increase due to featherbedding.

Another possible explanation for the absence of a union employment effect is union campaigns to increase the demand for the goods produced by their members. We sometimes see labels on products that proclaim them to be "union made" or "made with union labour." Unions also spend considerably on magazine and television advertising stressing the value of union labour. Some unions also lobby the government to restrict the import of foreign-made products in an attempt to increase Canadian consumers' demand for the domestic goods made with union labour. To the extent that these campaigns convince consumers to buy more union-made products than they otherwise would, the result will be an increase in demand for union labour.

Figure 14-8 shows how the combination of the union wage premium and the increases in demand for union labour (either through featherbedding or advertising) can explain the *absence* of an observed union employment effect.

FIGURE 14-8 The Union Employment Effect

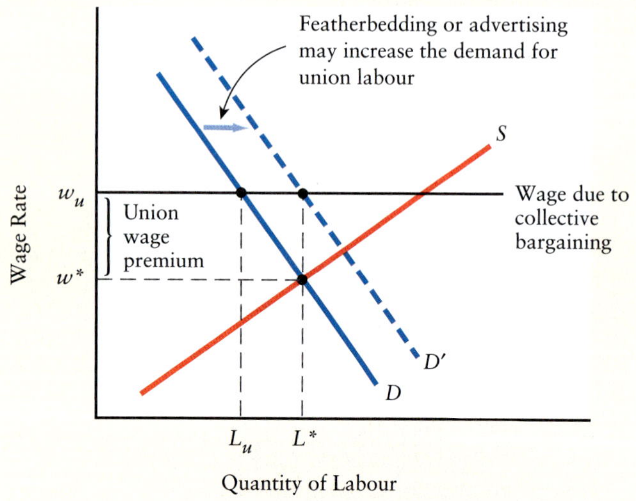

Featherbedding and advertising may explain the absence of a union employment effect even though there is a clear union wage effect. If the labour market is competitive, wages and employment will be given by w^* and L^*. The collective bargaining between firms and unions results in a wage of w_u, showing a clear premium above the competitive wage. If the demand for labour remains at *D*, employment would fall to L_u and there would be a reduction in employment caused by the union. If the collective agreement requires firms to use more labour, however, or if the union successfully promotes union-made products, the demand for labour shifts to *D′*. In this case, the combination of the higher wage and the greater demand for labour results in the competitive level of employment.

Unanswered Questions

Labour unions have played a significant role in the economies of Canada, the United States, and Europe for many years. It is therefore surprising how little economists actually know about how unions influence economic outcomes and, in particular, how unions affect long-run productivity.

Unions may reduce long-run productivity through a process known as the *hold-up* of capital. Much physical capital, once it is installed, is very difficult to move or resell. For this reason, *installed* capital has a very inelastic supply and, following the discussion from Chapter 13, a large part of its factor payment takes the form of economic rent. The union may be able to extract these rents from the firm in the form of higher wages. That is, once the firm has already installed its capital equipment the union may be able to *hold up* the firm by forcing it to pay higher wages; the firm is stuck with its installed capital and thus pays the higher wages and, in turn, receives lower profits. If firms are forward-looking, however, they can anticipate this sort of behaviour from unions *before* making such investments in physical capital. The possibility of being held up by union wage demands reduces the expected profitability of investment and may result in a reduction in investment. This decision to invest less would likely have negative implications for productivity growth in the industry.

There is some empirical evidence that the presence of a union does reduce investment by firms. It is not yet clear, however, whether such reduced investment has long-term effects on productivity. This issue is currently unresolved.

14.3 THE "GOOD JOBS–BAD JOBS" DEBATE

Figure 14-9 shows how the composition of Canadian employment has changed over the past century. The share of total employment in agriculture fell from 45 percent in 1891 to just over 2 percent today, while the share of total employment in services (including government) increased from 20 percent in 1891 to just over 75 percent today. The combined share for manufacturing and construction has been more variable over the last century, but has been on a clear downward trend for the past 50 years, falling from about 35 percent in 1951 to about 20 percent today.

The rise of service-sector employment, and the decline in the relative importance of the agriculture and manufacturing sectors as providers of jobs, is not just a

FIGURE 14-9 A Century of Change in the Composition of Canadian Employment

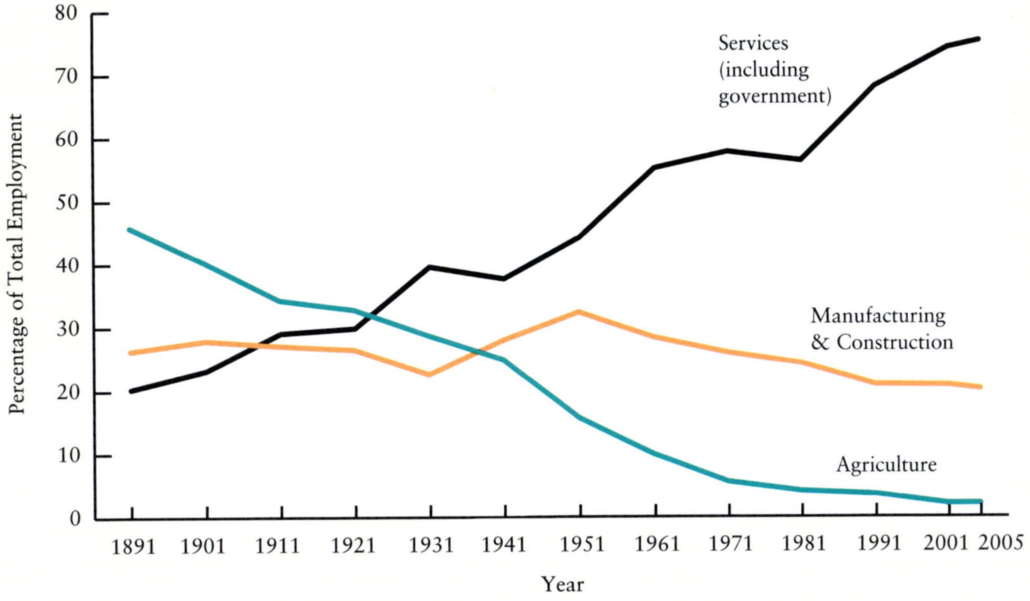

Over the past century, major shifts in employment have taken place between sectors of the economy. In 1891, over 45 percent of Canadian employment was in agriculture, and only 20 percent in services (including government). By 2005, agriculture accounted for only 2.1 percent of employment, while services had increased to over 75 percent. The share of employment in manufacturing and construction increased from 26 percent in 1891 to 32 percent just after the Second World War, and then declined back to 20 percent by 2005.

(*Source: Canadian Census*, various years, and authors' calculations. The most recent data are available on the Statistics Canada website at www.statcan.ca. Search for "Employment," and then choose "Employment by industry." Reprinted with permission of Statistics Canada.)

Canadian phenomenon—it has happened in all developed economies. Table 14-2 shows the percentage of total employment provided by the service sector in several developed countries in 2004.

The service sector contains an enormous variety of occupations. Many jobs in the service sector require considerable education and training and thus the workers in these jobs are highly paid. Obvious examples include lawyers, doctors, architects, design engineers, accountants, management consultants, and professors. On the other hand, the service sector also contains many jobs that require much less training and whose workers therefore receive much lower wages. Examples of these occupations include many

TABLE 14-2 The Importance of Service-Sector Employment, 2004

Country	Percentage of Employment in Services
Australia	74.9
Belgium	73.1
Canada	75.0
France	72.6
Japan	67.1
Sweden	75.2
United Kingdom	76.4
United States	78.4

(*Source: OECD in Figures*, 2005 Edition, www.oecd.org.)

restaurant waiters, fast-food employees, store clerks, flight attendants, telephone solicitors, janitors, and hotel maids.

In general, we can divide service-sector employment into two parts—the first part containing highly paid jobs and the second containing mostly low-wage jobs. The concerns sometimes heard about the growing importance of service-sector jobs are really concerns about this low-wage part of the service sector. In these jobs—many of which are in the retail sector—there are fewer possibilities for using more capital per worker, and thus fewer possibilities to increase the productivity of labour. Another concern is that many of these low-wage service-sector jobs offer workers little in the way of advancement or job security.

Are these dramatic changes in the composition of employment worrying? Is there something undesirable about the fact that fewer workers are now producing manufactured goods than forty years ago? Or that more workers are working in the service sector than forty years ago? Are good jobs being replaced by bad jobs? This final section of the chapter addresses this contentious issue.

Five Observations

There are five observations about the economy and the labour market that we must make when addressing the issue of the relative decline of manufacturing employment and the simultaneous rise of service-sector employment.

First, we need to keep a sense of perspective about the emergence of service-sector jobs. As is clear in Figure 14-9, this trend has been going on for many decades, yet real income per hour worked has been rising throughout this period; as a nation, Canadians are getting richer, not poorer.

Second, keep in mind that even the lowest-paying service jobs play an important role in the Canadian economy. The fast-food industry is often held up as an example of an industry in which employers provide bad jobs—low wages and little job security—to their workers. It *is* true that wages are low in this industry and, due to the part-time nature of the jobs, there are often no benefits and no job security. But it is also true that the vast majority of workers in the fast-food industry have little formal training and are between the ages of 15 and 20. Firms in this industry often provide young workers with their first paid jobs, helping them get their "foot in the door" of the labour market. After this first job, in which they acquire some skills and demonstrate responsibility, many young workers move on to jobs that are more demanding and for which they would not have qualified before their experience in the fast-food industry. In other words, some low-paying service-sector jobs provide employment to young, untrained individuals who would otherwise find it difficult to find a job at all.

Third, relating directly to the manufacturing sector, the decrease in the share of manufacturing in total employment is largely a result of that sector's dynamism. More and more manufactured goods have been produced by fewer and fewer workers, leaving more workers to produce services. This movement is analogous to the one out of agriculture in the twentieth century. At the turn of the twentieth century, nearly 45 percent of the Canadian labour force worked on farms. Today that number is just over 2 percent, yet they produce more total output than did the 45 percent in 1900. This movement away from agricultural employment

The reduction in manufacturing employment is partly the result of that sector's dynamism—more and more output can be produced with fewer and fewer workers.

freed workers to move into manufacturing, raising our living standards and transforming our way of life. In like manner, the movement away from manufacturing has been freeing workers to move into services, and by replacing the grimy blue-collar jobs of the smokestack industries with more pleasant white-collar jobs in the service industries, it has once again transformed our way of life.

Fourth, the decrease in the share of manufacturing in total employment also follows from consumers' tastes. Just as consumers in the first half of the century did not want to go on consuming more and more food products as their incomes rose, today's consumers do not wish to spend all of their additional income on manufactured products. Households have chosen to spend a high proportion of their increased incomes on services, thus creating employment opportunities in that sector. This simply reflects the fact that many products of the service sector—like restaurant meals, hotel stays, and airline flights—are products that have a high income elasticity of demand. Thus, as the income of the average Canadian household increases, so too does that household's demand for these products of the service sector.

Finally, it is easy to underestimate the scope for quality, quantity, and productivity increases in services. But these changes permit us to have a higher standard of living than we would otherwise have. As just one example of productivity increases, consider your ability to make an automatic cash withdrawal, at any time of the day or night, from your bank account in Nova Scotia, while you are on vacation in Brazil. Now compare that to the apprehension your parents faced 35 years ago when they had to get to their bank branch before 3:00 p.m. on a Friday afternoon to make sure they had enough cash for the weekend. It would have been simply impossible for them to cash a cheque in Brazil without having made elaborate prior arrangements.

Also, many quality improvements in services go unrecorded. Today's hotel room is vastly more comfortable than a hotel room of 40 years ago, yet this quality improvement does not show up in our national income statistics. Measuring such technological improvements is even more difficult when they take the form of entirely new products. Airline transportation, telecommunication, fast-food chains, and financial services are prominent examples. The resulting increase in output is not always properly captured in existing statistics.

A Mixed Blessing?

It is easy to become concerned when looking at the official statistics, which show low wages earned in some service jobs. Indeed, the shift in employment toward services is, like most changes that hit the economy, a mixed blessing. It entails a significant increase in the number of "bad" service-sector jobs with low pay or low job security. Further, such transitions often generate temporary unemployment as workers get laid off from a shrinking manufacturing sector and only slowly find jobs in the expanding service sector. Such transitions suggest a role for government policy to maintain the income of those workers temporarily unemployed (we will discuss employment insurance and other income-support programs in Chapter 18). However, if we focus on the *overall economy,* and consider the growth in the real living standards of the *average* Canadian household, we are reminded that average real income has continued to rise, not only throughout the shift from agriculture to manufacturing, but also throughout the shift from manufacturing to services. There is little reason to think that the continued growth of the service sector will stand in the way of this slow but steady improvement in Canadians' living standards.

SUMMARY

14.1 WAGE DIFFERENTIALS

LO 1 2 3

- In a competitive labour market, wages are set by the forces of supply and demand. Differences in wages will arise because some skills are more valued than others, because some jobs are more onerous than others, because of varying amounts of human capital, and because of discrimination based on such factors as gender and race.
- A union entering a competitive market can act as a monopolist and can raise wages, but at a predicted cost of reducing employment.
- A profit-maximizing monopsonistic employer entering a competitive labour market will reduce both the wage and the level of employment.
- A union in a monopsonistic labour market—a case of bilateral monopoly—may increase both employment and wages relative to the pure monopsony outcome. If the union sets wages above the competitive level, however, the prediction is that it will create a pool of workers who are unable to get the jobs that they want at the going wage.
- Governments set some wages above their competitive levels by passing minimum-wage laws. In competitive labour markets, a minimum wage is predicted to reduce employment and create some unemployment. In monopsonistic labour markets, a legislated minimum wage (as long as it is not too high) can raise both wages and employment.

14.2 LABOUR UNIONS

LO 4

- Labour unions seek many goals when they bargain with management. They may push for higher wages, higher fringe benefits, more stable employment, or less onerous working conditions. Whatever their specific goals, unless they face a monopsonist across the bargaining table, they must recognize the inherent conflict between the level of wages and the size of the union itself.
- There is clear evidence in Canada of a union wage premium: Unionized workers with a particular set of skills in particular types of jobs get paid 10 to 15 percent more than otherwise identical workers who are not union members.

14.3 THE "GOOD JOBS–BAD JOBS" DEBATE

LO 4

- The past half-century has witnessed an increase in the share of total employment in the service sector and a decline in the share of employment in manufacturing. One part of the service sector requires considerable skills and pays high wages, another part requires few skills and pays low wages. Some people are concerned that some "good" manufacturing jobs are being replaced by "bad" service jobs.
- The decline in manufacturing employment is partly due to the technological improvements in that sector and partly due to shifts in consumers' tastes toward services.
- Though the shift away from manufacturing and toward services involves some costs during the transition period, the ongoing growth in average per capita income (plus the hard-to-measure quality improvements) suggests that the shift is not a problem for the economy as a whole.

KEY CONCEPTS

Wage differentials in competitive labour markets
Effects of discrimination on wages and employment
Labour unions as monopolists
Single employer as monopsonist
Bilateral monopoly
Effects of legislated minimum wages
Collective bargaining
Union goals: wages versus employment
Union wage premium
"Good jobs" vs. "bad jobs"

STUDY EXERCISES

1. Fill in the blanks to make the following statements correct.

   a. If all workers were identical, all jobs had identical working conditions, and labour markets were perfectly competitive, then all wages would be __________.

   b. In reality there is wide variation in wages. Four reasons for wage differentials are __________, __________, __________, and __________.

   c. A country that invests in its public education and public health systems is improving the __________ of its population.

   d. If there are two groups of workers in a competitive labour market, and one group becomes discriminated against, the labour supply curve for jobs that remain available for that group will shift to the __________ and the wages for these jobs will __________.

2. Suppose there are only two industries in the economy. All workers have the same skills and the same preferences. But the jobs in the two industries are different. In the Pleasant industry, working conditions are desirable (quiet, safe, clean, etc.). In the Grimy industry, working conditions are awful (noisy, unsafe, dirty, etc.).

   a. Draw supply-and-demand diagrams for the labour market in each industry.

   b. In which industry are wages higher? Why?

   c. Now suppose the Grimy industry made its working conditions just as pleasant as in the Pleasant industry. Explain what happens in *both* labour markets.

3. Suppose there are two types of basketball players—black and white. Suppose also that, on average, black players are no better and no worse than white players. Furthermore, suppose there are only two types of basketball teams—good and bad. Good teams hire only good players; bad teams will hire both good and bad players. The two diagrams that follow show the initial outcomes in the labour markets for good teams and bad teams. Assume there is *no discrimination based on race.*

   a. As shown in the figures, the wage paid by good teams is higher than the wage paid by bad teams. What explains this wage differential?

   b. Do black players earn more or less than white players, on average? Explain.

   c. Now suppose the good teams discriminate against white players—rightly or wrongly they *believe* that black players are better than white players. Show in your diagram what happens in both labour markets.

   d. In the situation in part (c), what happens to the wage differential between good and bad teams?

   e. In the situation in part (c), what happens to the average black–white wage differential?

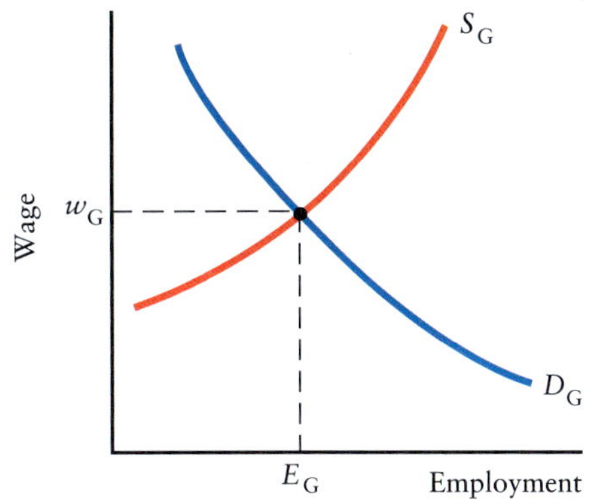

(i) Good teams

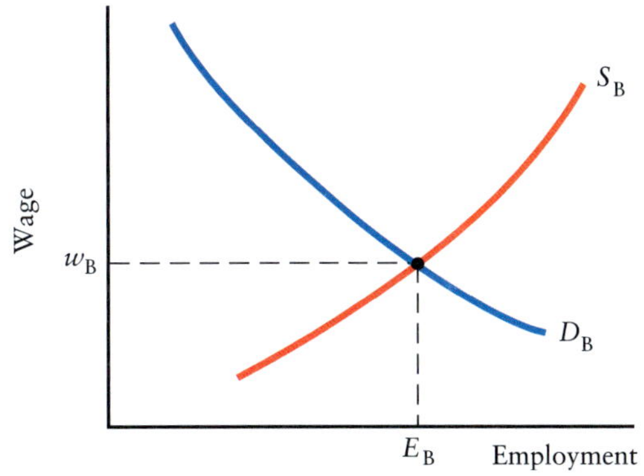

(ii) Bad teams

4. Suppose *in the real world* you observe that black basketball players get paid more than white basketball players. Do you conclude that discrimination is present? Explain why or why not.

5. Fill in the blanks to make the following statements correct.

   a. If workers in a competitive labour market join together to form a union, the effect will be a(n) __________ wage and __________ quantity of labour demanded.

   b. If firms in a competitive labour market form an employers' association and become a monopsonist, employment will be __________ and wages will be __________ than in the competitive outcome.

c. A legislated and binding minimum wage in a competitive labour market will lead to a(n) _________ in the quantity of labour demanded and a(n) _________ in the quantity of labour supplied. The actual number of workers employed will _________.

d. A legislated and binding minimum wage in a market where the employer has monopsony power and the wage is initially below the competitive level will lead to a(n) _________ in the number of workers employed.

6. myeconlab The table below shows how many workers are prepared to work at various hourly wages in the forestry industry. It also shows the workers' marginal revenue product (*MRP*).

Number of Workers	Wage ($)	Marginal Cost of Labour ($)	*MRP* ($)
50	10	—	50
100	12	14	40
150	14	18	30
200	16	—	24
250	18	—	22
300	20	—	20
350	22	—	18

a. On a diagram, draw the supply of labour curve and the demand for labour curve.
b. What is the equilibrium wage and level of employment if the labour market is competitive?
c. Now suppose there is only a single buyer for labour—a *monopsonist*. Compute the marginal cost of labour for each level of employment and fill in the table. (Recall that the *MC* of labour is the change in labour cost divided by the change in employment. The first two rows have been completed for you.)
d. What wage and level of employment would the monopsonist choose? Explain.

7. myeconlab The following diagram shows the market for labour in a particular industry. It shows both the supply of labour (the average cost of labour) and the marginal cost of labour.

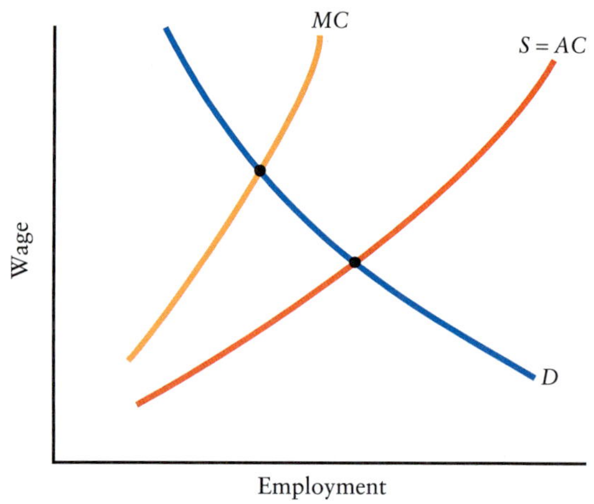

a. Suppose the labour market is competitive. What will be the equilibrium wage and level of employment (call them w^* and L^*)?
b. Now suppose the government imposes a minimum wage equal to $w^{min} > w^*$. Show what happens to wages and employment.
c. In the absence of a minimum wage, show the outcome if there is a monopsony buyer of labour services. Call this wage w^p.
d. Beginning with the monopsony outcome, show what happens if the government imposes a minimum wage above w^p but lower than w^*.
e. Do minimum wages always reduce employment? Explain.

8. Fill in the blanks to make the following statements correct.

a. In the case of labour unions, there is an inherent conflict between _________ and _________.
b. The union wage premium in Canada is estimated to be between _________ and _________ percent.
c. In Canada, the agricultural industry has a _________ rate of unionization and the public sector has a _________ rate of unionization.
d. The shift in employment from manufacturing jobs to service jobs in Canada has coincided with _________ real income per hour worked.
e. The decline in the share of total employment in the manufacturing sector in Canada is partly due to the _________ in the total output per worker in that sector.

9. The following diagram shows the market for labour in a particular industry. It shows both the supply of labour (the average cost of labour) and the marginal cost of labour. If the labour market were competitive, the outcome would be w^* and L^*.

   a. Suppose the workers in this industry form a union that is able to raise the wage above w^*. Show the expected outcome in the figure.
   b. Now suppose there is no union, but there is a monopsony buyer of labour. Show the expected outcome in this market.
   c. Now suppose there is both a union and a monopsony firm. What can you predict about the outcome in this case?

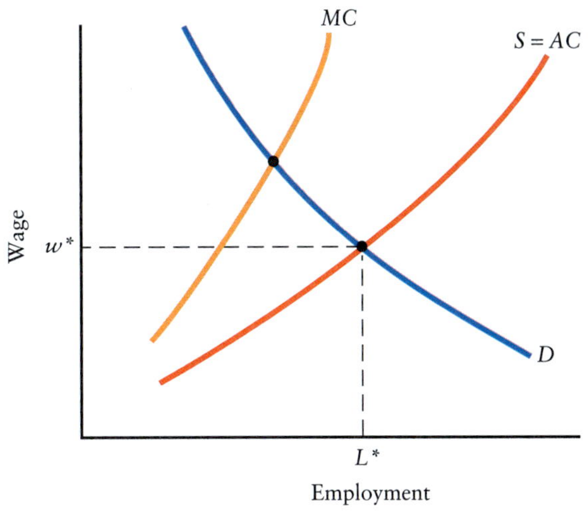

DISCUSSION QUESTIONS

1. "The great increase in the number of women entering the labour force for the first time means that relatively more women than men earn beginning salaries. It is therefore not evidence of discrimination that the average wage earned by females is less than that earned by males." Discuss.

2. Physicians are among the highest-paid of workers. However, in addition to a bachelor's degree, would-be physicians must attend four years of medical school, three years of residency, and up to seven additional years of residency to be specialists. How does this lengthy training change your perception with respect to how much physicians are paid? What additional information would you need to determine whether physicians' real pay is higher than that of other professionals?

3. In trying to measure the extent to which labour unions are responsible for increasing wages, economists use sophisticated statistical methods to compare the wages of unionized workers with those of non-unionized workers. Explain why it is not legitimate simply to compare the average wage across the two groups and attribute the difference to the effects of unionization.

4. "One can judge the presence or absence of discrimination by looking at the proportion of the population in different occupations." Does such information help? Does it suffice? Consider each of the following examples. Relative to their numbers in the total population, there are

   a. Too many blacks and too few Jews among professional athletes
   b. Too few male secretaries
   c. Too few female judges
   d. Too few female prison guards
   e. Too few male schoolteachers
   f. Too few female graduate students in economics

5. "Equal pay for work of equal value" is a commonly held goal, but "equal value" is hard to define. What would be the consequences of legislation that enforces equal pay for what turns out to be work of unequal value?

6. There is clear evidence of a union wage premium of between 10 and 15 percent. There is also clear evidence that firms' demand curves are downward sloping. Reconcile these two "facts" with the third fact that there is *no* clear evidence that unions lead to employment reductions.

7. One concern often expressed about the ongoing rise of services and decline of manufacturing is that the production of "things" is somehow better for wealth generation than the production of intangible services. Can you provide an argument in support of this view?

CHAPTER 15

Interest Rates and the Capital Market

LEARNING OBJECTIVES

In this chapter you will learn

1. how to compute the present value of an asset that delivers a stream of future benefits.
2. why the demand for investment is negatively related to the interest rate.
3. why the supply of saving is positively related to the interest rate.
4. how the equilibrium interest rate is determined and how it is affected by various economic events.

Economists use the word *capital* in three different ways. *Human capital,* which we discussed in Chapter 14, is the set of skills that workers acquire through education and on-the-job training. *Physical capital* is a produced factor of production, such as a machine, a factory, or a bridge. *Financial capital* refers to financial assets in the form of *loans, bonds,* or *stocks.* In this chapter, we focus on what economists call the "capital market," which involves both physical and financial capital, and the role played by the interest rate in this market.

15.1 A BRIEF OVERVIEW OF THE CAPITAL MARKET

Firms require physical capital to produce their goods and services. Their purchase of new capital equipment is called *investment* in physical capital. We saw in Chapter 7 that firms can finance their investment in one of four ways. First, they can use profits that are not remitted to shareholders—these are called *retained earnings.* Second, they can borrow from commercial banks or other financial intermediaries, such as credit unions and trust companies. Third, they can issue *bonds* (an IOU) and thereby borrow directly from lenders. Fourth, they can issue and sell *stock* (a share of the company) directly to shareholders. However firms choose to finance their investments, their demand for financial capital comes mostly from their demand for physical capital.

Firms' demand for financial capital is derived from their demand for physical capital.

The supply of financial capital comes mostly from households' saving decisions. Every year, millions of households decide how much of their income to save. These funds are often deposited into various types of accounts at commercial banks, each of which is a loan from the household to the bank. Sometimes the funds are used to buy bonds so that the household is lending directly to a nonbank borrower. The household may also decide to purchase stock, and thereby acquire a share of some firm. Whatever form households choose for their saving, their saving decisions determine their total supply of financial capital.

Households' supply of financial capital is derived from their supply of saving.

Figure 15-1 illustrates the interaction of firms and households in the market for financial capital. Note that some funds flow directly between firms and households (bond and stock purchases) whereas other funds flow through financial intermediaries (bank deposits and loans). Financial intermediaries play an important role in the economy for two reasons. First, they are specialists in assessing the *riskiness* of potential borrowers and thus are better suited than most households to making loans to firms. Second, they have the ability to *pool* the savings from a large number of households and thereby make large loans to firms. Despite the importance of financial intermediaries to the economy, in this chapter we will focus our attention on households and firms, thus focusing on the fundamental determinants of the demand for and supply of capital.

In this chapter, we look first at firms' demand for physical capital, which leads us to an understanding of their demand for financial capital. As we will see, the interest rate plays an important role in determining how much capital is demanded by firms. We then examine households' saving decisions and thus their supply of financial capital. The interest rate also plays an important role in determining how much financial capital households want to supply. Once we understand the demand and supply for financial capital, we will be ready to put the two sides of the capital market together to determine the equilibrium "price" of financial capital—the interest rate. Finally, we will look at how economic events or policies can affect the equilibrium levels of investment, saving, and the interest rate.

FIGURE 15-1 The Interaction of Firms and Households in the Capital Market

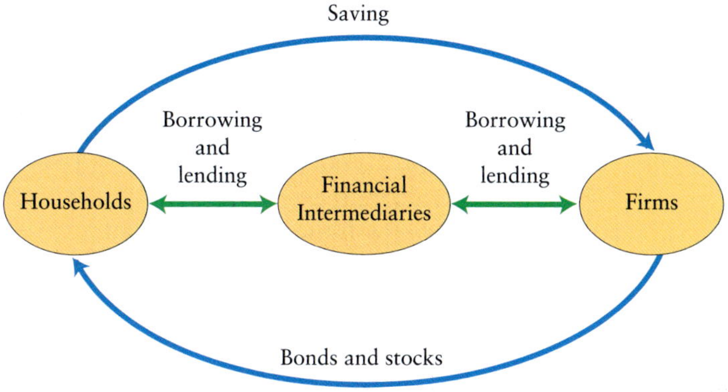

The capital market connects households' saving decisions with firms' borrowing decisions. Households save some part of their income. They can lend (make a deposit) to a commercial bank or other financial intermediary. They can lend directly to a firm by buying a bond. Or they can purchase stock and thereby become a part owner in a firm. Firms finance their investment (purchases of new capital equipment) either by using their retained earnings, borrowing from a bank, issuing a bond and borrowing directly from a lender, or issuing and selling stock.

myeconlab

Some people believe that the stock market is nothing more than a huge gambling casino. But economists argue that it is a vital economic institution without which much of our economic progress would be impossible. For a brief introduction to the stock market, look for "A Beginner's Guide to the Stock Market" in the *Additional Topics* section of this book's MyEconLab.

www.myeconlab.com

Before beginning our analysis of the demand for capital, it is necessary to clarify one important difference between labour and physical capital as factors of production. When economists speak of the demand and supply for labour, they are referring to the *flow* of labour services. For example, a firm considers hiring the services of a worker for a month, after which the firm and the worker go their separate ways. In contrast, when a firm considers its demand for physical capital, it is considering purchasing a new piece of equipment and thereby adding to its *stock* of capital. This piece of capital equipment will usually deliver services to the firm over many years before it eventually wears out. The durability of physical capital means that we must distinguish between the *stock* of capital and the *flow* of services that it delivers. We need a way to evaluate the flow of services that a piece of capital equipment delivers for many years into the future. Only then can we determine how much a firm would be willing to pay for the piece of capital equipment. This takes us to the concept of *present value.*

15.2 PRESENT VALUE

Suppose a firm buys a piece of capital equipment and thereby obtains the use of that equipment until it wears out. The capital equipment delivers a flow of benefits over its lifetime—that is, it delivers some benefit every year for many years. The benefit to the firm in any given year is the marginal revenue product (*MRP*) of that unit of capital. A given piece of capital may deliver different *MRP*s in different years—the *MRP* may change because of changes in market conditions or simply because the capital wears out slowly over time. In reality, the stream of future *MRP*s is uncertain. No firm can predict with certainty how its market will evolve, how consumers will respond to the product, or even how long the capital equipment will last.

How much would a firm be willing to pay today to purchase a piece of capital equipment that will deliver an uncertain stream of benefits into the future? In order to answer this question we introduce the concept of *present value*. The **present value** of a future amount is the most that someone would be prepared to pay today to get that amount in the future. The concept of present value is used extensively in financial analysis as well as in the analysis of economic policies where costs and benefits occur at different points in time.

present value The value today of a future stream of payments discounted using the market interest rate.

In what follows, we simplify our discussion by assuming that the future benefits from a piece of capital equipment are known with certainty. This allows us to develop the central insights about present value and the interest rate without dealing with complications arising from uncertainty.

The Present Value of a Single Future Payment

To begin our analysis, consider a very simple setting in which the piece of capital equipment produces an *MRP* only in one future period. Since most physical capital is durable and thus generates a *stream* of benefits, this assumption is quite unrealistic, but is only our starting point. In the first case, the *MRP* occurs one period from now. In the second, the *MRP* occurs several periods from now.

One Period in the Future How much would a firm be prepared to pay now to purchase a capital good that produces an *MRP* of $100 in one year's time, after which time the capital good will be useless? One way to answer this question is to ask a somewhat *opposite* question: How much would the firm have to *lend* now in order to be repaid

\$100 a year from now? Suppose for the moment that the interest rate is 5 percent per year, which means that \$1.00 loaned today will lead to a repayment of \$1.05 in one year's time.

If we use PV to stand for this unknown amount, we can write $PV \times (1.05) =$ \$100. Thus, $PV =$ \$100/1.05 = \$95.24. This tells us that the present value of \$100 receivable in one year's time is \$95.24 when the interest rate is 5 percent. Anyone who lends out \$95.24 for one year at 5-percent interest will receive \$95.24 back plus \$4.76 in interest, or \$100 in total. When we calculate this present value, the interest rate is used to *discount* (reduce to its present value) the \$100 to be received in one year's time.

The actual present value that we have calculated depended on our assumption that the interest rate was 5 percent. What if the interest rate is 7 percent? At that interest rate, the present value of the \$100 receivable in one year's time would be \$100/1.07 = \$93.46.

These examples are easy to generalize. In both cases, we have found the present value by dividing the sum that is receivable in the future by 1 plus the rate of interest.[1] In general, if the interest rate is i per year, then the present value of the MRP (in dollars) received one year hence is

$$PV = MRP/(1 + i)$$

Table 15-1 computes the present value of an MRP of \$500, received one year from now, under alternative assumptions of the interest rate. There is a negative relationship between present value and the interest rate.

TABLE 15-1 The Present Value of a Single Sum One Year in the Future

	MRP	Interest Rate Per Year	Present Value
1.	\$500	4% = 0.04	\$500/(1.04) = \$480.77
2.	\$500	5% = 0.05	\$500/(1.05) = \$476.19
3.	\$500	6% = 0.06	\$500/(1.06) = \$471.70
4.	\$500	7% = 0.07	\$500/(1.07) = \$467.29
5.	\$500	8% = 0.08	\$500/(1.08) = \$462.96

For any given sum at a given point in the future, the present value of the sum is negatively related to the interest rate. The firm earns an *MRP* of \$500 in one year's time. Using the formula developed in the text, it is clear that present value is lower when the interest rate is higher.

Several Periods in the Future Now we know how to calculate the present value of a single sum that is receivable one year in the future. The next step is to ask what would happen if the sum were receivable at a later date. For example, what is the present value of \$100 to be received *two* years hence when the interest rate is 5 percent? The answer is \$100/[(1.05)(1.05)] = \$90.70. We can check this by seeing what would happen if \$90.70 were lent out for two years. In the first year, the loan would earn interest of (0.05)(\$90.70) = \$4.54, and hence after one year, the outstanding loan would be worth \$95.24. If we assume that interest is compounded annually, then in the second year the interest earned would equal (0.05)(\$95.24) = \$4.76. Hence, after two years the firm would be repaid \$100.

In general, the present value of MRP dollars received t years in the future when the interest rate is i per year is

$$PV = MRP/(1 + i)^t$$

1 In this type of formula, the interest rate i is expressed as a decimal fraction where, for example, a 7-percent annual interest rate is expressed as 0.07, so that $1 + i$ equals 1.07. We also assume throughout our analysis that discounting by the interest rate occurs annually rather than semi-annually, monthly, or continuously.

This formula simply discounts the *MRP* by the interest rate, repeatedly, once for each of the t periods that must pass until the *MRP* becomes available. If we look at the formula, we see that the higher is i or t, the higher is the whole term $(1 + i)^t$. This term, however, appears in the denominator, so *PV* is *negatively* related to both i and t.

Table 15-2 computes the present value of an *MRP* of $500 received several years in the future. The table has two parts. In Part A, we keep the date of the *MRP* fixed and vary the interest rate. In Part B, we keep the interest rate fixed and vary the date of the *MRP*. This allows us to see the separate effects of varying i and t, and leads to the following conclusion.

Other things being equal, the present value of a given sum payable in the future will be smaller the more distant the payment date and it will be smaller the higher the rate of interest.

The Present Value of a Stream of Future Payments

Now consider the present value of a stream of payments that continues for many periods into the future. As we said earlier, the future benefits that a firm receives from a piece of capital equipment may not be constant. Changes in market conditions, technology, or the quality of the capital itself may result in different *MRP*s in different periods. For example, one new lathe may generate a marginal revenue product equal to $200 one year from now, $180 two years from now, and $210 in the third year—before it wears out and ceases to generate any further benefits.

TABLE 15-2 The Present Value of a Single Sum Several Years in the Future

Part A: Date Fixed; Interest Rate Variable

	MRP	Date	Interest Rate Per Year	Present Value
1.	$500	3 years	4% = 0.04	$\$500/(1.04)^3 = \$444.50$
2.	$500	3 years	5% = 0.05	$\$500/(1.05)^3 = \$431.92$
3.	$500	3 years	6% = 0.06	$\$500/(1.06)^3 = \$419.81$
4.	$500	3 years	7% = 0.07	$\$500/(1.07)^3 = \$408.15$

Part B: Date Variable; Interest Rate Fixed

	MRP	Date	Interest Rate Per Year	Present Value
1.	$500	2 years	6% = 0.06	$\$500/(1.06)^2 = \$445.00$
2.	$500	3 years	6% = 0.06	$\$500/(1.06)^3 = \$419.81$
3.	$500	4 years	6% = 0.06	$\$500/(1.06)^4 = \$396.05$
4.	$500	5 years	6% = 0.06	$\$500/(1.06)^5 = \$373.63$

The present value of a future sum is negatively related to the interest rate and negatively related to the length of time before the sum occurs. In all the rows in Part A, the firm receives an *MRP* of $500 in three years' time, but the interest rate varies. Using the formula from the text, we see that the higher is the interest rate, the lower is the present value of the future *MRP*. In all the rows in Part B, the interest rate is 6 percent per year, but the future date of the *MRP* varies. The computations show that the more distant in time is the *MRP*, the lower is the present value.

How do we compute the present value of such an uneven stream of *MRP*s? The answer is surprisingly simple. We just treat each future *MRP* as a single *MRP* that occurs at some point in the future. We then apply our earlier formula to each *MRP* and add them up. For example, suppose the interest rate is 6 percent per year and the capital generates *MRP*s equal to \$200 in one year, \$180 in two years, \$210 in three years, and nothing thereafter. The present value of this stream of *MRP*s is

$$
\begin{aligned}
PV &= \frac{\$200}{1.06} + \frac{\$180}{(1.06)^2} + \frac{\$210}{(1.06)^3} \\
&= \$188.68 + \$160.20 + \$176.32 \\
&= \$525.20
\end{aligned}
$$

In general, if MRP_t is the *MRP* that occurs *t* years from now, if *i* is the interest rate, and if the stream of *MRP*s lasts for *N* years, the present value of the stream of *MRP*s is

$$PV = \frac{MRP_1}{1+i} + \frac{MRP_2}{(1+i)^2} + \dots + \frac{MRP_N}{(1+i)^N}$$

Table 15-3 computes the present value of several streams of *MRP*s. It confirms the relationships we observed earlier. First, other things being equal, a higher interest rate leads to a lower present value. Second, for a given interest rate, a larger *MRP* leads to a larger present value. But now that we have a stream of *MRP*s that lasts for several periods, rather than just a single period, we can add a third general result: The longer a stream of *MRP*s lasts into the future, the greater is the present value.

Conclusions

The concept of present value can at first be confusing, but you should now see the straightforward way to evaluate a stream of benefits into the distant future. Let's summarize our findings.

1. A piece of capital is valuable because it generates a *stream* of benefits into the future. These benefits are the capital's marginal revenue product (*MRP*). The value to the firm of owning this capital now is what we have called its *present value.*
2. The larger is each future *MRP*, or the longer the stream of *MRPs* lasts, the greater is the present value of the capital.
3. For a given stream of future *MRP*s, the present value of the capital is negatively related to the interest rate. That is, when interest rates are higher, a given piece of capital is valued less. When interest rates are lower, the capital is valued more highly.
4. Capital that delivers its *MRP*s in the more distant future has a lower present value than capital that delivers the same stream of *MRP*s sooner.

Practise with Study Guide Chapter 15, Exercises 1 and 4.

We now go on to examine an individual firm's demand for capital goods. We will then consider the economy's overall demand for capital. Present value and the interest rate play a central role in our analysis.

TABLE 15-3 The Present Value of a Stream of Future Payments

Part A: Alternative Interest Rates

	MRP_1	MRP_2	MRP_3	Interest Rate Per Year	Present Value
1.	\$500	\$400	\$300	8% = 0.08	$\frac{500}{1.08} + \frac{400}{(1.08)^2} + \frac{300}{(1.08)^3} = \$1044.05$
2.	\$500	\$400	\$300	5% = 0.05	$\frac{500}{1.05} + \frac{400}{(1.05)^2} + \frac{300}{(1.05)^3} = \$1098.15$

Part B: Alternative *MRP*s

	MRP_1	MRP_2	MRP_3	Interest Rate Per Year	Present Value
3.	\$300	\$300	\$300	5% = 0.05	$\frac{300}{1.05} + \frac{300}{(1.05)^2} + \frac{300}{(1.05)^3} = \$816.97$
4.	\$400	\$400	\$400	5% = 0.05	$\frac{400}{1.05} + \frac{400}{(1.05)^2} + \frac{400}{(1.05)^3} = \$1089.30$

Part C: Alternative Lengths of Stream

	MRP_1	MRP_2	MRP_3	Interest Rate Per Year	Present Value
5.	\$500	\$500	\$0	5% = 0.05	$\frac{500}{1.05} + \frac{500}{(1.05)^2} + 0 = \$929.70$
6.	\$500	\$500	\$500	5% = 0.05	$\frac{500}{1.05} + \frac{500}{(1.05)^2} + \frac{500}{(1.05)^3} = \$1361.62$

The present value of a future stream of sums is negatively related to the interest rate, positively related to the size of each payment, and positively related to the length of time the stream continues. Part A presents a given stream of *MRP*s over three years but considers two different interest rates. The *PV* of the stream of *MRP*s is higher when the interest rate is lower.

Part B uses only a single interest rate of 5 percent but considers two different streams of *MRP*s. One is a stream of \$300 that lasts for three years; the other is a higher stream of \$400 that also lasts for three years. The stream with the higher *MRP*s has the higher present value.

Part C uses an interest rate of 5 percent and a constant stream of *MRP*s of \$500 per year. One stream lasts for two years, whereas the other lasts for three years. The longer-lasting stream of *MRP*s has the higher present value.

15.3 INVESTMENT DEMAND

As we said earlier, a firm's demand for financial capital comes from its demand for physical capital. Economists assume that the amount of physical capital the firm chooses to use comes from its objective of maximizing profit. We now examine this decision in detail.

The Firm's Demand for Capital

A profit-maximizing firm will purchase units of physical capital up to the point where the present value of the future stream of output produced by the last unit of capital equals its purchase price.

An individual firm faces a given interest rate and a given purchase price of capital goods. The firm can vary the quantity of capital that it employs, and as a result, the marginal revenue product of its capital varies. The hypothesis of diminishing marginal returns (see Chapter 7) predicts that the more capital the firm uses, the lower its *MRP*.

The Decision to Purchase a Unit of Capital

Consider a profit-maximizing firm that is deciding whether or not to add to its capital stock and is facing an interest rate of i at which it can borrow or lend money. The first thing the firm has to do is to estimate the expected stream of *MRP*s from the new piece of capital over its lifetime. Then it discounts this stream at the interest rate of i per year to find the present value of the stream of receipts the machine will generate. Having computed the *PV* of the stream of *MRP*s, the firm can then compare this *PV* with the purchase price of the capital good. The decision rule for a profit-maximizing firm is simple: If the *PV* is greater than or equal to the purchase price, the firm should buy the capital good; if the *PV* is less than the purchase price, the firm should not buy it.

Consider the following simple example. Suppose a computer has an *MRP* of \$1000 each year—that is, by buying this computer the firm can produce more output and thereby achieve a net addition to its revenues of \$1000 each year. Suppose further that the computer delivers benefits this year (now) and for two more years—after that, the computer is completely obsolete and worth nothing. Finally, suppose the interest rate is 6 percent per year. The *PV* of this stream of *MRP*s is then equal to

$$\begin{aligned} PV &= \$1000 + \$1000/(1 + 0.06) + \$1000/(1 + 0.06)^2 \\ &= \$2833.40 \end{aligned}$$

The present value tells us how much any flow of future receipts is worth now. If the firm can buy the computer for less than its *PV*—that is, for any amount less than \$2833.40—then this computer is a good buy. If it must pay more, the computer is not worth its price.

If a firm wants to maximize its profits, it is worthwhile to buy another unit of capital whenever the present value of the stream of future *MRP*s generated by that unit equals or exceeds its purchase price.

The Firm's Optimal Capital Stock Because of the law of diminishing marginal returns, the *MRP* of each unit of capital declines as the firm buys more capital. The profit-maximizing firm will thus go on adding to its stock of capital until the present value of the stream of *MRP*s generated by the *last unit* added is equal to the purchase price of that unit.

Practise with Study Guide Chapter 15, Exercises 2 and 3.

The profit-maximizing capital stock of the firm is such that the present value of the flow of *MRP*s that is provided by the last unit of capital is equal to its purchase price.

Figure 15-2 continues our earlier example of a firm considering the purchase of a computer. In this case, however, the firm is determining *how many* computers it wants to own, and so must compare the purchase price and the present value of the stream of *MRP*s produced by each successive computer. Because the *MRP* of each computer declines as the firm uses more of them, Figure 15-2 shows a negative relationship between the purchase price of the computer and the quantity the firm chooses to own.

What economic events, other than a change in the price of capital, might lead the firm to change its optimal capital stock? In terms of the example shown in Figure 15-2, anything that increases the *PV* of the future *MRP*s of computers will increase the height of the bars in the figure and, for a given purchase price of computers, lead the firm to purchase more computers. More generally, anything that increases the *PV* of the future *MRP*s of capital will lead firms to increase their desired capital stock. The future *MRP*s can increase in two ways.

Technological Improvement. If capital becomes more productive so that the stream of future *MRP*s increases, firms will choose to own more capital even if the purchase price of capital is unchanged. For example, in Figure 15-2, if a technological improvement increases the annual *MRP* for each computer by 20 percent, each computer's *PV* will also increase by 20 percent. The bars in the figure will increase in height and, for any given purchase price, the firm will increase its desired stock of computers.

Reduction in the Interest Rate. A second way in which the *PV* of the stream of *MRP*s will increase is if the interest rate falls. A lower interest rate means that future *MRP*s get discounted at a lower rate—and therefore have greater present value. Thus, as the interest rate declines, the firm's optimal capital stock increases. In Figure 15-2, imagine that the interest rate is 3 percent per year instead of 6 percent. In this case, the *PV*

FIGURE 15-2 The Firm's Optimal Capital Stock

	Annual *MRP*	Present Value
1st computer	\$1000	$1000 + \frac{1000}{1.06} + \frac{1000}{(1.06)^2}$ = \$2833.40
2nd computer	\$ 900	$900 + \frac{900}{1.06} + \frac{900}{(1.06)^2}$ = \$2550.06
3rd computer	\$ 800	$800 + \frac{800}{1.06} + \frac{800}{(1.06)^2}$ = \$2266.72
4th computer	\$ 700	$700 + \frac{700}{1.06} + \frac{700}{(1.06)^2}$ = \$1983.38
5th computer	\$ 600	$600 + \frac{600}{1.06} + \frac{600}{(1.06)^2}$ = \$1700.04

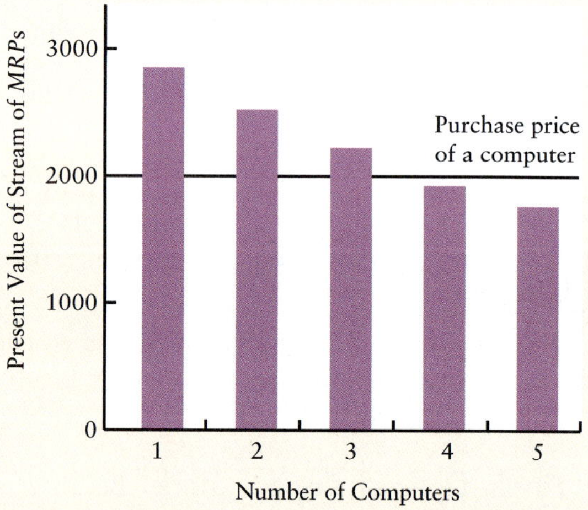

The firm's optimal capital stock is chosen so that the present value of the future *MRP*s on the last unit of capital is just equal to its purchase price. In this example, each computer delivers a stream of *MRP*s that begins now and lasts for two years, and the interest rate is 6 percent per year. The second column in the table shows the diminishing marginal product of capital—the annual *MRP* generated by each computer is less than for the previous one. The third column computes the *PV* of the stream of *MRP*s for each computer, and these are plotted in the accompanying figure. If the purchase price of a computer is \$2000, the firm will choose to own only three computers; any additional computer delivers a *PV* of *MRP*s that is less than the purchase price and thus is not profitable to the firm. An increase in the purchase price of a computer to \$2400 leads the firm to reduce its desired stock of computers to two.

of each computer's stream of future *MRP*s will rise, and each bar in the figure will increase in height. For a given purchase price of computers, the firm will therefore increase its desired stock of computers.

Anything that causes the present value of future *MRP*s of capital to increase—technological improvement or a reduction in the interest rate—leads firms to increase their desired capital stock.

From Capital Stock to Investment Demand We have just examined how a profit-maximizing firm determines its optimal stock of physical capital. It is important to emphasize again the distinction between *stocks* and *flows*—in this case the distinction between the firm's optimal *stock* of capital and its optimal *flow* of investment. In any given period, a firm can determine its optimal stock of capital. But if the economic environment changes either because of a change in technology or a change in interest rates, the firm's optimal capital stock will also change. In order for the firm to adjust its capital stock appropriately, it needs to carry out *investment.* A positive flow of investment—buying new capital—leads to an increase in the capital stock; a negative flow of investment—selling existing capital—leads to a decline in the capital stock.[2]

How do we get from the firm's optimal capital stock to its demand for investment? For any period, the firm's investment demand is determined by the *change* in the firm's optimal capital stock, which in turn is determined by changes in the economic environment. To illustrate, continue with our example of a firm with an optimal capital stock of 100 computers at the beginning of 2007. During the year 2007, suppose interest rates decline, thereby increasing the firm's optimal capital stock to 110 computers. For the year 2007, the firm would therefore have a demand for investment equal to the *change* in this optimal stock—in this case, 10 computers. After the firm carries out this investment (after it buys 10 new computers), it would again possess its optimal capital stock.

In any given period, the profit-maximizing firm's investment demand is given by the *change* in the firm's optimal capital stock.

Emphasis on the Interest Rate In Figure 15-2, there is a negative relationship between the purchase price of a computer and the desired stock of computers the firm wants to own. Firms use many types of physical capital, however, including buildings, furniture, computer equipment, and various types of tools and machines. Each different type of physical capital has a different price and therefore it is impossible to think of any individual firm's desired capital stock in terms of any single price. For this reason, economists focus on the negative relationship between the firm's desired capital stock and the interest rate. Indeed, since firms use financial capital to purchase their physical capital, it is natural to think of the interest rate as the "price" of financial capital.

Practise with Study Guide Chapter 15, Short-Answer Question 5.

We saw above that when the interest rate falls, the *PV* of the future stream of *MRP*s will rise. This increase in the present value of capital will lead firms to increase their desired capital stock, and thus the quantity of investment demanded. The opposite happens when the interest rate rises. We thus get a general prediction about firms' investment behaviour:

Other things being equal, firms' demand for investment (additions to physical capital) is negatively related to the interest rate.

[2] Positive investment may not add to the firm's capital stock if it is replacing obsolete capital. In this discussion, however, we make the simplifying assumption that all investment increases the firm's capital stock.

FIGURE 15-3 The Interest Rate and the Firm's Investment Demand

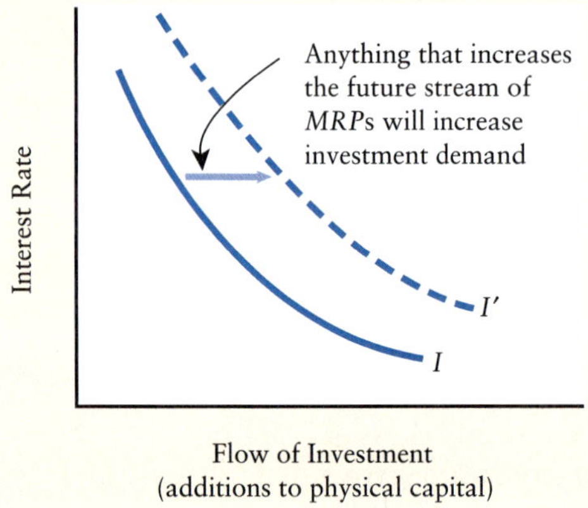

The lower the rate of interest, the larger is the firm's demand for investment. The lower the interest rate, the higher is the present value of any given stream of *MRP*s and hence the more capital that the firm will wish to use.

Anything that increases the future stream of *MRP*s produced by the capital leads the firm to demand more units of capital at any interest rate—the investment demand curve shifts to *I*′.

This relationship is shown in Figure 15-3. The negative relationship between the interest rate and the quantity of investment demanded can be thought of as the firm's demand curve for additional physical capital where the relevant "price" is the interest rate.

What would cause a firm's investment demand curve to shift? First, suppose the firm's expectations about future demand for its product improve. This optimism leads the firm to expect an increase in the future stream of *MRP*s produced by capital. With higher expected *MRP*s, the firm is prepared to purchase more units of capital (at any interest rate). Thus, the firm's investment demand curve shifts to the right. Second, suppose an improvement in technology increases the future stream of *MRP*s. Again, the higher future *MRP*s lead the firm to purchase more units of capital at any interest rate—a rightward shift in the firm's investment demand curve.

Any event that increases the expected future stream of *MRP*s leads to an increase in the firm's investment demand.

The Economy's Demand for Investment

The economy's overall demand for investment is determined from the demands of individual firms. Thus, there is a negative relationship between the interest rate and the desired *aggregate* investment for the same reasons that the negative relationship exists for any individual firm. The economy's demand for investment can therefore be represented by a downward-sloping curve just as in Figure 15-3.

The economy's investment demand curve shifts for the same reasons that individual firms' demand curves shift. Anything that increases the future stream of *MRP*s of capital leads to a rightward shift in the investment demand curve. Technological improvements are a key reason for such increases in the demand for investment. (We will say more about this later.)

15.4 THE SUPPLY OF SAVING

The supply of financial capital is determined by households' saving decisions. Saving is the difference between income and current spending. At any given time, households have a stock of *assets* that represents the accumulation of their past saving. During any given year, households modify their accumulated stock of assets by either saving or borrowing. (Saving leads to an increase in the accumulated stock of assets; borrowing leads to a reduction in the accumulated stock of assets.) Thus, the annual *flow* of saving by households leads to a change in the total *stock* of assets.

Households save because it allows them to spend in the future some of the income they earned today. They do this for several reasons. First, most people work for only part of their lives and, during their retirement, must live off their accumulated assets. Saving in the current year is a way of building up this retirement "nest egg." A second reason people save is that the future is uncertain. Next year they might become unemployed and thus lose their source of income, or they may have to provide for a relative who has lost a job or become incapacitated. In any case, uncertainty about the future provides a good reason to save. Finally, many households save in anticipation of specific large future expenditures. Young couples, for example, save in order to accumulate enough funds for a down payment on a house. Couples with young children save to help finance their children's university education.

Despite the many and varied reasons why any individual household chooses to save a lot or a little, to understand the economy's overall supply of financial capital, economists focus on three key determinants of saving—current income, expected future income, and the interest rate.

Saving and Current Income

Most people try to *smooth* their spending across time. Instead of spending a lot when income is high and spending only a little when income is low, most people prefer to spend a relatively constant amount from year to year. The result is that in high-income years people tend to save a lot, and in low-income years people tend to save only a little. (In years when income is very low, people may save a negative amount, meaning that they spend partially out of their accumulated assets.) When economists examine statistics across many households in the economy, they find that the positive relationship between total income and total saving is quite stable.

Household saving is positively related to current income. An increase in current income increases the supply of financial capital.

Saving and Expected Future Income

For any given level of current income, households tend to save less when their expected future income is higher. If people anticipate that their income will be higher in the near future, their desire to smooth their spending (between now and the future) means that they will want to spend some of that higher income now. An increase in their current spending, however, combined with an unchanged level of *current* income, means that their current saving must fall.

The best example of this behaviour is shown by many of you who are reading this book. Students are busy acquiring human capital and are usually earning little or no income. As we discussed in Chapter 14, people with university degrees earn more on average than people with only a high school diploma. Thus, students are examples of people whose expected future income is considerably higher than their current income. The result is that many students are spending at levels that would be unaffordable (and quite imprudent!) if they were to earn their current incomes permanently. These students are spending at relatively high levels precisely because they expect to have much higher incomes in the near future. They are borrowing now (from parents or through student loans) because their future income will be high enough to pay back these debts.

An increase in expected future income leads to a decline in current saving, and thus to a reduction in the supply of financial capital.

Saving and the Interest Rate

How does an increase in the interest rate affect households' desire to save, and thus their supply of financial capital?

The interest rate is the "price" of financial capital. Like any price, the interest rate represents an opportunity cost—it is the opportunity cost of spending now rather than in the future. For example, suppose the interest rate is 5 percent per year. Your decision to spend $100 now "costs" you $105 in forgone spending one year from now. An increase in the interest rate increases the "price"—or opportunity cost—of current spending. Households respond to an increase in the interest rate by substituting away from (relatively expensive) current spending and toward (relatively inexpensive) future spending.

FIGURE 15-4 The Economy's Supply of Saving

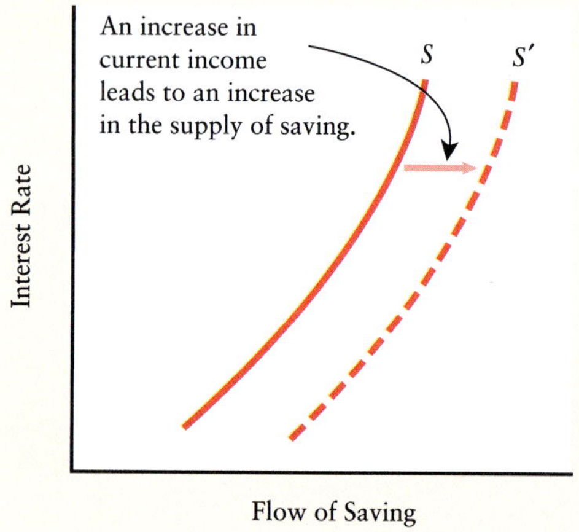

There is a positive relationship between the interest rate and the flow of saving supplied by households. An increase in the interest rate increases the opportunity cost of current spending and leads households to increase their desired saving.

An increase in the interest rate causes households to reduce their spending and increase their saving, thus increasing the quantity of financial capital supplied.[3]

The Economy's Supply of Saving

The economy's supply of saving is shown in Figure 15-4, and shows a positive relationship between the interest rate and the quantity of financial capital supplied by households. An increase in the interest rate leads the economy's households to increase their desired saving. This is a movement upward along the supply curve.

An increase in current income leads to an increase in households' desired saving *at any given interest rate* and thus causes the supply curve to shift to the right. An increase in expected future income (holding current income constant) leads to a decrease in households' desired saving *at any given interest rate* and thus causes the supply curve to shift to the left.

15.5 **INVESTMENT, SAVING, AND THE INTEREST RATE**

We have discussed how the economy's demand for financial capital is related to the interest rate; a rise in the interest rate leads firms to reduce their desired capital stock and thus reduce their need for financial capital. We have also discussed how the econ-

[3] This is the substitution effect of an increase in the interest rate and it works in the same direction for all individuals. There is also an income effect, which operates in one direction for households with negative net assets (debtors) and in the opposite direction for households with positive net assets (creditors). Economists usually assume that, when summed across all households in the economy, some of which are debtors and others creditors, the overall effect of a change in the interest rate is usually in the direction of the substitution effect.

omy's supply of financial capital is related to the interest rate; a rise in the interest rate leads households to increase their desired saving and thus provide more financial capital. We are now ready to put these two sides of the capital market together to examine market equilibrium.

There is an important difference between the analysis of individual firms and households, on the one hand, and the analysis of the overall capital market, on the other. Individual firms and households take the interest rate as given because they are so small relative to the entire economy that their own actions have no effect on the interest rate. For firms and households, the interest rate is *exogenous*. In the overall capital market, however, the interest rate is determined by the interaction of demand and supply—that is, the interest rate is *endogenous*. This important distinction is analogous to the one that exists in any competitive market; firms face a given market price for the product they sell, but the price is determined in equilibrium through the interaction of demand and supply.

One thing should be mentioned before we go on. In this chapter we have spent much time discussing the role of the interest rate in determining how firms and households behave. But we have ignored an important distinction between the *nominal* interest rate and the *real* interest rate. The *nominal* interest rate is the rate stated in the loan agreement. The *real* interest rate adjusts the nominal interest rate for the effects of inflation, and better represents the true cost of borrowing. (The real interest rate is approximately equal to the nominal interest rate minus the rate of inflation. The quality of this approximation is better, the lower are interest and inflation rates.) *Extensions in Theory 15-1* examines this distinction in more detail. In the discussion that follows, we restrict our attention to the real interest rate.

Figure 15-5 shows how the interest rate is determined in the market for financial capital. The intersection of the investment demand curve and the saving supply curve determines the equilibrium interest rate, i^*. If the interest rate were above i^*, there would be an excess supply of capital; households' desired saving would exceed firms' desired borrowing. This excess supply of financial capital would cause the interest rate—the price of financial capital—to fall. Conversely, if the interest rate were below i^*, there would be an excess demand for capital; firms' desired borrowing would exceed households' desired saving. This excess demand for capital would cause the interest rate to rise. Only at i^* is the market in equilibrium—the quantity of investment demanded by firms is just equal to the quantity of saving supplied by households.

FIGURE 15-5 The Market for Financial Capital

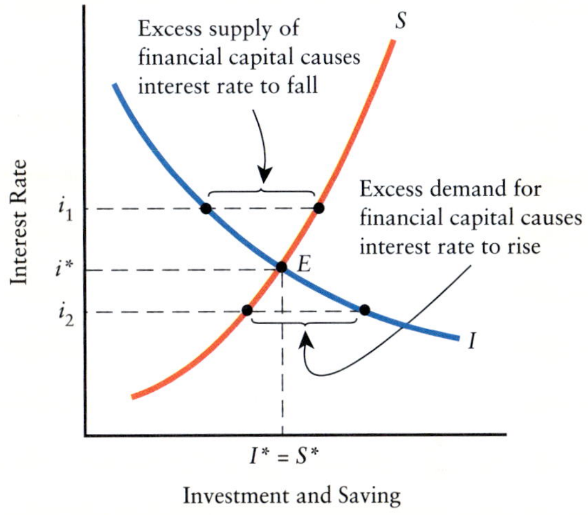

At the equilibrium interest rate, the quantity of investment demanded equals the quantity of saving supplied. The equilibrium interest rate is i^* where the quantity of investment demanded by firms equals the quantity of saving supplied by households (point E). At any interest rate above i^*, the excess supply of financial capital causes the interest rate to fall. At any interest rate below i^*, the excess demand for financial capital causes the interest rate to rise.

EXTENSIONS IN THEORY 15-1

Inflation and Interest Rates

Inflation means the prices of all goods in the economy are rising. More correctly, it means that the prices of goods are rising on *average*—some prices may be rising and others may be falling, but if there is inflation then the price of the average good is rising. Economists refer to the average price of all goods as the *price level*. When the price level is rising, inflation is positive; if prices are rising at a rate of 5 percent per year, the rate of inflation is 5 percent. When the price level is falling, inflation is negative. If prices are falling at a rate of 2 percent per year, the rate of inflation is −2 percent.

Real and Nominal Interest Rates

In the presence of inflation, we need to distinguish between the *real interest rate* and the *nominal interest rate*. The nominal interest rate is measured simply in dollars paid. If you pay me $7 interest for a $100 loan for one year, the nominal interest rate is 7 percent.

Consider further my one-year loan to you of $100 at the nominal rate of 7 percent. The real rate that I earn depends on what happens to the price level during the course of the year. If the price level remains constant over the year, then the real rate that I earn is also 7 percent—because I can buy 7 percent more real goods and services with the $107 that you repay me than with the $100 that I lent you. However, if the price level were to rise by 7 percent during the year, the real rate would be zero because the $107 you repay me will buy exactly the same quantity of real goods as did the $100 I gave up. If I were unlucky enough to have lent money at a nominal rate of 7 percent in a year in which prices rose by 10 percent, the real rate would be −3 percent. The real rate of interest concerns the ratio of the purchasing power of the money repaid to the purchasing power of the money initially borrowed, and it will be different from the nominal rate whenever inflation is not zero. *The real interest rate is the difference between the nominal interest rate and the rate of inflation.*

If lenders and borrowers are concerned with the real costs measured in terms of purchasing power, the nominal interest rate will be set at the real rate they require plus an amount to cover any expected rate of inflation. Consider a one-year loan that is meant to earn a real return to the lender of 3 percent. If the expected rate of inflation is zero, the nominal interest rate for the loan will also be 3 percent. If, however, a 10-percent inflation is expected, the nominal interest rate will have to be set at 13 percent in order that the real return be 3 percent.

Changes in the Capital-Market Equilibrium

Practise with Study Guide Chapter 15, Exercise 6.

We are now ready to examine some of the changes that occur in the market for financial capital, and how these changes affect the equilibrium interest rate and levels of investment and saving.

Increases in the Supply of Financial Capital Anything that increases the flow of households' desired saving *at the given interest rate* will shift the supply curve for saving to the right. At the initial interest rate, this increase in desired saving will lead to an excess supply of financial capital and thus to a decline in the equilibrium interest rate. As the equilibrium interest rate falls, firms will find it profitable to expand their capital stock and will therefore increase their quantity of investment demanded. The rightward shift in the saving supply curve will therefore lead to a movement downward along the investment demand curve. The effect of an increase in the supply of saving is illustrated in part (i) of Figure 15-6. Three possible causes of such an increase in the supply of saving are provided below.

This point is often overlooked, and as a result people are surprised at the high nominal interest rates that exist during periods of high inflation. But it is the real interest rate that matters more to borrowers and lenders. For example, as the accompanying figure shows, in 1981 the nominal interest rate on 3-month Treasury bills was almost 18 percent, but the high inflation rate at the time meant that the real interest rate was just over 5 percent. In contrast, a decade later in 1990, nominal rates had fallen to just below 13 percent but inflation had fallen further so that the real interest rate had actually *increased* to almost 8 percent. Thus, the period of lower nominal interest rates was actually a period of higher real interest rates.

Back to Capital

In this chapter we have examined investment demand by firms and the supply of saving by households. In both cases, the interest rate plays an important role. For firms, the interest rate reflects the cost of financial capital required to purchase physical capital. For households, the interest rate reflects the benefit of delaying their spending until the future and thus increasing their current saving. In both cases, though we did not say it, we were referring to the *real* interest rate.

When you go on to study *macroeconomics,* you will learn more about what causes inflation, and thus what forces us to make the distinction between real and nominal interest rates. For now, however, we assume in this chapter that there is no inflation; thus, real and nominal interest rates are the same.

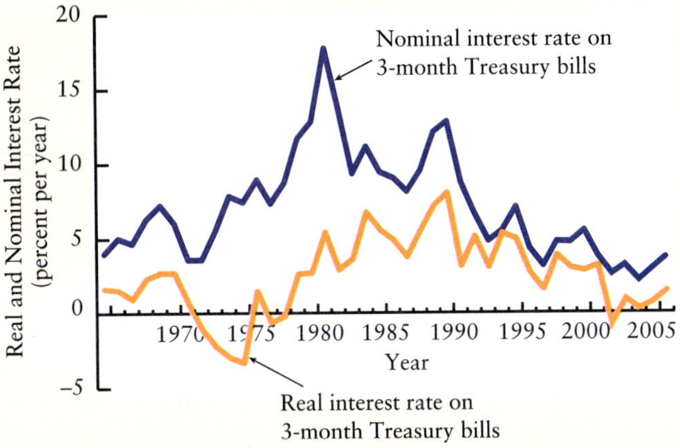

(*Source:* Nominal interest rate: 3-month treasury bill rate, CANSIM Series V122541. Real interest rate is based on authors' calculations of CPI inflation, Series PCPISA from www.bankofcanada.ca.)

Income Growth. As income increases, households desire to consume more, both now and in the future. The greater income leads to an increase in households' desired saving and thus to an increase in the supply of financial capital. Gradual but ongoing income growth over a period of many years is an important reason why the economy's supply of saving continues to increase.

Population Growth. An increase in the population—either through higher birth rates or greater immigration—leads to an increase in the supply of financial capital. The simple reason is that most households save, and so an increase in the number of households leads to an increase in the total amount of desired saving. For the effects on the capital market, there is little difference between an increase in the supply of capital due to an increase in the number of households, and an increase in the supply of capital due to higher income for an unchanged number of households. Both events will increase the economy's total income and thus total desired saving; both events will increase the economy's supply of financial capital.

FIGURE 15-6 Changes in Demand and Supply in the Market for Financial Capital

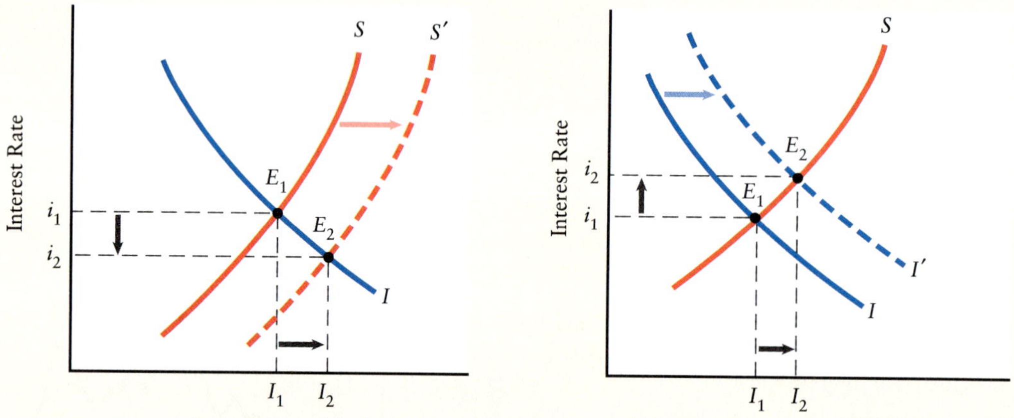

(i) An increase in the supply of saving

(ii) An increase in investment demand

Changes in the demand for or the supply of financial capital lead to changes in the equilibrium interest rate and levels of investment and saving. Part (i) illustrates an increase in the supply of saving. As households decide to increase the amount of their saving (at any given interest rate), the excess supply of capital leads to a reduction in the interest rate, from i_1 to i_2. As the interest rate falls, firms increase their quantity of investment demanded. The equilibrium level of investment (and saving) increases from I_1 to I_2.

Part (ii) illustrates an increase in investment demand. As firms decide to increase their desired investment, they require more financial capital (at any given interest rate). This leads to an excess demand for capital and to an increase in the interest rate, from i_1 to i_2. As the interest rate rises, households decide to increase their desired saving. The equilibrium level of investment (and saving) increases from I_1 to I_2.

Policies to Increase Desired Saving. Some Canadian government policies may increase households' desired saving. Registered Retirement Savings Plans (RRSPs), for example, offer tax benefits to households who contribute to special "registered" savings accounts. For every dollar contributed to an RRSP (up to a limit), the household reduces its taxable income by a dollar, and thus benefits by paying less income tax. While the funds remain in the registered account, the household does not pay any tax on the interest income earned. When the funds are eventually removed from the account at some point in the future, the full amount of the withdrawal gets added to the household's taxable income at that point. The scheme makes saving more attractive by offering the household a tax benefit for saving.

There is some debate about whether RRSPs actually increase the *total* amount of household saving. Many households have taken advantage of these plans and have a large stock of accumulated assets inside their registered accounts. The debate, however, centres on whether the funds inside these registered accounts would have been saved anyway through ordinary, non-registered savings accounts. Current economic research suggests that there is much substitution away from such "normal" saving and toward RRSP saving, but that the total amount of saving by households has also increased.

If RRSPs are successful in increasing the flow of total saving by households, the result is an increase in the economy's supply of financial capital and a reduction in the equilibrium interest rate. As the interest rate falls, firms will increase their planned investment. In the new equilibrium, the levels of both investment and saving will be higher.

Increases in the Demand for Financial Capital Anything that increases firms' desired investment *at the given interest rate* will shift the investment demand curve to the right. At the initial interest rate, this increase in the need for financial capital will lead to an excess demand for capital and thus to a rise in the equilibrium interest rate. As the equilibrium interest rate increases, households will find it desirable to reduce their current spending and increase their saving. The rightward shift in the investment demand curve will therefore lead to a movement upward along the saving supply curve. This case is illustrated in part (ii) of Figure 15-6. Let's briefly review some possible causes of an increase in the demand for financial capital.

Population and Income Growth. As the economy's total income grows, either through growth in population or in per capita income, the demand for goods and services increases. This increase in the demand for firms' products leads to an increase in the marginal revenue product (*MRP*) of capital. As we saw earlier in the chapter, an increase in capital's *MRP* leads to an increase in the economy's investment demand. The gradual but ongoing growth in the economy's total income is an important explanation for the gradual increase in the economy's investment demand.

Technological Improvement. Over time, there are technological improvements in the quality of factors of production. This is especially true for physical capital. Many of these improvements occur when worn-out capital is replaced by new and better capital. For example, dramatic improvements in computer and information technology have occurred over the past two decades. New desktop computers are hundreds of times faster and more powerful than two decades ago, and access to the Internet makes large quantities of information more readily available than it has ever been. Such improvements in computing power imply a large increase in the marginal product of capital, and thus to an increase in the economy's investment demand.

Policies to Encourage Investment. Over the years, Canadian federal and provincial governments have designed policies to encourage firms to increase their investment in physical capital. One effect of such policies is to increase firms' demand for financial capital. Reductions in corporate income-tax rates, special investment tax credits, and loans guaranteed by governments are three different policies that increase the profitability of investment to firms and lead to an increase in their demand for financial capital.

myeconlab

Our simple model of the capital market is based on the assumption that the economy is closed to international trade in financial capital. To see how the mobility of financial capital across international borders affects the analysis of investment, saving, and interest rates, look for "Investment and Saving in Globalized Financial Markets" in the *Additional Topics* section of this book's MyEconLab.

www.myeconlab.com

Long-Run Trends in the Capital Market Part (i) of Figure 15-7 shows the annual flow of non-residential investment from 1965 to 2005. It is quite volatile over time, though always positive. Part (ii) shows how this volatile flow of investment has led to an ever-increasing non-residential capital stock; it grew at an average annual rate of 3.2 percent over the period shown. Even in years when the flow of investment is relatively large, the growth rate of the overall capital stock rises only slightly, reflecting the small size of the investment *flow* relative to the large accumulated capital *stock*. Part (iii) of the figure shows the path of the real interest rate, which is quite volatile and displays no clear trend over the 40-year period. How can we use our model of the capital market to understand these data?

Over long periods of time, technological change and population growth can explain both a rising capital stock and an interest rate with no clear long-run trend. We have already stated that population growth leads to an increase in both the demand for and the supply of financial capital. A larger population implies more demand for goods and services, and thus greater investment demand by firms. A larger population, even

FIGURE 15-7 Investment, the Capital Stock, and the Real Interest Rate in Canada, 1965–2005

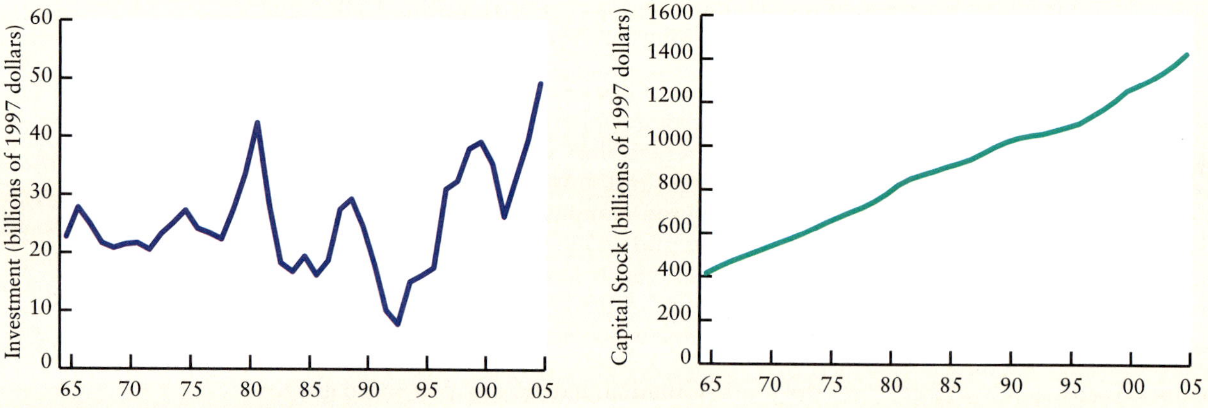

(i) Annual flow of non-residential investment

(ii) Non-residential capital stock

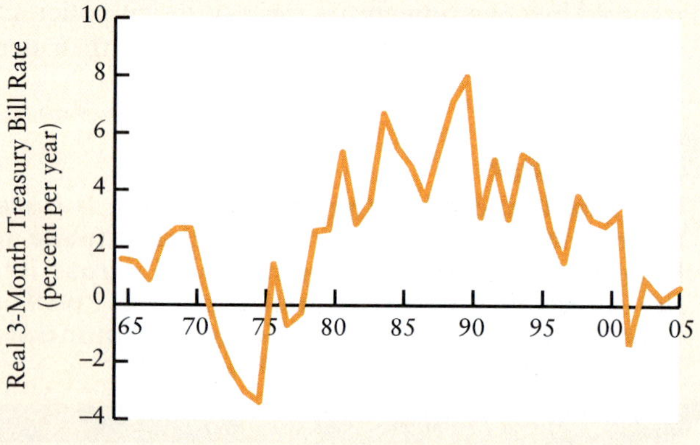

(iii) Real interest rate

The annual flow of investment is quite volatile, although the accumulated capital stock grows more steadily; the real interest rate is quite volatile and has no clear trend. Canada's non-residential capital stock has increased by over three times since 1965, an average annual growth rate of 3.2 percent. The real interest rate (here measured as the nominal interest rate on 3-month Treasury bills minus the annual rate of inflation) is much more volatile.

(*Source:* The capital stock is from Statistics Canada, series V1078482; the nominal interest rate is series V122541 and the rate of inflation is the rate of change of the CPI (all items), both from the Bank of Canada.)

with an unchanged level of income per person, leads to more income and greater saving by households. With both the demand and supply curves for financial capital shifting to the right due to population growth, there will be ongoing growth in the flow of investment, and an ever-rising capital stock; the effect on the interest rate will depend on the relative size of the demand and supply shifts.

Technological change also affects both sides of the capital market. Improvements in technology that increase capital's *MRP* lead firms to increase their investment demand. As we have said several times already in this book, technological change also lies at the heart of increasing productivity and growing per capita income. As income grows, so too does the supply of saving. Thus, through its effect on income, technological improvements that stimulate investment demand also lead to an increase in the supply of financial capital. With both the demand and supply curves shifting to the right due to technological improvements, there will be growth in the flow of investment and an ever-rising capital stock; the effect on the interest rate will again depend on the relative size of the demand and supply shifts.

Ongoing technological improvement and population growth, by increasing both the demand for and the supply of financial capital, explain a rising capital stock with no clear trend in the interest rate.

Our model of the capital market and the equilibrium interest rate can also be used to shed light on some *macroeconomic* issues—in particular, the nature of aggregate economic fluctuations. *Applying Economic Concepts 15-1* examines why during *recessions* and *booms* the demand for capital and the supply of capital often move in opposite directions, and why this helps to explain the volatility of the equilibrium interest rate.

APPLYING ECONOMIC CONCEPTS 15-1

The Capital Market and Macroeconomics

In the text we said that ongoing technological improvement and population growth can explain an upward trend in the capital stock with no clear trend in the interest rate. If this is the case, what explains fluctuations in the interest rate? The answer is that the demand and supply shifts in the market for financial capital are not happening at exactly the same time or in the same magnitude. In particular, firms' demand for investment can be quite volatile over relatively short periods of time.

In periods when the demand for financial capital is falling, the interest rate falls. An example is periods in which there is a slowdown in aggregate economic activity—what economists call a *recession.* The recession generates uncertainty for firms, which are then reluctant to embark on investment projects, thus reducing the demand for capital. During periods of slow economic activity, therefore, the demand for financial capital tends to decrease. The result is that the equilibrium interest rate falls and the flow of investment (and saving) declines.

The opposite is true during periods in which economic activity is growing quickly—what economists call *booms.* During booms, the level of production is high and growing in many industries, and there is growing demand for many factors of production. Firms are actively engaged in planning investment projects. These are times when the economy's demand for financial capital is growing. The result is that the equilibrium interest rate rises and the flow of investment (and saving) increases.

The topic of this box gets us into *macroeconomics*—the study of aggregate economic activity, including such things as unemployment, inflation, and business cycles. The study of macroeconomics is well beyond the scope of this chapter, but we will discuss it in detail in the second half of this textbook, beginning in Chapter 19. At this point, however, it is worth noting that when you go on to study macroeconomics, you will learn that the central bank (in Canada, it is called the Bank of Canada) also plays an important role in influencing the interest rate, at least over the short run.

SUMMARY

15.1 A BRIEF OVERVIEW OF THE CAPITAL MARKET

- The demand for financial capital comes from firms' need to finance their investment in new physical capital. The supply of financial capital comes from households' saving decisions.
- The capital market connects households' saving decisions with firms' financing requirements.
- Financial intermediaries—such as commercial banks—play an important role in bringing the two sides of the capital market together.

15.2 PRESENT VALUE

LO 1

- Since physical capital is durable, it delivers benefits to its owners over many years. As a result, firms need to evaluate the stream of future benefits produced by capital.
- *Present value* is the value today of any stream of future sums; it is computed by discounting the future sums using the rate of interest. The present value of X receivable in t years' time when the interest rate is i per year is:

$$PV = \frac{X}{(1+i)^t}$$

15.3 INVESTMENT DEMAND

LO 2

- Profit-maximizing firms will purchase capital up to the point where the present value of the future stream of *MRP*s generated by the last unit of capital equals its purchase price.
- Economists focus on the relationship between the interest rate and firms' desired capital stock; an increase in the interest rate reduces the present value of any given stream of future *MRP*s and thus reduces firms' desired capital stock.
- Since firms require financial capital to finance their investment in additional capital equipment, the economy's demand for financial capital comes from the many individual firms' demand for investment. An increase in the interest rate leads to a decline in firms' quantity of investment demanded.
- An increase in the marginal product of capital increases firms' desired capital stock at any given interest rate and therefore leads to an increase in the economy's demand for financial capital. This is represented by a rightward shift in the economy's investment demand curve.

15.4 THE SUPPLY OF SAVING

LO 3

- The economy's supply of capital comes from households' flow of desired saving.
- An increase in the interest rate increases the opportunity cost of current spending and thus leads households to increase their desired saving. This is a movement upward along the economy's supply of saving curve.
- An increase in aggregate income—either through population growth or growth in per capita income—leads to an increase in total household saving at any given interest rate. The result is a rightward shift in the economy's supply of saving curve.

15.5 INVESTMENT, SAVING, AND THE INTEREST RATE

LO 4

- Equilibrium in the market for financial capital is determined where the quantity of capital supplied by households equals the quantity of capital demanded by firms.
- Changes in the demand for capital or the supply of capital lead to changes in the equilibrium interest rate and equilibrium levels of investment and saving.
- Technological improvement and population growth lead to increases in both the demand for and the supply of capital. Continual technological improvement and population growth can therefore explain the ongoing growth in the capital stock with little or no trend in the interest rate.

KEY CONCEPTS

Physical capital and financial capital
Present value and the interest rate
A firm's optimal capital stock
The economy's demand for financial capital
Households' saving decisions
The economy's supply of financial capital
Equilibrium interest rate
Technological change and a rising capital stock

STUDY EXERCISES

1. Fill in the blanks to make the following statements correct.
   a. A firm's demand for financial capital is derived from its demand for ____________.
   b. A firm that decides to invest in additional machinery will ____________ its requirement for financial capital.
   c. An increase in the marginal product of capital will lead firms to ____________ their desired capital stock and therefore ____________ their demand for financial capital.
   d. An increase in the interest rate will ____________ the present value of capital's *MRP* and therefore ____________ firms' desired capital stock. The result will be a ____________ in the quantity of financial capital demanded by firms.
   e. An increase in capital's *MRP* results in a ____________ in the economy's investment demand curve, whereas an increase in the interest rate results in a ____________ the economy's investment demand curve.

2. Fill in the blanks to make the following statements correct.
   a. An increase in the interest rate leads households to ____________ their current spending and ____________ their current saving. The result is an ____________ in the quantity of financial capital supplied.
   b. An increase in current income leads to an ____________ in household saving at any given interest rate. This results in a ____________ in the economy's supply curve for capital.
   c. An increase in expected future income leads to an ____________ in current household spending. The result is a ____________ in household saving and therefore a ____________ in the quantity of capital supplied at any given interest rate. This is represented by a ____________ in the economy's supply curve for financial capital.

3. Fill in the blanks to make the following statements correct.

   a. The economy's equilibrium interest rate is determined where ____________. At an interest rate above the equilibrium interest rate, the quantity of capital supplied ____________ the quantity of capital demanded, and the result is a ____________ in the interest rate.
   b. At an interest rate below the equilibrium interest rate, the quantity of capital demanded ____________ the quantity of capital supplied, and the result is a ____________ in the interest rate.
   c. Beginning in equilibrium in the capital market, an increase in the supply of financial capital leads to a ____________ in the equilibrium interest rate, a ____________ in borrowing by firms, and an ____________ in the equilibrium level of investment and saving.
   d. Beginning in equilibrium in the capital market, an increase in the demand for financial capital leads to an ____________ in the equilibrium interest rate, an ____________ in desired saving by households, and an ____________ in the equilibrium level of investment and saving.
   e. Technological improvements lead to an ____________ in both the demand for and supply of financial capital. As a result, technological improvements can explain a ____________ capital stock and ____________ in the interest rate.

4. myeconlab The following table shows the stream of income produced by several different assets. In each case, P_1, P_2, and P_3 are the payments made by the asset in years 1, 2, and 3.

Asset	i	P_1	P_2	P_3	Present Value
A	8%	\$1000	\$0	\$0	—
B	7%	0	0	5000	—
C	9%	200	0	200	—
D	10%	50	40	60	—

   a. For each asset, compute the asset's present value. (Note that the market interest rate, i, is not the same in each situation.)
   b. In each case, what is the most a firm would be prepared to pay to acquire the asset?
   c. Suppose the listed purchase price for an asset were less than its present value. What would you expect to observe?

5. The following table shows how the present value of the future *MRPs* produced by each unit of capital changes as the firm's total capital stock increases.

Units of Capital	*PV* of future *MRPs*
100	\$10 000
101	9 000
102	8 000
103	7 000
104	6 000
105	5 000
106	4 000
107	3 000

   a. Notice that the present value of the *MRP* declines as more capital is used. What economic principle accounts for this?
   b. If a unit of capital can be purchased for \$5000, how many will the firm purchase? Explain.
   c. Suppose the market interest rate falls. Explain what happens to the *PV* of the stream of future *MRPs*. What happens to the firm's profit-maximizing level of capital?

6. The diagram below shows an individual firm's investment demand curve. The market interest rate is i_0.

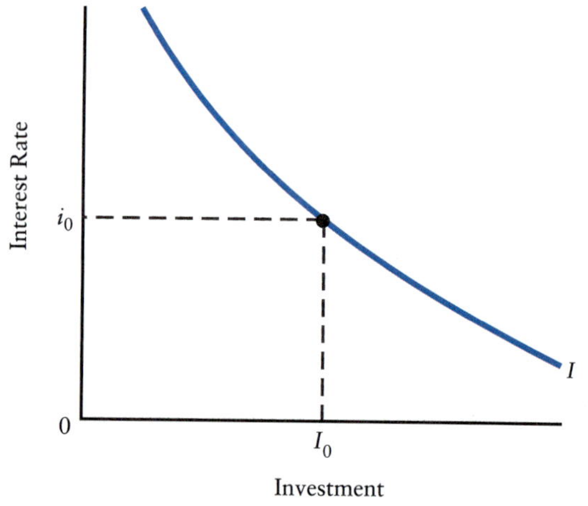

   a. Explain why the firm's investment demand curve is downward sloping.
   b. Suppose the firm now expects the market for its product to be especially good in the future. Explain what happens to its investment demand curve.
   c. Now suppose some technical problem leads to a reduction in the future stream of *MRPs* produced by capital. How does this affect the firm's investment demand curve?

7. myeconlab For each interest rate below, compute the opportunity cost (in terms of forgone spending next year) to a household of spending $1000 this year:

   a. The interest rate is 5 percent per year
   b. The interest rate is 7 percent per year
   c. The interest rate is 9 percent per year
   d. Explain why, other things being equal, households save more when the interest rate is higher.

8. The accompanying figure shows the economy's capital market, with the initial equilibrium at point *E*, with an interest rate of i^* and investment (and saving) equal to I^*.

   a. Suppose the government introduces a program of tax credits to firms that increase their desired investment in new physical capital. What is the effect on the equilibrium interest rate, investment, and saving of this policy? Show the effect of this policy in the diagram.
   b. In part (a), the policy has led to a higher interest rate *and* higher investment by firms. Does this contradict our discussion in this chapter about how changes in the interest rate affect firms' investment behaviour? Explain.
   c. Now suppose the government introduces a program of tax credits to households who save. What is the effect on the equilibrium interest rate, investment, and saving of this policy? Show the effect of this policy in the diagram.

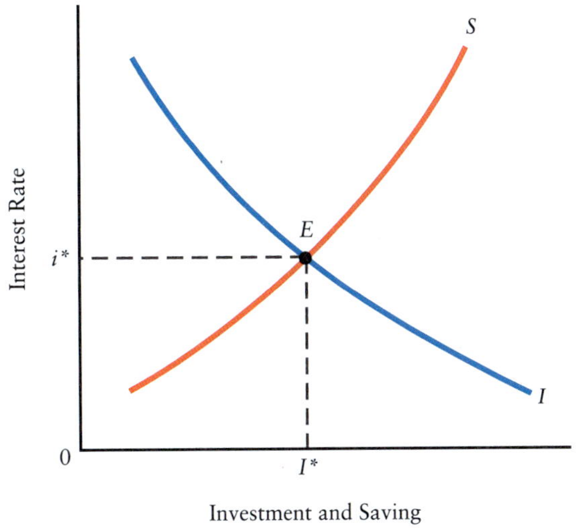

   d. In part (c), the policy has led to a lower interest rate *and* higher saving by households. Does this contradict our discussion in this chapter about how changes in the interest rate affect households' saving behaviour? Explain.

DISCUSSION QUESTIONS

1. How would you go about evaluating the present value of each of the following?

   a. The existing reserves of a relatively small oil company
   b. The total world reserves of an exhaustible natural resource with a known completely fixed supply
   c. A long-term bond, issued by a very unstable third-world government, that promises to pay the bearer $1000 per year forever
   d. A lottery ticket that your neighbour bought for $10, which was one of 1 million tickets sold for a drawing which will be held in one year's time paying $2 million to the single winner

2. Your parents argue that it makes more sense for you to take taxis and, on occasion, to rent a car while you are at university because you will be spending most of your time in the library and your need for a car should be minimal. Make an argument based on the rental price of transportation (not on the other advantages of having the car) that it may be cheaper for you to buy a car for use while you are at university.

3. "Profit-maximizing firms will reduce their desired investment when the interest rate rises, other things being equal. As a result, empirical economists should always expect to see a negative correlation between actual investment and the interest rate." Comment.

4. Since the interest rate is the price of financial capital, a change in the interest rate generates both an income effect and a substitution effect.

   a. Explain how the substitution effect of an increase in the interest rate influences households' desired saving.
   b. Explain how the income effect of an increase in the interest rate influences households' desired saving. Why does the direction of the income effect depend on whether the household is a net debtor or a net creditor?
   c. Explain why, for the economy as a whole, the substitution effect is likely to dominate the income effect.
   d. What is the importance of the result in part (c) for the economy's supply of financial capital?

5. For parts of this question, it is useful to read "Investment and Saving in Globalized Financial Markets" in the *Additional Topics* section of this book's MyEconLab.

   a. Suppose Canada were a closed economy, with no trade in financial capital with the rest of the world. In such a world, explain why a government that wished to encourage domestic saving could achieve this outcome *either* by designing a policy to increase saving or by designing a policy to increase investment.

   b. Now suppose financial capital is easily tradable between countries. What determines the Canadian real interest rate in such a setting?

   c. Explain why the government objective to increase saving now requires a policy aimed directly at increasing saving (and not investment).

PART 6: GOVERNMENT IN THE MARKET ECONOMY

CHAPTER 16

Market Failures and Government Intervention

LEARNING OBJECTIVES

In this chapter you will learn

1. about the "informal" defence of free markets.
2. about externalities and why they lead to allocative inefficiency.
3. why public goods are underprovided by private markets.
4. why free markets may not achieve some desirable social goals.
5. the direct and indirect costs of government intervention, and some of the important causes of government failure.

Many aspects of Canadian economic life are determined in free markets. Most of the goods and services that you buy are produced by privately owned profit-making firms, and the prices of those goods and services are determined in free markets. The incomes of most Canadian workers are also determined by free-market forces.

But government intervention and regulation are also pervasive. Canadian governments regulate the pricing of cable TV, land-line and cellular telephone service, and electricity. The Canadian government owns Canada Post, and dozens of other Crown corporations that sell goods or services to firms and households. Canadian governments also have extensive regulations regarding many aspects of our lives, including waste disposal, workplace safety, building codes, minimum wages, taxi service, and so on. And governments take a substantial portion of our incomes in the form of taxes, with which they finance their provision of services to us.

Which elements of the economy can be left to free markets and which elements require government intervention? Governments are clearly necessary to provide law and order and to define and enforce property rights. But beyond these basic functions—ones that we all too often take for granted—what is the case for government intervention in otherwise free markets?

The general case for some reliance on free markets is that allowing decentralized decision making is more desirable than having all economic decisions made by a centralized planning body. The general case for some government intervention is that almost no one wants to let markets decide *everything* about our economic affairs. Most people believe that there are areas in which markets do not function well and in which government intervention can improve the general social good.

The operative choice is not between an unhampered free-market economy and a fully centralized command economy. It is rather the choice of *which mix* of markets and government intervention best suits people's hopes and needs.

In this chapter, we discuss the role of the government in market-based economies, identifying why markets sometimes fail and why government policies sometimes fail. We begin by examining the basic functions of government.

16.1 BASIC FUNCTIONS OF GOVERNMENT

Governments are very old institutions. They arose shortly after the Neolithic Agricultural Revolution turned people from hunter–gatherers into settled farmers about 10 000 years ago. An institution that has survived that long must be doing something right! Over the intervening 100 centuries the functions undertaken by governments have varied enormously. But through all that time the function that has not changed is to provide what is called a *monopoly of violence*. Violent acts can be conducted by the military and the civilian police arms of government, and through its judicial system the government can deprive people of their liberty by incarcerating them or, in extreme cases, by executing them. This is a dangerous monopoly that is easily abused. For this reason satisfactory societies have systems of checks and balances designed to keep the government's monopoly directed to the general good rather than to the good of a narrow government circle.

The importance of having a monopoly of violence can be seen in those countries whose governments do not have it. Somalia in recent decades and China in the 1920s provide examples of countries in which individual warlords commanded armies that could not vanquish each other. Colombia and, to some extent, Russia provide examples of organized crime having substantial power to commit violence that the government cannot control. In extreme cases where many groups have almost equal ability to exert military violence, power struggles can create havoc with normal economic and social life. Life then becomes "nasty, brutish, and short"—to use the words of the seventeenth-century English political philosopher Thomas Hobbes (1588–1679).

The importance of having checks on the government's arbitrary use of its monopoly is seen in the disasters that ensue in the many dictatorships that misuse their power. The USSR under Stalin, Uganda under Idi Amin, Nigeria under Sanni Abacha, Cambodia under Pol Pot, Iraq under Saddam Hussein, and Liberia under Charles Taylor are a few of many examples from the past 75 years.

When the government's monopoly of violence is secure and functions with effective restrictions against its arbitrary use, citizens can safely carry on their ordinary economic and social activities.

A related government activity is to provide security of property. Governments define and enforce property rights that give people a secure claim to the fruits of their own labour. These property rights include clear definition and enforcement of the rights and obligations of institutions such as corporations, religious organizations, and non-profit enterprises.

As the founder of British classical economics, Adam Smith, put it a long time ago:

> *The first duty of the sovereign [is] that of protecting the society from the violence and invasion of other independent societies.... The second duty of the sovereign [is] that of protecting, as far as possible, every member of the society from the injustice or oppression of every other member of it.*[1]

[1] Adam Smith, *The Wealth of Nations* (1776; New York: Random House, 1937 ed., pp. 653, 669).

In a modern complex economy, providing these "minimal" government services is no simple task. Countries whose governments are not good at doing these things have seldom prospered economically.

The importance of these basic functions of government should not be underestimated. In recent years, economists and policymakers in rich, developed countries have come to a greater understanding of the challenges in developing countries that stem from their ineffective political structures. Local corruption, powerful warlords, and a lack of basic political infrastructure combine to make official development aid less effective than it would be in countries with more stable and representative political structures. As a result, a growing share of official assistance to developing countries is taking the form of *political* rather than *economic* assistance—a process often referred to as *institution building*.

16.2 THE CASE FOR FREE MARKETS

Within a secure framework of law and order, and well-defined and enforced property rights, a modern economy can function at least moderately well without further government assistance. In this section we review the case for free markets. In subsequent sections we study government functions that arise when free markets fail to produce acceptable results.

Free markets are impressive institutions. Consumers' tastes and producers' costs help to generate price signals. These signals coordinate separate decisions taken by millions of independent agents, all pursuing their own self-interest. In doing so, they allocate the nation's resources without conscious central direction. Markets also determine the distribution of income by establishing prices of factors of production, which provide incomes for their owners. Furthermore, modern market economies, where firms compete to get ahead of each other by producing better goods more cheaply, generate the technological changes that have raised average living standards fairly steadily over the past two centuries.

In presenting the case for free markets, economists have used two quite different approaches. The first of these may be characterized as the "formal defence," and is based on the concept of allocative efficiency, discussed in Chapters 5 and 12. The essence of the formal defence of free-market economies is that if all markets were perfectly competitive, and if governments allowed all prices to be determined by demand and supply, then price would equal marginal cost for all products and the economy would be allocatively efficient. Allocative efficiency is a worthy goal because it means resources are used in such a way that total surplus to society—consumer surplus plus producer surplus—is maximized. Since we discussed allocative efficiency extensively in earlier chapters, we will say no more about it at this point.

The other defence of free markets—what might be called the "informal defence"—is at least as old as Adam Smith and is meant to apply to market economies whether or not they are perfectly competitive. It is based on the theme that markets are a very effective mechanism for coordinating the decisions of decentralized decision makers. The informal defence is intuitive in that it is not laid out in a formal model of an economy, but it does follow from some hard reasoning, and over the years it has been subjected to much intellectual probing.

This informal defence of free markets is based on three central arguments.

1. Free markets provide automatic coordination of the actions of decentralized decision makers.

2. The pursuit of profits in free markets provides a stimulus to innovation and rising material living standards.
3. Free markets permit a decentralization of economic power.

Automatic Coordination

Defenders of the market economy argue that, compared with the alternatives, the decentralized market system is more flexible and adjusts more quickly to changes.

Suppose, for example, that the world price of oil rises. One household might prefer to respond by maintaining a high temperature in its house and economizing on its driving; another household might do the reverse. A third household might give up air-conditioning instead. This flexibility can be contrasted with centralized control, which would force the same pattern on everyone, say, by fixing the price, by rationing heating oil and gasoline, by regulating permitted temperatures, and by limiting air-conditioning to days when the temperature exceeded 27°C.

Furthermore, as conditions continue to change, prices in a market economy will also change, and decentralized decision makers can react continually. In contrast, government quotas, allocations, and rationing schemes are much more difficult to adjust. As a result, there are likely to be shortages and surpluses before adjustments are made. One great value of the market is that it provides automatic signals *as a situation develops* so that not all of the consequences of an economic change have to be anticipated and allowed for by a group of central planners. Millions of responses to millions of changes in thousands of markets are required every year, and it would be a Herculean task to anticipate and plan for them all.

A market system allows for coordination *without anyone needing to understand how the whole system works.* As Professor Thomas Schelling, who was awarded the Nobel Prize in economics in 2005, illustrated this idea:

> *The dairy farmer doesn't need to know how many people eat butter and how far away they are, how many other people raise cows, how many babies drink milk, or whether more money is spent on beer or milk. What he needs to know is the prices of different feeds, the characteristics of different cows, the different prices... for milk..., the relative cost of hired labor and electrical machinery, and what his net earnings might be if he sold his cows and raised pigs instead.*[2]

It is, of course, an enormous advantage that all the producers and consumers of a country collectively can make the system operate—yet not one of them, much less all of them, has to understand how it works.

Innovation and Growth

Technology, tastes, and resource availability are changing all the time, in all economies. Thirty years ago there was no such thing as a DVD player or a digital camera. Hybrid cars did not exist. Manuscripts existed only as hardcopy, not as electronic files in an ultralight, wireless, laptop computer. The Internet did not exist—nor did MP3 players, BlackBerrys, cellular phones, electronic airline tickets, cost-effective solar panels and wind turbines, income-tax software packages, computer-assisted design (CAD)

---

[2] T.C. Schelling, *Micro Motives and Macro Behavior* (New York: Norton, 1978).

programs, regional jets, standardized containers for transoceanic shipping, and a whole host of other goods and services that we now take for granted.

Digital cameras, personal computers, hybrid cars, and regional jets are all products that were invented or developed by individuals or firms in pursuit of profits. An entrepreneur who correctly "reads" the market and perceives that a demand for some product may exist or be created will be inclined to develop it.

Producers in market economies have the incentive to provide the goods and services that customers value, and the result is that line-ups like these rarely exist in these economies. In the former Soviet Union, however, the central planning system was very slow to respond, and line-ups like this were very common.

The next 20 years will also surely see changes great and small. Changes in technology may make an idea that is not practical today practical five years from now. New products and techniques will be devised to adapt to shortages, gluts, and changes in consumer demands and to exploit new opportunities made available by new technologies.

In a market economy, individuals risk their time and money in the hope of earning profits. Though many fail, some succeed. New products and processes appear and disappear. Some are fads or have little impact; others become items of major significance. The market system works by trial and error to sort them out and allocates resources to what prove to be successful innovations.

In contrast, planners in more centralized systems have to guess which innovations will be productive and which goods will be strongly demanded. Central planning may achieve wonders by permitting a massive effort in a chosen direction, but central planners also may guess incorrectly about the direction and put too many eggs in the wrong basket or reject as unpromising something that will turn out to be vital. Perhaps the biggest failure of centrally planned economies was their inability to encourage the experimentation and innovation that have proven to be the driving forces behind long-run growth in advanced market economies. It is striking that since the early 1990s most centrally planned economies abandoned their system in favour of a price system in one fell swoop while the only remaining large planned economy, China, is increasing the role of markets in most aspects of its economy.

Decentralization of Power

Another important part of the case for a free-market economy is that it tends to decentralize power and thus requires less coercion of individuals than any other type of economy. Of course, even though markets tend to diffuse power, they do not do so completely; large firms and large labour unions clearly have and exercise substantial economic power.

Though the market power of large corporations is not negligible, it tends to be constrained both by the competition of other large entities and by the emergence of new products and firms. This is the process of creative destruction that was described by Joseph Schumpeter and that we examined in Chapter 10. In any case, say defenders of the free market, even such concentrations of private power are far less substantial than government power.

Governments must coerce if markets are not allowed to allocate people to jobs and goods to consumers. Not only will such coercion be regarded as arbitrary (especially by those who do not like the results), but the power creates major opportunities for bribery, corruption, and allocation according to the tastes of the central administrators. If, at the going prices and wages, there are not enough apartments or coveted jobs to go around, the bureaucrats can allocate some to those who pay the largest bribe, some to those with religious beliefs or political views that they like, and only the rest to those whose names come up on the waiting list.

This line of reasoning has been articulated forcefully by the late Nobel laureate Milton Friedman (1912–2006), who was for many years a professor of economics at the University of Chicago. Friedman argued that economic freedom—the ability to allocate resources through private markets—is essential to the maintenance of political freedom.[3] Other economists and social theorists have challenged this proposition.

16.3 MARKET FAILURES

Free markets do all of the good things that we have just discussed in the informal defence; yet there are many circumstances in which the free market does not produce the allocatively efficient outcome. In these cases, economists say that markets have *failed.* The case for intervening in free markets turns in large part on identifying the conditions that lead to market failure. Much of the following discussion is devoted to this task.

We must be careful when using the expression *market failure* because the word *failure* may convey the wrong impression. Market failure does not mean that nothing good has happened. It means, instead, that the *best attainable outcome* has not been achieved. More precisely, **market failure** refers to a situation in which private markets, in the absence of government intervention, fail to achieve allocative efficiency. In other words, in some market or markets, the marginal benefit of the product differs from its marginal cost.

market failure Failure of the unregulated market system to achieve allocative efficiency.

Market failure describes a situation in which the free market, in the absence of government intervention, fails to achieve allocative efficiency.

It is useful to recall the distinction between normative and positive statements that we first encountered in Chapter 2. The statement that the economy is allocatively efficient (or not) is a *positive* statement. We can say that the economy has or has not achieved allocative efficiency without making any value judgement—the statement uses only an observation about the economy and the definition of allocative efficiency. It is important to note, however, that the allocatively efficient outcome may not be the most desirable outcome in a normative sense. For example, the economy may be allocatively efficient even though the distribution of income is judged by some to be undesirable. As we see later in the chapter, such concerns provide another motivation for government intervention.

We now examine four situations in which the free market fails to achieve allocative efficiency—*market power, externalities, non-rivalrous* and *non-excludable goods,* and *asymmetric information.* All of these market failures provide a justification, at least in principle, for government intervention in markets. We then discuss other reasons for government intervention that are not based on market failure—chief among these is intervention to achieve a more desirable distribution of income.

[3] Milton Friedman, *Capitalism and Freedom* (Chicago: The University of Chicago Press, 1982).

Market Power

Market power is inevitable in any modern market economy for at least two reasons. First, in many industries economies of scale are such that there is room for only a few firms to operate efficiently, each having some ability to influence market conditions. Second, in most manufacturing and service industries, firms sell differentiated products and thus have some ability to set price. As we saw in Chapters 10, 11, and 12, firms that have market power will maximize their profit at a level of output where price exceeds marginal cost. The result is allocative inefficiency.

Government policy is not aimed at *eliminating* firms' market power, however. Not only would this be impossible, given the pervasiveness of oligopoly and monopolistic competition, but it would also be undesirable since much of the innovation and productivity growth that our economy produces comes from firms with market power. Instead, the goal of government policy is to prevent firms from abusing their market power in a way that unduly harms consumers and reduces the amount of innovation. As we saw in Chapter 12, the government's standard approaches for this problem include regulation and competition policy.

Externalities

Recall from Chapter 12 that in order for the economy to be allocatively efficient, marginal benefit must equal marginal cost for all products. But whose benefits and costs are relevant? Firms that are maximizing their *own* profits are interested only in their own costs of production—they may not care about any benefits or costs their actions might create for others. Similarly, insofar as individual consumers are interested in the benefits *they* receive from any given product, they ignore any costs or benefits that may accrue to others. An **externality** occurs whenever actions taken by firms or consumers directly impose costs or confer benefits on others. When you smoke a cigarette in a restaurant, you might impose costs on others present; when you renovate your home, you might confer benefits on your neighbours by improving the general look of the neighbourhood. Externalities are also called *third-party effects* because parties other than the two primary participants in the transaction (the buyer and the seller) are affected.

externality An effect on parties not directly involved in the production or use of a commodity. Also called *third-party effects.*

The foregoing discussion suggests the importance of the distinction between *private cost* and *social cost.* **Private cost** measures the cost faced by the private decision maker, including production costs, advertising costs, and so on. **Social cost** includes the private cost (since the decision maker is a member of society) but also includes any other costs imposed on third parties. There is a similar distinction between *private benefit* and *social benefit.* To simplify things, however, we will discuss all externalities in terms of the distinction between private and social cost. But this does not limit our discussion in any way. If we want to consider a situation in which your listening to good music confers benefits to your nearby friends, we can think of your action as either increasing their benefits or, equivalently, as decreasing their costs. Similarly, your smoking of cigarettes can be viewed either as reducing their benefits or, equivalently, as increasing their costs. By expressing everything in terms of costs (rather than benefits), we merely simplify the discussion.

private cost The value of the best alternative use of resources used in production as valued by the producer.

social cost The value of the best alternative use of resources used in production as valued by society.

Discrepancies between private cost and social cost occur when there are externalities. The presence of externalities, even when all markets are perfectly competitive, leads to allocatively inefficient outcomes.

Practise with Study Guide Chapter 16, Exercise 1.

FIGURE 16-1 An Externality Leads to Allocative Inefficiency

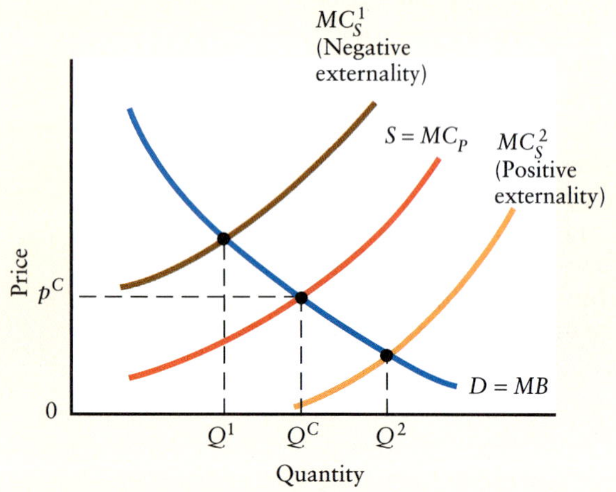

When there is an externality, either too much or too little of the good is produced. If the market for this good is perfectly competitive and there is no government intervention, the equilibrium is shown by p^C and Q^C. If there is no externality, social and private marginal cost are the same and so the outcome is allocatively efficient.

Now suppose the production or the consumption of the good imposes costs on third parties. This is a *negative* externality—social marginal costs are MC_S^1, above MC_P. The vertical distance between MC_P and MC_S^1 reflects the per-unit external cost. The allocatively efficient quantity is now Q^1 where MB equals MC_S^1. But the free market will produce Q^C, too much of the good.

If the production or consumption of the good instead confers benefits on third parties, this is a positive externality—social marginal costs are MC_S^2, below MC_P. The vertical distance between MC_P and MC_S^2 reflects the per-unit external benefit. The allocatively efficient quantity is now Q^2 where MB equals MC_S^2. But the free market will produce Q^C, too little of the good.

Externalities arise in many different ways, and they may be harmful or beneficial to the third parties. When they are harmful they are called *negative externalities;* when they are beneficial, they are called *positive externalities.* Figure 16-1 shows why an externality leads to allocative inefficiency, even though the market is perfectly competitive. Here are two examples.

Consider the case of a firm whose production process for steel generates harmful smoke as a byproduct. Individuals who live and work near the firm bear real costs as they cope with breathing (or trying to avoid breathing) the harmful smoke. When the firm makes its decision concerning how much steel to produce, it ignores the costs that it imposes on other people. This is a negative externality. In this case, because the firm ignores those parts of social cost that are not its own private cost, the firm will produce too much steel relative to what is allocatively efficient.

A second example involves an individual who renovates her home and thus improves its external appearance. Such improvements enhance the neighbours' view and the value of their property. Yet the individual renovator ignores the benefits that her actions have on the neighbours. This is a positive externality. In this case, because the renovator ignores those parts of social benefits that are not her own private benefits, there will be too little home renovation done relative to what is allocatively efficient.

With a positive externality, a competitive free market will produce too little of the good. With a negative externality, a competitive free market will produce too much of the good.

myeconlab

Ronald Coase, a Nobel-Prize-winning economist, presented the famous argument that as long as property rights are clearly assigned, externalities need not lead to allocative inefficiency. For more details and a numerical example, look for "Externalities and the Coase Theorem" in the *Additional Topics* section of this book's MyEconLab.

www.myeconlab.com

Non-Rivalrous and Non-Excludable Goods

Economists classify goods and services into four broad categories depending on the *rivalry* for the good and the *excludability* of the good. Table 16-1 shows these four types of goods.

A good or service is said to be **rivalrous** if one person's consumption of the good means that no one else can also consume it. For example, a chocolate bar is rivalrous because if you eat the entire bar, it cannot also be eaten by your friend. In contrast, a television signal is not rivalrous. You and your friend can sit in your separate living rooms and both receive the same signal, neither of you diminishing the amount available to the other.

A good is said to be **excludable** if people can be prevented from consuming it. A chocolate bar is excludable because you cannot eat it unless you buy it first. A regular TV signal is not excludable, but some speciality channels are because only those who pay for the special receivers can view them. Your use of the light produced by street lights is non-excludable, as is your access to the air you breathe.

The airborne emissions from coal-fired power plants are one important example of a negative externality. In this case, the social costs associated with the sulphur-dioxide emissions exceed the private costs.

Private Goods Most goods and services that you consume are both rivalrous and excludable. Your consumption of food, clothing, a rental apartment, a car, gasoline, CDs, airline tickets, and textbooks are only possible because you pay the seller for the right to own those goods or services. Furthermore, your consumption of those goods reduces the amount available for others. In Table 16-1 we simply refer to these goods as **private goods.**

rivalrous A good or service is rivalrous if, when one person consumes one unit of it, there is one less unit available for others to consume.

excludable A good or service is excludable if its owner can prevent others from consuming it.

private goods Goods or services that are both rivalrous and excludable.

Goods that are both rivalrous and excludable—private goods—pose no particular problem for public policy.

Common-Property Resources Goods that are rivalrous but non-excludable pose an interesting challenge for public policy. Note in Table 16-1 that the examples of these goods include such things as fisheries, common grazing land, wildlife, rivers and streams, and so on. These are called **common-property resources**. My use of river water reduces the amount available for you, but there is no practical way that my access to the water can be controlled. And since my access to the water cannot be controlled, there is no practical way to make me pay for it. The result is that there is a zero price. The zero price leads to the obvious result that, in the absence of government intervention, private users will tend to *overuse* common-property resources. In other words, private users will use these resources to the point where the marginal cost to society will exceed the marginal benefit to society. Society would be better off if less of these resources were used.

common-property resource A product that is rivalrous but not excludable.

Goods that are rivalrous and non-excludable are called common-property resources. They tend to be overused by private firms and consumers.

The overuse of common-property resources is especially noticeable in such cases as the Atlantic cod and Pacific salmon fisheries where individual fishermen have a natural incentive to overfish. After all, if they don't catch a particular fish, they will merely be leaving it to be caught by the next fisherman who comes along. It is this natural inclination to overuse the fisheries that has led the Canadian government over the years to develop a system of licences and quotas whereby individual fishermen must pay to have access to the common-property resource. *Applying Economic Concepts 16-1* examines the depletion of the world's fisheries.

TABLE 16-1 Four Types of Products

	Excludable	Non-Excludable
Rivalrous	*Private Goods* DVDs A seat on an airplane An hour of legal advice	*Common-Property Resources* Fisheries Rivers and streams Wildlife Clean air
Non-Rivalrous (up to capacity)	Art galleries Roads Bridges Cable or satellite TV signal	*Public Goods* National defence Public information Public protection Regular TV signal

Free markets cope best with rivalrous and excludable goods—what we here call "private" goods. The table gives examples of goods in each of four categories, depending on whether consumption of the good is rivalrous and whether one can be excluded from consuming the good.

Overfishing is a serious problem in Canada and many other countries, to the point where most of the world's fisheries have become significantly depleted and some have little chance of recovering. Recovery will require enforceable international agreements as well as difficult national political decisions.

Excludable But Non-Rivalrous Goods Goods that are excludable but not rivalrous are also interesting, and many of the obvious examples of these—art galleries, roads, and bridges—are typically provided by government. The non-rivalry for these goods means that the marginal cost of providing the good to one extra person is zero. As an example, just ask yourself what it costs for an extra person to walk through the Canadian Museum of Civilization in Hull, given that it is already open but not many people are there. Or, what is the cost for one more person to drive on an uncrowded road? The answer in both cases is zero. But if the marginal cost to society of providing one more unit of the good is zero, then allocative efficiency requires that the price also be zero. Any positive price would prevent some people from using it, but this would be inefficient. As long as their marginal benefit exceeds the social marginal cost of providing the good (zero in this case), it is efficient for these people to use the good.

To avoid inefficient exclusion, the government often provides non-rivalrous but excludable goods and services.

For this reason, art galleries, museums, libraries, roads, bridges, and national parks are often provided by various levels of government. In some cases, like libraries and roads, the price to consumers is usually zero. In others, like national parks and art galleries, there is usually some positive price.

The positive price in some of these cases can be explained by another feature of these goods. What happens in the Canadian Museum of Civilization on a summer Saturday morning? What happens on Highway 401 outside Toronto at rush hour? The answer is *congestion*. When congestion occurs on roads and bridges, or in art galleries and museums, it is no longer true that the marginal cost of providing the good to one more user is zero. By increasing the amount of congestion, providing the good to one more person imposes costs on those already using the good. If I enter an already-busy highway, I slow down all the existing traffic. If you visit an already-crowded museum, you make it less pleasant for everybody else. In these cases, a good that is non-rivalrous when uncongested becomes rivalrous when congested. At this point it becomes (in economic terms) a private good, and a positive price is appropriate.

APPLYING ECONOMIC CONCEPTS 16-1

The World's Endangered Fish

The fish in the ocean are a common-property resource, and theory predicts that such a resource will be overexploited if there is a high enough demand for the product and suppliers are able to meet that demand. In the past centuries there were neither enough people eating fish nor efficient enough fishing technologies to endanger stocks. Over the last 50 years, however, the population explosion has added to the demand for fish and advances in technology have vastly increased the ability to catch fish. Large boats, radar detection, and more murderous nets have tipped the balance in favour of the predator and against the prey. As a result, the overfishing prediction of common property theory has been amply borne out. Today, fish are a common-property resource; tomorrow, they could become no one's resource.

Since 1950 the world's annual capture of fish has increased by over four times, from 20 million tonnes in 1950 to over 80 million tonnes today (not including the "catch" from farmed fish, which raises the current annual haul to over 130 million tonnes). The increase was sustained only by substituting smaller, less desirable fish for the diminishing stocks of the more desirable fish and by penetrating ever further into remote oceans. Today, all available stocks are being exploited, and now even the total tonnage of captured fish is beginning to fall. The UN estimates that the total value of the world's catch could be increased by nearly $30 billion if fish stocks were properly managed by governments interested in the total catch, rather than exploited by individuals interested in their own catch.

The developed countries have so overfished their own stocks that Iceland and the European Union could cut their fleets by 40 percent and catch as much fish as they do today. This is because more fish would survive to spawn, allowing each boat in a smaller fleet to catch about 40 percent more than does each boat in today's large fishing fleet.

The problem has become so acute that Canada shut down its entire Atlantic cod fishing industry in 1992 and its Pacific salmon industry in 1998. Tens of thousands of Newfoundland and Labrador residents lost their livelihoods in an industry that had flourished for five centuries.

Canada and the European Union have since been in conflict over what Canada claims is predatory overfishing by EU boats just outside Canadian territorial waters. These tensions heightened in March 1995 when the Spanish fishing trawler *Estai* was fired at and forced into St. John's harbour by a Canadian fisheries-protection vessel for fishing turbot just outside Canada's 200-nautical-mile "economic zone." The EU (on behalf of Spain) accused Canada of piracy. Canada accused Spain of overfishing and depleting the value of Canada's turbot fishery.

Some developing countries are taking action to conserve their fish stocks but the majority are encouraging rapid expansion of their own fishing fleets with the all-too-predictable results that their domestic waters will soon be seriously overfished.

Worldwide action saved most species of whales. It remains to be seen how many types of fish will be caught to extinction and how many will recover as individual nations slowly learn the lesson of economic theory. Common-property resources need central management if they are not to be overexploited to an extent that risks extinction.

State of the World's Fish Stocks, 2004

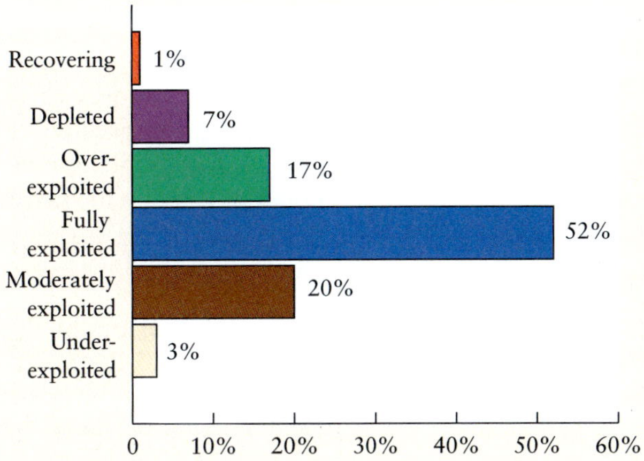

(*Source: Review of the State of World Marine Fishery Resources*, p. 10, FAO Fisheries Technical Paper #457, 2005. See: www.fao.org. © Food and Agriculture Organization of the United Nations (FAO), 2007.)

A near-empty road or highway has little rivalry in use, and is much like a public good. But once the crowds appear, there is considerable rivalry for space on the road and it therefore becomes more like a private good. Some jurisdictions have introduced financial charges to drivers to better allocate the scarce resource during peak hours.

Governments who provide such goods often charge a price to help ration the good when rivalry becomes significant. An excellent example of this is some toll highways that, with the aid of powerful cameras and computers, charge motorists a different amount per kilometre driven depending on the congestion of the highway. As the traffic slows down due to congestion, the price per kilometre increases to reflect the higher marginal cost. This higher price is indicated on electronic highway signs posted regularly along the highway. Drivers can then choose either to remain on the highway and pay the higher price, or exit the highway and take another (less expensive) route to their destination.

Public Goods Finally, there are some goods that are neither excludable nor rivalrous. These are called **public goods** or sometimes *collective consumption goods*. The classic case of a public good is national defence. All Canadians are equally protected and defended by the Canadian Forces. It is not possible to provide national defence to some Canadians and not to others.

public goods Goods or services that can simultaneously provide benefits to a large group of people. Also called *collective consumption goods.*

Information is also often a public good. Suppose a certain food additive causes cancer. The cost of discovering this fact needs to be borne only once. The information is then of value to everyone who might have used the additive, and the cost of making the information available to one more consumer is approximately zero. Furthermore, once the information about the newly discovered carcinogen is available, it is impossible to prevent people from using that information. Other public goods include street lighting, weather forecasts (a type of information), and some forms of environmental protection.

Practise with Study Guide Chapter 16, Exercise 2.

All of these examples raise what is called the *free-rider problem.* Since public goods are (by definition) not excludable, it is impossible to prevent anyone from using them once they are provided. If the provider charged a price, non-payers would take a *free-ride* at the expense of those individuals with a social conscience that do pay. But the existence of free riders, in turn, implies that the private market will generally not produce efficient amounts of the public good because once the good is produced, it is impractical (or impossible) to make people pay for its use. Indeed, free markets may fail to produce public goods at all. The obvious remedy in these cases is for the government to provide the good, financed from its tax revenues.

Because of the free-rider problem, private markets will not always provide public goods. Public goods must therefore be provided by government.

How much of a public good should the government provide? It should provide the public good up to the point where the *sum* of everyone's individual marginal benefit from the good is just equal to the marginal cost of providing the good. We add everyone's individual marginal benefit to get the total marginal benefit because a public good—unlike an ordinary private good—can be used simultaneously by everyone. It therefore generates value to more than one person at a time. Figure 16-2 shows the optimal provision of a public good in the simple case of only two individuals.

The optimal quantity of a public good is such that the marginal cost of the good equals the *sum* of all users' marginal benefits of the good.

Asymmetric Information

Information is, of course, a valuable commodity, and markets for information and expertise are well developed, as every student is aware. Markets for expertise are conceptually identical to markets for any other valuable service. They can pose special problems, however. One of these we have already discussed: Information is often a public good and when it is it tends to be underproduced by a free market.

Even where information is not a public good, markets for expertise are prone to market failure. The reason is that one party to a transaction can often take advantage of special knowledge in ways that change the nature of the transaction itself. Situations where one party to a transaction has special knowledge are called situations of **asymmetric information.**

The importance of asymmetric information to the operation of the economy has received considerable attention in recent years. In 2001, Professors George Akerlof, Michael Spence, and Joseph Stiglitz shared the Nobel Prize in economics for their insights about how asymmetric information can lead to market failures. The two important sources of market failure that arise from situations of asymmetric information are *moral hazard* and *adverse selection.*

FIGURE 16-2 The Optimal Provision of a Public Good

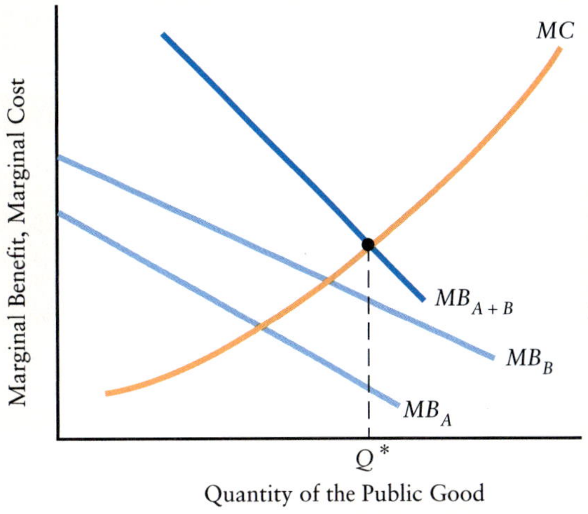

Determining the optimal provision of a public good requires adding together the marginal benefits for each individual. The figure shows marginal benefit curves for a public good for two individuals, Andrew and Brenda. By adding MB_A and MB_B *vertically* we derive society's marginal benefit curve, MB_{A+B}. The marginal cost of providing the public good is shown by *MC*. The allocatively efficient level of the public good is Q^*, where the marginal cost to society is just equal to the marginal benefit to society.

Moral Hazard In general, **moral hazard** exists when one party to a transaction has both the *incentive* and the *ability* to shift costs onto the other party. Moral hazard problems often arise from insurance contracts. The classic example is the homeowner who does not bother to shovel snow from his sidewalk because he knows that his insurance will cover the cost if the mail carrier should fall and break a leg. The costs of the homeowner's lax behaviour will be borne largely by others, including the mail carrier and the insurance company.

asymmetric information A situation in which one party to a transaction has more or better relevant information about the transaction than the other party.

moral hazard A situation in which an individual or a firm takes advantage of special knowledge while engaging in socially inefficient behaviour.

Individuals and firms who are insured against loss will often take less care to prevent that loss than they would in the absence of insurance. They do so because they do not bear all of the marginal cost imposed by the risk, whereas they do bear all of the marginal cost of taking action to reduce the risk.

With moral hazard, the market failure arises because the action by the insured individual or firm raises total costs for society. In the first example above, the decision not to shovel the sidewalk reduces costs for the individual but, in the event of an accident, increases by much more the costs to other individuals and firms.

Insurance is not the only context in which moral hazard problems arise. Another example is professional services. Suppose you ask a dentist whether your teeth are healthy or a lawyer whether you need legal assistance. The dentist and the lawyer both face moral hazard in that they both have a financial interest in giving you answers that will encourage you to buy their services, and it is difficult for you to find out if their advice is good. In both cases, one party to the transaction has special knowledge that he or she could use to change the nature of the transaction in his or her favour. Codes of professional ethics and licensing and certification practices, both governmental and private, are reactions to concerns about this kind of moral hazard.

Your auto mechanic probably knows far more about cars than you do, and is therefore able to benefit by convincing you to make unnecessary expenditures. This is an example of moral hazard caused by asymmetric information. One partial solution to this problem is to get a second (or third!) estimate before you spend any money.

Adverse Selection **Adverse selection** refers to the tendency for people who are more at risk than the average to purchase insurance and for those who are less at risk than the average to reject insurance. A person who has a heart condition may seek to increase his life insurance coverage by purchasing as much additional coverage as is available without a medical examination. People who buy insurance almost always know more about themselves as individual insurance risks than do their insurance companies. The company can try to limit the variation in risk by requiring physical examinations (for life or health insurance) and by setting up broad categories based on variables, such as age and occupation, over which actuarial risk is known to vary. The rate charged is then different across categories and is based on the average risk in each category, but there will always be much variability of risk *within* any one category.

adverse selection Self-selection, within a single risk category, of persons of above-average risk.

People who know that they are well above the average risk for their category are offered a bargain and will be led to take out more car, health, life, or fire insurance than they otherwise would. Their insurance premiums will also not cover the full expected cost of the risk against which they are insuring. Once again, their private cost is less than the social cost. On the other side, someone who knows that she is at low risk and pays a higher price than the amount warranted by her risk is motivated to take out less insurance than she otherwise would. In this case, her private cost is more than the social cost. In both cases, resources are allocated inefficiently because the marginal private benefit of the action (taking out insurance) is not equal to the marginal social cost.

An excellent and familiar example of market failure due to asymmetric information and adverse selection is the apparent overdiscounting of the prices of used cars because of the buyer's risk of acquiring a "lemon." See the discussion of this problem in *Applying Economic Concepts 16-2*.

Summary

Our discussion about market failures has covered a lot of ground. Before we move on to explore some details of government intervention, it is worthwhile to summarize briefly what we have learned. The following four situations result in market failures and, at least in principle, provide a rationale for government intervention.

1. Firms with market power will charge a price greater than marginal cost. The level of output in these cases is less than the allocatively efficient level.
2. When there are externalities, social and private marginal costs are not equal. If there is a negative externality, output will be greater than the allocatively efficient level. If there is a positive externality, output will be less than the allocatively efficient level.
3. Common-property resources will be overused by private firms and consumers. Public goods will be underprovided by private markets.

APPLYING ECONOMIC CONCEPTS 16-2

Used Cars and the Market for "Lemons"

It is common for people to regard the large loss of value of a new car in the first year of its life as a sign that consumers are overly style-conscious and will always pay a big premium for the latest in anything. Professor George Akerlof of the University of California at Berkeley suggests a different explanation. His theory, contained in his now-famous paper "The Market for Lemons," is based on the proposition that the flow of services expected from a one-year-old car that is *purchased on the used-car market* will be lower than that expected from an *average* one-year-old car on the road. Consider his theory.

Any particular model year of automobile will include a certain proportion of "lemons"—cars that have one or more serious defects. Purchasers of new cars of a certain year and model take a chance on their car turning out to be a lemon. Those who are unlucky and get a lemon are more likely to resell their car than those who are lucky and get a high-quality car. Hence, in the used-car market, there will be a disproportionately large number of lemons for sale. For example, maybe only 1 percent of all 2006 Toyota Corollas have a significant defect and are thus lemons. But, in the market for *used* 2006 Toyota Corollas, 20 percent of them may be lemons.

Buyers of used cars are therefore right to be on the lookout for lemons, while salespeople are quick to invent reasons for the high quality of the cars they are selling. Because it is difficult to identify a lemon or a badly treated used car before buying it, the purchaser is prepared to buy a used car only at a price that is low enough to offset the increased probability that it is a lemon.

The market failure in this situation arises because of the asymmetric information between the buyers and the sellers. If there were perfect information, prices would better reflect the quality of the used car. Good used cars would command higher prices than used cars known to be lemons. Buyers and sellers would then conduct more transactions, for two reasons. First, sellers of good used cars would be more likely to sell them since they know they will get a good price. In contrast, when information is poor, owners of good used cars are less inclined to sell their cars because the prices of used cars reflect the average quality, which of course is diminished by the presence of the lemons. Second, when information is good, consumers know precisely what it is they are buying. Consumers who wish to spend more on a good used car can do so; other consumers who want the bargain price on a car known to be a lemon can also be satisfied. A larger number of successful transactions between buyers and sellers means more surplus on both sides of the market—that is, a more efficient outcome.

Owners have an incentive to keep good-quality used cars because it is difficult to convince buyers that a used car is not a "lemon." As a result, lemons represent a larger proportion of used-car sales than of the total car population.

4. Situations in which there is asymmetric information—both moral hazard and adverse selection—can lead to allocative inefficiency.

These situations of market failure justify a role for government in a market economy. We now explore some reasons for government intervention that are *not* based on market failures.

16.4 BROADER SOCIAL GOALS

Suppose the market *did* generate the allocatively efficient outcome. That is, suppose all markets were perfectly competitive and there were no problems of market power, externalities, public goods, or asymmetric information. In such an extreme world, does the achievement of allocative efficiency mean that the government would have no reason to intervene in free markets? The answer, in general, is no.

Even if there are no market failures, the government may choose to intervene in markets to achieve broader social goals.

Practise with Study Guide Chapter 16, Exercise 3.

It should not be surprising that even if the free-market system were to generate an allocatively efficient outcome, it would be unlikely to achieve broader social goals. Some of these goals (for example, the desire for an "equitable" income distribution) are basically economic. Some, especially notions that people in a given society should have shared values, such as patriotism or a belief in basic human rights, are clearly not economic. In either set of cases, however, markets are not very effective, precisely because the "goods" in question are not of the kind that can be exchanged in decentralized transactions.

Income Distribution

As we saw in Chapter 13, an important characteristic of a market economy is the *distribution of income* that it determines. People whose services are in heavy demand relative to supply, such as good television news anchors, corporate CEOs, and outstanding hockey players, earn large incomes, whereas people whose services are not in heavy demand relative to supply, such as high school graduates without work experience, earn much less.

Such differentials in income, as we discussed in Chapter 13, can be either temporary or equilibrium phenomena. The temporary differentials, caused by changes in demand or supply in specific industries or regions, will eventually be eliminated by the mobility of workers. Equilibrium differentials will persist, whether they are created by differences in non-monetary aspects of the job or by differences in human capital or acquired or inherited skills.

Even equilibrium differences in income may seem unfair. A free-market system rewards certain groups and penalizes others. Because the workings of the market may be stern, even cruel, society often chooses to intervene. Should heads of households be forced to bear the full burden of their misfortune if, through no fault of their own, they lose their jobs? Even if they lose their jobs through their own fault, should they and their families have to bear the whole burden, which may include starvation? Should the ill and the aged be thrown on the mercy of their families? What if they have no families? Both private charities and a great many government policies are concerned with modifying the distribution of income that results from such things as where one starts, how able one is, how lucky one is, and how one fares in the labour market.

We might all agree that it is desirable to have a more equal distribution of income than the one generated by the free market. We would probably also agree that the pursuit of allocative efficiency is a good thing. It is important to understand, however, that the goal of a more equitable distribution of income often conflicts with the goal of allocative efficiency. To understand why this is so, see *Extensions in Theory 16-1*, which discusses Arthur Okun's famous analogy of the "leaky bucket."

EXTENSIONS IN THEORY 16-1

Arthur Okun's "Leaky Bucket"

Economists recognize that government actions can affect both the allocation of resources and the distribution of income. Resource allocation is easier to talk about simply because economists have developed precise definitions of *efficient* and *inefficient* allocations. Distribution is more difficult because we cannot talk about *better* or *worse* distributions of income without introducing value judgements.

To the extent that society chooses to redistribute income, allocative efficiency will often be reduced. Arthur Okun (1928–1980), who was a noted economist at Yale University, developed the image of a "leaky bucket" to illustrate this problem. Suppose we have a well-supplied reservoir of water and we wish to get some water to a household that is not able to come to the reservoir. The only vessel available for transporting the water is a leaky bucket; it works, in that water is deliverable to the intended location, but it works at a cost, in that some of the water is lost on the trip. Thus, to get a litre of water to its destination, more than a litre of water has to be removed from the reservoir. It may be possible to design better or worse buckets, but all of them will leak somewhat.

The analogy to an economy is this: The act of redistribution (carrying the water) reduces the total value of goods and services available to the economy (by the amount of water that leaks on the trip). Getting a dollar to the poor reduces the resources available to everyone else by more than a dollar. Thus, pursuing social goals—like the redistribution of income—conflicts with the goal of allocative efficiency.

Why is the bucket always leaky? Because there is no way to redistribute income without changing the incentives that private households and firms face. For example, a tax-and-transfer system that takes from the rich and gives to the poor will reduce the incentives of both the rich and the poor to produce income. This redistribution of income will often lead to less total income being generated. As another example, a policy of subsidizing goods that are deemed to be important, such as post-secondary education or daycare services, will cause the market prices of those goods to be lower than marginal costs, a result implying that resources used to produce those goods could be used to produce goods of higher value elsewhere in the economy.

Measuring the efficiency costs of redistribution is an important area of economic research. One result from this research is that some methods of redistribution are more efficient than others. For example, most economists agree that programs that directly redistribute income are more efficient (per dollar of resources made available to a given income group) than programs that subsidize the prices of specific goods. One reason for this is that price subsidies apply even when high-income households purchase the goods in question. These high-income households therefore benefit from the subsidy—an unintended (and perhaps undesirable) consequence of the program.

Redistribution often entails some efficiency cost. However, this inefficiency does *not* imply that such programs should not be undertaken. (That buckets leak surely does not imply that they should not be used to transport water, given that we want to transport water and that the buckets we have are the best available tools.) Whatever the social policy regarding redistribution of income, economics has an important role to play in measuring the efficiency costs and distributional consequences of different programs of redistribution. Put another way, it has useful things to say about the design and deployment of buckets.

Preferences for Public Provision

Police protection and justice could in principle be provided by private-market mechanisms. Security guards, private detectives, and bodyguards all provide policelike protection. Privately hired arbitrators, "hired guns," and vigilantes of the Old West represent private ways of obtaining "justice." Yet the members of society may believe that a public police force is *preferable* to a private one and that public justice is preferable to justice for hire. The question of the boundary between public and private provision of any number of goods and services became an important topic of debate during the late 1980s and early 1990s, and the debate shows no sign of waning. In Canada, the United States, and Western Europe, the issue is framed as *privatization*. In the formerly socialist countries of Eastern Europe, the disposition of much of the productive capacity of entire countries is currently under dispute. In all of these cases, part of the debate is about the magnitude of the efficiency gains that could be realized by private organization, and part is about less tangible issues, such as changes in the nature and distribution of goods and services that may take place when production is shifted from one sector to the other.

Protecting Individuals from Others

People can use and even abuse other people for economic gain in ways that the members of society find offensive. Child labour laws, minimum standards of working conditions, and laws against physical abuse and sexual harassment are responses to such actions. Yet direct abuse is not the only example of this kind of undesirable outcome. In an unhindered free market, the adults in a household would usually decide how much education to buy for their children. Selfish parents might buy no education, while egalitarian parents might buy the same education for all of their children, regardless of their abilities. The rest of society may want to interfere in these choices, both to protect the child of the selfish parent and to ensure that some of the scarce educational resources are distributed according to the ability and the willingness to use them rather than according to a family's wealth. The government requires all households to provide a minimum of education for their children, and a number of inducements are offered—through public universities, scholarships, and other means—for talented children to consume more education than they or their parents might choose if they had to pay the entire cost themselves.

A judicial system could be provided privately, with the judges levying charges to plaintiffs and defendants in order to hear their cases. But most people believe that for reasons of fairness and objectivity, it is better for the government to provide the judicial system, using money raised through general taxation.

Paternalism

paternalism Intervention in the free choices of individuals by others (including governments) to protect them against what is presumed to be their own ignorance or folly.

Members of society, acting through government, often seek to protect adult (and presumably responsible) individuals, not from others, but from themselves. Laws prohibiting the use of addictive drugs and laws prescribing the installation and use of seat belts are intended primarily to protect individuals from their own ignorance or shortsightedness. Other laws restrict the sale of medicinal drugs in Canada until they are approved by a government body, thus protecting individuals who are unlikely to be well-informed about the chemical composition of the drugs. These kinds of interference in the free choices of individuals are examples of **paternalism**. Whether such actions reflect the wishes of the majority in the society or whether they reflect the actions of overbearing governments, there is no doubt that the market will not provide this kind of protection. Buyers do not buy what they do not want, and sellers have no motive to provide it.

Social Responsibility

In a free-market system, if you can pay another person to do things for you, you may do so. If you persuade someone else to clean your house in return for $75, presumably both parties to the transaction are better off (otherwise neither of you would have voluntarily conducted the transaction). Normally, society does not interfere with people's ability to negotiate mutually advantageous contracts.

Most people do not feel this way, however, about activities that are regarded as social responsibilities. For example, in countries where military service is compulsory, contracts similar to the one between you and a housekeeper could also be negotiated. Some persons faced with the obligation to do military service could no doubt pay enough to persuade others to do their military service for them. Indeed, during the U.S. Civil War, it was common practice for a man to avoid the draft by hiring a substitute to serve in his place. Yet such contracts are usually prohibited by law. They are prohibited because there are values to be considered other than those that can be expressed in a market. In times when it is necessary, military service is usually held to be a duty that is independent of an individual's tastes, wealth, influence, or social position. It is felt that everyone *ought* to do this service, and exchanges between willing traders are prohibited.

Military service is not the only example of a social obligation. Citizens cannot buy their way out of jury duty or legally sell their voting rights to others, even though in many cases they could find willing trading partners.

Economic Growth

Over the long haul economic growth is the most powerful determinant of material living standards. Whatever their policies concerning efficiency and equity, people who live in economies with rapid rates of growth find their real per capita incomes rising (on average) faster than those of people who live in countries with low rates of growth. Over a few decades these growth-induced changes tend to have much larger effects on living standards than any policy-induced changes in the efficiency of resource allocation or the distribution of income.

For the last half of the twentieth century most economists viewed growth mainly as a macroeconomic phenomenon related to total saving and total investment. Reflecting this view, many textbooks do not even mention growth in the chapters on microeconomic policy.

More recently there has been a shift back to the perspective of earlier economists, who saw technological change as the engine of growth, with the individual entrepreneurs and firms as the agents of innovation. This is a microeconomic perspective, which is meant to add to, not replace, the macroeconomic emphasis on total saving and total investment.

Over the last decade or so, governments have placed considerable emphasis on this new microeconomic perspective on economic growth. Today few microeconomic policies escape being exposed to the question, "Even if this policy achieves its main goal, will it have unfavourable effects on growth?" Answering yes is not a sufficient reason to abandon a specific policy. But it is a sufficient reason to think again. Is it possible to redesign the policy so that it can still achieve its main micro objectives, while removing its undesirable side-effects on economic growth?

A General Principle

We have discussed how the free market may fail to achieve social goals that members of society deem to be desirable. This discussion suggests the following general principle:

Even if free markets generated allocatively efficient outcomes, they would be unlikely to generate outcomes consistent with most people's social goals. Furthermore, there is often a tradeoff between achieving these social goals and increasing allocative efficiency.

16.5 GOVERNMENT INTERVENTION

Private collective action can sometimes remedy the failures of private individual action. For example, volunteer fire departments can fight fires, firms in shopping centres can hire their own security staff, and insurance companies can guard against adverse selection by more careful classification of clients. However, by far the most common remedy for market failure is some form of government intervention.

Since markets sometimes *do* fail, there is a potential scope for governments to intervene in beneficial ways. Whether government intervention is warranted in any particular case depends both on the magnitude of the market failure that the intervention is designed to correct and on the costs of the government action itself.

The benefits of some types of government intervention—such as a publicly provided justice system—are both difficult to quantify and potentially very large. Further, government intervention often imposes difficulties of its own. For many types of government activity, however, *cost–benefit analysis* can be helpful in considering the general question of when and to what extent governments can successfully intervene.

cost–benefit analysis An approach for evaluating the desirability of a given policy, based on comparing total (opportunity) costs with total benefits.

The idea behind **cost–benefit analysis** is simple: Add up the (opportunity) costs of a given policy, then add up the benefits, and implement the policy only if the benefits outweigh the costs. In practice, however, cost–benefit analysis is usually quite difficult for three reasons. First, it may be difficult to ascertain what will happen when an action is undertaken. Second, many government actions involve costs and benefits that will occur only in the distant future; thus, they will be more complicated to assess. Third, some benefits and costs—such as the benefits of prohibiting actions that would harm members of an endangered animal species—are difficult to quantify. Indeed, some people argue that they cannot be and should not be quantified, as they involve values that are not commensurate with money. The practice then is to use cost–benefit analysis to measure the things that can be measured and to be sure that the things that cannot be measured are not ignored when collective decisions are made. By narrowing the range of things that must be determined by informal judgement, cost–benefit analysis can still play a useful role.

In this chapter, we have been working toward a cost–benefit analysis of government intervention. We have made a general case against government intervention, stressing that free markets are great economizers on information and coordination costs. We have also made a general case for government intervention, emphasizing that free markets fail to produce allocative efficiency when there are firms with market power, public goods, externalities, or information asymmetries, and may also fail to achieve broader social goals. We now turn to the more specific issues of how governments intervene, the costs of government intervention, and why government intervention sometimes fails to improve on imperfect market outcomes.

The Tools of Government Intervention

The legal power of governments to intervene in the workings of the economy is limited by the Charter of Rights (as interpreted by the courts), the willingness of Parliament and provincial legislatures to pass laws, and the willingness and ability of governments to enforce them. There are numerous ways in which one or another level of government can prevent, alter, complement, or replace the workings of the unrestricted market economy.

1. Public Provision National defence, the criminal justice system, public schools, universities, the highway system, and national parks are all examples of goods or services that are provided by governments in Canada. Public provision is the most obvious remedy for market failure to provide public goods, but it is also often used in the interest of redistribution (e.g., hospitals) and other social goals (e.g., public schools). We will consider public spending in detail in Chapter 18.

See the Government of Canada's web page to see how many federal government departments and Crown corporations exist: **www.gc.ca**.

2. Redistribution Programs Taxes and spending are often used to provide a distribution of income that is different from that generated by the free market. Government transfer programs affect the distribution of income in this way. We examine the distributive effects of the Canadian tax system in Chapter 18.

3. Regulation Government regulations are public rules that apply to private behaviour. In Chapter 12, we saw that governments regulate private markets to limit monopoly power. In Chapter 17, we will focus on regulations designed to deal with environmental degradation. Among other things, government regulations prohibit minors from consuming alcohol, require that children attend school, penalize racial discrimination in housing and labour markets, and require that new automobiles have seat belts. Government regulation is used to deal with all of the sources of market failure that we have discussed in this chapter; it applies at some level to virtually all spheres of modern economic life.

Almost all government actions, including the kinds we have discussed here, change the incentives that consumers and firms face. If the government provides a park, people will have a weakened incentive to own large plots of land of their own. Fixing minimum or maximum prices (as we saw in Chapter 5) affects privately chosen levels of output. If the government taxes income, people may have a reduced incentive to work.

The government can adjust the tax system to provide subsidies for some kinds of behaviour and penalties for others. For example, taxes on gasoline raise the price to consumers and may lead them to reduce the quantity used, especially over the long run. Tax exemptions for contributions to Registered Retirement Savings Plans (RRSPs) increase the rate of return to saving and may lead individuals to increase their total amount of saving. In both cases, the government policy alters prices and sends the household different signals from those sent by the free market.

The Costs of Government Intervention

Consider the following argument: The market system produces some particular outcome that is deemed to be undesirable; government has the legal means to improve the situation; therefore, the public interest will be served by government intervention.

Practise with Study Guide Chapter 16, Exercise 4.

At first glance the argument is appealing. But it is deficient because it neglects three important considerations. First, government intervention is itself costly since it uses scarce resources; for this reason alone, not every undesirable outcome is worth correcting because the cost of doing so may exceed the perceived benefits. Second, government intervention is generally imperfect. Just as markets sometimes succeed and sometimes fail, so government interventions sometimes succeed and sometimes fail. Third, deciding what governments are to do and how they are to do it is also costly and intrinsically imperfect.

Large potential benefits do not necessarily justify government intervention, nor do large potential costs necessarily make it unwise. What matters is the balance between benefits and costs.

There are several different costs of government intervention. Economists divide these costs into two categories—*direct costs* and *indirect costs*.

Direct Costs Government intervention uses real resources that could be used elsewhere. Civil servants must be paid and computer systems need to be purchased. Paper, photocopying, and other trappings of bureaucracy—the steel in the navy's ships, the fuel for the army's tanks, and the pilot of the prime minister's jet—all have valuable alternative uses. The same is true of the accountants who administer the Canada Pension Plan, the economists who are employed by the Competition Bureau, and the educators who retrain displaced workers.

Similarly, when government inspectors visit plants to monitor compliance with federally imposed standards of health, industrial safety, or environmental protection, they are imposing costs on the public in the form of their salaries and expenses. When regulatory bodies develop rules, hold hearings, write opinions, or have their staff prepare research reports, they are incurring costs. The costs of the judges, clerks, and court reporters who hear, transcribe, and review the evidence are also imposed by government regulation. All these activities use valuable resources that could have provided very different goods and services.

All forms of government intervention use real resources and hence impose direct costs.

The direct costs of government intervention are fairly easy to identify, as they almost always involve well-documented expenditures. In the 2004–2005 fiscal year, the total expenditures by all levels of governments (excluding transfer payments) in Canada were $304 billion, just over 21 percent of total national income.

Indirect Costs Most government interventions in the economy impose costs on firms and households over and above the taxes that must be paid to the government to finance its policies. The nature and the size of the extra costs borne by firms and households vary with the type of intervention. A few examples will illustrate what is involved.

1. Changes in Costs of Production. Government safety and emissions standards for automobiles have raised the costs of both producing and operating cars. Environmental policies that require firms to treat their waste products and emissions also increase the overall costs. In both cases, these costs are much greater than the direct budgetary costs of administering the regulations.

2. Costs of Compliance. Government regulation and supervision generate a flood of reporting and related activities that are often referred to collectively as *red tape*. The number of hours of business time devoted to understanding, reporting, and contesting regulatory provisions is enormous. Regulations dealing with occupational safety and environmental control have all increased the size of non-production payrolls. The legal costs alone of a major corporation sometimes can run into tens or hundreds of millions of dollars per year. While all this provides lots of employment for lawyers and economic experts, it is costly because there are other tasks these professionals could do that would add more to the production of consumer goods and services.

Households also bear compliance costs directly. A recent study found that the time and money cost of filling out individual income-tax returns was about 8 percent of the total revenue that is collected. In addition to costs of compliance, there are costs borne as firms and households try to avoid regulation. There is a substantial incentive to find loopholes in regulations. Resources that could be used elsewhere are devoted to the search for such loopholes and then, in turn, by the regulators to counteracting such evasion.

Farmers in Canada often request government assistance to offset the effects of low crop prices or bad weather. This is one example of "rent seeking."

myeconlab

***Red tape* is a problem in advanced, industrialized economies, but it is even more serious in some developing economies. For examples of how red tape can stand in the way of economic development, look for "How Excessive Regulation Hobbles Development" in the *Additional Topics* section of this book's MyEconLab.**

www.myeconlab.com

3. Rent Seeking. A different kind of problem arises from the mere existence of government and its potential to use its tools in ways that affect the distribution of economic resources. This phenomenon has been dubbed **rent seeking** by economists because private firms, households, and business groups will use their political influence to seek *economic rents* from the government in ways that do not advance the public interest. These valuable rents can come in the form of favourable regulations, direct subsidies, and profitable contracts that do not use public funds in a prudent manner. Democratic governments are especially vulnerable to manipulation of this kind because they respond to well-articulated interests of all sorts.

rent seeking Behaviour whereby private firms and individuals try to use the powers of the government to enhance their own economic well-being in ways that are not in the social interest.

Rent seeking is endemic to mixed economies. Because of the many things that governments are called on to do, they have the power to act in ways that transfer resources among private entities. Because they are democratic, they are responsive to public pressures of various kinds. If a government's behaviour can be influenced, whether by voting, campaign contributions, lobbying, or bribes, real resources will be used in trying to do so.

In the aggregate, the indirect costs of government intervention are substantial. But they are difficult to measure and are usually dispersed across a large number of firms and households.

Government Failure

Even in the cases where the benefits and costs of government intervention can be easily identified and measured, governments, like private markets, are imperfect. Often they will fail, in the same sense that markets do, to achieve their potential.

The reason for government failure is not that public-sector employees are less able, honest, or virtuous than people who work in the private sector. Rather, the causes of government failure are inherent in government institutions, just as the causes of market failure stem from the nature of markets. Importantly, some government failure is an inescapable cost of democratic decision making.

Decision Makers' Objectives By far the most important cause of government failure arises from the nature of the government's own objectives. Traditionally, economists did not concern themselves greatly with the motivation of government. The theory of economic policy implicitly assumed that governments had no objectives of their own. As a result, economists only needed to identify places where the market functioned well on its own, and places where government intervention could improve the market's functioning. Governments would then stay out of the former markets and intervene as necessary in the latter.

This model of government behaviour never fitted reality, and economists were gradually forced to think more deeply about the motivation of governments. Today economists no longer assume that governments are faceless robots doing whatever economic analysis suggests is in the social interest. Instead they are modelled just as are producers and consumers—as units with their own objectives, which they seek to maximize.

Governments undoubtedly do care about the social good to some extent, but public officials have their careers, their families, and their prejudices as well. As a result, public officials' own needs are seldom wholly absent from their consideration of the actions they will take. Similarly, their definition of the public interest is likely to be influenced heavily by their personal views of what policies are best. It is therefore often the case that the policies supported by the public are different from the policies advocated by policymakers.

Modelling governments as maximizers of their own welfare, and then incorporating them into theoretical models of the working of the economy, was a major intellectual breakthrough. One of the pioneers of this development was the American economist James Buchanan, who was awarded the 1986 Nobel Prize in economics for his work in this field. The theory that he helped to develop is called *public choice theory.* The key breakthrough was to view the government as just another economic agent engaging in its own maximizing behaviour.

Public Choice Theory Full-blown public choice theory deals with three maximizing groups. Elected officials seek to maximize their votes. Civil servants seek to maximize their salaries and their influence. Voters seek to maximize their own utility. To this end, voters look to the government to provide them with goods and services and income transfers that raise their personal utility. No one cares about the general interest!

On the one hand, this surely is not a completely accurate characterization of motives. Elected statesmen have acted in what they perceive to be the public interest, hoping to be vindicated by history even if they know they risk losing the next election. Some civil servants expose inside corruption—so-called whistleblowers—even though it can cost them their jobs. Some high-income individuals vote for the political party that advocates the most, not the least, income redistribution, and some poorer taxpayers vote for a party that advocates lower taxes on the rich and lower transfers to the poor.

On the other hand, the characterization is close to the mark in many cases. Most of us have read of politicians whose only principle is, "What will get me the most votes?" And many voters ask only, "What is in it for me?" This is why the theory can take us a long way in understanding what we see, even though real behaviour is more complex.

Here is one example relevant to Canada and many other developed economies. Why, in spite of strong advice from economists, have governments persisted in assisting agriculture for decades, until many governments now have major farm crises on their hands? Public choice theory looks at the winners and the losers among the voters.

Public choice theory seeks to explain how public officials make their decisions. They are assumed to act not in the best interests of their constituents but according to their own agendas that often conflict with the public interest.

The winners from agricultural supports are farmers. They are a politically powerful group, and are aware of what they will lose if farm supports are reduced. They would show their disapproval of such action by voting against any government that even suggests it. The losers are the entire group of consumers or taxpayers. Although they are more numerous than farmers, and although their total loss is large, each individual suffers only a small loss. Citizens have more important things to worry about, and so do not vote against the government just because it supports farmers. As long as the average voters are unconcerned about, and often unaware of, the losses they suffer, the vote-maximizing government will ignore the interests of the many and support the interests of the few. The vote-maximizing government will consider changing the agricultural policy only when the cost of agricultural support becomes so large that ordinary taxpayers begin to be concerned by the cost. What is required for a policy change, according to this theory, is that those who lose become sufficiently aware of their losses for this awareness to affect their voting behaviour.

Another example that we will see in Chapter 34 is the use of tariffs. When a tariff is imposed on an imported good, it increases the domestic price of the good. Tariffs therefore provide protection to the domestic firms producing competing products. This protection typically raises prices, profits, and wages in those firms. The costs of such tariffs are borne by a much larger number of consumers, each of whom is hurt a relatively small amount by the higher price. This concentration of benefits and the dispersion of costs explains to a large extent why tariffs, once in place, are so politically difficult to remove.

rational ignorance When agents have no incentive to become informed about some government policy because the costs of becoming informed exceed the benefits of any well-informed action the agent might take.

The ability of elected officials and civil servants to ignore the public interest is strengthened by a phenomenon called **rational ignorance**. Many policy issues are extremely complex. For example, even the experts are divided when assessing the pros and cons of Canada's maintaining a flexible exchange rate rather than pegging the value of the Canadian dollar to the U.S. dollar. Much time and effort is required for a layperson even to attempt to understand the issue. Similar comments apply to the evidence for and against capital punishment or lowering the age of criminal liability. Yet one person's vote has little influence on which party gets elected or on what they will really do about the issue in question once elected. So the costs of informing oneself are large, while the benefits of acting on that information are small. Thus, a majority of rational, self-interested voters will choose to remain innocent of the complexities involved in most policy issues.

Who will be the informed minority? The answer is those who stand to gain or lose a lot from the policy, those with a strong sense of moral obligation, and those policy junkies who just like thinking about these kinds of issues.

Democracy and Inefficient Public Choices At the core of most people's idea of democracy is the notion that all citizens' votes should have the same weight. One of the insights of the theory of public choice is that resource allocation, based on the principle of one vote per person, will generally be inefficient because it fails to take into account the *intensity of preferences*. Consider three farmers, Albert, Bob, and Charlene, who are contemplating building access roads to their farms. Suppose the road to Albert's farm is worth $7000 to him and that the road to Bob's farm is worth $7000 to him. Charlene's farm is on the main road, which already exists, and so an extra road is of no value to her. Suppose also that the cost of building each access road is $6000 and that under the current tax rules each of the three farmers would have to pay $2000 per road built.

The data for this example are summarized in Table 16-2, which shows each farmer's net benefits (benefits minus costs) from the construction of each road, and also the total net benefits for each road. For example, building the road to Albert's farm, and financing it by taxing each farmer $2000, generates net benefits of $5000 for Albert, and –$2000 each for Bob and Charlene. Total net benefits for this road are therefore $1000, revealing that the total benefits from building the road exceed the total costs. It is therefore efficient to build this road.

As the data in the table show, it is efficient to build roads to both Albert's and Bob's farms, but it is not efficient to build an (additional) road to Charlene's farm since it generates no benefits but costs $6000. The problem, however, is that both of the roads that should be built on the grounds of efficiency would be defeated 2–1 in a simple majority vote. Bob and Charlene would each vote against the road to Albert's farm, and Albert and Charlene would each vote against the road to Bob's farm. In this case, the democratic process leads to an inefficient outcome.

Now suppose we allow Albert and Bob to make a deal: "I will vote for your road if you will vote for mine." Although such deals are often decried by political commentators, the deal enhances efficiency: Both roads now get 2–1 majorities, and both roads get built. However, such deals can just as easily reduce efficiency. If the gross value of each road were $5000 instead of $7000, and Albert and Bob again make their deal, each road will still command a 2–1 majority, but building the roads will now be inefficient. (The gross value of each road is now only $5000, but the cost is still $6000.) Albert and Bob will be using democracy to appropriate resources from Charlene (the taxes she would have to pay) while reducing economic efficiency.

The possibility of inefficient public choices stems in large part from the problems inherent to a democratic system. *Extensions in Theory 16-2* discusses Kenneth Arrow's famous result in the theory of public choice. Arrow's somewhat unsettling theorem is that there is very often a tradeoff between democracy and efficiency.

Practise with Study Guide Chapter 16, Extension Exercise E1.

Governments as Monopolists Governments face the same problems of cost minimization that private firms do but often operate in an environment where they are

TABLE 16-2 Net Benefits from Road Construction

Build Road to	Net Benefits to Albert	Net Benefits to Bob	Net Benefits to Charlene	Total Net Benefits
Albert's Farm	$7000 – $2000 = $5000	$0 – $2000 = –$2000	$0 – $2000 = –$2000	$1000
Bob's Farm	$0 – $2000 = –$2000	$7000 – $2000 = $5000	$0 – $2000 = –$2000	$1000
Charlene's Farm	$0 – $2000 = –$2000	$0 – $2000 = –$2000	$0 – $2000 = –$2000	–$6000

EXTENSIONS IN THEORY 16-2

A Problem with Democracy

Nobel laureate Kenneth Arrow from Stanford University has shown that it is generally impossible to construct a set of rules for making public choices that is at once comprehensive, democratic, efficient, and consistent. This striking idea—called Arrow's Impossibility Theorem—has led to decades of work on the part of economists, philosophers, and political scientists, who have tried to find conditions under which democracy can be expected to yield efficient allocations of resources. The news is generally not good. Unless individual preferences or their distribution in the population meet fairly unlikely criteria, either democracy or efficiency must be sacrificed in the design of public-choice mechanisms.

The Arrow theorem can be illustrated by a simple case, depicted in the following table.

	Voter		
Density of Trees	A	B	C
Sparse (1)	3	1	2
Medium (2)	1	2	3
Dense (3)	2	3	1

Imagine we have a society that consists of three voters who are choosing how many trees to plant in the local park. The three possibilities are as follows: (1) Plant very few trees, in one corner. This would make the park suitable for playing Frisbee and soccer but not for walks in the woods. (2) Plant trees in moderate density throughout the park. In this case, the park would be nice for jogging but not usable for most sports. (3) Plant trees densely everywhere. This would make the park a pleasant place to get away from it all (for whatever reasons) but not a good place to jog. Voter A loves jogging, hates Frisbee, and likes walking in the woods. His ranking of the alternatives is 3–1–2. Voter B likes the wide open spaces. His ranking is 1–2–3. Voter C likes to play Frisbee, likes solitude even more, and has little taste for a park that provides neither. Her ranking is 2–3–1.

Now suppose the electorate gets to choose between alternatives that are presented two at a time. What does majority rule do? Unfortunately, there is no unique democratic outcome; the result of such voting depends on which two alternatives are presented. In a choice of 1 versus 2, 1 wins, getting votes from B and C. When the choice is between 2 and 3, 2 wins, getting votes from A and B. When 3 is pitted against 1, 3 wins with the support of A and C. Thus, the public-choice mechanism of majority rule is *inconsistent*. It tells us that 1 is preferred to 2, 2 is preferred to 3, and 3 is preferred to 1. There is no way to make a choice without arbitrarily—that is, undemocratically—choosing which set of alternatives to offer the electorate. This is the essence of Arrow's famous argument that, in general, democracy and efficiency cannot both be achieved in issues of public choice.

monopoly producers without shareholders. Large governments (provinces, big cities, the federal government) face all of the organizational problems faced by large corporations. They tend to use relatively rigid rules and hence respond slowly to change. Building codes are an example of this type of problem. Most local governments have detailed requirements regarding the materials that must go into a new house, factory, or office. When technology changes, the codes often lag behind. For example, plastic pipe, which is cheaper and easier to use than copper pipe, was prohibited by building codes for decades after its use became efficient. Changes in technology may make a regulation inefficient, but the regulation may stay in place for a long time.

In the private sector, market forces often push firms into revising their view of the problem at hand, whereas there is ordinarily no market mechanism to force governments to adopt relatively efficient regulations. Put another way, much government failure arises precisely because governments do not have competitors and are not constrained by the "bottom line."

How Much Should Government Intervene?

Do governments intervene too little, or too much, in response to market failure? This question reflects one aspect of the continuing debate over the role of government in the economy. While many economists might agree on the theoretical principles that should guide government intervention in selected cases, there is more disagreement about the broader role of government in the economy. Unfortunately, the issue is often framed ideologically. Those on the "right wing" tend to compare heavy-handed government with a hypothetical and perfectly operating competitive market. In contrast, those on the "left wing" tend to compare hypothetical and ideal government intervention with a laissez-faire economy rife with market failures. Both perspectives are in danger of missing the more relevant debate.

Evaluating the costs and benefits of government intervention requires a comparison of the private economic system as it actually works (not as it might work ideally) with the pattern of government intervention as it actually performs (not as it might perform ideally).

Over the last three decades in most of the advanced industrial countries, the mix of free-market determination and government ownership and regulation has been shifting toward more market determination. No reasonable person believes that government intervention can, or should, be reduced to zero. Do we still have a long way to go in reversing the tide of big intrusive government that flowed through most of the twentieth century? Or perhaps we have gone too far and have given some things to the market that governments could do better? This will be one of the great social debates of the early decades of the twenty-first century.

The cases we have made for the costs and benefits of government intervention are both valid, depending on time, place, and the values that are brought to bear. At this point, we turn to the issue of what government actually does, something that will perhaps illuminate the question of what it could do better. In Chapter 12, we discussed government action that is designed to affect monopoly and competition. In the next two chapters, we discuss in some detail three other important types of intervention in the Canadian economy today: environmental regulation, taxation, and public spending.

SUMMARY

16.1 BASIC FUNCTIONS OF GOVERNMENT

- The government's monopoly of violence gives it the ability to enforce laws and protect its citizens. But restrictions on the government's power are required to ensure that individuals' rights are not unnecessarily violated.

16.2 THE CASE FOR FREE MARKETS

LO 1

- The case for free markets can be made in two different ways. The "formal defence" is based on the concept of allocative efficiency. This was the basis for the appeal of competitive markets as discussed in Chapters 5 and 12.
- The "informal defence" of free markets is not specifically based on the idea of allocative efficiency, and thus applies to market structures other than just perfect competition. The informal defence of free markets is based on three central arguments:

1. Free markets provide automatic coordination of the actions of decentralized decision makers.
2. The pursuit of profits, which is central to free markets, provides a stimulus to innovation and economic growth.
3. Free markets permit a decentralization of economic power.

16.3 MARKET FAILURES

LO 2 3

- Market failure refers to situations in which the free market does not achieve allocative efficiency. Four main sources of market failure are
  1. market power
  2. externalities
  3. public goods
  4. information asymmetries
- Pollution is an example of an externality. A producer who pollutes the air or water does not pay the social cost of the pollution and is therefore not motivated to avoid the costs. Private producers will therefore produce too much pollution relative to what is allocatively efficient.
- National defence is an example of a public good. Markets fail to produce public goods because the benefits of such goods are available to people whether they pay for them or not.
- Information asymmetries cause market failure when one party to a transaction is able to use personal expertise to manipulate the transaction in his or her own favour. Moral hazard and adverse selection are consequences of information asymmetries.

16.4 BROADER SOCIAL GOALS

LO 4

- Changing the distribution of income is one of the roles for government intervention that members of a society may desire. Others include values that are placed on public provision for its own sake, on protection of individuals from themselves or from others, on recognition of social responsibilities, and on the promotion of economic growth.

16.5 GOVERNMENT INTERVENTION

LO 5

- Major tools of microeconomic policy include (a) public provision, (b) redistribution, and (c) regulation.
- Most government actions—especially taxes or subsidies—change incentives that consumers and firms face.
- The costs and benefits of government intervention must be considered in deciding whether, when, and how much intervention is appropriate. Among the costs are the direct costs that are incurred by the government, the costs that are imposed on the parties who are regulated, directly and indirectly, and the costs that are imposed on third parties. These costs are seldom negligible and are often large.
- The possibility of government failure, as well as the costs of successful intervention, must be balanced against the potential benefits of removing market failure. It is neither possible nor efficient to correct all market failure; neither is it always efficient to do nothing.

KEY CONCEPTS

Market failure
Externalities
Private and social cost
Excludable and non-excludable goods
Rivalrous and non-rivalrous goods
Private goods
Common-property resource
Public goods
Information asymmetries
Moral hazard and adverse selection
Cost–benefit analysis
Rent seeking
Government failure
Public choice theory

STUDY EXERCISES

1. Fill in the blanks to make the following statements correct.
   a. The "formal defence" of free markets is that, if all markets were perfectly competitive, then prices would equal ________ for all products and the economy would be ________.
   b. The "informal defence" of free markets is based on the following three central arguments:
      - ________
      - ________
      - ________
   c. A situation in which the free market, in the absence of government intervention, fails to achieve allocative efficiency is called ________.
   d. There are four major market failures that, in principle, justify government intervention in markets. They are:
      - ________
      - ________
      - ________
      - ________

2. Fill in the blanks to make the following statements correct.
   a. The marginal cost faced by the private decision maker is known as ________. The marginal cost faced by the private decision maker *plus* any other costs imposed on third parties is known as ________. If there is a divergence between these two marginal costs then we can say that ________ are present.
   b. An economic outcome is allocatively efficient when marginal social cost and marginal social benefit are ________.
   c. Suppose a potato chip plant is operating beside a residential neighbourhood and produces noise and an unpleasant odour. We can say that there is a ________ externality because the marginal social cost of producing potato chips is ________ the private cost of producing potato chips. As a result, the free market is producing too ________ potato chips.
   d. Suppose an apple orchard is operating beside a residential neighbourhood and provides beautiful blossoms and a pleasant fragrance. We can say that there is a ________ externality because the marginal social cost of apples is ________ the marginal private cost of apples. As a result, the free market is producing too ________ apples.

3. Fill in the blanks to make the following statements correct.
   a. A good or service that is rivalrous and excludable (e.g., a restaurant meal or a sofa) is known as a ________ good and is most efficiently provided by the ________.
   b. A good that is rivalrous and non-excludable (e.g., fish in the ocean, or common grazing land) is known as a ________ and tends to be overused by ________.
   c. Goods that are non-rivalrous and excludable (e.g., roads, museums, and parks) are often provided by government because the marginal cost of provision to society is ________ and so the allocatively efficient price is ________.
   d. Goods and services that are non-rivalrous and non-excludable (e.g., national defence, a lighthouse) are known as ________. Private markets will not provide these goods or services because of the ________ problem.
   e. If an auto mechanic tells you that your car needs a new transmission, there is the possibility of market failure in the form of ________.
   f. If you take up cliff diving as a new hobby and increase your life insurance, just in case, there is a possible market failure in the form of ________.

4. For each of the situations in the table below, indicate whether there is a positive or a negative externality. Indicate in each case whether social marginal cost (MC_S) is greater than or less than private marginal cost (MC_P).

	Positive or Negative Externality?	MC_S greater than or less than MC_P?
You smoke a cigarette and blow the smoke into others' faces.		
You cut your lawn early on a Sunday morning.		
A firm conducts R&D and generates useful "basic" knowledge that is freely available.		
A firm produces aluminum, but also produces toxic waste as a byproduct.		

5. myeconlab Consider the following diagram showing the perfectly competitive market for newsprint. The demand curve shows the marginal benefit to society of consuming an extra unit of newsprint. The supply curve shows the firms' marginal costs of producing an extra unit of newsprint.

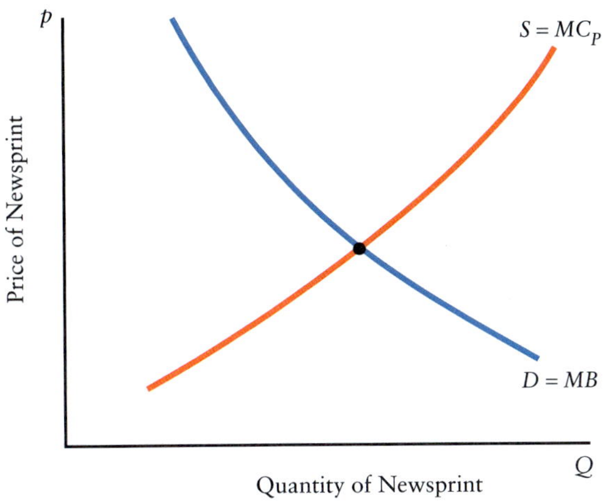

a. Describe the equilibrium in this competitive market.
b. Now suppose that, as a byproduct to producing newsprint, some toxic chemicals are also produced that get dumped in public streams and rivers. Suppose that for each unit of newsprint produced, one unit of toxic chemicals is also produced, imposing an external cost of $100. Show the social marginal cost curve in the diagram.
c. What is the allocatively efficient quantity of newsprint?

6. For each of the listed goods indicate whether they are rivalrous or non-rivalrous, and also indicate whether the use of them is excludable or non-excludable.

	Rivalrous?	Excludable?
CD player		
Clothing		
Library		
Lighthouse		
Medical services		
Published product safety information		
Pacific salmon		

a. Which of the goods in the table are public goods? Explain.
b. Which are common-property resources? Explain.

7. Art galleries, museums, roads, and bridges are usually provided by the government.

a. Explain why uncrowded goods of this sort should have a price of zero if allocative efficiency is to be achieved.
b. Would allocative efficiency be achieved if private firms provided these goods? Explain.
c. What happens when access to these goods becomes congested? Does efficiency still require a zero price? Explain.

8. myeconlab Consider a small town deciding whether to build a public park. The town council conducts a survey of its 100 residents and asks them how much they would each value the park. The survey results are as follows:

Number of people	Value of park per person	Total
10	$1000	$10 000
30	500	15 000
30	200	6 000
20	50	1 000
10	0	0
100		$32 000

a. Suppose it costs $35 000 to build the park. Should the town do it?
b. Suppose the park costs only $20 000 to build. Should the town build the park? If so, how should the town pay for building the park?
c. Suppose the town builds the park but charges people $50 for an annual pass. Does this present a problem for efficiency? Explain.

9. In the text we discussed how rent seeking is one of the costs of government intervention. Consider a group of pig farmers who are lobbying the federal government for some form of financial assistance (as they did in 1998 when the world price of pork declined steeply).

a. Explain why economists call such lobbying "rent seeking."
b. Suppose the farmers spend $500 000 in their lobbying efforts but have no effect on government policy. What is the cost to society of the rent seeking? Explain.
c. Suppose the $500 000 of lobbying *does* lead to a change in government policy. Now what is the social cost of the rent seeking?

DISCUSSION QUESTIONS

1. In each case, identify any divergence between social and private costs.
   a. Cigarette smoking
   b. Getting a university education
   c. Private ownership of guns
   d. Drilling for offshore oil

2. Consider the possible beneficial and adverse effects of each of the following forms of government intervention.
   a. Charging motorists a tax for driving in the downtown areas of large cities and using the revenues to provide peripheral parking and shuttle buses
   b. Prohibiting juries from awarding large malpractice judgements against doctors
   c. Mandating no-fault automobile insurance, in which the automobile owner's insurance company is responsible for damage to his or her vehicle no matter who causes the accident

3. The president of Goodyear Tire and Rubber Company complained that government regulation had imposed $30 million per year in "unproductive costs" on his company, as listed here. How would one determine whether these costs were "productive" or "unproductive"?
   a. Environmental regulation, $17 million
   b. Occupational safety and health, $7 million
   c. Motor vehicle safety, $3 million
   d. Personnel and administration, $3 million

4. Your local government almost certainly provides a police department, a fire department, and a public library. What are the market imperfections, if any, that each of these seeks to correct? Which of these are closest to being public goods? Which are furthest?

5. Suppose that for $100, a laboratory can accurately assess a person's probability of developing a fairly rare disease that is costly to treat. What would be the likely effects of such a test on health-insurance markets?

6. What market failures does public support of higher education seek to remedy? How would you go about evaluating whether the benefits of this support outweigh the costs?

7. This question is based on "Externalities and the Coase Theorem" on the book's MyEconLab at www.myeconlab.com. Consider a steel producer that dumps one litre of toxic waste into a river for every tonne of steel produced. A fishing camp located downstream bears the cost of cleaning up this toxic waste: $10 for every litre. Discuss how negotiations between the steel producer and the fishing camp may result in an allocatively efficient level of steel output even without direct government involvement. Does the nature of the negotiations depend on who owns the river?

CHAPTER 17

The Economics of Environmental Protection

LEARNING OBJECTIVES

In this chapter you will learn

1. how an externality can be internalized, and how this can lead to allocative efficiency.
2. why direct pollution controls are often inefficient.
3. how market-based policies such as emissions taxes and tradable pollution permits can improve economic efficiency.
4. about some of the most common arguments against market-based environmental policies.

In almost everything we do, we are subject to some form of government regulation. The system of criminal law regulates our interactions with people and property. Local zoning laws regulate the ways in which the land that we own or occupy may be used. Regulatory commissions set rates for electricity, natural gas, local telephone service, and a host of other goods and services. Seat belts, brake lights, turn signals, air bags, internal door panels, bumpers, and catalytic converters are compulsory and regulated in quality—all in a single industry. The list goes on and on. A good case can be made that various governments in Canada have more effect on the economy through regulation than through taxing and spending.

The focus in this chapter is on a specific type of government regulation, one that has become increasingly important in recent years. In particular, we examine the negative externalities that lead to environmental degradation and the various government policies designed to address them. As we will see, policies intended to protect the environment do not always do so in an efficient manner. One of the central themes in this chapter is that the information available to the regulatory agencies, especially regarding firms' technologies for reducing pollution, is generally incomplete. This lack of good information leads to the result that *market-based* environmental regulations are usually more successful than methods based on the government's *direct control*.

For information about the *Canadian Environmental Protection Act*, see Environment Canada's website: **www.ec.gc.ca**.

17.1 THE ECONOMIC RATIONALE FOR REGULATING POLLUTION

Pollution is a negative externality. As a consequence of producing or consuming goods and services, "bads" are produced as well. Steel plants produce smoke in addition to steel. Farms produce chemical runoff as well as food. Logging leads to soil erosion that contaminates fish-breeding grounds. Cars, trucks, and factories, by burning carbon-rich fossil fuels such as coal, oil, and natural gas, produce carbon dioxide and other "greenhouse" gases that contribute to global climate change. Households produce human waste and garbage as they consume goods and services. In all of these cases, the technology of production and consumption automatically generates pollution. Indeed, there are few human endeavours that do not have negative pollution externalities.

FIGURE 17-1 A Pollution Externality in a Competitive Market

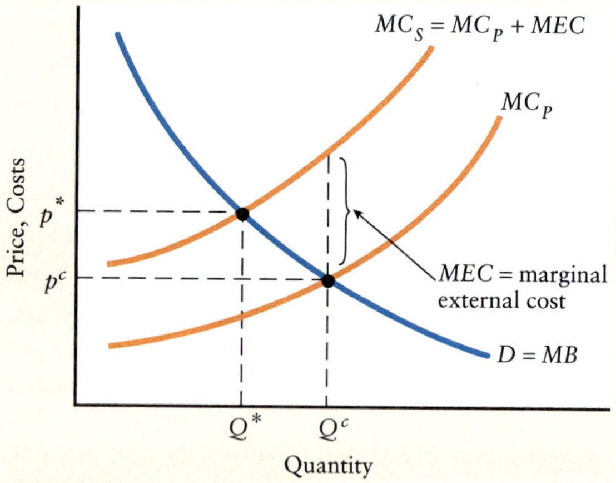

A negative externality implies that a competitive free market will produce more output than the allocatively efficient level. If the externality can be internalized, allocative efficiency can be achieved. A competitive free market will produce where the demand and supply curves intersect—that is, at Q^c and p^c. If each unit of output of this good also generates an external cost of *MEC*, then social marginal cost is greater than private marginal cost by this amount. The allocatively efficient level of output is where marginal benefit equals *social* marginal cost—that is, at Q^*. The competitive free market therefore produces too much output.

If firms in this industry are now required to pay a tax of \$*MEC* per unit of output, the private marginal cost curve, MC_P, shifts up to MC_S. The externality will thus be *internalized* because firms will now be forced to pay the full social cost of their production. The new competitive equilibrium will be p^*, Q^*, and allocative efficiency will be achieved.

Pollution as an Externality

Polluting firms do not regard a clean environment as a scarce resource and therefore fail to consider the full costs of using this resource when producing their product. When a paper mill produces newsprint for the world's newspapers, more people are affected than just its suppliers, employees, and customers. Its water-discharged effluent hurts the fishing boats that ply nearby waters, and its smog makes many resort areas less attractive, thereby reducing the tourist revenues that local motel operators and boat renters can expect. The profit-maximizing paper mill neglects these external effects of its actions because its profits are not directly affected by them.

As shown in Figure 17-1, allocative efficiency requires that the price (the value that consumers place on the marginal unit of output) be just equal to the marginal social cost (the value of the resources that society gives up to produce the marginal unit of output). When there are negative externalities, *social* marginal cost exceeds *private* marginal cost because the act of production generates costs for society that are not faced by the producer.

By producing where price equals private marginal cost and thereby ignoring the externality, the firms are maximizing profits but producing too much output. The price that consumers pay just covers the private marginal cost but does not pay for the external damage. The *social benefit* of the last unit of output (the market price) is less than the social cost (private marginal cost plus the extra cost to society from the externality). Reducing output by one unit would increase allocative efficiency and thus make society as a whole better off.

Making polluting firms bear the entire social cost of their production is called **internalizing the externality**. This leads them to produce a lower level of output, as shown in Figure 17-1. Indeed, at the optimal level of output, where the externality is completely internalized, consumer prices would just cover all of the *social* marginal cost of production. We would have the familiar condition for allocative efficiency that marginal benefits to consumers are just equal to the marginal (social) cost of producing these benefits.

internalizing the externality A process that results in a producer or consumer taking account of a previously external effect.

The socially optimal level of output is at the quantity where all marginal costs, private plus external, equal the marginal benefit to society.

Practise with Study Guide Chapter 17, Exercise 1.

In order to internalize the externality successfully, it is necessary to measure its size accurately. Looking at Figure 17-1, we must be able to measure the magnitude of the marginal external cost, *MEC*. In practice, however, external costs are quite difficult to measure. This measurement is especially difficult in the case of air pollution, where the damage is often spread over hundreds of thousands of square kilometres and can affect millions of people.

The Optimal Amount of Pollution Abatement

Notice from Figure 17-1 that the allocatively efficient outcome still has some pollution being generated. This is because the production of each unit of output in Figure 17-1 generates some pollution. It is simply impossible to produce goods and services without generating *some* environmental damage. The economic problem is then to determine how much environmental damage to allow or, equivalently, how much pollution abatement (reduction) to implement. In general it is not optimal to eliminate all pollution.

Zero environmental damage is generally not allocatively efficient.

The economics of determining how much pollution to prohibit, and therefore how much to allow, is summarized in Figure 17-2, which depicts the marginal benefits and marginal costs of pollution abatement. The analysis might be thought of as applying, for example, to water pollution in a specific watershed. It is drawn from the perspective of a public authority whose mandate is to maximize social welfare.

Note that the figure is drawn in terms of the amount of pollution that is prevented (or abated) rather than in terms of the total amount of pollution produced. We do this because pollution abatement (rather than pollution itself) is a "good" of economic value, and we are more familiar with applying the concepts of supply and demand for

FIGURE 17-2 The Optimal Amount of Pollution Abatement

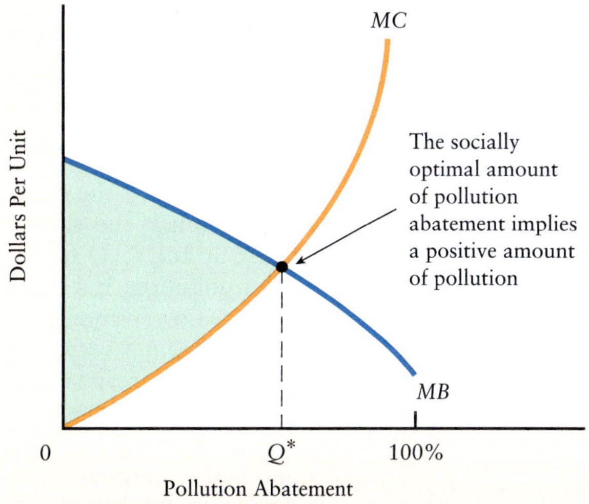

The optimal amount of pollution abatement occurs where the marginal cost of reducing pollution is just equal to the marginal benefits from doing so. *MB* represents the marginal benefit of reducing pollution by one unit. *MC* represents the marginal cost of reducing pollution by one unit. The optimal level of pollution abatement is Q^*, where $MB = MC$. *Notice that not all pollution is eliminated.* For each unit up to Q^*, the marginal benefit derived from pollution abatement exceeds the marginal cost. The total net benefit from the optimal amount of pollution abatement is given by the shaded area—the sum of the difference between marginal benefit and marginal cost at each level of abatement. Any further efforts to reduce pollution beyond Q^* would add more to social costs than to social benefits.

Pollution is an externality. Unless they are required by law to do so, most firms do not take the social costs of their pollution into account when they make their private profit-maximizing decisions.

goods with positive values. If no pollution is abated, the watershed will be subjected to the amount of pollution that would occur in an unregulated market. The greater the amount of pollution abated, the smaller the amount of pollution that remains. Thus, as we move to the right along the horizontal axis, there is more pollution abatement and therefore less remaining pollution. On the vertical axis, measured in dollars per unit, we show the marginal benefit and marginal cost of pollution abatement.

The marginal cost of abating pollution is likely to be small at low levels of abatement but to rise steeply after some point. This is the upward-sloping line shown in Figure 17-2. There are two reasons for believing that this shape is generally accurate. First is the familiar logic behind increasing marginal costs. Because some antipollution measures can be taken fairly easily, the first units of pollution abatement will be cheap relative to later units. In addition, it is likely that pollution prevention of any degree will be easier for some firms than for others. New facilities are likely to run more cleanly than old ones, for example. Pollution abatement in a factory that was designed in the era of environmental concern may be much easier than obtaining similar abatement in an older factory. After some point, however, the easy fixes are exhausted, and the marginal cost of preventing pollution further rises steeply.

The downward-sloping curve in Figure 17-2 is the "demand" for pollution abatement, and reflects the marginal benefit of pollution reduction. The curve slopes downward for much the same reason that the typical demand curve slopes downward. Starting at any level of pollution, people will derive some benefit from reducing the level of pollution, but the marginal benefit from a given amount of abatement will be lower, the lower the level of pollution (or the higher the level of abatement). Put another way, in a very dirty environment, a little cleanliness will be much prized, but in a very clean environment, a little more cleanliness will be of only small additional value.

The optimal amount of pollution abatement occurs where the marginal benefit is equal to the marginal cost—where "supply" and "demand" in Figure 17-2 intersect. In trying to reach this optimum, the pollution-control authority faces three serious problems.

First, although Figure 17-2 looks like a supply–demand diagram, we have already seen that the private sector will not by itself create a market in pollution control. Hence, the government must intervene in private-sector markets if the optimal level of control shown in Figure 17-2 is to be attained.

The second problem is that the optimal level of pollution abatement is not easily known because the marginal benefit and the marginal cost curves shown in Figure 17-2 are not usually observable. In practice, the government can only estimate these curves, and accurate estimates are often difficult to obtain, especially when the technology of pollution abatement is changing rapidly and the health consequences of various pollutants are not known. An excellent recent example of our ignorance regarding the marginal costs and benefits of pollution abatement is related to the debate on greenhouse-gas emissions and global warming. Though there is now a broad consensus among scientists that humankind's emissions of greenhouse gases are contributing to global warming, the estimates of the *magnitude* of the effects of the earth's warming vary considerably.

The third problem is that the available techniques for regulating pollution are themselves imperfect. Even if the optimal level of pollution abatement were known with precision, there are both technical and legal impediments to achieving that level through regulation.

17.2 POLLUTION-CONTROL POLICIES

We examine three different types of policies designed to bring about the optimal amount of pollution abatement (or the optimal amount of pollution). These are *direct controls, emissions taxes,* and *tradable pollution permits.*

Direct Controls

Direct control is the form of environmental regulation that is used most often in Canada and the United States, although it is often invisible to consumers. (Policies of direct control are sometimes referred to as *command-and-control* policies.) Automobile emissions standards are one example. The standards must be met by all new cars that are sold in Canada. They require that emissions per kilometre of a number of pollutants be less than certain specified amounts. The standards are the same no matter where the car is driven. The marginal benefit of reducing carbon monoxide emissions in rural Saskatchewan, where there is relatively little air pollution, is certainly much less than the marginal benefit in Montreal, where there is already a good deal of air pollution. Yet the standard is the same in both places.

Practise with Study Guide Chapter 17, Exercise 4.

Direct controls often require that specific *techniques* be used to reduce pollution. For example, coal-fired electric plants were sometimes required to use devices called "scrubbers" to reduce sulphur dioxide emissions, even in cases where other techniques could have achieved the same level of pollution abatement at lower cost.

Another form of direct control is the simple prohibition of certain polluting behaviours. For example, many cities and towns prohibit the private burning of leaves and other trash because of the air pollution problem (as well as the fire dangers) that the burning would cause. A number of communities have banned the use of wood-burning stoves for the same reason. Similarly, the Canadian federal government gradually reduced the amount of lead allowed in leaded gasoline and then eliminated leaded gasoline altogether.

Problems with Direct Controls The government can legislate a certain amount of pollution abatement through direct controls, and assuming that the legislation can be enforced, this amount of abatement will be achieved. An important problem with direct controls, however, is not with the amount of pollution abated, but rather with the total cost of achieving the given amount of abatement. In the terminology of Chapter 12, direct pollution controls are not *productively efficient* because the total cost of achieving a given amount of pollution abatement is not minimized.

Pollution is being abated efficiently when the marginal cost of pollution abatement is the same for all firms.

When firms are required to abide by direct pollution controls, however, the marginal cost of pollution abatement is usually *not* equated across firms. To see this, consider two firms that have different technologies and thus face different marginal costs of pollution abatement, as shown in Figure 17-3. These firms may be in the same

FIGURE 17-3 The Inefficiency of Direct Pollution Controls

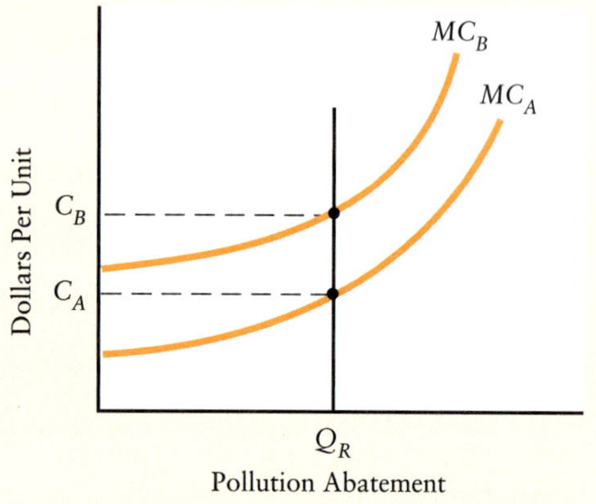

Requiring equal amounts of pollution abatement from different polluters is inefficient when the different polluters have different technologies of pollution abatement. Firm A is able to reduce its emissions according to the marginal cost curve MC_A. Firm B has a different abatement technology and has a higher marginal cost of abatement, MC_B. Suppose a regulatory authority requires that the two firms reduce pollution by the same amount, Q_R. Firm A will have a marginal cost of pollution abatement of C_A, whereas Firm B's marginal cost will be C_B, which is larger than C_A.

To see that this outcome is inefficient, consider what happens if Firm A increases its pollution abatement by one unit while Firm B decreases its abatement by one unit. Total pollution remains the same, but total costs fall.

industry, producing similar products, or they may be in different industries altogether. In either case, they are assumed to have different abilities to abate pollution. Suppose that, for any level of pollution abatement, Firm A's marginal costs of abatement are lower than those for Firm B.

In this situation, consider a system of direct pollution controls that requires Firm A and Firm B each to reduce pollution by a given amount, say Q_R. As shown in Figure 17-3, Firm A's marginal cost at Q_R (C_A) is less than Firm B's marginal cost (C_B). As long as C_A is less than C_B, it is possible to reduce the *total* cost of this amount of pollution abatement by reallocating it between the two firms. For example, suppose C_A is \$10 and C_B is \$18. If Firm A abated one more unit of pollution, its costs would rise by \$10; if Firm B abated one *less* unit of pollution, its costs would fall by \$18. By reallocating one unit of pollution abatement from Firm B to Firm A, total pollution abatement would be unaffected, but the total cost of the abatement would be reduced by \$8. As long as the two firms' marginal costs of abatement are not equal, it is possible to reduce total costs further by further redistributing the abatement between the firms. Only when marginal costs are equal across the two firms is the given level of pollution abatement being achieved at the lowest possible cost.

Direct pollution controls are inefficient because they do not minimize the cost of a given amount of pollution abatement.

Direct controls are also expensive to monitor and to enforce. The regulatory agency has to check—factory by factory, farm by farm—how many pollutants of what kinds are being emitted. It then also needs a mechanism for penalizing offenders. Accurate monitoring of all potential sources of pollution requires a level of resources that is much greater than has ever been made available to the relevant regulatory agencies. Moreover, the existing system of fines and penalties, in the view of many critics, is not nearly harsh enough to have much effect. A potential polluter, required to limit emissions of a pollutant to so many kilograms or litres per day, will take into account the cost of meeting the standard, the probability of being caught, and the severity of the penalty before deciding how to behave. If the chances of being caught and the penalties for being caught are small, the direct controls may have little effect.

Monitoring and enforcement of direct pollution controls are costly, and this costliness reduces the effectiveness of the controls.

Finally, some direct controls can have undesirable effects. For example, automobile manufacturers in the United States are required to achieve an average level of fuel efficiency on the entire fleet of cars they produce. Cars that could burn either ethanol or gasoline were first produced in 1997, and because fuel-efficiency is so much greater when burning ethanol, the production of these cars was much celebrated. However, because very few service stations sold ethanol, owners of these new cars soon turned to fuelling their cars with ordinary gasoline. But the regulations still counted these vehicles as fuel-efficient ethanol-burning cars even though they were, in practice, no more efficient than "normal" gasoline-burning cars. As a result, the manufacturers were able to produce *more* gasoline-guzzling SUVs and still achieve, at least on paper, their overall fuel-efficiency standards. Thus, the mere existence of cars that were able to (but didn't actually) burn ethanol contributed to an *increase* in the average per-vehicle consumption of gasoline.

Emissions Taxes

An alternative method of pollution control is to levy a tax on emissions at the source. The advantage of such a procedure is that it internalizes the pollution externality so that decentralized decisions can lead to allocatively efficient outcomes. Again, suppose Firm A can reduce emissions cheaply, while it is more expensive for Firm B to reduce emissions. And further suppose that all firms are required to pay a tax equal to \$*t* per unit of pollution emitted. Since firms must pay \$*t* for every unit of pollution they produce, they will save \$*t* for every unit of pollution they *do not produce*. It follows that the emissions tax of \$*t* is each firm's marginal benefit of pollution abatement. The goal of profit maximization will then lead firms to reduce emissions to the point where the marginal cost of further reduction is just equal to \$*t*. Firm A will reduce emissions much more than Firm B and both will then have the same marginal cost of further abatement, which is required in order to minimize the cost of a given total amount of pollution abatement. Such a situation is illustrated in Figure 17-4.

Practise with Study Guide Chapter 17, Exercise 2 and Extension Exercise E1.

Note that if the regulatory agency is able to obtain a good estimate of the marginal damage done by pollution, it could set the tax rate just equal to that amount. In such a case, polluters would be forced by the tax to internalize the full pollution externality and allocative efficiency would be achieved. In terms of Figure 17-1, each firm's private marginal cost curve would shift up by the full amount of the tax (set to equal the marginal external cost, *MEC*) and thus the allocatively efficient level of output (and pollution) would be produced.

A second advantage of using emissions taxes is that regulators are not required to specify anything about *how* polluters should abate pollution, and thus are not required to have expertise about the firms' technologies. Rather, polluters themselves can be left to find the most efficient abatement techniques. The profit motive will lead them to do so because they will want to avoid paying the tax.

FIGURE 17-4 The Efficiency of Emissions Taxes

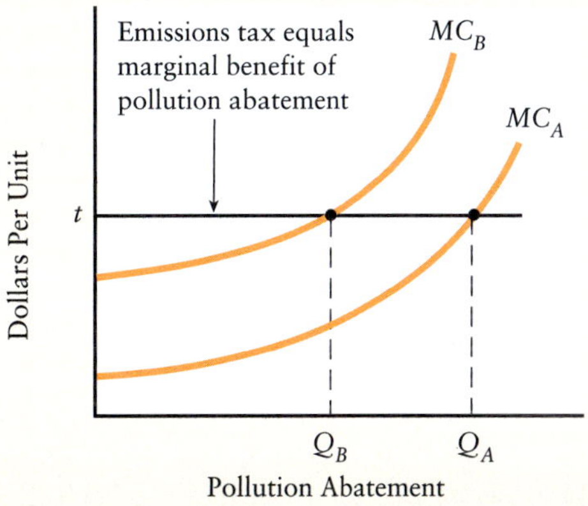

Emission taxes can lead to efficient pollution abatement. As in Figure 17-3, Firm A faces a lower marginal cost of pollution abatement than does Firm B. Suppose the regulatory authority imposes a tax of *t* dollars per unit of pollution. Since each firm must then pay *t* dollars for each unit of pollution it produces, *t* can be viewed as each firm's marginal benefit of pollution abatement.

Firm A chooses to reduce its pollution by Q_A. Up to this point, the tax saved (marginal benefit) from reducing pollution exceeds the marginal cost of reducing pollution. Firm B chooses to abate only a small amount of pollution, Q_B. Since the marginal cost of abatement is equated across firms, the total amount of pollution abatement ($Q_A + Q_B$) is achieved at minimum cost. This is efficient pollution abatement.

Emissions taxes can internalize pollution externalities so that profit-maximizing firms will produce the allocatively efficient amount of pollution abatement.

Applying Economic Concepts 17-1 discusses a simple type of pollution tax that is becoming more common in Canadian cities—charging for household garbage by the bag.

Problems with Emissions Taxes Emissions taxes can work only if it is possible to measure emissions with reasonable accuracy. For some kinds of pollution-creating activities, this does not pose much of a problem, but for many other types of pollution, good measuring devices that can be installed at reasonable cost do not exist. Obviously, in these cases, emissions taxes cannot work, and direct controls are the only feasible approach.

When there is good reason to prohibit a pollutant completely, direct controls are obviously better than taxes. Municipal bans on the burning of leaves fall in this category, as do the occasional emergency bans on some kinds of pollution that are invoked during an air pollution crisis in cities such as Los Angeles, Toronto, and Vancouver.

Another problem with emissions taxes involves setting the tax rate. Ideally, the regulatory agency would obtain an estimate of the marginal social damage caused per unit of each pollutant and set the tax equal to this amount. This ideal tax rate would perfectly internalize the pollution externality. However, the information that is needed to determine the marginal external cost (*MEC*) shown in Figure 17-1 is often difficult to obtain. If the regulatory agency sets the tax rate too high, too many resources will be devoted to pollution control. If the tax is set too low, there will be too little pollution abatement and thus too much pollution.

A disadvantage with emissions taxes is that information necessary to determine the optimal tax rate is often unavailable.

Tradable Pollution Permits

tradable pollution permits Government-granted rights to emit specific amounts of specified pollutants that private firms may buy and sell among themselves.

Practise with Study Guide Chapter 17, Exercise 3.

Like emissions taxes, tradable pollution permits can minimize the cost of a given amount of pollution abatement. **Tradable pollution permits** are permits that allow firms to emit a specified amount and type of pollution and which can be traded among firms at prices determined in a free market. For example, the government might issue permits for a total of 10 000 megatonnes of annual sulphur dioxide emissions and distribute to each of 20 firms a permit for 500 megatonnes. In any given year, a firm is restricted to emitting an amount of sulphur dioxide no greater than the amount allowed by the permits its holds. Firms can then trade the permits freely among themselves and a market-determined price will be established.

To see the efficiency of tradable pollution permits, consider starting from a situation similar to that with direct pollution controls. In Figure 17-5, both firms are abating pollution by Q_R units. (The inefficiency of this initial situation is reflected by the differential in marginal costs of the two firms.) Now suppose the government issues permits for a total amount of emissions consistent with the same total amount of pollution abatement ($= 2 \times Q_R$ in the figure). What should each of the firms do? Should they abate more pollution, or less?

Note that at Q_R units of pollution abatement, the marginal costs for Firm B exceed the marginal costs for Firm A—pollution abatement is more difficult for Firm B than for Firm A. Suppose the two firms could agree on a price p^* at which to buy and sell permits. Who would buy, and who would sell? Firm B, the high-abatement-cost firm, would rather buy permits at p^* and avoid having to reduce pollution at high marginal

APPLYING ECONOMIC CONCEPTS 17-1

Charging for Garbage by the Bag

One of the most common forms of pollution is household garbage. In bags or cans or just "bunches," it is typically removed from the curb by a municipally owned (or hired) garbage truck and transported to a landfill site outside the city. But landfills eventually become full, and new sites must be found. As a result, appropriate landfill sites are becoming scarce—and expensive. In some of the more populated regions of Canada and the United States, the garbage is transported for several hundred kilometres before it is dumped!

The cost of garbage removal and dumping is usually borne by the city, and financed through property taxes. The typical annual payment for this service is between $150 and $250 per Canadian household. But since individual households do not face a *direct* cost associated with each bag of garbage they put out, economic theory suggests this service will be overused, and the outcome will be allocatively inefficient. Too much garbage will be produced.

The externality in this case is the use of scarce landfill sites, which have a considerable, and rising, opportunity cost. When households throw out their garbage, they bear no direct cost associated with the use of these landfills. If households were charged directly for each bag of garbage they put out, economic theory suggests they would take more account of the value of this scarce resource (i.e., the externality would be internalized). As a result, households would reduce their production of garbage and come up with alternative means of dealing with their waste, including a greater emphasis on composting and recycling.

U.S. cities began introducing per-bag garbage-pricing policies in the late 1970s, and now over 6000 U.S. cities have them. Canadian cities have been much slower to adopt these policies, perhaps reflecting the greater availability and lower price of landfill sites. The first Canadian per-bag garbage-pricing policies appeared in 1991. Today, they exist in over 200 cities, mostly in Ontario and in the B.C. Lower Mainland.

The details of these programs differ from city to city. Some require households to purchase special stickers from the municipalities for between $1 and $2 each, and to affix these stickers to any garbage bags to be picked up. Other programs allow the household to pay a fee, such as $150 per year, giving the household the right to have one garbage bag picked up per week. In this case, a household that wants a second bag picked up on a regular basis must pay an additional $150 annual fee.

The theoretical proposition that charging for garbage by the bag leads to more recycling and less garbage being picked up is supported by recent evidence in both Canada and the United States. For example, in Peterborough, Ontario, a garbage-pricing program was introduced in 1993. By 2000, the annual amount of waste being collected had fallen by 21 percent and the annual amount of waste being recycled had increased by 49 percent. Similar results were observed in Markham, Barrie, and Orillia, all in Ontario, and in St. Albert, near Edmonton, Alberta.*

There are some difficulties with such garbage-pricing policies, however. First, it is difficult to determine the optimal price per bag of garbage. As long as landfill sites have some opportunity cost, however, it is obvious that the optimal price is greater than zero. Perhaps a more important problem relates to enforcement. Faced with the requirement to pay for each bag of garbage disposed, some households will choose the (privately) cheaper option of dumping their garbage in a park, in public garbage cans, or under a nearby bridge. In these cases, the households are simply *shifting* costs from themselves to society.

* These results do not control for changes in the amount of garbage and recycling that might have occurred even without the new pricing policies, such as what would be expected from the introduction of the free "blue box" programs designed to encourage recycling. For more details, see "Taking Out the Trash: How to Allocate the Costs Fairly," by M. Kelleher, J. Robins, and J. Dixie, C. D. Howe Institute *Commentary*, July 2005.

If a price is charged for every bag of garbage picked up from the curb, individuals have a strong incentive to reduce their garbage. This is one way to deal with the growing scarcity of landfill sites.

FIGURE 17-5 The Efficiency of Tradable Pollution Permits

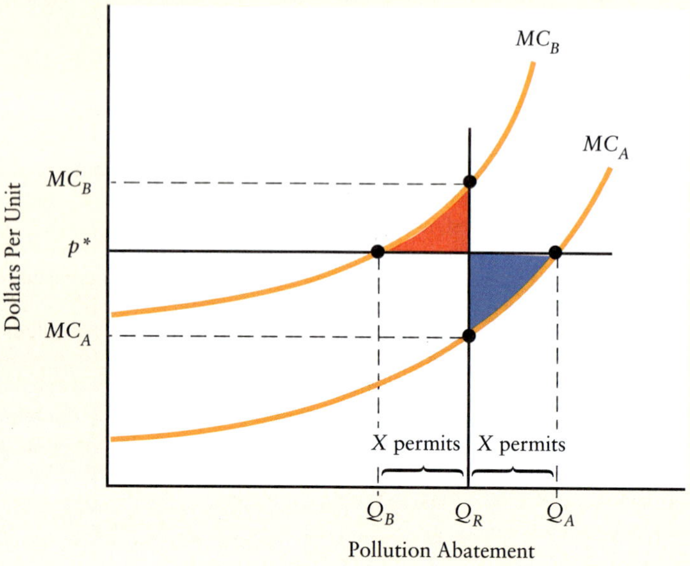

Tradable pollution permits are an efficient way to achieve a given amount of pollution abatement. As in Figure 17-3 and Figure 17-4, Firm A has lower marginal costs of pollution abatement than does Firm B. If each firm abates pollution by Q_R units, the firms' marginal costs are not equated and the pollution abatement is inefficient.

All firms can be better off if they are issued tradable pollution permits even though total pollution abatement remains unchanged. The price of the permits reflects firms' marginal benefit of pollution abatement. If the price is p^*, Firm A would sell X permits to Firm B. Firm B would reduce its abatement to Q_B and reduce its costs by the red area, while Firm A would increase its abatement to Q_A and increase its earnings by the blue area. Since the marginal costs of abatement are equated across firms, this is efficient pollution abatement.

costs. By buying X pollution permits from Firm A, Firm B ends up abating Q_B units of pollution and reduces its costs by the red shaded area. Firm A, the low-abatement-cost firm, would rather sell its permits at p^* and abate more pollution at low marginal cost. By selling X permits to Firm B, Firm A ends up abating Q_A units of pollution and increases its profits by the blue shaded area.

Therefore, with low-abatement-cost firms selling pollution permits to high-abatement-cost firms, both types of firms are better off than when they are subject to direct pollution controls even though the total amount of pollution abatement is unchanged. Since the marginal cost of abatement is now equal across firms, we know that the given amount of pollution abatement is being achieved at the lowest possible cost.

With tradable pollution permits, profit-maximizing firms will reduce pollution until their marginal abatement costs equal the price of pollution permits. The costs of a given amount of pollution abatement will be minimized.

What determines the equilibrium market price for pollution permits? The total supply of pollution permits is determined by the government policy. Let this amount be Q^S—it is represented by a vertical supply curve in Figure 17-6. The demand for pollution permits comes from firms and depends on their costs of pollution abatement.

For every unit of pollution that a firm abates, the firm requires one fewer pollution permit. The price of the pollution permit is therefore firms' marginal benefit of abatement. As the price of the permit increases, each firm decides to abate more pollution and therefore demand fewer pollution permits. Thus, the demand curve for pollution permits is downward sloping, as shown in Figure 17-6. At the equilibrium price for pollution permits, p^*, the number of permits demanded by firms will exactly equal the number of permits issued by the government.

In the market for pollution permits, the quantity is set by government policy. Given that quantity, the equilibrium price is determined by firms' demand for pollution permits.

Technological Change We said earlier that one problem with direct pollution controls is that they tend, like much government regulation, to respond only slowly to changes in technology or market conditions. In contrast, tradable pollution permits, because they are a market-based method of pollution control, maintain their efficiency even in the midst of frequent and substantial changes in technology. As technological advances occur that reduce firms' costs of pollution abatement, firms' demands for pollution permits will fall. The result will be a reduction in the equilibrium price of pollution permits. Whatever the market price for permits, profit-maximizing firms will equate the price to their marginal abatement costs, thus minimizing the total cost of a given amount of pollution abatement.

Improvements in abatement technology will lead to a reduction in the demand for emissions permits and thus a reduction in their equilibrium price. The total cost of a given amount of pollution abatement will still be minimized.

myeconlab

The U.S. *Clean Air Act* of 1990 created a national market for tradable permits for sulphur dioxide, the major cause of acid rain. For more details, look for "A Market for SO_2 Emissions in the United States" in the *Additional Topics* section of this book's MyEconLab.

www.myeconlab.com

FIGURE 17-6 The Market for Tradable Pollution Permits

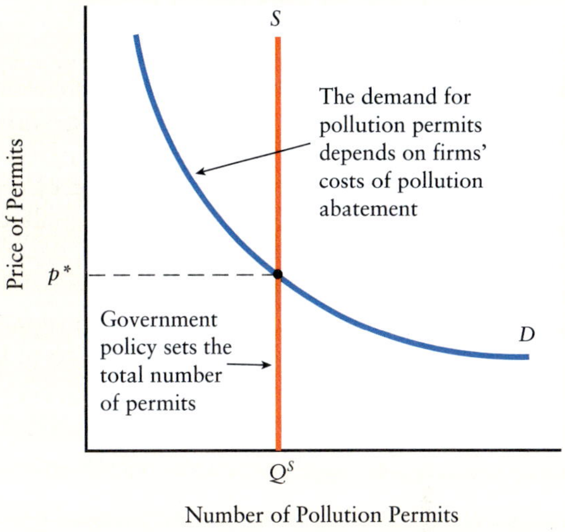

The equilibrium price in the market for pollution permits is determined by government policy and by firms' technology of pollution abatement. The government sets the total quantity of pollution permits at Q^S. This is the vertical supply curve. At a lower price for permits (the marginal benefit of abatement) firms decide to abate less pollution and they therefore require more pollution permits. The demand curve for permits is therefore downward sloping. At the equilibrium price, the quantity of permits demanded by firms is equal to the number issued by the government.

Problems with Tradable Pollution Permits Tradable permits pose some problems of implementation. Some of these involve technical difficulties in measuring pollution and in designing mechanisms to ensure that firms and households comply with regulations (some of these problems also exist for direct controls and emissions taxes). Furthermore, the potential efficiency gains arising from tradable permits cannot be realized if regulatory agencies are prone to change the rules under which trades may take place. Such changes have been a problem in the past, but they are a problem that can be corrected.

One problem with tradable permits is more political than economic, but it is certainly important in explaining why such policies are relatively rare. Opponents of tradable permits often argue that by providing permits, rather than simply outlawing pollution above some amount, the government is condoning crimes against society.

Direct controls, according to this argument, have much greater normative force because they say that violating the standards is simply wrong. Emissions taxes and markets for pollution make violating the standards just one more element of cost for the firm to consider as it pursues its private goals.

Most economists find arguments of this kind unpersuasive. An absolute ban on pollution is impossible because any production of goods and services generates at least some pollution. In choosing how much pollution to allow, society must recognize the tradeoff between devoting resources toward pollution abatement and other valuable things. Economic analysis has a good deal to say about how a society might minimize the cost of *any* degree of pollution abatement. By taking the moral attitude that pollution is wrong and pollution permits should not be allowed, the result is that *less* pollution gets abated for any given amount of society's scarce resources that are allocated toward this goal.

The creation of markets for pollution emissions may become one of the most promising strategies for efficiently overcoming the market failure that leads to environmental pollution.

17.3 THE POLITICS OF POLLUTION CONTROL

To see a copy of the Kyoto Protocol, go to the website for the United Nations Framework Convention on Climate Change: **www.unfccc.de**.

Tradable pollution permits increased in prominence after the 1997 conference on global warming held in Kyoto, Japan. At this conference, representatives for 166 countries met to discuss the need for reducing the emissions of greenhouse gases—gases that most scientists now believe are responsible for trapping the earth's heat and raising the earth's average surface temperature significantly. Thirty-eight countries initially signed the "Kyoto Protocol" and many more have signed since then. Canada signed the Protocol in 1997 and the Canadian Parliament ratified Canada's participation in the international agreement in 2002. By adopting the Kyoto standards, individual countries agree to reduce their emissions of carbon dioxide and other greenhouse gases by a specified amount by 2012. An important part of the Kyoto Protocol is its advocacy of tradable pollution permits, in particular between the participating countries.

There is considerable debate about whether the reduction of greenhouse-gas emissions as outlined in the Kyoto Protocol will have a significant effect in the overall effort to combat global climate change. Even among strong supporters of the Kyoto Protocol, and of environmental protection more generally, there is skepticism about the use of market-based pollution control policies—especially tradable pollution permits. To better understand this skepticism, we consider the respective views of producers, the public, and the environmentalists.

myeconlab

The social and economic implications of global warming are potentially disastrous. For a detailed discussion of the relationship between energy use and global climate change, as well as the technological challenges we face in limiting the emission of greenhouse gases, look for "Climate Change, Energy Use, and the Kyoto Emissions Targets" in the *Additional Topics* section of this book's MyEconLab.

www.myeconlab.com

Producers

Some firms object to the costs they are asked to pay in terms of emissions taxes or the purchase prices of emissions permits. However, there is no reason why payments to government (to purchase permits) under any market-based scheme need to be an unjustified "tax grab." Emissions taxes need not be in excess of the costs imposed on society by the industry's activities. If government uses the introduction of a market-based scheme to raise general revenue—and thus levies emissions taxes in excess of the costs generated by the pollution—firms can oppose the extra tax burden without opposing the market-based scheme itself.

The introduction of market-based measures may signal the end of a free ride that producers have been taking at society's expense. If the firms in an industry were bearing none of the cost of their pollution, any efficient antipollution scheme would impose a burden on them—but only to the extent of forcing them to bear the costs of their own activities. The difference between direct controls and the market-based solution, however, is that the former will cost the average firm in the industry more than the market solution. (This difference just reflects the fact that direct controls are generally less efficient than emissions taxes or tradable pollution permits.)

Under market-based schemes (rather than direct controls), many firms feel a sense of unfairness because their competitors continue polluting while they must clean up. Such complaints ignore the fact that those firms that continue to pollute have paid for the right to do so, either by paying effluent taxes or by buying pollution rights, and that the complaining firm could do the same if it wished (it does not do so because cleaning up is cheaper for it than paying to pollute, as the competitors are doing).

These points make clear a key issue in assessing market-based solutions: Such solutions must not be judged relative to a "no action" policy. Given a government's decision to reduce pollution, the market solution must be compared with other alternatives that reduce pollution by the same amount. When such a comparison is made, much of the opposition from producers fades away.

Some firms argue that environmental protection reduces overall welfare because output and employment will fall if firms are required to pay emissions taxes or the price of pollution permits. This argument is misleading. It is surely true, as is clear in Figure 17-1, that firms required to pay for the external cost of the pollution they create will experience an increase in marginal cost—this is precisely how the externality gets internalized. It is also true that the level of output and employment in such firms will fall. But there is no tradeoff here between the environment and overall welfare. The environment is part of overall welfare. When we say that one unit of pollution generates an external cost of $100, we are measuring the cost imposed on the environment (or, equivalently, the amount of resources required to clean up that environmental damage).

If steel-producing firms are required to pay the external cost of their pollution, the reduction in output and employment in those firms will indeed cause some pain. Profits will be lower, and some workers will be laid off. But this reduction in the amount of total resources devoted to the steel industry is part of the *solution* to the pollution externality. A negative externality in the steel industry means that too much steel is being produced. Thus, it will improve overall welfare—not reduce it—to reduce the amount of resources in the steel industry. The resources that are no longer used in the steel industry are now free to be used in other industries, producing goods and services that society values more at the margin, and that cause less environmental damage, than an extra unit of steel.

The General Public

Some members of the general public have a moral opposition to selling anyone the right to pollute. Since it involves human survival, dealing in the right to pollute seems evil to many people. As we said earlier, however, it is not possible simply to ban pollution outright since all production invariably generates some pollution. The relevant question then becomes: How best can society reduce pollution by a given amount? Economic analysis suggests that tradable pollution permits are an efficient way of reducing pollution, and are more efficient than direct pollution controls.

Opposition to the outcome where those who have the highest costs of cleaning up continue to pollute while those with the lowest costs do the cleaning up. Morality may dictate to many observers that the biggest polluters should do the cleaning up. Economists cannot show this reaction to be wrong; they can only point out the costs in terms of unnecessary resource use and less overall pollution abatement that follow from adopting such a position.

Environmentalists

Over the past decade or so, many environmental groups have accepted the logic of economists' argument that market-based schemes to reduce environmental damage are efficient and therefore desirable. These environmentalists continue to devote their energies to convincing governments as well as the rest of society that the problem of environmental damage must be seriously addressed. Other environmentalists, however, do not accept the efficiency arguments that we have developed in this chapter. What are some of the arguments commonly heard from these groups?

Many environmentalists are skeptical about the efficiency and desirability of markets. Some do not understand economists' reasoning as to why markets can be, and often are, efficient mechanisms for allocating scarce resources. Others understand the economists' case but reject it, although few complete their argument by trying to demonstrate that direct government controls will be more effective.

Many environmentalists do not like the use of self-interest incentives to solve what they regard as "social" rather than "economic" issues. Economists who point to the voluminous evidence of the importance of self-interest incentives are often accused of ignoring higher motives such as social responsibility, self-sacrifice, and compassion. Although such motives are absent from the simple theories that try to explain the everyday behaviour of buyers and sellers, economists since Adam Smith have been aware that these higher motives do exert strong influences on human behaviour.

Such higher motives are very powerful at some times and in some situations, but they do not govern many people's behaviour in the course of day-to-day living. If we want to understand how people behave in the aftermath of a flood, or an earthquake, or a war, we need motives in addition to self-interest; if we want to understand how people behave day after day in their buying and selling, we need little other than a theory of the self-interested responses to market incentives. Since control of the environment requires influencing the mass of small decisions, as well as a few large ones, the appeal to self-interest is the only currently known way to induce the required behaviour through voluntary actions.

Many environmentalists do not recognize that markets can be an efficient tool for protecting the environment.

Some environmentalists have the view that resources such as clean air and pure water are above mere monetary calculation and should thus be treated in special ways. The economist can point out that almost all human activity has an impact on the environment and that we all face tradeoffs between our environmental concerns and other wants and needs. To put clean air and water in a special category prevents us from seeking a socially desirable outcome through cost-benefit analysis. Moreover, attaching a monetary value to environmental quality may be the most convincing way to demonstrate that environmental factors can be valued more highly than material goods.

Summary

This chapter has examined the main economic issues, and some of the political issues, associated with pollution control. The fact that pollution is a byproduct of some other production process means that pollution is a negative externality. Producers think about their own private costs but ignore the pollution costs that their production imposes on the rest of society. The efficient solution to this problem involves *internalizing the externality*—that is, making sure that the producers of the pollution are made to bear its full external cost. In the chapter we reviewed two efficient ways of internalizing pollution externalities: emissions taxes and tradable pollution permits.

If properly designed, such market-based environmental policies can reverse the effects of the pollution externality. In terms of Figure 17-1, these policies have the effect of shifting the private marginal cost curve up by the full amount of the marginal external cost, thus equating private marginal cost with social marginal cost. When this occurs, firms will reduce the output of the goods that produce pollution as a byproduct, and the amount of pollution produced will also decline.

There is considerable opposition among some environmentalists and some of the general public to market-based environmental policies. Tradable pollution permits, especially, appear to generate much skepticism among non-economists. Much of this skepticism has the same source as skepticism toward other policies that advocate the use of markets: *the lack of understanding of how markets work to allocate resources efficiently.* In response, economists can only continue to explain how markets work, illustrate what happens when markets are not permitted to operate, and present the costs and benefits of various environmental policies. Eventually the message will get through.

SUMMARY

17.1 THE ECONOMIC RATIONALE FOR REGULATING POLLUTION (LO 1)

- Pollution can be analyzed as a negative externality. Polluting firms and households going about their daily business do harm to the environment and fail to take account of the costs that they impose on others.
- In a market that produces pollution as a byproduct, the external cost of the pollution implies that too much of the good is produced compared with what is allocatively efficient. Social marginal cost exceeds private marginal cost.
- The allocatively efficient level of pollution is generally not zero; it is the level where the marginal cost of further pollution reduction is just equal to the marginal benefit of pollution reduction.
- If a firm or a household faces incentives that cause it to internalize fully the costs that pollution imposes, it will choose the allocatively efficient level of pollution.

17.2 POLLUTION-CONTROL POLICIES

LO 2 3

- Pollution can be regulated either directly or indirectly. Direct controls are used most often. They are often inefficient because they require that all polluters meet the same standard regardless of the benefits and costs of doing so.
- Efficient pollution abatement requires that the marginal cost of abatement is equated across firms. This can be achieved with market-based policies, such as emissions taxes or tradable pollution permits.
- Emission taxes work by requiring polluters to pay a tax per unit of pollution produced. The tax becomes the marginal benefit of pollution abatement to the firms. Since all firms face the same tax per unit of pollution, their profit-maximizing behaviour will bring about efficiency in pollution abatement.
- Tradable pollution permits work by the government issuing permits to firms and then allowing those permits to be freely traded. The market price of the permit then represents firms' marginal benefit of pollution abatement. Efficiency in pollution abatement is achieved because firms' profit-maximizing behaviour leads their marginal abatement costs to be equated.

17.3 THE POLITICS OF POLLUTION CONTROL

LO 4

- There is considerable opposition by some of the public to the use of market-based environmental policies—especially the use of tradable pollution permits.
- Many firms oppose having to pay for pollution permits. But if the quantity of permits is chosen appropriately, the permit price will equal the marginal external cost of pollution, and thus firms will only pay the external cost that their production imposes on society.
- Some environmentalists and other members of the public oppose on moral grounds that firms should be able to pay for the "right to pollute." These criticisms ignore the fact that pollution is an important economic problem, and a strong case can be made for wanting to minimize the total cost of any given level of pollution abatement.

KEY CONCEPTS

Negative pollution externalities
Marginal external cost

Costs and benefits of pollution abatement
The efficient level of pollution

Direct pollution controls
Emissions taxes
Tradable pollution permits

STUDY EXERCISES

1. Consider the following costs and benefits associated with cleaning up a polluted city lake.

Cleanliness of Water (%)	Marginal Cost ($)	Marginal Benefit ($)
0	50 000	550 000
20	100 000	400 000
40	160 000	300 000
60	230 000	230 000
80	350 000	180 000
100	infinite	150 000

   a. Explain why the marginal cost of pollution reduction increases as the cleanliness of the water increases. Plot the *MC* curve in a diagram.
   b. Explain why the marginal benefit of pollution reduction falls as the cleanliness of the water increases. Plot the *MB* curve in the same diagram.
   c. What is the optimal level of water cleanliness?
   d. Explain why the efficient level of pollution is greater than zero.

2. Fill in the blanks to make the following statements correct.

   a. When there are pollution externalities associated with the production of steel, _______ marginal costs of steel production exceed _______ marginal costs of steel production.

b. By imposing a ________ on the production of steel, the externality can be ________.
c. If the tax is chosen to be exactly equal to the ________, the externality can be completely internalized. The result will be that private firms produce the ________ level of steel (and pollution).

3. Fill in the blanks to make the following statements correct.

a. Suppose the Canadian government announced that all homeowners must insulate their homes with R-40 insulation. As a pollution-control policy, this is an example of ________.
b. Suppose the Canadian government announced a tax of $2.50 per litre of home heating oil consumed. As a pollution-control policy, this is an example of ________.
c. Suppose the Canadian government distributed coupons to all homeowners allowing them to burn specified amounts of fossil fuels for home heating, and allowed homeowners to buy and sell these coupons. As a pollution-control policy, this is an example of ________. A ________ would develop for these coupons.

4. myeconlab Consider the market for lumber, which we assume here to be perfectly competitive.

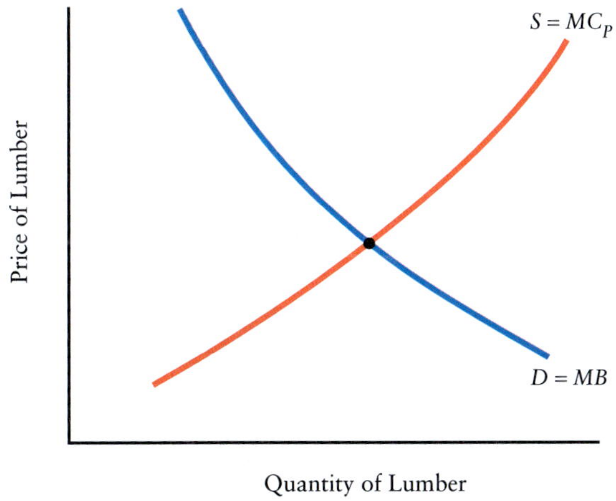

a. Suppose that for each unit of lumber produced, the firm also generates $10 of damage to the environment. Draw the social marginal cost curve in the diagram.
b. What is the allocatively efficient level of lumber output? Explain.
c. Describe and show the new market outcome if lumber producers are required to pay a tax of $10 per unit of lumber produced. Explain.
d. In part (c), does the equilibrium price of lumber rise by the full $10 of the tax? Explain.

5. The following diagram shows society's marginal benefit and marginal cost for abating a particular type of pollution—say greenhouse-gas emissions.

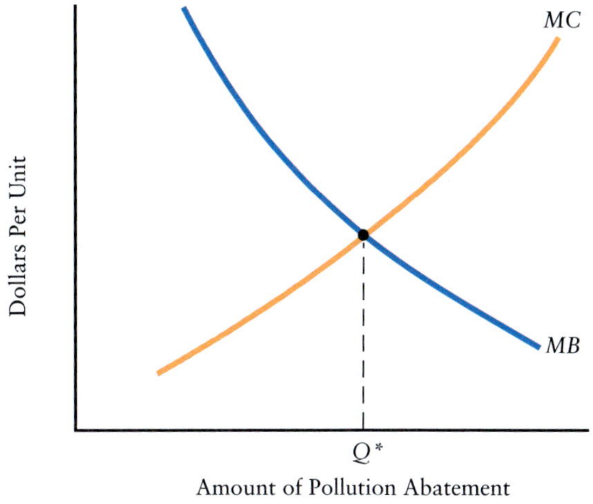

a. Explain why the marginal cost curve is upward sloping.
b. Explain why the marginal benefit curve is downward sloping.
c. At Q^*, are all greenhouse-gas emissions eliminated? Explain.
d. Is there an "optimal" level of greenhouse-gas emissions? Explain.

6. myeconlab Suppose there are only two firms—Softies Inc. and Cuddlies Inc.—producing disposable diapers. Both firms are releasing dioxins into the same river. To reduce the pollution, the regulatory agency must choose between using direct controls and emissions taxes. The diagrams on the next page show each firm's marginal cost of pollution abatement.

a. Suppose the regulatory agency requires that the two firms each abate Q_3 units of pollution. What is each firm's marginal abatement cost at Q_3?
b. Could the total cost of this amount of pollution abatement be reduced? Explain how.
c. Now suppose the regulatory agency instead imposes an emissions tax of $40 per unit of emissions. Explain why this tax can be thought of as each firm's "marginal benefit of abatement."
d. In part (c), how much pollution will each firm choose to abate?
e. Is it possible to reduce the total cost of the amount of abatement being done in part (d)?

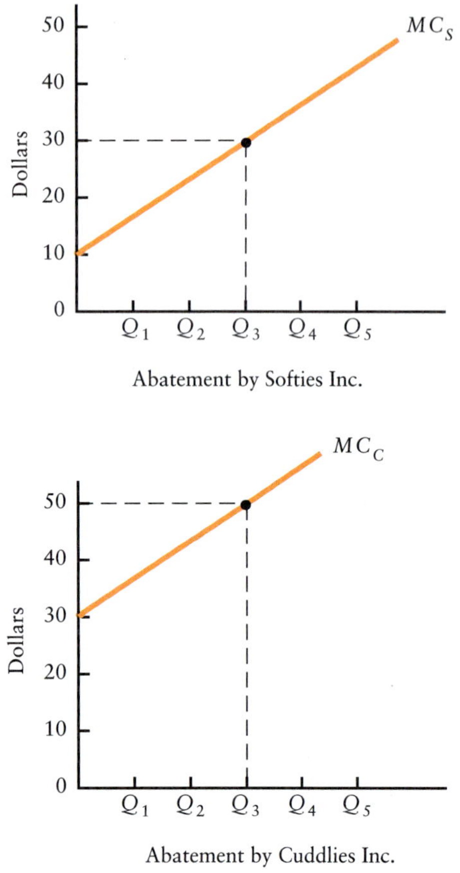

7. Suppose the government issues a fixed quantity, Q^*, of tradable pollution permits, each one permitting the emission of one tonne of sulphur dioxide. Use the accompanying figure to help answer the following questions.

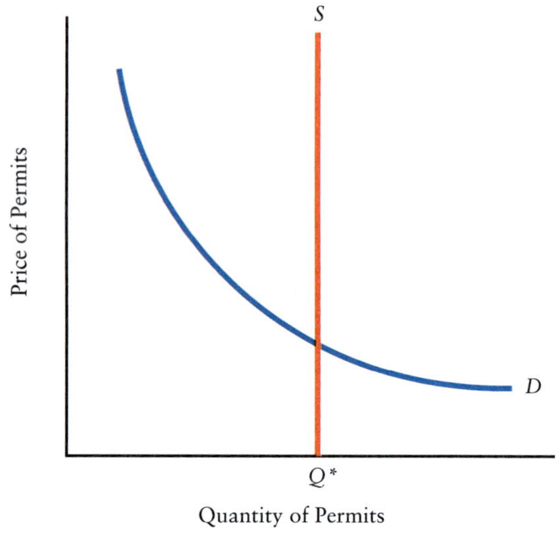

a. Explain what determines firms' demand for permits.
b. If there is a competitive market for pollution permits, explain why the equilibrium price of the permit will equal firms' marginal abatement cost.
c. Explain why the equilibrium price of permits will fall if polluting firms experience a technological improvement that reduces their marginal abatement costs.
d. One advantage of tradable pollution permits is that they allow the public to express their preferences for pollution reduction through the market. What happens if Greenpeace decides to buy a large number of pollution permits and "retire" them?

DISCUSSION QUESTIONS

1. "Pollution is wrong. When a corporation pollutes, it commits assault on the citizens of the country, and it should be punished." Comment on this statement in light of the discussion in this chapter.

2. Consider the following (alleged) facts about pollution control and indicate what influence they might have on policy determination.

   a. The cost of meeting government pollution requirements is about $300 per person per year.
   b. More than one-third of the world's known oil supplies lie under the ocean floor, and there is no known method of recovery that guarantees that large amounts of oil will not spill into the ocean.
   c. Sulphur-removal requirements and strip-mining regulations have led to the tripling of the cost of a tonne of coal used in generating electricity.
   d. Every million dollars that is spent on pollution control creates 47 new jobs in the economy.

3. Suppose you were given the job of drafting a law to regulate water pollution over the entire length of some river.
   a. How would you determine how much total pollution to permit?
   b. What control mechanism would you use to regulate emissions into the river? Why?
   c. Would you impose the same rules on cities as on farms?
   d. Would your answer to parts (a), (b), or (c) depend on the quality of information that would be available to you? How and why?

4. The federal government has imposed many regulations aimed at reducing the pollution that is generated by driving. The more familiar regulations are direct—catalytic converters, fuel efficiency, and the like. Given the discussion in the chapter, why do you think the government opted for such direct controls? Can you think of any indirect controls currently in use to reduce automobile pollution?

CHAPTER 18

Taxation and Public Expenditure

LEARNING OBJECTIVES

In this chapter you will learn

1. about the main taxes used in Canada.
2. why a tax can lead to allocative inefficiency.
3. about the concept of fiscal federalism in Canada.
4. how Canada's major social programs are financed.
5. some common pitfalls in evaluating government's role in the economy.

In Chapter 16, we saw some of the reasons why the scope of government is so extensive. Taxation is needed to raise money for public spending, and it can also play a policy role in its own right. Taxes and government expenditure both affect the distribution of income—some people get taxed more than others and some people benefit more from government spending programs than others. Moreover, taxation and public expenditure influence the allocation of resources. In some cases, government policy is carefully designed with such effects in mind; in other cases, the effects are unintentional byproducts of policies pursued for other purposes.

In this chapter, we examine the various sources of government tax revenues and the various types of government expenditures. We ask how taxation and public expenditure affect the allocation of resources and the distribution of income, and to what extent they are effective tools of public policy. We examine the basis on which to evaluate a tax system, emphasizing the distinction between equity and efficiency. The types of public expenditures in Canada are examined along with the important concept of fiscal federalism. Finally, we briefly discuss Canada's main social programs, which account for approximately 60 percent of combined government spending.

18.1 TAXATION IN CANADA

There is a bewildering array of taxes in Canada today. These are levied at the federal, provincial, and local levels. Some are highly visible, such as income taxes and the Goods and Services Tax (GST). Others are all but invisible because they do not show up on income-tax forms or on receipts for purchases. For example, there are special taxes levied on the sales of alcohol, cigarettes, and gasoline, but these taxes are levied directly on the producers (rather than the retailers) of these goods. People and firms are taxed on what they earn, on what they spend, and on what they own. Not only are taxes numerous, but taken together they raise a large amount of revenue. Table 18-1

For detailed information about the Canadian tax system, go to the website of the independent Canadian Tax Foundation: **www.ctf.ca**.

shows, for the federal, provincial, and local governments combined, the amount of revenue raised by the different types of taxes in 2005.

Canada lies roughly in the middle of other developed countries in terms of tax revenues as a share of GDP. Among the major industrialized countries, Denmark and Sweden collect roughly 50 percent of GDP in taxes. The lowest-tax industrialized country is Japan, which collects about 27 percent of GDP in taxes. Canada is in the middle of the pack, collecting taxes equal to approximately 38 percent of GDP.

TABLE 18-1 Tax Revenues of Canadian Governments, 2005

	Billions of Dollars	Percent of GDP
Income taxes	$205.1	14.5
Consumption taxes (GST, provincial sales taxes, and excise taxes)	104.1	7.4
Property and related taxes	46.8	3.3
Other taxes	17.7	1.3
Health and social insurance premiums	70.7	5.0
Total tax revenues	**$444.4**	**31.5**
Non-tax revenues (sales of goods and services, investment income)	86.2	6.1
Total government revenues	**$530.6**	**37.6**

Canadian governments (at all levels) collect over $530 billion in various taxes, over 37 percent of GDP. These data show total tax revenues for all levels of government combined. Notice that Canadian governments have considerable revenue, over $86 billion in 2005, from non-tax sources.

(*Source:* These data are available on Statistics Canada's website: www.statcan.ca. Search for "government" and then look for "consolidated government revenue and expenditure." Reprinted with permission of Statistics Canada.)

Progressive Taxes

Before discussing details about the Canadian tax system, we examine the concept of *progressivity* of taxes.

When the government taxes one income group in society more heavily than it taxes another, it influences the distribution of income. The effect of taxes on the distribution of income can be summarized in terms of *progressivity.* A **progressive tax** takes a larger percentage of income from high-income people than it does from low-income people. A **proportional tax** takes amounts of money from people in direct proportion to their incomes—for example, every individual might pay 10 percent of his or her income in taxes. A **regressive tax** takes a larger percentage of income from low-income people than it does from high-income people.

Note that the progressivity or regressivity of a tax is expressed in terms of *shares* of income rather than absolute dollar amounts. Thus, a tax that collects $1000 from each individual clearly collects the same dollar amount from everybody, though it collects a higher share of income from low-income people than from higher-income people. A tax of this type is therefore a regressive tax. It is often called a *lump-sum tax,* one that is the same at all levels of income.

Since a progressive tax takes a larger share of income from high-income people than it does from low-income people, progressive taxes reduce the inequality of income. A regressive tax increases the inequality of income.

The progressivity of a tax involves an important distinction between the average tax rate and the marginal tax rate. The **average tax rate** is the percentage of income that the individual pays in taxes. The **marginal tax rate** is the percentage *of the next dollar* earned that the individual pays in taxes. Progressivity of a tax requires an *average* tax rate that rises with income; we will see in this chapter that such progressivity can be achieved with either rising or constant marginal tax rates.

progressive tax A tax that takes a larger percentage of income the higher the level of income.

proportional tax A tax that takes a constant percentage of income at all levels of income.

regressive tax A tax that takes a lower percentage of income the higher the level of income.

average tax rate The ratio of total taxes paid to total income earned.

marginal tax rate The fraction of an additional dollar of income that is paid in taxes.

The Canadian Tax System

Taxes are collected by the federal government, by each of the provinces, and by thousands of cities, townships, and villages. Here is a brief guide to the most important of the various taxes.

Personal Income Taxes Personal income taxes are paid directly to the government by individuals. The amount of tax any individual pays is the result of a fairly complicated set of calculations. All types of income are included in what is called total income, although certain types of income qualify for total or partial exemption. Then a number of allowable deductions are subtracted from total income to determine taxable income. The most important deduction is called the "basic personal amount" and in 2006 was equal to $8839. Once taxable income is calculated, the amount of tax payable is then computed by applying different tax rates to different levels of income. There are four federal personal income tax rates, each applying within what is called a tax bracket. In 2006, the four **tax brackets** and marginal tax rates within each bracket were as follows:

tax bracket A range of taxable income for which there is a constant marginal tax rate.

- $0–$36 378: marginal tax rate = 15.5 percent
- $36 379–$72 756: marginal tax rate = 22 percent
- $72 757–$118 285: marginal tax rate = 26 percent
- $118 286 and over: marginal tax rate = 29 percent

To see how to compute the amount of taxes payable with this system of tax brackets, consider Christine, who has a taxable income of $75 000. To the federal government she pays at a rate of 15.5 percent on the first $36 378 of taxable income ($5639), at a rate of 22 percent on her next $36 378 ($8003), and at a rate of 26 percent on her last $2244 of income ($583). Since her taxable income is less than $118 285, she never enters the highest tax bracket and therefore does not face the 29-percent tax rate. Christine's total tax payable is therefore $14 225. Recalling the definition of average and marginal tax rates, Christine's *average* tax rate is $14 225/$75 000, or 19 percent. Her *marginal tax rate*—the rate on an additional dollar of income—is 26 percent.

The four federal personal income-tax rates do not represent the complete taxation of personal income in Canada because the provincial governments also tax personal income. Quebec and Alberta run their own income-tax systems, whereas the other eight provinces simply use the federal tax base (and federally distributed tax forms) and essentially "top up" federal taxes. In all provinces other than Quebec, taxpayers pay a single amount to the Canada Revenue Agency (CRA), which then distributes the total between the federal government and each province according to the amount collected from residents of that province.

The provincial taxation of income implies that Canada's highest marginal income-tax rate is not the highest *federal* rate, 29 percent. As of 2005, the highest combined (provincial plus federal) marginal tax rates varied from a low of 39 percent in Alberta to 53 percent in Quebec.

Corporate Income Taxes The federal corporate income tax is a flat-rate (proportional) tax on profits as defined by the taxing authorities—which includes the return on capital as well as economic profits. By 2006, following several years of reductions, the federal corporate income-tax rate for large businesses was 21 percent; provincial rates varied from a low of 8.9 percent in Quebec to a high of 16 percent in Nova Scotia and Prince Edward Island. Small businesses are taxed at lower rates by both the federal and (most) provincial governments.

Some corporate profits get distributed as dividends to shareholders. These dividends represent the shareholder's share of after-tax profits, and would ordinarily be taxed along with his or her other income. To avoid double taxation on this income, however, individual shareholders get a personal income-tax credit for their share of the corporate tax already paid by the firm. In this way, the corporate and personal income-tax systems are said to be *integrated.*

When governments in Canada consider changes to income-tax rates, a debate usually occurs regarding which taxes should be changed: personal income taxes or corporate income taxes. Some people argue that corporate income-tax rates are already too low and that firms are not paying their "fair share" of the tax burden. Others argue that corporate taxes end up being paid partly by firms' customers and employees, and partly by the individuals who own shares in firms, which now includes most individuals through some form of employer-sponsored or self-administered pension. In addition, they argue that corporate taxes, by reducing the rate of return on investment, impede the economy's long-run growth. *Extensions in Theory 18-1* discusses taxes on corporate income and highlights the important difference between taxing *accounting* profits and *economic* profits—a distinction we first saw in Chapter 7.

Excise and Sales Taxes As we first saw in Chapter 4, an *excise tax* is a tax levied on a particular commodity. In many countries, goods such as tobacco, alcohol, and gasoline are singled out for high rates of excise taxation. Because these goods usually account for a much greater proportion of the expenditure of lower-income than higher-income groups, the excise taxes on them are regressive. A *sales tax* applies to the sale of all or most goods and services. All provinces except Alberta impose a retail sales tax. Such a tax is mildly regressive, because poorer families tend to spend a larger proportion of their incomes than richer families. Both excise and sales taxes are often referred to as "indirect" taxes to contrast them with income taxes, which are levied directly on the income of individuals or firms.

Practise with Study Guide Chapter 18, Exercise 4.

Since 1991, Canada has had a country-wide tax that applies at the same rate (6 percent) to the sale of all goods and services (with a few exceptions, such as basic groceries). The main advantage of the Goods and Services Tax (GST) is that it taxes expenditure rather than income.

One problem with taxing income is that interest earnings from accumulated savings get taxed as well. Consider an example. Suppose you have after-tax earnings of \$1000, all of which you would like to save. You put your \$1000 in a bank account that offers to pay 5 percent interest, and at the end of the year you receive \$50 in interest income. But you must pay tax on this interest income. If the income-tax rate is 30 percent, you pay $0.3 \times \$50 = \$15.00$. You are left with only \$35.00 in after-tax interest earnings on your original saving of \$1000, which implies an after-tax rate of return of 3.5 percent. The income tax payable on your interest earnings has lowered your return from saving and thus reduced your incentive to save. As we saw in Chapter 15, any reduction in saving will imply less capital accumulation for the economy. In contrast, the GST only applies to the value of expenditure. Since the GST does not tax income (and therefore does not tax interest income) it does not discourage saving.

In introducing the GST, Canada followed the trend in almost all other developed nations (except the United States), which levy similar taxes; they are called *value added taxes* (VAT) in Europe.

In practice, the GST works by taxing a firm on the gross value of its output and then allowing a tax credit equal to the taxes paid on the inputs that were produced by other firms. Thus, the GST taxes each firm's contribution to the value of final output—its value added. The total tax collected is the same as if only *final* goods were taxed

EXTENSIONS IN THEORY 18-1

Who Really Pays the Corporate Income Tax?

As we saw in Chapter 7, there are two different measures of a firm's profit—*accounting* profit and *economic* profit. Accounting profit is the difference between the firm's revenues and its explicit costs such as labour, materials, overhead, and depreciation. The same firm's economic profit would also take into account the opportunity costs of the owner's time and financial capital. Since there are additional costs included, economic profits are less than accounting profits. As it turns out, the burden of the corporate income tax depends crucially on which measure of profit is used as the basis for the tax.

Let's examine two alternative taxes: one that applies to economic profits, and another that applies to accounting profits. To illustrate the two taxes, we consider an imaginary firm that produces hockey equipment—Canada Hockey Inc. (CHI), located in Brampton, Ontario. Suppose in 2007 CHI earns accounting profits of $1.5 million. Also suppose the opportunity cost of the owner's capital and time is $1.1 million. Once these opportunity costs are considered, CHI's economic profits are equal to $400 000.

A Tax on Economic Profits

Recall that *economic* profits are the return to the owner's capital over and above what could be earned elsewhere. In other words, CHI's $400 000 of economic profits represents the firm's return to its capital in excess of what that capital could earn in the (equally risky) next-best alternative investment. If CHI faces a 30-percent corporate tax that applies to its economic profits, it will pay $120 000 in corporate taxes, and it will still have after-tax economic profits equal to $280 000. Since CHI is still earning positive economic profits—that is, it is still earning more than it could earn elsewhere—it has no incentive to leave this industry.

In fact, the firm has no incentive to do anything differently than it was doing previously—the tax on the firm's economic profit has *no effect* on the firm's output, prices, employment, or long-run investment choices. Before the tax, CHI was making output, employment, price, and investment decisions to maximize its (economic) profits. With the tax, some fraction of these economic profits must be paid to the government, but CHI still chooses to maximize its profits by doing whatever it was doing before the tax.

The implication is that if the corporate income tax applies to *economic* profits, firms and their owners bear the entire burden of the tax. But the tax will have no effect on the allocation of resources, and in this sense the tax would be efficient.

A Tax on Accounting Profits

Now consider the alternative case in which the corporate income tax applies not to economic profit but to *accounting* profit. CHI's accounting profits are

when they were sold to consumers. Figure 18-1 shows how the GST is calculated at each stage from the mining of iron ore to the final retail sale of a washing machine.

Like sales and excise taxes, the GST is applied to expenditure rather than income. The GST taken alone would therefore be mildly regressive, because the proportion of income saved, and hence not taxed, rises with income. This regressivity is reduced by exempting food and, more importantly, by giving low- and middle-income households a refundable tax credit. For the lowest-income households, the GST is a progressive tax because the refundable tax credit exceeds the value of GST that they would pay even if they spent all of their incomes on taxable commodities.

Property Taxes The property tax is the most important Canadian tax that is based on wealth and is an important source of revenue for municipalities. It is different from any other important tax because it is not related directly to a current transaction. In contrast, income taxes are levied on the current payment to a factor of production (income) and sales taxes are levied on the value of a currently purchased good or service.

FIGURE 18-2 Direct and Excess Burdens of an Excise Tax

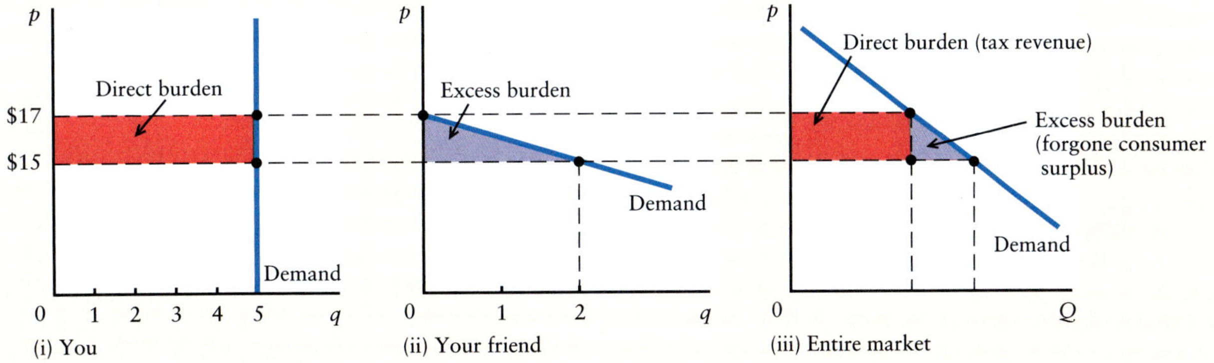

The allocative inefficiency of a tax is measured by its excess burden. The excess burden is greater the more elastic is demand. Part (i) shows your demand for CDs. It is perfectly inelastic at five CDs per month. When the government imposes an excise tax of $2 per CD, the price rises from $15 to $17. Your quantity demanded is unchanged, and so you pay $10 per month in taxes ($2 tax per CD × 5 CDs). The direct burden of the tax is $10; but because your quantity of CDs demanded is unchanged, there is no excess burden.

Part (ii) shows your friend's demand. Her quantity demanded falls from two CDs per month to zero as a result of the tax. Since she pays no tax (because she buys no CDs), she bears no direct burden of the tax. But because she has lost consumer surplus, she bears an excess burden from the tax.

Part (iii) shows the entire market demand. There is both a direct burden, the red shaded area, and an excess burden, the purple shaded area. The more elastic is the demand curve, the larger is the excess burden of the tax.

result of this tax. She is worse off by the amount of consumer surplus that she would have received had she made her usual purchases of two CDs per month. In this case, the direct burden is zero (because no tax is paid) but there *is* an excess burden. The excess burden is equal to her loss in consumer surplus from the two CDs per month that she no longer enjoys.

When an excise tax is imposed, some people behave like the music buff and do not change their consumption of the taxed good at all, others cease consuming the taxed good altogether, and most simply reduce their consumption. There will be an excess burden for those in the latter two groups. Thus, the revenue collected will understate the total cost to taxpayers of generating that revenue.

The same basic analysis applies to income taxes. Figure 18-3 shows the effect of levying a tax on workers' incomes. The income tax shifts the labour supply upwards because workers will only be prepared to supply any given amount of labour services if the pre-tax wage is increased to offset the effect of the tax.

The income tax generates both a direct burden and an excess burden. The tax raises revenue by collecting some percentage of workers' wages. This is a cost borne by both workers and firms. By reducing the equilibrium level of employment and creating a deadweight loss, the income tax also creates an excess burden. As with the case of excise taxes, the revenue collected by the tax understates the total cost of the tax.

Excise taxes and income taxes impose costs in two ways. By taking resources from market participants (consumers, firms, workers), they impose a direct burden. By reducing the volume of market transactions, they also generate a deadweight loss—this is the excess burden of the tax.

Practise with Study Guide Chapter 18, Exercise 2.

FIGURE 18-3 Direct and Excess Burdens of an Income Tax

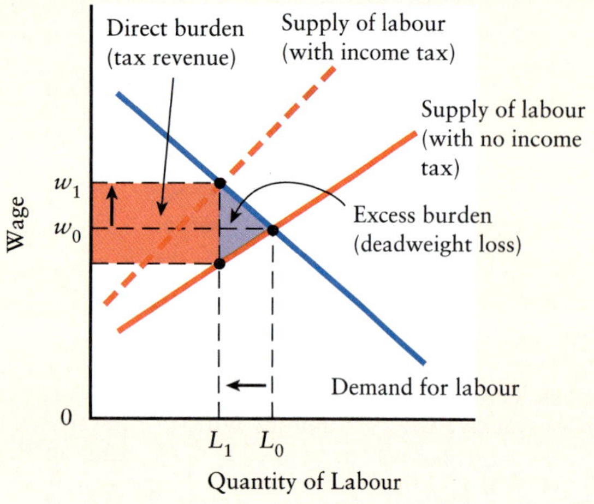

An income tax generates both a direct and an excess burden. Without an income tax, the labour-market equilibrium has employment of L_0 and a wage of w_0. A tax on workers' incomes shifts the supply of labour curve upward. The result is an increase in the pre-tax wage to w_1 and a reduction in the level of employment to L_1. The tax revenue generated is the red area; this is the direct burden of the income tax. The tax also generates a deadweight loss, as shown by the purple area; this is the excess burden of the income tax. (As our discussion of tax incidence in Chapter 4 showed, the less elastic is labour demand and supply, the lower will be the deadweight loss of the tax.)

Recall that our exercise in judging the efficiency of a tax is to hold constant the amount of revenue raised, and therefore to hold constant the direct burden of the tax. This leads us to the following important conclusion:

An efficient tax system is one that minimizes the amount of excess burden (deadweight loss) for any given amount of tax revenue generated.

As Figure 18-2 shows, the excess burden of an excise tax is smaller when the demand for the product is less elastic. In the extreme case of a perfectly inelastic demand, the excess burden of an excise tax is zero; the tax raises revenue but leads to no reduction in consumption of the product. Unfortunately, because the demand for many of life's necessities (such as food) is very inelastic, a tax system that was based only on imposing excise taxes on goods with inelastic demands would prove to be very regressive.

Many economists argue that taxing income is more efficient *and* more equitable than imposing large numbers of excise taxes on products. The greater efficiency of the income tax comes from the fact that the supply of labour is relatively inelastic with respect to the real wage. Figure 18-3 shows that an income tax does generate an excess burden. But if the labour supply curve is very steep—as most empirical evidence suggests—the excess burden is small, and the income tax is therefore relatively efficient. The greater equity of the income tax comes from the fact that the income tax can be designed to be either proportional or progressive, thus permitting some redistribution from high-income households to low-income households. The regressive effects of excise taxes can be reduced by greater reliance on income taxes.

Disincentive Effects of Income Taxes Our discussion of income taxes, and the illustration in Figure 18-3, shows how an income tax affects workers' incentives. If an increase in the income-tax rate leads to a reduction in the amount of work effort, it is possible that total tax revenue might actually *fall* as a result. This possibility is illustrated in Figure 18-4, which shows what economists call a *Laffer curve.*

The reasoning behind the general shape of the Laffer curve is as follows. At a zero tax rate, no revenue would be collected. As rates are raised above zero, some revenue will be gained. But as rates continue to rise, revenue will eventually fall because the very high tax rates will lead people to work less and less. At a tax rate of 100 percent, they will not bother to work at all (because all of their income would go to the government) and so tax revenue will be zero. It follows that there must be *some* tax rate, greater than zero and less than 100 percent, at which tax revenue reaches a maximum.

Figure 18-4 is drawn under the assumption that there is a steady increase in tax revenue as tax rates rise to t_0, and a steady decrease in tax revenues as tax rates continue to rise toward 100 percent. This particular shape—with a single peak in tax revenues—is not necessary. But the precise shape is beside the point. The key point is that there is *some* tax rate like t_0 that maximizes total tax revenue. And therefore tax rates above or below t_0 will raise less tax revenue than the amount raised at t_0.

Just where this maximum occurs—whether at average tax rates closer to 40 or to 70 percent—is currently unknown for either corporate or personal income taxes. Also, there will be a separate Laffer curve for each type of tax. The curve does, however, provide an important warning: Governments cannot increase their tax revenues to any desired level simply by increasing their tax rates. Sooner or later, further increases in the rates will reduce work incentives so much that total tax revenues will fall.

FIGURE 18-4 A Laffer Curve

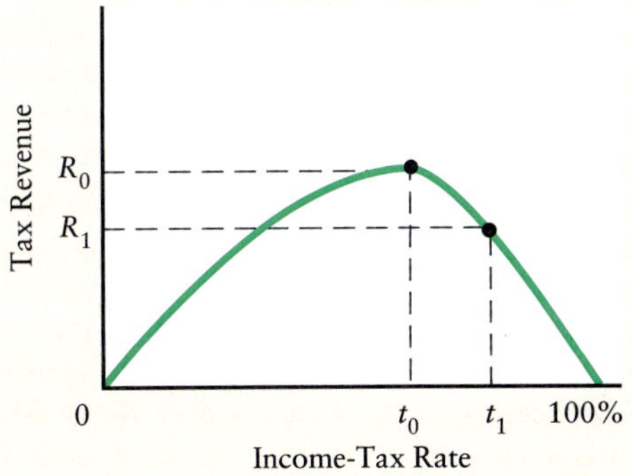

Increases in income-tax rates beyond some level will decrease rather than increase tax revenues. The curve relates the government's tax revenue to the tax rate. As drawn, revenue reaches a maximum level of R_0 at the tax rate t_0. If the tax rate were t_1, then *reducing* it to t_0 would increase the government's tax revenue.

18.3 PUBLIC EXPENDITURE IN CANADA

Spending by the consolidated public sector—which includes federal, provincial, and municipal governments—currently equals about 37 percent of Canadian GDP. Table 18-2 gives the distribution of consolidated government spending across a number of major *functions* for 2005. As can be seen, health care, education, and social services are very large items; collectively, they make up over 63 percent of the total spending of $519 billion. Interest on the public debt makes up about 9 percent of total spending. The remaining quarter covers everything else, from police protection and sanitation to general administration of government, environmental protection, and foreign aid.

Table 18-2 does not show which of the three levels of government actually do the spending. For example, of the $76.5 billion spent on education in 2005, the vast majority was spent by provincial and municipal governments. In contrast, expenditures on foreign affairs and foreign aid are made exclusively by the federal government. Expenditures on social services are about equally divided between the federal and provincial governments with only a small role played by the municipalities. Another thing that Table 18-2 does not show is the important distinction between the purchase of goods and services by government, and transfers that are made to individuals or firms.

Government Purchases of Goods and Services The government spends to provide goods and services to the public, as when the government pays for physicians' services, highway repair, primary and secondary education, and so on. Included in this category of expenditures are the salaries that the government pays to its employees. Also included is the interest that governments pay on their outstanding stock of debt. A government's stock of debt is equal to the accumulation of its past budget deficits, where the deficit is the excess of spending over revenues.

TABLE 18-2 Expenditures by Canadian Governments, 2005

Category of Spending	Billions of Dollars	Percent of GDP
General government services	16.7	1.2
Protection of persons and property	42.0	3.0
Transportation and communication	21.4	1.5
Health	96.2	6.8
Social services	154.8	11.0
Education	76.5	5.4
Resource conservation, environment, and industrial development	32.7	2.3
Recreation and culture	13.5	1.0
Housing	3.9	0.3
Labour, employment, and immigration	3.4	0.2
Foreign affairs and international aid	5.1	0.4
Debt charges	46.5	3.3
Other expenditures	5.9	0.4
Total spending	**518.6**	**36.7**

Expenditures on health, social services, and education together make up over 63 percent of total government expenditure. These data show the various categories of spending by all levels of government combined.

(*Source:* These data are available on the Statistics Canada website: www.statcan.ca. Search for "government" and then look for "consolidated government revenue and expenditures." Reprinted with permission of Statistics Canada.)

Transfer Payments The government also makes **transfer payments.** These are payments to individuals, firms, organizations, or other levels of government that are *not* made in exchange for a good or a service. For example, when the federal government pays employment insurance benefits to an unemployed individual, the government is not getting any good or service in return. Similarly, when the federal government transfers money to the provincial governments, it is not getting any good or service in return. Table 18-3 shows total government transfers to individuals, which totalled \$125 billion in 2003, about 26 percent of total government spending.

transfer payment A payment to an individual, firm, or organization that is not made in exchange for a good or service.

Fiscal Federalism

Canada is a federal state with governing powers divided between the central authority and the ten provinces and three territories. Municipalities provide a third level of government, whose powers are determined by the provincial legislatures. Understanding the fiscal interaction of the various levels of government is central to understanding the nature of government expenditure in Canada. In this section, we examine the concept of *fiscal federalism;* in the next section we examine how fiscal federalism affects the operation of Canada's social programs.

The Logic of Fiscal Federalism The essence of fiscal federalism is the recognition that Canada is a country with many different fiscal authorities (federal, provincial, and municipal governments) that need a certain amount of coordination to be responsive to the needs and desires of the citizens—who are free to move from one area to another. Four main considerations are important in understanding Canada's system of fiscal federalism.

1. Differences in Tax Bases. Canadian provinces vary considerably in terms of their average levels of prosperity. Newfoundland and Labrador and Quebec have for many years lagged the national average in terms of per capita real incomes, whereas Alberta and Ontario have for many years exceeded the national average. In order to provide services as varied as medical care, highways, and judicial systems, the provincial governments must levy various types of provincial taxes. Provinces that are more prosperous, and thus have larger tax bases, are able to provide a given amount of services while having relatively low tax rates. In contrast, less affluent provinces with smaller tax bases will be able to provide the same amount of services only by having higher tax rates.

One of the guiding principles in Canada's system of fiscal federalism is that individuals, no matter where they live, should have approximately the same access to what is regarded as a reasonable level and quality of public services and should face approximately the same tax rates to finance those services. Since revenue sources do not always match revenue needs at each level, *intergovernmental transfers* are required. This is the underlying motivation behind Canada's system of *equalization payments,* which transfers resources from the richer provinces to the poorer ones. We examine this shortly.

2. Geographic Scope of Services. Because the government of a province or a municipality is unlikely to be responsive to the needs of citizens outside its jurisdiction, some public services may not be provided adequately unless responsibility for them is delegated to the level of government appropriate to the scope of the service provided. For example, national defence is normally delegated to the central government because it provides benefits to all residents of the country. At the other extreme is fire protection. If fire protection is to be effective, it is necessary that there be fire stations serving small geographic areas. Accordingly, responsibility for fire stations lies with municipal governments.

3. Regional Differences in Preferences. The delegation of some functions to lower levels of government may provide a political process that is more responsive to regional differences in preferences for public versus private goods. Some people may prefer to live in communities with higher-quality schools and police protection, and they may be prepared to pay the high taxes required. Others may prefer lower taxes and lower levels of services. The differences in provincial tax rates that we noted earlier presumably reflect each provincial government's own view of the appropriate level of taxation.

TABLE 18-3 Government Transfer Payments to Individuals, 2003

	Billions of Dollars
Federal Government	**62.5**
Child Tax Benefit	8.1
War pensions and veterans' allowances	1.7
Employment Insurance benefits	13.4
Old Age Security payments	26.9
Grants to aboriginal persons	5.0
GST tax credit	3.3
Other transfers	4.1
Provincial Governments	**29.9**
Income maintenance	6.7
Other social assistance	3.1
Workers' Compensation benefits	5.2
Grants to benevolent associations	8.3
Other transfers	6.6
Local Governments	**3.8**
Canada/Quebec Pension Plan	**29.0**
Total Transfers	**125.2**

(*Source:* These data are available on the Statistics Canada website: www.statcan.ca. Search for "transfers" and then look for "government transfer payments to persons." Reprinted with permission of Statistics Canada.)

4. Administrative Efficiency. Administrative efficiency requires that duplication of the services provided at different levels of government be minimized and that related programs be coordinated. For this reason, in all provinces except Quebec and Alberta, income taxes are reported on a single form and paid to the federal government, which then remits the appropriate share of those taxes to the relevant provincial government. This coordination avoids the administrative burden that would exist if each province had its own tax-collection system.

Intergovernmental Transfers Canada's system of fiscal federalism requires transfers between various levels of government. For example, since income taxes are paid to the federal government (except in Quebec) but spending on hospitals, education, and highways is undertaken by provincial governments, federal–provincial transfers must be made. In addition, if some provinces have large tax bases, while others have much smaller tax bases, there is a role for transferring resources between provinces. Canada has two major programs in which cash is transferred from the federal to the provincial governments.

1. Canada Health and Social Transfers. The federal government makes two block grants to each provincial and territorial government every year—one to help finance expenditures on health care and the other to help finance expenditures on post-secondary education, social assistance, and early learning and childcare. Though the Canada Health Transfer (CHT) and the Canada Social Transfer (CST) are each described as being directed at these specific categories of expenditure, there is no practical way to prevent provincial governments from spending this money on whatever they deem to be appropriate. These block grants are therefore financial support with "no strings attached."

Until recently, the CHT and CST block grants were allocated to provinces on a per capita basis. In the last few years, however, wealthier provinces have received less in per capita terms than less wealthy provinces. For the fiscal year 2005–2006, the federal transfers to provinces under the CHT totalled \$20.3 billion, and those under the CST totalled \$8.4 billion. Both block transfers are scheduled to increase significantly over the next several years.

equalization payments Transfers of tax revenues from the federal government to the low-income provinces.

2. Equalization Payments. With the object of ensuring that citizens in all regions of the country have access to a reasonable level of public services, **equalization payments** are made out of federal government general revenues to provinces with below-average tax capacity. Since the federal government collects revenues from economic activity generated in *all* provinces, and uses this revenue to support only the lower-income ones, the equalization program is effectively a redistribution program from high-income to low-income provinces. In recent years, typically only Alberta and Ontario have *not* received equalization payments; the other provinces do receive equalization payments and are thus sometimes referred to as the "have not" provinces. Equalization payments are calculated by a complicated formula that involves 30 different revenue sources. From their inception in 1957, equalization payments have increased significantly. In the 2005–2006 fiscal year, total equalization payments were \$10.9 billion.

A Fiscal Imbalance? In recent years, many observers of Canadian fiscal federalism have noted a growing "fiscal imbalance" between the federal and the provincial governments. They point specifically to the large federal budget surpluses since 1998, indicating that the federal government is collecting more money than what is necessary to finance its program spending. During the same period, the provinces struggled to balance their books, partly because the fastest-growing categories of public spending have been health care, education, and other social services—all within provincial jurisdiction. Thus, tax revenue being collected at the federal level is increasingly necessary for public expenditures at the provincial level.

Some economists argue that this fiscal imbalance is indeed a problem and that it must be corrected through a change in *federal* policy. Specifically, they argue that the federal government should amend its CHT and CST block transfers (and perhaps its equalization formula as well) in ways that transfer more funds to the provinces. Alternatively, the federal government could reduce its personal and corporate income-tax rates, thereby creating more "tax room" within which the provinces would be free to raise their tax rates.

Other economists, while recognizing the basic facts of federal surpluses and growing provincial spending on health and social services, deny that the fiscal imbalance requires a significant change in federal policy. First, these economists note that the federal budget surpluses since 1998 are not simply "unnecessary money" being collected; on the contrary, these surpluses represent the gradual paying down of Canada's public debt that had become so large in the mid-1990s that merely making the interest payments on the debt threatened to crowd out other categories of government spending. They also note that in recent years the federal government has lowered both personal and corporate income-tax rates, and therefore the provinces could have increased their tax rates if they had chosen to do so. In their view, the correction of the fiscal imbalance requires provinces to make some difficult political decisions regarding their own spending and taxing policies.

Conservative Prime Minister Stephen Harper, elected early in 2006, campaigned partly on the promise to correct the fiscal imbalance between the federal and provincial governments. At the time this book went to press (late fall 2006), his precise policy approach to this issue was yet to be outlined.

Canadian Social Programs

Table 18-2 shows that government spending on health, education, and other social services represents over 63 percent of total government spending in Canada. Given their obvious fiscal importance, it is worth briefly reviewing Canada's major social programs.

Some social programs are universal, in the sense that they pay benefits to anyone meeting only such minimal requirements as age or residence. These are referred to as **demogrants**. Other programs are selective, in the sense that they pay benefits only to people who qualify by meeting specific conditions, such as by having young children or being unemployed. When these conditions are related to the individual's income, the term **income-tested benefits** is used. Some benefits are expenditure programs (including direct transfers to persons), while others are delivered through the tax system. Some programs are administered by the federal government, some by the provincial governments, and still others by the municipalities.

demograntsMARGIN

In this section we examine the five pillars of Canadian social policy: education, health care, income support, employment insurance, and retirement benefits. Each of these pillars, at various points in recent years, has been the focus of attention as financially strapped governments have explored new ways to provide these vital social services in a cost-effective manner.

demogrants Social benefits paid to anyone meeting only minimal requirements such as age or residence; in particular, *not* income-tested.

income-tested benefits Social benefits paid to recipients who qualify because their income is less than some critical level.

Education

Public education, one of the earliest types of social expenditure in Canada, remains one of the most important. It has been supplemented over the years by numerous other public programs aimed at developing human capital.

Basic Education. Primary and secondary schools are funded by provincial governments in Canada, but are managed by local school boards. Basic education is publicly financed for both efficiency and equity reasons. In terms of efficiency, a literate and numerate population is necessary for an informed electorate that can participate in democratic society. Society as a whole is therefore better off when all of its citizens have at least a basic level of education. The equity argument is based on the fact that basic skills acquired in primary and secondary schools are usually necessary in order for individuals to secure careers that can provide reasonable incomes. If basic education were not financed by the government, many low-income households could not afford to send their children to school. The result in many cases would be a vicious circle of poverty in which children from low-income families would lack basic education and thus secure only poor jobs, thus earning only low incomes themselves.

More than half of the operating revenues of Canadian universities come from provincial governments. Only 20 percent of revenues come from students' tuition fees. There is an active debate in Canada about how much students should be paying toward the full costs of their post-secondary education.

Post-secondary Education. Post-secondary education is a provincial responsibility in Canada. As discussed earlier in this chapter, however, the federal government makes large

For data on the financial position of Canadian universities, see Statistics Canada's website: **www.statcan.ca**. Click on "Canadian Statistics" and then type in "universities."

payments to the provinces to support post-secondary education as part of the Canada Social Transfer (CST).

In Canada, universities are public institutions, and university education is heavily subsidized by government. In 2005, total revenues for universities and colleges were $27.7 billion, with 57 percent coming from various levels of government. Only 20 percent came from student tuition fees. (The remaining 23 percent comes from various other sources—including those overpriced shirts that you can't afford to buy from your campus bookstore!) In addition, many students receive student loans from commercial banks where the loans are guaranteed by the federal government. In cases where students default on their loans, the repayment by the government amounts to a subsidy to the student.

Two arguments can be advanced for subsidizing higher education; one is an efficiency argument, and the other an equity argument. The efficiency argument is based on the claim that there are positive externalities from higher education—that is, that the country as a whole benefits when a student receives higher education. In many cases these externalities cannot be internalized by the students receiving the education, so, left to their own maximizing decisions, students who had to pay the full cost of their education would choose less than what is socially optimal. The equity argument is that if students were forced to pay anything like the full cost of the services they receive, a university education would become prohibitively expensive to low- and even middle-income families. Government subsidies help provide education according to ability rather than according to income.

Arguments that rely on higher tuition fees to finance a larger fraction of the costs of running universities start with the observation that the value of many kinds of post-secondary education is internalized and recaptured in higher incomes earned by the recipients later in their life. This is particularly true of professional training in such fields as law, medicine, dentistry, management, and computer science. Yet students in these fields typically pay a smaller part of their real education costs than students in the arts, where the argument for externalities is greatest. Also, subsidized education does represent a significant income transfer from taxpayers to students, even though the average taxpayer may have a lower income than the average post-secondary student can expect to earn in the future.

Health Care In Canada, basic health care is financed mainly by the provincial governments, with significant transfers from the federal government under the Canada Health Transfer (CHT). In most provinces, residents pay nothing to receive medical attention—health care is free to users and is financed out of the government's general tax revenues. Though health care is publicly financed, physicians and private (non-profit) hospitals working on a "fee for service" basis form the core of Canada's health-care delivery system. Thus, the Canadian health-care system is based on public *financing* but private *delivery*.

Health care is financed by government for reasons of both efficiency and equity. The efficiency argument is much the same as for basic education—a healthy population is as important to the smooth functioning of a democratic country as is an educated one. The equity argument is even more powerful: Most people believe that basic health care is so important that denying it to people who cannot afford it would be unacceptable.

Cost Containment. Taking federal and provincial payments into account, Canada's public health-care system is the country's single most expensive social program. In 2005, government expenditure on health care was $96.2 billion, about 19 percent of total government expenditure and 6.8 percent of GDP. Private spending on health care brought total spending up to over 10 percent of GDP. In other words, one out of every ten dollars in income produced in the Canadian economy gets spent on health care.

"Cost containment" in the health-care sector has become a priority for most provincial governments and the debate currently rages over what reforms would be practicable and acceptable. Most observers agree that some type of expenditure-controlling reform is urgently needed. Unfortunately, agreement stops there.

The Role of the Private Sector. Much of the debate over the reform of Canada's health-care system rests on the appropriate role of the private sector in what is a publicly financed system. Some provincial governments, notably Alberta, have suggested that allowing a greater role for private, for-profit hospitals and clinics can reduce waiting lists and therefore improve the overall quality of health care that citizens receive.

The main concern with allowing a greater role for private clinics and hospitals is that private hospitals may begin "extra billing" their patients. In this case there would develop a "two-tiered" health-care system in which individuals with higher incomes have faster access to health care than do individuals with lower incomes. If extra billing becomes a feature of private hospitals, then only those individuals who can afford to pay the extra fees will be able to use the private hospitals. Furthermore, many nurses and doctors that are currently within the financially strapped public health-care system may move to the private hospitals if salaries or working conditions are better there. The overall concern, therefore, is that the introduction of private hospitals into the existing public health-care system, while reducing waiting lists and providing more health-care services overall, may result in a high-quality system for the wealthy and a low-quality system for lower-income people. Many people think that such a two-tiered health-care system would destroy the equity that the public system was initially designed to promote.

Advocates of allowing a greater role for private hospitals and clinics, on the other hand, argue that to a significant extent, Canada already has a two-tiered system. For example, for services such as laser eye surgery and diagnosis with MRIs, private clinics have existed for several years; people have a choice between waiting in line for service in the public hospitals, sometimes for many months, or going to a private clinic immediately and paying for treatment. Even for more serious surgery, some Canadians, frustrated by the long waiting lists in the Canadian public health-care system, travel to the United States for medical treatment. Advocates of private for-profit hospitals also argue that the lack of public funding in the Canadian health-care system has already caused many doctors and nurses to leave Canada and move to the United States and that the introduction of private hospitals would help stem the flow of nurses and doctors out of Canada, thereby *improving* Canada's overall health-care system. Furthermore, they argue that two-tier systems do not seem to lead to major health-care inequalities in the countries of Western Europe, all of whom operate some form of two-tier system.

myeconlab

The debate over reforming Canada's health-care system continues to rage. For a more detailed discussion, including the recommendations of a recent Royal Commission, a Senate Report, and a Supreme Court decision, look for "Debate More Healthy than Health Care" in the *Additional Topics* section of this book's MyEconLab.

www.myeconlab.com

Income-Support Programs Canada has various programs that provide assistance for people in financial need—these programs constitute what is often called the "social safety net." The overriding objectives of this safety net are to reduce poverty and increase individuals' sense of economic security. Though nothing like the serious problem it was in Canada's past and still is in many other countries, poverty remains a matter of real concern to Canadian policymakers.

poverty line An estimate of the annual family income that is required to maintain a minimum adequate standard of living.

Statistics Canada defines the **poverty line** or *low-income cutoff* as the level of income below which the typical household spends more than 55 percent of its income on the three necessities of food, shelter, and clothing. Not surprisingly, this poverty line varies depending on the size of the family and where it lives. In 2004, Statistics Canada's estimated poverty line for a family of four living in a major urban centre was $37 253. Thus, a family of four with income less than this amount would be defined to be living in poverty. In 2004, 7.8 percent of Canadian families had incomes below Statistics Canada's estimated poverty line. This percentage includes some of the working poor, whether stuck in low-paying jobs or doing their first job; some whom were not working at all; and some whose incomes were only temporarily below the poverty line, such as students or other trainees.

There is considerable debate, however, about the methods used to estimate poverty. Central to this debate is whether poverty is best viewed as an *absolute* or a *relative* concept. If poverty is viewed as an absolute concept, then anybody without enough income to purchase a certain amount of food, shelter, and clothing is said to be in poverty. With such an absolute definition of poverty, sufficient growth in the economy could, at least in principle, eliminate poverty entirely as low-income households eventually see their income rise above the threshold level.

With a *relative* definition of poverty, however, there will *always* be some families defined to be impoverished. For example, suppose households are defined to be impoverished whenever their income is less than 25 percent of the economy's average household income. Since any realistic distribution of income will contain *some* households whose income is 25 percent of the average, there will always be some poverty when it is defined this way. Advocates of a relative measure of poverty argue that poverty is more than just the absence of enough food and clothing—it is also the social exclusion from mainstream society that typically comes from having much lower income than most households.

myeconlab

There is continuing debate in Canada about how best to measure poverty, and thus debate about how much poverty really exists. For a more detailed discussion of poverty in Canada, look for "Who Are Canada's Poor?" in the *Additional Topics* section of this book's MyEconLab.

www.myeconlab.com

Whatever the precise definition, all experts agree that many Canadians live in poverty. Canada has several income-support programs designed to address this important problem. They can be divided into three types. The first is designed to provide income assistance to those individuals whose incomes are deemed to be too low to provide an adequate standard of living. The second is designed to assist specifically those individuals who are in financial need because of temporary job loss—employment insurance. The third is designed to provide income assistance specifically to the elderly. In this subsection, we examine the first type. The next two subsections discuss employment insurance and elderly benefits, respectively.

Welfare. Social assistance for individuals below retirement age, usually called *welfare,* is mainly a provincial responsibility in Canada. The details of the programs vary considerably across the provinces even though they are partly financed by transfers received from the federal government under the Canada Social Transfer (CST).

Poverty and homelessness exist in Canada, though there is disagreement about how widespread these problems are.

One important problem with welfare occurs with what are called *poverty traps.* **Poverty traps** occur whenever the tax-and-transfer system results in individuals having very little incentive to increase their pre-tax income (by accepting a job, for example) because such an increase in their pre-tax income would make them ineligible for some benefits (such as welfare) and might even make them worse off overall. The presence of such poverty traps reflects a tax-and-transfer system that has been modified in many small steps over many years, the result of which is a plethora of programs often working at cross purposes. The elimination of such poverty traps requires that the tax-and-transfer system be examined in its entirety rather than on a piecemeal basis. *Applying Economic Concepts 18-1* discusses one possible reform of the tax-and-transfer system that maintains progressivity of the system while eliminating poverty traps. This is the idea of the negative income tax.

poverty trap Occurs whenever individuals have little incentive to increase their pre-tax income because the resulting loss of benefits makes them worse off.

Child Benefits. The support system for families with children has been evolving quite rapidly over the years. Prior to 1993, the system was a combination of universal family allowance payments and tax credits. In 1993, universality was eliminated. A Child Tax Benefit is now paid according to the number of children in the family and varies according to family income. For families with net incomes below about $23 000, the Child Tax Benefit pays approximately $200 per child per month. The amount declines as family income increases, finally reaching zero at an annual income of $79 000.

In 2006, the newly elected Conservative government implemented the Universal Child Care Benefit, a program which pays parents $100 per month for each child under the age of six. The payments are taxed in the hands of the lower-earning parent.

Employment Insurance Employment insurance (EI) is a federal program designed to provide temporary income support to workers who lose their jobs. Employers and employees remit EI premiums to the government equal to a small percentage of wages and salaries. These premiums then finance the EI payments to unemployed workers who qualify for the benefits. In boom times, when there is little unemployment, the total amount of EI premiums collected exceeds the total amount dispersed as EI benefits; in times of high unemployment, the benefits exceed the premiums. As a result, the EI program is approximately self-financing over the duration of the average business cycle (six to seven years).

For details on Canada's Employment Insurance program, go to the website for Human Resources and Social Development Canada: **www.hrsdc.gc.ca**. Then click on "financial benefits."

EI gives incentives to remain in seasonal jobs and in areas with poor employment prospects and to take EI-financed holidays. Saying that the EI system encourages behaviour that increases unemployment and reduces regional mobility does not say that the unemployed themselves are responsible for the "abuses" of the system that lead to these results. The responsibility lies with the people who designed the incentives and those who strive to preserve them. It is they who can alter the system to make it deliver the intended benefits with fewer incentives for undesired behaviour.

Retirement Benefits There are three components of the system of retirement benefits. These are the Canada Pension Plan (CPP), retirement income-support programs such as Old Age Security (OAS) and Guaranteed Income Supplement (GIS), and tax-assisted saving plans.

APPLYING ECONOMIC CONCEPTS 18-1

Poverty Traps and the Negative Income Tax

A tax is negative when the government pays the taxpayer rather than the other way around. The *negative income tax (NIT)* is designed to combat poverty by making taxes negative at very low incomes. Furthermore, the NIT potentially avoids some of the extreme disincentive effects that are caused by very high marginal tax rates. Finally, by combining taxes and transfers into a single system, the negative income tax also avoids the occurrence of poverty traps.

The underlying principle of the NIT is that a family of a given size should be *guaranteed* a minimum annual income. The tax system must be designed, however, to guarantee this income without eliminating the household's incentive to be self-supporting.

As an example, consider a system in which each household is guaranteed a minimum annual income of $10 000 and the marginal tax rate is 40 percent. Money can be thought of as flowing in two directions; the government gives every household $10 000, and then every household remits 40 percent of any *earned* income back to the government. The *break-even* level of income in this example is $25 000. All households earning less than $25 000 pay negative taxes overall; they receive more money from the government than they remit in taxes. Households earning exactly $25 000 pay no net taxes—their $10 000 from the government exactly equals the taxes they remit to the government on their earned income. All households earning more than $25 000 pay more than $10 000 in taxes and so they are paying *positive* taxes overall.

The figure shows the operation of this scheme by relating earned income on the horizontal axis to after-tax income on the vertical axis. The red 45° line shows what after-tax income would be if there were no taxes.

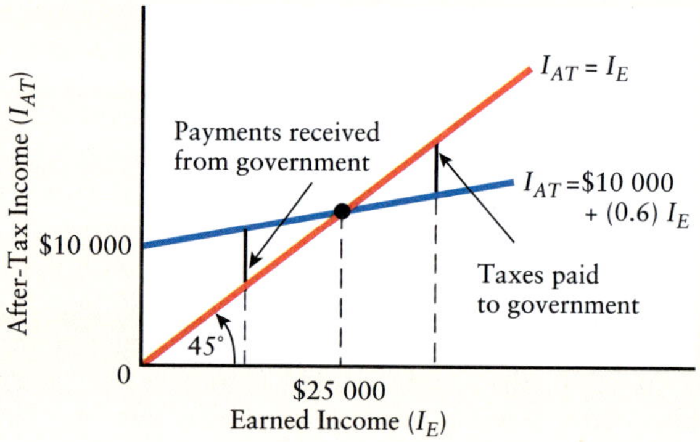

The Canada Pension Plan (CPP). The CPP provides a basic level of retirement income for all Canadians who have contributed to it over their working lives. A separate but similar scheme exists in Quebec—the Quebec Pension Plan or QPP. Unlike some private programs, the pension provided by the CPP is *portable*—changing jobs does not cause any loss of eligibility. Crucial to understanding the problems faced by the CPP is recognizing that the payments to current retirees are financed by the contributions made by those currently working.

Given the "pay-as-you-go" nature of the Canada Pension Plan, it is inevitable that the CPP will encounter financing problems as the population ages. As the oldest members of the baby boom begin to retire around 2010, the ratio of retirees to contributors will rise rapidly. As this ratio rises, working people must contribute more to the CPP in order to maintain a given level of benefits for the retirees. In 1996, the CPP was judged to be in a crisis situation—either contributions had to increase or retirement benefits had to fall in order to keep the CPP financially sound. In 1998, the Canadian government reformed the CPP by increasing the required level of contributions by both employers and employees. The system is now less vulnerable to demographic shifts than it was earlier.

The blue line shows after-tax income with a NIT. It starts at the guaranteed annual income of \$10 000, rises by 60 cents for every one dollar increase in earned income, and crosses the 45° line at the break-even level of income, \$25 000. The vertical distance between the two lines shows the net transfers between the household and the government.

Note that the NIT is a progressive tax, despite the *constant* marginal income-tax rate. To see this, note that a household's *average* tax rate is equal to the total taxes paid divided by total earned income. If I_E is earned income, then

$$\text{Average tax rate} = \frac{(0.40) \times I_E - \$10\,000}{I_E}$$

$$= (0.40) - \frac{\$10\,000}{I_E}$$

Thus, the average tax rate for the household rises as earned income rises, but the average tax rate is *always less* than the marginal tax rate (40 percent). That the average tax rate rises with earned income means that higher-income households pay a larger fraction of their income in taxes than is paid by lower-income households—that is, the NIT is progressive.

Supporters of the NIT believe that it would be an effective tool for reducing poverty. The NIT provides a minimum level of income as a matter of right, not of charity, and it does so without removing the work incentives for people who are eligible for payments; every dollar earned adds to the after-tax income of the family. Poverty traps are avoided.

One step toward the NIT was taken in 1987 when the personal income-tax system was substantially reformed. In those reforms, many personal exemptions were replaced with tax credits. An exemption reduces an individual's taxable income and hence is more valuable the higher the tax bracket. In contrast, a tax credit reduces taxes payable by the amount of the credit and hence is equally valuable at all levels of income. At present, however, the tax credit is not refundable—the credit can be used to reduce taxes payable to zero, but cannot be used to reduce taxes payable to a negative number. Thus, if an individual has taxes payable equal to \$5000 and then receives a \$6000 tax credit, total taxes payable fall only to zero—any remaining credit (\$1000) cannot be claimed back from the government. If the tax credit were fully refundable, however, someone whose taxes on earned income were less than the tax credit would receive the difference from the government. This would be a negative income tax.

Retirement Income-Support Programs. The existing public benefits system for the elderly is in many ways analogous to the child benefits system. There are two major parts to the system. First, a universal benefit called the Old Age Security (OAS) program acts much like the family allowance. Under the OAS program, the government sends out monthly benefit cheques to each Canadian over the qualifying age of 65. OAS payments to relatively wealthy individuals are fully recaptured by means of a tax "clawback."

Second, an income-tested program, called the Guaranteed Income Supplement (GIS), provides benefits targeted to the low-income elderly. (In some provinces this is supplemented by further targeted assistance.) The GIS provides for most of the progressivity that arises in the elderly benefits system.

Tax-Assisted Saving Plans. The CPP, OAS, and GIS are programs that involve direct spending on the part of the government. The government has also introduced programs that require no direct government spending but instead rely on *tax expenditures* (i.e., beneficial tax treatment). These tax expenditures are designed to provide incentives for individuals to save more for their retirement. There are two types of programs. The first is through Registered Retirement Savings Plans (RRSPs) and the second is through employer-sponsored Registered Pension Plans (RPPs).

RRSPs provide an incentive for individuals to provide for their own retirement, either because they are not covered by a company plan or because they wish to supplement their company plan. Funds contributed are deductible from taxable income (and accumulate year by year without any tax being paid) but they become fully taxable when they are withdrawn. It is thus a tax deferral plan, and as such it is more valuable the higher one's current taxable income and the lower one's expected future income.

Individuals without RRSPs may still receive some tax assistance for saving if their employer has a Registered Pension Plan. In this case, contributions to the company pension plan (which are often mandatory and are withdrawn directly from the regular paycheque) are tax deductible in a manner similar to an RRSP contribution.

18.4 EVALUATING THE ROLE OF GOVERNMENT

Earlier we pointed out that it is more informative to assess the progressivity of the overall tax system than any individual tax. It is even more informative to assess the progressivity of the combination of taxes and expenditures—that is, the entire tax-expenditure system. For example, a tax-expenditure system could be highly progressive even if all taxes were proportional, as long as government expenditures (including transfers) accounted for a higher portion of real incomes of the poor than of the rich. The evidence is that the overall Canadian tax-expenditure system is progressive and succeeds in successfully narrowing the inequalities of income generated by the market.

Even if there is widespread agreement that the Canadian tax-expenditure system is progressive, and that the resulting income redistribution is desirable, there is still considerable disagreement regarding the appropriate level of government activity in the economy.

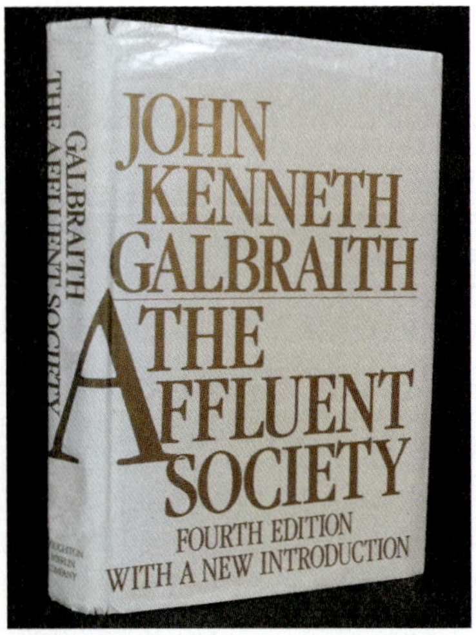

In this classic book, Galbraith argued that western democracies often undervalue public goods and place too much value on private consumption. He lamented the resulting contrast between "private affluence" and "public squalor."

Public Versus Private Sector

When the government raises money by taxation and spends it on an activity, it increases the spending of the public sector and decreases that of the private sector. Since the public sector and the private sector spend on different things, the government is changing the allocation of resources. Is this change good or bad? Should there be more schools and fewer houses or more houses and fewer schools?

For all goods that are produced and sold on the market, consumers' demand has a significant influence on the relative prices and quantities produced and thus on the allocation of the nation's resources. But no market provides relative prices for private houses versus public schools; thus, the choice between allowing money to be spent in the private sector and allowing it to be spent for public goods is a matter to be decided by Parliament and other legislative bodies.

John Kenneth Galbraith's 1958 bestseller, *The Affluent Society,* proclaimed that a correct assignment of marginal utilities would show them to be higher for an extra dollar's worth of public parks, clean water, and education than for an extra dollar's worth of television sets, shampoo, or automobiles. In Galbraith's view, the political process often fails to translate preferences for public goods into effective action; thus more resources are devoted to the private sector and fewer to the public sector than would be the case if the political mechanism were as effective as the market. He lamented the resulting "private affluence and public squalor."

An alternative view has many supporters, who agree with Nobel laureate James Buchanan that society has reached a point where the value of the *marginal* dollar spent by government is less than the value of that dollar left in the hands of households or firms. These people argue that because bureaucrats are spending other people's money, they care very little about a few million or billion dollars here or there. They have only a weak sense of the opportunity cost of public expenditure and, thus, tend to spend beyond the point where marginal benefits equal marginal costs.

Scope of Government Activity

One of the most difficult problems for the student of the Canadian economic system is to maintain the appropriate perspective about the scope of government activity in the market economy. On the one hand, there are thousands of laws, regulations, and policies that affect firms and households. Many people believe that a general reduction in the role of government is both possible and desirable. On the other hand, private decision makers still have an enormous amount of discretion about what they do and how they do it.

One pitfall is to become so impressed (or obsessed) with the many ways in which government activity impinges on the individual that one fails to see that these only make changes—sometimes large, but often small—in market signals in a system that basically leaves individuals free to make their own decisions. It is in the private sector that most individuals choose their occupations, earn their living, spend their incomes, and live their lives. In this sector too, firms are formed, choose products, live, grow, and sometimes die.

A different pitfall is to fail to see that a significant share of the taxes paid by the private sector is used to buy goods and services that add to the welfare of individuals. By and large, the public sector complements the private sector, doing things the private sector would leave undone or would do differently. For example, Canadians pay taxes that are used to finance expenditures on health and education. But certainly Canadians would continue to use hospitals and attend schools even if the various levels of government did not provide these goods, and instead left more money in people's pockets. Thus, in many cases, the government is levying taxes to raise money to finance goods that people would have purchased anyway. To recognize that we often benefit directly from government spending, however, in no way denies that it is often wasteful, and sometimes worse.

Evolution of Policy

Public policies in operation at any time are not the result of a single master plan that specifies precisely where and how the public sector shall seek to complement or interfere with the workings of the market mechanism. Rather, as individual problems arise, governments attempt to meet them by passing appropriate legislation to deal with the problem. These laws stay on the books, and some become obsolete and unenforceable. This pattern is generally true of systems of law.

Many anomalies exist in our economic policies; for example, laws designed to support the incomes of small farmers have created some agricultural millionaires, and commissions created to ensure competition between firms often end up creating and protecting monopolies. Neither individual policies nor whole programs are above criticism.

In a society that elects its policymakers at regular intervals, however, the majority view on the amount of government intervention that is desirable will have some considerable influence on the amount of intervention that actually occurs. Fundamentally, a free-market system is retained because it is valued for its lack of coercion and its ability to do much of the allocating of society's resources better than any known alternative. But we are not mesmerized by it; we feel free to intervene in pursuit of a better world in which to live. We also recognize, however, that sometimes government intervention has proved ineffective or even counterproductive.

SUMMARY

18.1 TAXATION IN CANADA

LO 1

- Although the main purpose of the tax system is to raise revenue, tax policy is potentially a powerful device for income redistribution because the progressivity of different kinds of taxes varies greatly.
- The most important taxes in Canada are the personal income tax, the corporate income tax, excise and sales taxes (including the nationwide GST), and property taxes.
- The progressivity of a tax is determined by how the average tax rate (taxes paid divided by income) changes as income changes. If the average tax rate rises as income rises, the tax is progressive. If the average tax rate falls as income rises, the tax is regressive.

18.2 EVALUATING THE TAX SYSTEM

LO 2

- Evaluating the tax system involves evaluating the efficiency and progressivity of the entire system, rather than of individual taxes within the system. For a given amount of revenue to be raised, efficiency and progressivity can be altered by changing the mix of the various taxes used.
- The total Canadian tax structure is roughly proportional, except for very low-income and very high-income groups (where it is mildly progressive).
- Taxes often generate allocative inefficiency. The allocative inefficiency of a tax is measured by the excess burden. Because of the excess burden, a tax is more costly than just the amount paid by the taxpayers (the direct burden).
- There are potentially important disincentive effects of taxation, as represented by a Laffer curve. A rise in the tax rate initially raises total tax revenue; after some point, however, further increases in the tax rate reduce the incentive to produce taxable income, and so total tax revenue falls. Thus, governments cannot always raise tax revenues by raising tax rates.

18.3 PUBLIC EXPENDITURE IN CANADA

LO 3 4

- A large part of public expenditure is for the provision of goods and services. Other types of expenditures including subsidies, transfer payments to individuals, and intergovernmental transfers are also important.
- Fiscal federalism is the idea that the various fiscal authorities should be coordinated in their spending plans and should have a mechanism for transfers between the various levels of government. Understanding the relationship between the federal government and the various provincial governments is of utmost importance in understanding many of Canada's most important government spending programs.
- The five pillars of Canadian social policy are:
  1. Education
  2. Health care

3. Income support programs (welfare and child benefits)
4. Employment insurance
5. Retirement benefits (CPP, GIS, OAS, and tax-assisted saving plans)

18.4 EVALUATING THE ROLE OF GOVERNMENT

LO 5

- Government taxation and expenditure have a major effect on the allocation of resources. The government determines how much of society's total output is devoted to education, health care, highways, the armed forces, and so on.
- The overall Canadian tax-expenditure system is progressive in that it reduces income inequalities produced by the market.
- When evaluating the overall role of government in the economy, we should keep three basic issues in mind:

1. What is the appropriate mix between public goods and private goods?
2. Much government activity is directed to providing goods and services that add directly to the welfare of the private sector.
3. We should continually re-evaluate existing programs; some that were needed in the past may no longer be needed; others may have unintended and undesirable side effects.

KEY CONCEPTS

Progressive, proportional, and regressive taxes
The benefit principle and the ability-to-pay principle
Vertical and horizontal equity
Direct and excess burdens of a tax
Disincentive effects of taxation
Transfer payments to individuals
Fiscal federalism
Intergovernmental transfers
Canadian social programs

STUDY EXERCISES

1. Fill in the blanks to make the following statements correct.
   a. Suppose you earn an annual income of \$22 500 and you paid a total of \$3600 in taxes. Your average tax rate is __________.
   b. Suppose you earn an annual income of \$22 500 and each dollar earned is taxed at the same rate. Your marginal tax rate is the same as __________.
   c. Suppose the marginal tax rate on the first \$25 000 of income is 20 percent, and on any income above that, the rate rises to 30 percent. If your annual income is \$42 000, you will pay total income tax of __________.
   d. Lower-income groups typically spend a higher proportion of their income than do higher-income groups. For this reason, excise and sales taxes are considered to be somewhat __________.
   e. The most important source of revenue for municipalities is the __________ tax. Rather than being a tax on income or expenditure, it is a tax on __________.

2. Fill in the blanks to make the following statements correct.
   a. Evaluating a tax system requires consideration of the following two aspects of taxation: __________ and __________.
   b. Taxation usually causes allocative inefficiency because it distorts the equality between marginal __________ and marginal __________ of a given activity.
   c. Economists refer to the revenue collected as a result of a tax as the __________ burden of taxation. Economists refer to other costs imposed on society because of the tax as the __________ burden of taxation.
   d. An efficient tax system is one that collects a given amount of revenue while minimizing the amount of __________.
   e. The Laffer curve suggests that above some tax rate, further increases in the tax rate will __________ tax revenue.

3. Consider an income-tax system that has four tax brackets. The following table shows the marginal tax rate that applies to the income in each tax bracket.

Earned Income	Tax Rate in Bracket
Up to \$20 000	0%
\$20 001–\$40 000	15%
\$40 001–\$80 000	30%
\$80 001 and higher	35%

   a. Compute the average income-tax rate at income levels \$10 000, \$20 000, and each increment of \$10 000 up to \$120 000.
   b. Compute the marginal income-tax rate for each level of income in part (a).
   c. On a graph with the tax rates on the vertical axis and income on the horizontal axis, plot the average and marginal tax rates for each level of income.
   d. Is this tax system progressive? Explain.

4. myeconlab The diagrams below show the market for gasoline in two countries, Midas and Neptune. In Midas, demand is perfectly inelastic; in Neptune, demand is relatively elastic. In both countries, supply is identical and upward sloping. The government in each country imposes an excise tax of \$*t* per litre on the producers of gasoline. This tax shifts the supply curve up by \$*t*.

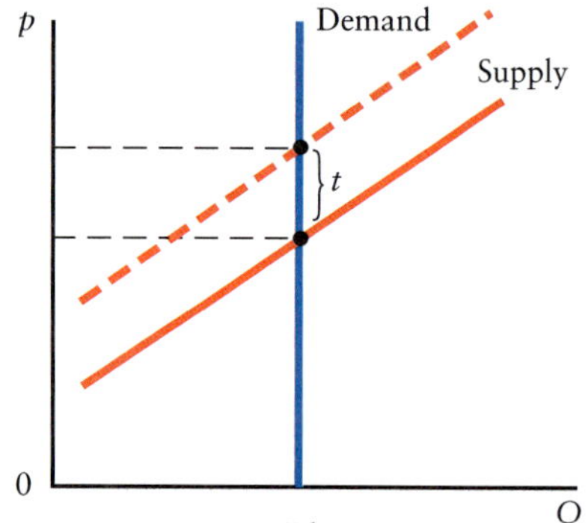

Midas

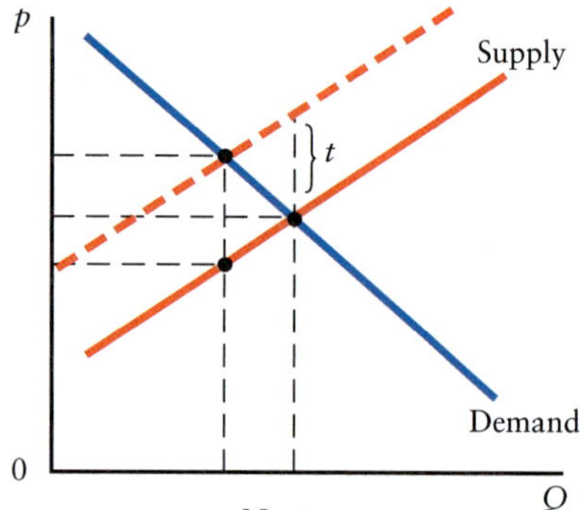

Neptune

   a. In each case, shade the area that is the direct burden of the tax.
   b. In each case, shade the area that is the excess burden of the tax.
   c. In which country does the tax cause the greater allocative inefficiency? Explain.

5. Rank the following taxes according to which has the highest excess burden relative to the direct burden. Start with the highest. Recall that the direct burden of the tax is equal to the revenue that the tax raises.
   a. An excise tax on one brand of breakfast cereal
   b. An excise tax on all breakfast cereals
   c. An excise tax on all food
   d. An excise tax on everything (which is basically what the GST is)

6. Classify each of the following government expenditures as either a transfer payment or a purchase of goods and services. Which ones clearly tend to decrease the inequality of income distribution?
   a. Payments of wages and family living allowances to Canadian soldiers overseas
   b. Employment insurance payments to unemployed workers
   c. Payments to provinces for support of highway construction
   d. Pensions of retired Supreme Court justices
   e. Salaries paid to government workers

7. Governments in Canada, at all levels, make considerable transfer payments to individuals and to businesses. This question will show you how significant these transfer payments are. Go to Statistics Canada's website (www.statcan.ca), click on "Canadian Statistics" and then type in "transfers." Then answer the following questions.
   a. For the years 2001–2005, what were the federal transfers for (un)employment insurance benefits?
   b. Have total government transfers been growing faster or slower than GDP?
   c. For the years 2001–2005, what were the total federal and provincial government transfers to universities and colleges?

8. myeconlab The Negative Income Tax has been proposed as a means of increasing both the efficiency and equity of Canada's tax system (see *Applying Economic Concepts 18-1*). The most basic NIT can be described by two variables: the guaranteed annual income and the marginal tax rate. Suppose the guaranteed annual income is \$8000 and the marginal tax rate on *every dollar earned* is 35 percent. With this NIT, after-tax income is given by:

After-tax income = \$8000 + (1 – 0.35) × (Earned income)

a. On a scale diagram with after-tax income on the vertical axis and earned income on the horizontal axis, draw the NIT relationship between earned income and after-tax income.
b. What is the level of income at which taxes paid on earned income exactly equal the guaranteed annual income?
c. The average tax rate is equal to total *net* taxes paid divided by earned income. Provide an algebraic expression for the average tax rate.
d. On a scale diagram with earned income on the horizontal axis and tax rates on the vertical axis, plot the average and marginal tax rates for the NIT. Is the NIT progressive?

DISCUSSION QUESTIONS

1. In Canada, capital gains are taxed at half the rates applicable to other income. Who are the likely beneficiaries of this policy? What are the likely effects on the distribution of income and the allocation of resources? Can you think of both equity and efficiency arguments supporting the special treatment of capital gains?
2. "Taxes on tobacco and alcohol are nearly perfect taxes. They raise lots of revenue and discourage smoking and drinking." In this statement, to what extent are the two effects inconsistent? How is the incidence of an excise tax related to the extent to which it discourages use of the product?
3. Suppose the government spends $1 billion on a new program to provide the poor with housing, better clothing, more food, and better health services.
   a. Argue the case for and against assistance of this kind rather than giving the money to the poor to spend as they think best.
   b. Should federal transfers to the provinces be conditional grants or grants with no strings attached? Is this issue the same as that raised in part (a) or is it a different one?
4. Is the tax deduction allowed for RRSPs progressive or regressive (or neither)?
5. In 1998, CPP contribution rates were increased to help secure the solvency of the system. An alternative proposal at the time was to reduce benefit rates. Who stood to lose and benefit from each proposal?
6. It is common to read articles in the newspapers by people who think Canadians pay too much in taxes. One popular concept is "tax freedom day," the day in the year beyond which you get to keep your income rather than pay it to the government as taxes. For example, if the government collects 33 percent of GDP in taxes, then "tax freedom day" is the 122nd day of the year, May 2.
   a. Does everyone in the economy have the same tax freedom day, no matter what their income?
   b. How sensible is the concept of "tax freedom day" in a country where the government provides some goods and services to the people that they would otherwise purchase on their own, such as primary education?
7. In 2001, the Alberta government permitted private, for-profit hospitals to exist within the public health-care system. Explain how private hospitals can make a profit if they receive the same payments for services that public hospitals receive.

PART 12: CANADA IN THE GLOBAL ECONOMY

CHAPTER 33

The Gains from International Trade

LEARNING OBJECTIVES

In this chapter you will learn

1. why the gains from trade depend on the pattern of comparative advantage.
2. how factor endowments and climate can influence a country's comparative advantage.
3. about the law of one price.
4. why countries export some goods and import others.

Canadian consumers buy cars from Germany, Germans take holidays in Italy, Italians buy spices from Africa, Africans import oil from Kuwait, Kuwaitis buy Japanese cameras, and the Japanese buy Canadian lumber. *International trade* refers to the exchange of goods and services that takes place across international boundaries.

The founders of modern economics were concerned with foreign trade problems. The great eighteenth-century British philosopher and economist David Hume (1711–1776), one of the first to work out the theory of the price system, developed his concepts mainly in terms of prices in foreign trade. Adam Smith (1723–1790), in *The Wealth of Nations,* attacked government restriction of international trade. David Ricardo (1772–1823) developed the basic theory of the gains from trade that is studied in this chapter. The repeal of the Corn Laws—tariffs on the importation of grains into the United Kingdom—and the transformation of that country during the nineteenth century from a country of high tariffs to one of complete free trade were to some extent the result of agitation by economists whose theories of the gains from international trade led them to condemn tariffs.

International trade is becoming increasingly important, not just for Canada but for the world as a whole. As Figure 33-1 shows, the volume of world trade has grown much faster than has world real GDP over the past half-century. Since 1950, the world's real GDP has increased by over six times, an average annual growth rate of 3.7 percent. Over the same period, however, the volume of world trade has increased by over *24* times, an average annual growth rate of 6.1 percent.

Figure 33-2 shows some data for Canadian trade in 2005. The figure shows the value of Canadian exports and imports of goods in several broad industry groupings. There are three important points to note from the figure. First, international trade is very important for Canada. In 2005, Canada exported $453 billion and imported over $388 billion in goods—if we added trade in services, the values would be higher by about $70 billion; each flow (exports and imports) amounts to over 40 percent of GDP. Second, exports and imports are roughly the same size, so that the *volume* of trade is

FIGURE 33-1 The Growth in World Trade, 1950–2004

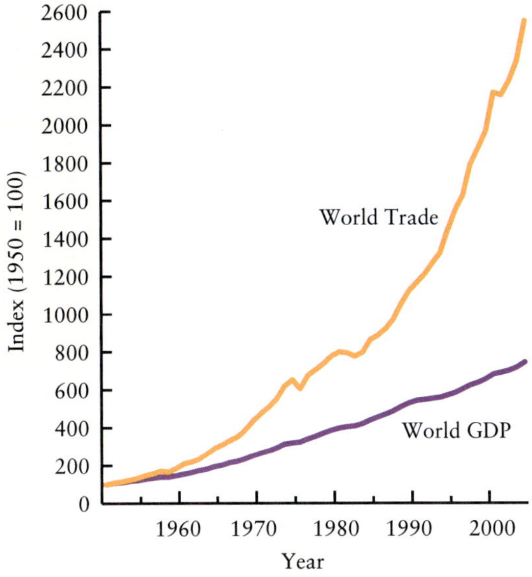

The volume of world trade has grown much faster than world GDP over the past 50 years. The figure shows the growth of real GDP and the volume of trade since 1950. Both are expressed as index numbers, set equal to 100 in 1950. Real world GDP has increased over six times since 1950; world trade volume has increased 24 times.

(*Source:* International Trade Statistics 2005, Chart 11.1, available at the World Trade Organization website: www.wto.org. Go to "Resources" and select "Trade Statistics." Then click on "International Trade Statistics, 2005" and go to "Selected Long-Term Trends." Choose Table 11.1. © World Trade Organization (WTO) 2007.)

FIGURE 33-2 Canadian Exports and Imports of Goods by Industry, 2005

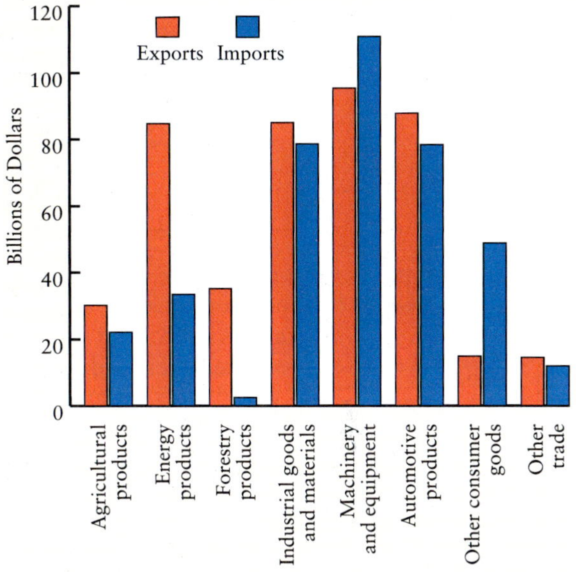

Canada exports and imports large volumes of goods in most industries. The data show the value of goods exported and imported by industry in 2005 (trade in services is not shown). The total value of goods exported was $453 billion; the total value of goods imported was $388 billion.

(*Source:* These data are available on Statistics Canada's website: www.statcan.ca. Search for "International trade." Reprinted with permission of Statistics Canada.)

much larger than the *balance* of trade—the value of exports minus the value of imports. Third, in most of the industry groupings there are significant amounts of both imports and exports. Such *intra-industry trade* will be discussed later in the chapter. Canada does not just export resource products and import manufactured goods; it also imports many resource products and exports many manufactured goods.

For information on world trade, see the World Trade Organization's website: **www.wto.org**.

In this chapter, we inquire into the gains to living standards that result from international trade. We find that the source of the gains from trade lies in differing cost conditions among geographical regions. World income is maximized when countries specialize in the products in which they have the lowest opportunity costs of production. These costs are partly determined by natural endowments (geographical and climatic conditions), partly by public policy, and partly by historical accident.

Canada trades with many countries, but most of our trade is with the United States, and the fraction of our total trade with the United States has been increasing in recent years. For more information on the location of Canada's trade, look for "Who Are Canada's Trading Partners?" in the *Additional Topics* section of this book's MyEconLab.

33.1 THE GAINS FROM TRADE

open economy An economy that engages in international trade.

closed economy An economy that has no foreign trade.

An economy that engages in international trade is called an **open economy**; one that does not is called a **closed economy**. A situation in which a country does no foreign trade is called one of *autarky*.

The benefits of trade are easiest to visualize by considering the differences between a world with trade and a world without it. Although politicians often regard foreign trade differently from domestic trade, economists from Adam Smith on have argued that the causes and consequences of international trade are simply an extension of the principles governing domestic trade. What are the benefits of trade among individuals, among groups, among regions, or among countries?

Interpersonal, Interregional, and International Trade

To begin, consider trade among individuals. Without trade, each person would have to be self-sufficient: Each would have to produce all the food, clothing, shelter, medical services, entertainment, and luxuries that he or she consumed. A world of individual self-sufficiency would be a world with extremely low living standards.

Trade among individuals allows people to specialize in activities they can do well and to buy from others the goods and services they cannot easily produce. A good doctor who is a bad carpenter can provide medical services not only for her own family but also for an excellent carpenter without the training or the ability to practise medicine. Thus, trade and specialization are intimately connected.

Without trade, everyone must be self-sufficient; with trade, people can specialize in what they do well and satisfy other needs by trading.

The same principle applies to regions. Without interregional trade, each region would be forced to be self-sufficient. With trade, each region can specialize in producing products for which it has some natural or acquired advantage. Prairie regions can specialize in growing grain, mountain regions in mining and forest products, and regions with abundant power can specialize in manufacturing. Cool regions can produce wheat and other crops that thrive in temperate climates, and hot regions can grow such tropical crops as bananas, sugarcane, and coffee. The living standards of the inhabitants of all regions will be higher when each region specializes in products in which it has some natural or acquired advantage and obtains other products by trade than when all regions seek to be self-sufficient.

This same basic principle also applies to nations. A national boundary is a political invention and rarely delimits an area that is naturally self-sufficient. Nations, like regions and individuals, can gain from specialization. More of some goods are produced domestically than residents wish to consume, while residents would like to consume more of other goods than is produced domestically. International trade is necessary to achieve the gains that international specialization makes possible.

With trade, each individual, region, or nation is able to concentrate on producing goods and services that it produces efficiently while trading to obtain goods and services that it does not produce efficiently.

Specialization and trade go hand in hand because there is no incentive to achieve the gains from specialization without being able to trade the goods produced for goods desired. Economists use the term **gains from trade** to embrace the results of both.

gains from trade The increased output due to the specialization according to comparative advantage that is made possible by trade.

Illustrating the Gains from Trade

Our discussion of individuals, regions, and countries emphasized the *differences* in their abilities to produce various products. In what follows we focus on trade between countries and, in order to focus on the differences across countries, we assume that within each country the average cost of production of any good is independent of *how much* of that good gets produced. That is, we are making the assumption of *constant costs*. Our example below involves only two countries and two products, but the general principles apply as well as to the case of many countries and many products.

Absolute Advantage One region is said to have an **absolute advantage** over another in the production of good X when an equal quantity of resources can produce more X in the first region than in the second. Or, to put it differently, one country has an absolute advantage in the production of good X if it takes fewer resources to produce one unit of good X there than in another country. Table 33-1 shows an example. The two "countries" are Canada and the European Union (EU) and the two goods are wheat and cloth. The table shows the *absolute cost* of producing one unit of wheat and one unit of cloth in each country. The absolute cost is the dollar cost of the labour, capital, and other resources required to produce the goods. Thus, the country that can produce a specific good with fewer resources can produce it at a lower absolute cost.

absolute advantage The situation that exists when one country can produce some commodity at lower absolute cost than another country.

In Table 33-1, the absolute resource cost for both wheat and cloth is less in Canada than in the EU. Canada is therefore said to have an *absolute advantage* over the EU in the production of both wheat and cloth. Canada has an absolute advantage over the EU in producing these goods because it is a more efficient producer—it takes less labour and other resources to produce the goods in Canada than in the EU.

TABLE 33-1 Absolute Costs and Absolute Advantage

	Wheat (kilograms)	Cloth (metres)
Canada	$1 per kilogram	$5 per metre
EU	$3 per kilogram	$6 per metre

Absolute advantage reflects the differences in absolute costs of producing goods between countries. The numbers show the dollar cost of the total amount of resources necessary for producing wheat and cloth in Canada and the EU. Note that Canada is a lower-cost producer than the EU for both wheat and cloth. Canada is therefore said to have an absolute advantage in the production of both goods.

The situation in Table 33-1 is hypothetical, but it is encountered often in the real world. Some countries, because they have access to cheap natural resources or better-trained workers or more sophisticated capital equipment, are low-cost producers for a wide range of products. Does this mean that high-cost countries stand no chance of being successful producers in a globalized world of international trade? Will the low-cost countries produce everything, leaving nothing to be done by high-cost countries? The answer is no. As we will see immediately, the gains from international trade do *not* depend on the pattern of absolute advantage.

Practise with Study Guide Chapter 33, Exercise 1.

comparative advantage The situation that exists when a country can produce a good with less forgone output of other goods than can another country.

Comparative Advantage The great English economist David Ricardo (1722–1823) was the first to provide an explanation of the pattern of international trade in a world in which countries had different costs. His theory of *comparative advantage* is still accepted by economists as a valid statement of one of the major sources of the gains from international trade. A country is said to have a **comparative advantage** in the production of good *X* if the cost of producing *X in terms of forgone output of other goods* is lower in that country than in another. Thus, the pattern of comparative advantage is based on *opportunity costs* rather than absolute costs. Table 33-2 illustrates the pattern of comparative advantage in the Canada–EU example. The opportunity cost in Canada for one kilogram of wheat is computed by determining how much cloth must be given up in Canada in order to produce an additional kilogram of wheat. From Table 33-1, the absolute costs of wheat and cloth were $1 per kilogram and $5 per metre, respectively. Thus, in order to produce one extra kilogram of wheat, Canada must use resources that could have produced one-fifth of a metre of cloth. So the opportunity cost of one kilogram of wheat is 0.2 metres of cloth. By exactly the same reasoning, the opportunity cost of one metre of cloth in Canada is 5.0 kilograms of wheat. These opportunity costs are shown in Table 33-2.

Even though a country may have an absolute advantage in all goods (as Canada does in Table 33-1), it *cannot* have a comparative advantage in all goods. Similarly, even though a country may be inefficient in absolute terms and thus have no absolute advantage in any goods (as is the case for the EU in Table 33-1) it *must* have a comparative advantage in some good. In Table 33-2, Canada has a comparative advantage in the production of wheat because Canada must give up less cloth to produce one kilogram of wheat than must be given up in the EU. Similarly, the EU has a comparative advantage in the production of cloth because the EU must give up less wheat in order to produce one metre of cloth than must be given up in Canada.

The gains from specialization and trade depend on the pattern of comparative, not absolute, advantage.

TABLE 33-2 Opportunity Costs and Comparative Advantage

	Wheat (kilograms)	Cloth (metres)
Canada	0.2 m of cloth	5.0 kg of wheat
EU	0.5 m of cloth	2.0 kg of wheat

Comparative advantages reflect opportunity costs that differ between countries. The first column shows the opportunity cost of a kilogram of wheat in terms of the amount of cloth that must be given up. The second column shows the opportunity cost of a metre of cloth in terms of the amount of wheat that must be given up. Canada has a comparative advantage in wheat production because it has a lower opportunity cost for wheat than does the EU. The EU has a comparative advantage in cloth because its opportunity cost for cloth is lower than that in Canada.

In our example, total world wheat production can be increased if Canada devotes more resources to the production of wheat and fewer resources to the production of cloth—that is, if it *specializes* in wheat production. Similarly, total world cloth production can be increased if the EU devotes more resources to the production of cloth and fewer to wheat—if it specializes in cloth production. Such reallocations of resources increase total world output because each country is specializing in the production of the good in which it has the lowest opportunity cost. The gains from specialization along the lines of comparative advantage are shown in Table 33-3.

World output increases if countries specialize in the production of the goods in which they have a comparative advantage.

Not *any* pattern of specialization, however, is beneficial for the world. In our example, if Canada were to specialize in cloth and the EU in wheat, total world output would *fall*. To see this, note that in order to produce one extra metre of cloth in Canada, 5.0 kilograms of wheat must be sacrificed (see Table 33-2). Similarly, in order to produce four extra kilograms of wheat in the EU, two metres of cloth must be sacrificed. Thus, if each country produced these additional units of the "wrong" good, total world output of wheat would fall by one kilogram and total output of cloth would fall by one metre.

Specialization of production *against* the pattern of comparative advantage leads to a decline in total world output.

TABLE 33-3 The Gains from Specialization

	Changes from each country producing more units of the product in which it has the lower opportunity cost	
	Wheat (kilograms)	Cloth (metres)
Canada	+5.0	−1.0
EU	−4.0	+2.0
Total	+1.0	+1.0

Whenever opportunity costs differ between countries, specialization can increase the production of both products. These calculations show that there are gains from specialization given the opportunity costs of Table 33-2. To produce five more kilograms of wheat, Canada must sacrifice 1.0 m of cloth. To produce two more metres of cloth, the EU must sacrifice 4.0 kg of wheat. Making both changes increases world production of both wheat and cloth.

We have discussed comparative advantage in terms of opportunity costs. We can also illustrate it by considering the two countries' production possibilities boundaries. Recall the connection between a country's production possibilities boundary and the opportunity costs of production. The slope of the production possibilities boundary indicates the opportunity costs. The existence of different opportunity costs across countries implies comparative advantages that can lead to gains from trade. Figure 33-3 illustrates how two countries can both gain from trade when they have different opportunity costs in production and those opportunity costs are independent of the level of production. An alternative diagrammatic illustration of the gains from trade appears in *Extensions in Theory 33-1* where the production possibilities boundary is concave (which means that the opportunity cost for each good is higher when more of that good is being produced).

Practise with Study Guide Chapter 33, Exercise 4.

The conclusions about the gains from trade arising from international differences in opportunity costs are summarized below.

1. Country *A* has a comparative advantage over Country *B* in producing a product when the opportunity cost of production in Country *A* is lower. This implies, however, that it has a comparative *dis*advantage in some other product(s).
2. The opportunity cost of product *X* is the amount of output of other products that must be sacrificed in order to increase the output of *X* by one unit.
3. When opportunity costs for all products are the same in all countries, there is no comparative advantage and there is no possibility of gains from specialization and trade.
4. When opportunity costs differ in any two countries and both countries are producing both products, it is always possible to increase production of both products by a suitable reallocation of resources within each country.

Practise with Study Guide Chapter 33, Extension Exercise E1.

The Gains from Trade with Variable Costs

So far, we have assumed that opportunity costs are the same whatever the scale of output, and we have seen that there are gains from specialization and trade as long as there are interregional differences in opportunity costs. If costs vary with the level of output, or as experience is acquired via specialization, *additional* gains are possible.

FIGURE 33-3 The Gains from Trade with Constant Opportunity Costs

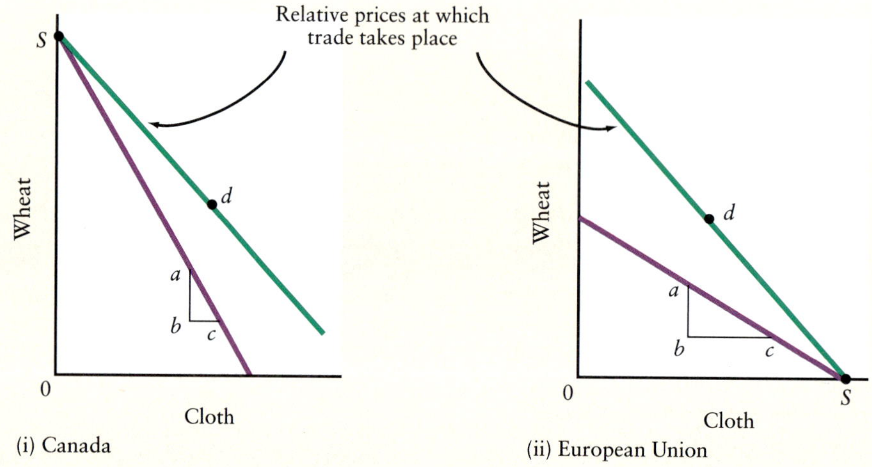

International trade leads to specialization in production and increased consumption possibilities. The purple lines in parts (i) and (ii) represent the production possibilities boundaries for Canada and the EU, respectively. In the absence of any international trade these also represent each country's consumption possibilities.

The difference in the slopes of the production possibilities boundaries reflects differences in comparative advantage, as shown in Table 33-2. In each part the opportunity cost of increasing production of wheat by the same amount (measured by the distance *ba*) is the amount by which the production of cloth must be reduced (measured by the distance *bc*). The relatively steep production possibilities boundary for Canada thus indicates that the opportunity cost of producing wheat in Canada is less than that in the European Union.

If trade is possible at some relative prices between the two countries' opportunity costs of production, each country will specialize in the production of the good in which it has a comparative advantage. In each part of the figure, the slope of the green line shows the relative prices at which trade takes place. Production occurs in each country at *S* (for specialization); Canada produces only wheat, and the EU produces only cloth.

Consumption possibilities for each country are now given by the green line that passes through *S*. Consumption possibilities are increased in both countries; consumption may occur at some point such as *d* that involves a combination of wheat and cloth that was not obtainable in the absence of trade.

Economies of Scale In many industries, production costs fall as the scale of output increases. The larger the scale of operations, the more efficiently large-scale machinery can be used and the more a detailed division of tasks among workers is possible. Small countries (such as Switzerland, Belgium, and Israel) whose domestic markets are not large enough to exploit economies of scale would find it prohibitively expensive to become self-sufficient by producing a little bit of everything at very high cost.

One of the important lessons learned from patterns of world trade since the Second World War has concerned imperfect competition and product differentiation. Virtually all of today's manufactured consumer goods are produced in a vast array of differentiated product lines. In some industries, many firms produce this array; in others, only a few firms produce the entire array. In either case, they do not exhaust all available economies of scale. Thus, an increase in the size of the market, even in a large economy, may allow the exploitation of some previously unexploited scale economies in individual product lines.

These possibilities were first dramatically illustrated when the European Common Market (now known as the European Union) was set up in the late 1950s. Economists had expected that specialization would occur according to the theory of comparative advantage, with one country specializing in cars, another in refrigerators, another in fashion and clothing, another in shoes, and so on. This is not the way it worked out. Instead, much of the vast growth of trade was in *intra-industry* trade—that is, trade of goods or services within the same broad industry. Today, one can buy French, English, Italian, and German fashion goods, cars, shoes, appliances, and a host of other products in London, Paris, Berlin, and Rome. Ships loaded with Swedish furniture bound for London pass ships loaded with English furniture bound for Stockholm, and so on.

Wine is a good example of an industry in which there is much intra-industry trade. Canada, for example, imports wine from many countries but also exports Canadian-made wine to the same countries.

The same increase in intra-industry trade happened with Canada–U.S. trade over successive rounds of tariff cuts that were negotiated after the Second World War, the most recent being those associated with the 1989 Canada–U.S. Free Trade Agreement, and its 1994 expansion into the North American Free Trade Agreement (NAFTA) which included Mexico. In several broad industrial groups, including automotive products, machinery, textiles, and forestry products, both imports and exports increased in each country. What free trade in Europe and North America did was to allow a proliferation of differentiated products, with different countries each specializing in different subproduct lines. Consumers have shown by their expenditures that they value this enormous increase in the range of choice among differentiated products.

In industries with significant scale economies, small countries that do not trade will have low levels of output and therefore high costs. With international trade, however, small countries can produce for the large global market and thus produce at lower costs. International trade therefore allows small countries to reap the benefits of scale economies.

Learning by Doing The discussion so far has assumed that costs vary with the *level* of output. But they may also vary with the *accumulated experience* in producing a product over time.

Early economists placed great importance on a concept that is now called **learning by doing**. They believed that as countries gained experience in particular tasks, workers and managers would become more efficient in performing them. As people acquire expertise, costs tend to fall. There is substantial evidence that such learning by doing does occur. It is particularly important in many of today's knowledge-intensive high-tech industries. The distinction between this phenomenon and economies of scale is illustrated in Figure 33-4. It is one more example of the difference between a movement along a curve and a shift of the curve.

learning by doing The reduction in unit costs that often results as workers learn through repeatedly performing the same tasks. It causes a downward shift in the average cost curve.

The opportunity for learning by doing has an important implication: Policymakers need not accept *current* comparative advantages as given. Through such means as education and tax incentives, they can seek to develop new comparative advantages. Moreover, countries cannot complacently assume that their existing comparative advantages will persist. Misguided education policies, the wrong tax incentives, or policies that discourage risk taking can lead to the rapid erosion of a country's comparative advantage in particular products and industries.

Sources of Comparative Advantage

David Ricardo's analysis taught us that the gains from trade arise from the pattern of comparative advantage. However, his analysis did not explain the *source* of a country's

EXTENSIONS IN THEORY 33-1

The Gains From Trade More Generally

Examining the gains from trade is relatively easy in the case where each country's production possibilities boundary is a straight line. What happens in the more realistic case where the production possibilities boundary is concave? As this box shows, the same basic principles of the gains from trade apply to this more complex case.

International trade leads to an expansion of the set of goods that can be consumed in the economy in two ways:

1. By allowing the bundle of goods consumed to differ from the bundle produced; and,
2. By permitting a profitable change in the pattern of production.

Without international trade, the bundle of goods produced is the bundle consumed. With international trade, the consumption and production bundles can be altered independently to reflect the relative values placed on goods by international markets.

Fixed Production

In each part of the figure, the purple curve is the economy's production possibilities boundary. In the absence of international trade, the economy must consume the same bundle of goods that it produces. Thus, the production possibilities boundary is also the consumption possibilities boundary. Suppose the economy produces and consumes at point *a*, with x_1 of good *X* and y_1 of good *Y*, as in part (i) of the figure.

Next suppose that with production point *a*, good *Y* can be exchanged for good *X* internationally. The consumption possibilities are now shown by the line *tt* drawn through point *a*. The slope of *tt* indicates the quantity of *Y* that exchanges for a unit of *X* on the international market—that is, the relative price of *X* in terms of *Y*.

Although production is fixed at point *a*, consumption can now be anywhere on the line *tt*. For example, the consumption point could be at *b*. This could be achieved by exporting y_2y_1 units of *Y* and importing x_1x_2 units of *X*. Because point *b* (and all others on line *tt* to the right of *a*) lies outside the production possibilities boundary, there are potential gains from trade. Consumers are no longer limited by their own country's production possibilities. Let us suppose that they prefer point *b* to point *a*. They have achieved a gain from trade by being allowed to exchange some of their production of good *Y* for some quantity of good *X* and thus to consume more of good *X* than is produced at home.

comparative advantage. Why do comparative advantages exist? Since a country's comparative advantage depends on its opportunity costs, we could also ask: Why do different countries have different opportunity costs?

Different Factor Endowments The traditional answer to this question was provided early in the twentieth century by two Swedish economists, Eli Heckscher and Bertil Ohlin. Ohlin was subsequently awarded the Nobel Prize in economics for his work in the theory of international trade. Their explanation for international differences in opportunity costs is now incorporated in the Heckscher-Ohlin model. According to their theory, the international cost differences that form the basis for comparative advantage arise because factor endowments differ across countries. This is often called the *factor endowment theory of comparative advantage.*

To see how this theory works, consider the prices for various types of goods in countries *in the absence of trade*. A country that is well endowed with fertile land but has a small population (like Canada) will find that land is cheap but labour is expensive. It will therefore produce land-intensive agricultural goods cheaply and labour-intensive goods, such as machine tools, only at high cost. The reverse will be true for

Variable Production

There is a further opportunity for the expansion of the country's consumption possibilities: With trade, production may be altered in response to international prices. The country may produce the bundle of goods that is most valuable in world markets. That is represented by the bundle d in part (ii). The consumption possibilities boundary is shifted to the line $t't'$ by changing production from a to d and thereby increasing the country's degree of specialization in good Y. For every point on the original consumption possibilities boundary tt, there are points on the new boundary $t't'$ that allow more consumption of both goods—for example, compare points b and f. Notice also that, except at the zero-trade point d, the new consumption possibilities boundary lies *everywhere above the production possibilities curve.*

The benefits of moving from a no-trade position, such as point a, to a trading position, such as points b or f, are the *gains from trade* to the country. When the production of good Y is increased and the production of good X decreased, the country is able to move to a point such as f by producing more of good Y, in which the country has a comparative advantage, and trading the additional production for good X.

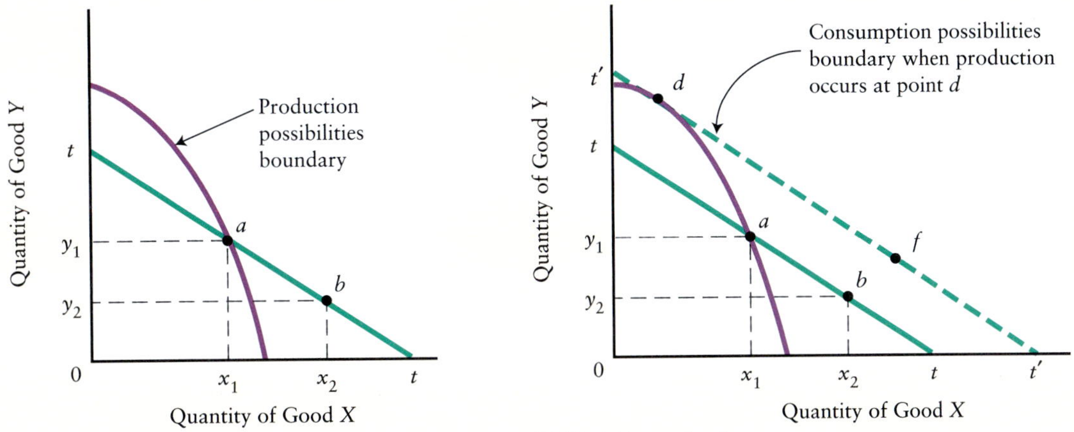

(i) Fixed production

(ii) Variable production

a second country that is small in size but possesses abundant and efficient labour (like Japan). As a result, the first country will have a comparative advantage in agricultural production and the second in goods that use much labour and little land.

According to the Heckscher-Ohlin theory, countries have comparative advantages in the production of goods that use intensively the factors of production with which they are abundantly endowed.

For example, Canada is abundantly endowed with forests relative to most other countries. According to the Hecksher-Ohlin theory, Canada has a comparative advantage in goods that use forest products intensively, such as newsprint, paper, raw lumber, and wooden furniture. In contrast, relative to most other countries, Canada is sparsely endowed with labour. Thus, Canada has a comparative disadvantage in goods that use labour intensively, such as cotton or many other textile products.

Canada is extremely well endowed with forests. It is no surprise, therefore, that it has a comparative advantage in a whole range of forestry products.

FIGURE 33-4 Economies of Scale vs. Learning by Doing

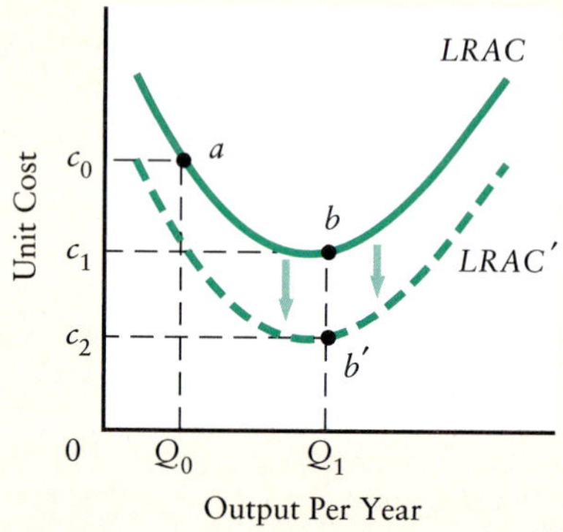

Specialization may lead to gains from trade through scale economies, learning by doing, or both. Consider a country that wishes to consume the quantity Q_0. Suppose it can produce that quantity at an average cost per unit of c_0. Suppose further that the country has a comparative advantage in producing this product and can export the quantity Q_0Q_1 if it produces Q_1. This may lead to cost savings in two ways.

First, the increased level of production of Q_1 compared to Q_0 permits it to *move along* its cost curve from *a* to *b*, thereby reducing costs per unit to c_1. This is an economy of scale.

Second, as workers and management become more experienced, they may be able to produce at lower costs. This is learning by doing and it shifts the cost curve from *LRAC* to *LRAC′*. At output Q_1, costs per unit fall to c_2. The movement from *a* to *b′* incorporates both economies of scale and learning by doing.

Different Climates The factor endowment theory has considerable power to explain comparative advantage but it does not provide the whole explanation. One additional influence comes from all those natural factors that can be called *climate* in the broadest sense. If you combine land, labour, and capital in the same way in Nicaragua and in Iceland, you will not get the same output of most agricultural goods. Sunshine, rainfall, and average temperature also matter. If you seek to work with wool or cotton in dry climates, you will get different results than when you work in damp climates. (You can, of course, artificially create any climate you wish in a factory, but it costs money to create what is freely provided elsewhere.)

Climate affects comparative advantage.

Of course, if we consider "warm weather" a factor of production, then we could simply say that countries like Nicaragua are better endowed with that factor than countries like Iceland. In this sense, explanations of comparative advantage based on different climates are really just a special case of explanations based on factor endowments.

Acquired Comparative Advantage Today it is clear that many comparative advantages are *acquired*. Further, they can change. Thus, comparative advantage should be viewed as being *dynamic* rather than static. Many new industries are seen to depend more on human capital than on fixed physical capital or natural resources. The skills of a computer designer, a videogame programmer, or a sound mix technician are acquired by education and on-the-job training. Natural endowments of energy and raw materials cannot account for Silicon Valley's leadership in computer technology, for Canada's prominence in communications technology, for Taiwan's excellence in electronics, or for Switzerland's prominence in private banking.

If comparative advantage can be acquired, it can also be *lost*. If firms within one country fail to innovate and adopt the latest technologies available in their industry, but competing firms in other countries are aggressively innovating and reducing their production costs, the first country will eventually lose whatever comparative advantage it once had in that industry. In recent years, for example, pulp and paper mills in Canada have been closing, driven out of the industry by Scandinavian firms that more aggressively pursue improvements in productivity.

With today's growing international competition, no country's comparative advantages are secure unless its firms innovate and keep up with their foreign competitors.

Contrasting Views? This modern view is in sharp contrast with the traditional assumption that cost structures based largely on a country's natural endowments lead to a given pattern of international comparative advantage. The traditional view suggests that a government interested in maximizing its citizens' material standard of living should encourage specialization of production in goods for which it *currently* has a comparative advantage. If all countries follow this advice, each will be specialized in a relatively narrow range of distinct products. The British will produce engineering products, Canadians will be producers of resource-based primary products, Americans will be farmers and factory workers, Central Americans will be banana and coffee growers, and so on.

There are surely elements of truth in both extreme views. It would be unwise to neglect resource endowments, climate, culture, social patterns, and institutional arrangements. But it would also be unwise to assume that all advantages are innate and immutable.

To some extent, these views are reconciled by the theory of human capital, which is a topic we discussed in Chapter 14. Comparative advantages that depend on human capital are consistent with traditional Heckscher-Ohlin theory. The difference is that this type of capital is acquired through conscious decisions relating to such matters as education and technical training.

33.2 THE DETERMINATION OF TRADE PATTERNS

Comparative advantage has been the central concept in our discussion about the gains from trade. If Canada has a comparative advantage in lumber and Italy has a comparative advantage in shoes, then the total output of lumber and shoes can be increased if Canada specializes in the production of lumber and Italy specializes in the production of shoes. With such patterns of specialization, Canada will naturally export lumber to Italy and Italy will export shoes to Canada.

For data on Canadian trade by industry and by country, go to Statistics Canada's website at **www.statcan.ca** and search for "trade."

It is one thing to discuss the potential gains from trade if countries specialized in the production of particular goods and exported these to other countries. But do *actual* trade patterns occur along the lines of comparative advantage? In this section of the chapter we use a simple demand-and-supply model to examine why Canada exports some products and imports others. We will see that comparative advantage, whether natural or acquired, plays a central role in determining actual trade patterns.

There are some products, such as coffee and mangoes, that Canada does not produce (and will probably never produce). Any domestic consumption of these products must therefore be satisfied by imports from other countries. At the other extreme, there are some products, such as nickel or potash, of which Canada is one of the world's major suppliers, and demand in the rest of the world must be satisfied partly by exports from Canada. There are also some products, such as houses, that are so expensive to transport that every country produces approximately what it consumes.

Our interest in this section is with the vast number of intermediate cases in which Canada is only one of many producers of an internationally traded product, as with beef, oil, copper, wheat, lumber, and newsprint. Will Canada be an exporter or an importer of such products? And what is the role played by comparative advantage?

The Law of One Price

Whether Canada imports or exports a product for which it is only one of many producers depends to a great extent on the product's price. This brings us to what economists call the *law of one price.*

The law of one price states that when a product is traded throughout the entire world, the prices in various countries will differ by no more than the cost of transporting the product between countries. Aside from differences due to these transport costs, there is a single world price.

Many basic products—such as copper wire, steel pipe, iron ore, and computer RAM chips—fall within this category. The world price for each good is the price that equates the quantity demanded worldwide with the quantity supplied worldwide. The world price of an internationally traded product may be influenced greatly, or only slightly, by the demand and supply coming from any one country. The extent of one country's influence will depend on how important its quantities demanded and supplied are in relation to the worldwide totals.

The simplest case for us to study arises when the country, which we will take to be Canada, accounts for only a small part of the total worldwide demand and supply. In this case, Canada does not itself produce enough to influence the world price significantly. Similarly, Canadian purchases are too small a proportion of worldwide demand to affect the world price in any significant way. Producers and consumers in Canada thus face a world price that they cannot influence by their own actions.

In this case, the price that rules in the Canadian market must be the world price (adjusted for the exchange rate between the Canadian dollar and the foreign currency). The law of one price says that this must be so. What would happen if the Canadian domestic price diverged from the world price? If the Canadian price were below the world price, no supplier would sell in the Canadian market because more money could be made by selling abroad. The absence of supply to the Canadian market would thus drive up the Canadian price. Conversely, if the Canadian domestic price were above the worldwide price, no buyer would buy from a Canadian seller because money could be saved by buying abroad. The absence of demand on the Canadian market would thus drive down the Canadian price.

The Pattern of Foreign Trade

Let us now see what determines the pattern of international trade in such circumstances.

Practise with Study Guide Chapter 33, Exercise 5.

An Exported Product To determine the pattern of Canadian trade, we first show the Canadian domestic demand and supply curves for some product, say, lumber. This is done in Figure 33-5. The intersection of these two curves tells us what the price and quantity would be *if there were no foreign trade.* Now compare this no-trade price with the world price of that product.[1] If the world price is higher, the actual price in Canada will exceed the no-trade price. In this situation there will be an excess of Canadian supply over Canadian demand. Domestic producers want to sell Q_2 units of lumber but domestic consumers want to buy only Q_1 units. If Canada were a closed economy, such excess supply would drive the price down to p_d. But in an open economy with a world price of p_w, this excess supply gets exported to Canada's trading partners.

Export Development Canada is a Crown corporation devoted to improving Canada's export prospects. For information about Canada's exports, check out its website: **www.edc.ca**.

Countries export products whose world price exceeds the price that would exist domestically if there were no foreign trade.

What is the role of comparative advantage in this analysis? We have said that Canada will export lumber if the world price exceeds Canada's no-trade price. Note that in a competitive market the price of the product reflects the product's marginal cost, which in turn reflects the opportunity cost of producing the product. That Canada's no-trade price for lumber is lower than the world price reflects the fact that the opportunity cost of producing lumber in Canada is less than the opportunity cost of producing it in the rest of the world. Thus, by exporting goods that have a low no-trade price, Canada is exporting the goods for which it has a comparative advantage.

Countries export the goods for which they are low-cost producers. That is, they export goods for which they have a comparative advantage.

FIGURE 33-5 An Exported Good

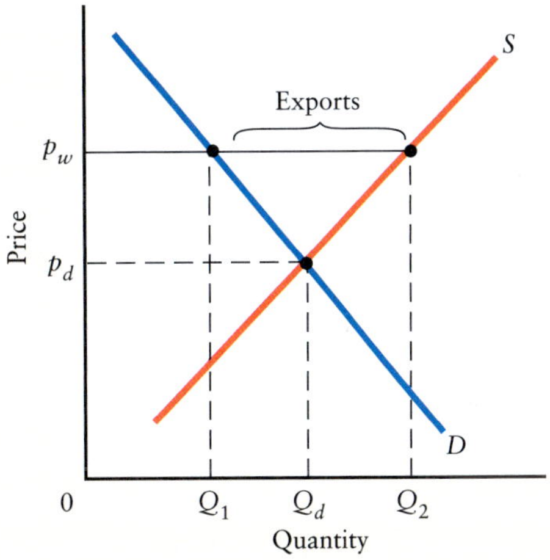

Exports occur whenever there is excess supply domestically at the world price. The domestic demand and supply curves are D and S, respectively. The domestic price in the absence of foreign trade is p_d, with Q_d produced and consumed domestically. The world price of p_w is higher than p_d. At p_w, Q_1 is demanded while Q_2 is supplied domestically. The excess of the domestic supply over the domestic demand is exported.

An Imported Product Now consider some other product—for example, computer RAM chips. Once again, look first at the domestic demand and supply curves, shown this time in Figure 33-6. The intersection of these curves determines the no-trade price that would rule if there were no foreign trade. The world price of RAM chips is below the Canadian no-trade price so that, at the price ruling in Canada, domestic demand is larger and domestic supply is smaller than if the no-trade price had ruled. The excess of domestic demand over domestic supply is met by imports.

[1] If the world price is stated in terms of some foreign currency (as it often is), the price must be converted into Canadian dollars using the current exchange rate between the foreign currency and Canadian dollars.

FIGURE 33-6 An Imported Good

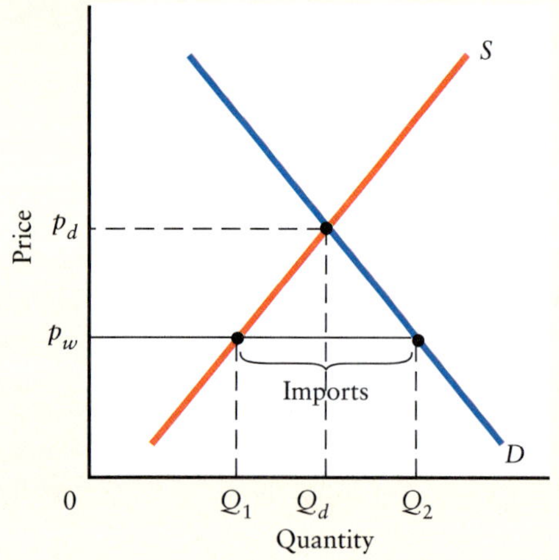

Imports occur whenever there is excess demand domestically at the world price. The domestic demand and supply curves are *D* and *S*, respectively. The domestic price in the absence of foreign trade is p_d, with Q_d produced and consumed domestically. The world price of p_w is less than p_d. At the world price Q_2 is demanded, whereas Q_1 is supplied domestically. The excess of domestic demand over domestic supply is satisfied through imports.

Countries import products whose world price is less than the price that would exist domestically if there were no foreign trade.

Again, this analysis can be restated in terms of comparative advantage. The high Canadian no-trade price of RAM chips reflects the fact that RAM chips have a higher opportunity cost in Canada than elsewhere in the world. This high cost means that Canada has a comparative disadvantage in RAM chips. So Canada imports goods for which it has a comparative disadvantage.

Countries import the goods for which they are high-cost producers. That is, they import goods for which they have a comparative disadvantage.

Is Comparative Advantage Obsolete?

In the debate preceding the signing of both the Canada–U.S. Free Trade Agreement and the North American Free Trade Agreement (NAFTA), some opponents argued that the agreements relied on an outdated view of the gains from trade based on comparative advantage. The theory of comparative advantage was said to be obsolete.

Contrary to such assertions, comparative advantage remains an important economic concept. At any one time—because comparative advantage is reflected in international relative prices, and these relative prices determine what goods a country will import and what it will export—the operation of the price system will result in trade that follows the current pattern of comparative advantage. For example, if Canadian costs of producing steel are particularly low relative to other Canadian costs, steel will be a Canadian export at international prices (which it is). If Canada's costs of producing textiles are particularly high relative to other Canadian costs, Canada will import textiles at international prices (which it does). Thus, there is no reason to change the view that Ricardo long ago expounded: *Current comparative advantage is a major determinant of trade under free-market conditions.*

What has changed, however, is economists' views about the *determinants* of comparative advantage. It now seems that current comparative advantage may be more open to change by private entrepreneurial activities and by government policy than used to be thought. Thus, what is obsolete is the belief that a country's current pattern of comparative advantage, and hence its current pattern of imports and exports, must be accepted as given and unchangeable.

The theory that comparative advantage determines trade flows is not obsolete, but the theory that comparative advantage is completely determined by forces beyond the reach of decisions made by private firms and by public policy has been discredited.

One caveat should be noted. It is one thing to observe that it is *possible* for governments to influence a country's pattern of comparative advantage. It is quite another to conclude that it is *advisable* for them to try. The case in support of a specific government intervention requires that (1) there is scope for governments to improve on the results achieved by the free market, (2) the costs of the intervention be less than the value of the improvement to be achieved, and (3) governments will actually be able to carry out the required interventionist policies (without, for example, being sidetracked by considerations of electoral advantage).

The Terms of Trade

We have seen that world production can be increased when countries specialize in the production of the goods for which they have a comparative advantage and then trade with one another. We now ask: How will these gains from specialization and trade be shared among countries? The division of the gain depends on what is called the **terms of trade**, which relate to the quantity of imported goods that can be obtained per unit of goods exported. The terms of trade are measured by the ratio of the price of exports to the price of imports.

terms of trade The ratio of the average price of a country's exports to the average price of its imports.

A rise in the price of imported goods, with the price of exports unchanged, indicates a *fall in the terms of trade;* it will now take more exports to buy the same quantity of imports. Similarly, a rise in the price of exported goods, with the price of imports unchanged, indicates a *rise in the terms of trade;* it will now take fewer exports to buy the same quantity of imports. Thus, the ratio of these prices measures the amount of imports that can be obtained per unit of goods exported.

The terms of trade can be illustrated along with the country's production possibilities boundary, as shown in Figure 33-7. The figure shows the hypothetical case in which Canada can produce only wheat and cloth. As we saw earlier, the slope of Canada's production possibilities boundary shows the relative opportunity costs of producing the two goods in Canada. A steep production possibilities boundary indicates that only a small amount of cloth must be given up to get more wheat; thus cloth is relatively costly and wheat is relatively cheap. A flatter production possibilities boundary indicates that a larger amount of cloth must be given up to get more wheat; thus cloth is relatively cheap and wheat is relatively expensive. Thus, the slope of the production possibilities boundary in Figure 33-7 shows the relative price of cloth (in terms of wheat) that Canada faces in the absence of international trade.

If, through international trade, Canada has access to different relative prices, Canada will be led to specialize in the production of one good or the other. In Figure 33-7, we show a case in which the

FIGURE 33-7 A Change in the Terms of Trade

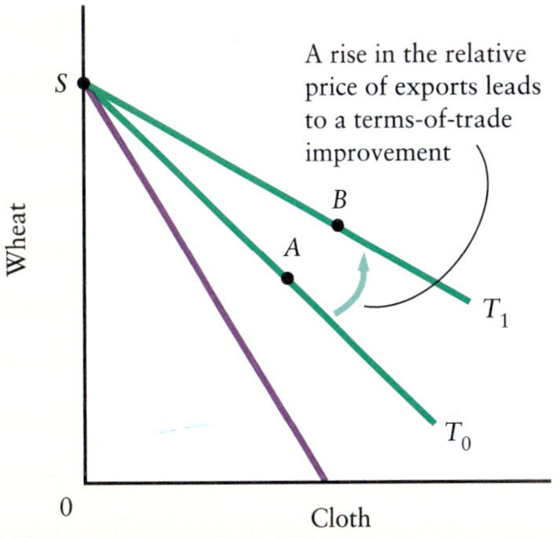

Changes in the terms of trade lead to changes in a country's consumption possibilities. The hypothetical production possibilities boundary is shown for Canada. With international trade at relative prices T_0, Canada specializes in the production of wheat, producing at point *S*, but is able to consume at a point like *A*. It pays for its imports of cloth with its exports of wheat. If the price of wheat rises relative to the price of cloth, production remains at *S* but the line T_1 shows Canada's new consumption possibilities. Consumption can now take place at a point like *B* where consumption of both wheat and cloth has increased. The increase in the terms of trade makes Canada better off because of the increase in consumption possibilities.

Practise with Study Guide Chapter 33, Exercise 3.

world relative price of cloth is lower than the relative price Canada would have if it did not trade. Faced with a lower relative price of cloth, Canada ends up specializing in the production of the relatively high-priced product (wheat), and importing the relatively low-priced product (cloth). This point of specialization is point *S* in Figure 33-7.

The *green* lines in the figure show alternative values of the world relative prices—that is, alternative values for Canada's terms of trade. A rise in the terms of trade indicates a fall in the relative price of cloth (or a rise in the relative price of wheat). This increase in the terms of trade is shown as an upward rotation of the green line from T_0 to T_1. A reduction in the terms of trade is shown as a downward rotation in the green line, from T_1 to T_0.

It should be clear from Figure 33-7 why changes in the terms of trade are important. Suppose the international relative prices are initially given by T_0. Canada specializes in the production of wheat (point *S*) but consumes at some point like *A* where it finances imports of cloth with exports of wheat. Now suppose there is a shift in world demand toward wheat and away from cloth, and this leads to an increase in the relative price of wheat. The terms of trade increase to T_1 and, with unchanged production at point *S*, Canada can now afford to consume at a point like *B* where consumption of both wheat and cloth has increased.

A rise in a country's terms of trade is beneficial because it expands the country's consumption possibilities.

Conversely, a reduction in the price of a country's exports (relative to the price of its imports) is harmful for a country. In Figure 33-7, this is shown as a change of the terms of trade from T_1 to T_0. Even though production may remain unchanged, the range of goods available to be consumed falls, and this reduction in consumption possibilities leads to an overall loss of welfare.

How do we measure the terms of trade in real economies? Because international trade involves many countries and many products, we cannot use the simple ratio of the prices of two goods as in Figure 33-7. The basic principle, however, is the same. A country's terms of trade are computed as an index number:

$$\text{Terms of trade} = \frac{\text{Index of export prices}}{\text{Index of import prices}} \times 100$$

A rise in the index is referred to as a *favourable* change in a country's terms of trade (sometimes called a terms of trade *improvement*). A decrease in the index of the terms of trade is called an *unfavourable* change (or a terms of trade *deterioration*). For example, the sharp rise in oil prices in the 1970s led to large unfavourable shifts in the terms of trade of oil-importing countries. When oil prices fell sharply in the mid-1980s, the terms of trade of oil-importing countries changed favourably. The converse was true for oil-exporting countries.

Canada's terms of trade since 1961 are shown in Figure 33-8. As is clear, the terms of trade are quite variable, reflecting frequent changes in the relative prices of different products. Note the dramatic increase (improvement) in Canada's terms of trade in the early 1970s, reflecting the large increase in oil prices caused by OPEC's output restrictions. Since Canada is a net exporter of oil, its terms of trade improve when the price of oil increases. An even larger increase occurred in the 2002–2005 period, when the world prices of most commodities, especially energy-related commodities, increased sharply.

FIGURE 33-8 Canada's Terms of Trade, 1961–2005

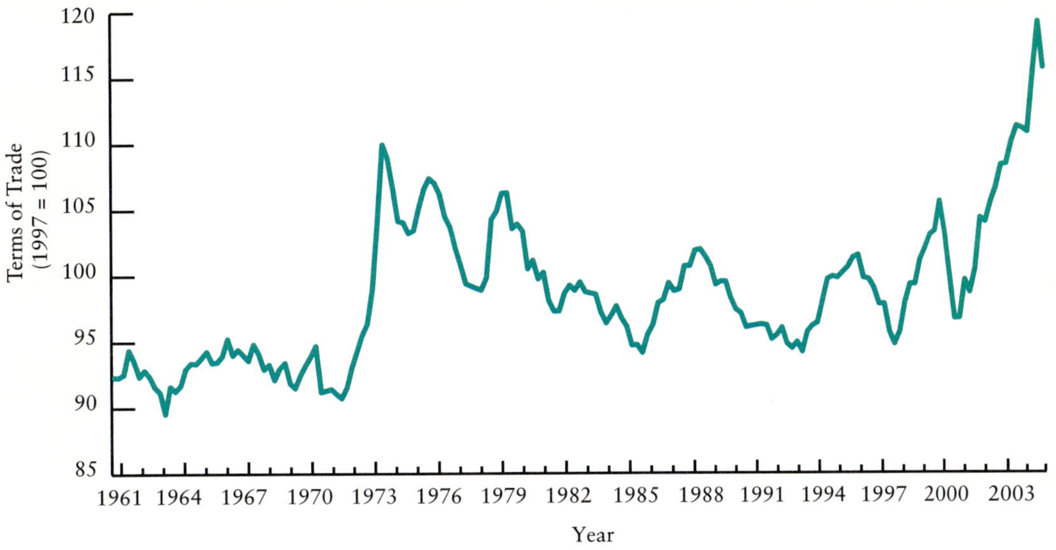

Canada's terms of trade have been quite variable over the past 40 years. The data shown are Canada's terms of trade—the ratio of an index of Canadian export prices to an index of Canadian import prices. As the relative prices of lumber, oil, wheat, electronic equipment, textiles, fruit, and other products change, the terms of trade naturally change.

(*Source:* Statistics Canada, CANSIM database, Series V1997754 and V1997751 and authors' calculations. Reprinted with permission of Statistics Canada.)

SUMMARY

33.1 THE GAINS FROM TRADE

LO 1 2

- Country A has an absolute advantage over Country B in the production of a specific product when the absolute resource cost of the product is less in Country A than in Country B.
- Country A has a comparative advantage over Country B in the production of a specific good if the forgone output of other goods is less in Country A than in Country B.
- Comparative advantage occurs whenever countries have different opportunity costs of producing particular goods. World production of all products can be increased if each country transfers resources into the production of the products for which it has a comparative advantage.
- Trade allows all countries to obtain the goods for which they do not have a comparative advantage at a lower opportunity cost than they would face if they were to produce all products for themselves; specialization and trade therefore allow all countries to have more of all products than they could have if they tried to be self-sufficient.
- A nation that engages in trade and specialization may also realize the benefits of economies of large-scale production and of learning by doing.
- Classical theory regarded comparative advantage as largely determined by natural resource endowments that are difficult to change. Economists now believe that some comparative advantages can be acquired and consequently can be changed. A country may, in this view, influence its role in world production and trade.

33.2 THE DETERMINATION OF TRADE PATTERNS

LO 3 4

- The law of one price says that the national prices of goods must differ by no more than the costs of transporting these goods between countries. After accounting for these transport costs, there is a single world price.
- Countries will export a good when the world price exceeds the price that would exist in the country if there were no trade. The low no-trade price reflects a low opportunity cost and thus a comparative advantage in that good. Thus, countries export goods for which they have a comparative advantage.
- Countries will import a good when the world price is less than the price that would exist in the country if there were no trade. The high no-trade price reflects a high opportunity cost and thus a comparative disadvantage in that good. Thus, countries import goods for which they have a comparative disadvantage.
- The terms of trade refer to the ratio of the prices of goods exported to the prices of those imported. The terms of trade determine the quantity of imports that can be obtained per unit of exports.
- A favourable change in the terms of trade—a rise in export prices relative to import prices—is beneficial for a country because it expands its consumption possibilities.

KEY CONCEPTS

Interpersonal, interregional, and international specialization
Absolute advantage and comparative advantage
Opportunity cost and comparative advantage
The gains from trade: specialization, scale economies, and learning by doing
The sources of comparative advantage
Factor endowments
Acquired comparative advantage
The law of one price
The terms of trade

STUDY EXERCISES

1. Fill in the blanks to make the following statements correct.

   a. A nation that engages in international trade is able to specialize in producing goods that it produces __________ and trade to obtain goods that it does not produce __________.
   b. The "gains from trade" refers to the increased __________ due to specialization and trade.
   c. Suppose Argentina can produce one kilogram of beef for $2.50 and Brazil can produce one kilogram of beef for $2.90. Argentina is said to have a(n) __________ in beef production over Brazil. The gains from trade do *not* depend on __________.
   d. Comparative advantage is based on __________ rather than absolute costs.
   e. It is possible for a country to have a comparative advantage in some good and a(n) __________ in none.
   f. If all countries specialize in the production of goods for which they have a comparative advantage, then world output will __________.
   g. If opportunity costs are the same in all countries, there is no __________ and no possibility of __________.

2. Fill in the blanks to make the following statements correct.

   a. A product such as coffee beans is cheaply transported and is traded around the world. The law of __________ tells us that it will tend to have __________ worldwide price.
   b. If the domestic price of copper wire in Canada (in the absence of trade) is $20 per unit and the world price is $24 per unit, then Canada will have an excess __________ which it will then __________. The opportunity cost of producing copper wire in Canada is __________ than the opportunity cost of producing it in the rest of the world.
   c. Canada will import goods for which it has an excess __________ at the world price. In the absence of trade, the __________ price of these goods would be less than the __________ price.
   d. A rise in Canada's terms of trade means that the average price of Canada's __________ has risen compared to the average price of Canada's __________. This change is referred to as a terms of trade __________.

e. The terms of trade determine the quantity of ________ that can be obtained per unit of ___________.

3. The following diagram shows the production possibilities boundary for Arcticland, a country that produces only two goods, ice and fish. Labour is the only factor of production.

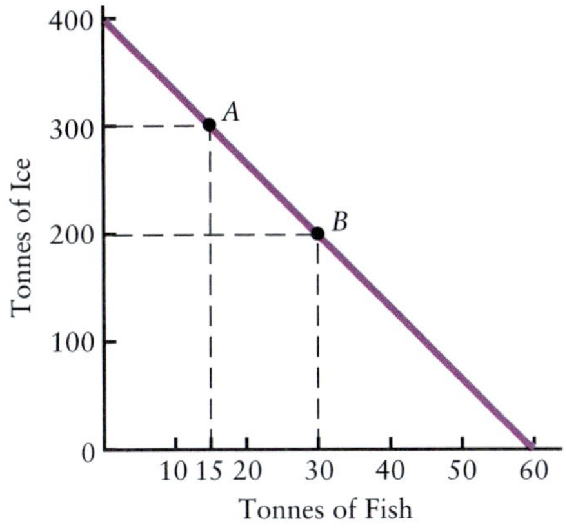

a. Beginning at any point on Arcticland's production possibilities boundary, what is the opportunity cost of producing 10 more tonnes of fish?
b. Beginning at any point on Arcticland's production possibilities boundary, what is the opportunity cost of producing 100 more tonnes of ice?

4. myeconlab The following table shows the production of wheat and corn in Brazil and Mexico. Assume that both countries have one million acres of arable land.

	Brazil	Mexico
Wheat	90 bushels per acre	50 bushels per acre
Corn	30 bushels per acre	20 bushels per acre

a. Which country has the absolute advantage in wheat? In corn? Explain.
b. Which country has the comparative advantage in wheat? In corn? Explain.
c. Explain why one country can have an absolute advantage in both goods but cannot have a comparative advantage in both goods.
d. On a scale diagram with wheat on the horizontal axis and corn on the vertical axis, draw each country's production possibilities boundary.
e. What is shown by the slope of each country's production possibilities boundary? Be as precise as possible.

5. myeconlab The following diagrams show the production possibilities boundaries for Canada and France, both of which produce only two goods, wine and lumber.

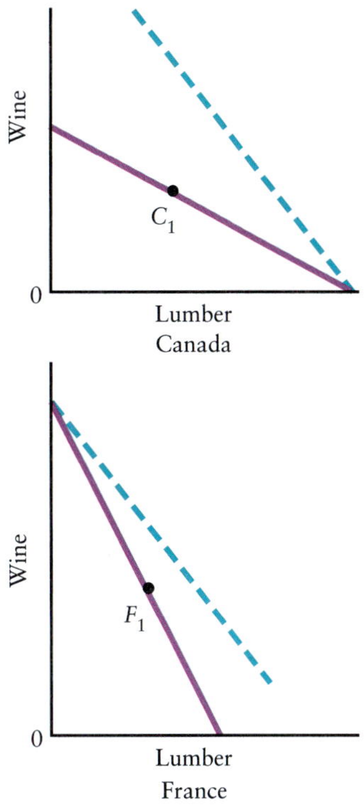

a. Which country has the comparative advantage in lumber? Explain.
b. Which country has the comparative advantage in wine? Explain.
c. Suppose Canada and France are initially not trading with each other and are producing at points C_1 and F_1, respectively. Suppose when trade is introduced, the free-trade relative prices are shown by the slope of the dashed line. Which combination of goods will each country now produce?
d. In this case, what will be the pattern of trade for each country?

6. The diagrams on the next page show the Canadian markets for newsprint and machinery, which we assume to be competitive.

a. Suppose there is no international trade. What would be the equilibrium price and quantity in the Canadian newsprint and machinery markets?
b. Now suppose Canada is open to trade with the rest of the world. If the world price of newsprint is higher than the price of newsprint from part (a), what will happen to the levels of domestic production and consumption? Explain.
c. If the world price of machinery is lower than the price of machinery from part (a), what happens to the levels of domestic consumption and production? Explain.

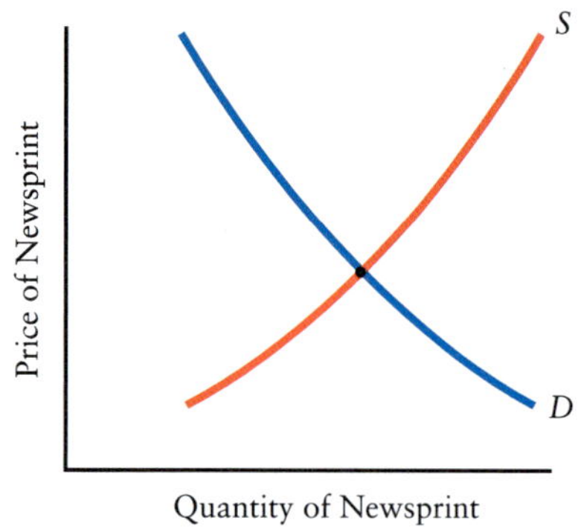

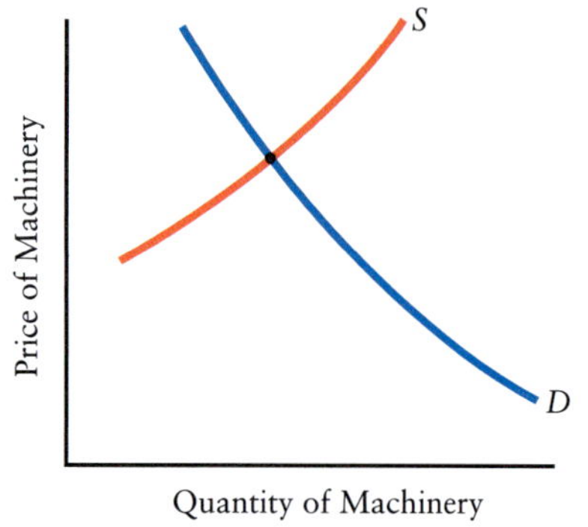

7. myeconlab The table below shows indexes for the prices of imports and exports over several years for a hypothetical country.

Year	Import Prices	Export Prices	Terms of Trade
2002	90	110	—
2003	95	87	—
2004	98	83	—
2005	100	100	—
2006	102	105	—
2007	100	112	—
2008	103	118	—

a. Compute the terms of trade in each year for this country and fill in the table.
b. In which years do the terms of trade improve?
c. In which years do the terms of trade deteriorate?
d. Explain why a terms of trade "improvement" is good for the country.

8. For each of the following events, explain the likely effect on Canada's terms of trade. Your existing knowledge of Canada's imports and exports should be adequate to answer this question.

a. A hurricane damages much of Brazil's coffee crop.
b. OPEC countries succeed in significantly restricting the world supply of oil.
c. Several new large copper mines come into production in Chile.
d. A major recession in Southeast Asia reduces the world demand for pork.

DISCUSSION QUESTIONS

1. Adam Smith saw a close connection between the wealth of a nation and its willingness "freely to engage" in foreign trade. What is the connection?

2. One critic of the North American Free Trade Agreement argued that "it can't be in our interest to sign this deal; Mexico gains too much from it." What does the theory of the gains from trade have to say about that criticism?

3. One product innovation that appears imminent is the electric car. However, development costs are high and economies of scale and learning by doing are both likely to be operative. As a result, there will be a substantial competitive advantage for those who develop a marketable product early. What implications might this have for government policies toward North American automobile manufacturers' activities in this area? Should the Canadian or U.S. governments encourage joint efforts by Chrysler, Ford, and GM, even if this appears to lessen competition among them?

4. Studies of Canadian trade patterns have shown that industries with high wages are among the largest and fastest-growing export sectors. One example is the computer software industry. Does this finding contradict the principle of comparative advantage?

5. Predict what each of the following events would do to the terms of trade of the importing country and the exporting country, other things being equal.

a. A blight destroys a large part of the coffee beans produced in the world.
b. The Koreans cut the price of the steel they sell to Canada.
c. General inflation of 4 percent occurs around the world.
d. Violation of OPEC output quotas leads to a sharp fall in the price of oil.

6. Are there always benefits to specialization and trade? When are the benefits greatest? Under what situations are there *no* benefits from specialization and trade?

CHAPTER 34

Trade Policy

LO LEARNING OBJECTIVES

In this chapter you will learn

1. the various situations in which a country may rationally choose to protect some industries.
2. the most common fallacious arguments in favour of protection.
3. the effects of a tariff or quota on imported goods.
4. why trade-remedy laws are sometimes just thinly disguised protection.
5. the distinction between trade creation and trade diversion.
6. the main features of the North American Free Trade Agreement.

trade policy A government's policy involving restrictions placed on international trade.

protectionism Any government policy that interferes with free trade in order to protect domestic firms and workers from foreign competition.

Conducting business in a foreign country is not always easy. Differences in language, in local laws and customs, and in currency often complicate transactions. Our concern in this chapter, however, is not with these complications but with government policy toward international trade, which is called **trade policy**. At one extreme is a policy of free trade—that is, an absence of any form of government interference with the free flow of international trade. Any departure from free trade designed to protect domestic industries from foreign competition is called **protectionism.**

We begin by briefly restating the case for free trade and then go on to examine various valid and invalid arguments that are commonly advanced for some degree of protection. We then explore some of the methods commonly used to restrict trade, such as tariffs and quotas. Finally, we examine the many modern institutions designed to foster freer trade on either a global or a regional basis. In particular, we discuss the North American Free Trade Agreement (NAFTA) and the World Trade Organization.

34.1 FREE TRADE OR PROTECTION?

tariff A tax applied on imports of goods or services.

nontariff barriers (NTBs) Restrictions other than tariffs designed to reduce imports.

Today, most governments accept the proposition that a relatively free flow of international trade is desirable for the health of their individual economies. But heated debates still occur over trade policy. Should a country permit the completely free flow of international trade, or should it sometimes seek to protect its local producers from foreign competition? If some protection is desired, should it be achieved by tariffs or by nontariff barriers? **Tariffs** are taxes designed to raise the price of imported goods. **Nontariff barriers (NTBs)** are devices other than tariffs designed to reduce the flow of imports; examples are import quotas and customs procedures that are deliberately more cumbersome than necessary.

The Case for Free Trade

The case for free trade was presented in Chapter 33. Comparative advantages arise whenever countries have different opportunity costs. Free trade encourages all countries to specialize in producing products in which they have a comparative advantage. This pattern of specialization maximizes world production and hence maximizes average world living standards (as measured by the world's per capita GDP).

Free trade does not necessarily make *everyone* better off than they would be in its absence. For example, reducing an existing tariff often results in individual groups receiving a smaller share of a larger world output so that they lose even though the average person gains. If we ask whether it is *possible* for free trade to improve everyone's living standards, the answer is yes because the larger total value of output that free trade generates could, at least in principle, be divided up in such a way that every individual is better off. If we ask whether free trade always does so in practice, however, the answer is, not necessarily.

Free trade makes the country as a whole better off, even though it may not make every individual in the country better off.

In today's world, a country's products must stand up to international competition if they are to survive. Over even so short a period as a few years, firms that do not develop new products and new production methods fall seriously behind their foreign competitors. If one country protects its domestic firms by imposing a tariff, those firms are likely to become complacent about the need to adopt new technologies, and over time they will become less competitive in international markets. As the technology gap between domestic and foreign firms widens, the tariff wall will provide less and less protection. Eventually, the domestic firms will succumb to foreign competition. Meanwhile, domestic living standards will fall relative to foreign ones.

Given that any country can be better off by specializing in those goods in which it has a comparative advantage, one might wonder why most countries of the world continue in some way to restrict the flow of trade. Why do tariffs and other barriers to trade continue to exist two centuries after Adam Smith and David Ricardo stated the case for free trade? Is there a valid case for some protection?

The Case for Protection

Two kinds of arguments for protection are commonly heard. The first concerns objectives *other than* maximizing national income; the second concerns the desire to increase one country's national income, possibly at the expense of the national incomes of other countries.

Objectives Other Than Maximizing National Income A country's national income may be maximized with free trade and yet it may still be rational to oppose free trade because of other policy objectives.

Advantages of Diversification. For a very small country, specializing in the production of only a few products—though dictated by comparative advantage—might involve risks that the country does not wish to take. One such risk is that technological advances may render its basic product obsolete. Another risk, especially for countries specialized in producing a small range of agricultural products, is that swings in world prices lead to large swings in national income. Everyone understands these risks, but there is debate about what governments can do about it. The pro-tariff argument is that the government can encourage a more diversified economy by protecting industries that otherwise could not compete. Opponents argue that governments, being naturally influenced by political motives, are poor judges of which industries can be protected in order to produce diversification at a reasonable cost.

Countries whose economies are based on the production of only a few goods face risks from fluctuations in world prices. For this reason, protection to promote diversification may be viewed as desirable.

Protection of Specific Groups. Although specialization according to comparative advantage will maximize *average* per capita GDP, some specific groups may have higher incomes under protection than under free trade. Of particular interest in Canada and the United States has been the effect that greater international trade has on the incomes of unskilled workers.

Consider the ratio of skilled workers to unskilled workers. There are plenty of both types throughout the world. Compared to much of the rest of the world, however, Canada has more skilled and fewer unskilled people. When trade is expanded because of a reduction in tariffs, Canada will tend to export goods made by its abundant skilled workers and import goods made by unskilled workers. (This is the basic prediction of the *factor endowment theory* of comparative advantage that we discussed in Chapter 33.) Because Canada is now exporting more goods made by skilled labour, the domestic demand for such labour rises. Because Canada is now importing more goods made by unskilled labour, the domestic demand for such labour falls. This specialization according to comparative advantage raises average Canadian living standards, but it will also tend to raise the wages of skilled Canadian workers relative to the wages of unskilled Canadian workers.

If increasing trade has these effects, then reducing trade by erecting protectionist trade barriers can have the opposite effects. Protectionist policies may raise the incomes of unskilled Canadian workers, giving them a larger share of a smaller total GDP. The conclusion is that trade restrictions can improve the earnings of one group whenever the restrictions increase the demand for that group's services. This is done, however, at the expense of a reduction in *overall* national income and hence the country's average living standards.

This analysis is important because it reveals both the grain of truth and the dangers that lie behind the resistance to trade liberalization (i.e., freer trade) on the part of some labour groups and some organizations whose main concern is with the poor.

Social and distributional concerns may lead to the rational adoption of protectionist policies. But the cost of such protection is a reduction in the country's average living standards.

Economists cannot say that it is irrational for a society to sacrifice average living standards in order to protect specific groups. But economists can do three things when presented with such arguments for adopting protectionist measures. First, they can ask if the proposed measures really do achieve the ends suggested. Second, they can calculate the cost of the measures in terms of lowered average living standards. Third, they can see if there are alternative means of achieving the stated goals at lower cost in terms of lost national income.

Maximizing National Income Next we consider several arguments for the use of tariffs when the stated objective is to maximize a country's national income.

Practise with Study Guide Chapter 34, Extension Exercise E1.

To Improve the Terms of Trade. Tariffs can be used to change the terms of trade in favour of a country that makes up a large fraction of the world demand for some product that it imports. By restricting its demand for that product through a tariff, it can force down the price that foreign exporters receive for that product. The price paid by domestic consumers will probably rise but as long as the increase is less than the tariff, foreign suppliers will receive less per unit. For example, a 20 percent U.S. tariff on the import of Canadian softwood lumber might raise the price paid by U.S. consumers by 12 percent and lower the price received by Canadian suppliers by 8 percent (the difference between the two prices being received by the U.S. treasury). This reduction in the price received by the Canadian suppliers of a U.S. import is a terms-of-trade improvement for the United States (and a terms-of-trade deterioration for Canada).

Note that not all countries can improve their terms of trade by levying tariffs on imported goods. A *necessary* condition is that the importing country has *market power,* in other words, that it is a large importer of the good in question, so that its restrictive trade policies lead to a decline in the world price of its imports. Small countries, like Canada, are not large enough importers of any good to have a significant effect on world prices. For small countries, therefore, tariffs cannot improve their terms of trade.

Large countries can sometimes improve their terms of trade by levying tariffs on some imported goods; small countries cannot.

infant industry argument The argument that new domestic industries with potential for economies of scale or learning by doing need to be protected from competition from established, low-cost foreign producers so that they can grow large enough to achieve costs as low as those of foreign producers.

To Protect Infant Industries. The oldest valid arguments for protection as a means of raising living standards concern economies of scale or learning by doing. It is usually called the **infant industry argument**. An infant industry is nothing more than a new, small industry. If such an industry has large economies of scale or the scope for learning by doing, costs will be high when the industry is small but will fall as the industry grows. In such industries, the country to first enter the field has a tremendous advantage. A developing country may find that in the early stages of development, its industries are unable to compete with established foreign rivals. A trade restriction may protect these industries from foreign competition while they grow up. When they are large enough, they will be able to produce as cheaply as foreign rivals and thus be able to compete without protection.

Most of the now industrialized countries developed their industries initially under quite heavy tariff protection. (In Canada's case, the National Policy of 1876 established a high tariff wall behind which many Canadian industries developed and thrived for many years.) Once the industrial sector was well developed, these countries moved to reduce their levels of protection, thus moving a long way toward freer trade. Electronics in Taiwan, automobiles in Japan, commercial aircraft in Europe (specifically the consortium of European governments that created Airbus), and shipbuilding in South Korea are all examples in which protection of infant industries was successful. In each case, the national industry, protected by its home government, developed into a major player in the global marketplace.

One practical problem with this argument for protection is that some infants "never grow up." Once the young firm gets used to operating in a protected environment, it may resist having that protection disappear, even though all economies of scale may have been achieved. This is as much a political problem as an economic one. Political leaders must therefore be careful before offering protection to infant industries because they must recognize the political difficulties involved in removing that protection in the future. The countries that were most successful in having their protected industries eventually grow up and succeed in fierce international competition were those, such as Taiwan and South Korea, that ruthlessly withdrew support from unsuccessful infants within a specified time period.

To Earn Economic Profits in Foreign Markets. Another argument for protectionist policies is to help create an advantage in producing or marketing some product that is expected to generate economic profits through its sales to foreign consumers. If protection of the domestic market, which might include subsidizing domestic firms, can increase the chance that one of the domestic firms will become established and thus earn high profits, the protection may pay off. The economic profits earned in foreign markets may exceed the cost to domestic taxpayers of the protection. This is the general idea behind the concept of *strategic trade policy.*

For many years, Canada and Brazil have been in a trade dispute centred around each country's alleged support of aerospace manufacturers. Canada's Bombardier and Brazil's Embraer both receive considerable financial assistance from their respective federal governments. Taxpayers in each country foot the bill.

Opponents of strategic trade policy argue that it is nothing more than a modern version of age-old and faulty justifications for tariff protection. Once all countries try to be strategic, they will all waste vast sums trying to break into industries in which there is no room for most of them. Domestic consumers would benefit most, they say, if their governments let other countries engage in this game. Consumers could then buy the cheap, subsidized foreign products and export traditional nonsubsidized products in return. The opponents of strategic trade policy also argue that democratic governments that enter the game of picking and backing winners are likely to make more bad choices than good ones. One bad choice, with all of its massive development costs written off, would require that many good choices also be made in order to make the equivalent in profits that would allow taxpayers to break even overall.

An ongoing dispute between Canada and Brazil illustrates how strategic trade policy is often difficult to distinguish from pure protection. The world's two major producers of regional jets are Bombardier, based in Montreal, and Embraer SA, based in Brazil. For several years, each company has accused its competitor's government of using illegal subsidies to help the domestic company sell jets in world markets. Brazil's Pro-Ex program provides Embraer's customers with low-interest loans with which to purchase Embraer's jets. Export Development Canada (EDC) provides similar loans to Bombardier's customers. In addition, the Canadian government's Technology Partnerships program subsidizes research and development activities in high-tech aerospace and defence companies. As the leading Canadian aerospace company, Bombardier benefits significantly from this program.

In 1999, the World Trade Organization (WTO) ruled that both the Brazilian and Canadian governments were using illegal subsidy programs to support their aerospace firms. Both countries, however, naturally view their respective programs as necessary responses to the other country's subsidization. Many economists believe that an agreement to eliminate both programs would leave a "level playing field" while saving Brazilian and Canadian taxpayers a considerable amount of money. As of 2006, however, both countries continue to support their respective aerospace firms and both sets of taxpayers continue to foot the bill.

For a list and discussion of many ongoing trade disputes, see the WTO's website: **www.wto.org**.

Fallacious Arguments for Protection

We have seen that free trade is generally beneficial for a country overall even though it does not necessarily make every person better off. We have also seen that there are some situations in which there are valid arguments for restricting trade. For every valid argument, however, there are many fallacious arguments—many of these are based, directly or indirectly, on the misconception that in every transaction there is a winner and a loser. Here we review a few arguments that are frequently heard in political debates concerning international trade.

Keep the Money at Home This argument says that if I buy a foreign good, I have the good and the foreigner has the money, whereas if I buy the same good locally, I have the good and our country has the money, too. This argument is based on a common misconception. It assumes that domestic money actually goes abroad physically when imports are purchased and that trade flows only in one direction. But when Canadian importers purchase Japanese goods, they do not send dollars abroad. They (or their financial agents) buy Japanese yen and use them to pay the Japanese manufacturers. They purchase the yen on the foreign-exchange market by giving up dollars to someone who wishes to use them for expenditure in Canada. Even if the money did go abroad physically—that is, if a Japanese firm accepted a bunch of Canadian $100 bills—it would be because that firm (or someone to whom it could sell the dollars) wanted them to spend in the only country where they are legal tender—Canada.

Canadian currency ultimately does no one any good except as purchasing power in Canada. It would be miraculous if Canadian money could be exported in return for real goods. After all, the Bank of Canada has the power to create as much new Canadian money as it wishes (at almost zero direct cost). It is only because Canadian money can buy Canadian products and Canadian assets that others want it.

Protect Against Low-Wage Foreign Labour This argument says that the products of low-wage countries will drive Canadian products from the market, and the high Canadian standard of living will be dragged down to that of its poorer trading partners. For example, if Canada imports cotton shirts from China, higher-cost Canadian textile firms may go out of business and Canadian workers may be laid off. Arguments of this sort have swayed many voters over the years.

As a prelude to considering this argument, think what the argument would imply if taken out of the international context and put into a local one, where the same principles govern the gains from trade. Is it really impossible for a rich person to gain by trading with a poor person? Would the local millionaire be better off if she did all her own typing, gardening, and cooking? No one believes that a rich person gains nothing by trading with those who are less rich.

Why, then, must a rich group of people lose when they trade with a poor group? "Well," some may say, "the poor group will price its goods too cheaply." Does anyone believe that consumers lose from buying in discount stores or supermarkets just because the prices are lower there than at the old-fashioned corner store? Consumers gain when they can buy the same goods at a lower price. If Chinese, Mexican, or Malaysian workers earn low wages and the goods they produce are sold at low prices, Canadians will gain by obtaining imports at a low cost in terms of the goods that must be exported in return. The cheaper our imports are, the better off we are in terms of the goods and services available for domestic consumption.

As we said earlier in this chapter, *some* Canadians may be better off if Canada places high tariffs on the import of Chinese goods. In particular, if the Chinese goods compete with goods made by unskilled Canadian workers, then those unskilled workers will be better off if a Canadian tariff protects their firms and thus their jobs. But Canadian income overall—that is, average per capita real income—will be higher when there is free trade.

Exports Are Good; Imports Are Bad Exports create domestic income; imports create income for foreigners. Thus, other things being equal, exports tend to increase our total GDP, and imports tend to reduce it. Surely, then, it is desirable to encourage exports by subsidizing them and to discourage imports by taxing them. This is an appealing argument, but it is incorrect.

Exports raise GDP by adding to the value of domestic output and income, but they do not add to the value of domestic consumption. The standard of living in a country depends on the level of consumption, not on the level of income. In other words, income is not of much use except that it provides the means for consumption.

If exports really were "good" and imports really were "bad," then a fully employed economy that managed to increase exports without a corresponding increase in imports ought to be better off. Such a change, however, would result in a reduction in current standards of living because when more goods are sent abroad but no more are brought in from abroad, the total goods available for domestic consumption must fall.

The living standards of a country depend on the goods and services consumed in that country. The importance of exports is that they provide the resources required to purchase imports, either now or in the future.

Create Domestic Jobs It is sometimes said that an economy with substantial unemployment, such as Canada during much of the 1990s, provides an exception to the case for freer trade. Suppose tariffs or import quotas reduce the imports of Japanese cars, Korean textiles, German kitchen equipment, and Polish vodka. Surely, the argument goes, this will create more employment in Canadian industries producing similar products. This may be true but it will also *reduce* employment in other industries.

The Japanese, Koreans, Germans, and Poles can buy from Canada only if they earn Canadian dollars by selling their domestically produced goods and services to Canada (or by borrowing dollars from Canada).[1] The decline in their sales of cars, textiles, kitchen equipment, and vodka will decrease their purchases of Canadian lumber, cars, software, banking services, and holidays. Jobs will be lost in Canadian export industries and gained in industries that formerly faced competition from imports. The major long-term effect is that the same amount of total employment in Canada will merely be redistributed among industries. In the process, living standards will be reduced because employment expands in inefficient import-competing industries and contracts in efficient exporting industries.

A country that imposes tariffs in an attempt to create domestic jobs risks starting a "trade war" with its trading partners. Such a trade war can easily leave every country worse off, as world output (and thus income) falls significantly. An income-reducing trade war followed the onset of the Great Depression in 1929 as many countries increased tariffs to protect their domestic industries in an attempt to stimulate domestic production and employment. Most economists agree that this trade war made the Great Depression worse than it otherwise would have been.

34.2 METHODS OF PROTECTION

We now go on to explore some specific protectionist policies. Two types of protectionist policy are illustrated in Figure 34-1. Both cause the price of the imported good to rise and the quantity demanded by domestic consumers to fall. They differ, however, in how they achieve these results.

[1] They can also get dollars by selling to other countries and then using their currencies to buy Canadian dollars. But this intermediate step only complicates the transaction; it does not change its fundamental nature. Other countries must have earned the dollars by selling goods to Canada or borrowing from Canada.

FIGURE 34-1 The Deadweight Loss of a Tariff

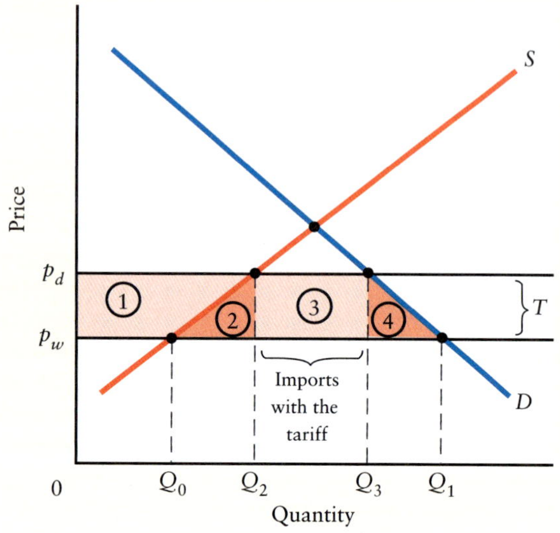

A tariff imposes a deadweight loss for the importing country. Before the tariff, the price in the domestic economy is the world price, p_w. Imports are Q_0Q_1. With a tariff of $\$T$ per unit, the domestic price rises to p_d. Domestic consumption falls to Q_3, and consumer surplus falls by areas ① + ② + ③ + ④. Domestic production rises to Q_2 and producer surplus increases by area ①. Imports fall to Q_2Q_3 and the government collects tariff revenue equal to area ③. The sum of areas ② and ④ represents the deadweight loss of the tariff.

Tariffs

A tariff, also called an *import duty,* is a tax on imported goods. For example, consider a Canadian firm that wants to import cotton T-shirts from India at \$5 per shirt. If the Canadian government levies a 20 percent tariff on imported cotton shirts, the Canadian firm pays \$5 to the Indian exporter *plus* \$1 (20 percent of \$5) in import duties to the Canada Revenue Agency. The immediate effect of a tariff is therefore to increase the domestic price of the T-shirt to \$6. This price increase has important implications for domestic consumers as well as domestic producers. The effect of a tariff is shown in Figure 34-1.

The initial effect of the tariff is to raise the domestic price of the imported product above its world price by the amount of the tariff. Imports fall. As a result, foreign producers sell less and must transfer resources to other lines of production. The price received on domestically produced units rises, as does the quantity produced domestically. On both counts, domestic producers earn more. However, the cost of producing the extra production at home exceeds the price at which it could be purchased on the world market. Thus, the benefit to domestic producers comes at the expense of domestic consumers. Indeed, domestic consumers lose on two counts: First, they consume less of the product because its price rises, and second, they pay a higher price for the amount that they do consume. This extra spending ends up in two places: The extra that is paid on all units produced at home goes to domestic producers, and the extra that is paid on units still imported goes to the government as tariff revenue.

Practise with Study Guide Chapter 34, Exercise 1.

The overall loss to the domestic economy from levying a tariff is best seen in terms of the changes in consumer and producer surplus. Before the tariff, consumer surplus was equal to the entire area below the demand curve and above the price line at p_w. After the tariff, the price increase leads to less consumption and less consumer surplus. The loss of consumer surplus is the sum of the areas ①, ②, ③, and ④ in Figure 34-1. As domestic producers respond to the higher domestic price by increasing their production and sales, they earn more producer surplus, equal to area ①. Finally, the taxpayers gain the tariff revenue equal to area ③. This is simply a redistribution of surplus away from consumers toward taxpayers. In summary:

Loss of consumer surplus	= ① + ② + ③ + ④
Gain of producer surplus	= ①
Gain of tariff revenue	= ③
Net loss in surplus	= ② + ④

The overall effect of the tariff is therefore to create a deadweight loss to the domestic economy equal to areas ② plus ④. Domestic consumers are worse off, while domestic firms and taxpayers are better off. But the net effect is a loss of surplus for the economy as a whole. This is the overall cost of levying a tariff.

A tariff imposes costs on domestic consumers, generates benefits for domestic producers, and generates revenue for the government. But the overall net effect is negative; a tariff generates a deadweight loss for the economy.

Quotas and Voluntary Export Restrictions (VERs)

The second type of protectionist policy directly restricts the quantity of an imported product. A common example is the **import quota**, by which the importing country sets a maximum quantity of some product that may be imported each year. Another measure is the **voluntary export restriction (VER)**, an agreement by an exporting country to limit the amount of a product that it sells to the importing country.

import quota A limit set on the quantity of a foreign commodity that may be imported in a given time period.

voluntary export restriction (VER) An agreement by an exporting country to limit the amount of a good exported to another country.

Figure 34-2 shows that a quantity restriction and a tariff have similar effects on domestic consumers and producers—they both raise domestic prices, increase domestic production, and reduce domestic consumption. But a direct quantity restriction is actually *worse* than a tariff for the importing country because the effect of the quantity restriction is to raise the price received by the foreign suppliers of the good. In contrast, a tariff leaves the foreign suppliers' price unchanged and instead generates tariff revenue for the government of the importing country.

Import quotas and voluntary export restrictions (VERs) impose larger deadweight losses on the importing country than do tariffs that lead to the same level of imports.

Practise with Study Guide Chapter 34, Exercise 2.

Canada, the United States, and the European Union have used VERs extensively, and the EU makes frequent use of import quotas. Japan has been pressured into negotiating several VERs with Canada, the United States, and the EU in order to limit sales of some of the Japanese goods that have had the most success in international competition. For example, in 1983, the United States and Canada negotiated VERs whereby the Japanese government agreed to restrict total sales of Japanese cars to these two countries for three years. When the agreements ran out in 1986, the Japanese continued to restrict their automobile sales by unilateral voluntary action. Japan's readiness to restrict its exports to North America partly reflects the high profits that Japanese automobile producers were making under the system of VERs, as explained in Figure 34-2. In recent years, such VERs have become less important because Japan's major automobile producers, Honda and Toyota, both have established manufacturing plants in Canada.

Tariffs Versus Quotas?

The dispute that raged for several years between Canada and the United States over Canadian softwood lumber exports illustrates an important distinction between tariffs and quotas. The United States protected its softwood lumber industry in two ways:

- by imposing tariffs on imports of Canadian softwood lumber
- by pressuring Canadian governments to place export quotas on Canadian softwood lumber shipments to the United States.

Analysis of Figures 34-1 and 34-2 reveals that the choice between tariffs and quotas matters greatly for Canadian producers.

In the case of a U.S. tariff on imported Canadian softwood lumber, Figure 34-1 illustrates the U.S. market. An import tariff raises the domestic price for U.S. lumber users and also increases the profits of U.S. lumber producers. Canadian lumber pro-

FIGURE 34-2 The Deadweight Loss of an Import Quota

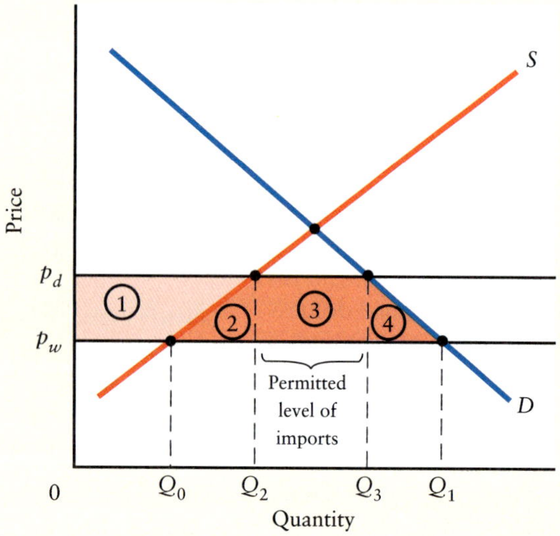

An import quota drives up the domestic price and imposes a deadweight loss on the importing country. With free trade, the domestic price is the world price, p_w. Imports are Q_0Q_1. If imports are restricted to only Q_2Q_3 (either through quotas or VERs), the domestic price must rise to the point where the restricted level of imports just satisfies the domestic excess demand. The rise in price and reduction in consumption reduces consumer surplus by areas ① + ② + ③ + ④. Domestic producers increase their output as the domestic price rises, and producer surplus increases by area ①. Area ③ does *not* accrue to the domestic economy; instead this area represents extra producer surplus for the *foreign* firms that export their product to this country. The net effect of the quota or VER is a deadweight loss for the importing country of areas ② + ③ + ④. Import quotas are therefore worse than tariffs for the importing country.

ducers are harmed because there is less demand for their product at the unchanged world price. Area ③ in the figure represents U.S. tariff revenue collected on the imports of Canadian lumber—revenue that accrues to the United States.

Figure 34-2 illustrates the U.S. market for softwood lumber when a quota is placed on the level of Canadian exports (U.S. imports). As with the tariff, the restricted supply of Canadian lumber to the U.S. market drives up the price to U.S. users and also raises profits for U.S. producers. But with a quota there is an important difference: The higher price in the U.S. market is received by the Canadian lumber producers, as shown by area ③ in the figure.

While a tariff and quota may lead to the same reduced volume of exports, the tariff permits some surplus to be captured by the importing country whereas the quota allows some surplus to be captured by the exporting country (area ③ in both cases). In the U.S.–Canadian softwood lumber dispute, both tariffs and quotas were used. And while both systems were to be preferred *overall* by a system of free trade, Canada had an interest in imposing quotas on Canadian lumber exporters rather than having the same export reduction accomplished by a U.S. tariff.

myeconlab

The trade dispute regarding Canada's softwood-lumber exports to the United States raged for almost 20 years. By 2006, a new agreement had been approved by the Canadian and U.S. governments. For details about the history, politics, and economics of this trade dispute, look for "The Continuing Saga of Softwood Lumber" in the *Additional Topics* section of this book's MyEconLab.

www.myeconlab.com

Trade-Remedy Laws and Nontariff Barriers

As tariffs in many countries were lowered over the years since the Second World War, countries that wished to protect domestic industries began using, and often abusing, a series of trade restrictions that came to be known as nontariff barriers (NTBs). The original purpose of some of these barriers was to remedy certain legitimate problems that arise in international trade and, for this reason, they are often called *trade-remedy laws*. All too often, however, such laws are misused to become potent means of simple protection.

dumping The practice of selling a commodity at a lower price in the export market than in the domestic market for reasons unrelated to differences in costs of servicing the two markets.

Dumping Selling a product in a foreign country at a lower price than in the domestic market is known as **dumping**. For example, if U.S.-made cars are sold for less in Canada than they are sold for in the United States, the U.S. automobile firms are said to be *dumping*. Dumping is a form of price discrimination studied in the theory of monopoly. Most governments have antidumping duties designed to protect their own industries against what is viewed as unfair foreign pricing practices.

Dumping, if it lasts indefinitely, can be a gift to the receiving country. Its consumers get goods from abroad at lower prices than they otherwise would.

Dumping is more often a temporary measure, designed to get rid of unwanted surpluses, or a predatory attempt to drive competitors out of business. In either case, domestic producers complain about unfair foreign competition. In both cases, it is accepted international practice to levy *antidumping duties* on foreign imports. These duties are designed to eliminate the discriminatory elements in their prices.

Unfortunately, antidumping laws have been evolving over the past three decades in ways that allow antidumping duties to become barriers to trade and competition rather than to provide redress for unfair trading practices.

Several features of the antidumping system that is now in place in many countries make it highly protectionist. First, any price discrimination between national markets is classified as dumping and is subject to penalties. Thus, prices in the producer's domestic market become, in effect, minimum prices below which no sales can be made in foreign markets, whatever the nature of demand in the domestic and foreign markets. Second, many countries' laws calculate the "margin of dumping" as the difference between the price that is charged in that country's market and the foreign producer's average cost. Thus, when there is a global slump in some industry so that the profit-maximizing price for all producers is below average cost, foreign producers can be convicted of dumping. This gives domestic producers enormous protection whenever the market price falls temporarily below average cost. Third, law in the United States (but not in all other countries) places the onus of proof on the accused. Facing a charge of dumping, a foreign producer must prove that the charge is unfounded. Fourth, U.S. antidumping duties are imposed with no time limit, so they often persist long after foreign firms have altered the prices that gave rise to them.

Antidumping laws were first designed to permit countries to respond to predatory pricing by foreign firms. More recently, they have been used to protect domestic firms against any foreign competition.

Countervailing Duties Countervailing duties, which are commonly used by the U.S. government but much less so elsewhere, provide another case in which a trade-remedy law can become a covert method of protection. The countervailing duty is designed to act as a means of creating a "level playing field" on which fair international competition can take place. Privately owned domestic firms rightly complain that they cannot compete against the seemingly bottomless purses of foreign governments. Subsidized foreign exports can be sold indefinitely at prices that would produce losses in the absence of the subsidy. The original object of countervailing duties was to counteract the effect on price of the presence of such foreign subsidies.

If a domestic firm suspects the existence of such a subsidy and registers a complaint, its government is required to make an investigation. For a countervailing duty to be levied, the investigation must determine, first, that the foreign subsidy to the specific industry in question does exist and, second, that it is large enough to cause significant injury to competing domestic firms.

Softwood lumber (spruce, pine, and fir) is extensively used in North America for the framing of houses and small buildings. For many years, the United States levied countervailing duties on Canadian softwood lumber exports, alleging that Canadian provinces unfairly subsidized production. In 2006, the Canadian and U.S. governments reached an agreement to end the dispute.

There is no doubt that countervailing duties have sometimes been used to counteract the effects of foreign subsidies. Many governments complain, however, that countervailing duties are often used as thinly disguised protection. At the early stages of the development of countervailing duties, only subsidies whose prime effect was to distort trade were possible objects of countervailing duties. Even then, however, the existence of equivalent domestic subsidies was not taken into account when decisions were made to put countervailing duties on subsidized imports. Thus, the United States levies some countervailing duties against foreign goods even though the foreign subsidy is less than the domestic subsidy. This does not create a level playing field.

Over time, the type of subsidy that is subject to countervailing duties has evolved until almost any government program that affects industry now risks becoming the object of a countervailing duty. Because all governments, including most U.S. state governments, have programs that provide direct or indirect assistance to industry, the potential for the use of countervailing duties as thinly disguised trade barriers is enormous.

The most well-known example in Canada of a U.S. countervailing duty is the 27-percent duty imposed between 2001 and 2005 on U.S. imports of Canadian softwood lumber. The U.S. justification for the duty was that Canadian provincial governments allegedly provided a subsidy to domestic lumber producers by charging artificially low *stumpage fees*—the fees paid by the companies to cut trees on Crown land. In 2006, the U.S. government agreed to eliminate the countervailing duty but only if restrictions were placed on Canadian lumber exports. Thus, a tariff was replaced by a combination of an export quota and an export tax.

34.3 CURRENT TRADE POLICY

In the remainder of the chapter, we discuss trade policy in practice. We start with the many international agreements that govern current trade policies and then look in a little more detail at the NAFTA.

Before 1947, any country was free to impose tariffs on its imports. However, when one country increased its tariffs, the action often triggered retaliatory actions by its trading partners. The 1930s saw a high-water mark of world protectionism as each country sought to raise its employment and output by raising its tariffs. The end result was lowered efficiency, less trade, but no more employment or income. Since the end of the Second World War, much effort has been devoted to reducing tariff barriers, both on a multilateral and on a regional basis.

The GATT and the WTO

One of the most notable achievements of the post-Second World War era was the creation of the General Agreement on Tariffs and Trade (GATT) in 1947. The GATT has since been replaced by the World Trade Organization (WTO). The principle of the GATT was that each member country agreed not to make unilateral tariff increases. This prevented the outbreak of "tariff wars" in which countries raised tariffs to protect particular domestic industries and to retaliate against other countries' tariff increases.

The Uruguay Round The Uruguay Round—the final round of trade agreements under GATT—was completed in 1994 after years of negotiations. It reduced world tariffs by about 40 percent. A significant failure of these negotiations was the absence of an agreement to liberalize trade in agricultural goods. The European Union and Canada both resisted an agreement in this area. The EU's Common Agricultural Policy (CAP) provides general support for most of its agricultural products, many of which are exported. The EU's position as a subsidized exporter causes major harm to agricultural producers in developing countries whose governments are too poor to compete with the EU in a subsidy war. Canada, which has free trade in many agricultural commodities, was concerned about maintaining its "supply management" over a number of industries including poultry, eggs, and dairy products. These schemes are administered by the provinces, who restrict domestic production and thus push domestic prices well above world levels. The federal government made such high domestic prices possible by imposing quotas on imports of these products at the national level.

Canada, the EU, and a number of other countries that lavishly protect some or all of their domestic agricultural producers were finally forced to agree to a plan to end all import quotas on agricultural products. In a process called "tariffication," these quotas were replaced by "tariff equivalents"—tariffs that restrict trade by the same amount as the quotas did. For example, a quota that restricted imports of some products to no more than 100 000 units per month and resulted in an increase in the domestic price by 20 percent was replaced by a tariff on that imported product of 20 percent. In the case of the Canadian poultry, egg, and dairy industries, some of the tariff equivalents were as high as several hundred percent, which illustrates the restrictiveness of the Canadian policy. The hope among countries that are pushing for freer trade in agricultural commodities is that pressure will build to reduce these very high tariffs over the next few decades.

Despite the failure to achieve free trade in agricultural products, the Uruguay Round is generally viewed as a success. Perhaps its most significant achievement was the creation of the World Trade Organization (WTO) to replace the GATT. An important part of the WTO is its formal dispute-settlement mechanism. This mechanism allows countries to take cases of alleged trade violations—such as illegal subsidies or tariffs—to the WTO for a formal ruling, and also obliges member countries to follow the ruling. The WTO's dispute-settlement mechanism is thus a significant step toward a "rules based" global trading system.

International trade negotiations sometimes generate considerable grass-roots opposition. There is some opposition to the reduction of tariffs in developed countries, and some controversy regarding the appropriate way to address the concerns of developing countries.

The Doha Round Agriculture also plays a central role in the current round of trade negotiations, which began in Doha, Qatar, in 2000. Many issues were discussed and negotiated in the period before the 2006 deadline, ranging from competition policy to antidumping and from environmental policies to electronic commerce. But one of the most contentious issues is agriculture. The WTO member governments claim to be committed to reducing export subsidies and other forms of government support to agriculture. Movements in this direction will naturally cause political friction within the developed economies that currently protect and support their agricultural producers, especially the United States and the European Union, which provide (by far) the most support to their farmers. A failure to reduce agricultural support in the developed countries, however, will increase the political frictions that already exist between developed and developing nations. For the many developing countries who have natural comparative advantages in agricultural products and who cannot afford to compete in a "subsidy war" with the developed countries, the liberalization of trade in agricultural products is crucial. They see the Doha round as central to their economic development.

At a set of WTO meetings in Cancún, Mexico, in September 2003, the developed countries began to backtrack on their commitment to reduce agricultural subsidies. In addition, the major developing countries, led by China, Brazil, and India, for the first time presented a united front and refused to back down on their position that further access to their own markets would not occur without significant cuts to agricultural subsidies by the rich countries. The Cancún meetings ended in a stalemate and many observers wondered how the Doha round would get back on track.

Late in 2005, another meeting in Hong Kong provided more positive results. Agreement was reached in principle to end all subsidies of agricultural exports by 2013, but the difficult bargaining over the all-important details was postponed. As this book went to press in the fall of 2006, there was still plenty of reason to be skeptical that a binding agreement to reduce agricultural subsidies would be reached.

myeconlab

Many countries, including Canada, provide generous financial support to their farmers and livestock producers. For some international comparisons of the generosity of agricultural subsidies, and for how these policies affect the ongoing WTO negotiations, look for "Farm Subsidies and the World Trade Organization" in the *Additional Topics* section of this book's MyEconLab.

www.myeconlab.com

Protests About the WTO Despite the successes of the WTO, it has its critics. In December 1999, trade ministers from the WTO member countries met in Seattle to set the agenda for what would become the Doha Round of trade negotiations. The Seattle meetings were delayed and interrupted by massive protests from environmental and labour groups, among others, who argued that the WTO's process of negotiating trade agreements pays insufficient attention to environmental and labour standards, especially in the developing countries. Many WTO officials and trade ministers, including those from the developing countries, recognized the importance of environmental and labour issues but questioned the wisdom of formally including these concerns in trade agreements. Reaching agreement on trade issues among the 155 (and growing) member countries of the WTO is difficult enough—it would be almost impossible if the issues were bundled with the even more contentious environmental and labour issues. The result would be an overall agreement that achieved very little in terms of either trade liberalization, environmental protection, or establishing labour standards. Instead, many trade officials argued that the existing International Labour Organization should be strengthened and a separate international organization like the WTO should be created to promote environmental issues. These organizations could then push ahead to achieve in their respective domains the same success that the GATT achieved over 50 years of negotiations.

Some of the protesters against the WTO process argue that paying greater attention to environmental and labour issues will improve the living standards in developing countries, where such standards typically fall far behind those in developed economies. One of the interesting ironies of the negotiations, however, is that the governments of the developing countries are among the strongest *opponents* of including environmental and labour issues in trade negotiations. They feel that developed countries would use stringent environmental and labour standards as a means of preventing imports from developing countries, thus protecting their own industries.

As it turned out, the work programme for the Doha Round includes very little on environmental issues and nothing on labour standards. Apparently, the view of the Doha negotiators was that many trade issues could usefully be discussed without getting embroiled in the very contentious but important environmental and labour issues. Perhaps the *next* round of WTO talks will include these broader issues.

For more information on the WTO, see its website at **www.wto.org**.

In any event, it seems a safe bet that these tensions between trade policy and environmental/labour policies will continue. At some point, further progress on trade liberalization will require that environmental and labour issues be addressed. Either domestic political pressures will push individual member countries to insist that these issues be included within the WTO negotiations, or other organizations like the WTO will be developed and/or strengthened to address the concerns. Whatever approach is followed, it appears that these will surely continue to be hot policy issues in the twenty-first century.

Applying Economic Concepts 34-1 addresses some of the often-heard criticisms of the WTO and argues that, as imperfect as the institution may be, it holds out much promise for continued progress in trade liberalization.

Regional Trade Agreements

Regional agreements seek to liberalize trade over a much smaller group of countries than the WTO membership. Three standard forms of regional trade-liberalizing agreements are *free trade areas, customs unions,* and *common markets.*

A **free trade area (FTA)** is the least comprehensive of the three. It allows for tariff-free trade among the member countries, but it leaves each member free to levy its own trade policy with respect to other countries. As a result, members must maintain customs points at their common borders to make sure that imports into the free trade area do not all enter through the member that is levying the lowest tariff on each item. They must also agree on *rules of origin* to establish when a good is made in a member country and hence is able to pass tariff-free across their borders, and when it is imported from outside the FTA and hence is subject to tariffs when it crosses borders within the FTA. The three countries in North America formed a free-trade area when they created the NAFTA in 1994. In 1997, Canada signed a bilateral FTA with Chile, and in 2001 negotiated an FTA with Costa Rica. It is currently in negotiations with Singapore.

free trade area (FTA) An agreement among two or more countries to abolish tariffs on trade among themselves while each remains free to set its own tariffs against other countries.

A **customs union** is a free trade area in which the member countries agree to establish a common trade policy with the rest of the world. Because they have a common trade policy, the members need neither customs controls on goods moving among themselves nor rules of origin. Once a good has entered any member country it has met the common rules and regulations and paid the common tariff and so it may henceforth be treated the same as a good that is produced within the union. An example of a customs union is Mercosur, an agreement linking Argentina, Brazil, Paraguay, and Uruguay.

customs union A group of countries who agree to have free trade among themselves and a common set of barriers against imports from the rest of the world.

A **common market** is a customs union that also has free movement of labour and capital among its members. The European Union is by far the most successful example of a common market. Indeed, the EU is now moving toward a full *economic union* in which all economic policies in the member countries are harmonized. The adoption of the euro as the EU's common currency in 1999 was a significant step in this direction.

common market A customs union with the added provision that labour and capital can move freely among the members.

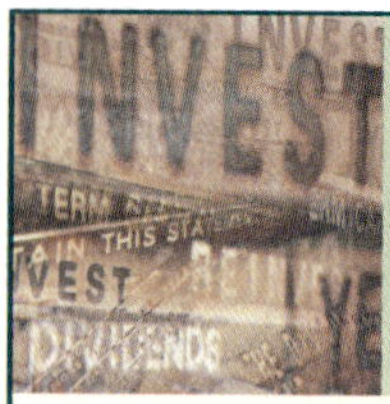

APPLYING ECONOMIC CONCEPTS 34-1

Should the WTO Be Abolished?

Globalization protesters often direct their wrath at the World Trade Organization. Extremists argue that all institutions supporting globalization should be abolished. Other critics admit that globalization is inevitable, but the WTO is so faulty in providing a rules-based system that it does more harm than good.

Supporters of the WTO argue that it is the best hope for poor countries who would be most oppressed in a lawless world where rich countries, particularly the United States and members of the European Union, could behave as they wished. Rather than allowing the poorer countries to flounder in a lawless world, the WTO provides a rules-based regime and has a dispute-settlement function that has heard more than 300 cases. Even if the rich countries do exert undue power over the negotiations, at least the WTO meetings provide a forum for poor nations to speak out and broker alliances. The alternative—no voice in a no-rules system—would be much worse.

Critics may respond that while the existence of the dispute-settlement mechanism may be beneficial, the enforcement of those settlements is undermined by disparities in economic power. Nations with large economies can use trade sanctions against small nations, but the small nation that attempts the same often inflicts the most harm on its own economy. Supporters of the WTO agree that this *is* a major defect, but the dispute-settlement mechanism has accomplished much, and to discard it because of imperfect enforcement would be a great loss. What is needed is *reform*—with larger economies agreeing to graduated enforcement mechanisms, including stiffer penalties for themselves.

Critics also claim that the WTO is a failure because it does not permit the imposition of trade sanctions against countries which pollute their own environments or exploit their own workers. But the poorest countries, many of whom are strong WTO supporters, fear that advanced countries would use environmental and labour standards written into the body of trade agreements as disguised non-tariff barriers. To the poorer countries it would be "policy imperialism" to argue that they should be forced to accept the standards of environmental and labour protection that the rich countries can only now afford.

Critics also complain that the WTO is undemocratic. In response, supporters point out that it is representatives of sovereign nations, usually elected ones, who conduct the negotiations, and that any agreements must be ratified by respective national parliaments before they come into effect. It is unlikely that any organization able to achieve agreement among 155 member-country governments could be any more democratic while still being effective.

Finally, some critics claim that the WTO is simply a tool for those who advocate a doctrinaire form of *laissez-faire* capitalism. It is true that some WTO supporters believe that unfettered free markets can meet all social requirements. A far larger number of supporters, however, believe that the market system needs government involvement if it is to meet societal needs for justice and growth. The vast majority of supporters agree that most, if not all, trade restrictions are harmful and that the WTO, with its mission of continued trade liberalization, can create significant benefits to rich and poor countries alike.

Trade Creation and Trade Diversion A major effect of regional trade liberalization is to reallocate resources. Economists divide these effects into two categories: *trade creation* and *trade diversion.* These concepts were first developed by Jacob Viner, a Canadian-born economist who taught at the University of Chicago and Princeton University and was a leading economic theorist in the first half of the twentieth century.

trade creation A consequence of reduced trade barriers among a set of countries whereby trade within the group is increased and trade with the rest of the world remains roughly constant.

Trade creation occurs when producers in one member country find that they can export to another member country as a result of the elimination of the tariffs. For example, when the North American Free Trade Agreement (NAFTA) eliminated most cross-border tariffs among Mexico, Canada, and the United States, some U.S. firms found that they could undersell their Canadian competitors in some product lines, and some Canadian firms found that they could undersell their U.S. competitors in other product lines. As a result, specialization occurred, and new international trade developed.

Trade creation represents efficient specialization according to comparative advantage.

Trade diversion occurs when exporters in one member country *replace* foreign exporters as suppliers to another member country. For example, trade diversion occurs when U.S. firms find that they can undersell competitors from the rest of the world in the Canadian market, not because they are the cheapest source of supply, but because their tariff-free prices under NAFTA are lower than the tariff-burdened prices of imports from other countries. This effect is a gain to U.S. firms and Canadian consumers of the product. U.S. firms get new business and therefore they clearly gain. Canadian consumers buy the product at a lower tariff-free price from the U.S. producer than they used to pay to the third-country producer (with a tariff), and so they are also better off. But Canada as a whole is worse off as a result of the trade diversion. Canada is now buying the product from a U.S. producer at a higher price with no tariff. Previous to the agreement, it was buying from a third-country producer at a lower price (and collecting tariff revenue).

trade diversion A consequence of reduced trade barriers among a set of countries whereby trade within the group replaces trade that used to take place with countries outside the group.

From the global perspective, trade diversion represents an inefficient use of resources.

One argument *against* regional trade agreements is that the costs of trade diversion may outweigh the benefits of trade creation. While recognizing this possibility, many economists believe that regional agreements, especially among only a few countries, are much easier to negotiate than multilateral agreements through the WTO. In addition, regional agreements may represent effective incremental progress in what is a very lengthy process of achieving global free trade.

The North American Free Trade Agreement

The NAFTA dates from 1994 and is an extension of the 1989 Canada–U.S. Free Trade Agreement (FTA). It is a free trade area and not a customs union; each country retains its own external trade policy, and rules of origin are needed to determine when a good is made within the NAFTA and thus allowed to move freely among the members.

National Treatment The fundamental principle that guides the NAFTA is the principle of *national treatment*. The principle of national treatment is that individual countries are free to establish any laws they wish, with the sole proviso that these laws must not discriminate on the basis of nationality. For example, Canada can have tough environmental laws, but it must enforce these laws equally on *all* firms located in Canada, independent of their nationality. In addition, Canada can have strict product standards, but it must enforce these equally on domestically produced and imported goods. The idea of national treatment is to allow a maximum of policy independence while preventing national policies from being used as trade barriers.

Other Major Provisions There are several other major provisions in NAFTA. First, all tariffs on trade between the United States and Canada were eliminated by 1999. Canada–Mexico and Mexico–U.S. tariffs are to be phased out by 2010. Also, a number of nontariff barriers are eliminated or restricted.

Second, the agreement guarantees national treatment to foreign investment once it enters a country while permitting each country to screen a substantial amount of inbound foreign investment before it enters.

Third, all existing measures that restrict trade and investment that are not explicitly removed by the agreement are "grandfathered," a term referring to the continuation of a practice that predates the agreement and would have been prohibited by the terms of the agreement were it not specifically exempted. This is probably the single most important departure from free trade under the NAFTA. Under it, a large collection of restrictive measures in each of the three countries are given indefinite life. An alternative would have been to "sunset" all of these provisions by negotiating dates at which each would be eliminated. From the point of view of long-term trade liberalization, even a 50-year extension would have been preferable to an indefinite exemption. In Canada, the main examples are supply-managed agricultural products and the cultural industries (both of which may be liberalized over time as a result of WTO negotiations).

For information about NAFTA, go to the website for the NAFTA Secretariat: **www.nafta-sec-alena.org**.

Fourth, trade in most nongovernmental services is liberalized by giving service firms the right of establishment in all member countries and the privilege of national treatment. There is also a limited opening of the markets in financial services to entry from firms based in the NAFTA countries.

Finally, a significant minority of government procurement is opened to cross-border bids.

Dispute Settlement From Canada's point of view, by far the biggest setback in the negotiations for the Canada–U.S. FTA was the failure to obtain agreement on a common regime for countervailing and antidumping duties. In view of that failure, no significant attempt was made to deal with this issue in the subsequent NAFTA negotiations. The U.S. Congress had been unwilling to abandon the unilateral use of these powerful weapons.

In the absence of such a multilateral regime, a NAFTA dispute-settlement mechanism was created. Under it, the justifications required for the levying of antidumping and countervailing duties are subject to review by a panel of Canadians, Americans, and Mexicans. This international review replaces appeal through the domestic courts. The panel has the power to suspend any duties until it is satisfied that the domestic laws have been correctly and fairly applied.

The establishment of the dispute-settlement mechanism in NAFTA was pathbreaking: For the first time in its history, the United States agreed to submit the administration of its domestic laws to *binding* scrutiny by an international panel that often contains a majority of foreigners.

Results The Canada–U.S. FTA aroused a great debate in Canada. Indeed, the Canadian federal election of 1988 was fought almost entirely on the issue of free trade. Supporters looked for major increases in the security of existing trade from U.S. protectionist attacks and for a growth of new trade. Detractors predicted a flight of firms to the United States, the loss of many Canadian jobs, and even the demise of Canada's political independence.

By and large, however, both the Canada–U.S. FTA and NAFTA agreements worked out just about as expected by their supporters. Industry restructured in the direction of greater export orientation in all three countries, and trade creation occurred. The flow of trade among the three countries increased markedly, but especially so between Canada and the United States. As the theory of trade predicts, specialization occurred in many areas, resulting in more U.S. imports of some product lines from Canada and more U.S. exports of other goods to Canada. In 1988, before the Canada–U.S. FTA took effect, Canada exported \$85 billion in goods to the United States, and imported \$74 billion from the United States. By 2005, the value of Canada–U.S. trade had more than quadrupled—Canadian exports of goods to the United States had increased to \$369 billion and imports from the United States had

APPLYING ECONOMIC CONCEPTS 34-2

Canadian Wine: A Free-Trade Success Story

Before the Canada–U.S. FTA was signed in 1989, great fears were expressed over the fate of the Canadian wine industry, located mainly in Ontario and British Columbia. It was heavily tariff protected and, with a few notable exceptions, concentrated mainly on cheap, low-quality products. Contrary to most people's expectations, rather than being decimated, the industry now produces a wide variety of high-quality products, some of which have won international competitions.

The nature of the pre-FTA protection largely explains the dramatic turnaround of the Canadian wine industry once the FTA took effect. First, Canadian wine producers were protected by high tariffs on imported wine, but were at the same time required by law to produce wine using only domestically grown grapes. The domestic grape growers, however, produced varieties of grapes not conducive to the production of high-quality wines, and with a captive domestic market, they had little incentive to change their behaviour. Thus, Canadian wine producers concentrated their efforts on "hiding" the attributes of poor-quality grapes rather than enhancing the attributes of high-quality grapes. The result was low-quality wine.

The second important aspect of the protection was that the high Canadian tariff was levied on a per unit rather than on an *ad valorem* basis. For example, the tariff was expressed as so many dollars per litre rather than as a specific percentage of the price. Charging a tariff by the litre gave most protection to the low quality wines with low value per litre. The higher the per-litre value of the wine, the lower the percentage tariff protection. For example, a $5-per-litre tariff would have the following effects. A low-quality imported wine valued at $5 per litre would have its price raised to $10, a 100 percent increase in price, whereas a higher quality imported wine valued at $25 per litre would have its price increased to $30, only a 20 percent increase in price.

Responding to these incentives, the Canadian industry concentrated on low-quality wines. The market for these wines was protected by the nearly prohibitive tariffs on competing low-quality imports, and also by the high prices charged for high-quality imports. In addition, protection was provided by many hidden charges that the various provincial governments' liquor monopolies levied in order to protect local producers.

When the tariff was removed under the FTA, the incentives were to move up-market, producing much more value per acre of land. Fortunately, much of the Canadian wine-growing land in the Okanagan Valley in B.C. and the Niagara Peninsula in Ontario is well-suited for growing the grapes required for good wines. Within a very few years, and with some government assistance to grape growers to make the transition from low-quality to high-quality grapes, Canadian wines were competing effectively with imported products in the medium-quality range. B.C. and Ontario wines do not yet reach the quality of major French wines in the $50–$70 (per bottle) range but they compete very effectively in quality with wines in the $15–$25 range, and sometimes even higher up the quality scale.

The success of the wine industry is a fine example of how tariffs can distort incentives and push an industry into a structure that makes it dependent on the tariff. Looking at the pre-FTA industry, very few people suspected that it would be able to survive, let alone produce a world-class product.

Prior to the FTA, the nature of protection encouraged the production of low-quality grapes and wine in Canada. The reduction in tariffs brought about by the FTA led to a successful restructuring of the Canadian wine industry.

increased to $260 billion. (Note that these figures exclude trade in services; with services included, the increase in Canada–U.S. trade between 1988 and 2005 would be even larger.)

It is hard to say how much trade diversion there has been and will be in the future. The greatest potential for trade diversion is with Mexico, which competes in the U.S. and Canadian markets with a large number of products produced in other low-wage countries. Southeast Asian exporters to the United States and Canada have been worried that Mexico would capture some of their markets by virtue of having tariff-free access denied to their goods. Most estimates predict, however, that trade creation will dominate over trade diversion.

Most transitional difficulties were initially felt in each country's import-competing industries, just as theory predicts. An agreement such as the NAFTA brings its advantages by encouraging a movement of resources out of protected but inefficient import-competing industries, which decline, and into efficient export industries, which expand because they have better access to the markets of other member countries. Southern Ontario and parts of Quebec had difficulties as some traditional exports fell and labour and capital were shifting to sectors where trade was expanding. By the late 1990s, however, Southern Ontario was booming again and its most profitable sectors were those that exported to the United States.

There were also some pleasant surprises resulting from free trade. Two Canadian industries that many economists expected to suffer from the FTA and NAFTA were winemaking and textiles. Yet both of these industries prospered as Canadian firms improved quality, productivity, and benefited from increased access to the huge U.S. market. *Applying Economic Concepts 34-2* discusses the success of the Canadian wine industry after the tariffs on wine were eliminated.

Finally, the dispute-settlement mechanism seems to have worked well. A large number of disputes have arisen and have been referred to panels. (Interested readers can read updated accounts of settled and ongoing disputes on the website for the Department of Foreign Affairs and International Trade at **www.dfait.gc.ca**.) Panel members have usually reacted as professionals rather than as nationals. Most cases have been decided on their merits; allegations that decisions were reached on national rather than professional grounds have been rare.

SUMMARY

34.1 FREE TRADE OR PROTECTION?

LO 1 2

- The case for free trade is that world output of all products can be higher under free trade than when protectionism restricts regional specialization.
- Trade protection may be advocated to promote economic diversification or to provide protection for specific groups. The cost of such protection is lower average living standards.
- Protection can also be urged on the grounds that it may lead to higher living standards for the protectionist country than would a policy of free trade. Such a result might come about by using a monopoly position to influence the terms of trade or by developing a dynamic comparative advantage by allowing inexperienced or uneconomically small industries to become efficient enough to compete with foreign industries.
- Some fallacious protectionist arguments are that (a) mutually advantageous trade is impossible because one trader's gain must always be the other's loss; (b) buying abroad sends our money abroad, while buying at home keeps our money at home; (c) our high-paid workers must be protected against the competition from low-paid foreign workers; and (d) imports are to be discouraged because they reduce national income and cause unemployment.

34.2 METHODS OF PROTECTION

LO 3 4

- A tariff raises the domestic price of the imported product and leads to a reduction in the level of imports. Domestic consumers lose and domestic producers gain. The overall effect of a tariff is a deadweight loss for the importing country.
- A quota (or voluntary export restriction) restricts the amount of imports and thus drives up the domestic price of the good. Domestic consumers lose and domestic producers gain. The overall effect is a *larger* deadweight loss than with a tariff because, rather than the importing country collecting tariff revenue, foreign producers benefit from a higher price.
- Antidumping and countervailing duties, although providing legitimate restraints on unfair trading practices, are often used as serious barriers to trade.

34.3 CURRENT TRADE POLICY

LO 5 6

- The General Agreement on Tariffs and Trade (GATT), under which countries agreed to reduce trade barriers through multilateral negotiations and not to raise them unilaterally, has greatly reduced world tariffs since its inception in 1947.
- The World Trade Organization (WTO) was created in 1995 as the successor to GATT. It has 155 member countries and contains a formal dispute-settlement mechanism.
- Regional trade-liberalizing agreements such as free trade areas and common markets bring efficiency gains through trade creation and efficiency losses through trade diversion.
- The North American Free Trade Agreement (NAFTA) is the world's largest and most successful free trade area, and the European Union is the world's largest and most successful common market.
- NAFTA is based on the principle of "national treatment." This allows Canada, the United States, and Mexico to implement whatever social, economic, or environmental policies they choose providing that such policies treat foreign and domestic firms (and their products) equally.

KEY CONCEPTS

Free trade and protectionism
Tariffs and import quotas
Voluntary export restrictions (VERs)
Countervailing and antidumping duties
The General Agreement on Tariffs and Trade (GATT)
The World Trade Organization (WTO)
Common markets, customs unions, and free trade areas
Trade creation and trade diversion
Nontariff barriers
The North American Free Trade Agreement (NAFTA)

STUDY EXERCISES

1. Fill in the blanks to make the following statements correct.
   a. The __________ argument provided the rationale for Canada's National Policy of 1876. A high tariff wall allowed many Canadian industries to develop where they may not have been able to compete otherwise.
   b. Advertisements that encourage us to "buy Canadian" are promoting a(n) __________ argument for protection. The reason is that money spent on imported goods must ultimately be spent on __________ goods and services anyway.
   c. Fallacious arguments for protection usually come from a misunderstanding of the gains from __________ or from the misbelief that protection can increase total __________.
2. Fill in the blanks to make the following statements correct.
   a. A tariff imposed on the import of leather shoes will cause a(n) __________ in the domestic price. Total quantity of leather shoes sold in Canada will __________. Domestic (Canadian) production of leather shoes will __________ and the quantity of shoes imported will __________.

b. The beneficiaries of the tariff described above are __________ because they receive a higher price for the same good and __________ because they receive tariff revenue. The parties that are clearly worse off are __________ because they now pay a higher price for the same good, and __________ because they sell less in the Canadian market.

c. The overall effect of a tariff on the importing country is a(n) __________ in welfare. The tariff creates a(n) __________ loss for the economy.

d. Suppose an import quota restricted the import of leather shoes into Canada to 20 000 pairs per year when the free trade imported amount was 40 000 pairs. The domestic price will __________, total quantity sold in Canada will __________, and domestic production will __________.

e. The beneficiaries of the quota described above are __________ and __________ because they both receive a higher price in the Canadian market. The party that is clearly worse off is __________ because they are now paying a higher price.

f. The overall effect of an import quota on the importing country is a(n) __________ in welfare. The quota imposes a(n) __________ loss for the economy.

3. Fill in the blanks to make the following statements correct.

a. A regional trade agreement such as NAFTA, or a common market such as the European Union, allows for __________, whereby trade within the group of member countries is increased.

b. A regional trade agreement such as NAFTA, or a common market such as the European Union, also results in __________, whereby trade within the group of member countries replaces trade previously done with other __________.

c. The fundamental principle that guides NAFTA is the principle of __________, which means that any member country can implement the policies of its choosing, as long as __________ and __________ firms are treated equally.

4. Canada produces steel domestically and also imports it from abroad. Assume that the world market for steel is competitive and that Canada is a small producer, unable to affect the world price. Since Canada imports steel, we know that in the absence of trade, the Canadian equilibrium price would exceed the world price.

a. Draw a diagram showing the Canadian market for steel, with imports at the world price.

b. Explain why the imposition of a tariff on imported steel will increase the price of steel in Canada.

c. Who benefits and who is harmed by such a tariff? Show these effects in your diagram.

5. myeconlab The diagram below shows the Canadian market for leather shoes, which we assume to be competitive. The world price is p_w. If the Canadian government imposes a tariff of t dollars per unit, the domestic price then rises to $p_w + t$.

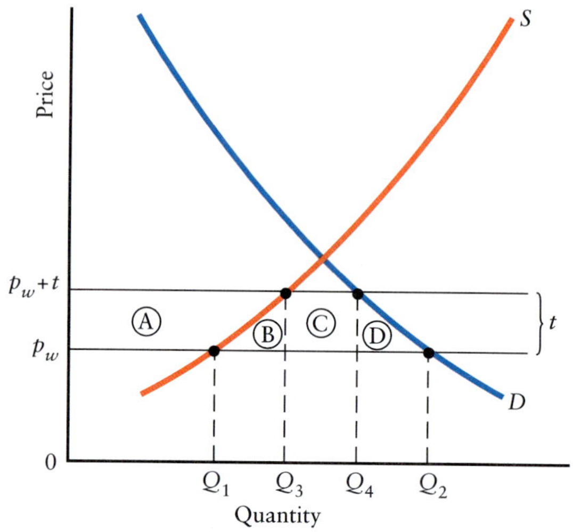

a. What quantity of leather shoes is imported before the tariff is imposed? After the tariff?

b. What is the effect of the tariff on the Canadian production of shoes? Which areas in the diagram show the increase in domestic producer surplus?

c. Which areas in the diagram show the reduction in domestic consumer surplus as a result of the higher Canadian price?

d. The Canadian government earns tariff revenue on the imported shoes. Which area in the diagram shows this tariff revenue?

6. Use the diagram from Question 5 to analyze the effects of imposing an import quota instead of a tariff to protect domestic shoe producers. Draw the diagram as in Question 5 and answer the following questions.

a. Explain why an import quota of Q_3Q_4 raises the domestic price to $p_w + t$.

b. With import quotas, the Canadian government earns no tariff revenue. Who gets this money now?

c. Is the import quota better or worse than the tariff for Canada as a whole? Explain.

7. Under pressure from the Canadian and U.S. governments in the early 1980s, Japanese automobile producers agreed to restrict their exports to the North American market. After the formal agreement ended, the Japanese producers decided unilaterally to continue restricting their exports. Carefully review Figure 34-2 and then answer the following questions.

a. Explain why such Voluntary Export Restrictions (VERs) are "voluntary."

b. Explain why an agreement to export only 100 000 cars to North America is better for the Japanese producers than a North American tariff that results in the same volume of Japanese exports.
c. Who is paying for these benefits to the Japanese producers?

8. Go to Statistics Canada's website: **www.statcan.ca.** Go to "Canadian Statistics," type in "international trade," and answer the following questions.

a. For the most recent year shown, what was the value of Canada's exports to the United States? To the European Union?
b. For the same year, what was the value of Canada's imports from the United States? From the European Union?
c. Compute what economists call the "volume of trade" (the sum of exports and imports) between Canada and the United States. How has the volume of trade grown over the past five years? Has trade grown faster than national income?

9. myeconlab The table below shows the prices *in Canada* of cotton towels produced in the United States, Canada, and Malaysia. Suppose cotton towels are identical.

Producing Country	Canadian Price (in $) Without Tariff`	Canadian Price (in $) With 20% Tariff
Canada	4.75	4.75
United States	4.50	5.40
Malaysia	4.00	4.80

a. Suppose Canada imposes a 20 percent tariff on imported towels from any country. Assuming that Canadians purchase only the lowest-price towels, from which country will Canada buy its towels?
b. Now suppose Canada eliminates tariffs on towels from all countries. Which towels will Canada now buy?
c. Canada and the United States now negotiate a free-trade agreement that eliminates all tariffs between the two countries, but Canada maintains the 20 percent tariff on other countries. Which towels now get imported into Canada?
d. Which of the situations described above is called trade creation and which is called trade diversion?

DISCUSSION QUESTIONS

1. Some Canadians opposed Canada's entry into NAFTA on the grounds that Canadian firms could not compete with the goods produced by cheap Mexican labour. Comment on the following points in relation to the above worries:

a. "Mexicans are the most expensive cheap labour I have ever encountered"—statement by the owner of a Canadian firm that is moving back to Canada from Mexico.
b. The theory of the gains from trade says that a high-productivity, high-wage country can gain from trading with a low-wage, low-productivity country.
c. Technological change is rapidly reducing labour costs as a proportion of total costs in many products; in many industries that use high-tech production methods this proportion is already well below 20 percent.

2. Should Canada and the United States trade with countries with poor human rights records? If trade with China is severely restricted because of its lack of respect for human rights, who will be the gainers and who the losers? Argue the cases that this policy will help, and that it will hinder, human rights progress in China.

3. Import quotas and voluntary export restrictions are often used instead of tariffs. What real difference, if any, is there between quotas, voluntary export restrictions (VERs), and tariffs? Explain why lobbyists for some import-competing industries (cheese, milk, shoes) support import quotas while lobbyists for others (pizza manufacturers, soft drink manufacturers, retail stores) oppose them. Would you expect labour unions to support or oppose quotas?

4. Over the past several years, many foreign automobile producers have built production and assembly facilities in Canada. What are some advantages and disadvantages associated with shifting production from, for example, Japan to Canada? Will these cars still be considered "imports"? What is beginning to happen to the definitions of "foreign made" and "domestic made"?

5. Consider a mythical country called Forestland, which exports a large amount of lumber to a nearby country called Houseland. The lumber industry in Houseland has convinced its federal government that it is being harmed by the low prices being charged by the lumber producers in Forestland. You are an advisor to the government in Forestland. Explain who gains and who loses from each of the following policies.

a. Houseland imposes a tariff on lumber imports from Forestland
b. Forestland imposes a tax on each unit of lumber exported to Houseland
c. Forestland agrees to restrict its exports of lumber to Houseland
d. Which policy is likely to garner the most political support in Houseland? In Forestland?

6. In March 1999, the Canadian government imposed antidumping duties of up to 43 percent on hot-rolled steel imports from France, Russia, Slovakia, and Romania. The allegation was that these countries were dumping steel into the Canadian market.
   a. Who benefits from such alleged dumping? Who is harmed?
   b. Who benefits from the imposition of the antidumping duties? Who is harmed?
   c. Is Canada as a whole made better off by the imposition of the duties? Explain.

Mathematical Notes

1. Because one cannot divide by zero, the ratio $\Delta Y/\Delta X$ cannot be evaluated when $\Delta X = 0$. However, as ΔX *approaches* zero, the ratio $\Delta Y/\Delta X$ increases without limit:

$$\lim_{\Delta X \to 0} \frac{\Delta Y}{\Delta X} = \infty$$

Therefore, we say that the slope of a vertical line (when $\Delta X = 0$ for any ΔY) is equal to infinity. (p. 39)

2. Many variables affect the quantity demanded. Using functional notation, the argument of the next several pages of the text can be anticipated. Let Q^D represent the quantity of a commodity demanded and

$$T, \overline{Y}, N, \hat{Y}, p, p_j$$

represent, respectively, tastes, average household income, population, income distribution, the commodity's own price, and the price of the *j*th other commodity.

The demand function is

$$Q^D = D(T, \overline{Y}, N, \hat{Y}, p, p_j), \qquad j = 1, 2, \ldots, n$$

The demand schedule or curve is given by

$$Q^D = d(p) \Big|_{T, \overline{Y}, N, \hat{Y}, p_j}$$

where the notation means that the variables to the right of the vertical line are held constant.

This function is correctly described as the demand function with respect to price, all other variables being held constant. This function, often written concisely as $Q^D = d(p)$, shifts in response to changes in other variables. Consider average income: if, as is usually hypothesized, $\partial Q^D/\partial \overline{Y} > 0$, then increases in average income shift $Q^D = d(p)$ rightward and decreases in average income shift $Q^D = d(p)$ leftward. Changes in other variables likewise shift this function in the direction implied by the relationship of that variable to the quantity demanded. (p. 48)

3. Quantity demanded is a simple and straightforward but frequently misunderstood concept in everyday use, but it has a clear mathematical meaning. It refers to the dependent variable in the demand function from note 2:

$$Q^D = D(T, \overline{Y}, N, \hat{Y}, p, p_j)$$

It takes on a specific value whenever a specific value is assigned to each of the independent variables. The value of Q^D changes whenever the value of any independent variable is changed. Q^D could change, for example, as a result of a change in any one price, in average income, in the distribution of income, in tastes, or in population. It could also change as a result of the net effect of changes in all of the independent variables occurring at once.

Some textbooks reserve the term *change in quantity demanded* for a movement along a demand curve, that is, a change in Q^D as a result *only* of a change in p. They then use other words for a change in Q^D caused by a change in the other variables in the demand function. This usage is potentially confusing because it gives the single variable Q^D more than one name.

Our usage, which corresponds to that in more advanced treatments, avoids this confusion. We call Q^D *quantity demanded* and refer to any change in Q^D as a *change in quantity demanded*. In this usage it is correct to say that a movement along a demand curve is a change in quantity demanded, but it is incorrect to say that a change in quantity demanded can occur *only because of* a movement along a demand curve (because Q^D can change for other reasons, for example, a *ceteris paribus* change in average household income). (p. 55)

4. Similar to the way we treated quantity demanded in note 2, let Q^S represent the quantity of a commodity supplied and

$$C, X, p, w_i$$

represent, respectively, producers' goals, technology, the product's price, and the price of the *i*th input.

The supply function is

$$Q^S = S(C, X, p, w_i), \qquad i = 1, 2, \ldots, m$$

The supply schedule or curve is given by

$$Q^S = s(p) \Big|_{C, X, w_i}$$

This is the supply function with respect to price, all other variables being held constant. This function, often written concisely as $Q^S = s(p)$, shifts in response to changes in other variables. (p. 56)

5. Equilibrium occurs where $Q^D = Q^S$. For *specified values of all other variables,* this requires that

$$d(p) = s(p) \qquad [5.1]$$

Equation 5.1 defines an equilibrium value of p; hence, although p is an *independent* or *exogenous* variable in each of the supply and demand functions, it is an *endogenous* variable in the economic model that imposes the equilibrium condition expressed in Equation 5.1. Price is endogenous because it is assumed to adjust to bring about equality between quantity demanded and quantity supplied. Equilibrium quantity, also an endogenous variable, is determined by substituting the equilibrium price into either $d(p)$ or $s(p)$.

Graphically, Equation 5.1 is satisfied only at the point where the demand and supply curves intersect. Thus, supply and demand curves are said to determine the equilibrium values of the endogenous variables, price and quantity. A shift in any of the independent variables held constant in the d and s functions will shift the demand or supply curves and lead to different equilibrium values for price and quantity. (p. 62)

6. The axis reversal arose in the following way. Alfred Marshall (1842–1924) theorized in terms of "demand price" and "supply price," these being the prices that would lead to a given quantity being demanded or supplied. Thus,

$$p^D = d(Q) \qquad [6.1]$$

$$p^S = s(Q) \qquad [6.2]$$

and the condition of equilibrium is

$$d(Q) = s(Q)$$

When graphing the behavioural relationships expressed in Equations 6.1 and 6.2, Marshall naturally put the independent variable, Q, on the horizontal axis.

Leon Walras (1834–1910), whose formulation of the working of a competitive market has become the accepted one, focused on quantity demanded and quantity supplied *at a given price.* Thus,

$$Q^D = d(p)$$

$$Q^S = s(p)$$

and the condition of equilibrium is

$$d(p) = s(p)$$

Walras did not use graphical representation. Had he done so, he would surely have placed p (his independent variable) on the horizontal axis.

Marshall, among his other influences on later generations of economists, was the great popularizer of graphical analysis in economics. Today, we use his graphs, even for Walras's analysis. The axis reversal is thus one of those historical accidents that seem odd to people who did not live through the "perfectly natural" sequence of steps that produced it. (p. 62)

7. The definition in the text uses finite changes and is called *arc elasticity.* The parallel definition using derivatives is

$$\eta = \frac{dQ}{dp} \cdot \frac{p}{Q}$$

and is called *point elasticity.* Further discussion appears in the Appendix to Chapter 4. (p. 76)

8. The propositions in the text are proved as follows. Letting TE stand for total expenditure, we can write

$$TE = p \cdot Q$$

It follows that the change in total expenditure is

$$dTE = Q \cdot dp + p \cdot dQ \qquad [8.1]$$

Multiplying and dividing both terms on the right-hand side of Equation 8.1 by $p \cdot Q$ yields

$$dTE = \left[\frac{dp}{p} + \frac{dQ}{Q}\right] \cdot (p \cdot Q)$$

Because dp and dQ are opposite in sign as we move along the demand curve, dTE will have the same sign as the term in brackets on the right-hand side that dominates—that is, on which percentage change is largest.

A second way of arranging Equation 8.1 is to divide both sides by dp to get

$$\frac{dTE}{dp} = Q + p \cdot \frac{dQ}{dp} \qquad [8.2]$$

From the definition of point elasticity in note 7, however,

$$Q \cdot \eta = p \cdot \frac{dQ}{dp} \qquad [8.3]$$

which we can substitute into Equation 8.1 to obtain

$$\frac{dTE}{dp} = Q + Q \cdot \eta = Q \cdot (1 + \eta) \qquad [8.4]$$

Because η is a negative number, the sign of the right-hand side of Equation 8.4 is negative if the absolute value of η exceeds unity (elastic demand) and positive if it is less than unity (inelastic demand).

Total expenditure is maximized when dTE/dp is equal to zero. As can be seen from Equation 8.4, this occurs when elasticity is equal to -1. (p. 80)

9. The distinction made between an incremental change and a marginal change is the distinction for the function $Y = Y(X)$ between $\Delta Y/\Delta X$ and the derivative dY/dX. The latter is the limit of the former as ΔX approaches zero. We shall meet this distinction repeatedly—in this chapter in reference to marginal and incremental *utility* and in later chapters with respect to such concepts as marginal and incremental *product, cost,* and *revenue.* Where Y is a function of more than one variable—for example, $Y = f(X,Z)$—the marginal relationship between Y and X is the partial derivative $\partial Y/\partial X$ rather than the total derivative, dY/dX. (p. 117)

10. The hypothesis of diminishing marginal utility requires that we can measure utility of consumption by a function

$$U = U(X_1, X_2, \ldots, X_n)$$

where $X_1, \ldots, X_n$ are quantities of the n goods consumed by a household. It really embodies two utility hypotheses: first,

$$\partial U/\partial X_i > 0$$

which says that the consumer can get more utility by increasing consumption of the commodity; second,

$$\partial^2 U/\partial X_i^2 < 0$$

which says that the utility of *additional* consumption of some good declines as the amount of that good consumed increases. (p. 118)

11. Because the slope of the indifference curve is negative, it is the absolute value of the slope that declines as one moves downward to the right along the curve. The algebraic value, of course, increases. The phrase *diminishing marginal rate of substitution* thus refers to the absolute, not the algebraic, value of the slope. (p. 136)

12. The relationship between the slope of the budget line and relative prices can be seen as follows. In the two-good example, a change in expenditure (ΔE) is given by the equation

$$\Delta E = p_C \cdot \Delta C + p_F \cdot \Delta F \qquad [12.1]$$

Expenditure is constant for all combinations of F and C that lie on the same budget line. Thus, along such a line we have $\Delta E = 0$. This implies

$$p_C \cdot \Delta C + p_F \cdot \Delta F = 0 \qquad [12.2]$$

and thus

$$\Delta C/\Delta F = -p_F/p_C \qquad [12.3]$$

The ratio $\Delta C/\Delta F$ is the slope of the budget line. It is negative because, with a fixed budget, one must consume less C in order to consume more F. In other words, Equation 12.3 says that the negative of the slope of the budget line is the ratio of the absolute prices (i.e., the relative price). Although prices do not show directly in Figure 6A-3, they are implicit in the budget line: Its slope depends solely on the relative price, while its position, given a fixed money income, depends on the absolute prices of the two goods. (p. 138)

13. *Marginal product,* as defined in the text, is really *incremental* product. More advanced treatments distinguish between this notion and marginal product as the limit of the ratio as ΔL approaches zero. Marginal product thus measures the rate at which total product is changing as one factor is varied and

is the partial derivative of the total product with respect to the variable factor. In symbols,

$$MP = \frac{\partial TP}{\partial L}$$

(p. 156)

14. We have referred specifically both to diminishing *marginal* product and to diminishing *average* product. In most cases, eventually diminishing marginal product implies eventually diminishing average product. This is, however, not necessary, as the accompanying figure shows.

In this case, marginal product diminishes after v units of the variable factor are employed. Because marginal product falls toward, but never quite reaches, a value of m, average product rises continually toward, but never quite reaches, the same value. (p. 157)

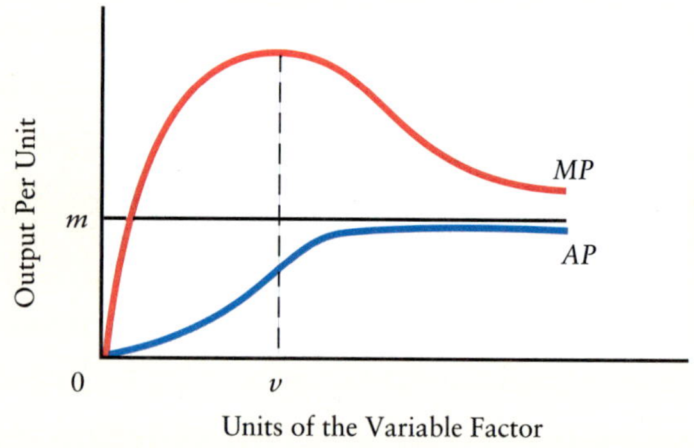

15. Let Q be the quantity of output and L the quantity of the variable factor. In the short run,

$$TP = Q = f(L) \qquad [15.1]$$

We now define

$$AP = \frac{Q}{L} = \frac{f(L)}{L} \qquad [15.2]$$

$$MP = \frac{dQ}{dL} \qquad [15.3]$$

We are concerned with the relationship between AP and MP. Where average product is rising, at a maximum, or falling is determined by its derivative with respect to L:

$$\frac{d(Q/L)}{dL} = \frac{L \cdot (dQ/dL) - Q}{L^2} \qquad [15.4]$$

This may be rewritten

$$\frac{1}{L} \cdot \left[\frac{dQ}{dL} - \frac{Q}{L}\right] = \frac{1}{L} \cdot (MP - AP) \qquad [15.5]$$

Clearly, when MP is greater than AP, the expression in Equation 15.5 is positive and thus AP is rising. When MP is less than AP, AP is falling. When they are equal, AP is neither rising nor falling. (p. 158)

16. The text defines *incremental cost.* Strictly, marginal cost is the rate of change of total cost with respect to output, Q. Thus,

$$MC = \frac{dTC}{dQ}$$

From the definitions, $TC = TFC + TVC$. Fixed costs are not a function of output. Thus, we may write $TC = Z + f(Q)$, where $f(Q)$ is total variable costs and Z is a constant. From this we see that $MC = df(Q)/dQ$. MC is thus independent of the size of the fixed costs. (p. 160)

17. This point is easily seen if a little algebra is used:

$$AVC = \frac{TVC}{Q}$$

but note that $TVC = L \cdot w$ and $Q = AP \cdot L$, where L is the quantity of the variable factor used and w is its cost per unit. Therefore,

$$AVC = \frac{L \cdot w}{AP \cdot L} = \frac{w}{AP}$$

Because w is a constant, it follows that AVC and AP vary inversely with each other, and when AP is at its maximum value, AVC must be at its minimum value. (p. 162)

18. A little elementary calculus will prove the point:

$$MC = \frac{dTC}{dQ} = \frac{dTVC}{dQ} = \frac{d(L \cdot w)}{dQ}$$

If w does not vary with output,

$$MC = \frac{dL}{dQ} \cdot w$$

However, referring to note 15 (Equation 15.3), we see that

$$\frac{dL}{dQ} = \frac{1}{MP}$$

Thus,

$$MC = \frac{w}{MP}$$

Because w is fixed, MC varies negatively with MP. When MP is at a maximum, MC is at a minimum. (p. 163)

19. Strictly speaking, the marginal rate of substitution refers to the slope of the tangent to the isoquant at a particular point, whereas the calculations in Table 8A-1 refer to the average rate of substitution between two distinct points on the isoquant. Assume a production function

$$Q = Q(K, L) \qquad [19.1]$$

Isoquants are given by the function

$$K = I(L, \overline{Q}) \qquad [19.2]$$

derived from Equation 19.1 by expressing K as an explicit function of L and Q. A single isoquant relates to a particular level of output, $\overline{Q}$. Define Q_K and Q_L as an alternative, more compact notation for $\partial Q/\partial K$ and $\partial Q/\partial L$, the marginal products of capital and labour. Also, let Q_{KK} and Q_{LL} stand for $\partial^2 Q/\partial K^2$ and $\partial^2 Q/\partial L^2$, respectively. To obtain the slope of the isoquant, totally differentiate Equation 19.1 to obtain

$$dQ = Q_K \cdot dK + Q_L \cdot dL$$

Then, because we are moving along a single isoquant, set $dQ = 0$ to obtain

$$\frac{dK}{dL} = -\frac{Q_L}{Q_K} = MRS$$

Diminishing marginal productivity implies $Q_{LL} < 0$ and $Q_{KK} < 0$, and hence, as we move down the isoquant of Figure 8A-1, Q_K is rising and Q_L is falling, so the absolute value of MRS is diminishing. This is called the *hypothesis of a diminishing marginal rate of substitution.* (p. 186)

20. Formally, the problem is to choose K and L in order to maximize

$$Q = Q(K, L)$$

subject to the constraint

$$p_K \cdot K + p_L \cdot L = C$$

To do this, form the Lagrangean,

$$\mathfrak{L} = Q(K, L) - \lambda(p_K \cdot K + p_L \cdot L - C)$$

where λ is called the Lagrange multiplier.

The first-order conditions for this maximization problem are

$$Q_K = \lambda \cdot p_K \qquad [20.1]$$

$$Q_L = \lambda \cdot p_L \qquad [20.2]$$

$$p_K \cdot K + p_L \cdot L = C \qquad [20.3]$$

Dividing Equation 20.1 by Equation 20.2 yields

$$\frac{Q_K}{Q_L} = \frac{p_K}{p_L}$$

That is, the ratio of the marginal products, which is -1 times the MRS, is equal to the ratio of the factor prices, which is -1 times the slope of the isocost line. (p. 188)

21. Marginal revenue is mathematically the derivative of total revenue with respect to output, dTR/dQ. Incremental revenue is $\Delta TR/\Delta Q$. However, the term *marginal revenue* is used loosely to refer to both concepts. (p. 195)

22. For notes 22 through 24, it is helpful first to define some terms. Let

$$\pi_n = TR_n - TC_n$$

where π_n is the profit when Q_n units are sold.

If the firm is maximizing its profits by producing Q_n units, it is necessary that its profits be at least as large as the profits at output zero. That is,

$$\pi_n \geq \pi_0 \qquad [22.1]$$

The condition says that profits from producing must be greater than profits from not producing. Condition 22.1 can be rewritten as

$$TR_n - TVC_n - TFC_n \geq TR_0 - TVC_0 - TFC_0 \qquad [22.2]$$

However, note that by definition

$$TR_0 = 0 \quad [22.3]$$

$$TVC_0 = 0 \quad [22.4]$$

$$TFC_n = TFC_0 = Z \quad [22.5]$$

where Z is a constant. By substituting Equations 22.3, 22.4, and 22.5 into Condition 22.2, we get

$$TR_n - TVC_n \geq 0$$

from which we obtain

$$TR_n \geq TVC_n$$

This proves Rule 1.

On a per-unit basis, it becomes

$$\frac{TR_n}{Q_n} \geq \frac{TVC_n}{Q_n} \quad [22.6]$$

where Q_n is the number of units produced.

Because $TR_n = Q_n \cdot p_n$, where p_n is the price when n units are sold, Condition 22.6 may be rewritten as

$$p_n \geq AVC_n$$

(p. 198)

23. Using elementary calculus, we may prove Rule 2.

$$\pi_n = TR_n - TC_n$$

each of which is a function of output Q. To maximize π, it is necessary that

$$\frac{d\pi}{dQ} = 0 \quad [23.1]$$

and that

$$\frac{d^2\pi}{dQ^2} < 0 \quad [23.2]$$

From the definitions,

$$\frac{d\pi}{dQ} = \frac{dTR}{dQ} - \frac{dTC}{dQ} = MR - MC \quad [23.3]$$

From Equations 23.1 and 23.3, a necessary condition for attaining maximum π is $MR - MC = 0$, or $MR = MC$, as is required by Rule 2. (p. 199)

24. To prove that for a negatively sloped demand curve, marginal revenue is less than price, let $p = p(Q)$. Then

$$TR = p \cdot Q = p(Q) \cdot Q$$

$$MR = \frac{dTR}{dQ} = Q \cdot \frac{dp}{dQ} + p$$

For a negatively sloped demand curve, dp/dQ is negative, and thus MR is less than price for positive values of Q. (p. 219)

25. The equation for a downward-sloping straight-line demand curve with price on the vertical axis is

$$p = a - b \cdot Q$$

where $-b$ is the slope of the demand curve. Total revenue is price times quantity:

$$TR = p \cdot Q = a \cdot Q - b \cdot Q^2$$

Marginal revenue is

$$MR = \frac{dTR}{dQ} = a - 2 \cdot b \cdot Q$$

Thus, the MR curve and the demand curve are both straight lines, and the (absolute value of the) slope of the MR curve ($2b$) is twice that of the demand curve (b). (p. 220)

26. The marginal revenue produced by the factor involves two elements: first, the additional output that an extra unit of the factor produces and, second, the change in price of the product that the extra output causes. Let Q be output, R revenue, and L the number of units of the variable factor hired. The contribution to revenue of additional labour is $\partial R/\partial L$. This, in turn, depends on the contribution of the extra labour to output $\partial Q/\partial L$ (the marginal product of the factor) and $\partial R/\partial Q$ (the firm's marginal revenue from the extra output). Thus,

$$\frac{\partial R}{\partial L} = \frac{\partial Q}{\partial L} \cdot \frac{\partial R}{\partial Q}$$

We define the left-hand side as marginal revenue product, MRP. Thus,

$$MRP = MP \cdot MR$$

(p. 301)

27. The proposition that the marginal labour cost is above the average labour cost when the average is rising is essentially the same proposition proved in note 15. Nevertheless, let us do it again, using elementary calculus.

The quantity of labour supplied depends on the wage rate: $L^s = f(w)$. Total labour cost along the supply curve is $w \cdot L^s$. The average cost of labour is $(w \cdot L^s) / L^s = w$. The marginal cost of labour is

$$\frac{d(w \cdot L^s)}{dL^s} = w + L^s \cdot \frac{dw}{dL^s}$$

Rewrite this as

$$MC = AC + L^s \cdot \frac{dw}{dL^s}$$

As long as the supply curve slopes upward, $dw/dL^s > 0$; therefore, $MC > AC$. (p. 332)

28. In the text, we define *MPC* as an incremental ratio. For mathematical treatment, it is sometimes convenient to define all marginal concepts as derivatives: $MPC = dC/dY_D$, $MPS = dS/dY_D$, and so on. (p. 502)

29. The basic relationship is

$$Y_D = C + S$$

Dividing through by Y_D yields

$$\frac{Y_D}{Y_D} = \frac{C}{Y_D} + \frac{S}{Y_D}$$

and thus

$$1 = APC + APS$$

Next, take the first difference of the basic relationship to get

$$\Delta Y_D = \Delta C + \Delta S$$

Dividing through by ΔY_D gives

$$\frac{\Delta Y_D}{\Delta Y_D} = \frac{\Delta C}{\Delta Y_D} + \frac{\Delta S}{\Delta Y_D}$$

and thus

$$1 = MPC + MPS$$

(p. 504)

30. The total expenditure over all rounds is the sum of an infinite series. If we let *A* stand for autonomous expenditure and *z* for the marginal propensity to spend, the change in autonomous expenditure is ΔA in the first round, $z \cdot \Delta A$ in the second, $z^2 \cdot \Delta A$ in the third, and so on. This can be written as

$$\Delta A \cdot (1 + z + z^2 + \ldots + z^n)$$

If *z* is less than 1, the series in parentheses converges to $1/(1 - z)$ as *n* approaches infinity. The total change in expenditure is thus $\Delta A/(1 - z)$. In the example in the box, $z = 0.80$; therefore, the change in total expenditure is

$$\frac{\Delta A}{1 - z} = \frac{\Delta A}{0.2} = 5 \cdot \Delta A$$

(p. 516)

31. This is based on what is called the "rule of 72." Any sum growing at the rate of *X* percent per year will double in approximately $72/X$ years. For two sums growing at the rates of *X* percent and *Y* percent per year, the *difference* between the two sums will double in approximately $72/(X - Y)$ years. (pp. 604, 613)

32. The time taken to break even is a function of the *difference* in growth rates, not their *levels*. Thus, if 4 percent and 5 percent or 5 percent and 6 percent had been used in the example, it still would have taken the same number of years. To see this quickly, recognize that we are interested in the ratio of two exponential growth paths:

$$\frac{e^{r_1 t}}{e^{r_2 t}} = e^{(r_1 - r_2)t}$$

(p. 616)

33. A simple example of a production function is $\text{GDP} = z(LK)^{1/2}$. This equation says that to find the amount of GDP produced, multiply the amount of labour by the amount of capital, take the square root, and multiply the result by the constant *z*. This production function has positive but diminishing marginal returns to either factor. This can be seen by evaluating the first and second partial derivatives and showing the first derivatives to be positive and the second derivatives to be negative.

For example,

$$\frac{\partial \text{GDP}}{\partial K} = \frac{z \cdot L^{1/2}}{2 \cdot K^{1/2}} > 0$$

and

$$\frac{\partial^2 \text{GDP}}{\partial K^2} = -\frac{z \cdot L^{1/2}}{4 \cdot K^{3/2}} < 0$$

(p. 624)

34. The production function GDP = $z(LK)^{1/2}$ displays contant returns to scale. To see this, multiply both L and K by the same constant, θ, and see that this multiplies the whole value of GDP by θ:

$$z(\theta L \cdot \theta K)^{1/2} = z(\theta^2 \cdot LK)^{1/2} = \theta z(LK)^{1/2} = \theta \cdot \text{GDP}$$

(p. 626)

35. This is easily proved. The banking system wants sufficient deposits (D) to establish the target ratio (v) of deposits to reserves (R). This gives $R/D = v$. Any change in D of size ΔD has to be accompanied by a change in R of ΔR of sufficient size to restore v. Thus, $\Delta R/\Delta D = v$, so $\Delta D = \Delta R/v$ and $\Delta D/\Delta R = 1/v$. This can be shown also in terms of the deposits created by the sequence in Table 27-7. Let v be the reserve ratio and $e = 1 - v$ be the excess reserves per dollar of new deposits. If X dollars are initially deposited in the system, the successive rounds of new deposits will be X, eX, e^2X, e^3X,. . . . The series

$$X + eX + e^2X + e^3X + \ldots = X \cdot [1 + e + e^2 + e^3 + \ldots]$$

has a limit of $X \cdot \dfrac{1}{1 - e}$

$$= X \cdot \frac{1}{1 - (1 - v)} = \frac{X}{v}$$

This is the total new deposits created by an injection of \$$X$ of new reserves into the banking system. For example, when $v = 0.20$, an injection of \$100 into the system will lead to an overall increase in deposits of \$500. (p. 661)

36. Suppose that the public wishes to hold a fraction, c, of deposits in cash, C. Now suppose that X dollars are injected into the system. Ultimately, this money will be held either as reserves by the banking system or as cash by the public. Thus, we have

$$\Delta C + \Delta R = X$$

From the banking system's reserve behaviour, we have $\Delta R = v \cdot \Delta D$, and from the public's cash behaviour, we have $\Delta C = c \cdot \Delta D$. Substituting into the above equation, we get the result that

$$\Delta D = \frac{X}{v + c}$$

From this we can also relate the change in reserves and the change in cash holdings to the initial injection:

$$\Delta R = \frac{v}{v + c} \cdot X$$

$$\Delta C = \frac{c}{v + c} \cdot X$$

For example, when $v = 0.20$ and $c = 0.05$, an injection of \$100 will lead to an increase in reserves of \$80, an increase in cash in the hands of the public of \$20, and an increase in deposits of \$400. (p. 662)

Timeline of Great Economists

1663
First gold guinea pieces are coined in England.

1670
Hudson's Bay Company is founded, with a monopoly over all rivers draining into Hudson Bay.

1687
Isaac Newton publishes *Principia Mathematica.*

1694
The Bank of England is created as a private venture to buy the government debt.

1698
Paper manufacturing begins in North America.

1718
First bank notes are circulated in England.

1721
J. S. Bach completes the Brandenburg Concertos.

1660 1670 1680 1690 1700 1710 1720 1730

ADAM SMITH *(1723–1790)*

Adam Smith was born in 1723 in the small Scottish town of Kirkcaldy. He is perhaps the single most influential figure in the development of modern economics, and even those who have never studied economics know of his most famous work, *The Wealth of Nations,* and of the terms *laissez-faire* and the *invisible hand,* both attributable to Smith. He was able to describe the workings of the capitalist market economy, the division of labour in production, the role of money, free trade, and the nature of economic growth. Even today, the breadth of his scholarship is considered astounding.

Smith was raised by his mother, as his father had died before his birth. His intellectual promise was discovered early, and at age 14 Smith was sent to study at Glasgow and then at Oxford. He then returned to an appointment as professor of moral philosophy at University of Glasgow, where he became one of the leading philosophers of his day. He lectured on natural theology, ethics, jurisprudence, and political economy to students who travelled from as far away as Russia to hear his lectures.

In 1759, Smith published *The Theory of Moral Sentiments,* in which he attempted to identify the origins of moral judgment. In this early work, Smith writes of the motivation of self-interest and of the morality that keeps it in check. After its publication, Smith left his post at the University of Glasgow to embark on a European tour as the tutor to a young aristocrat, the Duke of Buccleuch, with whom he travelled for two years. In exchange for this assignment Smith was provided with a salary for the remainder of his life. He returned to the small town of his birth and spent the next 10 years alone, writing his most famous work.

An Inquiry into the Nature and Causes of the Wealth of Nations was published in 1776. His contributions in this book (generally known as *The Wealth of Nations*) were revolutionary, and the text became the foundation of much of modern economics. It continues to be reprinted today. Smith rejected the notion that a country's supply of gold and silver was the measure of its wealth—rather, it was the real incomes of the people that determined national wealth. Growth in the real incomes of the country's citizens—that is, economic growth—would result from specialization in production, the division of labour, and the use of money to facilitate trade. Smith provided a framework for analyzing the questions of income growth, value, and distribution.

Smith's work marked the beginning of what is called the Classical period in economic thought, which continued for the next 75 years. This school of thought was centred on the principles of natural liberty (laissez-faire) and the importance of economic growth as a means of bettering the conditions of human existence.

1740 | 1750 | 1760 | 1770 | 1780 | 1790 | 1800

1749 Founding of Halifax.

1752 Benjamin Franklin demonstrates that lightning is electricity.

1771 *Encyclopaedia Britannica* is first published.

1775–1783 American Revolution; Declaration of Independence is signed in 1776.

1784 James Watt patents the steam locomotive.

1789 Start of the French Revolution.

1793 Eli Whitney invents the cotton gin.

THOMAS MALTHUS *(1766–1834)*

Thomas Malthus was born into a reasonably well-to-do English family. He was educated at Cambridge and from 1805 until his death he held the first British professorship of political economy in the East India Company's college at Haileybury. In 1798 he published *An Essay on the Principle of Population as It Affects the Future Improvement of Society,* which was revised many times in subsequent years until finally he published *A Summary View of the Principle of Population* in 1830.

It is these essays on population for which Malthus is best known. His first proposition was that population, when unchecked, would increase in a geometric progression such that the population would double every 25 years. His second proposition was that the means of subsistence (i.e. the food supply) cannot possibly increase faster than in arithmetic progression (increasing by a given number of units every year). The result would be population growth eventually outstripping food production, and thus abject poverty and suffering for the majority of people in every society.

Malthus's population theory had tremendous intellectual influence at the time and became an integral part of the Classical theory of income distribution. However, it is no longer taken as a good description of current or past trends.

DAVID RICARDO (1772–1823)

David Ricardo was born in London to parents who had immigrated from the Netherlands. Ricardo's father was very successful in money markets, and Ricardo himself had earned enough money on the stock exchange that he was very wealthy before he was 30. He had little formal education, but after reading Adam Smith's *The Wealth of Nations* in 1799, he chose to divide his time between studying and writing about political economy and increasing his own personal wealth.

Ricardo's place in the history of economics was assured by his achievement in constructing an abstract model of how capitalism worked. He built an analytic "system" using deductive reasoning that characterizes economic theorizing to the present day. The three critical principles in Ricardo's system were (1) the theory of rent, (2) Thomas Malthus's population principle, and (3) the wages-fund doctrine. Ricardo published *The Principles of Political Economy and Taxation* in 1817, which dominated Classical economics for the following half-century.

Ricardo also contributed the concept of comparative advantage to the study of international trade. Ricardo's theories regarding the gains from trade had some influence on the repeal of the British Corn Laws in 1846—tariffs on the importation of grains into Great Britain—and the subsequent transformation of that country during the nineteenth century from a country of high tariffs to one of completely free trade.

1805 Admiral Horatio Nelson's victory (and death) at Trafalgar.

1814 British forces burn Washington, D.C., in the War of 1812.

1815 Napoleon defeated at Waterloo and exiled to St. Helena; Corn Laws passed in Britain.

1822 First textile mills are built in Lowell, Massachusetts.

1831 The first horse-drawn buses appear in New York.

1837 Victoria becomes Queen of England (until 1901). Rebellions in Upper and Lower Canada.

1800 — 1810 — 1820 — 1830

JOHN STUART MILL (1806–1873)

John Stuart Mill, born in London, was the son of James Mill, a prominent British historian, economist, and philosopher. By age 12 he was acquainted with the major economics works of the day, and at 13 he was correcting the proofs of his father's book, *Elements of Political Economy*. J. S. Mill spent most of his life working at the East India Company—his extraordinarily prolific writing career was conducted entirely as an aside. In 1848 he published his *Principles of Political Economy,* which updated the principles found in Adam Smith's *The Wealth of Nations* and which remained the basic textbook for students of economics until the end of the nineteenth century. In *Principles,* Mill made an important contribution to the economics discipline by distinguishing between the economics of production and of distribution. He pointed out that economic laws had nothing to do with the distribution of wealth, which was a societal matter, but had everything to do with production.

Previous to Mill's *Principles* was his *System of Logic* (1843), which was the century's most influential text on logic and the theory of knowledge. His essays on ethics, contemporary culture, and freedom of speech, such as *Utilitarianism* and *On Liberty,* are still widely studied today.

KARL MARX (1818–1883)

Karl Marx was born in Trier, Germany (then part of Prussia), and studied law, history, and philosophy at the universities of Bonn, Berlin, and Jena. Marx travelled between Prussia, Paris, and Brussels, working at various jobs until finally settling in London in 1849, where he lived the remainder of his life. Most of his time was spent in the mainly unpaid pursuits of writing and studying economics in the library of the British Museum. Marx's contributions to economics are intricately bound to his views of history and society. *The Communist Manifesto* was published with Friedrich Engels in 1848, his *Critique of Political Economy* in 1859, and in 1867 the first volume of *Das Kapital.* (The remaining volumes, edited by Engels, were published after Marx's death.)

For Marx, capitalism was a stage in an evolutionary process from a primitive agricultural economy toward an inevitable elimination of private property and the class structure. Marx's "labour theory of value," whereby the quantity of labour used in the manufacture of a product determined its value, held the central place in his economic thought. He believed that the worker provided "surplus value" to the capitalist. The capitalist would then use the profit arising from this surplus value to reinvest in plant and machinery. Through time, more would be spent for plant and machinery than for wages, which would lead to lower profits (since profits arose only from the surplus value from labour) and a resulting squeeze in the real income of workers. Marx believed that in the capitalists' effort to maintain profits in this unstable system, there would emerge a "reserve army of the unemployed." The resulting class conflict would become increasingly acute until revolution by the workers would overthrow capitalism.

1840
Act of Union unites Upper and Lower Canada.

1844
Electric telegraph opens between Washington and Baltimore.

1846
Britain repeals the Corn Laws.

1859
Charles Darwin publishes *On the Origin of Species.*

1861–1865
The U.S. Civil War; Abraham Lincoln is assassinated in 1865.

1867
British North America Act establishes the Dominion of Canada. Alfred Nobel invents dynamite.

1869
Opening of the Suez Canal.

1840 | 1850 | 1860 | 1870

LEON WALRAS (1834–1910)

Leon Walras was born in France, the son of an economist. After being trained inauspiciously in engineering and performing poorly in mathematics, Walras spent some time pursuing other endeavours, such as novel writing and working for the railway. Eventually he promised his father he would study economics, and by 1870 he was given a professorship in economics in the Faculty of Law at the University of Lausanne in Switzerland. Once there, Walras began the feverish activity that eventually led to his important contributions to economic theory.

In the 1870s, Walras was one of three economists to put forward the marginal utility theory of value (simultaneously with William Stanley Jevons of England and Carl Menger of Austria). Further, he constructed a mathematical model of general equilibrium using a system of simultaneous equations that he used to argue that equilibrium prices and quantities are uniquely determined. Central to general equilibrium analysis is the notion that the prices and quantities of all commodities are determined simultaneously because the whole system is interdependent. Walras's most important work was *Elements of Pure Economics,* published in 1874. In addition to all of Walras's other accomplishments in economics (and despite his early poor performance in mathematics!), we today regard him as the founder of mathematical economics.

Leon Walras and Alfred Marshall are regarded by many economists to be the two most important economic theorists who ever lived. Much of the framework of economic theory studied today is either Walrasian or Marshallian in character.

CARL MENGER (1840–1921)

Carl Menger was born in Galicia (then part of Austria), and he came from a family of Austrian civil servants and army officers. After studying law in Prague and Vienna, he turned to economics and in 1871 published *Grundsatze der Volkswirtschaftslehre* (translated as *Principles of Economics*), for which he became famous. He held a professorship at the University of Vienna until 1903. Menger was the founder of a school of thought known as the "Austrian School," which effectively displaced the German historical method on the continent and which survives today as an alternative to mainstream Neoclassical economics.

Menger was one of three economists in the 1870s who independently put forward a theory of value based on marginal utility. Prior to what economists now call the "marginal revolution," value was thought to be derived solely from the inputs of labour and capital. Menger developed the marginal utility theory of value, in which the value of any good is determined by individuals' subjective evaluations of that good. According to Menger, a good has some value if it has the ability to satisfy some human want or desire, and *utility* is the capacity of the good to do so. Menger went on to develop the idea that the individual will maximize total utility at the point where the last unit of each good consumed provides equal utility—that is, where marginal utilities are equal.

Menger's emphasis on the marginal utility theory of value led him to focus on consumption rather than production as the determinant of price. Menger focused only on the demand for goods and largely ignored the supply. It would remain for Alfred Marshall and Leon Walras to combine demand and supply for a more complete picture of price determination.

1871 The Great Fire destroys much of Chicago.

1876 Alexander Graham Bell founds Bell Telephone Co.

1880 Thomas Edison invents the electric light bulb.

1885 The last spike is driven on the Canadian Pacific Railway. Louis Riel is hanged.

1870 *1875* *1880* *1885*

ALFRED MARSHALL (1842–1924)

Alfred Marshall was born in Clapham, England, the son of a bank cashier, and was descended from a long line of clerics. Marshall's father, despite intense effort, was unable to steer the young Marshall into the church. Instead, Marshall followed his passion for mathematics at Cambridge and chose economics as a field of study after reading J. S. Mill's *Principles of Political Economy.* His career was then spent mainly at Cambridge, where he taught economics to John Maynard Keynes, Arthur Pigou, Joan Robinson, and countless other British theorists in the "Cambridge tradition." His *Principles of Economics,* published in 1890, replaced Mill's *Principles* as the dominant economics textbook of English-speaking universities.

Marshall institutionalized modern marginal analysis, the basic concepts of supply and demand, and perhaps most importantly the notion of economic equilibrium resulting from the interaction of supply and demand. He also pioneered partial equilibrium analysis—examining the forces of supply and demand in a particular market provided that all other influences can be excluded, *ceteris paribus.*

Although many of the ideas had been put forward by previous writers, Marshall was able to synthesize the previous analyses of utility and cost and present a thorough and complete statement of the laws of demand and supply. Marshall refined and developed microeconomic theory to such a degree that much of what he wrote would be familiar to students of this textbook today.

It is also interesting to note that although Alfred Marshall and Leon Walras were simultaneously expanding the frontiers of economic theory, there was almost no communication between the two men. Though Marshall chose partial equilibrium analysis as the appropriate method for dealing with selected markets in a complex world, he did acknowledge the correctness of Walras's general equilibrium system. Walras, on the other hand, was adamant (and sometimes rude) in his opposition to the methods that Marshall was putting forward. History has shown that both the partial and the general equilibrium approaches to economic analysis are required for understanding the functioning of the economy.

THORSTEIN VEBLEN (1857–1929)

Thorstein Veblen was born on a farm in Wisconsin to Norwegian parents. He received his Ph.D. in philosophy from Yale University, after which he returned to his father's farm because he was unable to secure an academic position. For seven years he remained there, reading voraciously on economics and other social sciences. Eventually, he took academic positions at the University of Chicago, Stanford University, the University of Missouri, and the New School for Social Research (in New York). Veblen was the founder of "institutional economics," the only uniquely North American school of economic thought.

In 1899, Veblen published *The Theory of the Leisure Class,* in which he sought to apply Charles Darwin's evolutionism to the study of modern economic life. He examined problems in the social institutions of the day, and savagely criticized Classical and Neoclassical economic analysis. Although Veblen failed to shift the path of mainstream economic analysis, he did contribute the idea of the importance of long-run institutional studies as a useful complement to short-run price theory analysis. He also reminded the profession that economics is a *social* science, and not merely a branch of mathematics.

Veblen remains most famous today for his idea of "conspicuous consumption." He observed that some commodities were consumed not for their intrinsic qualities but because they carried snob appeal. He suggested that the more expensive such a commodity became, the greater might be its ability to confer status on its purchaser.

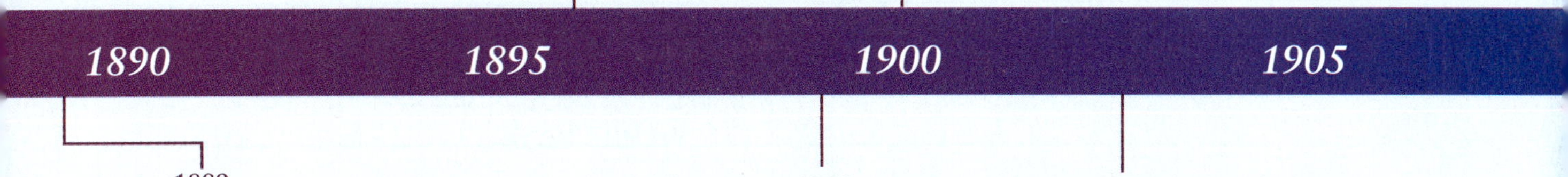

1889
Gustave Eiffel designs the Eiffel Tower for the Paris World Exposition.

1896
First modern Olympic Games are held in Athens. Klondike Gold Rush begins.

1898
Spanish-American War.

1900
J. P. Morgan buys out Andrew Carnegie, forming the biggest business in the world, U.S. Steel.

1903
The Wright Brothers' first successful flight.

VILFREDO PARETO (1848–1923)

Vilfredo Pareto was an Italian, born in Paris, and was trained to be an engineer. Though he actually practised as an engineer, he would later succeed Leon Walras to the Chair of Economics in the Faculty of Law at the University of Lausanne.

Pareto built upon the system of general equilibrium that Walras had developed. In his *Cours d'économie politique* (1897) and his *Manuel d'économie politique* (1906) Pareto set forth the foundations of modern welfare economics. He showed that theories of consumer behaviour and exchange could be constructed on assumptions of ordinal utility, rather than cardinal utility, eliminating the need to compare one person's utility with another's. Using the indifference curve analysis developed by F. Y. Edgeworth, Pareto was able to demonstrate that total welfare could be increased by an exchange if one person could be made better off without anyone else becoming worse off. Pareto applied this analysis to consumption and exchange, as well as to production. Pareto's contributions in this area are remembered in economists' references to *Pareto optimality* and *Pareto efficiency.*

JOSEPH SCHUMPETER (1883–1950)

Joseph Schumpeter was born in Triesch, Moravia (now in the Czech Republic). He was a university professor and later a Minister of Finance in Austria. In 1932, he emigrated to the United States to avoid the rise to power of Adolf Hitler. He spent his remaining years at Harvard University.

Schumpeter, a pioneering theorist of innovation, emphasized the role of the entrepreneur in economic development. The existence of the entrepreneur meant continuous innovation and waves of adaptation to changing technology. He is best known for his theory of "creative destruction," where the prospect of monopoly profits provides owners the incentive to finance inventions and innovations. One monopoly can replace another with superior technology or a superior product, thereby circumventing the entry barriers of a monopolized industry. He criticized mainstream economists for emphasizing the static (allocative) efficiency of perfect competition—a market structure that would, if it could ever be achieved, retard technological change and economic growth.

Schumpeter's best known works are *The Theory of Economic Development* (1911), *Business Cycles* (1939), and *Capitalism, Socialism and Democracy* (1943).

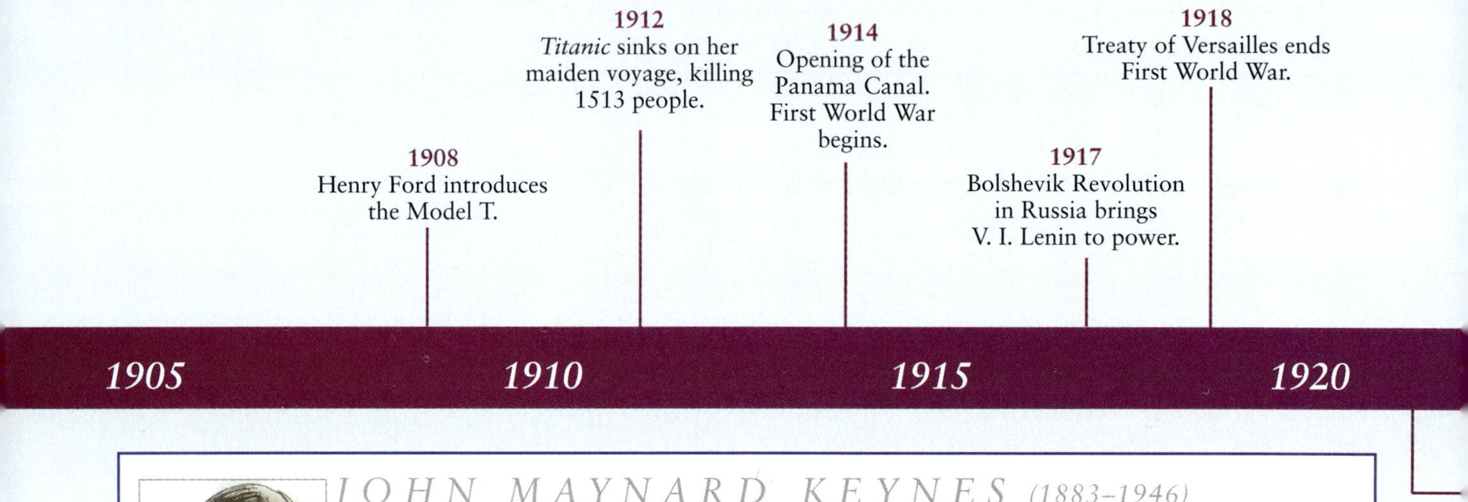

JOHN MAYNARD KEYNES (1883–1946)

John Maynard Keynes was born in Cambridge, England. His parents were both intellectuals, and his father, John Neville Keynes, was a famous logician and writer on economic methodology. The young Keynes was educated at Eton and then at Kings College, Cambridge, where he was a student of Alfred Marshall and Arthur Pigou. His career included appointments to the Treasury in Britain during both World Wars, a leading role in the establishment of the International Monetary Fund (through discussions at Bretton Woods, New Hampshire, in 1944), and editorship of the *Economic Journal* from 1911 to 1945, all in addition to his academic position at Kings College.

Keynes published extensively during his life but his most influential work, *The General Theory of Employment, Interest, and Money,* appeared in 1936. This book was published in the midst of the Great Depression when the output of goods and services had fallen drastically, unemployment was intolerably high, and it had become clear to many that the market would not self-adjust to achieve potential output within an acceptable period of time. Fluctuations in economic activity were familiar at this point, but the failure of the economy to recover rapidly from this depression was unprecedented. Neoclassical economists held that during a downturn both wages and the interest rate would fall low enough to induce investment and employment and cause an expansion. They believed that the persistent unemployment during the 1930s was caused by inflexible wages and they recommended that workers be convinced to accept wage cuts.

Keynes believed that this policy, though perhaps correct for a single industry, was not correct for the entire economy. Widespread wage cuts would reduce the consumption portion of aggregate demand, which would offset any increase in employment. Keynes argued that unemployment could be cured only by manipulating aggregate demand, whereby increased demand (through government expenditure) would increase the price level, reduce real wages, and thereby stimulate employment.

Keynes's views found acceptance after the publication of his *General Theory* and had a profound effect on government policy around the world, particularly in the 1940s, 1950s, and 1960s. As we know from this textbook, Keynes's name is attached to much of macroeconomics, from much of the basic theory to the Keynesian short-run aggregate supply curve and the Keynesian consumption function. His contributions to economics go well beyond what can be mentioned in a few paragraphs—for, in effect, he laid the foundations for modern macroeconomics.

EDWARD CHAMBERLIN (1899–1967)

Edward Chamberlin was born in La Conner, Washington, and received his Ph.D. from Harvard University in 1927. He became a full professor at Harvard in 1937 and stayed there until his retirement in 1966. He published *The Theory of Monopolistic Competition* in 1933.

Before Chamberlin's book (which appeared more or less simultaneously with Joan Robinson's *The Economics of Imperfect Competition*), the models of perfect competition and monopoly had been fairly well worked out. Though economists were aware of a middle ground between these two market structures and some analysis of duopoly (two sellers) had been presented, it was Chamberlin and Robinson who closely examined this problem of imperfect markets.

Chamberlin's main contribution was explaining the importance of product differentiation for firms in market structures between perfect competition and monopoly. Chamberlin saw that though there may be a large number of firms in the market (the competitive element), each firm created for itself a unique product or advantage that gave it some control over price (the monopoly element). Specifically, he identified items such as copyrights, trademarks, brand names, and location as monopoly elements behind a product. Though Alfred Marshall regarded price as the only variable in question, Chamberlin saw both price and the product itself as variables under control of the firm in monopolistically competitive markets.

1927 Charles Lindbergh flies *Spirit of St. Louis* nonstop from New York to Paris.

1929 Stock market crashes (October 29). Beginning of Great Depression.

1933 Adolf Hitler becomes German Chancellor.

1939 Germany invades Poland; Second World War begins.

1940 Unemployment Insurance begins as national program in Canada.

1925 **1930** **1935** **1940**

1922 The Soviet Union is formed; Joseph Stalin named Secretary General of the Communist Party.

FRIEDRICH AUGUST VON HAYEK (1899–1992)

Friedrich von Hayek was born in Vienna and studied at the University of Vienna, where he was trained in the Austrian tradition of economics (a school of thought originating with Carl Menger). He held academic positions at the London School of Economics and the University of Chicago. He returned to Europe in 1962 to the University of Freiburg in what was then West Germany and the University of Salzburg in Austria. He was awarded the Nobel Prize in Economics in 1974.

Hayek contributed new ideas and theories in many different areas of economics, but he is perhaps best known for his general conception of economics as a "coordination problem." His observation of market economies suggested that the relative prices determined in free markets provided the signals that allowed the actions of all decision makers to mesh—even though there was no formal planning taking place to coordinate these actions. He emphasized this "spontaneous order" at work in the economy as the subject matter for economics. The role of knowledge and information in the market process became central to Hayek, an idea that has grown in importance to the economics profession over the years.

Hayek's theory of business cycles provided an example of the breakdown of this coordination. A monetary disturbance (e.g., an increase in the money supply) would distort the signals (relative prices) by artificially raising the return to certain types of economic activity. When the disturbance disappeared, the boom caused by these distorted signals would be followed by a slump. Although Hayek's business-cycle theory was eclipsed by the Keynesian revolution, his emphasis on economics as a coordination problem has had a major influence on contemporary economic thought.

Hayek was also prominent in advocating the virtues of free markets as contributing to human freedom in the broad sense as well as to economic efficiency in the narrow sense. His *The Road to Serfdom* (1944) sounded an alarm about the political and economic implications of the then-growing belief in the virtues of central planning. His *Constitution of Liberty* (1960) is a much deeper philosophical analysis of the forces, economic and otherwise, that contribute to the liberty of the individual.

MILTON FRIEDMAN (b. 1912–2006)

Milton Friedman completed graduate studies in economics at the University of Chicago and at Columbia University, where he received his Ph.D. in 1946. Most of Friedman's academic career was spent as a professor at the University of Chicago, and after retiring in 1977 he was a senior research fellow at the Hoover Institution at Stanford University. Friedman is best known as one of the leading proponents of Monetarism and for his belief in the power of free markets. His work greatly influenced modern macroeconomics.

Friedman made his first significant mark on the profession with the publication of *The Theory of the Consumption Function* in 1957. There he developed the permanent income hypothesis, and argued that consumption depends on long-run average income rather than current disposable income, as it does in Keynesian analysis. This was an early example of a macroeconomic theory that emphasized the importance of forward-looking consumers. In 1963, he co-authored with Anna Schwartz his most influential book, *A Monetary History of the United States, 1867–1960,* where they presented evidence in support of the monetarist view that changes in the supply of money can cause dramatic fluctuations in the level of economic activity. Although this view was seriously challenged by subsequent research, Friedman helped the profession to understand the power of and the limitations of monetary policy. He also introduced (along with Edmund Phelps) the idea that in the long run the Phillips curve is vertical at the natural rate of unemployment. He argued that a tradeoff between inflation and unemployment exists *only* in the short run and that any attempt to maintain unemployment below this natural rate will lead to accelerating inflation.

Capitalism and Freedom (1962) and *Free to Choose* (1980), the latter co-written with his wife, Rose Friedman, are part of Friedman's attempts to communicate his ideas about economics and, in particular, the power of the free market, to a mass audience of non-economists. Both books became international bestsellers, and these books, in addition to his writing for newspapers and magazines, made Milton Friedman one of the most famous modern economists. He was awarded the Nobel Prize in Economics in 1976.

1941 United States enters war after the attack on Pearl Harbor (December 7).

1944 Bretton Woods Conference. IMF and World Bank are created.

1945 United States drops atomic bomb on Japan; Second World War ends.

1949 Mao Tse-tung's communists gain control of China.

1957 Treaty of Rome establishes the European Common Market.

1940 1945 1950 1955

JOHN KENNETH GALBRAITH (1908–2006)

John Kenneth Galbraith was born on a farm in Southeastern Ontario, to a family of Scottish-Canadian farmers. He began his undergraduate education at the Ontario Agricultural College in Guelph in 1926 where he studied agricultural economics and animal husbandry. He moved to California to study at the University of California at Berkeley and completed a Ph.D. in agricultural economics in 1934. Galbraith was hired by Harvard University in 1934 and, aside from his government and diplomatic postings, remained on staff there until his death.

Galbraith was heavily influenced by the ideas of John Maynard Keynes, Thorstein Veblen, and the "institutional" school of economics. He rejected the technical and mathematical approach of Neoclassical economics. Instead he emphasized the interplay of economics, politics, culture, and tradition, a combination that does not lend itself well to mathematical modelling. He was much more of a "political economist" in the style of the nineteenth century than a theoretical economist of the late twentieth century.

One of his earliest books was *American Capitalism: The Concept of Countervailing Power* (1952), in which he argued that the competitive model was not a good description of reality in the United States economy, nor was it an ideal to strive for. Rather, he described the U.S. economy as one where big corporations and big unions exert pressure on each other (countervailing power) and, along with an activist government, keep the nation's economy prosperous and stable. His most famous book was *The Affluent Society* (1958), where he argued that the United States had become obsessed with overproducing consumer goods and instead should be making large public investments in highways, education, and other public services. His expression "private opulence and public squalor" became well known, and many would agree is even more relevant today than it was when he wrote the words over 50 years ago. In a later book, *The New Industrial State* (1967), Galbraith argued that very few U.S. industries fit economists' model of perfect competition, and that the economy was dominated by large, powerful firms. In general, Galbraith continued to write about topics that he believed the economics profession had neglected—topics such as advertising, the separation of corporate ownership and management, oligopoly, and government and military spending.

Because of Galbraith's desire to focus on the interplay of economics, politics, and society, he was often criticized (or ignored) by mainstream economists. But he was undeterred. And while many economists disagreed with his approach and some of his political views, he was widely recognized as a gifted and insightful writer and speaker.

KENNETH ARROW (b. 1921)

Kenneth Arrow was born and educated in New York City. He began graduate work at Columbia University and received an M.A. in mathematics in 1941. Over the following ten years, after Arrow had completed his Ph.D. course work, he served in the U.S. Army Air Corps during the Second World War and held various research jobs while searching for a dissertation topic. His dissertation, which earned him his Ph.D. from Columbia in 1951, subsequently became a classic in economics, *Social Choice and Individual Values* (1951). Kenneth Arrow is currently Professor, Emeritus, at Stanford University.

In his 1951 book Arrow presented his "Impossibility Theorem," which we encounter in Chapter 16 of this book. His conclusion that it is not possible to construct a set of voting rules for making public choices that is simultaneously democratic and efficient has led to decades of work by economists, philosophers, and political scientists in the field of social choice theory.

Arrow also made significant contributions in other areas of economics. In 1954 (with Gerard Debreu) he constructed a mathematical model of an economy with many individual, inter-related markets, and proved the existence of a general market-clearing equilibrium. While his model was based on many unrealistic assumptions, including the presence of forward markets in all goods and services (that is, one can pay today to obtain a good or service in the future), many believe that Arrow's proof gave economists valuable insights into the workings of multi-market systems.

Arrow's work in the economics of uncertainty was also a major contribution. In *Essays in the Theory of Risk-Bearing* (1971), he introduced the concepts of moral hazard and adverse selection (among other ideas about risk), which we also encounter in Chapter 16 of this book. Arrow was one of the first economists to develop the idea of "learning by doing"; as producers increase their cumulative output of a product, they gain experience and are then able to produce that product at lower average costs. This idea has played an important role in modern theories of economic growth.

Arrow was awarded the Nobel Prize in 1972 (jointly with British economist John Hicks) and in 2004 was awarded the National Medal of Science, the United States' highest scientific honour.

1960 **1965** **1970** **1975**

1959 St. Lawrence Seaway officially opens.

1962 Cuban Missile Crisis.

1963 U.S. President John F. Kennedy assassinated.

1967 Canada celebrates its Centennial; Montreal hosts Expo '67.

1969 Neil Armstrong is first person to walk on the moon.

1973 First OPEC oil shock.

1975 Bill Gates and Paul Allen found Microsoft Corporation.

PAUL SAMUELSON (b. 1915)

Paul Samuelson was born in Gary, Indiana, the son of a drugstore owner. He received his Ph.D. in economics in 1941 from Harvard University and spent his academic career at the Massachusetts Institute of Technology (MIT), where he is currently Institute Professor of Economics, Emeritus.

Samuelson is generally regarded as one of the greatest economic theorists of the twentieth century. While still a graduate student at Harvard, Samuelson wrote most of *Foundations of Economic Analysis* (1947), which was path-breaking at the time and used mathematical analysis and constrained optimization techniques to shed insight into economic behaviour. He systematized economic theory into a more rigorous mathematical discipline, which has had enormous effects on the way economics is studied today.

Though Samuelson has made major contributions to many branches of economics, three are particularly notable. First, he showed how the central predictions of demand theory could be tested using the "revealed preferences" of consumers from observed market behaviour. Second, in international trade theory, he made important contributions in the analysis of the gains from trade and the effects of tariff protection on the distribution of income. Third, most familiar to readers of this book, he is credited with introducing the 45°-line model of short-run national income determination. This diagram, encountered throughout Chapters 21 and 22 of this book, has become the standard tool for teaching the Keynesian theory of national-income determination in the short run. Samuelson's work has also provided valuable insights in other areas of economics, including government taxation and expenditure, capital theory, and theories of economic growth.

Samuelson is also well known for his famous introductory economics textbook, *Economics,* first published in 1948, which provided a systematic treatment of both micro- and macroeconomics in a way that had not been presented before. In general, he is credited with raising the level of scientific and mathematical analysis in economics. Samuelson was awarded the Nobel Prize in Economics in 1970, and was the first American scholar to receive this honour.

Index

Key terms and their page references are in boldface. *f* denotes a figure, *t* denotes a table, and *n* denotes a footnote.

Photo Credits

Chapter 1 p. 2 Photo courtesy of the Adam Smith Institute, London, UK; p. 6 Getty Images/Stone/Daniel Bosler; p. 12 Photo Disc Inc.; p. 18 CP/Lionel Cironneau.

Chapter 2 p. 25 Hugues Siegenthaler/Bloomberg News/Landov; p. 26 Jose Luis Pelaez/Corbis Canada; p. 34 CP Photo/Sean Vokey.

Chapter 3 p. 49 Getty Images/Stone/Chris McCooey; p. 56 Saskatchewan Travel; p. 60 Copyright eBay Inc. All Rights Reserved; p. 67 Marc Serota/Reuters/Corbis Canada.

Chapter 4 p. 79 Imperial Oil Limited; p. 90 Richard Levine/Alamy.

Chapter 5 p. 103 Photo Disc Inc.

Chapter 6 p. 126 © Lee Hacker/Alamy; p. 128 Getty Images/Stone/Frank Siteman.

Chapter 7 p. 148 Courtesy of Alcan; p. 157 Chip East/Reuters/Landov.

Chapter 8 p.171 Photo Disc Inc.; p. 172 Tim Hall/Getty Images; p. 177 Magma; p. 181 Dick Hemingway Editorial Photographs.

Chapter 9 p. 192 Dick Hemingway Editorial Photographs; p. 193 © Sylvain Saustier/Corbis Canada; p. 206 Richard T. Nowitz/Corbis Canada; p. 210 Getty/Stone/Andy Sacks.

Chapter 10 p. 224 Celestica Inc.; p. 226 Dick Hemingway Editorial Photographs; p. 228 Photo Disc Inc.

Chapter 11 p. 248 Dick Hemingway Editorial Photographs; p. 250 Alene McNeil; p. 252 Wine Council of Ontario; p. 259 James Leynse/Corbis Canada; pp. 262, 263 Dick Hemingway Editorial Photographs.

Chapter 12 p. 273 Louie Psihoyos/Corbis Canada; p. 277 Mitch Gezar/Getty Images; p. 281 Peter Turnley/Corbis Canada; p. 285 Mike Dobel/Alamy; p. 286 Al Harvey/The Slide Farm, www.slidefarm.com; p. 288 CP/Adrian Wyld.

Chapter 13 p. 301 Courtesy of John Deere Company; p. 306 Kayte M. Deioma/Photo Edit; p. 308 Stockbyte/Getty Images; p. 310 Deborah Davis/PhotoEdit; p. 314 Aurora & Quanta Productions, Inc.; p. 315 Brownie Harris/Corbis Canada; p. 317 Gunter Marx Photography/Corbis Canada; p. 319 Jason Cohn/Reuters /Landov.

Chapter 14 p. 326 CP/Adrian Wyld; p. 330 Hulton Archive/Getty Images; p. 334 Luxner News; p. 337 Courtesy of Abitibi-Price; p. 340 N2762/Manitoba Archives; p. 344 Courtesy of Stelco.

Chapter 15 p. 357 Dana White/PhotoEdit.

Chapter 16 p. 379 Peter Turnley/Corbis Canada; p. 383 Peter Arnold Inc.; p. 384 Michael S. Yamashita/Corbis Canada; p. 386 Rommel/Masterfile; p. 388 Helen King/Corbis Canada; p. 389 Dick Hemingway Editorial Photographs; p. 392 Reuters/Chris Wattie/Landov; p. 397 CP/Roy Antal; p. 399 Reuters/Chris Wattie/Landov.

Chapter 17 p. 410 British Columbia Forest Service/Barbara Davies Photo; p. 415 Dick Hemingway Editorial Photographs; p. 420 Red Deer Advocate/Randy Fiedler.

Chapter 18 p. 432 Roy Ooms/Masterfile; p. 441 Brian Sytnyk/Masterfile; pp. 445, 448 Dick Hemingway Editorial Photographs.

Chapter 33 p. 809 Photo Disc Inc.; p. 811 British Columbia Forest Service/R.J. Challenger Photo.

Chapter 34 p. 825 Superstock; p. 827 Paulo Whitaker/Reuters/Landov; p. 834 Aaron Skinner/Bloomberg News/Landov; p. 835 © Christopher J. Morris/CORBIS/MagmaPhoto.com; p. 841 Courtesy of the Wine Council of Ontario.